Jenner 29th May 1995.

Comparative Economic Systems

Comparative Economic Systems

Fifth Edition

Paul R. Gregory
University of Houston

Robert C. Stuart
Rutgers University

HOUGHTON MIFFLIN COMPANY   **BOSTON**   **TORONTO**
Geneva, Illinois   Palo Alto   Princeton, New Jersey

Cover design: Judy Arisman/Arisman Design
Cover image: "Upward: Downward: Upward Movement" by Alfred Jensen, 1961.
Courtesy Edward Downe.

Sponsoring Editor: Denise Clinton
Development Editor: Joan Horan
Project Editor: Maria Morelli
Production/Design Coordinator: Jennifer Waddell
Senior Manufacturing Coordinator: Priscilla J. Bailey
Marketing Manager: Charles Baker

Printed in the U.S.A.

Library of Congress Catalog Card Number 94-76503

ISBN: 0-395-70867-2
Exam copy ISBN: 0-395-71674-8

1234567-XX-98 97 96 95

Contents

Preface

The first edition of this work was written in the mid-1970s, a period of stagflation, energy shocks, and general unease concerning the long-run future of market capitalism. Although planned socialist economies were experiencing their own troubles, the problems of capitalism appeared to be pressing. The second edition was written in the early 1980s, during the unexpectedly rapid reduction of inflation and the acceleration of economic growth in the West. The remarkable economic performance of Japan had become a topic of everyday conversation. These situations seemed to highlight the declining economic fortunes of parts of the East. Although talk of meaningful economic reform continued in the East, only the Chinese reform appeared to be yielding real benefits.

The third edition of this text was written in 1988. The mid to late 1980s was an era of conservative economic policy in the West. In virtually all major industrialized capitalist countries, conservative governments were pursuing policies of privatization and reducing the scope of government. Japan continued to be the envy of the West with its strong currency, rapid growth, low unemployment, and positive trade balances. The "four tigers" of Asia (Taiwan, Singapore, South Korea, and Hong Kong) had gained strong footholds in world manufacturing and threatened one day to replace Japan as the pacesetter. The major economic story of the late 1980s was the East's decision to attempt serious reform of planned socialism. It was much too early to know whether the attempts by then-Soviet General Secretary Gorbachev would lead to lasting change of the planned socialist economic systems.

The fourth edition was completed in 1992. By then the Soviet Union had collapsed. Reformers appeared to have had the upper hand in Russia. Eastern Europe, it appeared, had been freed of all constraints on its reform efforts. By 1992, it was clear that the former administrative-command economies had decided in favor of the market-economy alternative. The only questions were when, how, and how fast? The fourth edition asked the following questions:

1. Will the Soviet Union and its former Eastern Europe satellites succeed in transforming themselves into viable economies based on market allocation and non-state ownership? Will the economic decline of this region be reversed and the peoples involved gain access to a standard of living consistent with the resource base?
2. Will the Soviet Union and Eastern Europe become full-fledged members of the world economic community, opening up new product and technology markets for themselves and for their Western partners?

3. Will the Chinese embark on renewed economic and political reforms to rejuvenate their economy after the setbacks to reform that occurred in the late 1980s?
4. Will Western Europe and North America continue to move toward unification of world markets at the expense of national sovereignty? How will the industrialized West accommodate the desire of Eastern Europe to become part of this unification process?
5. Will the developing economies of Latin America, Asia, and Africa begin to make economic progress relative to the more industrialized countries of the world so that prosperity will cease to be limited to a small fraction of the world's population?
6. To what degree and in what ways will the new political and economic arrangements generate economic progress in the face of critical constraints such as energy requirements and the need to curtail environmental decay?

The above questions are relevant to the fifth edition. The new questions are:

1. Will the Chinese boom be of sufficient magnitude and duration to turn China into a developed country? Does the Chinese model of development plus dictatorship offer promise for other regions?
2. Is Western Europe going into a long-term decline or can policies be put in place to restore Europe's economic vitality?
3. Can Japan return to a pattern of rapid economic growth?

That the fifth edition of this book was written in 1994, only two years after the previous edition had been published, attests to the pace of change. Although interest in the capitalism–socialism dichotomy is waning and the Soviet-style administrative-command system has become discredited, the East has yet to find a way to respond to transition—how does it make the transition from the discredited administrative-command system to a market system? Moreover, the failures and costs of the transition have orchestrated a reaction against the transition. Former communist party bosses still rule in many of the former Soviet republics. Anti-reform forces dominated Russia's 1993 parliamentary elections. Former communist officials have formed democratically elected governments in Eastern Europe and the Baltic states. Public opinion polls throughout the region confirm people's dislike and distrust of market reform. How can transition take place in a democratic setting if it is not supported by the majority of the population?

The burgeoning growth of China has also presented the need for revision. China has reported growth rates in excess of 10 percent for the past several years with key regions reporting even more rapid growth. The world financial press has begun hailing China as the world's next great market and as an economic miracle. China, unlike Russia, remains a repressive political dictatorship under the communist party. The Chinese experience has caused people to ask whether, perhaps, the road to transition is through a strong dictatorship. In Russia and in China, talk is heard of the "iron colonels model"—namely the use of political power to impose change on an unwilling populace.

A third factor also explains why this book is being revised early. The 1990s have been characterized by "emerging markets." These emerging markets, located primarily in Asia and in Latin America, have raised the hope that affluence will not be limited to a small portion of the world's population. The rapid rise in living standards in Korea, Hong Kong, Taiwan, and Singapore appears to be spreading to Malaysia, Indonesia, and even the Philippines. In South America, the economic progress of Mexico and Chile has shown that emerging markets are not limited to Asia. These emerging markets have focused on a basic question of comparative economic systems: What changes in institutions brought about these dramatic transformations in economic performance? Were changes in policy responsible, such as the move to a more open economy? Were changes in institutions responsible, such as privatization?

Whereas Asia and Latin America were bright spots of the early 1990s, Western Europe and the United States both showed signs of wear-and-tear. The United States went into a mild recession from mid-1990 to mid-1991, but the recovery from this recession was prolonged and gradual. The recession ended the Republican Party's hold on the U.S. presidency, and for the first time since 1979, a Democratic president occupied the White House. The Western European economies went into more pronounced recessions in the mid-1990s—recessions exacerbated by structural problems, which became more evident in a recessionary setting. Unemployment rates in Western Europe had been rising since the 1970s; the recession of the mid-1990s pushed unemployment rates even higher. These events caused a reevaluation of Europe's economic institutions such as its more liberal welfare and unemployment systems and its emphasis on worker participation and guaranteed employment. Was Western Europe becoming the "sick man" of the world economy or was it suffering a "temporary cold" associated with the lingering recession?

In writing the fifth edition, our objective has been to examine the field of comparative economic systems in light of the developments outlined above. But, as any instructor of comparative economic systems knows, the subject matter is less well-defined today than it was, say, five years ago. Many would argue that, even in the past, the subject matter of comparative economic systems was not particularly well-defined. As we have emphasized above, the collapse of many of the planned socialist economic systems has lessened interest in the histories and the models that we have used to analyze their economic performance. Moreover, there has been a dramatic shift towards the use of organization theory to analyze what are now a broad spectrum of system variants, many of which are in fact in transition. This latter fact is of profound importance since economic theory is frequently of limited help as we attempt to analyze and to understand change. For the instructor, much of the material is contemporary, with limited theoretical bases and little or no analytical research on outcomes yet unfolding.

To assist the instructor in organizing the subject matter of comparative economic systems, we have sustained the general framework adopted in earlier editions of this book, but have introduced substantial variations within those sections.

In Part I, we begin with a familiar discussion of basic issues—the nature of the field, how systems are classified and analyzed and how we might assess the impact of differing systems on resource allocation. Finally, we discuss systemic change. While much of the material in this section will be familiar, there are two important changes. First, moving beyond the former dichotomies of plan and market, we emphasize the importance of organization theory for understanding economic systems along a continuum of variants. Second, while the earlier literature paid little attention to systemic change, we now must attempt to understand both the major shifts of plan to market and of decision-making arrangements within existing systems, for example, the appeal of privatization in market capitalist economic systems.

In Part II, we turn to the economic theory underlying system variants. While much of this theory seems to pre-date contemporary discussions of systemic change, these latter changes can only be understood and their effectiveness assessed if we have a clear understanding of basic and underlying principles of both market and non-market arrangements for resource allocation. What makes this understanding difficult, however, is our limited but emerging knowledge about systemic change and the resulting plethora of truly mixed systems.

In Part III, we begin a discussion of real world economic systems. Although the order is to some degree arbitrary, we begin with a discussion of the market capitalist economic systems in both developed and less developed countries. We then turn to a discussion of the formerly planned socialist systems focusing on the former Soviet Union as a major example of the administrative-command economy. We conclude this section with a discussion of performance, focusing on the reasons for the decline and ultimate collapse of the Soviet and East European command economies.

In Part IV we turn to a discussion of the essential characteristics of transition (economic systems at the starting block and the basic issues of the speed and sequencing of transition) and microeconomic and macroeconomic forces as well as the myriad of other important influences (the political, cultural, geographic and other factors). Here again, our discussion must be based on a contemporary and yet incomplete literature.

In Part V, we turn to the contemporary cases of transition, focusing on Russia, China, and the major ones of Eastern Europe. Once again, the treatment of these systems is very different from such discussions in the past; for we are judging systems in transition against the relatively new theory of transition, and outcomes against quite traditional performance indicators such as economic growth, consumer well-being and the like.

In Part VI we provide a summary of the contemporary systems experience, as well as some conclusions and projections for the future. This section undoubtedly reiterates much of what has been said at the end of each chapter. However, in this fifth edition, we are very much aware that as we watch the various transition experiences, we are presented with the evidence against which the approaches to transition will in fact be tested. It is important that beyond the individual country experiences treated in earlier chapters, reasonable generalizations be made from the accumulated evidence.

The fifth edition of *Comparative Economic Systems* is a bridge between the past and the present, but it must be much more. It has been structured and presented such that ongoing contemporary developments can be analyzed and interpreted anew to become the core of what will be the field of comparative economic systems in the future.

The reader of this book will quickly become aware of the fundamental changes taking place in the field of comparative economic systems. In light of these changes, our debts are many. In addition to those who assisted with past editions, we owe a debt to contemporary analysts whose work has greatly facilitated the preparation of this new edition.

We want to thank the following reviewers for their helpful suggestions and comments:

Berhanu Abegaz, *College of William and Mary*
Barry S. Clark, *University of Wisconsin–La Crosse*
John Knudsen, *University of Idaho*
Joseph B. Lear, *California Polytechnic State University*
Micke Meurs, *American University*
Michael A. Murphy, *Tufts University*
Ronald Soligo, *Rice University*

Finally, in addition to those who have commented directly on various aspects of this edition, the staff at Houghton Mifflin have provided major support, greatly facilitating the completion of this project at a very difficult time. Special thanks go to project editor, Maria Morelli, to our development editor, Joan Horan, and to our sponsoring editor, Denise Clinton.

P.R.G.
R.C.S.

PART I

Economic Systems: Issues, Definition, Comparisons

1. Economic Systems in an Era of Change
2. Definition and Classification
3. Evaluation of Economic Outcomes
4. Economic Reform: Evolution or Revolution

1

Economic Systems in an Era of Change

Comparative economic systems focuses on identifying and analyzing different economic systems and their impact on the allocation of resources. While comparative economics tends to focus on basic economic issues, comparative economic systems centers on the **economic system** or organizational arrangements. These differing arrangements, it is argued, combine with different economic policies in distinct natural and historical settings to influence resource allocation or the outcomes observed in each country setting. If differing economic systems and/or system components influence resource allocation in differing but identifiable ways, then one can think in terms of an optimal set of organizational arrangements to achieve desired objectives (for example, economic growth or full employment) from the endowment of scarce resources.

The economic system is the set of institutional arrangements used to allocate scarce resources. The limits of productive resources (labor, land, and capital) dictate the scarcity of resources. As a result of scarcity, societies must decide in an orderly way what is produced, how to produce it, and for whom it is produced. If such ordering arrangements are absent, anarchy and chaos will prevail.

Economic systems exist within countries both large and small, developed and less developed. Some countries are rich in human capital; others are rich in natural resources. These differences make it difficult to determine how the economic system will affect economic outcomes. Differences among countries and their endowments cloud the system's impact.

Economic systems are identified or classified according to their basic characteristics, such as ownership (private or nonprivate), information mechanisms (market or plan), levels of decision-making authority and responsibility (centralized or decentralized), and finally incentive arrangements (moral or material). Economic systems are constructed in various ways according to a spectrum of arrangements ranging from decentralized, market-driven, incentive-based "capitalist" systems to centralized, plan-directed "socialist" systems. Although systems change over time, the simple capitalist–socialist dichotomy proved viable as a way to model and to understand differences between the East and the West. The events of the 1980s and 1990s, however, have created so much diversity that the simple models and labels

3

of the past—**capitalism** and **socialism**—are now less relevant in the last decade of the twentieth century.

The New World

If Rip Van Winkle woke up in 1995 after a twenty-year sleep, he would be hard pressed to recognize the world he had last seen. In 1975, at the beginning of his sleep, life was more simple. About one-third of the world's population lived under Soviet-style or Chinese-style socialism dictated by the Communist party leadership. Although these economies were not prospering, they were muddling along without imminent threat of demise. The countries of Eastern Europe were held in the political and economic embrace of the Soviet Union. Although some reform of their Soviet-type economies had occurred, change was modest and often unsuccessful.

The Western world, in 1975, was recovering from energy shocks, recessions, and stagflation. How well they would deal with these issues remained open. The rest of the world, with the exception of Japan, appeared stuck at a low level of economic development. Latin America, South America, Africa, and Asia did not seem to be progressing satisfactorily towards long-term economic growth and development.

Imagine Rip Van Winkle's shock on waking in 1995. The Soviet empire has disintegrated; Germany has reunited; the Communist party no longer exists as a centralized, controlling organization; China has been experiencing phenomenal growth; the "developing markets" of Asia and Latin America are attracting large sums of capital. Even small investors are betting on emerging market funds. Not much has changed with the industrialized countries of Western Europe and North America. They are in or recovering from a recession after experiencing rapid growth in the 1980s. Let us consider these events in more detail.

The Collapse of Communism[1]

The year 1985 marked the starting point for serious change in the communist bloc. In this year, the newly selected general secretary of the Soviet Communist party, Mikhail Gorbachev, announced his intention to initiate "radical" reform of the Soviet political structure, society, and economy. Up until this point, the Soviet Union had been the most important example of a centrally planned socialist economic system that was experiencing serious problems in economic performance but had limited interest in economic reform. Gorbachev's call for radical reform was initially greeted with considerable skepticism. After all, Gorbachev rose through the party ranks and therefore could be expected to cling to past goals and methods. Few observers in 1985 could anticipate that five years later, Mikhail Gorbachev would receive the Nobel Peace Prize for his bold reforms, especially those related to Eastern Europe and the field of foreign policy.

As the Soviet leadership introduced one reform after another, even the most skeptical of observers came to see that real changes were intended. Thus, in spite of some discrepancies between the rhetoric of reform and the reforms actually instituted, the terms *glasnost, democratization,* and *perestroika* entered the Western vocabulary. They describe the radical reforms designed to change the economic and political systems of the Soviet Union and its Eastern European allies. Indeed, the pace of political and social change was rapid. Open criticism of the regime was tolerated; curbs on freedom of speech and of the press were significantly reduced; national and republican parliaments, city councils, and even factory managers were elected. Mass emigration of disaffected Soviet minorities was allowed, foreign travel became easier, religious activities were encouraged, and Marxist–Leninist ideology was disavowed. Most significant from a political and potentially economic perspective, the constitutionally guaranteed "leading role" of the Communist party became the subject of open discussion and debate. Indeed, political dominance of the Soviet Union by the Communist party would end in the summer of 1991.

The international consequences of liberalization in the Soviet Union were far-reaching. The lack of Soviet sympathy for conservative communist regimes in Eastern Europe became apparent. Soviet tanks would no longer be used to prop up unpopular dictatorships. Caught in the pincers of liberal reform in the Soviet Union and the attraction of consumer affluence in Western Europe, former communist dictatorships tumbled one after the other. As neighboring communist regimes granted access through their territories, East German citizens fled to West Germany, threatening to depopulate the former German Democratic Republic. The Berlin Wall was opened in November of 1989 and subsequently dismantled. The émigrés' "voting with their feet" became so pronounced that the unpopular regime of Erich Honecker fell in November of 1989, to be replaced by that of Lothar De Maiziere, the last leader of East Germany before full reunification in 1990.

The overthrow of the East German communist regime was followed by a series of mostly bloodless revolutions in Eastern and central Europe. By the end of 1989, the Communist political structure in Czechoslovakia (the Czech and Slovak Federal Republic) was toppled, as Václav Havel was elected president and Alexander Dubček, speaker of the parliament. Free popular elections held in 1990 sustained the mandate of Havel and his Civic Reform party. In Bulgaria, the Communist leader Todor Zhivkov was replaced in November of 1989. Finally, in the spring and summer of 1990, elections left a majority of communists in the Bulgarian parliament but resulted in the naming of a new president, Zhelyu Zhelev, a non-communist. In Hungary similar events unfolded. In the fall of 1989, agreement was reached on the creation of a multiparty system and on free elections to be held in 1990. In the spring of 1990, after elections were held, the United Democratic Front (a party in opposition to the reconstituted former Communist party) won, and Jozef Antall became prime minister. Events in Poland had generally anticipated those elsewhere. With the rise of Solidarity to political power in the summer of 1989, Tadeusz Mazowiecki became prime minister and General Wojciech Jaruzelski, president. These arrangements, however, were short-lived. In September of 1989, General Jaruzelski announced that he would step down, a move that led to the election of Lech Walesa, who replaced Tadeusz Mazowiecki as the Polish leader. Finally, the despotic dictator of Romania, Nicolae Ceausescu, was executed in a bloody uprising.

By the summer of 1990, elections placed Ion Ilies in the position of president, though unrest continued.

The process of political change in Eastern Europe typically followed a two-step pattern. First, the unpopular totalitarian communist regime was replaced by reform-minded communists, who formed coalition governments with non-communists. In this phase, the Communist party's monopoly on political power was broken. In the second stage, a non-communist coalition government was elected on a platform of closer alliance with the West and the establishment of a market economy. *Economic disarray resulting in popular discontent and the withdrawal of Soviet backing were two major forces that led to these developments.*

Events in China were equally dramatic, but they had quite different results. In the early 1980s, the aging Chinese communist leadership seemed determined to open the country to the West and to reform the Chinese planned economic system. The reintroduction of private incentives in agriculture and the initial influx of foreign investment boosted economic growth and brought about substantial improvements in living standards. However, liberalization quickly spilled over into political and social life. When, in the spring of 1989, opposition groups began to demand fundamental changes—an end to the Communist party monopoly, free speech, and democratic elections—the Communist regime decided to crack down on the reform movement. This decision culminated in the May 1989 Tiananmen Square massacre, the arrest of leading dissidents, and the introduction of sanctions by Western governments against the Chinese regime.

The Chinese retreat to political conservatism was in stark contrast to developments in the Soviet Union and Eastern Europe. Although the process of effecting economic reform in the Soviet Union has proved difficult, in Eastern Europe there was general acceptance of the long-term goals of reform: establishment of a market economy, multiparty elections, and free speech. In China there was instead a marked retrenchment in favor of traditional communist ideals: a slowing of economic reform and a return to dogmatic one-party rule.

By the start of the 1990s, conservative communist regimes were found only in China, Cuba, and Albania. And in 1990, the Albanian president Ramiz Alia responded to demonstrations with some concessions. Even Vietnam took preliminary steps toward reform and reconciliation with its archenemies in the West, resulting in the restoration of diplomatic relations in mid-1994.

In the 1990s, sober reality replaced the euphoria of the late 1980s. The leaders of once administratively planned economies realized that the transition to a market economy was not painless and, moreover, that blueprints were not established. Severe production declines replaced the stagnating growth of the 1980s; inflation at times accelerated to hyperinflation rates as prices were freed and budget deficits soared. The freeing of prices redistributed incomes from state employees and pensioners to entrepreneurs and black marketeers.

Lagging political support for reform compounded these difficulties. The people had only seen the negative side of transition; they had yet to see the positive consequences. Consequently, in some cases, former communist officials, promising order, returned to power. Elsewhere, political stalemates between conservative and reformist forces were created. Promising signs appeared in the Baltic States, which achieved balanced budgets and created stable currencies; Poland as well reduced inflation to reasonable levels and halted the production decline. In the meantime, China continued to boom under communist rule but with significant economic change.

The Industrialized West

Although change was less dramatic in the industrialized West, change did occur in the 1980s. With few exceptions, the 1980s witnessed voter repudiation of the more extreme forms of social democracy. The 1980s were dominated by Reaganism in the United States and by Thatcherism in England—both movements designed, at least in theory, to replace the ills of "big government" with the benefits of the market. In Germany, the conservative Christian Democratic party strengthened its hold over German politics at the expense of the waning Social Democratic and Environmentalist (Green) parties. Western conservatism put into motion policies designed to reduce the role of government in the economy and to shift existing government functions from federal to state and local levels. Tax reductions were used to improve incentives, welfare programs were cut, and privatization was encouraged in Great Britain, Germany, and France. Even Sweden, long a symbol of welfare statism, experienced a voter backlash against excessive social expenditures and high tax rates.

The conservative economic policies that characterized the industrialized West spread into Latin America, Africa, and Asia in the 1980s. In Latin America, programs were initiated to reestablish private enterprise, and experiments with planned socialism were largely aborted. In Asia, the remarkable rise of the "Four Tigers" (Singapore, South Korea, Taiwan, and Hong Kong) demonstrated that formerly poor Asian countries could industrialize rapidly and compete in world manufacturing markets by employing laissez-faire economic policies. The strong economic performance of the Four Tigers contrasted sharply with the continued stagnation of India and Pakistan, countries that continued to pursue economic policies of state interventionism and protection.

The 1980s also revealed the limits to conservative economic policies. United States political experience clearly showed public unwillingness to alter fundamentally the social security system put in place in the 1930s. Moreover, U.S. voters refused to accept pro-growth tax reforms that appeared to benefit the wealthy. And the British experience under Thatcher revealed a general unwillingness to abandon the national health service or to support growth-oriented tax reform that appeared to favor upper-income groups.

The 1980s saw a strong expansion of economic internationalism and an expanding role for multinational corporations. The West European governments agreed to a united European economy to become effective in 1992. The United States, Canada, and Mexico agreed to establish a barrier-free North American market (NAFTA). This decisive move toward economic integration has raised the issue of multinationalism versus national sovereignty—a divisive issue that must be resolved in the 1990s. Multinationalism threatens national identity and weakens sovereign control over economic destiny. How much autonomy should supranational European economic organizations enjoy? Should a European central bank be granted the authority to administer a common monetary policy and to issue a common European currency?

The highly publicized political movement toward economic multinationalism has been accompanied by a deeper and more gradual trend: the increased integration of the world economies. The major industrial firms of the West are no longer constrained by national boundaries. In fact, they are no longer national companies; rather, they have become multinational corporations. The IBMs, Siemens, and Sonys of the world are now equally at home in New York, Mexico City, Montreal, London, and Singapore. An oil venture in Indonesia may be carried out by a consortium of British Petroleum, Royal Dutch Shell, and Exxon and may be financed by funds from the Bank of Tokyo and the Deutsche Bank. A slight change in U.S. interest rates can cause billions of dollars to flow from Hong Kong, Zurich, and Toronto to New York. Transactions between Venezuela and Austria are conducted in U.S. dollars.

The 1990s have held fewer surprises for the industrialized West. The major change has been the shattering of the myth of Japanese invincibility. Japan's growth rates have tapered off, and Japan has been bogged down by a recession in the 1990s. Although Japan's trade performance has remained strong, doubt has begun to grow about the wisdom of Japan's touted industrial policy and its policy of lifetime employment.

The recession of the early 1990s, which hit Western Europe, raised Europe's already high unemployment rates. Basically Europe's hard times forced it to consider a restructuring of social welfare policies and policies to reestablish its competitive position in world markets.

The 1990s thus far have witnessed a move away from economic integration. Europe's attempts to create a common currency, with its European Monetary System of fixed internal exchange rates, fell apart in 1993.

The Third World

Comparative economic systems and economic development share some common ground, although the former overlaps the latter only when both low levels of economic development and differences between systems are encountered in the same case, as presently, for example, in China. When we examine China, our interest focuses primarily on the nature of the system and its influence on resource allocation; we are less concerned with development issues and the well-being of the population per se. After all, even in its most rigid forms, socialism has never been presented as an engine of economic progress for less developed countries (LDCs).

One of the most striking features of the world economy of the 1990s is that prosperity remains limited to a small proportion of the world's population. More than three-quarters of the world's population continues to live in poverty. The average citizen of Asia, Africa, and Latin America remains largely untouched by the industrial–technological revolutions that have created enormous affluence in North America, Western Europe, Australia, and parts of Asia. The twentieth century offers only a few examples of countries that have made the transition from relative poverty to relative affluence: Japan in the 1950s and Hong Kong, Singapore, South Korea, and Taiwan in the 1980s.

The challenge of the 1990s is to create—through aid, technical assistance, trade and enlightened government policy—conditions that will enable more countries to make the transition from relative poverty to relative affluence.

The basic questions for the 1990s are, will economic development continue to spread so that newcomers to affluence can enjoy higher living standards? Can such countries as Mexico, Chile, Thailand, and Indonesia join the elite group of affluent countries?

Economic Systems in a New Era

The dramatic events of the 1980s and 1990s—the end of the cold war, German reunification, the fall of communist political systems in Eastern Europe, and the dissolution of the Soviet Union—surprised most observers. These changes, unimaginable a few years earlier, raised new and challenging issues.

First, it had been commonly thought that the planned socialist economic systems would undergo slow, regime-directed reform designed to make the system work more effectively, rather than to replace it. Any change would involve using elements of the market system to improve the existing system. Although the outcome is still unknown, recent events have shown that system change can be so radical as to move from one economic system to another.

Second, if recent systemic change seems dramatic cast against past expectations, then the context of change has become ever more important, opening up new and complicated avenues of exploration. For example, while both the Ukraine and Poland are pursuing a transition from plan to market, their circumstances differ dramatically, a fact that will significantly impact transition. Many forces beyond the economic system (such as historical development patterns, foreign trade exposure, and cultural identities) affect the nature and outcome of transition—economic systems and system components are not neutral to the setting in which they arise.

Economists prefer to study general principles rather than become historical, sociological, or political experts on each country. If a country's "preconditions" affect the pattern and pace of transition, we must learn to deal with the "special circumstances" of each transition and perhaps to avoid generalized formulas.

Third, comparative economic systems, as traditionally studied, may be too narrow. Combining economic history, growth models, and comparative economics may be necessary to understand system change. For example, China is a large, relatively poorly planned socialist economy attempting to introduce market forces. Does understanding the Chinese experience thus require a look at comparative economic systems or the study of theories of economic development and growth? The messages may not differ dramatically, and yet being explicit about the approaches is useful if we are to take comfort in our projections.

Despite the importance of understanding starting points or initial conditions that may have a strong noneconomic content, remember that comparative economic systems is a branch of economics. It must therefore combine all those branches of economics that speak to the issues of economic systems: how they perform, where they come from, and which system performs the best.

The Economic Approach to Systemic Change

In the past, the purely economic content of economic systems was limited. After all, an economic system is a set of organizational arrangements, and such arrangements are studied in organization theory and behavior, largely of interest in business schools. Economists viewed the behavior of the firm usually as a black box in pursuit of profit. Of lesser importance was the internal organization of the firm, for example, whether it was centralized or decentralized. Although some economists had emphasized that different economic systems handle information differently, their ability to apply this insight productively to economic systems was limited.

Economists, for more than a century, assumed the task of analyzing how economies work in a setting of stable institutional arrangements. What happens, for example, if the money supply increases or if relative prices change? Only recently have economists become interested in the origins and evolution of the institutions themselves and have begun asking how property rights and constitutional law affect economic outcomes.

The number of economic subdisciplines that are now relevant to comparative economic systems has expanded, and this expansion has enriched but complicated the field. Instead of labels to describe different economic systems, it is more appropriate to look at the system and its components directly. In most societies (countries), people pursue objectives through the use of organizations. Economic systems, then, are organizations that can be analyzed and understood through organization theory, information economics, and contemporary microeconomic theory. Organizations have structure and guidance systems, both of which can differ in varying degrees. Figure 1.1 provides a schematic picture of traditional and modern approaches to differing economic systems.

The modern approach emphasizes the multidimensionality and the infinite gradations of economic systems rather than trying to sort them into several categories. The characteristics of an economic system are important, not the labels used. One economy may have more private ownership than another, but the other may have more government intervention in economic decision-making. One economy may allow worker participation in corporate decision-making, while another economy may allow government bodies to regulate prices. One economy may try to guide its long-term development by government industrial policy, and yet another may rely exclusively on private-enterprise decision-making.

FIGURE 1.1   The Spectrum of Economic Systems

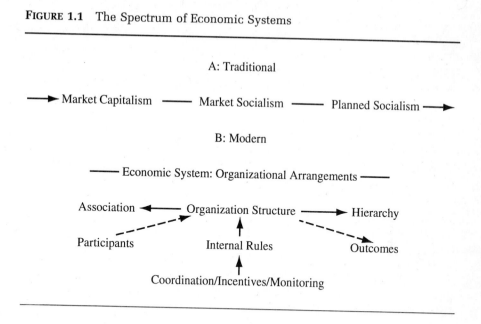

The Choice of Economic Systems

Recent history shows that we do have a choice of economic systems. The former Soviet Union and the countries of Eastern Europe are actively searching for their economic systems. The answers they will find are still unknown. The industrialized West has operated with fairly stable economic systems for decades if not centuries, but even these societies must make continuous and often subtle choices concerning the shape of their economic systems. The emerging worlds of Asia and Latin America must make crucial choices concerning the economic systems that will bring them to an appropriate level of affluence.

If choosing the economic system were not possible, the study of comparative economic systems would be less compelling. Insofar as people, through the ballot box and through their private and public lives, make choices that affect the economic system, it is important to stay informed about the strengths and weaknesses of alternate economic systems.

The first full-fledged experiment with economic systems began in the Soviet Union in the late 1920s, a decade after the October revolution of 1917. After World War II, the Soviet experiment expanded into Eastern Europe, China, North Korea, Cuba, and North Vietnam. At its peak, about one-third of the world's population lived in countries generally described as socialist economic systems dominated by Marxist–Leninist orthodoxy and communist political systems.

The spread of Soviet-style communism stimulated a debate about which economic system is "better." Viewed with hindsight, the answer to this question appears obvious. But the question of relative superiority has not always been easy to answer.

In the 1930s, the contrast between the depression-ridden West and the industrializing Soviet Union cast real doubt on the superiority of capitalism. At this time, the weaknesses of the capitalist system were all too evident, whereas the flaws of the Soviet system were hidden behind a veil of official secrecy and claims of extraordinary successes. The immediate postwar period of the 1950s saw the remarkable economic successes of West Germany and Japan, but the slow growth of the United States and Great Britain caused some to question the vitality of the capitalist system. In contrast, a confident Soviet Union launched the first piloted space vehicle and declared its intention to "bury" the West. Few will forget the flamboyant performances of then Soviet leader Nikita Khrushchev as he boasted about Soviet economic performance. Yet even Khrushchev warned the Soviet people that in the face of the Soviet ability to build basic industrial capacity, the system might well have "steel blinders" and might lack the ability to adjust and to diversify. The era of Leonid Brezhnev revealed to what degree the Soviet economy was, in fact, unable to adjust to change.

The gap between the economic performance of East and West became more pronounced in the 1980s. The West experienced a sustained recovery from the oil shocks of the 1970s and began its longest uninterrupted business expansion in 1981. The East, on the other hand, continued its secular decline. In the Soviet Union, this decline came to be called the "period of stagnation." Promises that things would be better in the future lost their meaning to people who had made considerable sacrifices from the 1930s through World War II, and even thereafter, in spite of the "thaw" of the Khrushchev years.

Even more troubling, was the lack of growth in productivity. In the face of limits to the growth of inputs, the call for greater reliance on "hidden reserves" proved fruitless. The search for greater efficiency became paramount.

The contrast between the economic growth and consumer affluence of the West and the secular stagnation and consumer poverty of the East set into motion the "radical" reform process that installed non-communist regimes in much of Eastern Europe. News publications in both East and West declared the final victory of capitalism over socialism and proclaimed Marxist–Leninist thought an historical dead end.

The Soviet experiment may be dead, but its appeal could be resurrected. If an appropriate path to transition cannot be found and the end result is chaos, enthusiasm for the old system could be revived. Some could claim that although it did not work well, it did work.

Summary

Comparative economic systems is a subfield of economics concerned with how differences in economic systems influence resource allocation. The **economic system** is the set of organizational arrangements that, along with differences in national economic policies and natural settings, influence the outcomes of economic activity. Economists interested in different economic systems attempt to define the nature of the system and system differences and to isolate their impact on resource allocation. The traditional "isms" of **capitalism, socialism**, and **communism** have been the defining characteristics in the field of comparative economic systems for many years. Recent events have, however, shifted concern away from the polar opposites of capitalism and communism toward an understanding of a broader spectrum of (mixed) organizational variants. These variants are defined in terms of the key features of the structure and functioning of organizations—specifically the **owner-ship** arrangements (private, public, or mixed), **information mechanisms** used within organizations (market, plan, or mix), levels of decision-making (**centralized, decentralized**, or mixed), and finally incentive arrangements designed to motivate system participants (**monetary, moral**, or mixed).

Economic systems arise in real-world (country) settings and can be changed and modified over time. Possibly the most important difference among various economic systems today (as opposed to, say, twenty years ago) is precisely the issue of change. An analyst of different economic systems studying the 1970s, for example, would have found useful the basic models of market capitalism and centrally planned socialism. The Soviet Union and the United States were often compared using such models, and although there were important variants of both polar models, nevertheless differences were often viewed as modest (the basic model of planned socialism was useful for understanding the Soviet Union, Hungary, or Cuba), and systemic change or "**reform**" was viewed as limited (the plan as a dominant alloca-tion mechanism remained, and planned economies did not shift to market arrange-ments). Thus the Soviet planned economy of the 1950s was viewed as pretty much the same as that of the 1970s. Market economic systems were often compared using a similar and generally limited framework of analysis.

The late 1980s and the 1990s thus far have witnessed changes of major histori-cal importance. Communism as a controlling political mechanism largely collapsed, and the planned socialist economic systems in the Soviet Union and Eastern Europe have been gradually replaced with market arrangements through the process termed **transition**. These changes, while dramatic in their own right, have led to a reassess-ment within the field of comparative economic systems. The two most important features of the new era are, first, the view that economic systems as organizations can be fully and appropriately characterized by the language and methods of organi-zation theory. Thus, rather than emphasizing polar extremes, we must consider that different systems can occupy a broad spectrum of arrangements that can be under-stood by examining the nature of the organization itself and the internal arrange-ments or rules used to coordinate and direct activity within the organization or system.

Second, while systemic change has traditionally been viewed as modest and often characterized within the mold of ideology (for example, the shift from capi-talism to socialism along an ideological spectrum of systems), contemporary systems analysts understand that change can be rapid (for example, the transition in Poland), and that, in theory, a wide spectrum of alternative arrangements for resource allo-cation is possible, implying a plethora of mixed systems, some of which arise as predominately market systems based on the formerly planned economies.

As differing economic systems in the 1990s are studied, more tools will be brought to bear on a greater variety of system alternatives. Yet the basic difficulties of comparison and analysis remain as we begin to assemble the evidence necessary to analyze the economic systems of a new and very different era.

Key Terms

economic system
capitalism
socialism
communism
ownership

information mechanisms
centralized
decentralized
monetary incentives
moral incentives

economic policies
reform
transition

Notes

1. The concept of communism as used here refers to the former political systems of the Soviet Union and Eastern Europe, while the economies of these former communist states were generally characterized as planned socialist economic systems.

Recommended Readings

Gale Stokes, *The Walls Came Tumbling Down: The Collapse of Communism in Eastern Europe* (New York: Oxford University Press, 1993).
Robert C. Stuart and Paul R. Gregory, *The Russian Economy: Past, Present, and Future* (New York: HarperCollins, 1995).

2

Definition and Classification

Comparative economic systems has always been more difficult to characterize than other fields of economics. Indeed it has been described as "a field in search of a definition."[1]

The field of comparative economic systems studies economic outcomes in different settings. The **economic system**, along with the conventional inputs of land, labor, and capital, is assumed to matter in observable and understandable ways. Beyond differing economic systems and the traditional inputs, however, economic outcomes are also influenced by social, economic, cultural, geographic, and random forces. The analyst of differing economic systems must develop methods to understand and to control (hold constant) all of the relevant variables in order to isolate and understand the influence of the economic systems.[2]

Relating the economic system and other inputs to the observed economic outcomes is a formidable task, and yet there are important cases where measurement is possible. Consider, for example, the importance of the level of economic development. The level of economic development can be measured, albeit imperfectly, by per capita gross domestic product and other such aggregates. We are aware of systematic and known relationships between, for example, shares of industry and agriculture in national product and the level of economic development, a feasible if imperfect way to control for differences in such factors. But what about the **nontraditional inputs**? One could argue that social, cultural, and historical forces are of even greater importance, and yet they are difficult to quantify and to relate to the development experience in a systematic fashion.[3]

Economic Systems: Definition

People generally seem to know what an economic system is, yet there is little agreement on a real-world definition that permits the isolation of the system as an input and thus the identification of its impact on observed outcomes. Traditionally, systems have been classified using an ideological spectrum from which the "isms" emerge—feudalism, capitalism, socialism, and communism. This classification identifies a

15

system by one or two important characteristics, such as ownership of the means of production.

The modern approach to classifying economic systems considers a system as a form of **organization**. Thus these systems can be understood by broadly defining the tools of organization theory, such as the nature of information mechanisms, behavior rules, decision-making arrangements, and property rights. While pure system types may be useful for this analysis, in the real world, organizational arrangement vary broadly. In the language of the "isms" it is therefore less likely to find pure capitalism or pure socialism than mixed systems with a variety of component characteristics.

This book's description and analysis relies on a mix of the traditional and modern approaches. First, it is difficult in a field undergoing rapid change to rely exclusively on a set of definitions and technical characteristics for describing different systems. Second, neglecting the lasting appeal of the capitalism–socialism dichotomy is also difficult.

> Capitalism, communism, socialism, and kindred terms, whatever system traits they may in actuality represent, have a life of their own. They live as symbols or clusters of symbols in the minds of participants in all modern systems . . . , and they may have a profound influence on the way actual systems change or on the reasons why they fail to change.[4]

A compromise to these problems is a definition proposed by Assar Lindbeck, one that while general in nature, emphasizes the multidimensional aspect of an economic system.[5]

An **economic system** is a set of mechanisms and institutions for decision making and for the implementation of decisions concerning production, income, and consumption within a given geographic area.

Broadly speaking, the economic system consists of mechanisms, organizational arrangements, and decision-making rules. An economic system can vary in any of its dimensions, particularly in its structure, its operation, and its adaptability to change through time. It "includes all those institutions, organizations, laws and rules, traditions, beliefs, attitudes, values, taboos, and the resulting behavior patterns that directly or indirectly affect economic behavior and outcomes."[6]

Economic systems are **multidimensional**, a feature that can be formalized in the following manner:

$$ES = f(A_1, A_2, \ldots, A_n) \tag{2.1}$$

As equation 2.1 indicates, an economic system (ES) is defined by its attributes (A_i) or characteristics, where there are n such attributes. An economic system cannot be defined fully in terms of a single characteristic such as property ownership; rather, the full set of characteristics must be known before ES is specified. We shall focus on four general attributes ($n = 4$) that are critical in differentiating economic systems:

1. Organization of decision-making arrangements: structure
2. Mechanisms for the provision of information and for coordination: market and plan
3. Property rights: control and income
4. Mechanisms for setting goals and for inducing people to act: incentives

These four characteristics have been chosen because economic systems differ within them. They have also been chosen because they affect economic outcomes. We do not list features that are relatively uniform across systems—for example, the organization of production in factory units.

Characteristics of Economic Systems

We shall now examine each of the four characteristics and explain why economic outcomes differ with respect to them. Initially, the characteristics appear to have little in common with characterizations of economic systems as capitalist or social-ist. However, later this chapter brings them together to formulate working definitions of capitalism and socialism based on the nature of organizational arrangements. This combines the contemporary and traditional approaches to understanding different economic systems.

The Organization of Decision-Making Arrangements

Nobel laureate Herbert Simon writes that "organization refers to the complex pattern of communications and other relations in a group of human beings."[7] According to J. M. Montias, "an organization consists of a set of participants (members) regularly interacting in the process of carrying on one or more activities. . . ."[8] The organi-zation must be allowed to have some turnover in its membership and must be able to change the activities it pursues. It is generally accepted that organized behavior has certain advantages over unorganized behavior. In an organization, goals exist, information is created, and assumptions and attitudes are formed, all of which play a part in the making of decisions.

In the language of organization theory, individuals participate in organized behavior, pursuing **self-interest** constrained by **bounded rationality**.[9] Self-interest may be construed as the maximization of some utility function constrained by a broad range of human limitations, such as the ability to generate, process, and utilize information. These characteristics of system participants lead to two major classes of organizational problems. The first, **technical–administrative problems**, derive from individuals who are limited in their ability to make decisions because of, for example, incomplete information. The second, **agency–managerial problems**, derive from individuals who, while pursuing self-interest, may pursue objectives differing from those established for the organization.

To handle these problems, an organization must establish a set of rules. These rules are concerned with setting up subgroups within the organization, assigning tasks, coordinating activities, monitoring activities, and describing the nature of incentive arrangements. These rules, along with such external factors as cultural and historical influences, largely determine the nature of the organization and lead to basic and important distinctions among economic systems.

The rules within an organization determine how the activities of the organization are carried out. The two extremes of organizational structure resulting from different rules are **hierarchy** and **association**. In an organization based on hierarchy, superiors (**principals**) establish objectives and issue orders to subordinates (**agents**) who are supposed to carry out assigned tasks leading to the achievement of organizational objectives.

In an association-based organization, decision making occurs among individuals where there is no superior–subordinate relationship but rather equality among the individuals.

Organizations typically exhibit a hierarchy to some degree, although within this form of organization there can be substantial differences in, for example, the number of levels in the hierarchy, the allocation of tasks among these levels, and the span of control or the number of subordinates directed by a superior. Armen Alchian and Harold Demsetz[10] suggest one reason that hierarchy exists. Technology requires members of the organization (say, a firm) to work together in "team production." Because the team effort produces output, it is difficult to assess each individual's contribution. Such a setting may cause some to slacken work effort unless a superior monitors work and relates rewards to this effort.

There are other reasons for hierarchy in organizations.[11] Some individuals are risk takers, while others avoid risk. Employees agree to work for an owner and to obey the owner's instructions. The owner reaps the rewards of profits if the business succeeds, but risks the losses if the business fails. Production is often carried out in a hierarchical setting because management problems are at times too complicated to organize production through markets.

The coordination of decision-making activities in markets has costs. The participants in market-coordinated activities must develop appropriate contracts based on market-generated information and must bear the legal and financial consequences of unfulfilled contracts. Business firms can limit the costs of market coordination. Consider, for example, the task of building a jet aircraft. Managerial coordination can reduce transaction costs and negotiations and can enforce a myriad of contracts through directing employees to fulfill required tasks limiting the need for subcontractors.

Thus far organizations have been treated in a general way, typically as business enterprises. Although economic systems are organizations, they are vastly more complex than a firm. Similar organizational characteristics, however, can be found across economic systems in differing countries.

An organization or economic system can be characterized by the levels at which resource-allocation decisions are made and executed. In a **decentralized** organization, decisions are made primarily at low levels of the organization, while a **centralized** organization implies that decisions are made at high levels.

Such characterizations are in fact simplistic, though as a practical matter, levels of decision making are important for assessing how organizations achieve objectives.

In most cases, decision-making levels are assessed in terms of the organization's structure, the manner in which the organization generates and utilizes information, and finally, the way in which it allocates authority and responsibility for decision making among the levels of the organization.[12]

In most organizations, a superior–subordinate (or principal–agent) relationship implies that agents are organized as groups, subunits, or smaller organizations. For example, as enterprise may be a branch of a larger company that is itself owned by a conglomerate. A government enterprise may be subordinated to a government department that in turn is subordinated to a ministry.[13]

Organizations enter into contractual relationships in which they can act either as a principal or as an agent. A **principal** is a party that has controlling authority and that engages an agent to act subject to the principal's control and instruction. An **agent** is a party that acts for, on behalf of, or as a representative of a principal.

Firm X is a principal when it enters into a contract with Firm Y. The contract requires that Firm Y (the agent) supply Firm X with specified amounts of a product at specified prices over a specified period of time. Firm X is also a principal when it signs a contract with an employee (the agent) that calls for the employee to perform specific services at a specified wage for a specified period of time. Once an agency relationship is established, the principal is responsible for monitoring performance to ensure that the agent is providing the services specified in the agreement. When both the principal and the agent are motivated toward the same goal, or when the performance of the agent can be easily monitored, conflicts between the principal and the agent are unlikely to arise. However, when the parties have different goals and when monitoring is difficult, conflicts between principal and agent are expected.

The physical allocation of resources takes place in the enterprise, yet the decisions that determine resource allocation may be made either at the enterprise level or above. The resource-allocation decision could be made at the lowest level (at the enterprise), at an intermediate level (the company or the branch department), or at a high level (the conglomerate corporation or the ministry).

Two factors determine the level of the resource-allocation decisions: the way **authority** is distributed within the hierarchy and how the hierarchy utilizes **information**.

In a perfectly centralized economy, the authority to make decisions rests in a single central command that issues orders to lower units in the organization. The perfectly decentralized case would be a structure where all decision-making authority rests with the lowest subunits (households and individual firms), independent of superior authorities. In the real world, authority is typically spread through various levels in the hierarchy.

The level of decision making depends on the handling of information. Perfect centralization of information means that a single decision maker possesses all information about all participants, their actions, and their environment. Decentralization means that decision makers possess less than complete information. An "informationally decentralized" system generates, processes, and utilizes information at the lowest level in the organization without exchanging information with higher levels in the organization. In a decentralized system, information on prices is exchanged only among the lowest units. Conversely, an "informationally centralized" system involves the generation, processing, and utilization of information by superior agencies and the subsequent transmission of only limited pieces of information to lower subunits.

Perfect centralization of information is not possible because of the mass of information on prices, locations, outputs, and technologies. Economic systems and their constituent organizations must have some degree of information decentralization. In fact, lower level units have an information advantage over their local circumstances compared with higher level organizations. Information advantages offer agents the opportunity to engage in **opportunistic behavior** relative to their principals. Opportunistic behavior means that the lower level unit can use its information advantage against the interests of its superiors.

Opportunistic behavior of this type can take two forms: moral hazard or adverse selection.[14] **Moral hazard** occurs when the lower level unit exploits an information advantage to alter its behavior after entering into a contract with the upper level unit. For example, a buyer may promise a supplier steady purchases at fixed prices if that supplier acquires specialized equipment suited only to that buyer's product. After the equipment has been installed, the buyer, as the sole buyer of that product, reduces its purchases or price. **Adverse selection** occurs when agents conceal information from the principals, making it impossible for their superiors to distinguish among them. For example, all enterprises may claim that they cannot adopt a new technology proposed by the ministry. Some can and others cannot, but those that can conceal this fact from the ministry. The ministry therefore may be forced into inefficient decision making, such as requiring all firms to adopt the technology.

Information disadvantages require careful consideration of incentive systems to limit the effects of moral hazard and adverse selection.

Identifying levels of decision making from organization charts can be misleading. Figure 2.1 shows why. In column A, there are three levels in the hierarchy. In column B, there are two—resulting, say, from eliminating the intermediate level or from combining the lower and intermediate levels. At first glance, the change from A to B appears to be a move toward the centralization of decision making. The removal of the intermediate organization seems to concentrate decision-making authority at the center. But elimination of the intermediate organization *might* cause authority to devolve to the subunits.

Market and Plan

The **market** and the **plan** are the two major mechanisms for providing information and for coordinating decisions in economic systems. It is common to identify centralization with plan and decentralization with market, but there is no simple relationship between the level of decision making and the use of market or plan as a coordinating mechanism. In market economies, it is possible to combine a considerable concentration of decision-making authority and information in a few large corporations with substantial state involvement, and yet to have no system

FIGURE 2.1   Levels of Decision Making in an Economic System

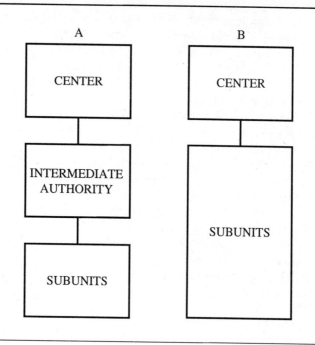

of planning as such.[15] On the other hand, economies that are characterized as planned can vary substantially: Witness the centralized planning of the former Soviet Union, the "indicative" planning system of France, and the combination of plan and market that exists in other countries. To identify an economy as planned does not necessarily reveal the prevalent coordinating mechanism or, for that matter, the degree of centralization in decision making. Both depend on the *type* of planning mechanism.

A **planned economy** is one wherein subunits are coordinated by specific instructions or directives formulated by a superior agency (a planning board) and disseminated through a plan document (sometimes termed directive planning). The participants are induced to carry out the directives via appropriate incentives or threats, which are designed by the planning authorities. The specifics differ from one case to another. The basic point, however, is that in a planned economy, economic activity is guided by instructions or directives devised by higher units and subsequently transmitted to lower units. Rewards depend on the achievement of plan directives. A planned economy and a **market economy** are mutually exclusive: in the former, resources are allocated in accordance with the instructions of planners, who thereby usurp the role of the market as an allocator of resources.

In the case of a market economy, the market—through the forces of supply and demand—provides signals that trigger organizations to make decisions on resource utilization. The market thereby coordinates the activities of decision-making units. Households earn income by providing land, labor, and capital, and with this income they buy the goods that firms supply. Firms and households respond to the market. Other mechanisms for information or coordination are not necessary, and decision-making authority is vested at the lowest level of the economic system.

In **indicative planning**, the market serves as the principal instrument for resource allocation, but a plan is prepared to guide decision making. An indicative plan is one in which planners seek to project aggregate or sectoral trends and to provide information beyond that normally supplied by the market. An indicative plan is *not* broken down into directives or instructions for individual production units; enterprises are free to apply the information in the indicative plan as they see fit, though indirect means are often used to influence economic activity.

The ultimate decision makers are different in planned and market economies. In a market economy, the consumer can "vote" in the marketplace and exercise **consumer sovereignty**. If consumer sovereignty prevails, then the basic decision of what to produce is dominated by consumers in the marketplace. In a planned economy, on the other hand, decisions are made by the planners, and hence **planners' preferences** prevail. Where planners' preferences dominate, the basic decision of what to produce is made by planners.

In a planned economy, planners must base their instructions to production units on some social preference function (that is, some known ordering of society's desires). For political reasons or to promote incentives, however, planners may well have to take into account consumers' preferences. It is difficult to envision a pure planners' preference system, where the wishes of the consumer are totally disregarded.

Neither would one expect pure consumer sovereignty to prevail in a market economy. In market economies, governments can exercise considerable influence over what goods and services are produced. Furthermore, factors such as public goods, externalities, and the market power of large concentrated firms abridge the consumer's ability to dictate resource allocation.

Property Rights: Control and Income

"*Ownership* refers to an amalgam of rights that individuals may have over objects or claims on objects or services" and that "these rights may affect an object's disposition or its utilization."[16] Ownership rights may be divided into three broad types. First is the *disposition* of the object in question—the transfer of ownership rights to others, as in the selling of a privately owned automobile. Second, ownership may include the right to *utilization*, whereby the owner can use the object in question in a manner deemed appropriate. Third, ownership implies the **right to use the products and/or services** generated by the object in question.

Ownership rights may be temporary or permanent, and they may well rest with different individuals at any time. The individual who rents an automobile has the right to the *utilization* of that automobile, but not to its *disposition*. The owners of a private firm have a claim over the profits of the firm, even though the operation may be significantly circumscribed by government rules and regulations. De jure ownership rights may differ significantly from de facto rights. For example, although members of Soviet collective farms (*kolkhoz*) "owned" the assets of the farm, departing members could not sell their share of these assets.

There are three broad forms of property ownership—**private**, **public**, and **collective** (cooperative). Under private ownership, each of the three ownership rights ultimately belongs to individuals, whereas under public ownership, these rights belong to the state.

Differences in ownership rights affect economic outcomes. Consider an economic system in which all three ownership rights belong to individuals. As the owners seek to maximize their lifetime incomes, capital will be disbursed so as to yield the highest rate of return commensurate with the risk involved. If capital is owned by the state, the rules of capital allocation may be different. Greater attention may be paid to long-term social rates of return. Moreover, time preferences may differ according to whether individuals or the state owns the capital. The distribution of income will differ according to state or private ownership: Property income will accrue to private owners in the one case, to the state in the other. Finally, because the allocation of capital ultimately determines the direction of economic activity, the ownership of capital will determine whether allocation is done by private individuals or by the state.

Clearly, ownership arrangements are important in the classification of economic systems. As previously noted, in the traditional classification in terms of the "isms," ownership arrangements are a distinguishing characteristic among the different systemic arrangements. Moreover, in the Marxian schema, changes in ownership of the means of production signalled changes in the economic system. Additionally, unlike differing levels of decision making in an organization, it is possible to identify and to measure differences in property ownership arrangements among different groups in a society.

In the contemporary era, it is widely argued that if markets replace plans as decision-making frameworks, then private ownership must be the basis of market allocation mechanisms. The nature of ownership and its influence on resource allocation is a complex subject. Indeed, in terms of the broad ownership arrangements we have identified, most economic systems are, in fact, mixed systems. Even in economic systems that may be classified as market or capitalist systems, not only are there major differences in the nature of private ownership, but also major segments of the economy are likely dominated by what has been broadly termed as public ownership, where traditional ownership rights are much less well established. We know much more about decision making in the private sector.[17] The nature of decision making and its impact on resource allocation in a state enterprise or a state bureaucracy is much less well understood in both theory and practice. An economic system must organize both private and public decisions. Ultimately, identifying the nature of differing mixes of decision-making arrangements, especially the effect these differences have on resource allocation, is a major challenge for the field of comparative economic systems.

Incentives

An economic system can also be characterized in terms of the incentives that motivate people. "Goals and incentives are . . . vital links in understanding the transformation of property rights and informational inputs into effective actions."[18]

An incentive mechanism should induce participants at lower levels to fulfill the
directives of participants at higher levels. An effective mechanism must fulfill three
conditions.[19] First, the person who is to receive the reward must be able to influence
the outcomes for which the reward will be given. Second, the superior (principal)
must be able to check on the subordinate (agent) to see whether tasks have been
executed properly. Third, the potential rewards must matter to the agent.

In a hierarchy in which superiors issue binding directives to their subordinates,
incentives would not be necessary if the principal had perfect information. Armed
with perfect information, the principal would automatically know whether the agent
was carrying out designated tasks properly. In complex organizations, however,
principals typically lack such perfect information. The subordinate knows much
more about local circumstances than the superior, and the superior cannot issue
perfectly detailed instructions to the subordinate. Because of the imperfect information of the principal, the agent gains local decision-making authority in a number
of realms. The principal needs to devise an incentive system that will induce the
agent to act in the interests of the superior when the subordinate makes such local
decisions. If the principal's incentive system is flawed, the agent will not act in the
interest of the superior.

The information disadvantage of superior organizations relative to their agents
affects the way the system is organized. If it is not possible to devise incentive systems that cause agents spontaneously to work in the interests of superior organizations, a more centralized solution may be required. If incentive systems do not elicit
information (such as from Soviet-type enterprises on their technical possibilities),
the superior organization may impose decisions on the subordinate organization
without even consulting them. If private insurance companies cannot elicit in a cost-
effective way information on disabilities or on driving habits, government agencies,
rather than private markets, may have to provide disability or automobile insurance.
Information disadvantages explain why governments instead of private markets
handle unemployment and poverty insurance.

The superior can devise and use either material or moral incentives to motivate
the subordinate. Material incentives have typically been dominant in modern economic systems, yet some systems have attempted to emphasize moral rewards.
Material incentives promote desirable behavior by giving the recipient a greater
claim over material goods. **Moral incentives** reward desirable behavior by appealing
to the recipient's responsibility to society (or the company) and accordingly raising
the recipient's social stature within the community. Moral incentives do not give
recipients greater command over material goods. In simpler terms, the difference
between material and moral incentives is the difference between giving an outstanding performer a cash bonus and bestowing a medal.

Different justifications for material rewards have been advanced. According to
the neoclassical theory of distribution, those who provide inputs to the system

(private owners in a market system) are rewarded according to their productivity. Material incentives are a reward for higher productivity. A case for material incentives can be made even when capital is not privately owned. Marx argued that material rewards are necessary for socialist societies to progress. When ownership of the means of production becomes public and socialism is attained, differential material rewards should persist, but moral incentives (to build socialism for future generations) will become more important. Eventually, when a stage of material abundance is reached, distribution can be based on the notion "from each according to his ability, to each according to his needs." In the Marxian framework, one would expect material rewards to be gradually replaced by moral incentives.

The issue of incentives in the contemporary analysis of different economic systems remains complex.[20] First, from the perspective of the "isms" much of the early literature deals with the equity aspects of differing reward systems and makes particular assumptions about individual behavior and how that behavior changes as systems evolve, for example, in the Marxian schema. Indeed, one of the most critical features of socialism is achieving a distribution of income more equitable than under capitalism. Second, much of the contemporary literature on incentives focuses on incentive compatibility or on designing incentive systems for complex organizations such that participant behavior achieves system objectives in the most efficient manner. Much of this research has been cast within the framework of organization theory focusing on firm (enterprise) behavior. In this latter case, the variety of special circumstances arising in real-world organizations is immense, and the difficulties of relating organization features to economic system features is great.

Comparing Economic Systems: A Mode of Classification

This chapter has examined the attributes that characterize economic systems. Figure 2.2 summarizes the alternative options available for each attribute. Four criteria for distinguishing among economic systems have been selected. Although additional criteria could have been introduced, these four are especially useful. They result in a threefold classification of economic systems: *capitalism, market socialism*, and *planned socialism*. As Figure 2.3 shows, each system is characterized multidimensionally in terms of the four criteria we have established.

Capitalism is characterized by private ownership of the factors of production. Decision making is decentralized and rests with the owners of the factors of production. Their decision making is coordinated by the market mechanism, which provides the necessary information. Material incentives are used to motivate participants.

Market socialism is characterized by public ownership of the factors of production. Decision making is decentralized and is coordinated by the market mechanism. Both material and moral incentives are used to motivate participants.

Planned socialism is characterized by public ownership of the factors of production. Decision making is centralized and is coordinated by a central plan,

FIGURE 2.2   Attributes of Economic Systems

Attribute:	Options:
Organization of Decision Making	Centralization Decentralization } MIXED
Provision of Information and Coordination	Market Plan } MIXED
Property Rights	Private Cooperative Public } MIXED
Incentive System	Moral Material } MIXED

which issues binding directives to the system's participants. Both material and moral incentives are used to motivate participants.

These definitions raise as many questions as they answer. They merely state the most important characteristics of economic systems; they do not tell us how and how well each system solves the economic problem of resource allocation. Under capitalism, how do the owners of the factors of production actually allocate their resources, according to what rules, and with what results? Under market socialism, how can public ownership of the factors of production be made compatible with market coordination? In fact, is public ownership ever compatible with market coordination? Under planned socialism, how is information gathered and processed to allocate resources effectively? How is it possible to ensure that the system's participants will follow the center's directives?

The "Isms" and Organizations

This chapter has introduced some basic ideas about different economic systems, using both the traditional models of capitalism and socialism and the contemporary framework of organization theory. As succeeding chapters pursue these themes in greater depth, it will be useful to focus on the simple system variants in familiar schematic form.

FIGURE 2.3   The Classification of Economic Systems

	CAPITALISM	MARKET SOCIALISM	PLANNED SOCIALISM
Decision-making Structure	Primarily Decentralized	Primarily Decentralized	Primarily Centralized
Mechanisms for Information and Coordination	Primarily Market	Primarily Market	Primarily Plan
Property Rights	Primarily Private Ownership	State and/or Collective Ownership	Primarily State Ownership
Incentives	Primarily Market	Material and Moral	Material and Moral

Figure 2.4 presents the traditional circular flow diagram (panel A) to represent the market capitalist economy. In panel B, a typical hierarchy represents the socialist economy of the planned or market type.

These system types are similar in the process of resource allocation. Both have major system variants that arise in a geographic (country) setting with political governance arrangements. Both face scarcity and opportunity costs and need to allocate resources rationally to achieve societal objectives. Both use organized behavior as a fundamental framework for coordinating the activities of system participants as they pursue the allocation of resources. But, for the similar economic problem facing different system variants and mixed systems, the settings, objectives, and the systems used to achieve the objectives differ as do many of the economic outcomes.

The market capitalist economy (Figure 2.4, panel A) typically has a relatively decentralized economy in which association, driven by economic gain, results in organized behavior to achieve system objectives determined largely in the marketplace. Markets for factors and for products are based on private property and the "invisible hand" to provide information necessary for making and coordinating decisions about resource allocation as participants respond to material incentives. Market forces drive the basic decisions about production, distribution, and accumulation. When examining the contemporary transition systems of Eastern Europe, we will see that there is a faith that markets are efficient, though government intervention "regulates" most market capitalist systems to offset perceptions of market failure.

FIGURE 2.4   System Variants: Capitalism and Socialism

Panel A
The Circular Flow: Markets

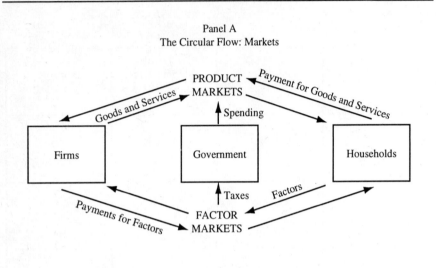

Panel B
The Hierarchical Command Economy

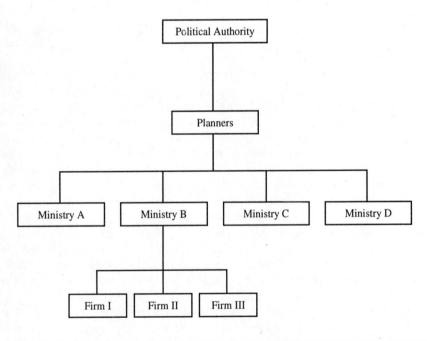

The socialist economy (Figure 2.4, panel B) is typically some variant of the hierarchical form of organization. In the planned variant, decision making is relatively centralized and a planning mechanism generates information that it uses to coordinate decision making. In this system, the state directs the basic decisions about production, distribution, and accumulation. These decisions are then formulated and executed through the planning system using state-owned resources. Superiors issue plan directives to subordinates generally through intermediate ministries, and participants respond to the directives, influenced by both material and moral incentives.

In the market socialist variant, market mechanisms can be substituted for various components of the allocation process, but in such models the state generally retains a central role in many facets of resource allocation.

After considering these simple schematic representations, the reader might well ask why, if the market is a generally efficient mechanism for resource allocation requiring minimal intervention, would anyone wish to construct the hierarchical system presented in Figure 2.4, panel B? After all, many of the basic problems of relating organizations to resource allocation introduced in this chapter are abundantly evident in the hierarchical model. If one finds the classical Marxian schema a useful approach to explaining historical evolution, then socialism is inevitable and indeed would be viewed as a superior system, especially from the perspective of equity. But, in terms of the contemporary theory of organizations, the hierarchical model cannot be dismissed, for its structure and its features are embedded in the capitalist economic system as firms both large and small. In fact, many corporate entities in market economies have larger and more complex structures than individual small countries. In essence, as this chapter has emphasized, both costs and benefits can be discovered in a variety of different organizational arrangements. Thus it is not surprising that an optimal economic system in any given setting comprises a variety of differing organizational arrangements and guidance mechanisms for the purpose of resource allocation.

Summary

The field of comparative economic systems focuses on identifying the differences in economic systems and the impact of these differences, along with the effect of traditional inputs (land, labor, and capital) and nontraditional inputs (culture, history, and geography) on the allocation of resources in a given geographic (country) setting.

An economic system is the organizational arrangements used to make decisions about resource allocation and can be identified in terms of a variety of important system characteristics, such as system organization (structure), use of market or plan for generating information, and for coordination of ownership arrangements and incentives.

Traditionally, pure systems have been classified as market capitalist, market socialist, or planned socialist, depending on the prevailing configuration of the key defining factors. While sustaining this classification helps understand real-world systems, in the contemporary setting, the focus is on understanding the defining organizational arrangements occurring in the real world in differing mixes, thus influencing resource allocation in a variety of ways.

Organizations involve individuals pursuing objectives. In an organization, individuals may function in groups or singly, and objectives can be formulated in a variety of ways. However, the organizational rules guiding system participants in the pursuit of these objectives define the structure of the organization. The structural extremes are hierarchy (where superiors issue orders to subordinates) or association (where individuals have roughly equal rights). The function of an economic system is the pursuit of objectives, generating and using information for decision making—understanding alternatives for the best use of available resources and coordinating this use of resources.

Having defined the structure of an organization, decision making is often characterized in terms of levels, that is whether decision making is centralized (made at upper levels in the hierarchy) or decentralized (made at lower levels in the hierarchy). Levels of decision making are often characterized in terms of information (sources and uses) and/or the authority and responsibility to make decisions. Planned economies are often viewed as hierarchical in structure and centralized in that superiors or principals give instructions to subordinates or agents. Market systems are often defined by association in structure, where impersonal markets rather than instructions are the dominant source of information and the mechanism used for the coordination of economic activities. In fact, both mechanisms have costs and benefits and can both be found in varying degrees in most modern real-world economic systems.

Control over resource use is important, and thus differences in ownership arrangements or property rights (private property versus state or social ownership) are critical to understanding allocational arrangements and differing economic outcomes in different economic systems. Private property is associated with the functioning of markets and has always been a major characteristic of capitalist economic systems. Some form of state or social ownership of property is associated with socialism, a fact that alters both the way property is used and the distribution of rewards from that use.

Finally, for participants in economic systems to achieve objectives, they must be appropriately motivated. Incentive arrangements can differ broadly (moral or material) and technically, but must induce system participants to achieve system objectives efficiently with available scarce resources.

Key Terms

economic system

nontraditional inputs

organization

self-interest

bounded rationality

technical–administrative problems

agency–managerial problems

hierarchy

association

principal

agent
market
directive plan
indicative plan
decentralized
centralized
authority
information

opportunistic behavior
moral hazard
adverse selection
market economy
property rights
material incentives
moral incentives

Notes

1. Alexander Eckstein, "Introduction" in Alexander Eckstein, ed., *Comparison of Economic Systems: Theoretical and Methodological Approaches* (Berkeley: University of California Press, 1971) p. 1; John Michael Montias, *The Structure of Economic Systems* (New Haven: Yale University Press, 1976).
2. This issue is discussed in Appendix 3A.
3. Relatively little attention has been given to the relationship between the nontraditional inputs (social, cultural, and historical forces), the traditional inputs (land, labor, and capital), the economic system, and the resulting outcomes. See, for example, Douglass C. North, *Institutions, Institutional Change and Economic Performance* (Cambridge: Cambridge University Press, 1990). To see how other social sciences approach the study of organizations, see, for example, Terry M. Moe, "Politics and the Theory of Organization" *The Journal of Law, Economics and Organization*, 7 (1991), Special Issue, 106–129; Christopher Winship and Sherwin Rosen, eds., "Organizations and Institutions: Sociological and Economic Approaches to the Analysis of Social Structure," *American Journal of Sociology*, 94 (1988), Supplement.
4. Montias, *The Structure of Economic Systems*, p. 8.
5. Assar Lindbeck, *The Political Economy of the New Left: An Outsider's View* 2nd ed. (New York: Harper & Row, 1977), p. 214.
6. Frederic Pryor, *Property and Industrial Organization in Communist and Capitalist Nations* (Bloomington: Indiana University Press, 1973), p. 337. Adapted from T. C. Koopmans and J. M. Montias, "On the Description and Comparison of Economic Systems" in Eckstein, *Comparison of Economic Systems*, pp. 27–28.
7. Herbert A. Simon, *Administrative Behavior*, 2nd ed. (New York: Free Press, 1966), p. xvi.
8. Montias, *The Structure of Economic Systems*, p. 8.
9. This discussion is based on the excellent survey by Avner Ben–Ner, John Michael Montias, and Egon Neuberger, "Basic Issues in Organizations: A Comparative Perspective," *Journal of Comparative Economics* 17 (1993), 207–242. For an early discussion, see Benjamin Ward, "Organization and Comparative Economics: Some Approaches" in Eckstein, *Comparison of Economic Systems*, pp. 103–133.
10. A. A. Alchian and H. Demsetz, "Production, Information, Costs and Economic Organizations," *American Economic Review*, 62 (December 1972), 777–795. A classic in the study of organizations is Simon, *Administrative Behavior*; for a contemporary survey see Paul Milgrom and John Roberts, *Economics, Organization and Management*, (Englewood Cliffs, N.J.: Prentice-Hall, 1992); see also the classic work of Oliver E. Williamson, *The Economic Institutions of Capitalism: Firms, Markets, Relational Contracting* (New York: The Free Press, 1985) and Armen A. Alchian and Susan Woodward, "The Firm

is Dead; Long Live the Firm: A Review of Oliver E. Williamson's 'The Economic Institutions of Capitalism,'" *Journal of Economic Literature*, 26, (March 1988), 65–79; Alfred D. Chandler, "Organizational Capabilities and the Economic History of the Industrial Enterprise," *Journal of Economic Perspectives*, 6, (Summer 1992), 79–100.

11. For a different approach, see Raaj Kumar Sah and Joseph E. Stiglitz, "The Architecture of Economic Systems: Hierarchies and Polyarchies," *American Economic Review*, 76, 4 (September 1986), 716–727; see also Roy Radner, "Hierarchy: The Economics of Managing," *Journal of Economic Literature*, 30, (September 1992), 1382–1415.

12. There is a large body of literature concerned with issues of centralization and decentralization. For early contributions, see, for example, Leonid Hurwicz, "Centralization and Decentralization in Economic Processes," in Eckstein, *Comparison of Economic Systems* pp. 79–102; Leonid Hurwicz, "Conditions for Economic Efficiency of Centralized and Decentralized Structures," in Gregory Grossman, ed., *Value and Plan* (Berkeley: University of California Press, 1960), pp. 162–183. Thomas Marschak, "Centralization and Decentralization in Economic Organizations," *Econometrica*, 27 (1959), 399–430; A summary of different meanings can be found in Pryor, *Property and Industrial Organization*, Ch. 8; for a recent discussion of the issues, see Robert G. Lynch, "Centralization and Decentralization Redefined," *Journal of Comparative Economics*, 13, (March 1989), 1–14; Donald Chisholm, *Coordination Without Hierarchy* (Berkeley: University of California Press, 1989).

13. Much attention has been paid to the principal–agent relationship. See, for example, Stephen A. Ross, "The Economic Theory of Agency: The Principal's Problem," *American Economic Review Papers and Proceedings* (May 1973); Glen MacDonald, "New Directions in the Economic Theory of Agency," *Canadian Journal of Economics*, 17 (1984), 415–440; George Baker, Michael Jensen, and Kevin Murphy, "Compensation and Incentives: Practice vs. Theory," *Journal of Finance*, 43 (1988), 593–616; Bengt Holmstrom and Paul Milgrom, "Multitask Principal–Agent Analyses: Incentive Contracts, Asset Ownership, and Job Design," *The Journal of Law, Economics, & Organization*, 7 (1991), Special Issue, 34–52; John Pratt and Richard Zeckhauser, eds., *Principals and Agents: The Structure of Business* (Cambridge: Harvard Business School, 1985).

14. It is argued that with the presence of adverse selection and moral hazard, incentive arrangements must be altered. For an early discussion of incentive arrangements in a systems context, see David Conn, ed., "The Theory of Incentives," *Journal of Comparative Economics*, 3, (September 1979); for a discussion of incentives in simple cases, see for example Bernard Caillaud, Roger Guesnerie, Patrick Rey, and Jean Tirole, "Government Intervention in Production and Incentives Theory: A Review of Recent Contributions," *Rand Journal of Economics*, 19, (1988), 1–26; Nahum D. Melumad and Stefan Reichelstein, "Value of Communication in Agencies," *Journal of Economic Theory*, 47 (1989), 334–368; David E. M. Sappington, "Incentives in Principal–Agent Relationships," *Journal of Economic Perspectives*, 5 (Spring 1991); for a discussion of incentive arrangements under adverse selection and moral hazard, see for example Liang Zou, "Threat-Based Incentive Mechanisms Under Moral Hazard and Adverse Selection," *Journal of Comparative Economics*, 16 (March 1992), 47–74.

15. A classic example of this view is John Kenneth Galbraith, *Economics and the Public Purpose* (Boston: Houghton Mifflin, 1973).

16. Montias, *The Structure of Economic Systems*, p. 116; for an early survey of the literature, see Erik Furubotn and Svetozar Pejovich, "Property Rights and Economic Theory: A Survey of Recent Literature," *Journal of Economic Literature*, 10 (December 1972), 1137–1162; for a discussion in the comparative context, see Pryor, *Property and*

Industrial Organization; for a recent discussion, see Alan Ryan, "Property" in John Eatwell. Murray Milgate, and Peter Newman, eds., *The New Palgrave: Dictionary of Economics* (New York: Stockton Press, 1987), pp. 1029–1031; Louis Putterman, "Ownership and the Nature of the Firm," *Journal of Comparative Economics*, 17 (1993), 243–263; John P. Bonin, Derek C. Jones, and Louis Putterman, "Theoretical and Empirical Research on Producers' Cooperatives: Will Ever the Twain Meet?" *Journal of Economic Literature*, 31 (September 1993), 1290–1320.

17. For a discussion of decision making in the public sector, see for example V. V. Ramanadham, *Public Enterprise: Studies in Organizational Structure* (London: Frank Cass, 1986); for a discussion of nonprofit organizations, see Avner Ben–Ner and Theresa Van Hoomissen, "Nonprofit Organizations in the Mixed Economy: A Demand and Supply Analysis," *Annals of the Public and Cooperative Economy*, 62, 4 (October–December, 1991), 519–550; Susan Rose-Ackerman (ed.), *The Economics of Nonprofit Institutions: Studies in Structure and Policy* (New York: Oxford University Press, 1986); Burton A. Weisbrod, *The Nonprofit Economy* (Cambridge: Harvard University Press, 1988); Jean–Jacques Laffont and Jean Tirole, "Privatization and Incentives," *Journal of Law, Economics & Public Organization*, 7 (1991) Special Issue, 84–105.

18. Pryor, *Property and Industrial Organization*, p. 338.
19. Montias, *The Structure of Economic Systems*, Ch. 13.
20. For a broader approach to the relationship between participants in an organization and those who make decisions, see Paul Milgrom and John Roberts, "An Economic Approach to Influence Activities in Organizations," *American Journal of Sociology*, 94 (1988) Supplement, s154–s179.

Recommended Readings

A. Traditional Sources

A. A. Alchian and H. Demsetz, "Production, Information, Costs and Economic Organizations," *American Economic Review*, 62 (December 1972), 777–795.

David Conn, ed., "The Theory of Incentives," *Journal of Comparative Economics*, 3 (September 1979).

H. Demsetz, "Toward a Theory of Property Rights," *American Economic Review*, 57 (May 1967), 347–359.

Alexander Eckstein, ed., *Comparison of Economic Systems: Theoretical and Methodological Approaches* (Berkeley: University of California Press, 1971).

Erik Furobotn and Svetozar Pejovich, "Property Rights and Economic Theory: A Survey of Recent Literature," *Journal of Economic Literature*, 10 (December 1972), 1137–1162.

John Michael Montias, *The Structure of Economic Systems* (New Haven: Yale University Press, 1976).

Egon Neuberger, "Classifying Economic Systems," in Morris Bornstein, ed., *Comparative Economic Systems: Models and Cases*, 4th ed. (Homewood, Illinois: Richard D. Irwin, 1978).

Frederic Pryor, *Property and Industrial Organization in Communist and Capitalist Nations* (Bloomington: Indiana University Press, 1973).

——, *A Guidebook To The Study of Economic Systems* (Englewood Cliffs, N.J.: Prentice–Hall, 1985).

Herbert A. Simon, *Administrative Behavior*, 2nd ed. (New York: Free Press, 1966).

P. J. D. Wiles, *Economic Institutions Compared*, (New York: Halsted, 1977).

———, "What is Comparative Economics?" *Comparative Economic Studies*, 31 (Fall 1989), 1–32.

Oliver E. Williamson, *Markets and Hierarchies* (New York: Free Press, 1975).

B. Basic, General, Contemporary Sources

Armen Alchian and Susan Woodward, "The Firm is Dead; Long Live the Firm: A Review of Oliver E. Williamson's 'The Economic Institutions of Capitalism,'" *Journal of Economic Literature*, 26 (March 1988), 65–79.

Avner Ben–Ner, John Michael Montias, and Egon Neuberger, "Basic Issues in Organizations: A Comparative Perspective," *Journal of Comparative Economics*, 17 (1993), 207–242.

Paul Milgrom and John Roberts, *Economics, Organization and Management* (Englewood Cliffs, N.J.: Prentice–Hall, 1992).

Frederic L. Pryor, "Corporatism as an Economic System: A Review Essay," *Journal of Comparative Economics*, 12 (September 1988), 317–344.

Oliver E. Williamson, *The Economic Institutions of Capitalism: Firms, Markets, Relational Contracting.* (New York: The Free Press, 1985).

———, ed., *Organization Theory: From Chester Barnard to the Present and Beyond.* (Oxford: Oxford University Press, 1990).

C. Organizations: Historical Aspects

Alfred D. Chandler, "Organizational Capabilities and the Economic History of the Industrial Enterprise," *Journal of Economic Perspectives*, 6 (Summer 1992), 79–100.

James S. Coleman, "Constructed Organization: First Principles," *The Journal of Law, Economics, & Organization*, 7 (1991), Special Issue, 7–23.

R. R. Nelson and S. G. Winter, *An Evolutionary Theory of Economic Change* (Cambridge: Harvard University Press, 1982).

Douglass C. North, *Institutions, Institutional Change and Economic Performance* (Cambridge: Cambridge University Press, 1990).

D. The Structure of Organizations

Sanford Grossman and Oliver Hart, "The Costs and Benefits of Ownership: A Theory of Vertical and Lateral Integration," *Journal of Political Economy*, 94 (August 1986), 691–719.

Raaj Kumar Sah and Joseph E. Stiglitz, "The Architecture of Economic Systems: Hierarchies and Polyarchies," *American Economic Review*, 76 (September 1986), 716–727.

Paul Milgrom, "Employment Contracts, Influence Activities and Efficient Organizational Design," *Journal of Political Economy*, 96 (February 1988), 42–60.

Herbert A. Simon, "Organizations and Markets," *Journal of Economic Perspectives*, 5 (Spring 1991), 25–44.

Joseph E. Stiglitz, "Symposium on Organizations and Economics," *Journal of Economic, Perspectives*, 5 (Spring 1991), 15–24.

E. Principal–Agent Relationships

Joseph Farrell, "Information and the Coase Theorem," *Journal of Economic Perspectives*, 1, (Fall 1987), 113–129.

Bengt Holmstrom and Paul Milgrom, "Multitask Principal–Agent Analyses: Incentive Contracts, Asset Ownership and Job Design," *The Journal of Law, Economics, & Organization*, 7 (1991), Special Issue, 34–52.

Glen MacDonald, "New Directions in the Economic Theory of Agency," *Canadian Journal of Economics*, 17 (1984), 415–440.

John Pratt and Richard Zeckhauser, eds., *Principals and Agents: The Structure of Business* (Cambridge: Harvard Business School, 1985).

F. Incentive Arrangements

David Conn, "Effort, Efficiency, and Incentives in Economic Organizations," *Journal of Comparative Economics*, 6 (September 1982), 223–234.

Jean–Jacques Laffont and Eric Maskin, "The Theory of Incentives: An Overview," in Werner Hildenbrand, ed., *Advances in Economic Theory* (Cambridge: Cambridge University Press, 1982).

Louis Putterman and Gil Skillman, "The Incentive Effects of Monitoring Under Alternate Compensation Schemes," *International Journal of Industrial Organization*, 6 (March 1988), 109–120.

Yingyi Qian, "Equity, Efficiency, and Incentives in a Large Economy," *Journal of Comparative Economics*, 16 (March 1992), 27–46.

David E. M. Sappington, "Incentives in Principal–Agent Relationships," *Journal of Economic Perspectives*, 5 (Spring 1991), 45–66.

Liang Zou, "Threat-Based Incentive Mechanisms Under Moral Hazard and Adverse Selection," *Journal of Comparative Economics*, 16 (March 1992), 47–74.

G. Property Rights

H. Demsetz and K. Lehn, "The Structure of Corporate Ownership: Causes and Consequences," *Journal of Political Economy*, 93 (December 1985), 1155–1177.

Louis Putterman, "Ownership and the Nature of the Firm," *Journal of Comparative Economics*, 17 (1993), 243–263.

Alan Ryan, "Property," in John Eatwell, Murray Milgate and Peter Newman, eds., *The New Palgrave: Dictionary of Economics* (New York: Stockton Press, 1987), pp. 1029–1031.

Xiaoki Yang and Ian Wills, "A Model Formalizing the Theory of Property Rights," *Journal of Comparative Economics*, 14 (June 1990), 177–198.

H. The Theory of Cooperatives

John P. Bonin, Derek C. Jones, and Louis Putterman, "Theoretical and Empirical Research on Producers' Cooperatives: Will the Twain Ever Meet?" *Journal of Economic Literature*, 31 (September 1993), 1290–1320.

I. Nonprofit Organizations

Susan Rose–Ackerman, ed., *The Economics of Nonprofit Institutions: Studies in Structure and Policy* (New York: Oxford University Press, 1986).

Walter Powell, ed., *The Nonprofit Sector: A Research Handbook* (New Haven:; Yale University Press, 1987).

Burton A. Weisbrod, *The Nonprofit Economy* (Cambridge: Harvard University Press, 1988).

J. The Public Sector

Abram Bergson, "Managerial Risks and Rewards in Public Enterprises," *Journal of Comparative Economics*, 2 (September 1978), 211–225.

A. Boardman and A. Vining, "Ownership and Performance in Competitive Environments: A Comparison of the Performance of Private, Mixed, and State-Owned Enterprises," *Journal of Law and Economics*, 32 (1989), 1–33.

Estelle James, Egon Neuberger, and Robert Willis, "On Managerial Rewards and Self-Selection: Risk Taking in Public Enterprises," *Journal of Comparative Economics*, 3 (December 1979), 395–406.

Jean-Jacques Laffont and Jean Tirole, "Privatization and Incentives," *The Journal of Law, Economics, & Organization*, 7 (1991), Special Issue, 84–105.

3

Evaluation of Economic Outcomes

This chapter considers how observed economic outcomes can be systematically related to variations in the economic system. This, after all, is the central focus of comparative economic systems. Selected criteria are used to judge which economic systems perform best and thus how to alter economic systems or system components to improve performance. The task of relating outcomes to systems presents a number of important methodological issues.

Models versus Reality

The previous chapter examined in abstract terms three types of economic systems: capitalism, planed socialism, and market socialism. Each exhibits different organizational arrangements and decision-making rules. In the real world, however, actual systems tend to be mixed systems, a fact that complicates an assessment of outcomes.

The field of comparative economic systems can be structured on two levels: models and reality.[1] The justification for examining and comparing **system models** is the same as that made for economic theory. Theories or models allow us to abstract from reality to understand basic issues; they provide a means to make comparisons in simple ways; they provide a means for predicting outcomes to establish a "norm" for assessing ultimate real-world outcomes.

Having justified the use of abstract system models, it is now important to understand that the economic outcomes observed are those of real-world systems working in actual geographic settings influenced by a variety of system and nonsystem forces.[2] Most important, however, is that these real-world systems are typically mixed. Thus there are a number of basic and important issues to bear in mind while attempting to relate outcomes to systems.

First, to the extent that theoretical system models are used, it is important to compare model with model, or the reality of a given model (say market capitalism) with the model of market capitalism. Comparing the outcomes of, say, a planned socialist economic system with the model of market capitalism is not generally useful, though models of planned socialist systems are generally much less developed

37

than those of market capitalist systems, making cross-comparisons appealing in some cases.

Second, comparing real-world outcomes with system models is difficult in that it is generally difficult, if not impossible, to quantify measures of economic systems and system differences. While outcomes are generally measurable, system characteristics are much less so.

Third, as previously emphasized, many forces beyond the economic system influence outcomes. Although this issue is discussed in greater depth in Appendix 3A, it is important to emphasize that while some nonsystem forces are measurable, others are not, thus making generalizations about system and nonsystem forces and their relationships to outcomes difficult.

Fourth, most real-world systems are mixed systems, which is of great importance in the contemporary analysis of economic systems in an era when market-type systems seem to dominate over the historically observed contrasts of plan and market. Is the United States more "capitalistic" than Germany or Singapore, and if so, by how much?

Such questions cannot be answered satisfactorily. More subtle and difficult to assess, moreover, is the variability of system components. For example, it has generally been noted that different economic systems all use the firm as a basic unit of industrial production. But firms can differ significantly in terms of ownership, for example. Public- or government-owned corporations are very different from private corporations, and both differ from cooperative arrangements. These differences are difficult to isolate and to measure such that their impact on outcomes can be assessed.

The Forces Influencing Economic Outcomes

To capture some of the ideas outlined above, we propose some simple notation. If we could measure the **economic system (ES)** in a manner that provides ordinal or cardinal rankings, we would still have to measure economic **outcomes (O)** in a meaningful manner.

Economic outcomes depend on factors other than the economic system—natural resource endowments, the level of economic development, the size of the economy, labor and capital inputs, random events, and so on. These are termed **environmental factors (ENV)**. Finally, economic outcomes depend on the **policies (POL)** that the policy makers in economic systems choose to follow.

$$O = f(\text{ES, ENV, POL}) \tag{3.1}$$

where

$$
\begin{array}{ll}
\text{O} & \text{denotes economic outcomes} \\
\text{ES} & \text{denotes the economic system} \\
\text{ENV} & \text{denotes environmental factors} \\
\text{POL} & \text{denotes policies pursued by the economic system}
\end{array}
$$

Equation 3.1 and Figure 3.1 highlight the methodological problems of determining the impact of the economic system (ES) on the observed outcomes (O)—the *ceteris paribus* ("other things being equal") problem. Insofar as the outcomes observed depend on factors in addition to the economic system, one cannot isolate the impact of the system without first controlling for or holding constant the influence of the environmental (ENV) factors and the policy variables (POL). But how is this problem handled, and to what extent can ENV and POL factors be identified? To illustrate the problem, some basic examples from the real world can be used.

Labor productivity (an "outcome") in the former Soviet Union was relatively low compared with Western Europe and the United States.[3] Assuming accurate measurement, is the observed outcome the result of the economic system (planned socialism), environmental factors, policy factors, or some combination of these forces? This question cannot be easily answered. For example, the level of economic development in the former Soviet Union (as measured, say, by per capita domestic product) was well below levels in the United States and Western Europe, and historical evidence shows that the level of productivity is positively associated with the level of economic development. In this case, is the productivity gap observed in the former Soviet Union a function of the economic system, or are other factors involved?

Consider another example. Agricultural performance in the former Soviet Union was the subject of continuing concern to a series of Soviet leaders. To take a specific instance of agricultural performance, grain yields in the former Soviet Union were low compared with yields in western countries. But is it reasonable to compare grain yields in the former Soviet Union with, say, grain yields in England? The answer of course is yes, but beyond system differences, there were other important differences. For example, would it not be reasonable to expect that in England,

FIGURE 3.1   Forces Influencing Economic Outcomes

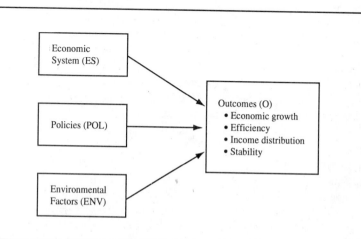

where fertile agricultural land is in relatively short supply, that land would be intensively used in combination with fertilizer, multiple croppings, and the like? On the other hand, might the former Soviet Union, a country with vast (albeit some inhospitable) land areas, be expected to use land extensively with less fertilizer and related inputs? In short, given differing levels of economic development and very different factor endowments, the same grain yields should not be expected, complicating the measurement problems.

Appendix 3A, contains simple statistical techniques to handle these sorts of measurement problems, and yet basic difficulties remain because many of the variables of interest (notably the economic system) are in fact difficult to measure in any meaningful manner.

This discussion of measurement problems has focused on the nature of the economic system and environmental factors. But how is it possible to identify the policy (POL) differences across economic systems? Again, examples are useful.

It is well known that the planned socialist economic systems pursued a strategy of rapid economic growth. If both the levels of investment in these systems and the distribution of investment resources by sector were examined, the emphasis on economic growth would be evident. Another example is the perceived aversion to foreign trade. It has been widely argued that, for a variety of reasons, the planned socialist economic systems of the former Soviet Union and Eastern bloc pursued a policy of avoiding trade. Although the trade mechanisms and the policies of these systems, and indeed simple measurement of trade participation ratios, seemed to support the hypothesis of trade aversion, the issue is in fact more complex in theory and in practice. If trade participation ratios were somewhat low, relative to other (market) economic systems at similar levels of economic development, would this necessarily support the view of trade aversion? Could such an outcome be considered a policy variable? Or might trade aversion be inherent in the systematic features of planned socialist system.

A factor is classified as **policy** if it can be significantly changed without changing the underlying economic system. It is a direct attribute of the economic system if it cannot conceivably be altered without an alteration of the economic system. Such an approach provides us with some conception of how policy influences and system influences might differ.

Policies tend to be closely intertwined with the economic system. They are nonetheless important to the evaluation of economic systems. In most instances, trade aversion leads to a lower standard of living than would have prevailed had there been international specialization. The standard of living is often used as a performance indicator. Should this weakness be attributed to the economic system or to policies pursued by the economic system?

To understand the impact of the economic system on economic outcomes, one must understand the impacts of all other significant environmental and policy factors. In other fields of economics, the economic system is taken as "given," and one can more easily isolate the effect of changes in a particular variable on economic outcomes. Appendix 3A, at the end of this chapter, discusses the statistical methods for analyzing the effect of the economic system on economic outcomes.

The Evaluation of Outcomes: The Success Criteria Problem

When the outcomes of differing economic systems are compared, we wish to determine which economic system performs "best" in achieving its goals. How are we to evaluate the differing outcomes in order to decide which is "best"? Two crucial problems arise.

First, to evaluate the outcomes of differing economic systems, we must select a set of performance criteria. Because people typically do not agree on the appropriate criteria, the selection tends to be subjective.

Second, even if agreement could be reached on a list of criteria for evaluating outcomes, how will the criteria be added together if economic systems yield different results? In such instances, the disparate results must be somehow added together by assigning *weights* for aggregation. This produces a single index of achievement, which can then be used to compare systems. Clearly, the weights selected will determine the value of the index of achievement, but they are themselves subjective and depend on the values held by the particular observer.[4]

It is logical to think that the economic system should have as its objective the achievement of a maximal value of the economic outcome (O), subject to the constraints imposed by the economic system (ES), policies (POL), and environmental factors (ENV), which include technology and resource constraints. The objective is to

Maximize: O

Subject to (ES, ENV, POL)   **(3.2)**

From this, it would seem that evaluating the performance of economic systems would be (theoretically at least) a rather simple matter. After adjusting for differences in environment and policy, one would have only to determine which system achieved the highest economic outcome. If there were agreement on the measurement of outcomes, it would work this way. Instead, the economic outcome (O) is a function of a series of performance indicators:

$$O = \sum_{j=1}^{k} a_j o_j$$ **(3.3)**

where

o_j = desirable (or undesirable if negative) economic outcomes
a_j = the relative importance of the various outcomes

Consider the following example in which two economic systems designated A and B are judged according to two criteria. A receives a score of 1 and 2 on the two criteria. B receives a score of 2 and 1 on the two criteria. Which system has outperformed the other depends on the relative weights applied to the two criteria.

Just as individuals assign different weights (a_j) to different economic goals, so one would expect economic systems to assign different weights to those goals.[5]

Moreover, the evaluation of these goals changes over time. One need only note the changing priority of economic goals in the United States or that capitalist societies attach different weights to the items on a rather similar list of economic goals or objectives.

Equation 3.3 summarizes the crux of the problem. Because different societies assign different subjective weights (a_j) to economic outcomes (o_j), the measurement of economic performance depends not only on o_j but also on a_j, which must remain subjective. For example, one economic system may assign priority to economic growth and allocate resources accordingly. In so doing, it attaches relatively low weights to the other goals. Another economic system may attach a dominant weight to price stability and allocate its resources accordingly. It is likely, in this scenario, that the first system will perform better in terms of the growth objective and that the second system will perform better in terms of price stability. Which system has outperformed the other? The answer depends on one's personal judgment of which goal is more important.

The Determination of System Priorities

How are **national priorities** determined in practice? The involvement of substantial subjective elements does not mean that priorities are not in fact established, although they do change over time partly as a function of change in the economic system itself.

The determination of national priorities differs from system to system. In societies where political power is largely centralized, the prevailing political authority exercises decisive control over the formation of national goals. In the former Soviet Union, for example, the Communist party historically played a dominant role in goal formation.[6] This does not mean that other forces had no influence, but their roles were relatively limited. (In socialist societies, where political power was substantially concentrated, the process of modernization itself led to some pluralization of the society and to the formation of influential interest groups.)[7]

In democratic capitalist societies, establishing priorities is more complicated. This complexity is reflected in the various arrangements through which individuals can express preferences by voting. The vote may indicate a preference among political candidates with differing positions on major national issues, or it may be a "vote" cast in the marketplace indicating what goods and services are desired. However, pressure groups such as trade unions, manufacturers' associations, and professional associations can and do exert substantial influence. Even though majority voting prevails, legislation that advances minority interests may be passed.[8] Also, even in a pluralistic democratic society, as power becomes concentrated (whether in the hands of individuals in the form of wealth or in the hands of lobby groups or corporations), there is a tendency for the goal formation process to change.[9] In a democratic society, the change may take place slowly. In a society where power is centralized, change may be more sudden, though not necessarily revolutionary.

If various goals are laudable, why not pursue all of them? Specific goals can often be achieved only by sacrificing other, less important goals. The necessity of choosing to pursue some goals at the expense of others is a consequence of the fundamental scarcity of resources, which prevents every economic system from producing unlimited quantities of goods and services. Instead, choices must be made among goals.

The nature of the tradeoffs is not always clearly defined. Can unemployment in the United States be lowered without increasing inflation? Is sustained economic growth compatible with a cleaner environment? Could the Soviet Union have sustained rapid growth of both GDP and military power? The existence of tradeoffs is important in at least two dimensions. First, we cannot assess the performance of economic systems without some insight into the nature of the tradeoff among alternatives that has been made. Second, when one goal must in some degree be sacrificed to achieve another, we should not criticize a system for not achieving a goal that it has, in effect, decided not to pursue.

Performance Criteria

We have selected those performance criteria that can be generally applied to assess economic outcomes. We realize that any such list will omit some criteria (military power, for instance, or environmental quality) that are important. We shall use the following criteria to evaluate economic outcomes:

1. Economic growth
2. Efficiency
3. Income distribution
4. Stability (cyclical stability, inflation, unemployment)
5. Viability of the economic system

Economic Growth

Probably the most widely used indicator of economic performance is economic growth. **Economic growth** refers to increases in the volume of output that an economy generates over time or to increases in output per capita.[10] We are interested in economic output and its growth because, for a particular economic system at a particular time, the material well-being or welfare of its population can be approximated by the volume of goods and services per capita at its disposal.[11] Changes in the volume of output per capita over time normally bring about changes in the welfare of the population in the same direction. Using this interpretation, we can compare levels of well-being of different systems at any time, or over time, to evaluate the rate at which economic progress is being made.

Because economic growth is so widely employed as a performance indicator, it is useful to spell out some complications. First, measurement problems arise in assessing economic growth, especially when different economic systems are compared. These sorts of problems are discussed in specialized literature on economic growth.[12] Second, it is difficult to untangle the causes of differences in economic growth. Such differences may be a consequence of the economic system, but they may also result from environmental and policy factors. The process of economic growth is so complex that it defies easy description; therefore, we can never be sure of the system's impact on growth. For example, economic growth appears related to level of development. If one compares the growth of two economic systems over time, when each system begins with a different base, one may expect, *ceteris paribus*, differences in growth performance.

Third, the uncertain link between the growth of output and increases in quality of life should be emphasized. Economic growth is enhanced by capital formation, but to expand the capital stock, saving (refraining from current consumption) is required. It may well be that the savings of the present generation will bear fruit in the form of living standard improvements only for later generations. The decision to postpone present consumption in favor of future consumption must be confronted in any economic system, whether the choice is made primarily by consumer or by planner. The outcome of this decision has an impact on growth performance and on current living standards.

It has been argued that capitalist systems consistently underrate the merits of future consumption and hence save too little to make adequate provision for the future.[13] Thus we anticipate higher savings ratios in socialist systems and, accordingly, a more rapid rate of growth of the capital stock and, *ceteris paribus*, a higher rate of growth of output.

Finally, it is important to understand that economic growth and economic development are different concepts. The former refers to increases in output or per capita output, while the latter refers to the broad socioeconomic changes beyond increases in output per se. In all cases, the relationship between these changes and improvements in the well-being of the population are complex issues, a defining basis of the field of economic development.

Efficiency

A second measure of system performance is economic efficiency. **Efficiency** refers to the effectiveness with which a system utilizes its available resources (including knowledge) at a particular time (**static efficiency**) or through time (**dynamic efficiency**).[14] Static and dynamic efficiency are interrelated in a complex manner, but both are multidimensional in the sense that they depend on a wide variety of factors.

The concept of efficiency can be conveniently illustrated by the production possibilities schedule shown in Figure 3.2. The initial production possibilities schedule (*AB*) illustrates all feasible combinations of producer and consumer goods that a particular economic system is capable of producing at a particular time by using all available resources at maximal efficiency. The production possibilities schedule shows that, given its existing resources, the system has a menu of production choices open to it. Economic systems must choose where to locate on the schedule.

FIGURE 3.2   The Production Possibilities Schedule

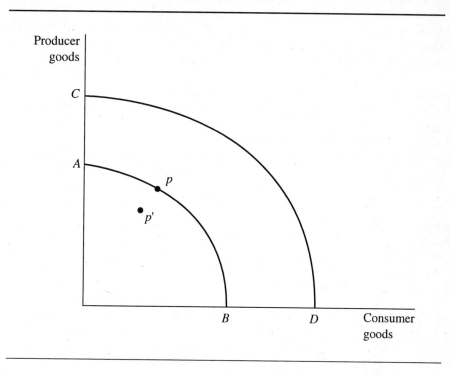

In capitalist societies, the consumer–voter dominates this choice. In planned socialist societies, planners make the decision.

The labels we have attached to the axes in Figure 3.2 are arbitrary. We could have chosen other goals and could have examined a number of possible tradeoffs. However, the *shape* of the production possibilities frontier is not accidental. The fact that it is a curve convex from the origin illustrates a basic fact of economic life: As one attempts to produce increasing amounts of, say, consumer goods, one has to give up ever larger amounts of producer goods to obtain identical increases in consumer goods. In more technical terms, there is a diminishing marginal rate of technical substitution between the production of consumer goods and the production of producer goods.

The production possibilities schedule is a useful device for illustrating the concept of efficiency. We have already indicated that *AB* represents the capacity of a particular economic system at a particular time. Static efficiency requires an economic system to be operating on its production possibilities frontier—for example, at point *p*. Output combinations beyond *AB* are impossible at that time; combinations inside *AB* are feasible but inefficient. An economic system that has the capacity *AB* but is producing at point *p'* is statically inefficient, because it could move to point *p* and produce *more of both* goods with no increase in available resources.

Dynamic efficiency refers to the ability of an economic system to enhance its capacity to produce goods and services over time without an increase in capital and labor inputs. Dynamic efficiency is indicated by movement of the frontier outward from *AB* to *CD* (without an underlying increase in resources); the distance of this movement indicates the change in efficiency.

Like other indicators of system performance, static and dynamic efficiency are subject to complex measurement problems. The basic approach to measuring static efficiency is to make productivity calculations, as measured by the ratio of the output to inputs. Dynamic efficiency is measured by the ratio of the growth of output to the growth of inputs.

Economic growth and dynamic efficiency are not the same. The output of a system may grow by increasing efficiency (finding better ways of doing things with the same resources) or by expanding the amount of, say, labor but using that labor at a constant rate of effectiveness. The former is often termed **intensive growth**, the latter **extensive growth**.

The concepts of intensive and extensive growth have been important to an understanding of the growth experiences of different economic systems. Later chapters show that the former planned socialist systems of the Soviet Union and Eastern Europe tended toward high-growth systems in their early years, with substantial and continuing slowdowns in their later years. Although the growth slowdown is an outcome for later discussion, the early rapid-growth experience has been widely attributed to a strategy of extensive growth—a growth-oriented policy supported by an economic system designed to harness inputs and to allocate those inputs to growth-generating sectors such as heavy industry. It is important to realize, however, that one cannot characterize extensive or intensive economic growth as "good" or "bad," although historical experience tells us that as systems reach higher levels of economic development, growth in output is increasingly derived from intensive economic growth, a major problem in the contemporary historical experiences of the formerly planned socialist economic systems.

Income Distribution

How well an economic system distributes income among households is the third criterion for assessing economic performance. Technically, **income distribution** is measured by the **Lorenz curve** or **Gini coefficient**, as shown in Figure 3.3. Our ability to measure income distributions does not, however, answer the question of what constitutes a good distribution. There may be substantial agreement on the definition of bad income distributions (for example, where 1 percent of the population receives 95 percent of all income); judgments about intermediate cases are more difficult to make.

What constitutes an equitable distribution of income?[15] Equity involves fairness, though what is considered fair differs from case to case and over time. One criterion of fairness might involve reward according to contribution to the production process. In a capitalist society, personal income is determined by the human and physical capital one owns and by their prices as determined by factor markets. Income

FIGURE 3.3 Measuring Income Inequality: The Lorenz Curve

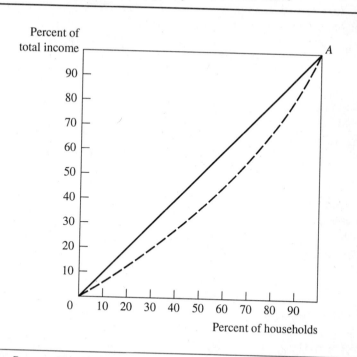

Explanation: Percent of households is measured on the horizontal axis, percent of income on the vertical axis. Perfect equality would be, for example, where 10 percent of households received 10 percent of all income. This would be illustrated by a 45-degree line between the origin (O) and point *A*. Inequality can be illustrated by the dashed line. The further the dashed line bows away from the 45-degree line, the more unequal the distribution of income. In the diagram, for example, the bottom 20 percent of households receive 10 percent of income. A comprehensive measure, known as the *Gini coefficient*, is typically used to measure income inequality. The Gini coefficient is the area between the 45-degree line and the dashed line divided by the entire area under the 45-degree line.

differences reflect differences in effort (provision of labor services), differences in frugality (provision of capital), inheritance of physical and human capital, luck, and so on. The market distribution of income may be modified by the tax system and the provision of social services. The extent to which government redistributive action is justified on equity grounds is a matter of continuing controversy in capital- ist societies. Under socialism, the factors of production are, with the exception of labor, publicly owned. Capital and land are both socially owned in a socialist society; hence, their remuneration belongs to the state, not directly to individuals.

Stability

The fourth criterion is economic stability. By **stability** we mean the absence of significant fluctuations in growth rates, the maintenance of acceptable rates of unemployment, and the avoidance of excessive inflation. Economic stability is a desirable objective for two reasons. The first is that various segments of the population are damaged by instability. Individuals on fixed incomes are hurt by unanticipated inflation; the poorly trained are hurt by unemployment. Second, cyclical instability can lead to losses of potential output, making the economic system operate inside its production possibilities schedule.

Capitalist economies have historically been subject to fluctuations in the level of economic activity—in other words, to business cycles.[16] In planned socialist economies, aggregate economic activity (including investment) had been subject to the control of planners. Although cyclical activity could have occurred in planned socialist economics—through planning errors or transmission through the foreign sector—the economic growth of a socialist society was less likely to suffer cyclical fluctuations.

Stability of economic growth is of practical importance. Potential lost at any particular time is lost forever. A system that, because of cyclical instability, does not reach its potential cannot be expected to achieve its potential rate of growth through time. Thus the matter of cyclical instability, the length and the severity of cycles, and the forms in which they find expression are important indicators of the relative success of economic systems.

Inflation, a second manifestation of instability, may appear in open form as a general rise in the price level, or it may occur in repressed form as lengthening lines for goods and services, regional and sectoral shortages, and the like. In capitalist economies, inflation typically occurs in the first form; in the planned socialist economies (where planners set prices), it historically manifested itself in repressed form. In any event, excessive inflation is viewed as an undesirable phenomenon; it can distort economic calculation (where relative prices are used as sources of information), cause increased use of barter, and alter the income distribution.

Excessive **unemployment** is also undesirable. It implies, along with the personal hardships of those unemployed, less than full utilization of resources. It is difficult, however, to measure causal factors and to compare unemployment rates across economic systems, because the planned socialist economies for many years did not maintain records on unemployment (which was said to have been "liquidated"). Moreover, the standard definition of unemployment (the unemployed are those seeking employment but unable to find jobs) leaves room for differences in interpretation. There are different types of unemployment, ranging from unemployment associated with the normal changing of jobs to chronic, hard-core unemployment.

These definitions, however, fail to account for the more subtle but important concept of **underemployment**, or the employment of individuals on a full-time basis at work in which they utilize their skills at less than their full potential. Underemployment (which was common in the planned socialist economies) is less visible than unemployment, but it can have a similarly adverse effect on capacity utilization. It typically takes the form of overstaffing, a situation in which ten people are employed for a job that could be accomplished just as well by five.

Viability of the Economic System

The ultimate test of an economic system is its long-term viability. The basic premise of Marxian economics is that over the course of history, "superior" economic systems replace "inferior" ones. In the Marxian scheme, capitalism replaces feudalism and then socialism replaces capitalism. Inferior systems are beset by internal contradictions that make it impossible for them to survive over the long term. Marx depicted capitalism as an unstable system suffering from a number of insurmountable internal contradictions. These internal contradictions, he believed, ensured the eventual demise of capitalism and its replacement by the "superior" system of socialism.

Since the beginning of the Soviet experiment with planned socialism (and its eventual expansion to one-third of the world's population), there had been little discussion of the long-term viability of the planned socialist variant. Rather, discussion had focused on the *relative* economic performance of planned socialism. Most experts felt that planned socialism, though inefficient, would be able to muddle along—to survive, but at relatively low levels of efficiency and consumer welfare.

Events of the late 1980s highlighted the issue of the long-term viability of planned socialism. Significantly, the goal of the reform movements in the former Soviet Union and in Eastern Europe is transforming the planned economic system into a market economic system. The rejection of the planned socialist system by the political leadership casts serious doubt on this economic system's ability to deliver an economic performance strong enough to ensure its continued existence.

Among the other basic performance criteria—economic growth, efficiency, income distribution, and stability—the long-term viability of the economic system itself stands out as the dominant test of performance. If an economic system cannot survive, it has clearly proven itself inferior to those systems that can.

It may be premature to declare the planned socialist system dead. The move away from socialism in the former Soviet Union and in Eastern Europe could be reversed. Socialism continues to have appeal in China, which is combining Communist dictatorship with market reform and the opening up of the economy to international trade and investment.

Tradeoffs

The four performance criteria are not all-inclusive. Other criteria could be added such as military power, environmental quality, or democratic political institutions. The four criteria we have selected are those typically used to measure economic performance.

If all performance criteria were compatible, the measurement of economic performance would be less complicated. If the achievement of higher growth meant the automatic achievement of the other goals, countries need only aim for one goal and expect to achieve the others spontaneously. This is not the way the world works. Frequently, the achievement of one goal requires the sacrifice of another.

Consider a society that sets a "fair" distribution of income as its overriding economic goal, where "fairness" requires an equal distribution of income. Dividing output equally among families means that those who have worked harder, more effectively, or who have taken risks receive the same as those who have not. If unequal effort receives equal reward, this society would have no incentives for hard and effective work, risk taking, and innovations, and in the long run these activities would no longer occur. An equal distribution of income would therefore harm both efficiency and economic growth.

Consider a society that establishes rapid growth as its overriding goal, and it seeks to achieve this growth by requiring all teenagers and retired persons to work and by forcing households to save unreasonably large sums for capital formation. Such policies would create economic growth through extensive means (growth through expansion of inputs), but it would likely reduce static efficiency and dynamic efficiency. The capital and labor employed at the margin would not be effective; the loss of household production might make people work less effectively.

Consider a society that wishes to guarantee employment to all those able to and willing to work. This guarantee is made in the form of an implicit *job rights* contract, which declares that the state will, as a last resort, provide a job and an income to all.[17] Such a job rights contract would mean that workers have a job no matter how ineffectively and unconscientiously they work. Under such an arrangement, effort would slacken, absenteeism would rise, and employee discipline would fall. These events would depress economic efficiency and cause the society to produce below its production possibilities.

Economic Systems and Performance

Societies do have a choice of economic systems. The countries of the former Soviet Union and Eastern Europe are currently searching for a new economic system. China is experimenting with the combination of political dictatorship, planning, public ownership, and market reform. The industrialized West is faced with ever-changing choices of tax systems, industrial policies, and privatization.

Comparative economic systems addresses the effect of the system on economic performance. The big issue is the effect radically different economic systems—market economies or planned socialist economies—have on economic performance. Although the countries of the former Soviet Union and Eastern Europe appear to have rejected this socialist model, it is still important to evaluate its performance, both to complete the historical record and to judge those countries continuing its use in modified form, such as China.

It is more difficult to judge the effect of differences in institutional arrangements on performance in countries that use basically the same economic system. What is the effect, for example, of worker participation in management on German economic performance? What has been the effect of exceptionally high marginal tax rates in Sweden? With interest in the planned socialist economy declining, comparative economics will focus much more on such issues. In fact, a number of studies have been done that relate differences in institutional arrangements and policies—such as the independence of the central bank and the generosity of the social safety net—to economic performance.

Social experiments, both broad and small, can be costly if erroneously performed. Consider the United States's effort to reform health care in the mid-1990s. America's eventual choice will be enriched by the availability of social experiments that have been conducted in Canada, the U.K., and Germany, which reveal consequences of the choice of various policies. Japan, in its reexamination of its industrial policies in the mid-1990s, can find guidance from the experiments with industrial policies in other countries. The poor countries of Asia and Africa can take guidance from the privatization and free-trade experiments of Hong Kong and South Korea.

Performance Comparisons: The 1990s

A number of issues have complicated performance comparisons in the 1990s. Much of the assessment of the performance of different systems since World War II has been based on the assumption that systemic change has not been great in either capitalist or socialist economic systems. Change or reform in the planned socialist economic systems, for example, was viewed as modest. The era of transition presents the need to examine economic systems that are really not in place. In this new setting, the tendency is to look more at transition indicators (for example, the implementation of privatization) as an outcome of the transition process rather than basic performance indicators per se. Moreover as performance across economic systems is assessed, classification, as previously emphasized, will be more subtle and thus more difficult. What model should be used to assess the progress of economic development in Uzbekistan? Against which other countries should the progress in Uzbekistan be judged? In such a setting, the framework of economic development may be more useful than that of comparative economic systems.

Finally, the issue of data availability has taken on new importance. Those formerly planned socialist economies now in transition, have steadily shifted away from the old definitions and concepts toward standard international concepts in, for example, national income accounting. But as subsequent chapters will show, data availability and reliability remains a serious problem and complicates attempts to understand contemporary performance, let alone to make accurate comparisons with the past. These complications are especially important in an era of evolving efforts to improve the nature of basic international economic comparisons.

Summary

The central focus of comparative economic systems is the characterization of differences in economic systems and the influence of those differences on outcomes. The field of comparative economic systems sustains comparative analysis using both theoretical or abstract system models and real-world variants. In the former, it is important to compare theoretical variants, while in the latter, complicated measurement problems limit the ability to relate observed outcomes to theoretical ideals.

In addition to the influence of the economic system (ES), outcomes are influenced by a variety of forces conveniently aggregated as environmental factors (ENV) and policy factors (POL). As outcomes are related to differences in these three major forces, it is difficult though important to isolate the impact of each while holding constant the influence of the others. While Appendix 3A discusses statistical means to achieve such results, problems of method and measurement limit such efforts in the real world.

As outcomes of economic activity in different economic systems are evaluated, it is important to identify clear performance criteria and develop some (generally subjective) weighting criteria to aggregate these criteria. Although the result of such an exercise is necessarily subjective, there is nevertheless a considerable measure of agreement on the criteria that might be used to assess economic performance.

Although most observers of different economic systems would recognize the importance of a variety of both economic and noneconomic criteria, the focus remains on the four most-basic economic performance criteria: economic growth, efficiency, income distribution, and stability. All are critical to economic growth and economic development, though in real-world economic systems, the formation of societal objectives is a complex social process, the nature of which changes through time.

Economic growth refers to increases in the output of goods and services produced in a system (country) and/or to increases in output per capita. Economic development is a broader concept that includes societal changes and improvements in the well being of the population.

The second criterion, efficiency, refers to the effectiveness with which a system uses its resources at a point in time (static efficiency) or through time (dynamic efficiency). Though difficult to measure with precision, the concept of efficiency is frequently related to the concepts of extensive economic growth (growth achieved through the expanded use of inputs) and intensive growth (growth achieved through the better use of available inputs). Experience suggests that as economic systems grow and develop, they typically rely increasingly on intensive growth as a source of expanded output and as a means to raise the well-being of the population.

The third criterion of economic performance is the nature of the resulting income distribution. Apart from extremes, the matter of a "good" distribution of income is inherently subjective, though economists argue that the nature of the income distribution is related to the effectiveness with which participants pursue system objectives.

The fourth criterion of economic performance is stability, which refers to the ability of an economic system to grow without such significant cyclical fluctuations, a shifts in price levels (inflation), and unemployment.

Possibly the ultimate test of an economic system is its viability. In the contemporary setting, relating the system characteristics in the preceding chapter to the performance criteria is an important but difficult task. As previously emphasized, most systems are in fact mixed systems where system characteristics are difficult to identify and to measure, and the tradeoffs among differing outcomes are subtle and not always well known.

Key Terms

system models	national priorities	income distribution
economic system (ES)	economic growth	Lorenz curve
outcomes (O)	efficiency	Gini coefficient
environmental factors (ENV)	static efficiency	stability
policies (POL)	dynamic efficiency	inflation
success criteria	intensive growth	unemployment
aggregation	extensive growth	underemployment

Notes

1. For a survey of issues relating to system models, see Morris Bornstein (ed.) *Comparative Economic Systems: Models and Cases*, 7th ed. (Homewood, Illinois: Irwin, 1994), chapters 1–2. The use of deductive models has been criticized in a work by Trevor Buck. Buck argues that the predictions derived from utopian models (in particular those of perfect capitalism, central planning, and self-management) are identical, and that "empirical evidence cannot test utopian models." For an elaboration of these views, see Trevor Buck, *Comparative Industrial Systems* (New York: St. Martin's, 1982), chapter 1.
2. The approach used here is suggested in Tjalling C. Koopmans and John Michael Montias, "On the Description and Comparison of Economic Systems" in Alexander Eckstein (ed.), *Comparison of Economic Systems: Theoretical and Methodological Approaches* (Berkeley: University of California Press, 1971), chapter 2; see also John Michael Montias, *The Structure of Economic Systems* (New Haven: Yale University Press, 1976).
3. For a discussion of the productivity issue in this case, see, for example, the work of Abram Bergson, especially, "Comparative Productivity," *American Economic Review*, 77 (June 1987), 342–357.
4. See Koopman and Montias, "On the Description and Comparison of Economic Systems," pp. 27–78.
5. For the matter of goals or objectives as viewed within the field of comparative economic systems, see, for example, Montias, *The Structure of Economic Systems*, chapter 3; G. M. Heal, *The Theory of Economic Planning* (New York: North Holland, 1973), chapter 2.
6. For a brief treatment of the role of the Communist party in the formation of national economic objectives in the former Soviet Union, see Paul R. Gregory and Robert C. Stuart *Soviet and Post-Soviet Economic Structure and Performance*, 5th. ed. (New York: HarperCollins, 1994).

7. For a discussion of the various paradigms of political economy, see Barry W. Poulson, *Economic Development: Private and Public Choice* (New York: West Publishing Company, 1994), Part II.

8. The literature on modern public choice has reached some disturbing conclusions about the rationality of majority-rule voting procedures in single and multi-issue settings. See James Buchanan and Gordon Tullock, *The Calculus of Consent* (Ann Arbor: University of Michigan Press, 1962); James M. Buchanan and Robert Tollison, eds., *The Theory of Public Choice II* (Ann Arbor: University of Michigan Press, 1984); for a summary of issues, see Barry W. Poulson, *Economic Development* (New York: West Publishing Company, 1994), chapter 4.

9. This is a standard element in the socialist critique of capitalism, namely that under capitalism the impact of the consumer is in fact quite limited, constrained by powerful lobby groups, large corporations and the like. For a classic treatment, see, for example, John Kenneth Galbraith, *The New Industrial State* (Boston: Houghton Mifflin, 1967); Assar Lindbeck, *The New Left: An Outsider's View*, 2nd. ed. (New York: Harper & Row, 1977); Samuel Bowles, David M. Gordon and Thomas E. Weisskopf, *Beyond the Waste Land: A Democratic Alternative to Economic Decline* (New York: Anchor Press/ Doubleday, 1983); for a brief summary of issues, see Poulson, *Economic Development*, chapter 1.

10. There is much literature on the subject of economic growth. For an introduction, see, for example, Malcolm Gillis, Dwight H. Perkins, Michael Roemer, and Donald R. Snodgrass, *Economics of Development*, 3rd. ed. (New York: W. W. Norton, 1992; Bruce Herrick and Charles P. Kindleberger, *Economic Development* (New York: McGraw-Hill Book Company, 1983), chapter 2.

11. The contemporary literature on economic development in fact looks well beyond simple indicators such as per capita output. See, for example, Poulson, *Economic Development*, chapter 1.

12. The methodological problems of cross-country comparisons have received a great deal of attention in the literature. For early discussions in the U.S.–Soviet context, see Robert W. Campbell, N. Mark Earle Jr., Herbert S. Levine, and Francis W. Dresch, "Methodological Problems Comparing the U.S. and U.S.S.R. Economies," in United States Congress, Joint Economic Committee, *Soviet Economic Prospects for the Seventies* (Washington, D.C.: U.S. Government Printing Office, 1973), 122–146; for an analysis of growth patterns, see Hollis Chenery and Moshe Syrquin, *Patterns of Development 1950–1970* (London: Oxford University Press, 1975); Moshe Syrquin and Hollis Chenery, "Patterns of Development, 1950–1983," World Bank, Working Papers Series No, 41, 1989; Ross Levine and David Renelt, "A Sensitivity Analysis of Cross-Country Growth Regressions," *American Economic Review*, 82, 4 (September 1992), 942–963.

13. This is a rather standard socialist criticism of capitalism. See, for example, the classic work by A. C. Pigou, *Socialism versus Capitalism* (London: Macmillan, 1960), Chapter 8 or the extended discussion in Maurice Dobb, *Welfare Economics and the Economics of Socialism* (Cambridge: Cambridge University Press, 1969); see also Janos Kornai, *The Socialist System* (Princeton: Princeton University Press, 1992).

14. A great deal of attention has been given to the issue of efficiency in connection with the growth analysis of the former planned socialist systems. For a summary of this literature and its application to the Soviet case, see Paul R. Gregory and Robert C. Stuart, *Soviet and Post-Soviet Economic Structure and Performance*, 5th ed. (New York: Harper-Collins, 1994), chapter 10.

15. For an introductory discussion of income distribution, see, for example, Roy Ruffin and Paul Gregory, *Economics* (New York: HarperCollins, 1993); for a development perspective on the distribution of income and wealth, see Poulson, *Economic Development*, chapter 7.
16. The basic theory of business cycles can be found in any basic work on macroeconomics. See, for example, Andrew W. Abel and Ben S. Berkake, *Macroeconomics* (New York: Addison-Wesley Publishing Company, 1992), chapter 11; there has been a great deal of interest in the issue of cycles in the formerly planned socialist economic systems. For a summary, see Paul R. Gregory and Robert C. Stuart *Soviet and Post-Soviet Economic Structure and Performance*, 5th ed., chapter 11.
17. David Granick, *Job Rights in the Soviet Union: Their Consequences* (Cambridge: Cambridge University Press, 1987).

Recommended Readings

A. Traditional Sources

Kenneth Arrow, *Social Choice and Individual Values*, 2nd. ed. (New York: Wiley, 1963.

Trevor Buck, *Comparative Industrial Systems* (New York: St. Martins, 1982).

Edward F. Denison, *Why Growth Rates Differ* (Washington, D.C.: The Brookings Institution, 1967).

————, *Accounting for Slower Economic Growth* (Washington, D.C.: The Brookings Institution, 1979).

John W. Kendrick, *Understanding Productivity* (Baltimore: Johns Hopkins University Press, 1977).

Etienne, S. Kirschen and Lucien Morrisens, "The Objectives and Instruments of Economic Policy," in Morris Bornstein (ed.), *Comparative Economic Systems: Models and Cases*, 7th. ed. (Homewood, Illinois, Irwin, 1994), 49–66.

Simon Kuznets, *Modern Economic Growth: Rate, Structure and Spread* (New Haven: Yale University Press, 1966).

John Michael Montias, *The Structure of Economic Systems* (New Haven: Yale University Press, 1977).

P. J. D. Wiles, *Distribution of Income East and West* (Amsterdam: North Holland, 1974).

B. Economic Growth and Productivity

Robert J. Barro, "Economic Growth in a Cross Section of Countries," *Quarterly Journal of Economics*, 106 (May 1991), 407–444.

"Empirical Evidence in Economic Growth Theory," *American Economic Review: Papers and Proceedings*, 83, 2 (May 1993), 415–430.

Malcolm Gillis, Dwight H. Perkins, Michael Roemer and Donald R. Snodgrass, *Economics of Development*, 3rd. ed. (New York: W. W. Norton, 1992), chapters 2–3.

Bruce Herrick and Charles P. Kindleberger, *Economic Development*, 4th. ed. (New York: McGraw-Hill, 1985).

Ross Levine and David Renelt, "A Sensitivity Analysis of Cross-Country Growth Regression," *American Economic Review*, 82, 4 (September 1992), 942–963.

Angus Maddison, "Growth and Slowdown in Advanced Capitalist Economics," *Journal of Economic Literature*, 25, 2 (June 1987), 649–698.

E. Wayne Nafziger, *The Economics of Developing Countries*, 2nd. ed. (Englewood Cliffs, N.J.: Prentice Hall, 1990), chapter 3.

Robert Summers and Alan Heston, "A New Set of International Comparisons of Real Product and Price Levels: Estimates for 130 Countries, 1950–1985," *Review of Income and Wealth*, 34 (March 1988), 1–25.

C. Income Distribution

Malcolm Gillis, Dwight H. Perkins, Michael Roemer and Donald R. Snodgrass, *Economics of Development*, 3rd. ed. (New York: W. W. Norton, 1992), chapter 5.

Margaret E. Grosh and E. Wayne Nafziger, "The Computation of World Income Distribution," *Economic Development and Cultural Change*, 34 (January 1986).

Jacques Lecaillon, Felix Paukert, Christian Morrison and Dimitri Germidis, *Income Distribution and Economic Development: An Analytical Survey* (Geneva: International Labor Office, 1984).

E. Wayne Nafziger, *The Economics of Developing Countries*, 2nd. ed. (Englewood Cliffs, N.J.: Prentice-Hall, 1990), chapter 6.

Barry W. Poulson, *Economic Development* (New York: West Publishing Company, 1994) chapter 7.

D. Cyclical Stability

Morris Bornstein, "Unemployment in Capitalist Regulated Market Economies and Socialist Centrally Planned Economies," in Morris Bornstein, ed., *Comparative Economic Systems: Models and Cases*, 7th. ed. (Homewood, Illinois: Irwin, 1994), 597–605.

Carlo Frateschi, ed., *Fluctuations and Cycles in Socialist Economies* (Brookfield, Vermont: Avebury Publishers, 1989).

David Granick, *Job Rights in the Soviet Union: Their Consequences* (Cambridge: Cambridge University Press, 1987).

Paul R. Gregory and Robert C. Stuart, *Soviet and Post-Soviet Economic Structure and Performance*, 5th. ed. (New York: HarperCollins, 1994), chapter 11.

Barry W. Ickes, "Cyclical Fluctuations in Centrally Planned Economies: A Critique of the Literature," *Soviet Studies*, 38, 1 (January 1986), 36–52.

Appendix 3A: Measuring The Impact of the Economic System

The analyst of differing economic systems is interested in isolating and measuring the impact of the economic system on economic outcomes for two major reasons. First, if differing system arrangements matter in the process of resource allocation, it is critical to understand the relationship between system or system characteristics and outcomes such that the former can be altered to influence the latter. Historically, much of the interest in differing system arrangements has focused on this issue, namely that resource allocation differs in knowable ways among system variants, especially the capitalist–socialist comparison. Second, in this era of transition, the nature and success of transition from plan to market is in part determined by the starting point from which the transition process begins. Put another way, many analysts have argued that indeed the planned socialist system did matter, and that its procedures of resource allocation resulted in a set of structural distortions compared with the outcomes that might have resulted under different allocation procedures. Thus it has been widely argued that the formerly planned socialist systems emphasized economic growth through forced saving and investment, the latter directed towards industry and especially heavy industry to a degree not generally observed in market economic systems. Can these sorts of differences be measured such that economic structures at the beginning of transition can be better understood?

To measure the system effect, differences in patterns of urbanization have been chosen as an example for two reasons. First, there is a large body of evidence relating levels of urbanization to levels of economic development for a large number of countries that differ in known and measurable ways. Second, it has been widely argued that the planned socialist systems in fact exercised a great deal of control over the urbanization process. Thus, while the case of urbanization seems important for understanding system differences, it is also an approach that can be generalized to understand other differences, such as those of industrial structure, consumption, international trade patterns, and the like.

Comparative Urbanization Patterns: System Influences

The relationship between economic development, as measured by per capita gross domestic product (GDP) and the proportion of a country's population living in urban areas (URB) is depicted in Figure 3.4, which shows that urbanization is positively related to GDP per capita.

Suppose we wish to determine whether urbanization patterns differ systematically between socialist and capitalist systems. Data for the late 1980s revealed that about 65 percent of the Soviet population lived in urban centers, whereas the

FIGURE 3.4 Urbanization and Economic Development

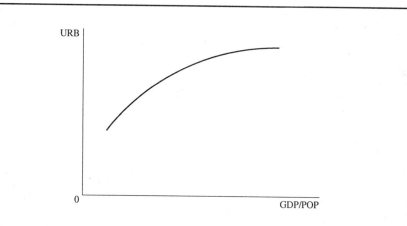

equivalent figure for the United States was about 75 percent. Can we conclude that the Soviet Union was less urbanized than the United States? According to Figure 3.4, lower Soviet urbanization should be expected because the Soviet Union was at a lower level of economic development than the United States. There are two possible explanations for these patterns, each developed in Figure 3.5.

Panel A of Figure 3.5 provides one possible explanation of the observed urbanization pattern: Urbanization patterns have been similar in socialist and capitalist economic systems and differences accounted for simply because urbanization *levels* have been related to levels of economic development. Because the Soviet Union was at a lower level of economic development than the United States, the Soviet level of urbanization was also lower. Had the Soviet Union suddenly achieved the same level of development, the two countries would have had the same urbanization rate.

Panel B suggests a different interpretation: Socialist and capitalist urbanization patterns are systematically different. Even when we control for the level of economic development, socialist systems are less urbanized, suggesting that there are characteristic features of socialism—possibly aspects of the economic system or policies—that systematically influence urbanization.

Chapter 2 outlined an approach to isolating the impact of the economic system and assessing that impact (both its direction and its magnitude) on observed outcomes. In notational form, the following approach was suggested:

$$O = f(\text{ES, ENV, POL}) \qquad (3\text{A.1})$$

Outcomes (O) are a function of the economic system (ES), the environment in which the economic system functions (ENV), and, finally, policy (POL). Can we, in practice, empirically estimate the foregoing relationship for real-world economic systems? In this particular case, the outcome (O) is the level of urbanization, the environmental or controlling factor (ENV) is the level of economic development, measured by per capita gross domestic product; the economic system (ES) is considered explicitly—it is either capitalist or socialist:

$$\text{URB}_i = a + b(\text{GNP/POP})_i + u_i \qquad (3\text{A.2})$$

This relationship, which is assumed to have the usual characteristics (a positive relationship between per capita income and urbanization), allows the examination of statistical regularities across a number of systems. In practice, there are several ways to estimate equation 3A.2 to capture the economic system. Statistically, the task is to observe a particular relationship (in this case, urbanization) in samples drawn from two populations (capitalist and socialist) and to determine whether the results obtained can be assumed to have come from two different populations.

The Forecasting Approach

Equation 3A.2 can be estimated from data drawn from a sample of capitalist or market systems. Deriving estimates for the parameters of the equation (the constant *a* and the coefficient *b*), results in a simple model from which predictions can be made. Specifically, using sample data on per capita gross domestic product from

FIGURE 3.5   Urbanization in Different Economic Systems

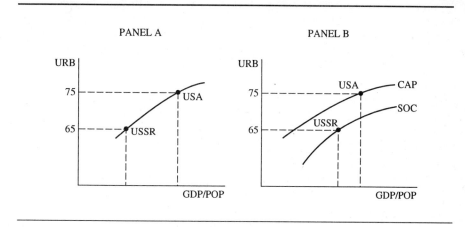

capitalist systems, we would use the predictive equation to forecast values for URB_i in socialist systems. The forecast values provides the expected level of urbanization of each socialist country, assuming that they follow the "normal" capitalist relationship between income and urbanization. The actual socialist values of URB_i can then be compared with those predicted by our equation. Assuming that our predictive equation captures the "normal" capitalist relationship, differences between predicted and actual values of URB_i would indicate whether socialist countries are, relative to capitalist countries, underurbanized, overurbanized, or about the same.

This approach has the distinct advantage of indicating how particular socialist countries behave relative to "normal" patterns. As it stands, however, we have no test of the statistical significance of our results. Finally, should we observe that the deviations are not uniformly positive or negative, some additional criterion of evaluation would be necessary.

The Dummy Variable Approach

An alternate method is to use dummy variables.[1] In this approach, equation 3A.2 is respecified as follows:

$$URB_i = a + b(GDP/POP)_i + cDUM + u_i \qquad (3A.3)$$

We assign the dummy variable the value 1 for socialist systems and the value 0 for capitalist systems, and then we estimate it by using an aggregated sample of socialist and capitalist countries. The statistical importance of the economic system in influencing urbanization levels is assessed by determining the significance and magnitude of the coefficient attached to the dummy variable.

A variant of the dummy variable approach is used to isolate differences in *both* the intercept and the slope, thus providing a better explanation of why the socialist and capitalist patterns differ. Were we to use this variant in our present example, the dummy variable would be defined as before: 1 for socialist systems and 0 for capitalist systems. A second dummy variable would be defined as follows:

$$DUMG = (DUM)(GNP/POP)$$

In this variant, the equation to be tested would be

$$URB_i = a + b(GNP/POP)_i + cDUM + dDUMG + u_i \qquad (3A.4)$$

As before, we would make this estimate by using data from capitalist and socialist systems, and the results would be assessed by examining the magnitude and significance of the coefficients. The c coefficient captures differences between intercepts, and the d coefficient differences between slopes, in the urbanization—income relationship.

The Chow Test

A third method for examining system differences in a relationship such as equation 3A.2 is the Chow test.[2] In this approach, equation 3A.2 is estimated separately, once using capitalist and once, socialist sample data. Two sets of parameter estimates exist, one for the socialist, the other for the capitalist sample. The Chow test is used to determine whether the coefficients (for example, the coefficient b in equation 3A.2) are in fact statistically different in the sense that they can be said to come from different populations. If the Chow test shows the parameters to be statistically different, the conclusion is that the economic system acts to render the relationship between per capita income and urbanization different.[3] The empirical evidence on urbanization patterns seems to support the outcome postulated in Panel B of Figure 3A.2.[4] However, although considerable emphasis is placed on this sort of analysis in our characterization of different outcomes across economic systems, the analysis presents a number of problems. The modeling of the relationship between systems and outcomes remains simplistic. Moreover, econometric issues such as appropriate specification, along with the usual problems of data availability in the international context, complicate our attempts to analyze these relationships.[5]

Notes

1. The problem posed in this appendix is of a basic and general nature. For the techniques of analysis, see, for example, William H. Greene, *Econometric Analysis*, 2d. ed. (New York: Macmillan Publishing Company, 1993), pp. 3–32.
2. For a discussion of the Chow test, see *Econometric Analysis*, 211–212.
3. For a useful comparison of various approaches, see Edward A. Hewett, "Alternative Econometric Approaches for Studying the Link Between Economic Systems and Economic Outcomes," *Journal of Comparative Economics*, 4 (September 1980), 274–294. Also see John Michael Montias, *The Structure of Economic Systems* (New Haven: Yale University Press, 1976), Ch. 5.
4. See Gur Ofer, "Economizing on Urbanization in Socialist Countries: Historical Necessity or Socialist Strategy?" in Alan A. Brown and Egon Neuberger, eds., *Internal Migration:*

A Comparative Perspective (New York: Academic, 1977), Ch. 16. For a broader discussion, see Henry W. Morton and Robert C. Stuart, *The Contemporary Soviet City* (Armonk, N.Y.: M. E. Sharpe, 1984).

5. For a recent alternative to traditional approaches, see Peter Murrell and Randi Ryterman, "A Methodology for Testing Comparative Economic Theories: Theory and Application to East-West Environmental Policies," *Journal of Comparative Economies*, 15, 4 (December 1991), 582–601.

4

Economic Reform: Evolution or Revolution

The economic system, the environment in which the system functions, and the economic policies all influence economic outcomes. Most of these influencing forces can, however, be changed. Although the terminology lacks precision, it is useful to think of **economic reform** as attempts to modify an existing system, while **transition** refers to the shift from one system to another, for example, the contemporary replacement of plan by market in the countries of Easter Europe.

Reform of Economic Systems

Although the concept of economic reform applies to both capitalist and socialist economic systems, change is usually viewed differently in different systems. For example, economic reform in capitalist systems is generally evolutionary in nature, gradual in pace, and, to a significant degree, introduced on a decentralized basis through market-type institutions. In socialist systems, however, change is viewed as revolutionary in nature and abrupt in approach and is usually introduced by a central authority, for example, the former communist parties of Eastern Europe and the Soviet Union.

No matter how systemic change is classified, modifications that economic systems undergo do change their character. The introduction of command planning and collectivized agriculture in the Soviet Union at the end of the 1920s and the subsequent introduction of such arrangements into Eastern Europe and China after World War II are examples of fundamental and rapid changes in economic systems. In these cases, decision-making arrangements were centralized, the market was replaced by the plan, state ownership supplanted private ownership, and moral incentives became increasingly important. The replacement of command planning by worker-managed socialism in Yugoslavia in the 1950s is another case of fundamental change. Finally, in recent times Eastern Europe and the Soviet Union are attempting to shift from plan to market allocation.

If economic reforms in socialist economic systems can generally be identified as "packages" introduced by a central authority, the reforms of capitalist systems are more difficult to characterize. Today's industrialized countries operate differently from those of 100 years earlier. These changes have occurred gradually, without clear milestones. When resources are allocated through markets, changes in allocation procedures are less visible than they are when a central authority makes sweeping changes by fiat. Some milestones can be identified. Britain's passage of the Cornu Laws in the nineteenth century turned the English economy into the world's first open economy. Bismarck's introduction of social security legislation changed Germany's economic system as did the passage of social security laws in the United States during the Great Depression. Further examples include privatization during the Thatcher years in Great Britain and, in the United States, the Full Employment Act of 1946 and the Great Society of Lyndon Johnson in the 1960s.

Measuring the implementation of economic reform is a complex task. Economic reform attempts to change system characteristics, but the ultimate intent is to change economic outcomes. Should the implementation of economic reform be judged by looking at outcomes, or should we look directly at the changes made in the characteristics of the economic system? If neither outcomes nor characteristics change, has the reform been a failure or has it been less than a full-blown economic reform? As previously emphasized, this problem is especially complex in the 1990s as a number of countries move through the transition from plan to market.

The fundamental problem, however, is that systemic change is part of a much broader process of socioeconomic change and economic development. This broader spectrum goes well beyond the confines of comparative economic systems and yet, as we are emphasizing in the 1990s, is directly relevant to the field.

Economic Development and Systemic Change

This characterization of systemic change is in part influenced by the models or frameworks used for interpreting change. The work of the classical economists in the nineteenth century made our view of economic development appear pessimistic despite the perceived merits of the invisible hand for the allocation of resources. Economic development, they argued, required capital accumulation, which would be insufficient to offset the impact of diminishing returns. At best, a circular flow or continuing reproduction of an existing state was possible, and more likely, stagnation would result. In the twentieth century, the era of neoclassical economics spawned a variety of explanations, some focusing on the technical underpinnings of economic growth and structural change, others focusing more broadly on social change, with many cast in historical perspective. In many of the different approaches to understanding change, a point of contrast has been between those who have argued within a framework of static general equilibrium theory and those who attempt a more general dynamic framework to understand why, in fact, an equilibrium at a particular point in time may not be sustained.

Karl Marx, who sought to demonstrate the inevitability of change through the natural evolution of one system into another, formulated the most famous theory of system change. Whether the Marxian approach is used as a framework in which to interpret change, or as a set of tools to understand the underpinnings of contemporary socialist objectives, classical Marxian analysis deserves attention.

Within the broader framework of theories attempting to understand the dynamics of systemic change, the contributions of Joseph Schumpeter and the contemporary evolutionary approaches are of special importance. Both approaches attempt to move beyond the static framework of neoclassical economic theory, including emphasis on the importance of organizational change.

Marx's Theory of Change

Karl Marx (1818–1883) concluded in *Das Kapital* that capitalism is an unstable economic system, whose lifespan is inevitably limited.[1]

Marx's theory of capitalism is based on his materialist conception of history,[2] which teaches that economic forces (called **productive forces**) determine how production relations, markets, and society itself (the **superstructure**) are organized. Weak productive forces (underdeveloped human and capital resources) result in one arrangement for producing goods and services (**production relations**), and strong productive forces lead to different, more advanced production arrangements. A society with underdeveloped economic resources has underdeveloped production relations and superstructure (manifested in barter exchange, serf labor, a rigid social hierarchy, and religious biases against commerce). As the productive forces improve, new economic and social relationships emerge (such as hired rather than serf labor and monetary rather than natural exchange). These new arrangements are not compatible with the old economic, cultural, and social relationships. When they come into contact, tensions and conflicts mount.

Eventually, incompatibilities become so great that a quantitative change (usually the result of violent revolution or war) occurs. New production relations and a new superstructure, compatible with the new productive forces, replace the old order. These **qualitative changes** are inevitable because societies are destined to evolve from a lower to a higher order.

The engine of change is the conflict between the old and new, primarily in the form of class antagonisms (the emerging capitalist class versus the landed gentry in feudal societies, the worker versus the capitalist in capitalist societies). The process of evolutionary and inevitable qualitative change through the competition of opposing forces (**thesis versus antithesis**) is the foundation of Marx's theory of **dialectical materialism**, which was based on the teachings of the German philosophers George Wilhelm Hegel and Ludwig Feuerbach.

The upshot of Marx's materialist conception of history was his contention that societies evolve according to an inevitable pattern of social and economic change in which lower systems are replaced by more advanced systems. In this manner, feudalism is bound to replace slavery, capitalism inevitably displaces feudalism, and socialism eventually replaces capitalism.

The victory of capitalism over feudalism represented a qualitative step forward for society. A highly efficient productive machine (capitalism) replaced an inefficient one (feudalism) based on semiservile labor and governed by traditional landed interests. Two landmarks signaled the emergence of capitalism. The first was the initial accumulation of capital by the emerging capitalist class—a process Marx called **primitive capitalist accumulation**. The second indicator was the formation of a "free" labor force at the disposal of capitalist employers. Laborers, were separated from control over land, tools, and livestock and were left with only their own labor to sell. At this point the capitalist, who now controlled the means of production, hired this free labor, and capitalist factories were established. In this manner, the basic class conflict of capitalism was created—the conflict between the working class and the capitalist, who "owns" the labor services of the worker.

The feature that distinguishes labor from the other factors of production is that the employer can compel workers to produce a value that exceeds the value that workers require to maintain themselves. Yet the employer is not required to pay workers the full value of their production—only enough to allow them to subsist. One worker may have to perform 8 hours of work to produce a value sufficient to meet subsistence needs; yet the employer can force the worker to create a surplus, which will accrue to capitalists, by working 12 hours—4 hours more than are required to satisfy subsistence needs. The exploitation of labor is the source of capitalist profits, which Marx called **surplus value**.

Marx pictured capitalism, in its early stages, as a world of cut-throat competition. The capitalist was driven to maximize profits (surplus value) and to accumulate more capital out of profits. Capitalists, operating in intensely competitive markets, are forced to introduce cost-saving innovations lest their competitors do so first and drive them out of business. One capitalist introduces a new labor-saving technology, attracts competitors' customers through lower prices, and experiences a temporary increase in profits above "normal" levels. The profits are short-lived, however, because competitors respond by introducing the same cost-saving techniques, and new competitors enter the market in response to windfall profits. Excess industry profits are eliminated, and no capitalist ends up better off. But when fixed capital is substituted for labor, the profit rate will decline. There is an inherent tendency to substitute capital for labor, even though labor is the sole source of surplus value. Marx predicted the profit rate would fall, with disastrous consequences for capitalism.

As the profit rate falls, capitalism's internal contradictions and weaknesses become apparent. In an effort to halt the decline in profits, capitalists increase the exploitation of their workers, and alienation and exploitation intensify. The declining profit rate leads to the failure of marginal businesses, and bankrupt capitalists now swell the ranks of the unemployed. Those fortunate enough to be employed are exploited and alienated; the unemployed are in even worse shape.

A more ominous phenomenon is the tendency toward overproduction. Workers are kept at subsistence wages by high unemployment; capitalists, driven by the desire to accumulate capital, are not willing to increase their spending on luxury goods. Moreover, the ranks of the capitalists are thinning, as monopolies drive out smaller capitalists. Yet all the while, the productive capacity of the economy is growing because of the growing capital-intensity of industry. Aggregate demand falls chronically short of aggregate supply; recessions and then depressions occur, and worldwide crises become commonplace. The declining profit rate leads to declines in investment spending and to further shortfalls in aggregate demand.

Marx described only generally the final stages of the **capitalist breakdown**. Overproduction, underconsumption, disproportions, and the exploitation and alienation of workers combine to create the conditions necessary for the violent overthrow of capitalism.[3] Workers unite against the weakened capitalist class and, through a violent *world* revolution, establish a new socialist order. Marx had little to say about this new order. Implicit in Marx's writings on the final stage of capitalism is the point that the contradictions will be more intense in the most advanced capitalist countries; the socialist revolution would be initiated there.

Joseph A. Schumpeter: The Evolution of Capitalism

The views of Joseph Schumpeter are important for the student of differing economic systems.[4] Although Schumpeter was pessimistic about the survival of capitalism as an economic system and predicted its replacement with socialism, he nevertheless viewed this demise rather differently than Marx.[5]

Schumpeter argued that the capitalist economy could not be understood within the framework of static economic analysis—that is, the pursuit of objectives by existing institutions. Capitalism, he argued, is fundamentally dynamic in character and can only be understood if change is understood. The important issues, therefore, are not how an organization functions at a point in time, but rather how that organization comes into being and how it evolves over time as a mechanism generating economic growth.

The driving force of evolution in the capitalist system, according to Schumpeter, is innovation, or the development and implementation of new products, new ideas, and new ways of doing things. This drive, he argued, is the function of an entrepreneurial class, driven by and rewarded through a profit motive. Indeed, the development of new ideas broadly defined was for Schumpeter a process termed **creative destruction**, as the new replaced the old.

Schumpeter viewed the capitalist economy not in terms of the competitive ideal, but rather characterized by concentration. This concentration—the routinization of the entrepreneurial spirit and a lack of social willingness to reward this type of activity—would lead to a decline in entrepreneurial activity, which would be a fundamental reason for the decline of capitalism.

Thus while there are similarities between the Schumpeterian and Marxian interpretations of capitalism (the importance of classes, the cyclical nature of economic activity, the importance of profit, and a tendency for profit rates to decline), the Schumpeterian focus is really different. But, for both views, the focus on dynamics or change is important.

The Evolutionary View of Capitalism

There are a wide variety of approaches to economic development and specifically to the nature of capitalism as an economic system through which economic development may proceed. In recent years, emphasis has been renewed on the need to view the economic system in dynamic terms, focusing on change rather than achievements at a given point in time.

Although a variety of views and perspectives are perhaps first associated with the views of Schumpeter, the evolutionary approach is fundamentally dynamic in character, emphasizing that, as individuals (or participants in an economic system) pursue objectives, they do so in a special environment.[6]

Specifically, individuals are likely to pursue a variety of (changing) goals in an environment of uncertainty and limited information. In this setting of uncertainty and continually emerging new information, it is argued that both the objectives being pursued and the organizational arrangements through which they are pursued are likely to change over time. The importance of the evolutionary perspective lies, in part, in its emphasis on a dynamic process, but this also makes the development and change of organizations a fundamental component of that process. In this sense, there is a close affinity between the evolutionary perspective and what was once termed the organizational theory of the firm. But, more important, the evolutionary perspective relates organizational structure and organizational behavior to the growth of the economy, and especially the importance of innovation as a source of growth, a view consistent with the earlier Schumpeterian focus. Thus in a number of dimensions, the evolutionary perspective differs markedly from the traditional neoclassical perspective. Moreover, these differences are of major importance to the analyst of differing economic systems. The importance of these differences will be evident as subsequent chapters look more closely at the process of transition from plan to market.

Marx and Schumpeter were interested primarily in system change. Marx focused attention on the interrelationship among economics, culture, and politics that remain valid to the present day. In Marx's view the demise of capitalism and the rise of socialism were inevitable. In this regard, Marx was a poor predictor of the future.

Marx's theory of system change, while severely flawed, remains the most serious model of system change. Its primary hypothesis is that capitalism is inherently unstable. Capitalism's internal contradictions ordained it to failure.

The Instability of Socialism

Whereas Marx and others believed in the inherent instability of capitalism, a number of critics argued the exact opposite: socialism is an inherently unstable economic system. Socialism's critics warned against socialist experiments on the grounds that, once started, they might be difficult to stop.[7] If a socialist economy was indeed established, it would prove unworkable and destined either to collapse or to operate at very low levels of efficiency.

Mises and Hayek

The Austrian economists, Ludwig von Mises and Nobel laureate Friederich von Hayek, argued that capitalism develops its institutions in an efficient manner.[8] If an attempted institutional change does not improve the efficiency of the system, it will disappear. In capitalism's early years, it encountered problems of raising capital for projects of great risk. To solve this problem, the limited liability corporation was invented. The corporation proved its durability by effectively raising capital for risky projects. Similarly, capitalism discovered that without effective common law to protect private property, privately owned resources could not be effectively allocated. Out of this need, common laws emerged, which made it possible to honor contracts and to obey property laws. Capitalism's institutions emerged according to a **spontaneous order** and were thus able to withstand the test of time.

Experiments with socialism, such as took place in Russia after the Bolshevik revolution of 1917, created an economic system of planned socialism that contained a number of internal contradictions. The ideas of Mises and Hayek will be discussed in a later chapter. For now, it is sufficient to note that they felt a socialist economy would be too complex to plan from the center and would require more information on technology, prices, quantities, and assortments than a central planning board could digest. Moreover, they felt that the task of planning and management could not be effectively decentralized because, in the absence of private property, even the best-intentioned managers of state enterprises could not make economically correct decisions.

For these reasons, Mises and Hayek felt that such socialist experiments as those in the Soviet Union, would fail and that eventually the experiment would be abandoned. In this sense, the theories of Mises and Hayek are models of change of socialism back to capitalism on the grounds of socialism's inferiority as an economic system.

Kornai: The Economics of Shortage

The Hungarian economist, Janos Kornai, also argued that socialism was inherently unstable because of its natural tendency to generate shortage.[9]

Kornai argued that the planned socialist economy is a **system of shortage**, where shortage is a systemic, perpetual, and self-reproducing condition. Others argued that persistent shortages or excess demand in the socialist systems are functions of identifiable, though not necessarily easily corrected, forces. Consumer goods are simply not a high priority but rather are supplanted by producer goods and military production. Errors in planning, inadequate incentives, and other system characteristics lead to continuing shortages.

From a very different perspective, Kornai argued that the economy of shortages arises from the nature of the enterprise in the planned socialist system. The socialist enterprise operates under fundamentally different rules from the capitalist enterprise. The capitalist enterprise is motivated to maximize profits. It makes its input and output decisions on the basis of prices established in markets. As a profit maximizer, the capitalist enterprise has little incentive to overdemand resources. If it employs more resources than technology requires, its profits suffer. The capitalist enterprise operates under a **hard budget constraint**. Faced with input prices and output prices, the capitalist enterprise must cover its costs while earning an acceptable rate of return on invested capital. If it fails to meet its budget constraint, the capitalist firm will fail in the long run. The capitalist firm must live within its means. The hard budget constraint polices capitalist enterprise activities and effectively eliminates shortage (in the sense of excess demand for inputs).

The socialist firm operates in a supply-constrained economy. Socialist planners have as their objective the rapid expansion of outputs, and they judge the performance of socialist enterprises on the basis of output expansion. The manner in which socialist enterprises select inputs to meet their output objectives is of less importance than the output targets themselves. Although socialist enterprises face prices for inputs and outputs, their resource-allocation decisions are aimed at meeting output targets. Relative prices play only a minor role.

The capitalist enterprise that fails to live within its means is punished by bankruptcy. The socialist enterprise that fails to cover costs plus a rate of return on the state's invested capital does not suffer the same consequences. Socialist planners value enterprises for their outputs; socialist enterprises that make losses remain in business by virtue of state subsidies. Accordingly, socialist enterprises face a **soft budget constraint**. Socialist enterprises can live beyond their means, if necessary, over the long run.

The hard budget constraint forces capitalist enterprises to limit their demands for inputs. The soft budget constraint on socialist enterprises fails to reward them for restricting their input demands. Hence the socialist system generates continuous excess demands for inputs. The supply of inputs falls chronically short of the demand for inputs, and persistent shortages or imbalances result.

Economic systems must allocate resources in an orderly fashion. Persistent imbalances and chronic shortages detract from the orderly allocation of resources. With imbalances, those who obtain resources may be those who will not put them to their best and highest use. Kornai's analysis of socialism is related to the complexity and motivation issues raised by Mises and Hayek. Kornai's conclusion is that the socialist motivation system and inattention to relative prices disrupt the orderly allocation of resources under socialism.

Changes in Capitalist Economies

Change in capitalist economies is more gradual and less visible than change in socialist economies, which tends to come from above. Careful analysis of long-run changes can, however, reveal the process of change in capitalist economies.

Property Rights: Private versus Public

The ownership of property is a fundamental distinguishing characteristic of economic systems that can be measured, albeit imperfectly. Significant changes in the shares of public and private ownership of property can alter the nature of a capitalist economic system. Indeed, if the state owned a major share of existing property, we would no longer classify the system as capitalist.

Real-world capitalist systems are mixed, some having higher shares of public ownership than others. **Privatization** occurs when property that had previously been publicly owned is sold to private owners.[10] Public ownership increases when property that had previously been privately owned becomes publicly owned, or **nationalized**. The shares of public and private ownership can be changed either by government spending programs that create new government-owned capital (such as the U.S. government's Tennessee Valley Authority project initiated during the Great Depression) or by direct government buying or selling of existing facilities. By selling its shares of British Air, for example, the British government increased the share of private ownership in the United Kingdom. And by buying a failing steel company, the British government increases the share of public ownership.

Public sentiment in favor of public ownership was highest in the United States during the Great Depression. In the United Kingdom, the election of labor governments in the 1940s and 1950s provided political support for nationalization, whereas the lengthy tenure of a conservative government from the mid-late 1970s to the mid-1990s showed support for privatization. Alternating socialist and conservative governments in France also reflect rising and falling sentiment for privatization or nationalization. In Germany, both socialist and conservative governments have consistently favored privatization since the end of the Second World War. The German government has sold its shares of major corporations to private owners throughout the postwar era.

In the United States, government shares of structures and land have not changed noticeably since the early 1930s, nor has the share of output produced by government enterprises. After a rise in public ownership in the early 1930s, the share of government ownership has remained fairly stable, despite a substantial increase in output shares consumed by government.

Table 4.1 shows the government shares of fixed capital in 1955, 1980, and 1987 in seven industrialized capitalist countries including Greece. The differences in ownership shares partially result from different accounting procedures, but even so, substantial changes in government ownership shares within each country cannot be observed from these figures. In some countries, government ownership shares have fallen (Canada and Greece). In others, they have risen (United Kingdom and Sweden). In the majority of countries, government shares of capital have been stable over the 25-year period. In France, West Germany, and Finland, government ownership shares either were unchanged or changed only slightly.

Table 4.1 reveals that overall there has been little change in private and public ownership shares in capitalist countries, suggesting that these countries have reached a basic consensus on the distribution of public and private ownership. Changes in governments over the years have not notably altered this consensus.

The conservative governments elected in the United States and Western Europe in the 1980s brought a rising tide of privatization. It is difficult to tell whether this trend will continue long enough to fundamentally change the shares of private and

TABLE 4.1   Share of Government Ownership of Fixed Capital,
Capitalist Countries (percentages of total)

	1955	1980	1987
Canada	22	24	23
Finland	—	16	16
France	16	17	—
Greece	3	1	—
Sweden	4	7	—
United Kingdom	11	14	—
West Germany	7	8	8
Unweighted average	11.2	9.9	—

Source: OECD, *Flows and Stocks of Fixed Capital, 1955–1980* (Paris: OECD, 1983); OECD, *Flows and Stocks of Fixed Capital, 1962–1987* (Paris, OECD, 1989).

public ownership in the industrialized capitalist countries, but in view of the long-term stability of ownership shares, this outcome seems unlikely.[11] It is, however, important to be aware that assessing the role of government in the economy would require evidence beyond simple ownership arrangements. For example, the evidence in Table 4.2 suggests expansion of government influence as measured by the relative importance of central government spending.

Trends in Competition

Changes in **competition** alter the nature and operation of a capitalist economy, but they do not result in the system's ceasing to be capitalist. A capitalist economy in which monopoly is the prevalent form may operate inefficiently and may cause consumers to pay high prices, but it is still a capitalist economy.

The degree of competitiveness in a capitalist economy is affected by antitrust laws, regulations, and trade policies. It is difficult to generalize about trends in state policy toward competition. The best-documented trend is the postwar relaxation of international trade barriers. The industrialized capitalist countries created international arrangements for dismantling the restrictive trade barriers that were put in place during the Great Depression, and there is little doubt that the degree of international competition expanded at a rapid rate throughout the postwar period. Trade barriers were lowered in both product markets and factor markets (see Figure 4.1). In the 1990s, one can speak of a world capital market in which financial capital flows freely and quickly among Europe, North America, and the industrialized Asian countries.

Deregulation is another visible indicator of state policy toward competition. When a potentially competitive industry is regulated by the state, the degree of competition is reduced. The trend toward deregulation started in the United States in the late 1970s, and it spread from North America to Western Europe and Japan in the

TABLE 4.2   Central Government Expenditure as
a Percentage of GNP

	1972	1990
Canada	20.2	23.4
Finland	24.3	31.1
France	32.3	43.0
Greece	27.5	50.9 [a]
Sweden	27.7	42.3
United Kingdom	32.0	34.8
Germany (West)	24.2	29.4

[a] 1986

Source: The World Bank, *World Development Report 1992* (New York: Oxford University Press, 1992), Table II.

1980s. Deregulation has been most prominent in transportation, communications, and banking, but it remains to be seen whether other capitalist countries will deregulate to the extent of the United States and whether the deregulation experiment will continue in the United States through the 1990s.

The least visible aspect of state competition policy—and the most difficult to characterize—is antitrust policy and the mechanisms designed to implement these policies. Most industrialized capitalist countries allow more exemptions from antitrust laws than the United States, which exempts primarily farming operations and labor unions; however, antitrust laws that prevent abuse of monopoly power exist in nearly every capitalist country. Unlike the U.S. laws, which declare all formal price-fixing agreements illegal, other industrialized capitalist countries judge price-fixing arrangements on the basis of whether they result in reasonable prices.

In the United States, there have been few major changes in antitrust legislation since the 1930s. The changes that have occurred have taken place in the courts. Initially, the courts interpreted the antitrust laws as outlawing anticompetitive behavior, but in the early 1950s, antitrust laws were interpreted as outlawing monopoly power per se, whether this power was abused or not. The 1970s and 1980s have seen a move toward a more liberal interpretation of antitrust laws, stemming from the recognition that businesses must compete in international markets against close substitutes and that antitrust laws should not be used to penalize competitive successes.

Growing international competition and deregulation should increase the degree of competition in capitalist countries. Moreover, rapid technological progress produces a wider variety of competitive products and promotes competition. William Shepherd has attempted to measure the changing degree of competition in the U.S. economy. He concludes that the American economy became more competitive after 1960 as a consequence of growing international competition and deregulation.[12] According to Shepherd, the share of the U.S. economy that was effectively competitive remained fairly stable at 52 to 54 percent between 1939 and 1958 but rose to

FIGURE 4.1   Average U.S. Import Duties, 1900–1990

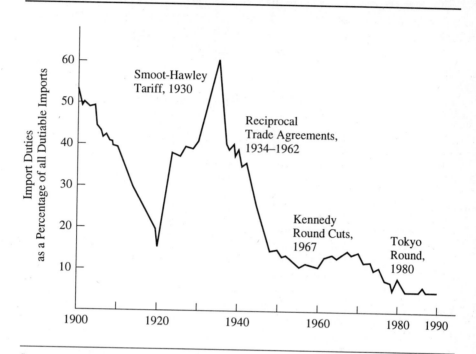

Sources: *Historical Statistics of the United States; Statistical Abstract of the United States.*

77 percent by 1980. Similar studies have not been conducted for the other industrialized capitalist countries, so we do not know whether the American experience is representative. However, because virtually all industrialized capitalist countries have been subject to growing international competition, the impact of this development may be equally strong in other capitalist countries.

An important perspective on deregulation in the American economy is provided by the major changes in airlines, telecommunications, trucking, and other important sectors of the economy during the 1980s.[13] According to a recent survey of the outcomes of this deregulation, in 1977 fully regulated industries produced 17 percent of gross national product, while by 1988 this share had decreased to 6.6 percent.[14] Although the results of this deregulation experience have often been controversial, economic analysis suggests that, for the most part, the benefits have outweighed the costs with significant net gains for the American public.

Income Redistribution

Capitalism uses material incentives to motivate economic behavior, and a move away from material incentives would signal a fundamental change in the capitalist economic system. If a capitalist state altered the distribution of income earned in factor markets, earnings in factor markets would become less decisive in determining command over resources. For example, if the tax system equalized the distribution of income after taxes, material rewards would cease to guide economic decision making. Changes in tax policy can indeed change the nature of the capitalist economic system.

For a tax system to have a large impact on the reward system, taxes must make up a large share of factor income, and the tax system must redistribute income. Income is redistributed via either a **progressive tax** (which redistributes proportionally away from high-income earners) or a **regressive tax** (which redistributes proportionally away from low-income earners). In a progressive tax system, the tax's share of income rises with income; in a regressive system, that share falls. In order to substantially redistribute income away from high-income earners, the tax system must take up a large share of factor income and must be highly progressive.

Table 4.3 gives information on changes in the tax system's shares of income and in the shares of income taken by several different taxes. The table shows that in all the capitalist countries surveyed, taxes rose as a percentage of GDP. The most modest rise was in the United States—from 27 to 29 percent; the largest rise was in Sweden—from 28 to 49 percent.

The shares of income taxes and taxes on goods provide indirect information on the redistributive role of the tax system. Taxes on income tend to be progressive, whereas taxes on goods are regressive. Assuming no significant changes in income tax rates by income bracket, the tax system would become more progressive as a whole when the share of income taxes rose. The tax system would become more regressive as a whole when the share of taxes on goods rose. Table 4.3 reveals a mixed picture. In five of the countries, the income tax share of total taxes remained stable or fell. In the other three countries, the income tax share rose. In only two countries (Italy's rising share and Sweden's falling share) were the changes substantial. The table also shows a generally declining reliance on taxes on goods. The share of taxes on goods fell substantially in France, Italy, and Japan. Only Canada and the United Kingdom recorded small increases in the share of taxes on goods.

Not having readily available information on income tax rates, we can draw only cautious conclusions about Table 4.3. There has been a substantial increase in the share of taxes of factor income in the industrialized capitalist countries, but there has not been a substantial shift in the form of taxation. Although there has been a slight drift away from taxes on goods and toward taxes on income (which should increase progressivity), these changes have been relatively minor, except in Italy. The overall conclusion is that the redistributive role of the tax system has not changed much in capitalist economies, even though the share of taxes has been rising.

What have capitalist governments done with the increasing tax share of GDP? The last columns show the dramatic rises in the shares of social security transfers as a percentage of GDP. The effect of social security transfers on economic rewards depends on how these transfers are distributed. If they are distributed according to contributions, they do not alter the factor distribution of income. If they are

TABLE 4.3 Changes in the Capitalist Tax System

| | Taxes as a Percentage of GDP | | | Share of Total Taxes | | | | | | Social Security Transfers as Percentage of GDP | | |
| | | | | Income Taxes[a] | | | Taxes on Goods | | | | | |
	1960	1980	1989	1970	1985	1989	1970	1985	1989	1960	1981	1988
United States	27	29	30	48	42	44	19	18	16	5.0	11.1	10.6
Canada	24	32	35	45	43	47	32	33	30	7.9	9.9	12.0
France	32	42	44	18	18	17	38	29	29	13.5	20.3	21.7
Italy	27	30	38	17	36	37	38	26	27	9.8	5.7	17.3
Japan	20	25	31	41	46	49	22	15	13	3.8	10.6	11.8
Sweden	28	49	56	54	42	43	29	25	24	8.0	18.2	15.1[b]
United Kingdom	28	35	37	40	38	39	29	31	31	6.8	12.9	16.0
West Germany	30	38	38	32	33	35	32	27	26	12.0	17.2	—

[a] individual and corporate
[b] 1987

Sources: *Statistical Abstract of the United States* (international comparisons); OECD, *Historical Statistics* (Paris: OECD, 1990).

distributed in a manner unrelated to contributions (such as in poverty programs), they do alter the distribution of income.

The evidence that has been collected for the United States shows that, although the tax system does not materially alter the distribution of income, the distribution of transfers does.[15] The major instrument of state income redistribution in the United States is the distribution of transfer payments to low-income recipients. The growing GDP share of social security transfers suggests that a significant alteration in material rewards may have occurred in capitalist economic systems through the distribution of social security transfers to the less advantaged.

Worker Participation

A basic characteristic of capitalism is that the owners of capital (individual proprietors, partners, or corporate shareholders) are rewarded out of profits.[16] Workers are paid wages that do not vary directly with profits. Capitalism can change its character by sharing profits and management control with workers. Such a change would require new incentive arrangements.

Because profits fluctuate more than wage income, the owners of capital are, in effect, making a deal with workers that as long as the business remains solvent, workers will receive their contracted wages. Owners of capital, who bear risk in the form of fluctuating returns on capital, earn a return to reward them for risk taking. The worker accepts a contractual wage and, in return, is prepared to follow the directions of management.

The fundamental nature of the relationship between worker and owner of capital can be altered by profit sharing. If rewards to workers depend in part on the profits of the business, the worker becomes a partial capitalist and bears a part of the risk of fluctuating profits. If workers' incomes depend entirely on the profits of the enterprise, then they basically become capitalists.

The advantages of a profit-sharing economy are that workers are more materially interested in the profitability of the enterprise. They will be more inclined to work in the interests of the enterprise than before, and they will be less inclined to shirk work. A profit-sharing economy has another advantage: If workers' pay rises and falls with profits, the economy becomes more flexible. Recessions cause wages to drop, and falling wages stimulate employment.

The notion of profit sharing is not new, but it has gained increasing attention in capitalist economies because of the large-scale use of profit sharing in postwar Japan.[17] In Japan, worker bonuses average about one-quarter of annual earnings, and they are paid out of profits. Although the relationship between profits and worker bonuses is not clear-cut, Japanese workers certainly benefit from higher profits in the form of higher year-end bonuses.

Government Intervention

Capitalist economic systems rely on the market mechanism to provide information for decision makers. At the same time, there is much debate over the extent to which various failures of the market mechanism might be reduced or eliminated by state intervention.

An important change in policy has been widespread acceptance of the notion that government is responsible for macroeconomic stability. This change—called the **Keynesian revolution**—took place in the period since World War II, especially in the 1960s and thereafter. Capitalist governments use fiscal and monetary policies to pursue stabilization. Most capitalist systems have put in place a variety of monetary and fiscal mechanisms designed to implement stabilization policies. Although the role of the state in macroeconomic stabilization remains a subject of discussion and controversy, capitalist countries have generally experienced greater macroeconomic stability in the second half of the twentieth century despite major energy shocks in the 1970s than in the first half of the twentieth century or in the nineteenth century. Business cycles have become less severe.

A different sort of change in capitalist systems is represented by the introduction of some sort of planning mechanism—and thus a reduction in reliance on the market mechanism. Great Britain, a country known for the important role government plays in its market economy, has had very limited experience with national economic planning. France, on the other hand, is well known for its application of **indicative planning**, an approach to planning designed to achieve better decision making based on more and better information without being vulnerable to the possibility of authoritarian control in an otherwise democratic system.

Japan is yet another case of a market capitalist economy where the state plays an important role. But, as in Great Britain, the state's role is exercised by means other than planning per se. And these patterns of state influence do not seem to have changed significantly in recent years.

There are cases where market capitalist systems have developed some form of planning to supplement and/or modify market outcomes. The Scandinavian countries are cases in point. In the United States, there is no planning in the sense of utilizing a national economic planning mechanism, though one could argue that a great deal of planning does occur through large government branches, powerful corporate entities, and the like. Recent discussion has focused on the perceived need for an **industrial policy**, to develop and implement policies designed to promote the health of the capitalist economy—for example, through technological change.[18] The concept of industrial policy is not recent. For many years it has focused on the potential role of government (through both policies and institutions) to stimulate growth sectors in what has been viewed as an aging U.S. economy. It is, therefore, part of the much broader issue of long-term growth performance of the American economy.

Change in Socialist Economies

Contemporary **socialist economic reform** programs have been driven by pragmatic issues. The predominant force promoting economic reform in the former Soviet Union and Eastern Europe was concern about economic performance. The Soviet and East European systems slipped significantly over the past three decades.

Specifically, rates of growth of output declined steadily between the late 1950s and the mid-1980s. For countries whose hallmark was once rapid economic growth, such a trend had important implications. Without improvements in productivity, the growth of consumer well-being had to lag. And even in less-developed socialist systems such as China, reform was motivated by poor performance.

Many reasons have been advanced to explain the general slackening of economic performance, but the fact remains that the planned socialist economies found the transformation from extensive to intensive growth very difficult. The basic Stalinist model, though draconian and costly, nevertheless served to bring idle and underused resources into the production process. However, the luxury of idle resources was, for many socialist systems, over by the late 1960s. Economic growth and the expansion of consumer well-being had to come from improved productivity, or what socialist systems described as **intensification**.

We do not know exactly why intensification in socialist systems proved so difficult. Clearly there were consumer pressures in these systems, and clearly they grew more complex over time. Advances in planning methods did not keep pace with the demands on the planning system. But most important, the diffusion of technology was inadequate. These systems were not demand driven, and enterprise rules generally did not stimulate growth in productivity and cost reduction. Efficiency was simply not a hallmark of the Stalinist command economy. Moreover, in contrast to the cyclical nature of productivity problems in market systems, socialist systems seemed to experience long, steady declines of productivity growth through the 1980s.

Interest in socialist reform began in the 1960s and grew in the 1980s and 1990s. By the mid-1980s, performance in most socialist systems had slipped to the point where demand could not be met. With inadequate incentives, there appeared to be little hope for improved productivity. Moreover, most socialist countries had not been able to compete well enough in export markets to afford significant imports of consumer products. Seen in this perspective, the imperative of reform was evident, although the sudden spread of radical economic reform in the late 1980s caught most observers by surprise.

Socialist Economic Systems: Reform Models

Reform of planned socialist economic systems has focused on changes in some or all of the system components.[19] However, prior to the dramatic changes of the late 1980s and 1990s, most reform in socialist systems was very modest and was characterized as an attempt, by means of very limited changes, to make the existing system work better. Recent reforms, however, which can be characterized as radical, have the potential to change system components significantly. Many of the reform programs envisioned propose the elimination of central planning and its replacement by market forces.

Much of the literature on socialist economic reform has focused on reform models that differ in intensity. We characterize socialist reform in terms of three basic variants: attempts to make planning work better, **changes in organizational arrangements**, and **decentralization** of decision making.

Improving the Planning Mechanism   Improving planning is a weak alternative—one that signals unwillingness to make serious changes in the economic system. The arguments in support of this alternative are that problems of economic performance arise largely because planning has not been perfected and that planning can be improved through the application of more sophisticated computer technology. To the extent that enterprise managers make bad decisions because they lack information, ready access to accurate information through an advanced computer network would alleviate the problem. Better planning methods, better information channels, and more attention to incentive compatibility, can perfect the planning system and improve economic performance. The 1970s were devoted to a number of attempts to improve planning both in the Soviet Union and in Eastern Europe.

Organizational Reform   Changing the organizational arrangements of the existing plan structure represents a second reform alternative. A typical organizational reform is the introduction of intermediate organizations into the organizational hierarchy. Ministries, it was argued, are too distant from the enterprises they supervise. Moreover, each ministry supervises enterprises that produce too diverse an array of products. Ministries cannot keep in touch with enterprise behavior and do not truly understand the problems peculiar to the enterprises they oversee. Thus an intermediate agency or association should be placed between the ministries and groups of enterprises that produce similar products. The intermediate association, it is argued, could understand and manage a particular group of firms more successfully.

Another way to implement organizational reform would be to shift the emphasis from sectoral to regional planning. An economy planned on a sectoral basis may place the interests of the branch over national interests. A shift to regional planning might loosen the grip of an entrenched bureaucracy and encourage a better flow of information among units in the economy. It was this type of reform that Nikita Khrushchev tried, without success, in the Soviet Union in the late 1950s and early 1960s. Most—though not all—past reform attempts in socialist systems have been organizational in nature.

Decentralization   Decentralization, the third broad category of socialist economic reform, is a shifting of decision-making authority and responsibility from upper to lower levels. Decentralization is often viewed as "real" reform that can fundamentally change the nature of economic systems and, especially, reduce the role of central planning.

Decentralization implies that decisions about resource allocation will be shifted downward in the economic hierarchy. Most important, in a decentralized economy, decisions are not made by planners but are reached at lower levels by means of what are frequently termed **economic levers**—prices, costs, profits, rates of return, and the like. Decentralization of decision making entails both the devolution of decision-making authority and responsibility *and* the use of different decision-making tools in the process. To put it another way, although planning still exists, decentralization implies that local decision makers pay less attention to planners and more attention to market signals.

This type of economic reform has been characterized as real reform or significant reform to distinguish it from organizational change. In contemporary terms, it is likely to be called radical reform. Its existence raises new and difficult questions about the development of markets—and thus market signals—in systems previously dominated by planners, by state-ownership of property, and by an absence of market signals.

Reform versus Transition

As applied to the planned socialist economies, **reform** refers to generally serious efforts to make the existing system work better. The most serious reform is decentralization, which seeks to introduce market-type elements into a centrally planned economy. **Transition** refers to the process of moving from one economic system to another. In this case, transition involves the transformation of formerly planned socialist economies into market capitalist economies. Presumably, transition results in an economic system with the basic characteristics of but different from existing capitalist economies.

Overview of Socialist Reform and Transition

The latter part of this book is devoted to reform and transition. This chapter presents a broad overview of this process.

The Soviet experiment with planned socialism began in earnest in the late 1920s with the introduction of command planning to industry and forced collectivization to agriculture. The economic system that Stalin created in the late 1920s and early 1930s proved durable. It was introduced into Eastern Europe by Soviet troops at the end of World War II, and it found its way into China with the victory of communist forces there.

Prior to the early 1960s, reform of the Stalinist economic system was not possible. According to Stalinist dogma, the system was perfect. Any failures encountered were the result of human error or sabotage. Such thinking did not provide fertile ground for reform. The death of Stalin and the ensuing mild liberation allowed discussion of reform to begin. The problems of the planned socialist economy were apparent, and it was natural to consider improving the system.

The Soviet Communist Part officially approved such discussion when *Pravda* published the reform proposals of Evsei Liberman in 1962. In this fashion, reform discussion was initiated in the Soviet Union and Eastern Europe. Although official reforms in the Soviet Union were modest, reforms in Eastern Europe were more substantial. Hungary, for example, initiated a long and careful reform process designed to orient its economy more towards the consumer. But none of these reforms, either in thought or in content, were designed to replace the planned socialist economy with a market capitalist economy.

Declining economic performance in the Soviet Union and Eastern Europe in the 1970s and early 1980s convinced the leadership of the Soviet Communist Party that radical change was necessary. They appointed a relatively young and vigorous general secretary, Mikhail Gorbachev, to lead this reform effort, which Gorbachev immediately described as radical, to distinguish it from the modest reforms of the past. Internationally, Gorbachev relaxed Soviet control over Eastern Europe. As a result, these countries gained their political independence and their freedom to experiment with reform and transition. The collapse of the Soviet Union in December 1991 allowed an additional 15 former republics of the Soviet Union freely to select their economic systems.

Although Part III discusses these matters in detail, the basic results of the reform/transition process can be described as follows:

First, a consensus has emerged that transition rather than reform is the appropriate path. With few exceptions, there is realization that problems are not resolved by reform. They must be resolved by a change in the system itself.

Second, transition is not easy. Although Poland, Hungary, the Czech Republic, and the Baltic states have shown signs of success, no country has yet to complete the process of transition. Transition has been costly both politically and economically. Each country undergoing transition has experienced substantial declines in output, dramatic changes in the distribution of income, and rampant inflation. These costs have created political backlashes that have returned to power those favoring the old system.

Third, there is no single path to transition. Some countries have tried a gradual approach, while others have tried "shock therapy." Although the results are inconclusive, it appears that the result of either approach is similar.

Fourth, the combination of transition and a young democracy has proven to be difficult. Politicians in newly democratic countries must somehow enact transition policies that are costly in terms of lost political support. This difficult combination has created considerable interest in the Chinese reform model, which has combined market-oriented reforms with communist party dictatorship.

Although the final outcome is still not known, the former Soviet Union and Eastern Europe have taken the first steps of dismantling the power structure on which their planned economic systems were based. The planned socialist economy no longer exists. What has yet to happen is the replacement of the old system with a new, stable economic system.

Summary

The central focus of this chapter is change. Although the use of terminology is somewhat imprecise, economic reform usually refers to change, wherein attempts are made to improve the functioning of an economic system that basically remains unchanged. Transition, on the other hand, refers to the replacement of one economic system with another, for example replacing plan with market in contemporary Eastern European. If it is difficult to classify systemic change precisely, it is equally difficult to assess results. Typically, in cases of major changes, such as privatization in Eastern Europe, there is a tendency to examine the degree of privatization at a stage when the impact on resource allocation (the outcome) is tenuous.

Systemic change is part of the more general process of economic development, though among the many approaches to understanding economic development, those that attempt to focus on institutional (systemic) change are of special interest in the field of comparative economic systems. In the 1800s, Karl Marx proposed the most famous theory of system change. Marx argued from a materialist/determinist/ revolutionary perspective that revolutionary system change was an inevitable product of class struggle in an efficient but inequitable system (capitalism) that would result in socialism and ultimately communism. Although the conflict between the economy (productive forces) and the organization of the society (production relations) would inevitably lead to change, capital accumulation and the exploitation of labor under capitalism would nevertheless build an economic base from which the more equitable socialist system could emerge.

Although the classical Marxian schema and its modifications by Lenin and others remains important, contemporary theories of socioeconomic change have focused on the role of institutions—how they emerge, why they differ in different systems, and how they change through time. The **Austrian school**, notably Ludwig von Mises and Friedrich von Hayek, argued that the task of planning in the planned socialist economy is too complex to be reasonable, and that in the absence of private property, decentralization of decision making would not be effective as a means to allocate resources.

In recent years, new emphasis has been placed on the evolutionary approach to understanding economic development. The evolutionary approach, like the earlier views of the Schumpeterian school, focuses on uncertainty and disequilibrium and the importance of institutional change as society responds to uncertainty in the building and changing of institutions.

Janos Kornai has developed a general theory of the socialist economy. He argues that the socialist system is fundamentally a shortage economy largely because enterprise rules in such a system differ from those in market capitalist economies and do not present the firm with a hard budget constraint, or the need to use scarce resources effectively.

Change in capitalist systems is viewed as evolutionary and can be analyzed by examining changes in property rights, trends in competition, income distribution, the role of government, and the organization of the workplace, notably worker participation.

In the past, socialist economic reform was viewed as an attempt to make the planning system function effectively. Although most observers would argue that such reforms in socialist economic systems have been of minimal value, transition in the contemporary era, or the shift from one system to another, remains difficult and important cases of modified reform (China) remain important to our understanding of systemic change.

Key Terms

economic reform
transition
Marx's theory of capitalism
superstructure
productive forces
production relations
qualitative changes
thesis versus antithesis
dialectical materialism
primitive capitalist accumulation
surplus value
capitalist breakdown
creative destruction
spontaneous order
economics of shortage
hard budget constraint
soft budget constraint
privatization
nationalization

property rights
competition
income redistribution
progressive tax
regressive tax
worker participation
role of government
Keynesian revolution
indicative planning
industrial policy
socialist economic reform
intensification
changes in organizational arrangements
decentralization
economic levers
reform
transition
the Austrian school

Notes

1. Karl Marx, *Capital* (Chicago: Charles Kerr and Company), Vol. I, 1906; Vols. II and III, 1909. Two works that seek to describe the basics of Marx's economics in the language of conventional economic theory are Oskar Lange, "Marxian Economics and Modern Economic Theory," *Review of Economic Studies*, Vol. II (June 1935); and Murray Wolfson, *A Reappraisal of Marxian Economics* (New York: Columbia University Press, 1966).

2. Our discussion of the economic theories of Marx and Engels is based primarily on the following sources: Paul Sweezy, *The Theory of Capitalist Development* (New York: Monthly Review Press, 1968); Wolfson, *A Reappraisal of Marxian Economics*; Alexander Balinky, *Marx's Economics: Origin and Development* (Lexington, Mass.: Heath, 1970); John Gurley, *Challengers to Capitalism: Marx, Lenin, Mao* (San Francisco: San Francisco Book Company, 1976); William Baumol, Paul Samuelson, and Michio Morishima, "On Marx, the Transformation Problem, and Opacity—A Colloquium," *Journal of Economic Literature*, 12 (March 1974), 51–77; *Grundlagen des Marxismus–Leninismus: Lehrbuch*, German translation of the 4th Russian edition (Berlin: Dietz Verlag, 1964); Karl Marx and Friedrich Engels, *The Communist Manifesto*, in Arthur Mendel, ed., *Essential Works of Marxism* (New York: Bantam Books, 1965), pp. 13–44; Paul Samuelson, "Understanding the Marxian Notion of Exploitation: A Summary of the So-called Transformation Problem Between Marxian Values and Competitive Prices," *Journal of Economic Literature*, 9 (June 1971), 399–431; and Leon Smolinsky, "Karl Marx and Mathematical Economics," *Journal of Political Economy*, 81 (September–October 1973), 1189–1204.

3. According to Sweezy, *The Theory of Capitalist Development*, Ch. 11, the Marx-Engels description of the end of capitalism and the coming of socialism was scattered and sketchy. Their failure to deal more thoroughly with the breakdown of capitalism led to the breakdown controversy among socialist writers—Eduard Bernstein, M. Tugan-Baranovsky, Karl Kautsky, Rosa Luxemburg, and others. The central issue of this controversy was whether a violent overthrow of capitalism was obviated by reform of the capitalist system and the capitalist government. For Lenin's view of Kautsky and "revisionism," see V. I. Lenin, *State and Revolution*, in Mendel, *Essential Works of Marxism*, pp. 103–198; and V. I. Lenin, *Izbrannye proizvedeniia, Tom I* (Moscow: Gospolitizdat, 1960), pp. 56–63 ("Marxism and Revisionism").

4. The basic works are Joseph Schumpeter, *Capitalism, Socialism, and Democracy*, 3rd ed. (New York: Harper, 1950) and Joseph Schumpeter, *The Theory of Economic Development* (Cambridge: Harvard University Press, 1934).

5. A useful point by point comparison of the views of Marx and Schumpeter can be found in Richard L. Carson, *Comparative Economic Systems* (New York: Macmillan, 1973), Table 13-1.

6. See Richard R. Nelson and Sidney G. Winter, *An Evolutionary Theory of Economic Change* (Cambridge: Harvard University Press, 1982); for a discussion of the contemporary transition experience from an evolutionary perspective, see, for example, Peter Murrell, "Can Neoclassical Economics Underpin the Reform of Centrally Planned Economies?" *Journal of Economic Perspectives*, 5, 4 (Fall 1991), 59–76; Peter Murrell, "Evolution in Economics and in the Economic Reform of the Centrally Planned Economies," in Christopher C. Clague and Gordon Rausser, eds., *Emerging Market Economies in Eastern Europe* (Cambridge: Blackwell, 1992).

7. F. A. Hayek, *The Road to Serfdom*

8. F. A. Hayek, ed., *Collectivist Economic Planning*, 6th ed. (London: Routledge and Kegan Paul, 1963), Ludwig von Mises, "Economic Calculation in Socialism," in Morris Bornstein, ed., *Comparative Economic Systems*, rev. ed. (Homewood, Ill.: Irwin, 1969), pp. 61–68.

9. See Janos Kornai, *Economics of Shortage*, Vols. A and B (New York: North-Holland, 1980); "Resource Constrained Versus Demand Constrained Systems," *Econometrica*, 47 (July 1979), 801–819; *Anti-Equilibrium: On Economic Systems Theory and the Tasks of Research* (Amsterdam: North-Holland, 1971); and Janos Kornai, *Rush Versus Harmonic Growth* (Amsterdam North-Holland, 1972); *Overcentralization in Economic Administration* (London: Oxford University Press, 1959); and *Growth, Shortage, and Efficiency: A Macrodynamic Model of the Socialist Economy* (Berkeley: University of California Press, 1983).

10. There is a large and growing body of literature on privatization most notably pertaining to the transition from plan to market in the planned socialist systems of the former Soviet Union and Eastern Europe. Part III of this book discusses privatization in some detail.

11. If privatization is a focal theme of economic policy in the 1990s, why might we not expect significant changes in ownership arrangements? The former socialist systems will clearly undergo important ownership changes; however, in market capitalist systems, privatization is usually more subtle and more difficult to measure. For example, rather than the sale of a public asset to a private owner, privatization in the United States frequently occurs when services provided in the public sector are subsequently arranged on a contractual basis through private vendors. The impact of this type of privatization on equity arrangements is less clear than the case of the outright sale of assets.

12. William G. Shepherd, "Causes of Increased Competition in the U.S. Economy, 1939–1980," *Review of Economics and Statistics* (November 1982), 613–626.
13. Clifford Winston, "Economic Deregulation: Days of Reckoning for Microeconomists," *Journal of Economic Literature*, 31.3 (September 1993), 1263–1289.
14. Clifford Winston, "Economic Deregulation," 1263.
15. Edgar K. Browning, "The Trend toward Equality in the Distribution of Net Income," *Southern Economic Journal*, 43 (July 1976), 914.
16. The theoretical foundation of a profit-sharing capitalist economy is provided by Martin L. Weitzman, *The Share Economy* (Cambridge: Harvard University Press, 1984) and Martin L. Weitzman, "The Simple Macroeconomics of Profit Sharing," *American Economic Review*, 75 (December 1985), 937–953; for an excellent survey of recent developments in the theory of producer cooperatives, see John P. Bonin, Derek C. Jones and Louis Putterman, "Theoretical and Empirical Studies of Producer Cooperatives: Will the Twain Ever Meet?" *Journal of Economic Literature*, 31, 3 (September 1993), 1290–1320.
17. For an analysis of Japanese profit sharing, see Merton J. Peck, "Is Japan Really a Share Economy?" *Journal of Comparative Economics*, 10 (December 1986), 427–432.
18. For a discussion of industrial policy in the American contemporary American context, see R. D. Norton, "Industrial Policy and American Renewal," *Journal of Economic Literature*, 24, 1 (March 1986), 1–40.
19. There is a large body of literature on reform in the former planned socialist economies. For a summary with emphasis on the Soviet case, see Paul R. Gregory and Robert C. Stuart, *Soviet and Post-Soviet Economic Structure and Performance*, 5th ed. (New York: HarperCollins, 1994), Chs. 12–13.

Recommended Readings

A. Traditional Sources

Paul A. Baran, *The Political Economy of Growth* (New York: Monthly Review Press, 1957).
William Baumol, Paul Samuelson and Michio Morishima, "On Marx. The Transformation Problem and Opacity—A Colloquium," *Journal of Economic Literature*, 12 (March 1974), 51–77.
John Gurley, *Challengers to Capitalism: Marx, Lenin, Mao* (San Francisco: San Francisco Book Company, 1976).
Oskar Lange, "Marxian Economics and Modern Economic Theory," *Review of Economic Studies*, 2 (June 1935).
Karl Marx, *Capital* (Chicago: Charles Kerr and Company), Vol. I, 1906; Vols. II and III, 1909.
Ernest Mandel, *Marxist Economic Theory* (New York: Monthly Review Press, 1970).
Arthur Mendel, ed., *Essential Works of Marxism* (New York: Bantam Books, 1965).
Joan Robinson, *An Essay on Marxian Economics* (New York: Macmillan, 1966).
Paul Samuelson, "Understanding the Marxian Notion of Exploitation: A Summary of the So-Called Transformation Problem between Marxian Values and Competitive Prices," *Journal of Economic Literature*, 9 (June 1971), 399–431.
Joseph Schumpeter, *Capitalism, Socialism and Democracy*, 3rd ed. (New York: Harper, 1950).
————, *The Theory of Economic Development* (Cambridge: Harvard University Press, 1934).

Leon Smolinsky, "Karl Marx and Mathematical Economics," *Journal of Political Economy*, 81 (September–October 1973), 1189–1204.

Paul Sweezy, *The Theory of Capitalist Development* (New York: Monthly Review Press, 1968).

Murray Wolfson, *A Reappraisal of Marxian Economics* (New York: Columbia University Press, 1966).

B. Economic Development: Background

Malcolm Gillis, Dwight H. Perkins, Michael Roemer and Donald R. Snodgrass, *Economics of Development* 3rd ed. (New York: W. W. Norton, 1992).

E. Wayne Nafziger, *The Economics of Developing Countries*, 2nd. ed. (Englewood Cliffs, N.J.: Prentice Hall, 1990).

Barry W. Poulson, *Economic Development*, New York: West Publishing Company, 1994.

C. Economic Development: Special Approaches

Janos Kornai, *Anti-Equilibrium: On Economic Systems Theory and the Tasks of Research* (Amsterdam: North-Holland, 1971).

———, *Economics of Shortage*, Vols. A and B (New York: North-Holland, 1980).

———, *Growth, Shortage, and Efficiency: A Macrodynamic Model of the Socialist Economy* (Berkeley: University of California Press, 1983).

———, "Resource Constrained versus Demand Constrained Systems," *Econometrica*, 47 (July 1979), 801–819.

———, *Rush versus Harmonic Growth* (Amsterdam: North-Holland, 1972).

———, *The Road to a Free Economy* (New York: W. W. Norton, 1990).

———. *The Socialist System: The Political Economy of Communism* (Princeton. N.J.: Princeton University Press, 1992).

Richard R. Nelson and Sidney G. Winter, *An Evolutionary Theory of Economic Change* (Cambridge: Harvard University Press, 1982).

D. The Capitalist Economy: Selected Aspects of Change

Richard R. Nelson and Sidney G. Winter, *An Evolutionary Theory of Economic Change* (Cambridge: Harvard University Press, 1982).

R. D. Norton, "Industrial Policy and American Renewal," *Journal of Economic Literature*, 24, 1 (March 1986), 1–40.

Nitin Nohria and Robert G. Eccles, eds., *Networks and Organizations: Structure, Form, and Action* (Boston: Harvard Business School Press, 1993).

Richard B. Freeman, "Unionism Comes to the Public Sector," *Journal of Economic Literature*, 24, 1 (March 1986), pp. 41–86.

William G. Shepherd, "Causes of Increased Competition in the U.S. Economy, 1939–1980," *Review of Economics and Statistics*, (November 1982), 613–626.

Grahame Thompson, Jennifer Frances, Rosalind Levacic and Jeremy Mitchell, eds., *Markets Hierarchies and Networks: The Coordination of Social Life* (London: Sage Publications, 1991).

Michael L. Vasu, Debra W. Stewart and S. David Garson, *Organizational Behavior and Public Management*, 2nd. ed., revised and expanded (New York: Marcel Dekker, Inc., 1990).

Leonard W. Weiss and Michael W. Klass, eds., *Regulatory Reform: What Actually Happened* (Boston: Little, Brown, 1986).

Oliver E. Williamson and Sidney G. Winter, eds., *The Nature of the Firm: Origins, Evolution and Development* (Oxford: Oxford University Press, 1991).

Clifford Winston, Economic Deregulation: Days of Reckoning for Microeconomists, *Journal of Economic Literature*, 31, 3 (September 1993), 1263–1289.

E. The Socialist Economy: Selected Aspects of Change

Robert W. Campbell, *The Socialist Economies in Transition: A Primer on Semi-Reformed Systems* (Bloomington: Indiana University Press, 1991).

Sabastian Edwards, "The Sequencing of Economic Reform: Analytical Issues and Lessons from the Latin American Experience," *World Economy*, 1 (1990).

Paul R. Gregory and Robert C. Stuart, *Soviet and Post-Soviet Economic Structure and Change*, 5th ed. (New York: HarperCollins, 1994), Ch. 12.

Peter Murrell, "Public Choice and the Transformation of Socialism," *Journal of Comparative Economics*, 14 (June 1991), 203–210.

PART **II**

Economic Systems in Theory

5

Theory of Capitalism

This chapter is about the *theory* of capitalism. Subsequent chapters discuss capitalism in practice. This chapter asks: How well should capitalist market economies *in theory* resolve the problem of allocating scarce resources among competing ends? This issue is important for two reasons. The first is that the theories of capitalism and socialism yield hypotheses concerning expected differences in performance, and those hypotheses can be tested against real-world experience. The second is that one may be most interested in what the theoretical models themselves suggest about the performance of economic systems under *ideal conditions*. Because actual economies diverge from the ideal, it could be argued that they cannot be used as a test of the system's "true" performance and that the performance issue must be resolved at the theoretical level.[1]

How Markets Work

The theory of capitalism focuses on *markets* in which the interaction of demand and supply determine prices for factors such as labor (factor markets) and products such as consumer goods (product markets). These markets (see Figure 2.4A) provide a mechanism for harmonizing consumer desires with producers' ability to meet these desires.

Equilibrium and the "Invisible Hand"

The pioneering analysis of market capitalism is Adam Smith's *The Wealth of Nations*, published in 1776.[2] Speaking against the mercantilist position that free trade could lead to a country's ruin, Adam Smith argued that a highly efficient and harmonious economic system would emerge if competitive markets were left to function freely without government intervention.

Smith's underlying notion was that if individuals were given free rein to pursue their own selfish interests, the **invisible hand** of competitive markets would cause them to behave in a socially responsible manner. Products desired by consumers would be produced in the appropriate assortments and quantities, and the most efficient means of production would be used. No government or social action would be required, for individuals acting in their own interests could be counted on to do the right thing. In fact, government action would probably interfere with this natural process, so government should be limited to providing essential public services—national defense, a legal system to protect private property, and highways—that private enterprise could not produce on its own. An equilibrium of consumers and producers would be created spontaneously in the competitive marketplace, for if the actions of consumers and producers were not in harmony, the market price would adjust to bring the two groups into equilibrium.

Smith's notion of a natural tendency toward an efficient economic equilibrium was the foundation for the liberal economic thought of the nineteenth century. In the words of one authority, Smith's most important triumph was that "he put into the center of economics the systematic analysis of the behavior of individuals pursuing their self-interest under conditions of competition," and this remains "the foundation of the theory of resource allocation."[3] Most of the later theorizing aimed at a further elaboration of Smith's vision of market capitalism.

Market Equilibrium

Adam Smith's description of markets was incomplete. Partial equilibrium assumes that two motivating forces drive market capitalism: the desire of producers to maximize profits and the desire of consumers to maximize their own welfare (utility) subject to the constraint of limited income.[4] Under competitive conditions, producers will be prepared to supply larger quantities at higher prices, combining inputs to minimize costs. Consumers, seeking to maximize their welfare, will purchase less at higher prices. The producer and consumer meet in the marketplace, where their conflicting objectives are brought into equilibrium. If the quantity demanded exceeds the quantity supplied at the prevailing price, the price automatically rises, squeezing out some demand and evoking a larger supply until all those willing to buy and all those willing to sell at the prevailing price can do so. At this point, an equilibrium price is established, the market clears, and there is no tendency to depart from the equilibrium unless it is disrupted by some exogenous change (see Figure 5.1).

This description underscores how market resource allocation works under competitive conditions. All other things being equal, an increase in consumer demand for a particular product disrupts the established equilibrium, and the price starts to rise. As the price rises, producers find it in their interest to supply larger quantities. If larger profits can be obtained at the new price, additional producers enter the market. On the demand side, the rise in the price causes substitution of now less-expensive commodities and income effects, thereby reducing the quantity demanded (see Figure 5.2). The increase in demand causes resources to be shifted automatically to the product in greater demand, and the wants of the consuming public are met without intervention from outside forces. Consumers are said to be sovereign because the economy responds to changes in their demand.

FIGURE 5.1   Market Equilibrium in a Competitive Economy

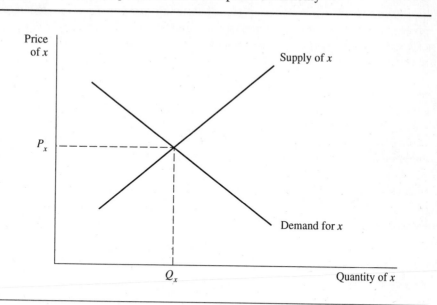

Explanation: In a competitive market economy, the price at which x sells will be P_x. If the price were *below* this level, the quantity demanded would exceed the quantity supplied. The *shortage* of x would cause the price of x to rise. If the price were *above* P_x, the quantity supplied would exceed the quantity demanded. The surplus of x would then cause the price of x to fall. Only at P_x is the quantity supplied equal to the quantity demanded (Q_x).

Efficiency of Market Allocation

There are two arguments for the **efficiency of market allocation**. One depends on the market being competitive—that is, consisting of a large number of buyers and sellers, none of whom has the power to influence the market price. The other efficiency argument rests on the ability of markets to use information effectively.

The first argues that in perfectly competitive markets, production will take place to the point where the marginal cost of society's resources equals the marginal benefit or utility to consumers. Firms that operate in competitive markets produce the level of output that equals the price of their marginal costs, and that price is set in the marketplace. When costs and benefits are not equal at the margin, society can gain by producing more or less of the product. For example, if price exceeds marginal cost, the product yields more benefits than costs and society can gain by producing more. If marginal costs exceed price, too much of the product has been produced and production should be reduced.

The Austrian economists, Friedrich Hayek and Ludwig von Mises wrote about the *relative* superiority of market economies over planned socialist economies.[5] Their arguments rest on the efficient manner in which market economies mobilize and utilize information, in contrast to the inefficient use of information in socialist economies. Hayek wrote that the principal economic problem is not how to allocate given resources, but "how to secure the best use of resources known to any member of society, for ends whose relative importance only these individuals know. Or, to put it briefly, it is a problem of the utilization of knowledge not given to anyone in its totality." Economic agents (consumers and producers) specialize in information about prices, products, and location that is relevant to them in their daily lives. Economic agents need not know all prices, products, and locations to behave efficiently in the marketplace. According to Hayek and Mises, the fact that market economies efficiently generate information in the form of market prices, which enable producers and consumers to plan their actions in a rational manner, is the principal advantage of capitalism and will ensure its relative superiority over planned socialism. This is their argument for the theoretical and practical superiority of capitalism. The planned socialist economies would prove too difficult to manage because of the complexity of information and incentive problems.

FIGURE 5.2   Consumer Sovereignty in a Competitive Economy

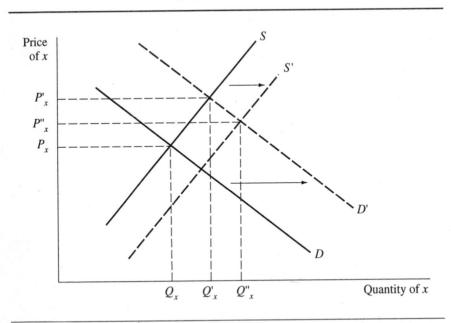

Explanation: We begin with the market for *x* in equilibrium at price P_x and quantity Q_x. *There is an increase in consumer demand from D to D'.* As a consequence, the price of *x* rises to P'_x and the equilibrium quantity *rises* to Q'_x. If economic profits are being made at this new price, new firms will enter the market and the supply curve will eventually shift to *S'*. Now a new long-run equilibrium is established at price P''_x and quantity Q''_x. An increase in consumer demand *automatically* leads to an increase in the quantity produced. The long-run effect on market prices depends on the entry of new firms at the higher price.

State Intervention

The picture of capitalism that we have developed is one of a harmonious and efficient resource allocation system, strongly inclined toward equilibrium in production especially under competitive conditions. This harmony occurs without the benefit of government intervention and control. Critics of the harmonious model point to the need for **state intervention** to deal with monopoly power, externalities, public goods, and income distribution problems. They also stress the inherent cyclical instability of capitalism and the problems of making rational public choices.

The appropriate level of state intervention into the affairs of private enterprise is one of the most disputed issues in economics. The neoclassical position, descended directly from Adam Smith, is that in the absence of monopoly power, and in the absence of external effects, the economic role of the state should be strictly limited. The state should supply only those public goods—such as national defense, public roads, a legal system, and foreign policy—that private enterprise on its own would not be able to provide in optimal proportions. The theory of public goods explains why laissez-faire capitalism will underproduce such goods.[6] The question under consideration here is in what instances is state intervention required to correct deficiencies in market allocation.

Monopoly Power

The nonoptimality of monopoly has been emphasized since, and even before, publication of *The Wealth of Nations*.[7] The crux of the monopoly problem is the monopolist's inclination to restrict output below the level that would prevail in a competitive situation. Monopolists underproduce and overcharge relative to competitive producers. Monopoly causes a deadweight loss, in that the gains of the monopolist are less than the losses to consumers. Figure 5.3 demonstrates that monopolies produce less and charge higher prices than competitive markets.

Monopoly behavior is not explained by extraordinary greed on the part of the monopolist, who is simply attempting to maximize profits. By definition, the monopolist is the sole producer in a particular market. Therefore, to sell a large volume of output, the monopolist must lower the price. Perfectly competitive producers, as price takers, can sell all they desire at the market price. Monopolists fail to expand their output to the point where the marginal cost (which measures the marginal cost of output in terms of society's resources) equals price (which measures the marginal benefit of output to society). Rather, monopolists who wish to maximize profits must restrict their output.

Economic theory suggests four approaches to the control of monopoly, three of which require state intervention. The first is to use the state's authority to *tax and subsidize* to correct the underutilization of resources by monopolistic producers. The basic idea is to combine subsidization with consumer and producer **taxation** to induce the monopolist to expand output to the competitive level, while at the same time producing a social tax dividend for society. The obvious difficulty is that tax

FIGURE 5.3   The Competitive and Monopolistic Models

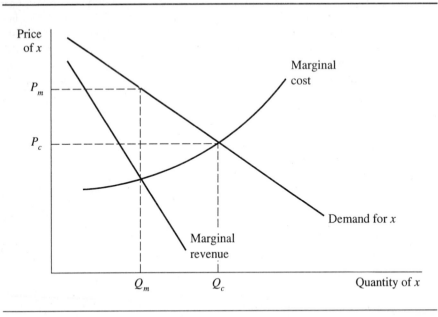

Explanation: This diagram presents the models of price and output determination under conditions of perfect competition and monopoly.

Let us suppose that industry X could be organized either as a monopoly (with a single producer) or as a competitive industry (with a large number of producers). The marginal costs are the same whether the industry is a monopoly or is perfectly competitive. The industry demand schedule and the industry marginal-cost schedule are given in the diagram. The latter is the marginal-cost schedule of the monopolist (in the case of the monopolistic industry) or the sum of the individual marginal-cost schedules of producers (in the case of the competitive industry).

Because the demand schedule is negatively sloped, the monopolist's marginal revenue is less than the product price. To maximize profits, the monopolist produces that output (Q_m) at which marginal cost and marginal revenue are equated and sells this output at the price dictated by the market (P_m). Competitive producers produce output levels at which the product price and marginal costs are equal; therefore, the supply schedule of the competitive industry is the industry marginal-cost schedule. The competitively organized industry produces Q_c, and the product sells for P_c.

The monopoly produces less than the competitive industry and charges a higher price. The monopolist charges a price greater than the marginal costs of production, whereas the competitive industry equates price and marginal cost. Because price and marginal revenue are not equal, an economy made up of monopolies is not Pareto-optimal.

authorities must make quite sophisticated calculations in order to implement it. The use of **subsidies** and taxes to obtain an optimal allocation of resources from a monopolist does not seem too practical, although the theory of how to do so is clear.

The second form of state intervention is **direct regulation** of monopoly. Theoretically, state regulatory authorities could dictate that the regulated monopoly produce the efficient quantity of output at which *P* equals *MC* and force the monopolist to charge a regulated price equal to marginal costs. In this manner, the regulators could dictate directly an efficient allocation of resources. There are two practical difficulties with this approach, however. How are regulators to know market demand and monopoly marginal costs? The monopoly might be tempted to inflate its costs by lax management or other means in order to obtain a higher regulated price. The second difficulty is that marginal-cost pricing would probably force the monopolist to operate at a loss, if marginal costs were still declining at the output where *P* equals *MC*. The existence of regulated losses would require a system of subsidization, which would tend to disrupt the optimal allocation of resources.

The third approach is that recommended by Milton Friedman—to *leave* **natural monopolies** *alone* because regulation is poorly managed and encourages monopolists to be inefficient.[8] The unregulated monopoly, prompted by the desire to maximize profits and keep potential competitors out of the market, would supply a larger quantity at a lower price than that charged by a regulated monopoly. Moreover, even monopolists must face some form of competition in the long run and cannot get by indefinitely with an inefficient use of resources.

The final collective approach applies to cases where competitive production is also possible. The state, through enforcement of antitrust and anticartel legislation and through the removal of legal obstacles to competition could *transform the industry from monopolistic to competitive.*

Modern theory has pondered whether there are natural limitations on monopoly power. Unless freedom of entry were highly restricted, monopolists would avoid charging monopoly prices for fear of attracting competitors in the long run.

External Effects and Collective Action

External effects refer to situations where the actions of one producer or consumer directly affect the costs or utility of a second producer or consumer.[9] External effects, are effects that take place outside of the price system. These external effects may be harmful, in which case they are called an **external diseconomy**, or they may be salutary, in which case they are known as an **external economy**. An example of an external diseconomy of production is the dumping of wastes into a river by one producer, requiring a producer downstream to increase costs by installing water purification equipment.

When external effects are present, the allocation of resources is not optimal, even if the economy is perfectly competitive. Producers of the external effect are not required to take the external impact of their actions into account when making decisions. Rather they seek to maximize their private profit on the basis of the **private costs** of production, not on the basis of **social costs**. The producer of an external harmful effect therefore produces an output level in excess of the optimum, for the private producer tends to underestimate the true social costs of production (Figure 5.4).

Economic theory suggests remedies to correct for misallocations caused by external effects. One is the internalization of such effects—for example, by merging both the enterprises producing and those being affected by external effects. Consider the example of the waste-dumping factory. If it merged with the downstream factory, the water purification costs would become private costs for the combined enterprise, and waste dumping would be limited as a natural consequence of profit maximization.

In the absence of opportunities for internalization, remedies may require state action, such as taxation and subsidies, to equate private and social costs. If an excise tax equal to the external diseconomy could be levied on the producer, private costs would equal social costs. To maximize private profits, the producer would be forced to limit output to the level at which price and marginal *social* costs are equal—the condition required for an efficient allocation of resources.

When appropriate taxes and subsidies cannot be levied, one alternative is state regulation. Government regulators determine the optimal allocation of resources and administratively decree that producers supply the optimal output. The major drawback is that enforcement and policing costs may be quite high, for it is not clear how one would obtain compliance with regulations. Moreover, there is the enormous problem of calculating private and social marginal costs—the data required for effective regulation.

FIGURE 5.4   The Inefficiency of External Costs

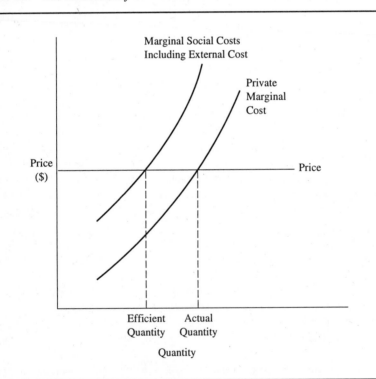

Explanation: When externalities are present, enterprises base their decisions on private marginal costs. This perfectly competitive firm produces where *P* = private marginal costs, not where *P* = full marginal cost. Thus externalities cause competitive firms to produce more than the optimal quantity.

A third approach to the externality problem is voluntary agreements among the parties involved. This notion was first suggested by Ronald Coase.[10] He contends that under certain conditions the creator and recipient of the external effect can come to a mutually satisfactory agreement that restores an optimal allocation of resources. Whenever harmful externalities exist, the affected parties have opportunities for gains from trade by striking deals. In the absence of legal obstacles, the amount of shared gains from an agreement must exceed the costs of transacting the agreement. Coase's novel conclusion, therefore, is that if the transaction costs of reaching an agreement are small, private agreements can correct the misallocation of resources caused by external effects. If mutually acceptable bargains are not reached in the presence of small transaction costs, the divergence between private and social costs is probably inconsequential.

The most important drawback to voluntary agreements is exactly the problem of transaction costs and other impediments to agreement, especially when the number of parties involved is large. When a small number of parties are involved, voluntary agreements are feasible. When a large number of parties must participate in the agreement, some of whom have relatively small stakes in the matter, the probability of reaching a mutually acceptable agreement is small.

Problems of Public Choice

Public goods—national defense, police protection and a legal system, dams, flood control projects, and the like— will not be supplied in efficient quantities by the private economy for two principal reasons: Nonpayers (called free riders) cannot be prevented from enjoying the benefits of the public good; and one person's use of the good does not generally prevent others from using it. Both of these features make it difficult for the private sector to produce public goods.

How efficiently will government supply such public goods? How rational is public choice? Public-choice theorists, such as Nobel laureate James Buchanan, have concluded that certain factors prevent public choices in a democratic (majority-rule) society from being made in an efficient manner.[11]

Efficiency in the case of a public good requires, at a minimum, that the marginal benefits enjoyed by users of the good equal or exceed its marginal costs. Will this necessarily be the case in a society in which public-choice decisions are made by majority-rule voting? Public-choice theory outlines a number of potential problems: First, **majority voting** fails to take into consideration the intensity of preferences among voters. A number of voters may have intense feeling about a specific public-expenditure decision, whereas others may be virtually indifferent. Yet each person's vote counts equally, and changes in preferences typically do not change the voting outcome. This is called the **median voter rule**. Second, there may be a tendency toward vote trading when voters must decide on a number of public-choice issues. A group that wishes one public-expenditure program may offer its support for the public-expenditure program of a second group, if that group will form a majority coalition. Through such logrolling techniques, public-expenditure programs may be enacted where marginal costs exceed marginal benefits. Moreover, politicians are in the business of getting reelected and are likely to serve special-interest groups that are instrumental in financing election campaigns. The voter, on the other hand, does not have a great incentive to be well informed about public-choice issues. Individual voters are aware that their votes are unlikely to change any outcome, and the costs of gathering information on the large number of technically detailed government programs are high. It is therefore in the rational voter's economic interest to remain "rationally ignorant." Logrolling, vote trading, and rational ignorance cause governments to authorize public programs that are not economically efficient.

Income Distribution

In a capitalist economy, people who own resources that command a high price have higher incomes than those who own resources that command low prices. How equally or unequally should income be distributed? To what extent should the state redistribute income?

The marginal productivity theory of **income distribution** follows from the fact that the private owners of labor, land, and capital are paid the marginal revenue product of their factor. If the factor market is perfectly competitive, the owner receives the actual value of the marginal product of the factor. Thus, argue some economists, the resulting distribution of income is "just" because factor owners receive a reward that is equal to the factor's marginal contribution to society's output. Bestowing rewards according to marginal productivity encourages the owners of the factors of production to raise the productivity of their factors. If the state were to alter this distribution, there would be less incentive to raise the marginal productivity of one's own factors. There would be less investment in human capital and less risk taking, and accordingly society's output would be less.

Critics of this "natural justice" view point out that the marginal productivity of any factor depends on the presence of cooperating factors. An American coal miner may work with millions of dollars of capital equipment, whereas the Indian coal miner works just as hard with only a pick and shovel. The marginal productivity of the American coal miner is therefore many times that of the Indian coal miner. Moreover, marginal productivity is affected by human capital investment, and not everyone has equal access to education.

There are a number of arguments in favor of a redistributive role for the state. First, people are not indifferent to the welfare of others, and their own welfare is diminished by poverty around them. Yet despite altruistic motives, there are strong incentives against charitable contributions. Any one person's contribution can have only a negligible effect on poverty. The insignificance of any one donor creates a substantial free-rider problem, which means that it is unlikely for voluntary contributions to have a significant impact on the distribution of income. Government income redistribution programs eliminate the free-rider problem. Only the state is in a position to alter the distribution of income.

The philosopher John Rawls has advanced another argument in favor of state intervention.[12] Rawls argues that an unequal distribution of income persists because those who benefit from income inequality are unwilling to accept changes that favor the poor. People are unwilling to agree to redistribution because those who will be rich know fairly early in life their chances of being rich. For this reason, a social consensus can never be formed whereby the rich agree to redistribute income to the poor.

Rawls asks: How would people behave if they did not know in advance their lifetime endowment of resources? How would they react if they operated behind a "veil of ignorance"? Rawls maintains that under this condition, people would naturally act to minimize the risks of being poor and would therefore reach a social consensus in favor of a fairly equal distribution of income. If people, operating behind a veil of ignorance, would naturally favor an equal distribution of income, then society should have an equal distribution of income. Insofar as voluntary charitable giving will not effect this result, the state is justified in redistributing income from the rich to the poor.

Macroeconomic Instability

A major challenge to the neoclassical vision of self-regulating capitalism was mounted by John Maynard Keynes in *The General Theory of Employment, Interest, and Money*, published in 1936 against the backdrop of the world depression.[13] The depression seemed to deny neoclassical notions of an automatic tendency toward equilibrium over time. Keynes's assertion that activist government action was required to stabilize capitalist economics has come to be called the **Keynesian revolution**.

Keynes Keynes disputed the mainstay of classical equilibrium theory, Say's Law.[14] According to **Say's Law**, there can be no lasting deficiency of aggregate demand because the act of producing a given value of output creates an equivalent amount of income. If that income were not spent directly on consumer goods, it would be saved. The savings would end up being spent as well, for interest rates would adjust to equate *ex ante* savings and *ex ante* investment. Accordingly, depressions could not be caused by deficiencies in aggregate demand. If one were only patient, eventually prices and wages would adjust to bring about an equilibrium at full employment. If unemployment did exist, it would be because workers were unwilling to accept the lower real wages required for labor market equilibrium. As long as prices and wages are flexible, there will be an automatic adjustment mechanism to restore full employment.

Keynes argued that there is no assurance that equilibrium will occur at full employment or that the automatic adjustment mechanism will work with reasonable speed. Thus—and this is the foundation of the Keynesian revolution—it is the responsibility of government to ensure full employment.

Keynes disputed the conclusions of the neoclassical school in the following manner. First, he argued that wages and prices are not nearly so flexible (especially downward) as the neoclassical economists believed. He pointed out that despite considerable unemployment, money wages were not falling in England in the 1920s and 1930s. Second, he argued that aggregate saving is not significantly affected by the interest rate; rather, it is principally dependent on the level of income. According to Keynes, the investment–savings relationship would be especially troublesome because of the cyclical instability of investment expenditures; only by chance would enough investment be forthcoming to guarantee full employment.

Keynes saw no reason why macroequilibrium should occur at a rate of output sufficient to ensure full employment. Therefore, it is the responsibility of government, by appropriately raising or lowering its spending and taxes (**fiscal policy**) or by controlling investment spending (through **monetary policy**), to ensure that equilibrium occurs near full employment. Because investment spending is quite unstable, government must be prepared to counteract investment fluctuations with compensatory actions.

After the Second World War, Keynes's advocacy of discretionary monetary and fiscal policy became widely accepted by economists and public officials, who felt justified in abandoning the traditional hands-off policies favored by the neoclassical school. Federal budgets could be openly in deficit in order to stimulate the economy. In the United States, for example, tax cuts and tax increases were imposed for the express purpose of manipulating aggregate demand. The practice of demand management became standard procedure in Western Europe, Japan, and Canada. Monetary policy also became an instrument of macroeconomic regulation. In the height of optimism in the mid-1960s there was talk of being able to "fine-tune" the economy, and the business cycle was declared dead.

Self-Correcting Capitalism: Monetarism and Rational Expectations

Keynes and his contemporary followers questioned the cyclical stability of capitalism. Without government intervention to moderate business cycles, there will be a significant loss of output and employment. Keynesian economics advocates **policy activism**—the discretionary use of monetary and fiscal policy to try to prevent or ameliorate the business cycle. Activist monetary and fiscal policy is required to keep the economy on an even keel.

The **monetarists**, under the intellectual leadership of Milton Friedman, and rational expectations economists, led by Robert Lucas, argue against the use of activist macroeconomic policy to combat capitalism's cyclical instability.[15] They argue that capitalism is considerably more stable than Keynes had thought. In fact, the Great Depression was an aberration caused in large part by blunders in economic policy. The capitalist economy has a built-in self-correcting mechanism that will restore it to full employment or to the natural rate of unemployment. If the economy is operating at an unemployment rate above the natural rate, a slowing down of the inflation rate (or even deflation in extreme cases) will restore the economy to full employment. Lower prices raise aggregate supply, and aggregate employment rises until the natural rate is reached.

The monetarists argue against the use of activist policy. Because fiscal policy is decided primarily by politics rather than economics, monetary policy has been the most flexible tool of activist policy. Monetarists maintain that activist monetary policy is as likely to do harm as good. Lengthy and indeterminate lags separate the recognition of a macroeconomic problem, the taking of necessary monetary action, and realization of the effect of that action on the economy. An anti-inflationary policy adopted during a period of rising prices may begin to affect the economy at the very time an expansionary monetary policy is required. Rather than running the risk of policy mistakes, the monetarists favor a fixed-monetary-growth rule, which would bind monetary authorities to expand the money supply by a fixed rate each year (roughly equal to the real growth of the economy) regardless of the state of the economy.

Advocates of the **rational expectations theory** also argue against activist policy. They maintain that activist policy will have the desired effect on the economy only if the policy catches people off guard. If taxes are lowered for the purpose of stimulating employment, and people know from experience that lower taxes raise inflation, people will take actions to defeat the policy. If monetary authorities expand the money supply to raise employment, and workers and employees know that more monetary growth means more inflation, the higher wages and prices will not raise employment or real output.

The basic message of the monetarists and rational expectations economists is that capitalism is much more stable than Keynes had thought and that activist policies are likely to harm the economy. It is better to rely on the self-correcting forces of the capitalist economy to restore it to equilibrium than to count on government policy makers to do so.

Growth and State Policy

An economy must grow for living standards to rise. Will a market economy grow appropriately on its own or is state action required to promote and direct growth?

The Austrian economist, Joseph Schumpeter, argued that market economies are well suited to create growth.[16] Schumpeter saw growth as a process of **creative destruction**. A particular company or industry will find new ways to produce products or find new products to develop. Such adaptability can become the engine of growth for the entire economy, pulling along laggard branches. The company's success, however, will result in its eventual decline as competitors create substitutes and invent improved technologies.

To prove that economic growth follows the path of creative destruction, Schumpeter pointed out that no company or industry has been able to maintain a dominant position over the long run. The railroads were dominant in the nineteenth century; now they face tough competition from superior technologies, such as truck and air transport. IBM dominated computer production until new technologies allowed smaller, more efficient companies to grab IBM's market share.

Although economists such as Schumpeter argue that market economies can grow on their own devices and can be trusted to select those industries that will grow more rapidly than others, a significant number of economists believe **industrial policy** can manage growth. Industrial policy uses the state to promote, subsidize, and generally manage the economic growth of a country. The proponents of industrial policy argue that private markets cannot effectively produce growth. Returns from research and development are insufficient to encourage private sector financing. The state must therefore fund R&D, perhaps in partnership with private industry. The proponents of industrial policy also argue that private industries are not farsighted; they are unable to identify growth industries of the future. Therefore government must find, support, and subsidize the growth industries of the future. The real-world model for industrial policy is Japan, which apparently used industrial policy to develop its automobile and electronics industries.

The Performance of Capitalist Economic Systems: Hypotheses

Chapter 3 discussed criteria by which to judge the performance of economic systems: economic growth, efficiency, income distribution, and stability. What hypotheses, if any, follow from the theory of capitalism in each of these areas? First, let us say that it is difficult to formulate hypotheses at this point, because our principal concern is the efficiency of capitalism vis-à-vis other economic systems; these hypotheses would best be stated in relative terms. (See Table 5.1.)

Efficiency

Capitalism should provide a high level of efficiency, especially in the static case. The more competitive the economy, the more efficient the economy. The producer's desire to maximize profits and the consumer's desire to maximize utility lead to a maximal output from available resources under conditions of perfect competition. Imperfect competition and external effects reduce this efficiency. Another point promoting static efficiency is capitalism's apparent ability to process and utilize information more effectively than an economic system in which the market is lacking. Probably the most important point is that profit maximization, under all market arrangements, strongly encourages the efficient (least-cost) combination of resources to produce output.

Stability

Stability is the ability of an economic system to grow without undue fluctuations in the rate of growth and without excessive inflation and unemployment. Of course, it is a subjective judgment what "undue" and "excessive" mean in such a context. Keynes argued that capitalist economies are not stable, at least in terms of short-run automatic equilibrating forces. Monetarists and rational expectations theorists believe that capitalist economies are (or could be) inherently more stable if left to their own devices; so there is considerable disagreement on this point. However, capitalism continues to suffer periodic bouts of inflation, unemployment, and growth fluctuations, which the general public regards as troubling.

TABLE 5.1   Hypothesis on the Performance of Capitalist
Economic Systems

Criterion	Performance
Efficiency	Good
Stability	Potentially poor; debate over government role
Income distribution	Unequal in the absence of state action
Economic growth	No clear *a priori* hypothesis; greater efficiency versus potentially lower capital formation

Income Distribution

The theory of capitalism cannot make definitive judgments about equity and how resources should be divided among the members of capitalist societies. Only value judgments can provide answers. We lack a consensus about "fairness," and without an agreed-upon definition it is difficult to arrive at hypotheses. Instead, we can only consider empirical measures of income distribution and make statements like the following: Income is distributed more equally in society X than in society Y. It is difficult to proceed further and say income is distributed "better" ("more fairly") in X or in Y.

The theory of capitalism, however, does suggest the likelihood of significant inequalities in the distribution of income. The factors of production are owned predominantly by private individuals, and the relative value of these factors is determined by the market. Insofar as human and physical capital and natural ability are not likely to be evenly distributed, especially when such things can be passed from one generation to another, private ownership of the factors of production raises the likelihood of an uneven distribution of income and wealth among the members of capitalist societies. Exactly how unevenly income and wealth are distributed will depend on the distribution of human and physical capital and also on the redistributive role of the state.

Economic Growth

One of the supposed advantages of planned socialist economies is their ability to direct resources to specific goals, such as economic growth and military power. To a greater extent than capitalist economies, they can marshal resources for economic growth, if they so desire, by controlling the investment rate and the growth rate of the labor force. Although capitalist governments can and do affect the investment rate, the amount saved is largely a matter of individual choice, and it is likely that individual choice will result in lower savings rates than a planned socialist economy. Thus if the growth of factor inputs is left to individuals, one would hypothesize a slower rate of growth of factor inputs and hence of economic growth, *ceteris pari-bus*, under capitalism.

A counterbalancing factor must be considered: the hypothesized efficiency of capitalist economies. Static efficiency means that a maximal output is produced from available resources and (with a given saving rate) a greater volume of savings is available relative to less efficient production methods. Moreover, there is the unresolved matter of the dynamic efficiency of capitalist economic systems. Up to this point, capitalist theory has had relatively little to say about dynamic efficiency. It is conceivable that the greater static and dynamic efficiency of capitalism can compensate for the lesser control over the growth of productive resources.

Viability of the Capitalist System

The viability of capitalism has been demonstrated by both theory and historical experience. Capitalist theory points to its inherent tendencies toward equilibrium. And historical experience shows that capitalism has survived several centuries and that there are no signs of impending collapse.

Summary

This chapter focuses on the theory of resource allocation in the market capitalist economic system, in particular, the way resources are allocated and the role that the state should play in the allocation process. The traditional neoclassical model maintains that capitalist economies have a strong tendency towards equilibrium and generate and process information efficiently. Under competitive conditions, they use resources efficiently. Market capitalism promotes consumer sovereignty, which allows consumers to determine what will be produced. From a policy perspective, in the perfectly competitive market capitalist economy, the role of government would be very limited, avoiding interference in the operation of business.

Critics of this model of self-regulating market capitalism have focused on several perceived weaknesses. In his classic work dating from the late 1930s, John Maynard Keynes attempted to demonstrate that such an economy could establish a stable macroeconomic equilibrium at less than (or greater than) full employment. Thus with the possibility of persistent and unacceptable unemployment, Keynes argued that it is the responsibility of government through fiscal and monetary policies to bring about an appropriate (full-employment) equilibrium.

A major line of criticism focuses on the argument that in the real world, perfectly competitive markets are likely to be replaced, in part, by imperfectly competitive markets, where resources are misallocated and that regulation and taxation are required to offset potential abuses arising from monopoly power.

The outcomes of the market economy have also been criticized from the perspective of externalities. As seen in this chapter, the basic neoclassical model assumes that all costs and benefits, both private and social, can be measured and accounted for in the resource-allocation process. Economists have demonstrated that in a variety of circumstances, there are likely to be externalities—that is, costs or benefits—external to and thus not accounted for by the decision maker as resource allocation takes place. In this setting, it is argued that government intervention may be necessary to achieve an optimal allocation of resources.

Despite the above criticism, the notion of self-regulating market capitalism remains controversial. For example, the monetarist view of the market economy has been a major counterattack against the Keynesian revolution, arguing that, on balance, government intervention in the economy is not necessarily stabilizing and thus should be minimized. Indeed, some have argued that capitalism is capable of handling problems of market imperfections and externalities without significant, if any, government intervention.

What hypotheses can be put forward concerning the economic performance of the market capitalist economy? The traditional view holds that the markets tend to result in an efficient allocation of resources but that economic activity remains unstable or cyclical. It is usually argued that the distribution of income will be less even than in those systems where greater degrees of social ownership or government redistributive effort are present; however, the matter of an appropriate distribution of income is controversial on both equity and efficiency grounds. No firm hypotheses are suggested regarding economic growth in the market capitalist economy.

Key Terms

invisible hand
consumer sovereignty
efficiency of market allocation
state intervention
monopoly
taxation
subsidies
direct regulation
natural monopoly
external effects
external diseconomies
external economies
private costs
social costs

public goods
majority voting
the median voter rule
income distribution
Keynesian revolution
Say's law
fiscal policy
monetary policy
policy activism
monetarists
rational expectations theory
creative destruction
industrial policy

Notes

1. Examples of how the latter approach has been applied are found in Abram Bergson, *The Economics of Soviet Planning* (New Haven: Yale University Press, 1964); Jaroslav Vanek, *The Participatory Economy* (Ithaca, N.Y.: Cornell University Press, 1971), Chs. 2–3; and Benjamin Ward, *The Socialist Economy* (New York: Random House, 1967),

Chs. 8–9. We also refer the reader to our discussion of the socialist controversy in Chapter 7.

2. Adam Smith, *The Wealth of Nations*, ed. Edwin Cannan (New York: Modern Library, 1937).

3. George Stigler, "The Successes and Failures of Professor Smith," *Journal of Political Economy*, 84 (December 1976), 1199–1214.

4. It is difficult to single out a few individuals and claim that they are the major contributors to partial-equilibrium analysis, but these three would appear on most lists: Alfred Marshall, *Principles of Economics*, 8th ed. (New York: Macmillan, 1948); J. R. Hicks, *Value and Capital*, 2nd ed. (Oxford, England: Oxford University Press, 1946); and Paul Samuelson, *Foundations of Economic Analysis* (Cambridge, Mass.: Harvard University Press, 1948).

5. Friedrich Hayek, "The Price System as a Mechanism for Using Knowledge," *American Economic Review*, 35 (September 1945), 519–530; and Ludwig von Mises, *Socialism: An Economic and Sociological Analysis* (New Haven: Yale University Press, 1951).

6. Paul Samuelson, "The Pure Theory of Public Expenditure," *Review of Economics and Statistics*, 36 (November 1954), 26–30.

7. For a brief but lucid discussion of monopoly theory, see George Stigler, *The Theory of Price*, rev. ed. (New York: Macmillan, 1952), pp. 204–222.

8. Milton Friedman, "Monopoly and Social Responsibility of Business and Labor," in Edwin Mansfield, ed., *Monopoly Power and Economic Performance*, 3rd ed. (New York: Norton, 1974), pp. 57–68; and George J. Stigler, "The Government of the Economy," in Paul Samuelson, ed., *Readings in Economics*, 7th ed. (New York: McGraw-Hill, 1973), pp. 73–77.

9. The discussion of externalities is based on the following sources: E. J. Mishan, "The Postwar Literature on Externalities: An Interpretive Essay," *Journal of Economic Literature*, 9 (March 1971), 1–28; George Daly, "The Coase Theorem: Assumptions, Applications, and Ambiguities," *Economic Inquiry*, 12 (June 1974), 203–213; and Eirik Furobotin and Svetozar Pejovich, "Property Rights and Economic Theory: A Survey of Recent Literature," *Journal of Economic Literature*, 12 (December 1972), 1137–1162.

10. R. H. Coase, "The Problem of Social Costs," *Journal of Law and Economics*, 3 (October 1960), 1–44.

11. James Buchanan and Gordon Tullock, *The Calculus of Consent* (Ann Arbor: University of Michigan Press, 1974); Kenneth Arrow, *Social Choice and Individual Values* (New Haven: Yale University Press, 1976); for a discussion of differing views of the state, see Barry W. Poulson, *Economic Development: Private and Public Choice* (New York: West Publishing, 1994).

12. John Rawls, *Theory of Justice* (Oxford, England: Clarendon Press, 1976).

13. John Maynard Keynes, *The General Theory of Employment, Interest, and Money* (New York: Harcourt, 1936). The most important early work to interpret Keynes's general theory for nonspecialists was Alvin Hansen, *A Guide to Keynes* (New York: McGraw-Hill, 1953).

14. There is considerable controversy over what Keynes actually meant to say in *General Theory*, and some authorities argue that the more popular interpretations of Keynes are incorrect. For discussion of this controversy, see Don Patinkin, *Money, Interest, and Prices*, 2nd ed. (New York: Harper & Row, 1965); Axel Leijonhufvud, *On Keynesian Economics and the Economics of Keynes* (New York: Oxford University Press, 1968); Herschel Grossman, "Was Keynes a 'Keynesian'? A Review Article," *Journal*

of Economic Literature, 10 (March 1972), 26–30; and Alan Coddington, "Keynesian Economics: The Search for First Principles," *Journal of Economic Literature*, 14 (December 1976), 1258–1338. For a historical perspective on the Keynesian revolution, see Alan Sweezy *et al.*, "The Keynesian Revolution and Its Pioneers," *American Economic Review, Papers and Proceedings*, 62 (May 1972), 116–141.

15. The discussion of the monetarist school is based on the following sources: Milton Friedman, ed., *Studies in the Quantity Theory of Money* (Chicago: University of Chicago Press, 1956); Milton Friedman and A. J. Schwartz, *A Monetary History of the United States* (Princeton, N.J.: Princeton University Press, 1963); Milton Friedman, *Dollars and Deficits* (Englewood Cliffs, N.J.: Prentice-Hall, 1968); Franco Modigliani, "The Monetarist Controversy, or, Should We Forsake Stabilization Policies?" *American Economic Review*, 67 (March 1977), 13; Edmund Phelps, *Microeconomic Foundations of Employment and Inflation Theory* (London: Macmillan, 1974); and Milton Friedman, "Inflation and Unemployment," *Journal of Political Economy*, 85 (June 1977), 451–472.

16. For a contemporary view of the Schumpeterian contribution, see F. M. Scherer, "Schumpeter and Plausible Capitalism," *Journal of Economic Literature*, 30 (September 1992), 1416–1433. For a discussion of contemporary issues in economic growth, see Paul M. Romer et al., "New Growth Theory," *Journal of Economic Perspectives*, 8 (Winter 1994), 3–72.

Recommended Readings

A. Traditional Sources

F. M. Bator, "The Simple Analytics of Welfare Maximization," *American Economic Review*, 47 (March 1957), 22–59.

Abram Bergson, "A Reformulation of Certain Aspects of Welfare Economics," *Quarterly Journal of Economics*, 52 (February 1938), 310–334; reprinted in R. V. Clemence, ed., *Readings in Economic Analysis* (Reading, Mass.: Addison Wesley, 1950), Vol. I, pp. 61–85.

James Buchanan and Robert Tollison, eds., *Theory of Public Choice: Political Applications of Economics* (Ann Arbor: University of Michigan Press, 1972).

James Buchanan and Gordon Tullock, *The Calculus of Consent* (Ann Arbor: University of Michigan Press, 1974).

Edward Chamberlin, *The Theory of Monopolistic Competition*, 6th ed. (Cambridge, Mass.: Harvard University Press, 1948).

R. H. Coase, "The Problem of Social Costs," *Journal of Law and Economics*, 3 (October 1960), 1–44.

Alan Coddington, "Keynesian Economics: The Search for First Principles," *Journal of Economic Literature*, 14 (December 1976), 1258–1338.

A. S. Eicher and J. A. Kregel, "An Essay on Post-Keynesian Theory: A New Paradigm in Economics," *Journal of Economic Literature*, 13 (December 1975), 1293–1314.

Milton Friedman, *Dollars and Deficits* (Englewood Cliffs, N.J.: Prentice-Hall, 1968).

————, ed., *Studies in the Quantity Theory of Money* (Chicago: University of Chicago Press, 1956).

Robert J. Gordon, "What Is New Keynesian Economics?" *Journal of Economic Literature*, 28 (September 1990), 15–71.

J. de V. Graaff, *Theoretical Welfare Economics* (London: Cambridge University Press, 1957).

Herschel Grossman, "Was Keynes a 'Keynesian'? A Review Article," *Journal of Economic Literature*, 10 (March 1972), 26–30.

J. R. Hicks, *Value and Capital*, 2nd ed. (Oxford, England: Oxford University Press, 1946).

Axel Leijonhufvud, *On Keynesian Economics and the Economics of Keynes* (New York: Oxford University Press, 1968).

John Maynard Keynes, *The General Theory of Employment, Interest, and Money* (New York: Harcourt, 1936).

E. J. Mishan, "The Postwar Literature on Externalities: An Interpretive Essay," *Journal of Economic Literature*, 9 (March 1971), 1–28.

Franco Modigliani, "The Monetarist Controversy, or, Should We Forsake Stabilization Policies?" *American Economic Review*, 67 (March 1977), 1–19.

A. C. Pigou, *The Economics of Welfare*, 4th ed. (London: Macmillan, 1946).

John Rawls, *Theory of Justice* (Oxford, England: Clarendon Press, 1976).

Joan Robinson, *The Economics of Imperfect Competition* (London: Macmillan, 1959).

Paul Samuelson, "The Pure Theory of Public Expenditure," *Review of Economics and Statistics*, 36 (November 1954), 26–30.

————, *Foundations of Economic Analysis* (Cambridge, Mass.: Harvard University Press, 1948).

Tibor Scitovsky, *Welfare and Competition*, rev. ed. (Homewood, Ill.: Irwin, 1971), Chs. 20–21.

Adam Smith, *The Wealth of Nations*, ed. Edwin Cannan (New York: Modern Library, 1937).

B. The Neoclassical Model

David M. Krebs, *A Course in Microeconomic Theory* (Princeton N.J.: Princeton University Press, 1990).

Eugene Silberberg, *The Structure of Economics: A Mathematical Analysis*, 2nd ed. (New York: McGraw-Hill, 1990).

Hal R. Varian, *Intermediate Microeconomics: A Modern Approach*, 2nd ed. (New York: Norton, 1990).

C. Macroeconomic Theory

Andrew B. Abel and Ben S. Bernake, *Macroeconomics* (New York: Addison-Wesley, 1992).

William H. Branson, *Macroeconomics: Theory and Policy*, 3rd. ed. (New York: Harper-Collins, 1989).

Richard T. Froyen, *Macroeconomics: Theories and Policies*, 4th ed. (New York: Macmillan Publishing Company, 1993).

Robert J. Gordon, "What is the New Keynesian Economics?" *Journal of Economic Literature*, 28 (September 1990), 15–71.

————, *Macroeconomics*, 5th ed. (Glenview, Illinois: Scott Foresman, 1990).

Robert E. Hall and John B. Taylor, *Macroeconomics*, 3rd ed. (New York: Norton, 1991).

N. Gregory Markiw, "A Quick Refresher Course in Macroeconomics," *Journal of Economic Literature*, 28 (December 1990), 1645–1660.

N. Gregory Mankiw et al., "Keynesian Economics Today" *Journal of Economic Perspectives*, 7 (Winter 1993), 3–82.

Paul M. Romer et al., "New Growth Theory," *Journal of Economic Perspectives*, 8 (Winter 1994), 3–72.

D. Market Failure: Imperfect Competition, Income Distribution, and Public Choice

Nicholas Barr, "Economic Theory and the Welfare State: A Survey and Interpretation," *Journal of Economic Literature*, 30 (June 1992), 741–803.

Dennis W. Carlton and Jeffrey M. Perloff, *Modern Industrial Organization* (New York: HarperCollins, 1990).

Douglas F. Greer, *Business, Government, and Society*, 2nd ed. (New York: Macmillan, 1987).

F. M. Sherer and David Ross, *Industrial Market Structure and Economic Performance*, 3rd ed. (Boston: Houghton Mifflin, 1990).

R. D. Norton, "Industrial Policy and American Renewal," *Journal of Economic Literature*, 24 (March 1986), 1–40.

Barry W. Poulson, *Economic Development: Private and Public Choice* (New York: West Publishing, 1994).

Leonard W. Weiss and Michael W. Klass, eds., *Regulatory Reform: What Actually Happened* (Boston: Little, Brown, 1986).

Clifford Winston, "Economic Deregulation: Days of Reckoning for Microeconomists," *Journal of Economic Literature*, 31 (September 1993), 1263–1289.

6

Theory of Planned Socialism

Chapter 2 introduced two variants of the socialist economy: centrally planned socialism and market socialism. This chapter discusses the former, after which Chapter 7 looks at market socialism. Before the two major organizational variants of the socialist economy are discussed, it is important to introduce the basic ideas that define the nature of **socialism**.

The Socialist Economy

The characterization of the socialist economy in Chapter 2 focused on the nature of decision-making arrangements, property rights, and incentive arrangements. Much of the literature on socialism focuses on the impact of these arrangements, which along with different policies and a different political system, lead to outcomes different from those generally observed under capitalism. Appreciating these differences is important because unlike the neoclassical paradigm of the market capitalist economy, no widely accepted theoretical paradigm of the socialist economy exists.[1] Much of the literature on socialism focuses on noneconomic aspects and especially the nature of socialist society. Indeed, many socialists characterize their economic system as one not only based on fundamental social changes with special emphasis on issues of equity but designed to improve the capitalist system.

If the four fundamental tasks of any economic system from basic economics are recalled (what to produce, how to produce, who gets the product, and how to provide for the future), the socialist idea immediately becomes apparent.

First, although the output mix could in theory be the same in the capitalist and socialist systems, such an outcome is unlikely. Typically, the socialist economic system is accompanied by a strong central state, which along with state ownership of resources allows considerable state influence over deciding what will be produced. It is therefore not surprising that in most socialist economies, the output mix favors public goods, defense goods, and the socialization of consumption as opposed to the expansion of private consumer goods.

Second, the structure of the socialist economy, through state controls and ownership arrangements, can be dictated by forces that may or may not resemble those of the market. Thus the state dictates the nature of sectoral expansion and, within sectors, the arrangements for production. Moreover, socialists have viewed the technology of production as much simpler than that thought to prevail in the market economy. As a result, the appropriate mix of factor inputs (capital and labor, for example) appear quite limited and constrained by technology, making an assumption of constant-factor proportions over extended periods of time is quite reasonable. In such a setting, information problems are not serious, and engineers rather than economists can resolve the factor proportions issue. Not surprisingly, in such a setting, factor prices are of limited importance for deciding the appropriate input mix.

Third, the state ownership of the means of production has fundamental and important implications for distribution. For the household, the primary source of income is labor. Moreover, in a system where the socialization of consumption is an objective, one would expect a more equitable distribution of income than in a market capitalist economy. This expectation—one of the strongest basic tenets of socialism—relies on important assumptions concerning basic human needs, human participation in the economy, and how these basic needs ought to be fulfilled. It is therefore often argued that under socialism, human needs change, that their fulfillment can, in fact, be socialized, and that no major differences exist in the ability to benefit from increases in income, all of which supports an egalitarian distribution of income.[2]

Finally, the manner in which an economy provides for the future of its participants differs in the socialist case. A socialist frequently argues that the capitalist market economy tends to overstate the worth of present consumption at the expense of future consumption. Thus the socialist economy follows policies that expand present savings and present investment, arguing that such policies can offset individual shortsightedness and expand participant well-being in the future.

In a sense, its advocates view socialism as an economic system that can offset the perceived faults of the market capitalist economy. The socialist economy places greater emphasis on economic equality and socialization and in doing so uses a variety of state controls and policies to offset the problems of unemployment, inflation, and slow economic growth, all perceived as inevitable under capitalism.

Although a look at historical experience helps judge the relative merits of different economic and associated political systems, it is difficult to compare the paradigm of the market with that of the socialist economy because there is no single dominant paradigm of the latter system. Indeed, it is for this reason that so little attention is given to socialist economic thought in the general history of economic thought. Views of the socialist economy have varied through history. Beyond the economic aspects of socialism, a great deal of attention has focused on the nature of a socialist society and its evolution. Not surprisingly, therefore, as we focus on how systems evolve through time and the social and political settings that emerge, a great deal of attention is paid to Marx and subsequent Marxian thinkers. As will be seen, Marx analyzed capitalism, but in doing so, he envisioned socialism (and ultimately communism) as an inevitable outcome of the process of social change.

The Marxist-Leninist View of Socialism

Although Marx did not analyze socialist working arrangements, he did develop a framework for predicting the triumph of socialism over capitalism. For Marx, the historical evolution from primitive societies to communism was inevitable.[3] Capitalism, because of its exploitation of workers and internal contradictions, would be replaced by socialism. Capitalism would be an engine of economic progress, the results of which would be more evenly shared under socialism.

Socialism itself would be an intermediate step, a system ultimately to be replaced by communism. **Communism**, the highest stage of social and economic development, would be characterized by the absence of markets and money, distribution according to need, abundance, and the withering away of the state. In the meantime, under socialism, vestiges of capitalism would continue and some familiar institutions would remain. The state would be transformed into a **dictatorship of the proletariat**. Marx emphasized a strong role for the state, a role that was subsequently strengthened by Lenin.[4] Under socialism, though, the state would be representative of the masses and therefore noncoercive. The state would own the means of production as well as rights to surplus value. Under socialism, each individual would be expected to contribute according to capability, and rewards would be distributed according to that contribution. Subsequently, under communism, the basis of reward would be need. However, need would presumably have a meaning rather different from the one assigned to it under capitalism, where wants are continually expanding.

Many changes and additions have been made to the Marxian model originally developed in the nineteenth century. Lenin wrote extensively on the role of the state under socialism, especially on the tactics of revolution.

Lenin emphasized that inequalities and capitalist vestiges would still exist under socialism and that, accordingly, coercive actions by the state would be necessary.[5] Indeed, during the war communisim period in the former Soviet Union, Lenin promoted a peculiar view of the state in which the task of administering the economy's affairs was viewed as simple, capable of being handled by anyone.[6] There was no need, Lenin argued, for specialists, because the tasks of management were regarded as quite routine. These views were subsequently modified, although they form the basis of later Soviet thinking on management.

Marx, Engels, and Lenin wrote about the role of the state and income distribution under socialism. They did not deal with the more fundamental issue of how scarce resources were to be allocated during the socialist phase.

The Socialist Controversy: The Feasibility of Socialism

There is no single socialist economic paradigm. Socialist economics must be assembled partly from theory and partly from historical experience.

Resource allocation under socialism has been widely discussed over the past 75 years, a discussion loosely termed the **socialist controversy**. Socialist economic theory must explain how resources are to be allocated under socialism. If the socialist economy is planned, how will planners make rational decisions about the use of scarce resources? Is private ownership necessary for the proper functioning of markets?

Barone: A Theoretical Framework

The first consistent theoretical framework of resource allocation under socialism was developed by the Italian economist Enrico Barone. In 1907, Barone published "The Ministry of Production in the Collectivist State."[7] Here he argued, though in a limited and purely theoretical way, that prices, understood as **relative valuations**, are not bound to the market. A **central planning board** (hereafter designated CPB) could establish prices, or "ratios of equivalence" among commodities.

Barone's model consisted of simultaneous equations relating inputs and outputs to the ratios of equivalence. When solved (Barone admitted that a real-world solution would be impractical), the equations could provide the appropriate relative valuations of resources required to balance demand and supply. A CPB armed with perfect computation techniques would require perfect knowledge of all relevant variables, specifically (1) individual demand schedules, (2) enterprise production functions, and (3) existing stocks of both producer and consumer goods. Barone's principal conclusion was that the CPB's computed resource allocation would be similar to that of competitive capitalism. In fact, he saw no reason for substantial differences.

One could question the practicality of this approach, both at the time Barone was writing and even in the present state of improved computer technology. Nevertheless, it demonstrated that the relative valuations of resources essential for rational resource allocation could be discovered by imputation (solving equations) rather than through the particular institutional arrangements of the market.

The Challenge of Ludwig von Mises

The discussion of this matter went little further until the 1920s and 1930s, when three important developments took place. First, Ludwig von Mises mounted a formidable and now famous attack against the case for rational resource allocation under socialism.[8] Second, a number of Soviet authors made significant contributions to the theory of planning, then in its formative stages. Third, the noted Polish economist Oskar Lange set forth his famous model of market socialism, to be discussed in the next chapter.[9]

Mises's challenge was directed toward the problem of allocating producer goods in a socialist economic system, a task presumably in the hands of the state (with the allocation of consumer goods left to the market). Mises argued that for a state to direct available resources rationally toward the achievement of given ends, even if resource availabilities and ends are known, a knowledge of relative valuations (prices) would be essential. Mises maintained that the only way to establish these valuations would be through the market mechanism, absent in a socialist state where producer goods are owned and allocated by the state. If prices are the vehicle by which relative scarcities are reflected, why not artificially simulate prices via a system of equations as proposed by Barone? Mises argued that it would be difficult if not impossible to separate the allocation function from the workings of the market. Both, he suggested, are tied together through the profit motive and the existence of private property.

Much has been written about the profit motive and private property.[10] Mises argued that individuals are motivated by the urge for material self-betterment, which translates into utility and profit maximization. Second, individuals and enterprises are motivated to produce goods and services as efficiently as possible so as to increase profits. Third, the drive for achievement cannot be socialized; that is, the urge for betterment cannot be translated from the individual to the group. Furthermore, if resources are owned by the state, profits accrue to the state, not to individuals. Thus, Mises argued, the motivation for utilizing available resources in the most efficient way is lost.

The responses to Mises's original position have varied. There have been two main interpretations. The first is that Mises was saying that socialism could not "work" in the sense that resource allocation would be impossible in the absence of a market mechanism. The second and more common interpretation of Mises is that socialism cannot work *efficiently*. In fact, the debate over the relative merits of socialism and capitalism has focused on the question of relative efficiency.[11]

The Planned Economy: Organizational Arrangements

Figure 2.4 (Panel B) presents a rather typical chart depicting the hierarchical nature of a planned socialist economic system. Unlike the market economy, where the resource allocation process takes place on a relatively decentralized basis through the market arrangements of supply and demand, allocation here is guided by the planning mechanism. What is planning, and how does it differ from other mechanisms as it handles the problem of resource allocation?

Typically, the political authority exercises a good deal of control over the broad economic objectives. But, having characterized these objectives, it is the planning authority that is responsible for developing a plan or document outlining how resources will be used to achieve the objectives. The task of developing a plan is a complex and sophisticated task, a matter dealt with at some length in this chapter.

Once a plan is developed, it is disseminated to the participants (enterprises) in the economy, whose responsibility it is to execute or carry out the plan. These instructions tell the enterprises what to produce, how to organize production (technology), and to whom to distribute the products (through the state distribution system). In this setting, the flow of information and commands is from enterprise to planner and vice versa, with only limited interaction among enterprises. Typically agencies (ministries) between the planners and the enterprises coordinate the information flows by the nature of the product, for example, steel, agricultural products, and the like. Ideally, the directives of the plan, based on adequate and appropriate information, are complete and clear to the enterprises, and the incentive structure is such that local enterprise actions are in fact harmonized with central directives. When real-world planning systems are examined, it will be evident that real-world market economies differ from the ideals of perfect competition as do the planned economies differ from the ideals of a perfectly administered economy. In both theory and practice, the two mechanisms for allocating resources are very different, though in both cases the basic task of efficiently utilizing resources to achieve desired objectives is fundamentally the same.

Resource Allocation Under Planned Socialism

The socialist controversy raised the key issues of resource allocation under conditions of socialism. On the one hand, it raised the complexity issue for planned socialism. Barone showed that the CPB would, in theory, have to gather data and solve simultaneous equations for millions of products. Such a task would be beyond the capabilities of any real-world CPB. On the other hand, the socialist controversy raised the motivation issue for both planned and market socialism. If the means of production are owned by society at large, how are managers to be motivated to combine resources efficiently and to take innovative risks?

The discussion that follows pursues these questions for planned socialism. It begins with the origins of the theory of planned socialism in its first real-world experiment, the Soviet Union in the 1930s, and then proceeds to the theory of planning.

Origins: The Soviet Union in the 1920s

The 1920s have been described as "the golden age of Soviet mathematical economics."[12] There was relatively open discussion in the Soviet Union, including discussion about the appropriate path and mechanisms for economic growth under socialism.[13] The emphasis was on formulating a socialist path of development, guided by Marxist–Leninist ideological principles. Pioneers in mathematical economics, a key area for the subsequent development of the theory of economic planning, were very active. Under these conditions, it is not surprising that prior to the Stalinist crackdown of the late 1920s, Soviet planners and theoreticians pursued the theory of planning under conditions of social ownership. Possibly the most important practical work of this period was the development of **balances of the national economy**, forerunners of the input–output analysis of Wassily Leontief, and of **material balances**, the planning system later used in planned socialist economies. The development of the material balance approach remains a major (though simple) contribution of considerable practical importance.[14]

The material balances formulated by Soviet economists focused on the need to determine aggregate demands and supplies for basic industrial commodities and to bring them in balance without relying on market forces. More specifically, the theoretical underpinning of the material balance approach (input–output analysis) demonstrated that the productive relations of an economic system could be approximated by a system of simultaneous equations along the lines suggested by Barone.

A significant omission in the Soviet discussion of the 1920s was the matter of how enterprises might be guided at the micro level. Some Soviet economists even argued that the whole discussion of relative values (prices) under socialism was irrelevant because the **law of value** would not exist under socialism.

Although there is no necessary inconsistency between Marxian economics and mathematical economics, Stalin thought otherwise. This view ended open discussion in the Soviet Union, a situation that did not change until after Stalin's death in the early 1950s.

Economic Planning: A Paradigm for Planned Socialism

It is not surprising that the Soviet discussions of the 1920s focused on **national economic planning**. If market-resource allocation is to be eliminated, some alternative arrangement must be used in its place.

There has been a tendency to associate national economic planning with socialism in both a political and an economic context. Actually, planning is consistent with a wide variety of organizational and ideological arrangements. Nevertheless, the idea that an economic system could be centrally planned stems in large part from the experience of the former Soviet Union. Even in the countries where most national planning was done—for example, the Soviet Union—the theory of planning was only a set of pragmatic principles; there was no "theory" comparable to the paradigm of the market economy. In this sense, most real-world national planning is a pragmatic exercise.

Planning is a term with widely differing connotations. Different authors have used different definitions, but there are basic elements in common. Gerald Sirkin writes, "Planning is an attempt, by centralizing the management of the allocation of resources sufficiently, to take into account social costs and social benefits which would be irrelevant to the calculus of the decentralized decision maker."[15] The emphasis here is the appropriate *level* of decision making and the social versus the private element in the decisions taken.

Abdul Qayum defines planning as "a systematic and integrated program covering a definite period of time, approved or sponsored by the state to bring about a rationalization of resources to achieve certain national targets using direct and indirect means with or without state ownership of resources."[16] Here we have a broader and more inclusive definition, which nonetheless includes elements of the previous definition—notably, the implication of centralization in the decision-making process.

Michael Todaro, writing in the context of development planning, defines planning as follows: "Economic planning may be described as the conscious effort of a central organization to influence, direct, and, in some cases even control changes in the principal economic variables (e.g., GDP, consumption, investment, savings, etc.) of a certain country or region over the course of time in accordance with a predetermined set of objectives."[17] Todaro further emphasizes that the key concepts are influence, direction, and control, and he defines an economic plan "as a specific set of quantitative targets to be reached in a given period of time."

The concept of plan formulation has been described succinctly by G. M. Heal, who writes that it can be viewed as "solving a constrained maximization problem."[18] Plan formulation involves doing the best one can to achieve objectives, albeit with limitations on available resources.

In contrast to the increasing specificity of these definitions, it is interesting to consider the following Soviet definition:

> Socialist planning is based upon strict scientific foundations; it demands the continuous generalization of the practical experience of the construction of Communism as well as the utilization of the accomplishments of science and technology. To operate the economy according to plan means to foresee. Scientific foresight rests on the reconciliation of the objective economic laws of socialism. Plans carry in socialism the character of objectives. The planned direction of the economy requires that priorities be established and the main priorities of the economic plan are the branches of heavy industry, for they determine the development of all industrial branches as well as the economy as a whole.[19]

Although some of the elements of this definition (for example, the "objective economic laws of socialism") may be difficult to interpret, the definition contains some familiar concepts, such as the ability to foresee and the existence of objectives.

These definitions, though differing in specifics, differ relatively little in terms of substance. A **national economic plan** is a mechanism to guide the activity of an economy through time toward the achievement of specified goals or objectives. The notion of *control* is fundamental to the concept of planning. Planning is more than forecasting. Although forecasting involves projections of future economic activity, planning is substantively different: The planner attempts to *alter* the economy's direction of movement and hence to change economic outcomes. It is convenient to categorize planning as either indicative or directive. In the case of **indicative planning**, targets are set in the hope of affecting economic outcomes by providing information external to the market; typically, individual firms receive no directives from planners. In the case of **directive planning**, however, targets are set by planners with the expectation of directly altering outcomes, because plan targets are legally binding on enterprises. A popular expression in the Soviet Union was that "the plan is law." Indicative planning will be discussed in more detail in a later chapter.

If the economic activity of a country is to be planned, three basic steps are required. First, a plan has to be constructed that specifies the goals or objectives to be achieved and the means for achieving those goals. A time frame must also be specified. Second, there must be an organizational mechanism for executing the plan and, in particular, a means to guarantee that the participants in the economic system will in fact attempt to achieve plan goals. In short, there must be an incentive system to harmonize the behavior of participants with goal achievement. Finally, there must be a means to evaluate outcomes and, where they differ from targets, to ensure appropriate feedback to adjust the direction of future economic activity.

The literature on national economic planning can be conveniently divided into two categories. First, there is the literature devoted to the planning methods actually utilized in the planned socialist economic systems. This literature describes material balance planning, the Soviet origins of which have already been discussed. Second, there is the literature devoted to national economic planning models, which usually employ some optimizing procedure. Although the basic principles of planning are common to both lines of thought, the planned socialist economies have utilized the material balance approach.

Material Balance Planning

The material balance approach to national economic planning has been widely used in the planned socialist economic systems. The central planning board specifies a list of goods and services that are to be produced in the plan period. Once the CPB determines the inputs (land, labor, capital, and intermediate products) needed to produce one unit of output (generally on the basis of historical input–output relationships), it can draw up a list of input requirements necessary for meeting the specified output objectives. Obviously the CPB would like to produce as much output as possible, but the availability of inputs limits how much can be produced given available technology.

The CPB must ensure a **balance** between outputs and inputs. For each factor input and intermediate good, the amount needed to produce output (the demand) must be equated with the amount available (the supply). If a balance between the two sides does not exist, then administrative steps must be taken to reduce demand and/or expand supply. A balance must exist for each item, and there must also be an aggregate balance of demand and supply.

On the supply side, there are three main sources of inputs: production, stocks on hand, and imports. On the demand side, there are two main elements: inter-industry demand, where the output of one industry (for example, coal) is used as the input for another industry (for example, steel); and final demand, consisting of output that will be invested, consumed by households, or exported. Thus adjustment is possible on both the demand and supply sides, and it is through administrative adjustment that demand and supply are balanced. This procedure is in basic contrast to the operation of the market in market economies, where prices adjust to eliminate imbalances.

For a modern economic system, maintaining an appropriate balance between the supplies and demands for all products would be an enormous task, a point empha-sized by Hayek and Mises. In fact, the planned economies that use the material–balance approach plan only the most important inputs and outputs, handling others on a more decentralized basis. Although this means that only a portion of total output is within the control of central planners, it is nevertheless sufficient to exert a major degree of influence over the economic outcomes.

Even in this more limited context, Barone's question—how to solve the equations—remains a problem. The problem of balancing supply and demand can be conveniently formalized in the following manner:

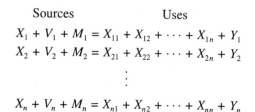

$$
\begin{aligned}
\text{Sources} & \qquad\qquad \text{Uses} \\
X_1 + V_1 + M_1 &= X_{11} + X_{12} + \cdots + X_{1n} + Y_1 \\
X_2 + V_2 + M_2 &= X_{21} + X_{22} + \cdots + X_{2n} + Y_2 \\
&\ \ \vdots \\
X_n + V_n + M_n &= X_{n1} + X_{n2} + \cdots + X_{nn} + Y_n
\end{aligned}
$$

where n items are included in the balance, and

X_i = planned output of commodity i
V_i = existing stocks of commodity i
M_i = planned imports of commodity i
X_{ij} = interindustry demand; that is, the amount of commodity i required to produce the planned amount of commodity j
Y_i = the final demand for commodity i; that is, for investment, household consumption, or export

Table 6.1 depicts a simplified material balance. Note that for each commodity a balance exists. In the case of steel, there are three sources on the supply side: production of 2,000 tons, no stocks on hand, and imports of 20 tons, for a total supply of 2,020 tons. On the demand side, there are six users of steel: the coal industry using 200 tons, the steel industry using 400 tons, the machinery industry using 1,000 tons, the consumer goods industry using 300 tons, exports of 100 tons, and domestic use of 20 tons, for a total demand of 2,020 tons. In this example, supply and demand are balanced at 2,020 tons.

Computational, administrative, and data-gathering limitations set an upper limit on the number of items that can be handled by material balance planning. Which items will be planned and which unplanned? Typically, the items that are of major significance to the achievement of state objectives are included in the plan. Items not included in the plan are planned at a lower level in the hierarchy. Plan authorities have discovered that the economy can be effectively controlled by manipulating a relatively small number of important inputs.

How does the CPB know how much of each input (X_{ij}s) will be necessary to produce a unit of output? The coefficient relating input to output is typically derived from the previous year's planning experience and adjusted somewhat (usually upward) to allow for investment and productivity improvements. Moreover, these coefficients are normally assumed to be constant over varying ranges of output—an assumption that causes problems when an industry is expanding and experiencing increasing (or decreasing) returns to scale. Gathering the information necessary to keep the coefficients up to date is a real problem. Most planned socialist systems rely on communications with enterprises, a process that is time-consuming and not necessarily reliable.

TABLE 6.1 Sample Material Balance

| | Sources | | | Intermediate Inputs Required by | | | | Final Uses | |
	Output	Stocks	Imports	Coal Industry	Steel Industry	Machinery Industry	Consumer Goods Industry	Exports	Domestic Uses
Coal (tons)	1,000	10	0	100	500	50	50	100	210
Steel (tons)	2,000	0	20	200	400	1,000	300	100	20
Machinery (units)	100	5	5	20	40	10	20	10	10
Consumer goods (units)	400	10	20	0	0	0	100	100	230

Demonstration that a balance exists:

Sources of coal: 1,010 tons   = uses of coal: 1,010 tons
Sources of steel: 2,020 tons   = uses of steel: 2,020 tons
Sources of machinery: 110 units   = uses of machinery: 110 units
Sources of consumer goods: 430 units = uses of consumer goods: 430 units

Source: Paul R. Gregory and Robert C. Stuart, *Soviet Economic Structure and Performance* (New York: Harper & Row, 1986), p. 169. Reprinted by permission of Harper & Row. Copyright © 1974 by Paul R. Gregory and Robert C. Stuart.

Material balance planning must deal with the interrelatedness of economic sectors. Suppose, for example, that during the process of plan formulation or execution, a need arises to expand the output of a particular commodity or a previously unknown input shortage is discovered. If more steel is needed, so also will more coal be needed for the production of the steel. But to produce more coal, more electricity is needed, and on, and on, and on. These so-called second-round effects reverberate throughout the economic system, making it very difficult to obtain a balance. To what degree can planners take second-round effects into account? In theory, a number of reformulations of the plan would be necessary. In practice, most planners allow for the initial or most serious repercussions, leaving the remainder to be absorbed as shocks by the system.

The balancing of demands with supplies is the essence of material balance planning. But what about optimality? **Optimality** implies selecting the *best* plan of all those with which it would be possible to achieve a balance. The best plan is the one that maximizes the planners' objectives. Although it is mathematically possible to elaborate the criteria for selecting an optimal plan from among a number of feasible variants, most planned socialist economies are able to prepare two or three variants at best, and there is no reason for the selected variants to be optimal.

When we examine Soviet planning in practice, we shall have a chance to consider further aspects of material balance planning. At this juncture, let us simply observe that material balance planning was a mechanism that worked, albeit at a low level of efficiency. Furthermore, it enabled the planners to select key areas on which pressure can be applied to seek rapid expansion, regional economic growth, or whatever. On the other hand, it is cumbersome, and achieving a balance frequently requires the existence of buffer or low-priority sectors (typically consumer goods) that can absorb planning mistakes.

Raymond Powell examined how economies that operate through material balance planning have been able to survive and generate growth.[20] Powell pointed out that material balance planning does not prevent participants in the economy (managers, ministers, and planners) from responding to nonprice scarcity indicators. Because there will inevitably be planning errors (imbalances between output targets and the inputs allocated to produce these targets), managers and planners will be confronted with various indicators of scarcity. Managers will recognize that some materials are harder to acquire than others or that some materials held by the enterprise are scarcer than others. Ministries will receive warnings from their enterprises concerning production shortfalls and material shortages and will have to assess the reliability of this information. On the basis of this nonprice information, resources will be reallocated within the firm according to perceived indicators of relative scarcity. Managers may allocate internal resources (personnel and trucks) to seek out and transport scarce materials. Ministries and central planners will reallocate materials to enterprises that, according to the scarcity indicators they receive, have relatively high marginal products. According to Powell, these natural responses to scarcity indicators introduce into material balance planning the rationality that allows it to function and survive.

The Input–Output Model[21]

The **input–output model** offers an alternative approach to administrative material balance planning. In theory, it gives planners an opportunity to determine balances quickly (through high-speed computers) and hence to explore alternative resource allocations.

An input–output table is a graphical presentation of the national accounts of an economy and illustrates the flows among the various sectors. The economy is divided into **sectors** of which there are two broad types—those that produce output (final output for consumption or intermediate output) and those that use final output (either as an intermediate input to further production or as a final consumption item). Sectors may correspond to industries, the number of which depends on the degree of disaggregation. Naturally, the greater the number of sectors, the more accurately the table reflects real economic interrelationships. At the same time, data and computational problems normally place severe limits on size. A simple input–output table is presented in Figure 6.1.

The sum total of goods and services produced (gross domestic product) is equal to the sum total of factor incomes (gross domestic income) used to produce this output. This concept is illustrated in the input–output table. The sum of all inputs used in, say, agriculture (sum of entries in the second column) is numerically equal to the total output of the agricultural sector (sum of entries in the second row). Each column in the input–output table illustrates both the source and the amount of input that will be used from each source in producing output. The inputs are of two types, **primary inputs** (labor, capital, and land) and **intermediate inputs** (steel, agricultural products). At the same time, each row shows how the output of the particular sector (agriculture in this case) is distributed among the various users (of agricultural products). In this table, there are two types of users: industries that use agricultural products as intermediate inputs for manufacturing, and final consumers who use agriculture products directly without further processing.

The input–output table is a simple yet highly useful picture of resource flows in an economic system. We should emphasize, however, that input–output economics relies on several crucial and limiting assumptions.

1. *Aggregation:* Obviously, the fewer the sectors, the easier it is to manipulate the table. The larger the number of branches, the more realistic the table, but the more difficult it is to compile and manipulate. On the other hand, generalized branches such as "agriculture" and "manufacturing" tell us little about the real working arrangements of an economy.
2. *Time frame:* The simple model presented here is *static* and does not, therefore, allow for change through time. The amount of labor required to produce a unit of steel is assumed not to change over time.
3. *Returns to scale:* We are assuming constant returns to scale. That is, the input–output ratios are the same, regardless of the *volume* of output being produced.

Our interest focuses largely on Quadrant I, for here are the **technical coefficients** relating inputs to outputs. Specifically, this quadrant tells us how much of a

FIGURE 6.1   Schematic Input–Output Table

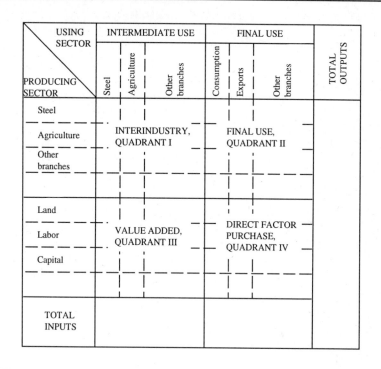

particular input is required to produce a unit of a particular output. Clearly this technical relationship is crucial for specifying what will be produced and what inputs will be available for this production activity. How are these coefficients determined?

If there are *i* rows and *j* columns in the input–output matrix, then any cell can be described as a_{ij}, which represents the amount of *i* that is used to produce a unit of *j* as a proportion of the total output of *j*. These technical coefficients are defined in the following manner:

$$a_{ij} = \frac{x_{ij}}{X_j}$$

where:

x_{ij} = the amount of input *i* used in industry *j*
X_j = the total output of industry *j*

What is the relationship between the input–output framework and material balance planning? First, knowledge of the matrix of technical coefficients is crucial to the development of a plan, whether that plan is constructed by a simple material balance technique or by more sophisticated methods. For example, if a plan is to be feasible, input availabilities must be sufficient to produce desired outputs. Clearly, knowledge of the technical coefficients can assist in making such a determination.

Second, if one knows the relationship between inputs and outputs, then with a given feasible objective, one in effect knows the relative worth (value) of different inputs in the production process. Thus a set of **relative prices** can be determined from the input–output model.

Third, the basic input–output model, even with a fair degree of aggregation, provides the planner with important information about the relationship between inputs and outputs.

Suppose the technical coefficients (a_{ij}) are known. How can the planner determine whether a particular objective is possible with available inputs? The input–output model says that for n sectors, the total production of each sector is the sum of intermediate demand and final demand. In notational form, this relationship can be expressed as follows:

$$\sum_{j=1}^{n} x_{ij} + Y_i = X_i \tag{6.1}$$

But we know something about the amount of i needed to produce a unit of j. Specifically, this relationship is as follows:

$$x_{ij} = a_{ij} X_j \tag{6.2}$$

Substituting equation 6.2 into equation 6.1, we derive the following relationship:

$$\sum_{j=1}^{n} a_{ij} X_j + Y_i = X_i \tag{6.3}$$

Rearranging terms, we get

$$Y_i = X_i - \sum_{j=1}^{n} a_{ij} X_j \tag{6.4}$$

Equation 6.4 expresses the basic relationship among final demand, interindustry demand, and total production. This basic relationship can be more conveniently expressed in matrix notation as follows:

$$X = AX + Y \tag{6.5}$$

or by rearranging terms

$$Y = (I - A)X \tag{6.6}$$

where:

I = identity matrix
X = a vector of planned outputs
A = the matrix of technical coefficients
Y = a vector of final outputs

If the matrix of technical coefficients (A) is known to the planner, then the feasibility of a given vector of plan targets (X) can be readily determined by the matrix multiplication. Clearly, even if the focus of the planner should change, knowing any two of the three components of this relationship makes it easier to determine the third component.

How useful is this model in practice? Although aggregation reduces the realism and the practical applicability of the model, it nevertheless remains useful as a method of checking the feasibility of alternative scenarios. The input–output model performs a number of functions: it provides a mathematical formulation of material balances, and it shows how supply–demand balances can be achieved mathematically via computers. Although problems that arise in the real-world collection and manipulation of data limit its applicability, the input–output model supplies the theoretical underpinnings of material balance planning.

Optimization and Economic Planning

Soviet material balance planning was the actual planning method used by the Soviets to allocate resources. As we have noted, Soviet material balance planning was a pragmatic method for planning an economy by administrative means. Its objective was to provide a rough balance between supplies and demands of a relatively limited number of key industrial commodities. Because of its administrative complexity, Soviet material balance planning aimed at achieving a balance; it did not aim at achieving the optimal balance.

The theory of economic planning focuses on the problem of achieving an *optimal* balance. It shows how, in theory, planners can plan for the economy to produce the optimal combinations of outputs, subject to the constraint of limited land, labor, and capital resources. No present-day economy actually allocates resources by using administrative planning techniques that select detailed optimal combinations of outputs. Although the solution to such a planning problem is evident in theory, in practice it is elusive.

The planning problem can be expressed in the following manner:

$$\text{Maximize } U = U(X_1, X_2, \ldots, X_n) \qquad i = 1, \ldots, n \qquad (6.7)$$

Here X_i are products that are produced subject to existing technology:

$$X_i = f(u_1, u_2, \ldots, u_m) \qquad (6.8)$$

where u_j are resources (land, labor, materials, and others) and are subject to

$$u_j \leq b_j \qquad j = 1, \ldots, m \qquad (6.9)$$

where b_j represents resource availabilities, and u_j represents the total amount of resource j used by all producers. Moreover, resources are employed at zero or positive levels:

$$u_j \geq 0 \qquad (6.10)$$

The goal of planning is to achieve the maximal value of equation 6.7, which is termed the **objective function**. The objective function summarizes the planners' economic objectives and provides a precise relationship between the utility derived by society (U) and the output of goods and services (X_i) from which that social utility, or satisfaction, is derived. In turn, the magnitude of goods and services available is a function of resource availabilities (u_j) with given technology. Resources cannot be used beyond their available supplies (b_j), either in the aggregate or for any individual resource.

The critics of the Barone model explained why such optimal planning is virtually impossible in practice. First, an economy produces millions of distinct products and factor inputs. Even with powerful computers, it is not possible to solve the millions of simultaneous equations for the optimal combinations of inputs and outputs. To reduce the computational problem to manageable proportions, planners would have to work with aggregations of distinct commodities (such as tons of steel or square meters of textiles). Real-world economies do not operate with aggregated commodities. Factories require steel goods of specific grades and qualities. To go from a planning solution based on aggregate inputs or outputs to real production and distribution processes is an extremely complicated problem. Second, even if planners could gather the necessary information and make the complicated calculations, it is still not clear how to get enterprises actually to produce the planned commodities by using optimal combinations of inputs. This is the problem of creating an incentive scheme that encourages firms to implement the optimal production and distribution computed by planners. A related problem is the generation and processing of data. The information burden on planners is already excessive even if there is accurate and unbiased reporting by the enterprises. However, planners might find it difficult to elicit accurate information from enterprises, because their success or failure might hinge on these statistical reports.

A final problem with optimal planning is obtaining agreement on the objective function of society. How are planners to know what goods and services are more important than others? Presumably, planners would have some insights on this issue, but the more complex the economy becomes, the more difficult it might be to determine the relative social valuations of different goods and services. In a complex economy, planners must know whether industrial plastics are more important than stainless steel or ceramics, all of which might serve similar functions as substitutes.

Coordination: How Much Market? How Much Plan?

In our discussion of planning, two themes emerge. First, there is the matter of how much control the central planning board is to exercise over economic outcomes. Should all decisions be made from above by planners, or should there be some decentralization to lower levels? Second, there is the matter of actually solving the plan to achieve both consistency and optimality. In most planned socialist systems, the practical approaches to these problems involve simplification through limitation of the formal planning procedures to important outputs and inputs, and a downgrading of the optimality criterion. Furthermore, mistakes are typically absorbed by low-priority (buffer) sectors. Also, most real-world systems utilize intermediate arrangements that combine plan and market. For sectors viewed by the planners as crucial to the achievement of state objectives (for example, steel), the CPB plays an important role; for sectors viewed as substantially less important (for example, light industrial goods), the CPB may play a minor role. Most approach planning as only a partial means for the allocation of resources. The "priority principle" (that is, focusing on important sectors such as steel and chemicals) serves to limit the range of inputs and outputs planned at the center. Plan techniques are of the material balance type; they are substantially distant from the more sophisticated and theoretically elegant optimization models that we have described.

Critics of the planned socialist system argue that the complexities of the real world make it impossible for the CPB to handle its tasks, let alone to expect the individual firm to follow its directives. The supporters of planned socialism, on the other hand, have argued that choices in production and consumption are generally much simpler than neoclassical economic theory implies. These sorts of issues remain at the center of the debate over the relative merits of the plan versus the market.

The theory of planning stresses the **formulation of a plan**, consisting of a set of objectives and the means for achieving the objectives. However, plans are of little value unless they are implemented. Implementation calls for incentives that induce economic agents to achieve the goals planners have set. The record of the Soviet Union and other planned socialist economic systems shows that ensuring appropriate motivation is a serious problem. Managers frequently work with plan objectives that are poorly specified, if not contradictory. When managers are asked to **execute plans** with limited information under such conditions, a large element of informal (and often dysfunctional) decision making takes over where plan directives were intended to be dominant.

The Performance of Planned Socialism: Hypotheses

Chapter 5, put forth several hypotheses concerning the expected performance of capitalist economic systems in terms of the performance criteria of economic growth, efficiency, and income distribution. We shall now attempt to do the same for socialist economic systems.

Because we have no paradigm of socialist economic systems, the formulation of hypotheses is especially difficult. Moreover, it is difficult to formulate hypotheses independently of the performance of real-world socialism. We now know a great deal about the efficiency problems of planned socialism in practice. Although it does not constitute a scientific approach to hypotheses formulation, real-world experience is hard to ignore.

Income Distribution

The first hypothesis is obvious. Income should be more equally distributed under planned socialism than under capitalism. The state (society) owns capital and land,

and the returns on these assets go to the state. It is conceivable, but not likely, that the state will distribute this nonlabor income *less* equitably than capitalist societies. Presumably, authorities in planned socialist economies attach considerable importance to the "fair" distribution of income. We therefore expect income to be distributed relatively equally in a planned socialist economy.

Efficiency

The critics of planned socialism believe that planned socialist economies have difficulty in efficiently allocating resources. Planners, they feel, would have great difficulty in processing information, constructing a plan, and motivating participants. Moreover, the planned socialist economy would not automatically generate relative prices that would enable participants to make good use of resources. These theoretical difficulties suggest the hypothesis that planned socialist economies operate at relatively low levels of efficiency. Planning techniques that aim at optimality still have limited real-world applicability, and planned socialist economies have had to use material balance planning procedures that are unlikely to place them on their production possibilities schedules (see Figure 3.2). In fact, the aim of material balance planning is consistency, not optimality. Thus the hypothesis that the planned socialist economies do not perform well in terms of both dynamic and static efficiency appears to be a fairly safe one.

Economic Growth

In planned socialism, the state is able to exercise greater control over the investment and savings rates than under capitalism. This is true because virtually all nonlabor income accrues to the state. One would therefore expect a higher savings rate under both forms of socialism, because the socialist state is likely to adopt rapid growth as a priority objective (the building of socialism).

In the planned socialist economies, rapid growth is promoted both by the high savings rate and by the direction of resources by planners into growth-maximizing pursuits. At first glance, therefore, it would appear that one should hypothesize a higher growth rate for the planned socialist economies. The complicating factor, however, is the hypothesized lower efficiency of the planned socialist economies. Thus we must again refrain from stating a strong hypothesis about the relative growth of planned socialism, which must be left as an empirical issue.

Stability

We hypothesize that the planned socialist economies will be more stable than their capitalist counterparts. In making this statement, we do not deny the fact that significant concealed instabilities (repressed inflation, underemployment) will be present in the planned socialist economies. We base our hypothesis of greater stability on the following considerations. First, investment spending will be subject to the control of planners and will probably be maintained at a fairly stable rate. Thus fluctuations in investment spending (a major source of instability in capitalist economies) will probably be small. Second, material balance planning will lead to an approximate balance of labor supplies and demands. Third, supplies and demands for consumer goods will be subject to a great deal of state control (planners set industrial wages and determine the output of consumer goods). Moreover, the state will be less subject to popular pressures to pursue inflationary monetary policies. Fourth, firms operating under pressure to meet output targets will provide workers with guaranteed jobs.

Summary

This chapter examines socialism with special emphasis on central planning as a mechanism to organize resource allocation. Although there is no single dominant paradigm of the socialist economy, socialism typically combines a strong state with public ownership and a set of policies designed to change economic outcomes that are typically associated with market capitalism. The socialist system focuses on an output mix distributed largely through labor incomes and socialized consumption to pursue an egalitarian distribution of benefits. The socialist system also maintains substantial state control over the nature and expansion of industry, especially economic growth.

In the absence of a theoretical paradigm of the socialist economy, emphasis is placed on the evolution of systems and especially the views of Marx and Lenin that contend socialism is an inevitable outcome of social and economic progress. Much of the twentieth century has witnessed a continuing debate about the feasibility of socialism as an economic system. Indeed, at the beginning of the century Barone demonstrated the theoretical feasibility of socialist resource allocation, but he failed to provide a workable real-world scheme for such a system. While a fundamental objective of socialism is equity based on an egalitarian distribution of income, much of the criticism rests on the efficiency of resource allocation in an economy where markets do not exist.

Mises and Hayek argued that socialism would be inefficient if not unworkable, largely owing to computational problems, evaluation difficulties, and fundamental incentive problems.

In the socialist economy where central planning is used, resources are allocated through a national economic plan. Typically the economy is organized in a hierarchical fashion using a central planning board (CPB). The CPB is responsible for preparing a plan document—basically a sources and uses statement—that directs producing enterprises as they allocate inputs to produce goods and services. While input–output analysis is a theoretical basis of planning, most real-world planned socialist systems use a system of balances, or material balance planning. The former Soviet Union pioneered the development and implementation of the balance approach to planning.

In a sense, the theory of planning could serve as a theoretical paradigm for the socialist economy. Planning, however, is a general approach to the basic problem of rational resource allocation, emphasizing the development of an optimal plan that maximizes an objective function subject to a variety of constraints, especially resources. Although the theory of planning is a general paradigm, real-world applications have typically suffered from both information and incentive problems.

These latter difficulties have led to modifications of planning arrangements and the use of mixed systems in real-world socialist applications. Thus an attempt is often made to combine the perceived equity of socialist arrangements with the efficiency of the market, the latter serving as a way to limit the burdens placed on planning agencies.

Key Terms

socialism	balance
communism	optimality
dictatorship of the proletariat	input–output model
socialist controversy	sectors
relative valuations	primary inputs
central planning board	intermediate inputs
balances of the national economy	aggregation
material balances	technical coefficients
law of value	relative prices
national economic plan	objective function
indicative planning	plan formulation
directive planning	plan execution

Notes

1. See A. C. Pigou, *Socialism Versus Capitalism* (New York: St. Martin's, 1960), Ch. 1. For a brief definition, see Benjamin N. Ward, *The Socialist Economy* (New York: Random House, 1967), Ch. 1; for a broader definition, see J. Wilczynski, *The Economics of Socialism* (London: Unwin Hyman, 1970), Ch. 1; for a contemporary summary, see Tom Bottomore, *The Socialist Economy: Theory and Practice* (New York: Harvester Wheatsheaf, 1990).
2. If the marginal utility of income is identical and declining for all individuals, then an equal distribution of income would maximize social benefit.
3. In the Marxian schema, capitalism is the engine that was to create the developed and industrialized economy; socialism would be concerned with providing an "equitable" distribution of the productive capacity developed under capitalism. Although socialism was not intended to be the mechanism for economic development, this is precisely the role in which it has been cast.
4. For a survey, see R. N. Carew Hunt, *The Theory and Practice of Communism* (Harmondsworth, England: Penguin Books, 1963), Chs. 6, 15.
5. Lenin's views on this matter are elaborated in his *State and Revolution*, published in 1917.

6. This view, though largely discredited during the period of war communism in the Soviet Union, has remained influential in present-day Soviet attitudes toward industrial and agricultural management. This attitude is used to support the argument for technical rather than managerial training in large enterprises.

7. The important articles on this debate can be found in F. A. Hayek, ed., *Collectivist Economic Planning*, 6th ed. (London: Routledge and Kegan Paul, 1963).

8. See Ludwig von Mises, "Economic Calculation in Socialism," in Morris Bornstein, ed., *Comparative Economic Systems*, rev. ed. (Homewood, Ill.: Irwin, 1969), pp. 61–68.

9. The best source for the original article by Oskar Lange and related discussion is Benjamin Lippincott, ed., *On the Economic Theory of Socialism* (Minneapolis: University of Minnesota Press, 1938), reprinted by McGraw-Hill in 1964.

10. Pigou, *Socialism versus Capitalism*, Ch. 1.

11. Abram Bergson, *Essays in Normative Economics* (Cambridge, Mass.: Harvard University Press, 1966), Ch. 9; also see Abram Bergson, "Market Socialism Revisited," *Journal of Political Economy*, 75 (October 1967), 663–675; for contemporary views, see Don Lavoie, *Rivalry and Central Planning: The Socialist Calculation Debate Reconsidered* (New York: Cambridge University Press, 1985); Peter Murrell, "Did the Theory of Market Socialism Answer the Challenge of Ludwig Von Mises? A Reinterpretation of the Socialist Controversy," *History of Political Economy*, 15 (September 1981), 261–276.

12. See Leon Smolinski, "The Origins of Soviet Mathematical Economics," in Franz-Lothar Altmann, ed., *Jahrbuch der Wirtschaft Osteuropas* [Yearbook of East European Economics], Band 2 (Munich: Gunter Olzog Verlag, 1971), pp. 137–154.

13. The most famous Soviet growth model is by P. A. Feldman and is discussed in Evsey Domar, *Essays in the Theory of Economic Growth* (New York: Oxford University Press, 1957), pp. 233–261. The classic work on the Soviet industrialization debate is Alexander Erlich, *The Soviet Industrialization Debate, 1924–1928* (Cambridge, Mass.: Harvard University Press, 1962).

14. R. W. Davies and S. G. Wheatcroft, eds., *Materials for a Balance of the National Economy 1928/29* (Cambridge, England: Cambridge University Press, 1985).

15. Gerald Sirkin, *The Visible Hand: The Fundamentals of Economic Planning* (New York: McGraw-Hill, 1968), p. 45.

16. Abdul Qayum, *Techniques of National Economic Planning* (Bloomington: Indiana University Press, 1975), p. 4.

17. Michael P. Todaro, *Development Planning: Models and Methods* (Nairobi: Oxford University Press, 1971), p. 1.

18. G. M. Heal, *The Theory of Economic Planning* (New York: American Elsevier, 1973), p. 5.

19. *Political Economy: A Textbook*, 4th ed. (Berlin: Deitz, 1964), pp. 496, 499.

20. Raymond Powell, "Plan Execution and the Workability of Soviet Planning," *Journal of Comparative Economics*, 1 (March 1977), 51–76.

21. H. B. Chenery and P. G. Clark, *Interindustry Economics* (New York: Wiley, 1959); R. Dorfman, P. Samuelson, and R. Solow, *Linear Programming and Economic Analysis* (New York: McGraw-Hill, 1958); W. W. Leontief, *Input–Output Economics* (New York: Oxford University Press, 1966); Michael P. Todaro, *Development Planning: Models and Methods* (Nairobi: Oxford University Press, 1971); and Vladimir Treml, "Input–Output Analysis and Soviet Planning," in John Hardt *et al.*, eds., *Mathematics and Computers in Soviet Planning* (New Haven: Yale University Press, 1967); for a discussion in the development context, see E. Wayne Nafziger, *The Economics of Developing Countries*, 2nd ed. (Englewood Cliffs, N.J.: Prentice Hall, 1990), Ch. 19.

Recommended Readings

A. Traditional Sources

Abram Bergson, "Socialist Economics" in Howard Ellis, ed., *A Survey of Contemporary Economics* (Philadelphia: Blakiston, 1948).

———, "Market Socialism Revisited," *Journal of Political Economy*, 75, (October 1967), 655–673.

R. N. Carew-Hunt, *The Theory and Practice of Communism* (Harmondsworth, England: Penguin, 1963).

G. D. H. Cole, *Socialist Economics* (London: Gollancz, 1950).

Maurice Dobb, *Welfare Economics and the Economics of Socialism* (Cambridge: Cambridge University Press, 1969).

F. A. Hayek, ed., *Collectivist Economic Planning*, 6th ed. (Routledge and Kegan Paul, 1963).

Michael P. Todaro, *Development Planning: Models and Methods* (Nairobi: Oxford University Press, 1971).

Benjamin N. Ward, *The Socialist Economy* (New York: Random House, 1967).

B. The Socialist Economy

Pranab K. Bardhan and John E. Roemer, eds., *Market Socialism: The Current Debate* (New York: Oxford University Press, 1993).

Tom Bottomore, *The Socialist Economy: Theory and Practice* (New York: Harvester Wheatsheaf, 1990).

Bernard Crick, *Socialism* (Minneapolis: University of Minnesota Press, 1987).

Don Lavoie, *Rivalry and Central Planning: The Socialist Calculation Debate Reconsidered* (New York: Cambridge University Press, 1985).

Andrew Levine, *Arguing for Socialism: Theoretical Considerations* (London: Routledge and Kegan Paul, 1984).

Peter Murrell, "Did The Theory of Market Socialism Answer the Challenge of Ludwig von Mises? A Reinterpretation of the Socialist Controversy," *History of Political Economy*, 15 (September 1984), 261–276.

———, "Incentives and Income Under Market Socialism," *Journal of Comparative Economics*, 8 (September 1984), 261–276.

Alec Nove, *The Economics of Feasible Socialism* (Winchester, Mass.: Unwin Hyman, 1983).

S. Pejovich, *Socialism: Institutional, Philosophical, and Economic Issues* (Norwell, Mass.: Kluwer Academic Publishers, 1987).

James A. Yunker, *Socialism Revised and Modernized: The Case for Pragmatic Market Socialism* (New York: Praeger, 1992).

C. Economic Planning

John Bennett, *The Economic Theory of Central Planning* (Cambridge, Mass.: Blackwell, 1989).

Morris Bornstein, ed., *Economic Planning, East and West* (Cambridge, Mass.: Ballinger, 1975).

Roger A. Bowles and David K. Whynes, *Macroeconomic Planning* (London: Unwin Hyman, 1979).

Phillip J. Bryson, *Scarcity and Control in Socialism* (Lexington, Mass.: Heath, 1976).

Parkash Chander and Ashok Pavikh, "Theory and Practice of Decentralized Planning Procedures," *Journal of Economic Surveys*, 4 (1990), 19–58.

G. M. Heal, *The Theory of Economic Planning* (New York: American Elsevier, 1973).

Zoltan Kenessey, *The Process of Economic Planning* (New York: Columbia University Press, 1978).

Don Lavoie, *National Economic Planning: What Is Left* (Cambridge, Mass.: Ballinger, 1985).

Abdul Qayum, *Techniques of National Economic Planning* (Bloomington: Indiana University Press, 1975).

Gerald Sirkin, *The Visible Hand: The Fundamentals of Economic Planning* (New York: McGraw-Hill, 1968).

Nicolas Spulber and Ira Horowitz, *Quantitative Economic Policy and Planning* (New York: Norton, 1976).

7

Theory of Market Socialism

Market socialism is, as the term suggests, a hybrid of market and state ownership. It is an economic system that combines social ownership of capital with market allocation. As such, it offers the potential of combining the "fairness" of socialism with the efficiency associated with market allocation. The state owns the means of production, and returns to capital accrue to society at large. Because resources are allocated primarily by markets, many of the problems of planned socialism—the administrative and computational burdens and the problem of valuing resources—appear to be avoided.

This chapter presents the theory of market socialism. Unlike the perfectly competitive model of capitalism, there is no single paradigm of market socialism. Instead, there are alternative visions of market socialism, one characterized by state ownership of the means of production, the other by worker ownership. Both visions rely on markets (or at least artificial markets) to do the job of resource allocation.

Whereas it has been possible to study the actual workings of both market capitalism and planned socialism, the world has little experience with market socialism. This lack of real-world practice makes the theory of market socialism even more important. We must rely heavily on theory to understand the properties of this type of economic system. As this chapter shows, market socialism has both advantages and drawbacks. The major problems appear to be how to motivate participants to use resources efficiently and how to make markets work when private individuals do not own capital.

The appeal of market socialism is obvious. The widespread rejection of planned socialism in the late 1980s and early 1990s has elevated market socialism to the status of the major alternative to capitalism. The reform leadership of the Soviet Union and Eastern Europe may find market socialism a more palatable solution than market capitalism insofar as it promises to avoid the more negative features of market capitalism. Put another way, the demise of communism in Eastern Europe does not mean the demise of socialist thought and especially democratic variants of socialism. The latter will sustain, especially in poor countries striving to achieve improved levels of living.

136

Market Socialism: Theoretical Foundations

The problems of optimal planning—computational difficulty and motivation—make market socialism appealing. Permitting the market to direct a number of resource-allocation decisions reduces the burden on the **central planning board** (CPB). Also, by allowing individual participants to respond to market incentives, market socialism may offer greater inducements to combine resources efficiently at the local level.

Advocates of market socialism have had to answer two questions raised by Hayek and Mises (see Chapter 6). If the means of production are owned by society, what assurances are there that capital will be used efficiently? And will the social ownership of capital distort incentives or lead to perverse economic behavior?

The Lange Model

The most famous theoretical model of market socialism is the **trial-and-error model** proposed by the Polish economist Oskar Lange.[1] This model focuses on the use of a general equilibrium framework (emphasized in the writings of Barone, Pareto, and Walras), approaching a "solution" through a number of sequential stages (emphasized by Walras).

A number of economists (most notably H. D. Dickinson and Abba Lerner) contributed to the Lange model, and a number of variants of the model exist.[2] Furthermore, the **Lange model** of market socialism differs from our definition of market socialism in that Lange envisioned only some indirect usage of the market.

What are the essential features of the Lange-type market socialist model? The model posits three levels of decision making (see Figure 7.1). At the lowest level are firms and households; at the intermediate level, industrial authorities; and at the highest level, a CPB. The means of production, with the exception of labor, are state owned. Consumer goods are allocated by the market.

The CPB would set the prices of producer goods. Producing firms would be informed of these prices and would be instructed to produce in accordance with two rules: Produce the level of output at which price is equal to marginal cost, and minimize the cost of production at that output. Households would be left alone to make their own decisions about how much labor to supply.

Because the initial prices of producer goods would be arbitrarily set by the CPB, there is no reason to believe that as firms followed the rules (assuming that they did in fact follow the rules), the "right" amount of goods and services would be produced and supplies and demands would be in balance. What would the planners do if there were an imbalance?

If there were an excess supply of a particular good, its price would be lowered by the CPB. If there were excess demand, its price would be raised by the CPB. Thus, in a sequential process, the CPB would adjust prices until they were at the "right" levels—that is, where supply and demand were balanced.

In addition to setting prices, the central planning board would also allocate the social dividend (rents and profits) earned from the use of productive resources

FIGURE 7.1   The Organization of Market Socialism in the Lange Framework

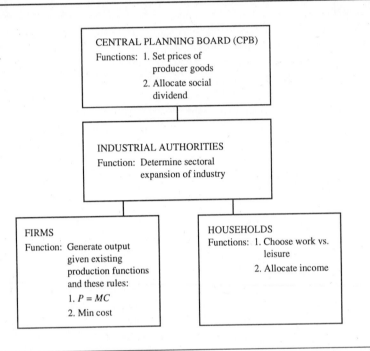

owned by the state. This dividend could be distributed in the form of public services or investment, the latter decision made in conjunction with the intermediate industrial authorities. The state would have a substantial degree of power because it could determine both the magnitude and the direction of investment, though Lange argued that investment funds should be generally allocated to equalize marginal rates of return in different applications. Considerable central control over the economic system would be maintained by the CPB. At the same time, prices would be used for decision making to relieve the CPB of a substantial administrative task.

Let us examine some of the proposed advantages of the Lange model. Lange envisioned that with the means of production owned by the state, both the *rate* and the *direction* of economic activity would in large part be determined by the state. Thus the returns from and the influence of private ownership would be removed. Accordingly, the distribution of income would be substantially more even than under capitalism. Furthermore, the mix of output would be different, and insofar as the investment ratio would be a major determinant of the rate of economic growth, this rate too would be largely state determined. Both these features of the Lange model (a more even distribution of income and state control over investment) are presumed advantages.

Lange argued that externalities could be better accounted for because the state could manipulate resource prices. Other economists—for example, Jan Tinbergen and Maurice Dobb—have argued that, in general, decisions made at higher levels rather than lower levels are likely to be "better" in terms of preventing undesirable environmental effects.[3] Lange further presumed that state control over savings and investment would reduce cyclical instability, a mainstay in the socialism critique of capitalism.

Real-world market systems depart from the perfectly competitive model. Simulation of the market, argued Lange, would utilize the positive aspects of the market while eliminating its negative characteristics. In this context, it is ironic that Lange said little about the problems that would arise when difficulties of entry, economies of scale, or changes in technology were present. These forces are crucial in determining the degree of competition in a capitalist economic system. Might not some of these problems arise in the real-world operation of a Lange-type model?

Critics of the Lange Model

The Lange model captured the fancy of many observers over the years, but it has not been without critics. Lange himself recognized that the many tasks assigned to the CPB could lead to a large bureaucracy, long considered a negative feature of socialism. The most outspoken critic on this score has been the Nobel laureate F. A. Hayek. Hayek has suggested that although the task set for the CPB might be manageable in theory, it would probably be unmanageable in practice.[4]

Abram Bergson and others have pointed to a key problem in the Lange model: that of ensuring appropriate managerial motivation.[5] How would the intermediate authorities, and especially enterprise managers, be motivated to follow Lange's rules of conduct even if they knew marginal costs? The problem of establishing a workable incentive structure has been a major theme in modern socialist economic systems.

Bergson also emphasized the possibility of monopolistic behavior in the Lange framework—if not at the enterprise level, then at the intermediate level. This problem and the matter of relating one level to another are substantially neglected in the original formulation of the Lange model.

Although the Lange model uses features of capitalism, it is also characterized by many elements normally associated with socialism. The scholarly literature, therefore, has tended to focus on whether the Lange model can operate in reality and, if so, how effectively. The Lange model has also sparked great interest because most existing socialist systems use a crude form of trial and error for the setting of prices, at least for consumer goods. Real-world reliance on the trial-and-error methods is important, for mathematical models of planning (and price formulation) have been of limited practical use in spite of their theoretical elegance.[6]

Market Socialism: The Cooperative Variant

A second variant of market socialism is the **cooperative economy**, or **labor-managed economy** or, more specifically, the **producer cooperative**.[7] The interest in worker participation stems from both the theory of cooperative economic behavior elaborated in this section and the systems of worker management used in Yugoslavia, Western Europe, and now Eastern Europe.

The cooperative model of market socialism stems from the notion that people should participate in making the decisions that affect their well-being. Jaroslav Vanek, a major early advocate of the **participatory economy**, emphasizes this theme:

> The quest of men to participate in the determination and decision-making of the activities in which they are personally and directly involved is one of the most important sociopolitical phenomena of our times. It is very likely to be the dominant force of social evolution in the last third of the twentieth century.[8]

Vanek uses five characteristics to identify the participatory economy:

1. Firms will be managed in participatory fashion by the people working in them.
2. Income sharing will prevail and is to be equitable—that is, "equal for labor of equal intensity and quality, and governed by a democratically agreed-upon income-distribution schedule assigning to each job its relative claim on total net income."[9]
3. Although the workers may enjoy the fruits of the operation, they do not own, and must therefore pay for, the use of productive resources.
4. The economy must always be a market economy. Economic planning may be used through indirect mechanisms, but "never through a direct order to a firm or group of firms."[10]
5. There is freedom of choice in employment.

In essence, resources are state owned but are managed by the workers in the enterprises, whose objective is to create a maximum dividend per worker. Cooperative socialism belongs to the more general category of market socialism, because there is state ownership of the means of production but also an exchange of goods and services in the market without intervention by central planners. Producer goods would use market prices, as opposed to prices manipulated by the CPB in the Lange framework. The cooperative form of socialism has been viewed as an important and path-breaking addition to socialist thinking, especially by those who would identify with democratic socialism as a political system.

Theoretical analysis of the cooperative model dates from an article by Benjamin Ward published in 1958 and the subsequent early elaboration of the participatory economy by Vanek and thereafter by many authors.[11] Resources (with the exception of labor) are owned by the state and will be used by each firm, for which a fee will be paid to the state. Prices for both producer goods and consumer goods will be determined by supply and demand in the market. Enterprises will be managed by the workers (who may hire a professional manager responsible to them), who will attempt to maximize the dividend per worker (**net income per worker**) in the enterprise. With this objective, management must decide on input and output combinations.

In addition to levying a charge for the use of capital assets and for land, the state will administer the public sector of the economy and may levy taxes to finance cultural and industrial development. In this environment, how will the cooperative firm behave? Let us examine two cases: first, the short run, where there is a variable supply of labor but capital is fixed; second, the long run, where both labor and capital are variable.

The cooperative model assumes that the enterprise manager wishes to maximize net earnings per worker (Y/L), and that output (Q) is solely a function of the labor input (L) in the short run. The output can be sold on the market at a price (P) dictated by *market* forces. The firm must pay a fixed tax (T) on its capital. In the short-run variant, capital is fixed; so is the tax. Under these conditions, the firm will seek to maximize the following expression:

Maximize
$$Y/L = \frac{PQ - T}{L} \tag{7.1}$$

where

Y/L = net income per worker
P = price of the product
Q = quantity produced
T = fixed tax levied on capital
L = labor input

Maximum net income per worker in equation 7.1 will be achieved when the amount of labor hired (L) is such that the value of the marginal product of the last worker hired is the same as average net earnings per worker or, in terms of the notation of equation 7.1, when the following balance is achieved:

$$P \cdot MP_L = \frac{(PQ - T)}{L} \tag{7.2}$$

where

MP_L = marginal product of labor

The logic of this solution is quite simple. If the enterprise can increase average net revenue by hiring another worker—that is, if the marginal product of the last worker hired is greater than average net revenue—then the worker should be hired and average net revenue can be increased. The addition of workers should continue until the value of the marginal product of the last person hired and the average net revenue are the same. If the manager were to hire, at the margin, a worker the value of whose marginal product were less than the average net revenue per worker, then the net income of remaining workers would fall.

In the *long run*, the cooperative must select its optimal capital stock (K), on which it will pay a rental charge (r) per unit of capital used. The firm now seeks to maximize its average net revenue as given by the following expression:

Maximize
$$Y/L = \frac{PQ - rK}{L} \qquad (7.3)$$

where

$$K = \text{amount of capital}$$
$$r = \text{the charge per unit of capital}$$

The maximum value of this expression (average net revenue per worker) will be achieved in a manner similar to that of the short-run case. As long as the value of the marginal product of capital $(P \cdot MP_K)$ is greater than the rental rate (r) paid on capital, more capital should be hired and utilized until the return and the cost are equalized $(P \cdot MP_K = r)$. This rule applies to the perfectly competitive capitalist firm and the Lange-type firm as well. The same rule as equation 7.2 would apply for the hiring of labor, except that the charge for variable capital would have to be deducted as follows:

$$P \cdot MP_L = \frac{PQ - rK}{L} \qquad (7.4)$$

These two cases, the short run and the long run, are both simple variants of the cooperative model. The short-run case is elaborated diagrammatically in Figure 7.2. Note that the model assumes that both product and factor markets are perfectly competitive and that there is no interference by the state.

The cooperative model works through product and factor markets. Households supply labor services as a consequence of maximizing household utility in the choice of work versus leisure. In this way labor supply schedules are determined, as are demand schedules for consumer goods. Firms maximize net revenue per worker and in so doing are prepared to supply goods and services at various prices and at the same time purchase inputs at various prices.

There is a close relationship between the cooperative model and the competitive capitalist and Lange models. In essence, the cooperative model captures the efficiency features of both. In the Lange model, the firm follows two rules, equating price and marginal cost and minimizing average cost of production. In the cooperative model, these two rules are replaced by a single rule (in the short run represented by equation 7.2). In the case of the capitalist market economy, the firm follows the rule of equating marginal cost and marginal revenue, which in the case of perfect competition reduces to the Lange rule; so here too, the cooperative variant simply replaces this rule with equation 7.2.

There is now a considerable body of literature on the cooperative model and its variants. Many pertinent issues have been raised by the model's critics as well as by its admirers.

Criticism of the Cooperative Model

The cooperative model has been analyzed in detail by Benjamin Ward. Ward notes that the two key features of the model are "individual material self-interest as the

FIGURE 7.2   The Cooperative Model

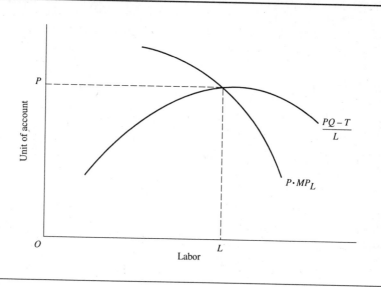

Explanation:

$$\frac{PQ - T}{L} = net \text{ receipts per worker}$$

$$P \cdot MP_L = \text{marginal value product of labor}$$

If the cooperative wishes to maximize the value of net receipts per worker, it should hire labor until the value of the marginal product of the last worker hired is the same as the net receipts per worker. In the diagram, the cooperative would hire *OL* labor, and each worker would receive *OP*.

dominant human motivation" and "the resort to markets as the means of allocating resources."[12] Ward devoted considerable attention to analyzing the response of the cooperative to various changes in capital charges, taxes, input prices, and product prices.[13] For the capitalist and the Lange-type firm, an increase in price will induce an increase in output (that is, a positively sloped supply curve). Ward demonstrated that the cooperative supply curve may well be negatively sloped (that is, an increase in price generates a *decrease* in output), especially in the short run.[14] If true, this would certainly be a perverse and undesirable result, especially in an economy where resources are allocated by the market. Such a result might (though it would not necessarily) threaten both the existence and the stability of equilibrium in product markets.

Ward also argued that if two cooperatives producing an identical product use different technologies, there will be a misallocation of labor and capital that would not occur if the two were capitalist firms.[15] In the case of the capitalist firms, both would hire labor until the wage was equal to the value of the marginal product ($W = P \cdot MP_L$), for both would face the same market-determined wage (W) and hence would generate the same value of marginal product. In the case of the cooperative, however, unless the production functions are identical, the average net revenue per worker will differ between the two cooperatives. Although each cooperative equates average net revenue per worker with the marginal product of the last worker hired, overall output could be increased by moving workers to the cooperatives where the value of the marginal product is higher.

Ward also argued that the cooperative might be undesirable if it existed in a noncompetitive environment.[16] Specifically, he contends that the monopolistic cooperative would be less efficient than either its competitive cooperative twin or its monopolistic capitalist twin. The monopolistic cooperative would hire less labor, produce less output, and charge a higher price than either the competitive cooperative or the monopolistic capitalist firm.

Critics of the Lange model raised the issue of how to ensure appropriate managerial motivation. To the extent that the cooperative utilizes hired professional management, the problem of how to motivate and regulate managers will exist. Ward noted that in some cases the cooperative will have the incentive to expand, although in the absence of private property holding, it is not clear who the entrepreneur will be.[17] It is possible that the state would play an important role here because it would control some of the investment funds.

Advantages of the Cooperative Model

Strong support for the cooperative model comes from Jaroslav Vanek, who argues that the participatory economy is an element of social evolution that will be especially important in future years.[18] In addition to prescribing the participatory economy for present-day economies, Vanek also argues that it is the best alternative for developing economies.

Vanek does not agree with Ward's criticisms. He argues that if two cooperative firms have access to identical technology, and if there is free entry and exit, the input–output decisions of the cooperatives will be identical to those of two capitalist firms operating under the same condition.[19] Moreover, Vanek argues, the result will be much more desirable socially, because in the capitalist case the workers are rewarded according to the value of the marginal products, whereas under the cooperative case, workers are rewarded according to the decision of the collective, which they themselves control.

Vanek also maintains that under certain likely cases, the supply curve of the cooperative firm will not be negatively sloped as Ward suggests. If the cooperative is a multiproduct firm, or if it faces an external constraint (for example, a limited supply of labor), Vanek shows that the firm's supply curve will be positively sloped.

Vanek argues that the imperfectly competitive cooperative firm will be superior to the imperfectly competitive capitalist firm because it will have no incentive to grow extremely large and hence to dominate a particular market. Further, the cooperative will have no incentive to act in a socially wasteful manner—to create artificial demand for a product through advertising. Finally, Vanek maintains that both the demand for investment and the supply of savings will tend to be greater in the cooperative than in the competitive capitalist environment.

Many of the issues surrounding the comparative performance of cooperative and capitalist firms seem highly abstract and theoretical. They are, however, of basic importance to the efficiency of each system. The response of the cooperative firm to market signals determines the extent to which it can meet consumer goals and, in the long run, the extent to which an appropriate industrial structure is established in line with long-term development goals and aspirations.

Many of the supporters of the cooperative model, especially Vanek, argue that beyond these specific performance characteristics, the crucial features of the cooperative are its "special dimensions." Among the most important would be the elimination of the capitalist dichotomy between management and labor. It is also argued that there would be greater social justice in the distribution of rewards.[20]

The Participatory Economy in the 1990s

The pioneering work of Benjamin Ward in the late 1950s and the subsequent elaboration by Jaroslav Vanek in the late 1960s spawned a large and ever-growing body of literature devoted to the broad concepts of labor management and, more specifically, producer cooperatives as a means to organize production in an economy. A recent discussion of this literature by John Bonin, Derek Jones, and Louis Putterman provides an excellent basis for understanding the state of the cooperative idea in the 1990s.[21]

The body of literature on cooperatives is large but diverse and mainly theoretical with only limited attention to empirical verification. At the same time, the practical use of cooperatives in real-world economies has been limited, though it has grown in recent years. The lack of empirical work on cooperatives in part reflects the absence of appropriate data for evaluation purposes; it also reflects the nature of the theoretical models, which tend to be highly abstract, and the great deal of diversity among cooperatives in real-world economies.

In addition, many of the outcomes of the earlier simple models are evidently not robust under more realistic circumstances. For example, contemporary research demonstrates that the existence of a negatively sloped supply curve depends heavily on the original assumptions of early models and is not generally found in contemporary specifications where ". . . the focus shifts to the membership as the constituent decision-making body or when reasonable labor supply considerations are added. . . ."[22] Moreover, limited empirical evidence seems to support the contemporary view.

Contemporary empirical evidence on issues relating to worker effort and productivity in producer cooperatives does not provide clearcut answers. Bonin et al., in their survey of this empirical literature, found that participation variables are important when explaining differences in outcomes. There seems to be a positive relation between profit sharing and productivity; however, isolating the impact of other types of participation has proven difficult.

Finally, the literature places considerable emphasis on the potential problems of self-financing of producer cooperatives based on the notion that members will distribute internal funds to themselves rather than expand the capital stock in the absence of appropriate property rights. Based on existing empirical evidence, Bonin et al. conclude that no econometric evidence supports this proposition.[23]

Despite the relatively few producer cooperatives in contemporary market economies, their existence provides growing evidence that presents them much more favorably than would have been the case if based only on the early and simple models of cooperative behavior. Furthermore, future empirical research will undoubtedly reveal at least partial answers to as yet unanswered questions and will shed more light on the evolutionary aspects of cooperatives in market economies.

Feasible Socialism in the 1990s

Some might argue that the demise of the major planned socialist economic systems of the former Soviet Union and Eastern Europe significantly reduces the potential appeal of socialism as an economic system. There is, however, great interest in the reasons for the demise of these systems and thus the possibility of defining a socialist system that not only eliminates these reasons but sustains the basic tenets of socialism—most notably an egalitarian distribution of benefits. As a result, in the 1990s the discussion of **feasible socialism** and the socialist economy continues.

For example, in a detailed argument, James Yunker presents what he terms a case for "pragmatic socialism" based on public ownership and a bureau of public ownership ". . . to enforce upon the executives who manage the publicly owned business corporations a strong profit motivation."[24] This board will also oversee disbursement of the social dividend in an egalitarian manner. In addition to dealing with issues such as transition, Yunker devotes substantial attention to such critical areas as investment, growth, and entepreneurship in the socialist economy.

In another contribution to the discussion of market socialism, Pranab Bardhan and John Roemer argue that the economies that failed were characterized by public or state ownership of the means of production, noncompetitive and nondemocratic politics, and command/administrative allocation of resources and commodities.[25] Bardhan and Roemer argue that what they term "competitive socialism" could be envisioned through the negation of the latter two characteristics of the failed economies.

In their approach to defining the socialist economic system, Bardhan and Roemer focus on competitive markets but include an important role for the state, a system using banks for insider monitoring to solve the traditional problems of enterprise decision making, and the development of political accountability for a state that supervises the banking structure.

In a further discussion of market socialism, Andrei Schleifer and Robert W. Vishny argue that the Bardhan–Roemer approach would not work primarily because of the characterization of the state.[26] Specifically, Schleifer and Vishny argue that under market socialism, the state's objectives will dominate over those of firms, that the state will not necessarily pursue economic efficiency, and that government's pursuit of its objectives will be less destructive under capitalism than under socialism.

These ongoing discussions are meant neither to characterize market socialism in any detail nor to assess its positive and negative features. Rather, these discussions send several important signals. First, as previously emphasized, the demise of socialist economic systems in the former Soviet Union and the countries of Eastern Europe does not end discussions about socialism in general and market socialism in particular. Second, much of the discussion here focuses on the nature of the state in a socialist system and how agency and incentive problems can be resolved. Contemporary organization theory provides useful insights into these problems. Finally, the appeal of a more egalitarian distribution of income remains, and yet limited attention is given to the noneconomic aspects of socialism that many argue are of basic importance to understanding the nature of socialism.

Hypotheses Concerning Market Socialism

Yugoslavia, a small country beset by a wide range of problems, experimented with worker-managed socialism. But for the most part, we lack real-world experience with market socialism either of the Lange or of the worker-managed type. Consequently, we do not have the advantage of long historical experience to test hypotheses concerning the economic performance of market socialism. The following paragraphs represent our best analytical—though somewhat speculative—efforts.

Income Distribution

The easiest hypothesis to formulate concerns the distribution of income under market socialism. Inasmuch as capital continues to belong to society, we would expect income to be distributed more nearly equally under market socialism than under capitalism. Even in the case of worker-managed enterprises, the state must be paid a fee for the use of capital, and presumably, the state would divide such income among the population on a fairly equal basis. Some reservations must be expressed, however. As critics have pointed out, prosperous worker-managed firms might protect extraordinarily high earnings by excluding outsiders. This type of behavior could lead to significant inequality in wage income.

Economic Growth

Proponents of market socialism claim that market socialism would yield relatively high rates of growth, primarily because society would plow earnings from capital back into the economy. This conclusion, however, assumes that the socialist state would not be pressured into putting the "social dividend" into current consumption in the form of subsidies and social services. Such pressure would be particularly strong in the case of democratically elected socialist governments. For these reasons, we believe it risky to presume that market socialism will yield higher investment rates—and hence higher rates of growth—than the capitalist model. The outcome is far from certain.

Efficiency

The theory of market socialism does not yield strong propositions concerning economic efficiency. Arguing that market socialism can indeed be more efficient than capitalism, its advocates cite the lack of monopoly, the greater attention to externalities, and individual participation in decision making. Its critics, however, mount equally convincing arguments about the inefficiency of market socialism: motivation problems, perverse supply curves, and the difficulty of finding equilibrium prices. Accordingly, we cannot venture any hypotheses about the relative efficiency of market socialism.

Stability

Advocates of market socialism make the following case for greater economic stability: The state will have greater control over the investment rate, so sharp fluctuations in investment can be avoided. Counterarguments exist, however. If market socialist economies (we are using the Lange model) have trouble adjusting prices to equilibrium, macroeconomic instabilities associated with nonequilibrium prices might be experienced. Moreover, democratically elected officials will be under strong pressure to pursue "popular" economic policies (the political business cycle), while feeling less pressure from market forces to tighten the reins on economic policy. Again, we cannot propose any strong hypotheses concerning the relative stability of market socialism.

Market socialism has sufficient appeal to make it a serious model for discussion —Western Europe has experimented with programs of partial worker management and major corporations in the United States now have employees as their majority shareholders. Market socialism has appeal for Eastern Europe because it combines the elements of market and socialist economies.

Summary

Market socialism has significant appeal because it promises to combine attractive features of capitalism (especially the efficiency of the market mechanism) with similarly attractive features of socialism (a more equitable distribution of income). Although there is no generally accepted paradigm of the market socialist economy, the positive and negative features of market socialism (the socialist controversy in Chapter 6), along with specific variants suggested by various authors, presents a picture of the market socialist idea that culminates in the contemporary discussion of the "economics of feasible socialism."

Probably the most famous model of market socialism is that suggested many years ago by the Polish economist Oskar Lange. The Lange model combines public ownership with a "trial-and-error" approach to establishing equilibrium and determining output as individual enterprises are expected to follow market-type rules, specifically producing where price and marginal cost are equal and by minimizing cost. Households supply labor services and the state distributes the social dividend. Sectoral expansion is also dictated by the state.

Although the original model developed by Lange was simple, its considerable appeal focuses on a number of key issues, especially those raised in the socialist controversy. Critics, however, have generally viewed the model as computationally inefficient, lacking appropriate and necessary managerial motivation, and possibly suffering from monopoly problems.

The general idea of a participatory economy is very appealing, especially in less-developed countries. Unlike other suggested models of the socialist economy, there is much theoretical rigor in the contemporary theory of the cooperative, and yet its real-world application is quite limited.

Although the specifics of different variants of the cooperative idea vary greatly, the basic construct typically involves worker management in enterprise decision making. Workers share profits and pay a rental charge for the use of productive assets that society at large owns. The cooperative differs fundamentally from the typical capitalist firm, which maximizes profits (or some variant of profits). The cooperative, however, maximizes profit per worker, usually termed a dividend.

Advocates of the cooperative model argue that such a system would be fair, efficient, and stable and would offer the population a number of less-quantifiable yet potentially attractive features, such as the possibility of substantial participation in economic decision making.

Critics of the cooperative model maintain that such an economic system would be unstable, offer no potential efficiency advantages, and suffer from problems of **managerial motivation**.

Although there are relatively small numbers of producer cooperatives in contemporary market economies, the significant body of theory combined with recent if limited empirical research suggests that some of the negative features of the early cooperative models (the negatively sloped supply curve, difficulties of generating capital internally, etc.) are not evident in models with differing and reasonable specifications and such negative features cannot be confirmed by empirical evidence.

Key Terms

market socialism	labor-managed economy	short-term equilibrium
central planning board	producer cooperative	long-term equilibrium
Lange model	participatory economy	feasible socialism
trial-and-error model	net income per worker	managerial motivation
cooperative economy		

Notes

1. Benjamin Lippincott, ed., *On the Economic Theory of Socialism* (Minneapolis: University of Minnesota Press, 1938).
2. See, for example, F. M. Taylor, "The Guidance of Production in a Socialist State," *American Economic Review*, 19 (March 1929); reprinted in Lippincott, *On the Economic Theory of Socialism*, pp. 39–54; H. D. Dickinson, *Economics of Socialism* (London: Oxford University Press, 1939); and Abba P. Lerner, *The Economics of Control* (New York: Macmillan, 1944).
3. See the discussion in Maurice Dobb, *The Welfare Economics and the Economics of Socialism* (Cambridge, England: Cambridge University Press, 1969), p. 133 and footnotes thereto.
4. F. A. Hayek, "Socialist Calculation: The Competitive Solution," *Economica*, n.s. 7 (May 1940), 125–149; reprinted in Bornstein, *Comparative Economic Systems*, pp. 77–97.
5. Abram Bergson, *Essays in Normative Economics* (Cambridge, Mass.: Harvard University Press, 1966), Ch. 9.
6. The sophisticated works of Soviet mathematical economists have been brought to Western readers by Zauberman, Ellman, and others. See, for example, Alfred Zauberman, *The Mathematical Revolution in Soviet Economics* (London: Oxford University Press, 1975); Michael Ellman, *Soviet Planning Today* (Cambridge, England: Cambridge University Press, 1971); Martin Cave, Alastair McAuley, and Judith Thornton, eds., *New Terms in Soviet Economics* (Armonk, N.Y.: M. E. Sharpe, 1982).
7. For a recent discussion of the state of the literature on producer cooperatives, see John P. Bonin, Derek C. Jones, and Louis Putterman, "Theoretical and Empirical Studies of Producer Cooperatives: Will The Twain Ever Meet?" *Journal of Economic Literature*, 31 (September 1993), 1290–1320.
8. Jaroslav Vanek, *The Participatory Economy* (Ithaca, N.Y.: Cornell University Press, 1971), p. 1.
9. Ibid., p. 9.
10. Ibid., p. 11.
11. For Ward's original contribution, see Benjamin Ward, "The Firm in Illyria: Market Syndicalism," *American Economic Review*, 48 (September 1958), 566–589. See also E. Domar, "The Soviet Collective Farm as a Producer Cooperative," *American Economic Review*, 56 (September 1966), 734–757; and Walter Y. Oi and Elizabeth M. Clayton, "A Peasant's View of a Soviet Collective Farm," *American Economic Review*, 58 (March 1968), 37–59. For a general treatment of Vanek's argument, see Vanek, *The Participatory Economy*; and for a detailed analysis, see Jaroslav Vanek, *The General Theory of Labor-Managed Market Economies* (Ithaca, N.Y.: Cornell University Press, 1970). Since these early contributions, the literature has expanded rapidly. For a survey, see John P. Bonin and Louis Putterman, *Economics of Cooperation and the Labor-Managed Economy* (New York: Harwood Academic Publishers, 1987); see also John P. Bonin, Derek C. Jones, and Louis Putterman, "Theoretical and Empirical Studies."
12. Ward, *The Socialist Economy*, p. 183.
13. Ibid., Chs. 8–10.
14. Ibid., pp. 191–192.
15. Ibid., pp. 184 ff.
16. Ibid., pp. 201 ff.
17. Ibid., Ch. 9.
18. For the general treatment, see Vanek, *The Participatory Economy*.

19. See Vanek, *The General Theory.*
20. For background on participatory socialism, see, for example, Ellen Turkish Comisso, *Worker's Control Under Plan and Market* (New Haven: Yale University Press, 1979), Chs. 1–2; Hans Dieter Seibel and Ukandi G. Damachi, *Self-Management in Yugoslavia and the Third World* (New York: St. Martin's, 1982); Howard M. Wachtel, *Workers' Management and Workers' Wages in Yugoslavia* (Ithaca, N.Y.: Cornell University Press, 1973), Ch. 2.
21. John P. Bonin, Derek C. Jones, and Louis Putterman, "Theoretical and Empirical Studies."
22. Ibid., 1299.
23. Ibid., 1316.
24. James A. Yunker, *Socialism Revised and Modernized: The Case for Pragmatic Market Socialism* (New York: Praeger, 1992), p. 38.
25. Pranab Bardhan and John E. Roemer, "Market Socialism: A Case for Rejuvenation," *Journal of Economic Perspectives*, 6 (Summer 1992), 101–116.
26. Andrei Schleifer and Robert U. Vishny, "The Politics of Market Socialism," *Journal of Economic Perspectives*, 8 (Spring 1994), 165–176; for the Bardhan/Roemer reply, see Pranab Bardhan and John Roemer, "On the Workability of Market Socialism," *Journal of Economic Perspectives*, 8 (Spring 1994), 177–181.

Recommended Readings

A. Traditional Sources

H. D. Dickinson, *The Economics of Socialism* (London: Oxford University Press, 1938).

Abba P. Lerner, *The Economics of Control* (New York: Macmillan, 1944).

Benjamin Lippincott, ed., *On The Economic Theory of Socialism* (New York: McGraw-Hill, 1964).

Jaroslav Vanek, *The General Theory of Labor-Managed Economies* (Ithaca, N.Y.: Cornell University Press, 1970).

———, *The Labor-Managed Economy* (Ithaca, N.Y.: Cornell University Press, 1971).

———, *The Participatory Economy* (Ithaca, N.Y.: Cornell University Press, 1971).

Benjamin N. Ward, "The Firm in Illyria: Market Syndicalism," *American Economic Review*, 48 (September 1958), 566–589.

———, *The Socialist Economy* (New York: Random House, 1967).

B. The Lange Model

Abram Bergson, "Market Socialism Revisited," *Journal of Political Economy*, 75 (October 1967), 663–675.

Benjamin Lippincott, ed., *On The Economic Theory of Socialism* (New York: McGraw-Hill, 1964).

C. Market Socialism: The Labor-Managed Variant

Katrina V. Berman, "An Empirical Test of the Theory of the Labor-Managed Firm," *Journal of Comparative Economics*, 13 (June 1989), 281–300.

John P. Bonin, Derek C. Jones, and Louis Putterman, "Theoretical and Empirical Studies of Producer Cooperatives: Will the Twain Ever Meet?" *Journal of Economic Literature*, 31 (September 1993), 1290–1320.

John P. Bonin and Louis Putterman, *Economics of Cooperation and the Labor-Managed Economy* (New York: Harwood Academic Publishers, 1987).

Saul Estrin, "Some Reflections on Self-Management, Social Choice and Reform in Eastern Europe," *Journal of Comparative Economics*, 15 (June 1991), 349–361.

Derek C. Jones and Jan Svenjar, eds., *Advances in the Economic Analysis of Participatory and Labor Managed Firms*, Vols. 1–4 (Greenwich: JAI Press, various years).

Kathryn Nantz, "The Labor-Managed Firm Under Imperfect Monitoring: Employment and Work Effort Responses," *Journal of Comparative Economics*, 14 (March 1990), 33–50.

Hugh Neary, "The Comparative Statics of the Ward–Domar Labor-Managed Firm: A Profit–Function Approach," *Journal of Comparative Economics*, 12 (June 1988), 159–181.

V. Rus and R. Russell, eds., *International Handbook of Participation in Organization* (New York: Oxford University Press, 1989).

Fernando B. Saldanha, "Fixprice Analysis of Labor-Managed Economies," *Journal of Comparative Economics*, 13 (June 1989), 227–253.

D. Feasible Socialism: Contemporary Views

Pranab Bardhan and John E. Roemer, "Market Socialism: A Case for Rejuvenation," *Journal of Economic Perspectives*, 6 (Summer 1992), 101–116.

———, eds., *Market Socialism: The Current Debate* (New York: Oxford University Press, 1993).

———, "On the Workability of Market Socialism," *Journal of Economic Perspectives*, 8 (Spring 1994), 177–181.

Alec Nove, *The Economics of Feasible Socialism* (Winchester, Mass.: Unwin Hyman, 1983).

S. Pejovich, *Socialism: Institutional, Philosophical and Economic Issues* (Norwell, Mass.: Kluwer Academic Publishers, 1987).

Andrei Schleifer and Robert W. Vishny, "The Politics of Market Socialism," *Journal of Economic Perspectives*, 8 (Spring 1994), 165–176.

James A. Yunker, *Socialism Revised and Modernized: The Case for Pragmatic Market Socialism* (New York: Praeger, 1992).

8

The American Economy: Market Capitalism

Now that the basic models of market capitalism, planned socialism, and market socialism have been outlined, the real-world variants of these different economic systems will be examined. This examination looks at several variants of market capitalism and gives special attention to the economy of the United States.

As one of the world's most advanced industrial nations, the United States serves as an important representative of market capitalism. It is an economy with a high per capita income and the largest total output of goods and services of any country. This study of the American economy begins with the nature of resource allocation through markets and an analysis of the structure and operation of product and factor markets as well as changes in market structure over time.

Next, the focus turns to the role government plays in the American economy and why the public sector generates such considerable controversy. This includes an examination of the provision of public goods and the impact government has on regulation and on antitrust policy. Finally, the role of the government in the macroeconomy and especially stabilization policies and policies with regard to the distribution of income are examined.

Why study the American economy in a book devoted to the analysis of different economic systems? For many, the American economy is immediately familiar because it is the system within which we work. The American economy is a large and wealthy economy that has enjoyed considerable success. But it is a mixed system relying predominately on markets with much less government intervention than is common in many other market capitalist economies. Moreover, it is an economy whose participants continuously focus on economic issues, such as the problems of debt, health, or poverty. Resource allocation in the American economy provides an important example of market capitalism.

Resource Allocation in the Private Sector

The American economy can be divided into two major sections: the **private sector** and the **public sector**. How important is the role of government (the public sector) in the American economy? The role of government in the United States is more

limited than the role many other governments play in other market capitalist economies. Even in the case of natural monopolies, the U.S. government has a limited
role and has no apparatus for economic planning. Most resource-allocation decisions
are made in the private sector, though in areas such as public utilities government
predominates.

The term *private sector* refers to the business sector in which private ownership
prevails and government regulation or intervention is limited. Although a more
general discussion of the importance of the government sector occurs later in this
chapter, the focus here centers on the private sector. Such a concept is difficult to
measure, although estimates are available.

According to estimates developed by Milton Friedman, roughly 25 percent of
economic activity in the United States in 1939 was government operated or government supervised, leaving roughly 75 percent conducted in the private sector.[1]
Frederic Scherer has noted that in 1965, the government-regulated sector accounted
for 11 percent of the GNP, with the government-operated sector accounting for
another 12 percent. The resulting total of 23 percent is very close to that for 1939.[2]

In a recent study of deregulation in the American economy, Clifford Winston
argues that in 1977, 17 percent of United States GNP "was produced by fully regulated industries," while in 1988, this share was 6.6 percent.[3] Assuming no significant
changes in government ownership, one might estimate a contemporary private sector
amounting to roughly 80 percent of the American economy.

Figure 2.4 presents a simple circular-flow diagram to represent the organization
of a typical market capitalist economy. That diagram contains three main actors:
namely firms, households, and the government that interact through product and
factor markets. In that process, households provide factor inputs and earn income
(factor markets), and firms respond to household demand, producing goods and
services that are paid for with household incomes (product markets). As previously
emphasized, government intervenes in this setting for a variety of reasons, but
fundamentally markets provide the information (primarily through prices) used to
guide decision making on a decentralized basis. As any student of market economics
knows, the organizational arrangements within and among the actors (the economic
system) are critical to understanding the observed outcomes. It is therefore important
to closely examine the major actors in the market economy.

Business Organization

Business enterprises in the United States are divided into three categories on the
basis of legal organization: sole proprietorships, partnerships, and corporations.

The **sole proprietorship** is owned by one individual, who makes all the
business decisions and absorbs the profits (or losses) that the business earns. A
partnership is owned by two or more partners, who make all the business decisions
and share in the profits and losses. The major advantages of these forms of business
organization are their relative simplicity (the proprietorship is simpler than the
partnership) and that, under existing tax law, their profits are taxed only once. They
have two major disadvantages: (1) the owners are personally liable for the debts of

the business, and (2) the ability to raise capital is limited, dependent as it is on the owners' ability to borrow against personal assets.

The third form of business organization, the **corporation**, is owned by its stockholders and has authorization to act as a legal person. A board of directors, elected by the stockholders, appoints a management team to run the corporation. The advantages of the corporation are (1) that its owners (the stockholders) are not personally liable for the debts of the corporation (limited liability), (2) that its management team can be changed if necessary, and (3) that it has more options for raising capital (through the sale of bonds and additional stock). A major disadvantage of the corporation is that its income is taxed a second time when corporate earnings are distributed to stockholders as dividends. Double taxation gives American corporations an incentive to reinvest earnings rather than pay out dividends.

These three forms of business organization are supplemented in the United States by innovative legal arrangements (such as limited liability partnerships) designed to circumvent a variety of weaknesses, yet the threefold classification remains valid. Figure 8.1 and Table 8.1 show the distribution of U.S. enterprises according to the legal form of business organization. Although sole proprietorships account for the bulk of American businesses, they account for only a small percentage of business revenues. Corporations, though few in number (about 20 percent of the total), account for 90 percent of business revenues. The larger size of the corporation is explained by limited liability and the greater ability of the corporation to raise capital. The sole proprietorship is important in agriculture, retail trade, and services; the partnership

FIGURE 8.1   Proprietorships, Partnerships, and Corporations, 1990

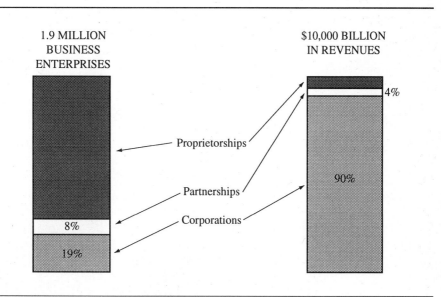

Source: *Statistical Abstract of the United States.*

TABLE 8.1 Proprietorships, Partnerships, and Corporations, by Industry, 1989

Industry	Number (in thousands)			Business Revenues (in billions of dollars)		
	Proprietorships	Active Partnerships	Active Corporations	Proprietorships	Active Partnerships	Active Corporations
Total	14,298	1,635	3,628	693.0	405.0	10,440
Agriculture, forestry, and fishing	342	131	123	15.0	8.0	81.0
Mining	155	46	42	7.0	20.0	88.0
Construction	1,757	62	393	101.0	30.0	505.0
Manufacturing	431	26	301	25.0	55.0	3,276.0
Transportation, public utilities	623	22	156	31.0	27.0	844.0
Wholesale and retail trade	2,438	173	1,012	234.0	90.0	3,095.0
Finance, Insurance, Real Estate	1270	853	592	50.0	71.0	1,868.0
Services	7,039	299	109	226.0	162.0	680.0

Source: *Statistical Abstract of the United States.*

is important in finance, insurance, real estate, and services; the corporation is the dominant form in other sectors.

The Product Market

Resource-allocation arrangements depend on the degree of **market power** in different product markets. There is no accurate measure of market power, but the most frequently used measure is the **concentration ratio**. The concentration ratio gives the percentage of industry sales accounted for by the largest 4, 8, or 20 firms. For example, a 4-firm concentration ratio of 80 percent means that the 4 largest firms account for 80 percent of industry sales. An industry with a very low concentration ratio is generally a "competitive" industry; one with a very high concentration ratio is an "oligopoly" or near-monopoly. The comparison is not exact for various reasons: the difficulties of defining industry boundaries; the availability of competitive substitutes; the fact that some firms operate in regional and local markets, others in national and international markets; and so on.

The degree of **competition** in the U.S. economy is hard to measure. Most concentration studies focus on manufacturing, which, although it is the most visible branch of U.S. industry, accounts for only one-fourth of national income. Many industries that produce raw materials, such as agriculture, forest products, and coal, are organized competitively. Yet government price-support programs in agriculture have affected the behavior of agricultural producers, and the owners of coal mines often band together in associations. Retail stores and most services operate in local markets and in a competitive environment.

Estimates of the overall level of competitiveness (including agriculture, manufacturing, trade, and services) are few and far between. Milton Friedman's estimates for the year 1939 indicate that the private sector was then between 15 and 25 percent "monopolistic" and between 75 and 85 percent "competitive."[4] A contemporary study finds that the degree of competition has increased for the U.S. economy as a whole since the 1960s,[5] see Table 8.2.

Competitive Industries   Competitive producers are **price takers**. They cannot influence prices, so they maximize profits by expanding their output to the point where marginal cost is equal to the product price. If for some reason (say, an unexpected shift in demand) above-normal profits are made, excess profits disappear as new firms enter the market.

Prices are formed in competitive industries by supply and demand. Take the case of basic agricultural products (wheat, pork bellies, soy beans, frozen orange juice), which are traded on commodity markets. These markets are called **perfect markets** because at any time, all buyers pay the same price. All potential buyers and sellers are participants in the market, and information concerning prices is available almost instantaneously. All participants know, for example, the price of a bushel of wheat at any time.

Producers and users of commodities, however, are not the only participants in the market. Commodity speculators buy and sell in the hope of buying at a low

TABLE 8.2   Trends in Competition in the U.S. Economy, 1939–1980

Sectors of the Economy	Share of Each Sector That Was Effectively Competitive (percent)		
	1939	1958	1980
Agriculture, forestry, and fisheries	91.6	85.0	86.4
Mining	87.1	92.2	95.8
Construction	27.9	55.9	80.2
Manufacturing	51.5	55.9	69.0
Transportation and public utilities	8.7	26.1	39.1
Wholesale and retail trade	57.8	60.5	93.4
Finance, insurance, and real estate	61.5	63.8	94.1
Services	53.9	54.3	77.9
Total	52.4	56.4	76.7

Note: In this table, an effectively competitive industry is one in which the 4-firm concentration ratio was below 40 percent, entry barriers were low, market shares were unstable, and prices were flexible. The extent of oligopoly in the economy is the measure of the combined shares of dominant-firm and tight-oligopoly industries.

Source: William G. Shepherd, "Causes of Increased Competition in the U.S. Economy, 1939–1980," *Review of Economics and Statistics*, November 1982, 613–626. Used by permission of Elsevier Science Publishers, Amsterdam.

price and then selling high. Commodity markets establish not only prices of commodities for immediate delivery, but also prices (called **futures prices**) for deliveries at some specified date in the future. An American wheat farmer can contract, even before the crop has been planted, to sell next year's harvest at a specified price in the commodity market.

In the real world of the U.S. economy, most competitive industries are not perfectly competitive because they sell slightly differentiated products. Most of the practices just described, however, apply in general terms. Even though a product is differentiated, producers have little control over price. In each market, prices are established by supply and demand, and **arbitrage** (buying in the cheap market and reselling in the expensive market) prevents large price disparities between markets. Although these markets are not perfectly competitive, they closely approximate perfect competition.

Imperfectly Competitive Industries   Competitive markets work in a fairly invisible and low-key manner. Highly concentrated, noncompetitive industries follow a wide variety of behavior patterns.

The surprising feature of U.S. manufacturing is that the degree of concentration appears to have scarcely changed since the turn of the century (see Table 8.3). According to G. Warren Nutter's famous study, in 1900 roughly one-third of manufacturing net output came from industries wherein the four largest firms accounted

TABLE 8.3   Trends in Concentration in American Manufacturing: Two Measures

Year	Percentage of Output by Firms with 4-Firm Concentration Ratio of 50 percent or Above (1)	Percentage of Output of 100 Largest Firms (2)
1895–1904	33	n.a.
1947	24	23
1954	30	30
1958	30	32
1972	29	33
1977	28	33
1982	24	33

Sources: G. Warren Nutter, *The Extent of Enterprise Monopoly in the United States, 1899–1939* (Chicago: University of Chicago Press, 1951); pp. 35–48, 112–140; F. M. Scherer, *Industrial Market Structure and Economic Performance* (Boston: Houghton Mifflin, 1980), pp. 68–69; *Concentration Ratios in Manufacturing, 1977 Census of Manufacturing,* MC77-SR-9; *1982 Census of Manufacturers,* MC82-S-7.

for one-half or more of industry output. In 1963 and 1982, the figure was still one-third. Morris Adelman reports similar findings for the period 1947–1958, when the average concentration ratio of the four largest firms in each industry rose only from 35 to 37 percent. Between 1931 and 1960, the share of the 117 largest manufacturing firms in total manufacturing assets remained stable at 45 percent.[6]

Economic theory suggests that concentrated industries with a great deal of market power will enjoy larger profit rates. Joe S. Bain and H. Michael Mann have shown that profit rates in the 1930s and 1950s tended to rise with concentration and with barriers to entry, although this effect was more pronounced in the 1950s.[7] More recent studies find that at concentration ratios above 70 percent, concentration is strongly related to profit rates. Barriers to entry appear to have an even stronger positive effect on profit rates. At lower rates of concentration, the relationship among profits, concentration, and entry barriers appears weak or even nonexistent.[8]

Another gauge of the degree of competition in the U.S. economy is how much output would increase if monopoly were eliminated. Researchers—notably Arnold Harberger and David Schwartzman—have calculated such "monopoly welfare losses."[9] They conclude that if monopoly were to disappear, national income would increase by less than 1 percent. These calculations do not deny that the distribution of income between the monopolist and the consumer is distorted by monopoly. Rather, what is calculated is the "deadweight loss" of monopoly—that is, the net loss of output due to monopoly.

Critics of monopoly such as Gordon Tullock and Anne Krueger have pointed out that monopoly rent-seeking raises society's losses above dead-weight losses.[10]

Examples of monopoly rent-seeking include bribing public officials to gain monopoly franchises and lobbying to gain protection from foreign imports. Because substantial profit gains accrue to the monopolist, people are prepared to expend substantial resources to turn a competitive industry into a monopoly. Harvey Leibenstein has emphasized the "organizational slack" or "X-inefficiency" of monopoly. Because monopolists are faced with less competition, they are under less pressure to minimize costs of production. The competitive firm that fails to minimize costs may be forced out of business, but the monopoly can relax. If one takes monopoly rent-seeking and X-inefficiency into account, society's losses from monopoly may be considerable.

Harold Demsetz argues in a different vein that the higher profits of large enterprises result from their superior cost performance.[11] If prices are set competitively so that each firm acts like a price taker, then economic profits accrue to those firms that have lower costs of production. The higher profit rates found in highly concentrated industries are the result of the superior efficiency of large firms.

The Labor Market[12]

Labor is allocated largely through labor markets in the United States. In competitive labor markets, employers demand larger quantities of labor at low wages. The supply of labor is a positive function of the wage rate offered, and a wage rate equating the supply and demand for labor is established automatically in the marketplace.

There are no measures to indicate how competitive the U.S. labor market is. Obvious examples of highly competitive labor markets include markets for domestic help, farm labor, most white-collar occupations, and banking employees. Labor market analysis focuses on the causes of deviations from the competitive model: union power, government intervention, and discrimination.

Unions   Only 20 percent of the U.S. labor force belongs to labor unions. In the 1930s, union members accounted for 6 to 7 percent of the labor force. Union membership rose in the 1940s and peaked at 25 percent in the mid-1950s. Since then the percentage has declined—despite the notable increase in union membership among public employees—largely because of the rapid growth of white-collar employment. The American trade union movement is more decentralized than its counterparts in Europe. More authority rests with local unions, and the movement has failed to produce its own political party. The American union movement consists of loose federations of local unions banded into national unions. With notable exceptions, bargaining over wages proceeds on a company-by-company basis. In recent years, however, the trend has been toward collective bargaining at the national level and bargaining over local issues at the local level.

Most American unions are associated with the AFL-CIO (American Federation of Labor–Congress of Industrial Organizations). The AFL-CIO accounts for almost 80 percent of all union members.

American workers were slower to organize than their European counterparts, because unfavorable legislation existed until the early 1930s: The Sherman Antitrust

Act of 1890 was initially applied against "monopolistic" labor unions, court orders prohibited union activity, and "yellow dog" contracts required employees to agree not to join a union. The Norris–LaGuardia Act of 1932 and the Wagner Act of 1935 laid the legislative foundation for the growth of unionism.

How much have unions altered the process of labor allocation? There are wide differences of opinion. Some (Milton Friedman, for example) argue that unions have had only a minimal impact on employment and wages. Unions act as highly visible **intermediaries** between the forces of supply and demand, and the pattern of wages and employment is virtually identical to that which would have prevailed without unions. Collective bargaining cannot negate the forces of demand over the long term, because too-high wages would result in a substitution of other factors for labor.

Most studies show that unions raise wages in unionized industries. Unions control wages through their power to strike and to control the supply of (and in some cases, through work rules, the demand for) labor. Unions raised wages in the unionized sector some 25 percent during the mid-1930s, 5 percent during the late 1940s, and some 10 to 15 percent during the 1950s. The most recent studies show that union wages are 15 to 18 percent higher than they would have been in the absence of unions. For the entire economy, the impact of unionization is probably small. Union wages are emulated in the nonunionized sector, and higher union wages reduce employment in the unionized branches and hence place downward pressure on wages in nonunionized branches.

What has been the effect of unions on productivity? Economists have traditionally believed that unions have a negative effect on productivity. Unions were thought to limit output per worker through disruptive strikes, featherbedding practices that kept employers from using labor efficiently, and distortion of union–nonunion wages. Some economists have questioned this view. Albert Hirschman, Richard Freeman, and James Medoff maintain that unions actually raise productivity by giving union members a collective voice. Without union representation, the only voice workers have against bad employers is to exit—that is, to leave the enterprise. With unions, workers can gain effective representation and can work from within to improve conditions. Unions can have a positive effect on productivity in three ways: Unions reduce worker turnover and thus limit hiring and training costs. In the union setting, senior workers are more likely to provide informal training and assistance. And the union provides for an improved information flow between workers and managers.

Government Intervention in the Labor Market   A second extramarket force in the labor market is government. Government affects wages through licensing and other procedures that regulate the supply of labor in particular occupations. It also affects the supply of labor in the long run through its policies toward public education and job training. Moreover, antidiscrimination legislation, hiring quotas, and the like also affect employment practices. Probably the most disputed role of government is minimum wage legislation. Its opponents argue that minimum wages disrupt the market process and create unemployment among the poor workers the legislation seeks to assist. Supporters argue that minimum wages are unlikely to have a significant effect on employment and are necessary to protect weak workers, who are at a disadvantage in the bargaining process.

Discrimination   The third extramarket force in the labor market is **discrimination** by race and gender, which excludes particular races and sexes from particular occupations (such as specific craft unions) and channels them into overpopulated occupations. An example is the channeling of women into public school teaching. A great deal of research has attempted to estimate the effect of discrimination on earnings of African Americans, Mexican-Americans, and women. The general consensus is that discrimination does exist, once other factors such as background and education are held constant, but that its overall effect on wages in the United States has been limited. Within specific occupations, the discrimination effect on the observed minority wage differential is small. The most significant impact of race and sex discrimination results from the exclusion of minorities from specific occupations.

The Capital Market

The **capital market** brings together suppliers and users of credit. Businesses undertake investment projects as long as the anticipated risk-adjusted rate of return exceeds the cost of acquiring capital funds. At the margin, projects are undertaken wherein the rate of return just equals the cost of borrowing. Accordingly, the lower the cost of acquiring investment funds, the higher the demand for investment will be.

The supply of investment funds to the capital market depends on the savings of individuals, government surpluses or deficits, retained profits, and depreciation. In the U.S. capital market, the supply of investment funds is seldom channeled directly from the saver to the investor. Such transactions are normally handled by **financial intermediaries**, such as commercial banks, savings banks, and insurance companies. In the corporate sector (which accounts for some three-fourths of business borrowing), there are three sources of investment finance. The corporation can raise capital by issuing debt, by issuing additional stock, or by using retained earnings. The supply of investment funds varies positively with the interest rate.

A striking feature of American capital markets (and capital markets in general in industrialized capitalist countries) is the prevalence of financial intermediation. Financial intermediaries borrow funds from one set of economic agents (people or companies with savings) and lend to other economic agents. Financial intermediaries serve a useful purpose by making it unnecessary for borrowers and lenders to seek each other out. A commercial bank, for example, borrows from its depositors (by accepting checking and savings account deposits) and then lends to a corporation building a new plant. If borrowers and lenders had sought each other out, the lender would have received a higher rate of interest and the borrower would have paid a lower rate of interest. The fact that lenders and borrowers pay for financial intermediation suggests that the service performed is a valuable one. Of the private domestic funds advanced for private investment in the early 1980s, about 90 percent was supplied through financial intermediaries.

The U.S. capital market is a well-organized market in the sense that national securities markets (the New York and American Stock Exchanges, markets for federal funds, and others) bring together all potential borrowers and suppliers of investment funds, and information concerning investment alternatives is readily and almost instantaneously available to all participants. It is misleading to speak of a U.S. capital market, for there is an *international* capital market. The huge amount of international data in the financial section of the daily newspaper demonstrates this fact. The net result is an approximate equalization of rates of return on all investments *at the margin* once they are adjusted for risk.

This equalization of rates of return at the margin is considered to be an important positive feature of capital markets, because it leads to an efficient allocation of capital resources. If rates of return were not equal at the margin, then capital funds could be redistributed from projects with a lower rate of return to those with higher rates, and output could be increased without an increase in capital resources.

Government in the American Economy

When examining socialist economic systems, it is usual to study the role of market forces and in particular to determine how such forces arise in the socialist economy and how they contribute to the overall performance of the economy. Similarly, it is important to discover how and why government becomes involved in a predominantly market economy and the results of such a system.

Government intervention in the American economy is usually justified as a response to various types of market failure. As Chapter 5 emphasized, markets can fail in a variety of ways. Similarly, government response can take a variety of forms, usually involving some mix of direct production (**public goods**), redistribution of income, and/or regulation.

Although many would agree that some degree of government activity is necessary in the contemporary American economy, beyond this limited consensus there is much disagreement.[13] Public choice theory does not provide significant guidance in determining how much government involvement is appropriate, and yet an examination of most market capitalist economies indicates that government activity has been growing over time.[14] Both the measurement of that activity (its size and influence in the economy) and explanations for its growth are complex.

The Scope of the Public Sector

The data presented in Figure 8.2 shed light on the role of government in the American economy. The government's claim on labor and capital resources indicates how productive resources are divided between government and business uses. Government (federal, state, and local) employs approximately 16 percent of the American labor force and owns approximately 18 percent of the stock of structures, one-eighth of all land, and one-twentieth of all inventories. Government owned approximately

FIGURE 8.2   Indicators of Government Participation in Economic Activity and
Wealth in the United States, 1900–1990

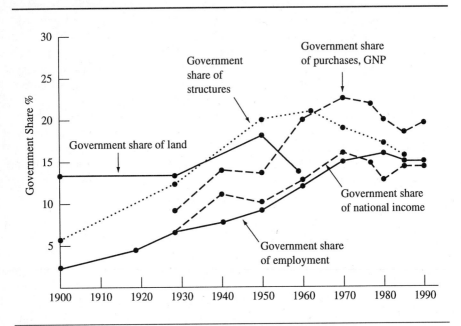

The dots (•) indicate the years of observations.

Source: *Handbook of Economic Statistics 1992*, CPAS 92–10005, September 1992.

15 percent of the national wealth and accounted for some 7 percent of total labor,
capital, and land inputs in the late 1950s.

Government's share of productive resources has increased steadily over the last
hundred years. At the turn of the century, government accounted for some 4 percent
of employment and owned 6 percent of the stock of structures and 13 percent of the
stock of land. By 1939, the government's share had increased substantially (to 18
percent of structures and 19 percent of land), while its share of the labor force rose
to about 10 percent. Since the late 1930s, government's share of employment has
increased by 80 percent, but its share of national wealth has risen only slightly. The
United States appears to have reached a national consensus on the distribution of
wealth, which has remained fairly stable for about 50 years. There is now little
serious talk of large-scale nationalizations, and most of the major decisions in this
area (broadcasting, communication satellites, atomic energy) have come down on
the side of private ownership.

Government produces about 15 percent of national income, of which the overwhelming portion is produced not by government enterprises but by "general government." The business sector accounts for more than 80 percent of national income; the
remainder is accounted for by government and nonprofit institutions. The encroachment of government enterprises on private business has been minimal. Government

enterprises account for less than 2 percent of the national income. Rather than government enterprises supplanting private enterprises, it has been the expansion of general government activities that has accounted for rising government output.

The government's share of national income has been rising steadily over the last hundred years (4 percent in 1869 to 8.5 percent in 1919 to 15 percent in 1985). Since the 1930s, the increase in the federal government's share has been more substantial than that of state and local government. Since 1929, business's share of national income has fallen from 91 to 81 percent at the expense of the rise in general government and nonprofit institutions.

Government purchases account for about one-fifth of the total. Interestingly, most of the historical increase in the share of government purchases has been due to rising state and local government spending and federal defense spending.

It is important to put these U.S. developments in perspective. An examination of other industrialized capitalist countries (Figure 8.3) shows that the scope of the public sector in the United States is average or even below average if one considers

FIGURE 8.3 The Size of Government in the United States and Other Countries, 1960 and 1990

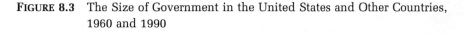

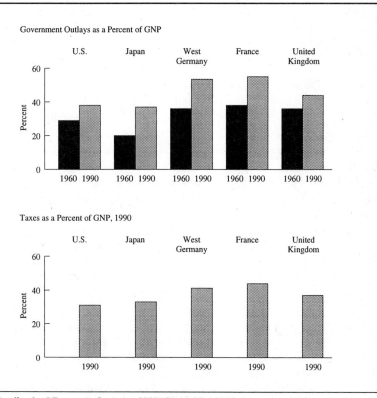

Source: *Handbook of Economic Statistics 1992*, CPAS 92–10005, September 1992.

that most countries do not bear a substantial defense burden. If one looks only at nondefense spending, the U.S. government's share of total spending appears relatively small by international standards. The rising share of government output and expenditures is also unexceptional; it has characterized the economic growth of capitalism for more than a century. The U.S. tax burden is also relatively modest.

Some people view the rising share of government with alarm; others consider it too small. All one can say for sure is that in the United States, the allocation of resources between the public and private sectors is basically a matter of public choice.

Public Goods: The Case of National Defense

Government bears the principal responsibility for providing public goods, although it must be noted that in the real world there are few "pure" public goods. The activity that dominates the so-called public goods market in the United States is national defense, which is also the best theoretical example of a public good; we shall therefore use it to illustrate how the U.S. government deals with public goods.

Two issues must be considered. The first is how decisions are reached concerning national defense's share of total public resources. The second issue is the market structure under which defense goods are produced.

Resource Allocation by the Defense Industry   The share and product mix of national defense are decided by the political process. The connection between the government and the large manufacturers of military hardware has been called the **military–industrial complex**. Three explanations of weapons procurement have been offered: the strategic, the bureaucratic, and the economic.[15]

The strategic explanation is that defense planners determine weapons procurement on the basis of rational calculations about the foreign military threat. The bureaucratic explanation is that defense spending is the product of a disorganized tug of war among the various interests that make up the military–industrial complex, not of any rationally calculated plan of national security. One branch of the military exerts pressure for its weapons system, while a rival branch applies similar pressure in favor of its project. Or one system manufacturer exerts, through strategic members of Congress or lobbyists, pressure in favor of its design for a weapons system. According to the bureaucratic explanation, the overall distribution of resources depends on the outcome of this struggle of vested interests.

Economics provides the final explanation. According to this view, defense spending is based on its impact on the overall economy. In the view of the New Left, an expanding defense budget is necessary to preserve full employment and economic stability. According to another view, contracts for major weapons systems will be granted, not on the basis of which company will produce the most effective system, but to preserve established contractors located in politically important states.[16]

A related consideration is the extent to which the private defense contractors themselves are able to determine, or at least influence, defense spending. According to some, the economic and political power of the major defense contractors is sufficient to exert significant control over the allocation of defense resources.[17] Although these observers have probably overrated the power of defense contractors, there is evidence that their view is at least partially true.[18]

The Market Structure of the Defense Industry   Most observers agree that defense contracting procedures violate the principle that national defense should be provided at a minimum cost of resources. Some authorities, in fact, argue that the current system leads to excessive cost and subsidies. The market structure of the U.S. military–industrial complex consists of the U.S. government, as a monopsonistic buyer, purchasing from a small number of defense contractors. The government purchases a weapons system from a single supplier, who is granted a monopoly to develop the system. Often there is no serious negotiation with potential competitors. Defense contracts are typically let on a cost-plus basis, whereby the manufacturer agrees to supply a particular weapons system at a negotiated cost plus an agreed-upon profit margin. Because there is little competition among producers, and because the manufacture of a new weapons system is characterized by technological uncertainty, the government cannot judge whether the manufacturer is operating efficiently.

Most suggestions for reform of the military procurement system center on either the nationalization of the defense industry or the introduction of more competition into the existing system.[19] The major disadvantage of nationalization is that the monopoly of new weapons systems would then reside directly with the U.S. government; pressure to seek out cost-effective techniques would still be lacking. The second approach does not appear to be politically feasible because strong vested interests favor the existing system of protecting and subsidizing established defense contractors.

Personnel and National Defense   Until 1973, the personnel needs of the armed forces were met by a national draft operated by the Selective Service System. Conscription was employed to fill the gap between the number of volunteers joining the military at established wage rates (the supply) and the quotas established by the armed services (the demand). The costs of maintaining the armed forces therefore consisted of payments to armed service personnel *plus* the loss of income incurred by those draftees who had to forgo higher incomes outside the military. To some extent, however, individuals with higher earning capacities were excluded from the draft by educational and occupational exemptions.

Military personnel prior to 1973 were handled largely outside of the labor market. With the winding down of the Vietnam War, the U.S. government turned to a voluntary army in 1973. Military personnel needs were to be met by raising military pay and benefits to the level required to bring the supply of and demand for military personnel into approximate balance. This use of the market represents a return to the practice of using hired troops. It has the advantage of relying on freedom of choice of occupation and avoiding the economic inefficiency of conscripting individuals with high earning capacities. Its disadvantages are that the armed forces are made up primarily of the disadvantaged, for whom military pay scales are attractive, and that the whole notion of national service is circumvented. The effectiveness of the volunteer army was tested in the Persian Gulf War with apparently favorable results.

Health, Education, and Welfare

U.S. government public assistance has been limited to public education, some low-cost health care for the poor, and social security insurance for retirement, disability, and unemployment. Such services are typically supplied on a mixed private-enterprise–public-service basis with the user paying a portion of the cost.

The mix of private versus public support has been shifting toward public provision, and it reflects a changing public attitude toward government responsibility. Over the last half-century, this change has been most dramatic in the areas of health expenditures, social welfare expenditures, and social insurance (Table 8.4), which had been regarded as private or charitable obligations. Prior to the 1930s, almost all retirement, health, and unemployment insurance was purchased on a voluntary

TABLE 8.4   Expenditures on Public Assistance in the United States, 1890–1990

Year	Public Social Welfare Expenditures as a Percent of GNP[a]	Public Social Insurance Expenditures as a Percent of GDP	National Health Care Expenditures as a Percent of GDP	Public Higher Education Expenditures as a Percent of Total
1990	19.1	9.3	13.2[b]	64.0
1987	18.4	10.8	—	—
1985	18.4	10.1	10.5	65.0
1980	18.6	8.0	9.2	66.3
1970	14.8	5.7	7.4	67.5
1955	8.6	2.6	5.3[c]	64.0
1929	3.9	.2	10	41.0
1920	—	—	—	38
1900	—	—	—	—
1890	2.4	—	—	—

[a] Social welfare expenditures include social insurance and public aid, education, veterans' programs, child nutrition, and rehabilitation programs. Cited as a percent of GDP after 1970.
[b] 1991
[c] 1960

Source: U.S., Department of Commerce, *Historical Statistics of the United States: Colonial Times to 1970* (Washington, D.C.: Government Printing Office, 1975), Series B236-247, H1–31, H412–432, H716–727; *Statistical Abstract of the United States.*

private basis; in 1929 only 10 percent of personal health expenditures were funded by governmental agencies. Public elementary and secondary education has dominated the American education system for quite a while, but the government share of support for higher education has increased substantially over the last 50 years. During that time, public universities have supplanted private universities as the dominant institutions in higher education.

Two general rules have governed public assistance. The first is that, if feasible, goods should be provided on an "in-kind" basis (for example, subsidized school lunches and food stamps) rather than as income payments. This suggests an unwillingness to rely on freedom of choice and a feeling that the poor are not to be trusted to allocate their incomes wisely. The second general rule is that families should not have the power to shop around for education or public health, despite arguments that making such choice possible would force suppliers to be more efficient and responsive to the consumer.

U.S. Government Policy Toward Monopoly

In the United States, monopoly policy has been neither uniform nor consistent. In some instances, government policy restricts competition (tariffs, licensing, agricultural price supports); in others, it seeks to restrain monopoly power and to promote competitive behavior.

Government Ownership

Several options are open to government with regard to natural monopolies, which for a variety of reasons must serve as the sole suppliers of a product. The government can nationalize them in the "public interest." It can also tax them in order to transfer monopoly profits to the state and to guarantee an output/price combination more consistent with competitive standards. A third alternative is government regulation. A fourth is for the government to auction exclusive franchises to operate natural monopolies. This option would transfer much of the monopoly return to the state.[20]

In the United States, all of these approaches have been employed, though discriminatory monopoly taxation and franchise auctions are rare. Public ownership of natural monopolies is common at the local and state levels but rare at the federal level. Municipal services such as local transportation, garbage collection, water, electricity, gas, public wharves, and state transit authorities are often owned and operated by state and municipal government. More than 20 percent of all electrical energy is generated by government or cooperative arrangements, and 10 percent of all utility payments go to government enterprises. In only 2 of the 10 largest cities is the municipal transit system privately owned. Approximately 3 percent of all residential housing construction has been undertaken by public authorities.[21]

Government enterprise operated by the federal government is more limited: operating the postal services (now a semigovernmental operation), administering public lands (the Forest Service), lending and guaranteeing loans (the FHA and VA programs), providing insurance against various risks (social security), generating electricity (the Tennessee Valley Authority), and engaging in limited manufacturing activities (Redstone Arsenal, the U.S. Government Printing Office).[22]

Local, state, and federal government enterprises account for less than 2 percent of national income. The public's decision to leave natural monopolies in the hands of private owners has been in marked contrast to the European pattern, where the state owns and operates most natural monopolies—and even enterprises that are not natural monopolies (such as automobile manufacturing, national airlines, and railroads).

Despite their small scope, it is nevertheless important to consider how well U.S. public enterprises perform. In public enterprises, the incentive to restrict output and raise prices should not be so strong as under private ownership. On the other hand, the pressures to reduce costs and to innovate are generally weaker. Moreover, red tape and civil service restrictions may impede efficiency in the public enterprise. At the empirical level, the evidence is mixed. One authority concludes (after reviewing the European experience as well) that "the evidence is presently insufficient to support a sharp choice between the alternatives on straightforward economic performance grounds."[23]

In industries where public and private enterprises coexist, the former represent a potential yardstick for evaluating the private sector. The prime example is the Tennessee Valley Authority (TVA), the largest electrical utility in the United States. The exceptionally low costs of the TVA have been used to challenge the rates of private utilities. Yet TVA's lower costs do not unambiguously establish the greater efficiency of public ownership, for, as the private utilities point out, the TVA enjoys certain privileges not accorded the private companies.

Public enterprise could conceivably improve resource allocation by forcing private producers to behave more competitively and efficiently. Strategies available to the public enterprise include price undercutting and the threat to expand capacity. According to one authority, these strategies have rarely been used because of the opposition of private enterprises and the reluctance of managers of public enterprises to compete with private industry.

Regulation

The overwhelming political choice has been to regulate industries that possess monopoly power rather than to use public ownership.[24] **Regulation** has been exercised by a wide variety of local, state, and federal agencies. Other kinds of regulation—control by the courts or by the terms of franchises, charters, and city ordinances—have proved ineffective in the United States, and the public has turned instead to administrative regulation, either by an official of executive government or by semi-independent commissions operating under general legislative authority.[25]

Regulation at the state and local level is principally directed at natural monopolies—specifically, the electric, gas, and telephone companies. At the national level, federal commissions have regulated both monopolistic industries (such as local telephone service) and those with a potentially significant degree of competition (such as trucking and airlines). The stated rationale for federal regulation has been to ensure quality of service and to guarantee the public "reasonable" prices without unfair discrimination among users. A degree of monopoly power, however, is generally a necessary but insufficient condition for regulation. Buyers have to be at a disadvantage in bargaining by virtue of the fact that the service is an essential, non-postponable one for which there are few good substitutes. Although the American automobile industry is more concentrated than the natural gas or rail industry, the latter two have been regulated, whereas the other has remained free from direct regulation. There are historical reasons for regulation as well. The railroads were placed under the supervision of the Interstate Commerce Commission at a time when they possessed considerable monopoly power. Motor and air transport lessened this power, yet the commission could not continue to regulate railroads without extending federal regulation to other forms of transport.

Generally, the regulatory commissions have controlled entry into the industry by granting franchises and licenses—for a new airline route, say, or a new interstate natural gas pipeline. Rarely are these licenses or franchises actually sold (for the purpose of diverting the ensuing profits to the public). Rather, it is assumed that regulation will prevent excessive profits.

It is the responsibility of the regulators to set "reasonable" rates for the services of regulated producers. In this, the regulatory commissions have been guided by the principle, guaranteed by the Fifth and Fourteenth Amendments protecting private property, that rates should be sufficient to cover operating costs plus a "proper" rate of return on invested capital. A second principle is that the rate structure should not discriminate among buyers, except when such discrimination is justified by cost differences.

Before this pricing formula can be applied, several important matters must be resolved: How are operating costs to be defined? What is an appropriate rate of return on invested capital? How is the rate base (the value of tangible and intangible assets of the company) to be measured? The regulated price is essentially a cost-plus price, and additions to cost will, in time, be passed on to the user. This may well reduce the incentive to seek out cost economies. Moreover, there is the problem of dealing with illegitimate or padded costs, such as buying materials from an unregulated affiliate at inflated prices in order to increase that company's profits.

Determining an appropriate rate of return to regulated firms has been another area of controversy. The rate of return should be high enough to attract new capital; hence, the interest rate on recently floated debt has often been used as the rate of return. According to one authority, however, the rates of return that regulatory commissions and the courts have historically allowed have been "conventional or arbitrary, bearing no apparent relation to any statement of principles . . . usually based on expert testimony with little pretense of economic analysis."[26] The rates allowed have varied from state to state and from time to time, ranging between 5½ percent in the 1940s and 11 percent and higher during the 1970s and 1980s.

An Assessment of Regulation

Most authorities give regulation relatively poor marks, especially in industries that are not natural monopolies.[27] Regulation of natural monopolies has had a remarkably small effect on the prices charged consumers. Opponents of regulation argue that operating costs will fall when potentially competitive industries are freed from regulation (deregulated).

Why have the regulatory commissions not had a more beneficial impact on the industries they regulate? There are several possible explanations. The first is that the balance of power between the regulators and the regulated is uneven. The regulated industries have well-paid staffs, whereas the regulatory commissions (the state commissions particularly) are understaffed and underpaid. Regulated industries appear able to circumvent regulations if necessary. Moreover, the commissioners themselves tend to keep in close contact with the industries they regulate, not with the consumers they are supposed to represent. The very *methodology* of regulation also remains a problem. A commission has no way of knowing what operating costs would be if the most efficient production techniques were used. Even if it did know, it would lack the authority to mandate use of these techniques. Instead, it must simply accept the actual operating costs of the utilities as given, except in obvious cases of corruption or gross mismanagement.

To show that regulation has been less than optimal does not establish that a superior alternative exists, especially in the case of natural monopolies. Because they cannot be organized on competitive bases, they will possess significant monopoly power. Despite its weaknesses, direct regulation may be the best alternative.

Deregulation[28]

A substantial amount of **deregulation** in the American economy has occurred in recent years. The Airline Deregulation Act, signed in October 1978, allowed the airlines rather than the Civil Aeronautics Board (which went out of existence in 1984) to set fares and choose routes, according to the availability of landing slots at airports. In 1980, the Motor Carrier Act curbed the role of the Interstate Commerce Commission in interstate trucking. Also in 1980, the Staggers Rail Act led to major changes in railroad transport, and the Depository Institution Deregulation and the Monetary Control acts significantly changed the way the banking sector sets charges, enters markets, and the like. The AT&T Settlement of 1982 and the Cable Television Deregulation Act of 1984 brought major and well-known changes in the telecommunications and cable television industries, respectively.

Much of this deregulation was motivated by the message of microeconomic theory, namely that the development of competitive markets could provide benefits that would outweigh associated costs. At the same time, the opponents of deregulation warned of deteriorating service, pricing wars, and general instability in deregulated industries.

U.S. experience has shown that deregulation leads to lower prices for most—but not all—consumers. Consumers in small markets characterized by high costs are no longer protected and now have to pay prices closer to costs. Deregulation has increased the diversity of services offered and has given consumers more freedom of choice. Firms that had been protected by regulation have lowered their costs substantially, and these lower costs are being passed on to their customers. Deregulation has also had its losers. Firms that could not meet competitive pressures have gone out of business or have been acquired by more successful firms. Employees have seen their earnings fall as firms have sought ways to lower their costs.

In the airline industry, the problems of high fuel prices, terrorism, and high debt resulted in the concentration of the industry in the hands of a few giant airlines. In banking, a number of problems (such as corruption and the inflation of the 1970s and 1980s) led to massive failures both in the savings and loan industry and in commercial banking. These negative experiences have caused some to question the wisdom of deregulation.

Antitrust Legislation

The major alternative to direct regulation of monopoly is legislation to control market structure and market conduct.[29] The most important piece of federal **antitrust legislation**, the Sherman Antitrust Act of 1890, confronts these issues. The Sherman Act was the government's reaction to public hostility toward the trust movement of the late nineteenth century in the transportation, steel, tobacco, and oil industries. The Sherman Act contains two sections. Section 1 declares "every contract, combination . . . or conspiracy" in restraint of interstate commerce illegal. Section 2 makes the attempt to monopolize interstate commerce a federal offense. Section 1 prohibits a particular type of market *conduct* (conspiring to restrain trade), whereas Section 2 enjoins a particular market *structure* (monopoly). The language of Section 2 is vague, and this imprecision has led to varying court interpretations over the years. According to the language of Section 2, **monopolization** is prohibited, not **monopolies**. The Sherman Act clearly bans the act of creating a monopoly but is ambiguous on the legality of existing monopolies.

The Sherman Antitrust Act of 1890 forms the foundation of American antitrust legislation. The Clayton and Federal Trade Commission acts of 1913 established a commission to investigate "unfair" business practices (the Federal Trade Commission) and prohibited specific illegal business practices. The Wheeler–Lea Act of 1938 gave the Clayton Act more teeth by declaring unfair or deceptive business practices illegal. The Celler–Kefauver Act of 1950 tightened up the antimerger provisions of the Clayton Act. (See Table 8.5.)

American antitrust policy is made by Congress and by the courts, for it is in the courts that actual antimonopoly policy has been set. The basic issue confronting the courts was whether certain forms of market conduct were prohibited or whether the monopoly market structure was illegal per se. If so, it was then up to the courts to decide what constituted a monopoly. In the early court rulings (the American

TABLE 8.5   An Overview of U.S. Antitrust Legislation

Act	Date	Provisions
Sherman Act	1890	Section 1: restraint of interstate commerce illegal
		Section 2: attempt to monopolize illegal
Clayton Act	1914	Declared specific business practices illegal
Federal Trade Commission Act	1914	Established the FTC to secure compliance with Clayton Act
Wheeler–Lea Act	1938	Banned deceptive business practices
Celler–Kefauver Act	1950	Broadened ban on mergers

Tobacco and Standard Oil cases of 1911 and the U.S. Steel case of 1920), the courts interpreted the Sherman Act as enjoining anticompetitive market conduct (price cutting to eliminate competition, mergers, price fixing) but not the existence of monopoly per se. This became known as the "rule of reason."[30]

The rule of reason appeared to be reversed when the courts ruled in 1945 that Alcoa was in violation of the Sherman Act because it controlled more than 90 percent of U.S. aluminum output. Although Alcoa had not used its monopoly power to restrain trade unfairly, the courts ruled that size alone was a violation of antitrust statutes. Thus an important inconsistency appeared to be removed. The rule of reason had implied that companies engaging in practices that would ultimately lead to monopoly were in violation of the Sherman Act but that existing monopolies, if they behaved well, were not in violation.

The Alcoa ruling was gradually eroded by court decisions of the 1970s and 1980s. The basic problem with the Alcoa decision was that it appeared to punish all monopolies, even those that became monopolies by means of superior innovation and management. The Eastman Kodak case of 1972 and the FTC ruling in favor of DuPont in 1978 established that monopolies created through superior management and innovation were not in violation of the Sherman Act. The Alcoa decision was also weakened when the Justice Department dropped its thirteen-year-old suit against IBM in 1982.

Price Fixing and Mergers

In the United States, the courts have generally found **price-fixing** agreements among producers and **mergers** of large companies engaged in the same line of business to be in violation of the antitrust laws.[31] Formal arrangements for fixing prices have consistently been ruled illegal restraints of trade. The United States stands virtually alone among the industrialized capitalist countries in holding that formal arrangements for price fixing are illegal per se, even if the resulting prices are "reasonable."

The courts have thus avoided the difficult issue of distinguishing "reasonable" from "unreasonable" price fixing.

The more difficult enforcement issue, however, has been collusion without outright agreement on pricing policy. Prior to 1948, the courts held that informal price coordination was illegal even if a formal price conspiracy could not be shown. After 1948, in order to demonstrate an illegal conspiracy, it had to be shown that the pattern of pricing could not conceivably have occurred if each firm had acted independently in its own self-interest.

The basic legislation against mergers is found in the Clayton Act of 1914 and in the Celler–Kefauver Act of 1950. Especially since 1950, the courts have adopted a virtual prohibition of mergers between firms with substantial market shares. The only exceptions appear to be (1) mergers wherein one firm takes over another that is on the verge of bankruptcy and (2) conglomerate mergers wherein one firm takes over another that is in a different line of business. In various rulings, the courts have decided that mergers involving combined market shares of 20 percent and even lower constitute an undue lessening of competition.

In its strict interpretation of antimerger statutes, the United States stands alone among the industrialized capitalist countries, most of which encourage mergers that serve to increase the scale of production. In Western Europe, for example, the burden of proof is on the government to establish that the social costs of a proposed merger exceed its benefits. In the United States the burden of proof lies with the merging firms, and if significant market shares are involved, the merger will be declared illegal per se.

An Evaluation of Antitrust Policy

The most relevant criterion for evaluating government policy toward monopoly is its effect on U.S. economic structure and performance. Since the antitrust laws have been in effect, there has not been a significant increase in the concentration of American industry, whereas the second half of the nineteenth century witnessed a substantial increase in concentration. (The government's inability to prevent the conglomerate mergers of the 1960s and 1970s, however, has probably led to an increased concentration of ownership.) Many have speculated on the manner in which the antitrust laws contributed to the stability of concentration in the twentieth century. According to one authority, antitrust legislation made three important contributions to the maintenance of workable competition: It prevented European-type cartelization of American industry, it prevented consolidations that would have led to dominant industries, and it helped to preserve freedom of entry and equality of opportunity.[32]

Although it does appear that government policy has contributed to the maintenance of workable competition in the U.S. economy, not all such policy has been consistent. In fact, a great many government activities have been designed to *reduce* the competitiveness of the American economy: protective tariffs for selected industries, price supports for agricultural products, the patent system, licensing, and so on.

Government and Macroeconomic Stability

Planning for macroeconomic stability in the United States is limited to the use of indirect tools of monetary and fiscal policy. No national economic plan is drafted by government. In this, the United States deviates significantly from other industrialized capitalist countries, most of which have some form of national economic planning. (The case studies of capitalist variants in Chapter 9 focus on national economic planning in France and Britain.) Congressional proposals to introduce a rather mild form of economic planning have generated considerable controversy.[33]

Prior to the Great Depression, the prevailing notion in government circles was that monetary and fiscal policy should be as neutral as possible. "Neutral" meant interfering as little as possible with private economic activity. After the Great Depression and the acceptance of Keynesian economics, this view changed; by the 1960s both major political parties came to accept the view that discretionary monetary and fiscal policy should be used to counter cyclical unemployment and inflation. Although some American monetarists and rational-expectations theorists have spoken out in favor of a return to the traditional neutralist view, monetary and fiscal planners continue to engage in countercyclical policy.

The Federal Reserve System (the Fed) is in charge of formulating monetary policy. Established in 1913, the Federal Reserve System consists of twelve Federal Reserve district banks coordinated by the board of governors in Washington, D.C. In the United States the "central bank" is more decentralized along regional lines than is common for central banks, but it nonetheless performs the functions of a central bank—regulating the money supply through open market operations, managing the discount rate, setting reserve requirements, and so on.

Authority over fiscal policy is diffused among the various executive and legislative bodies in charge of government spending and taxation, and the balance of authority has tended to shift over time. It is therefore difficult to describe briefly how important fiscal decisions are made. The president can propose budgets, but only Congress can approve them. The Treasury Department can propose changes in the tax structure, but it is the Congress that amends and approves such executive suggestions.

One point emerges clearly when we compare the existing machinery for conducting monetary and fiscal policy: The conduct of monetary policy is more divorced from the business of day-to-day politics than is that of fiscal policy. Members of the Board of Governors of the Fed are appointed for fourteen-year terms and, although they owe their ultimate responsibility to the Congress, a tradition of independence for the Fed has evolved. Recurring proposals call for greater congressional control of the Fed, and there is evidence that the Fed does seek to pursue a monetary policy consistent with that of the current administration. The conduct of fiscal policy is very much a matter of politics, so it has proved difficult to conduct countercyclical fiscal policy. This is especially true during periods of inflation, when politically unpopular budget cuts and tax increases are shunned.

On the whole, the distinctive feature of economic planning in the United States is its virtual absence. Price and wage controls have been applied during periods of inflation, in the form of either voluntary guidelines or mandatory wage and price limitations. The most dramatic examples of this were the price freezes of 1971–1973, after which the economy returned to measures that were more voluntary.

Government Activity and Externalities

In an economic system using price signals for resource allocation decisions, incorrect signals (signals that do not recognize both public and private costs and benefits) can lead to incorrect decisions in the sense of not recognizing **external costs and benefits**. Thus, externalities, like pollution, are permitted because their full cost is not always recognized. Benefits are lost because their value is not recognized. Government can play a role in lessening these imbalances. No comprehensive program for dealing with externalities exists at the federal level, and the responsibility for environmental protection is diffused among a wide variety of federal, state, and local agencies. Some of these agencies have an exceptional record of environmental protection; an example is the U.S. Soil Conservation Service. Others, such as the U.S. Environmental Protection Agency, lack sufficient authority to correct serious cases of misallocation.

Three themes should be stressed in assessing the role of the state in dealing with the externality problem. The first is that the division of authority and responsibility among local, state, and national agencies (control of air pollution, for example) has made it difficult to devise effective programs. In many cases, external effects transcend local political boundaries; dealing with them requires some form of national or regional coordination. The second theme has been the general reluctance to use market forces (such as taxes on polluters). Fines, prohibitions, and other administrative orders have been the principal means of enforcement. The third theme is the general unwillingness to consider "optimal" levels of environmental disruption—that is, the level of pollution reduction one should aim for, given the fact that it can be attained only at the expense of society's resources.[34]

The record of environmental protection varies by locality and region. In some areas, heavy emphasis has been placed on environmental protection with strict enforcement of meaningful pollution regulations. Examples include the efforts to prohibit development of additional refining capacity and offshore drilling in the Northeast and the furor over the generation of nuclear power in different parts of the country.

Government Policies and the Distribution of Income

To what extent does government in the United States redistribute income through taxation and the distribution of social services? The distribution of income is measured by the Lorenz curve (defined in Chapter 3), which compares family income by rank (say, the lowest to the highest fifth of all families) with percentage share of income either before or after taxes. Some studies "tailor" the Lorenz curve by adjusting for age differences, for differences in family size, and for the distribution of government services.[35]

As measured by the Lorenz curve before taxes and any other adjustments, the U.S. distribution of income seems to have changed little since 1950. In 1950, the lowest and the highest fifth of families accounted for 5 and for 45 percent of all income, respectively. By 1982, those figures were 5 and 42 percent. The change since 1929 has been more substantial: The share of the highest fifth of U.S. families declined from 54 to 43.5 percent in all income between 1929 and 1985.[36] It has been argued that if one adjusts these figures for differences in age and family size, then the trend toward greater equality is even more evident.[37]

The traditional view is that government has not played a significant role in redistributing income from upper-income to lower-income groups. Although the federal tax system is progressive (upper-income families pay a higher percentage of their income in taxes than do lower-income families), state and local taxes are regressive (upper-income families pay a lower percentage of income). On balance, therefore, the total tax system is roughly proportional (each income group pays the same percentage of its income in taxes), and the after-tax distribution of income is little different from the before-tax distribution. Remember, though, that all such calculations are inexact because of the difficulty of determining what proportion of business and property taxes are passed on to the consumer in the form of higher prices. Joseph Pechman and Benjamin Okner have found that if one assumes such taxes are almost entirely passed on to the consumer, then the tax system is proportional. If one assumes they are borne by the producer, however, Pechman and Okner found that the tax system becomes progressive, but only at the very top and very bottom of the income distribution.[38]

According to some, the state plays a greater redistributive role than is commonly thought.[39] The basis for such claims is that lower-income groups receive larger shares of government in-kind benefits (food stamps, welfare, public education) than their shares of money income. If one includes the value of these benefits in income and then subtracts income and payroll taxes, the distribution of disposable income is much more nearly equal than the unadjusted figures suggest. Figure 8.4 shows calculations from a study by Edgar Browning to illustrate this position. The redistributive role of government in the United States is probably much less significant than in other industrialized capitalist countries. Thus, relatively speaking, the government plays a modest role in the redistribution of income in the United States.

Privatization

In recent years, interest has been growing in **privatization** which is the shift of economic activity from the public sector to the private sector.[40] In part, this new interest stems from the vast privatization efforts taking place in the former planned socialist economies and elsewhere in Europe. In this sense, privatization represents one way to reduce the role of government in a market economy. But the contemporary American economy focuses more on efficiency or the notion that goods and services can be more efficiently provided (that is at lower cost) in the private sector than in the public sector.

FIGURE 8.4   Lorenz Curves: U.S. Income Distribution Before and After Income and Transfer Payments

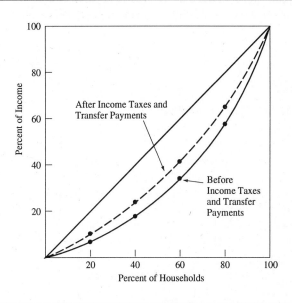

Source: Data from 1972 based on Edgar K. Browning, "The Trend Toward Equality in the Distribution of Net Income," *Southern Economic Journal*, 43 (July 1976), 914.

Thus, while privatization in Eastern Europe primarily refers to changes in equity arrangements from public to private, privatization in the United States more likely refers to government contracting for the private production of traditionally public-sector goods and services, such as trash collection, homes for the elderly, local transportation services, and the like.

Privatization is a matter of considerable controversy in the contemporary American economy. Accordingly, it is easy to find strongly held views on both sides of the subject. Those who favor privatization in the provision of municipal services, for example, argue that beyond immediate cost reduction, quality will improve as a result of competitive markets, and in the long term, the role of government in the economy will be reduced. Those who oppose privatization argue that, in fact, only limited empirical evidence indicates actual cost reductions. Moreover, because measuring its impact is difficult, the role of government might not be reduced, competitive provision of services might not prevail, and quality might, in fact, be threatened. Inevitably, privatization threatens government employees who will most likely oppose the trend.

What is the status of privatization in the United States in the mid-1990s? First, although past trends have been toward contracting, there are publicly owned facilities, such as airports, roads, water systems, and sports centers, to which the privatization discussion has been applied. Second, although considerable variation exists from one city or region to another, there is nevertheless a substantial amount of private initiative in the provision of local services. Finally, the message from the scholarly literature remains divided. However, as more case studies are examined, doubtless empirical evidence will help in understanding privatization, in determining whether it is a realistic alternative for cost savings, and in sorting out the preconditions that are necessary to achieve such savings.

Economic Systems and American Capitalism

At the outset, this book noted that much of the literature in contemporary neoclassical economics paid relatively little attention to the economic system as a construct influencing outcomes in different settings. It is equally true that much of the literature on the American economy is not cast within a systems framework, let alone a comparative framework. As the systems of the former Soviet Union and Eastern Europe undergo a transition to markets, it is perhaps ironic that our view of American capitalism is changing. Themes that once were primarily of interest to the systems economist are now taking center stage in discussions of the American market economy.

For example, the fundamental unifying theme of comparative economic systems, namely the organizational arrangements comprising the economic system are now of growing importance in mainstream contemporary economic theory. The nature of the firm, the importance of the principal–agent relationship, and the relation of the firm to the market now hold great interest in understanding how the market economy functions and how it changes through time. Although some economists have focused on these issues for many years, recent attempts to extend the frontiers of traditional neoclassical economic theory will undoubtedly lead to empirical evidence that shows how organizational arrangements in the American economy might be changed to better achieve desired national objectives.

Consider also the case of industrial policy, an issue discussed in Chapter 5. Although planning in any form has typically been viewed as inappropriate and unnecessary for the American economy, a kernel of interest in some planning mechanism always remains to guide and influence resource allocation in key sectors of the American economy. One example of this involves the resources necessary for commanding technological change and thereby for capturing world markets. Although most major corporations within the American economy conduct something usually termed "planning," the macroeconomic impetus of the 1980s, which was derived from cases such as Japan, has largely faded. Thus the focus in the mid-1990s is on less control and the encouragement of competitive market arrangements.

The issue is not the popularity of a particular policy option at a given point of time, but the potential effectiveness of that option for achieving national economic goals. Basically, the current approach to resource allocation in the American economy is now more familiar to the analyst of differing economic systems than in the past. The experiences of different economic systems therefore become much more relevant to the United States and both the theory and the reality of these different systems and system components become increasingly important.

Summary

Three main actors comprise the American economy: firms, households, and the government. The private sector refers to that economic activity in which private ownership prevails, whereas the public sector refers to economic activity influenced by government. The coordination of economic activity is determined primarily by relatively decentralized product and factor markets in which the forces of supply and demand interact to produce relative factor and product prices. This structure conforms quite well to the theoretical model of market capitalism, with important exceptions to the existence of competitive markets both for products and for factors of production.

Government plays an important role in the American economy, although direct government ownership is more limited in the United States than in other market economies. The American government does, however, play an important role in the regulation and control of industries in which some degree of concentration of market power is said to exist. Although measuring the size of the government sector is difficult, traditionally some 25 percent of economic activity in the United States has been directly affected by such involvement as government spending and regulatory activity. The percentage of that government activity was reduced in the 1980s as a result of significant deregulation, especially in airlines, trucking, and telecommunications. Activity not influenced by government regulation is considered to be in the private sector.

The principal mechanisms of government influence in the American economy are regulation and antitrust policy. Antitrust policy in the United States is spelled out in four main acts: the Sherman Act, the Clayton Act, and Federal Trade Commission Act, and the Celler–Kefauver Act. These date from the late 1800s and are subject to varying court interpretations over time.

The American government, in spite of important social programs, does not play a major role in the redistribution of income. Some, however, would argue that the actual impact is greater than the visible impact mostly because of difficulties measuring the effect of in-kind transfers. Certainly the redistributive role of the American government in the American economy is less than that typically found in other industrialized market economies.

In recent years, interest has increased in the privatization of government activity. Privatization is controversial largely because of the relatively limited empirical evidence of its costs and benefits. In the American economy, privatization is generally achieved not through changes in ownership but through local government attempting to reduce costs through private contracting for services.

Key Terms

public sector	price takers	military–industrial complex
private sector	perfect markets	regulation
sole proprietorship	arbitrage	deregulation
partnership	imperfect competition	antitrust legislation
corporation	intermediaries	monopolization
product market	discrimination	monopolies
factor market	capital market	price fixing
market power	future prices	mergers
concentration ratio	financial intermediaries	external costs and benefits
competition	public goods	privatization

Notes

1. Milton Friedman, "Monopoly and Social Responsibility of Business and Labor," in Edwin Mansfield, ed., *Monopoly Power and Economic Performance*, 3rd ed. (New York: Norton, 1974), pp. 57–68.
2. Frederic Scherer, *Industrial Structure and Economic Performance*, 2nd ed. (Boston: Houghton Mifflin, 1980), p. 519.
3. Clifford Winston, "Economic Deregulation: Days of Reckoning for Microeconomists," *Journal of Economic Literature*, 31, 3 (September 1993), 1263–1289.
4. Milton Friedman, "Monopoly and Social Responsibility of Business and Labor," pp. 57–68.
5. William G. Shepherd, "Causes of Increased Competition in the U.S. Economy, 1939–1980," *Review of Economics and Statistics* (November 1982), 613–626.
6. See Scherer, *Industrial Market Structure*, pp. 68–70; James V. Koch, *Industrial Organization and Prices*, 2nd ed. (Englewood Cliffs, N.J.: Prentice-Hall, 1980), p. 181; and Morris Adelman, "Changes in Industrial Concentration," in Mansfield, *Monopoly Power and Economic Performance*, pp. 83–88.
7. Joe S. Bain, *Barriers to New Competition*, pp. 192–200; H. Michael Mann, "Seller Concentration, Barriers to Entry, and Rates of Return in Thirty Industries," *Review of Economics and Statistics*, 58 (August 1966), 296–307.
8. Leonard W. Weiss, "Quantitative Studies of Industrial Organization," in Michael D. Intrilligator, ed., *Frontiers of Quantitative Economics* (Amsterdam: North Holland, 1971); Leonard Weiss, "Concentration-Profits Relationship and Antitrust," in Goldschmidt et al., eds., *Industrial Concentration: The New Learning* (Boston: Little, Brown, 1974), pp. 184–233.
9. The Harberger results can be found in Arnold Harberger, "Monopoly and Resource Allocation," *American Economic Review*, 44 (May 1954), 77–87.
10. Anne Krueger, "The Political Economy of the Rent-Seeking Society," *American Economic Review*, 64 (June 1974), 291–303; Gordon Tullock, "The Welfare Cost of Tariffs, Monopolies, and Theft," *Western Economic Journal*, 5 (June 1967), 224–232; Harvey Leibenstein, "Allocative Efficiency vs. X-Inefficiency," *American Economic Review*, 56 (June 1966), 392–415.
11. Harold Demsetz, "Industry Structure, Market Rivalry, and Public Policy," *Journal of Law and Economics*, 16 (April 1973), 1–10.

12. Our discussion of the U.S. labor market and the figures cited are from the following sources: William Bowen and Orley Ashenfelter, eds., *Labor and the National Economy*, rev. ed. (New York: Norton, 1975); H. Gregg Lewis, *Unions and Relative Wages in the United States* (Chicago: University of Chicago Press, 1963); Stanley Masters, *Black–White Income Differentials* (New York: Academic, 1975); Cynthia Lloyd, ed., *Sex, Discrimination and the Division of Labor* (New York: Columbia University Press, 1975); Michael Boskin, "Unions and Relative Real Wages," *American Economic Review*, 62 (June 1972), 466–472; George Johnson, "Economic Analysis of Trade Unionism," *American Economic Review, Papers and Proceedings*, 65 (May 1975), 23–28; Albert Rees, *The Economics of Trade Unions* (Chicago: University of Chicago Press, 1963); C. J. Paisley, "Labor Union Effects on Wage Gains: A Survey of Recent Literature," *Journal of Economic Literature*, 18 (March 1980), 1–31; and Richard Freeman and James Medoff, "The Two Faces of Unionism," *The Public Interest*, 57 (Fall 1979), 73–80; and Ronald G. Ehrenberg and Robert S. Smith, *Modern Labor Economics*, 3rd ed. (Glenview, Ill.: Scott, Foresman, 1988); "Rising Wage Inequality in the United States: Causes and Consequences," *American Economic Review: Papers and Proceedings*, 84, 2 (May 1994), 10–33; "Lessons from Empirical Labor Economics: 1972–1992," *American Economic Review: Papers and Proceedings*, 83, 2 (May 1993), 104–121.

13. The original statement of the merit goods (wants) concept is found in Richard Musgrave, *The Theory of Public Finance* (New York: McGraw-Hill, 1959).

14. For a classic debate over the proper scope of government and "nongovernment," see Paul Samuelson, "The Economic Role of Private Activity," *A Dialogue on the Proper Economic Role of the State*, in Paul Samuelson, ed., *Readings in Economics*, 7th ed. (New York: McGraw-Hill, 1973), pp. 78–84; and George J. Stigler, "The Government of the Economy," *A Dialogue on the Proper Economic Role of the State*, ibid., 73–77; for a discussion of public choice, see Harvey S. Rosen, *Public Finance* 3rd ed. (Homewood, Ill.: Irwin, 1992), Ch. 7.

15. For more on the various explanations of the U.S. weapons procurement system, see James Kurth, "The Political Economy of Weapons Procurement: The Follow-On Imperative," *American Economic Review, Papers and Proceedings*, 62 (May 1972), 304–311.

16. Seymour Melman, *Pentagon Capitalism* (New York: McGraw-Hill, 1970); and Kurth, "The Political Economy of Weapons Procurement," pp. 304–311.

17. For Galbraith's view, see John Kenneth Galbraith, "Power and the Useful Economist," *American Economic Review*, 63 (March 1973), 1–11.

18. For a more moderate view of the power of the military–industrial complex, see Adam Yarmolinsky, "The Industrial–Military Complex: II," in Edwin Mansfield, ed., *Defense, Science, and Public Policy* (New York: Norton, 1968), pp. 42–43.

19. For suggestions on how to improve the current procurement system, see Carl Kaysen, "Improving the Efficiency of Military Research and Development" with comments by Paul Cherington, in Mansfield, *Defense, Science, and Public Policy*, pp. 114–131.

20. For arguments in favor of the fourth approach, see Friedman, "Monopoly and Social Responsibility of Business and Labor," pp. 57–68; and George Stigler and Claire Friedland, "What Can Regulators Regulate? The Case of Electricity," in Paul MacAvoy, ed., *The Crisis of the Regulatory Commissions* (New York: Norton, 1970), pp. 39–52.

21. These statistics are from Department of Commerce, *Historical Statistics of the United States: Colonial Times to 1970* (Washington, D.C.: Government Printing Office, 1975), Series N15–29, S86–94, 6416–469, Y505–521; and Clair Wilcox, *Public Policies Toward Business*, 3rd ed. (Homewood, Ill.: Irwin, 1966).

22. Wilcox, *Public Policies Toward Business*, Ch. 20.

23. Scherer, *Industrial Structure and Economic Performance*, p. 421.

24. The following discussion of regulation is based on these sources: Wilcox, *Public Policies Toward Business*, part III; Scherer, *Industrial Structure and Economic Performance*, Ch. 18; and Paul MacAvoy, "The Rationale for Regulation of Field Prices of Natural Gas," in MacAvoy, *The Crisis of the Regulatory Commissions*, pp. 152–168; Robert E. Litan and William D. Nordhaus, *Reforming Federal Regulation* (New Haven: Yale University Press, 1983); and Lawrence J. White, *Reforming Regulation* (Englewood Cliffs, N.J.: Prentice-Hall, 1981).

25. The first of these commissions was established in New England before the Civil War, with authority over the railroads, and in the Midwest in the 1870s. Commissions for the regulation of public utilities were set up only in the early twentieth century (1907); in some instances, public utility supervision was entrusted to the already established railroad commissions. Federal regulation was initiated first in 1887 with the Interstate Commerce Commission, the first major federal regulatory commission.

   State commissions in almost all states have jurisdiction over railroads, motor carriers, water, electricity, gas, and telephones, and about one-half have the authority to regulate urban transit, taxicabs, and gas pipelines. Commissioners are either elected or appointed by the governor of the state. The staffs of the commissions are generally small and are generally poorly funded compared to the legal staffs of the industries they regulate.

   There are five federal commissions. The Interstate Commerce Commission (established in 1887) regulates railroads, interstate oil pipelines, and interstate motor and water carriers. The Federal Power Commission (established in 1920) has jurisdiction over power projects and the interstate transmission of electricity and natural gas. The Federal Communications Commission (established in 1933) regulates interstate telephone and telegraph and broadcasting. The Securities and Exchange Commission (established in 1934) regulates securities markets. The Civil Aeronautics Board (established in 1938) supervises domestic and international aviation. These federal commissions are staffed by commissioners appointed by the U.S. president for terms of five to seven years, and their staffs range from 1000 to 2000 employees. In general, the professional staffs on the federal commissions are better paid and better qualified than their state counterparts, but their salaries are not competitive with those paid by the regulated industries.

26. Wilcox, *Public Policies Toward Business*, p. 326.

27. See, for example, the selections by Merton Peck (on transportation), Richard Caves (on air transport), and Paul MacAvoy and E. W. Kitch (on natural gas) in MacAvoy, *The Crisis of the Regulatory Commissions*, pp. 72–93, 131–151, 152–186.

28. This discussion is based on Roy J. Ruffin and Paul R. Gregory, *Principles of Microeconomics*, 3rd ed. (Glenview, Ill.: Scott, Foresman, 1988), Ch. 14; Elizabeth E. Bailey, "Price and Productivity Change Following Deregulation: The U.S. Experience," *The Economic Journal*, 96 (March 1986), 1–17. See also C. Winston, "Conceptual Developments in the Economics of Transportation," *Journal of Economic Literature*, 23 (1985), 57–94; T. Keeler, *Railroads, Freight, and Public Policy* (Washington, D.C.: Brookings, 1983); A. F. Friedlander and R. H. Spady, *Freight Transport Regulation* (Cambridge, Mass.: M.I.T. Press, 1981); Clifford Winston, "Economic Deregulation: Days of Reckoning for Microeconomists," *Journal of Economic Literature*, 31, 3 (September 1993), 1263–1289.

29. This discussion is based on Scherer, *Industrial Structure and Economic Performance*, Ch. 19 and pp. 469–494; A. D. Neale, *The Antitrust Laws of the United States of*

America (Cambridge, England: The University Press, 1962), pp. 2–5; Eugene Singer, *Antitrust Economics* (Englewood Cliffs, N.J.: Prentice-Hall, 1968), Ch. 2; Marshall C. Howard, *Antitrust and Trade Regulation* (Englewood Cliffs, N.J.: Prentice-Hall, 1983); Oliver Williamson, *Markets and Hierarchies: Analysis and Antitrust Implications* (New York: The Free Press, 1975); and Howard, *Antitrust and Trade Regulation.*

30. The landmark cases were the Standard Oil and American Tobacco cases of 1911. In both instances, the courts ruled that these companies, both accounting for some 90 percent of industry output, should be dissolved into smaller companies. The courts' reasoning, however, was that Standard Oil and American Tobacco were in violation of the Sherman Act not because they accounted for such a large share of industry output (that is, not because they were monopolies), but because they had engaged in "unreasonable" restraints of trade. The implication of this ruling was that if these companies had behaved better toward their competitors, they would not have been held in violation of the Sherman Act. This so-called rule of reason was the prevailing interpretation of the Sherman Act until 1945. The rule of reason was upheld in 1920 with the U.S. Steel case. The company controlled over half of industry output yet had not treated its competitors unfairly or sought to control steel prices. In this case, the courts upheld the rule of reason, stating that the law does not make mere size or the existence of unexerted power an offense.

31. This discussion is based on material in Wilcox, *Public Policies Toward Business*, Ch. 11; and Mansfield, *Monopoly Power and Economic Performance*, pt. II.

32. These conclusions are from Simon Whitney, *Antitrust Policies*, Vol. II (New York: Twentieth Century Fund, 1958), p. 429; summarized in Wilcox, *Public Policies Toward Business*, p. 281.

33. Richard Musgrave, "National Economic Planning: The U.S. Case," *American Economic Review, Papers and Proceedings*, 67 (February 1977), 50–54; see also R. D. Norton, "Industrial Policy and American Renewal," *Journal of Economic Literature*, 24, 1 (March 1986), 1–40.

34. Edwin Mills, "Economic Incentives in Air-Pollution Control," in Marshall Goldman, ed., *Controlling Pollution: The Economics of a Cleaner America* (Englewood Cliffs, N.J.: Prentice-Hall, 1967), pp. 100–108.

35. See, for example, Morton Paglin, "The Measurement and Trend of Inequality: A Basic Revision," *American Economic Review*, 65 (September 1975), 598–609; and Edgar Browning, "The Trend Toward Equality in the Distribution of Income," *Southern Economic Journal*, 43 (July 1976), 912–923.

36. These figures are from Department of Commerce, *Historical Statistics of the United States*, series G; and *Statistical Abstract of the U.S.*

37. Paglin, "The Measurement and Trend of Inequality," pp. 598–609.

38. Joseph Pechman and Benjamin Okner, *Who Bears the Tax Burden?* (Washington, D.C.: Brookings, 1974).

39. Browning, "The Trend Toward Equality," pp. 912–923. Also see Edgar Browning and William R. Johnson, *The Distribution of the Tax Burden* (Washington, D.C.: American Enterprise Institute, 1979).

40. For background, see Janet Rotherberg Pack, "Privatization of Public Sector Services in Theory and Practice," *Journal of Policy Analysis and Management*, 6 (1987), 523–540; John B. Donahue, *The Privatization Decision* (New York: Basic Books, 1989); a useful summary of the American experience can be found in Richard L. Worsnop, "Privatization," *Congressional Quarterly Researcher* (November 13, 1992), 979–999.

Recommended Readings

A. Traditional Sources

F. M. Bator, "The Simple Analytics of Welfare Maximization," *American Economic Review*, 47 (March 1957), 22–59.

———, "The Anatomy of Market Failure," *Quarterly Journal of Economics*, 72 (August 1958), 351–379.

H. G. Lewis, *Unionism and Relative Wages in the United States* (Chicago: University of Chicago Press, 1963).

Paul MacAvoy, ed., *The Crisis of Regulatory Commissions* (New York: Norton, 1970).

B. Product Markets

William J. Baumol, John C. Panzar and Robert D. Willig, *Contestable Markets and the Theory of Industry Structure* (New York: Harcourt Brace Jovanovich, 1982).

Oliver Williamson, *The Economic Institutions of Capitalism* (New York: The Free Press, 1985).

C. Factor Markets

Ronald Ehrenberg and Robert Smith, *Modern Labor Economics* 3rd ed. (Glenview, Ill.: Scott Foresman, 1988).

Richard B. Freeman, "Unionism Comes to The Public Sector," *Journal of Economic Literature* 24, 1 (March 1986), 41–86.

"Lessons from Empirical Labor Economics: 1972–1992," *The American Economic Review: Papers and Proceedings*, 83, 2 (May 1993), 104–121.

James B. Rebitzer, "Radical Political Economy and the Economics of Labor Markets," *Journal of Economic Literature*, 31, 3 (September 1993), 1394–1434.

D. Government and the Economy

Andrew B. Abel and Ben S. Bernanke, *Macroeconomics* (New York: Addison-Wesley, 1992).

Douglas H. Blair and Robert A. Pollack, "Rational Collective Choice," *Scientific American*, 249, 2 (August 1983), 88–95.

John B. Donahue, *The Privatization Decision* (New York: Basic Books, 1989).

Frank Levy and Richard J. Murname, "U.S. Earning Levels and Earnings Inequality: A Review of Recent Trends and Proposed Explanations," *Journal of Economic Literature* 30, 3 (September 1992), 1333–1381.

N. Gregory Mankiw, "Symposium on Keyneseian Economics Today," *Journal of Economic Literature*, 7, 1 (Winter 1993), 3–82.

Robert Moffitt, "Incentive Effects of the U.S. Welfare System: A Review," *Journal of Economic Literature* 30, 1 (March 1992), 1–61.

Janet Rotherberg Pack, "Privatization of Public Sector Services in Theory and Practice," *Journal of Policy Analysis and Management*, 6 (1987), 523–540.

Joseph Pechman, *Who Paid the Taxes, 1966–85?* (Washington, D.C.: Brookings Institution, 1985).

Harvey S. Rosen, *Public Finance* 3rd ed. (Homewood, Ill.: Irwin, 1992).

F. M. Scherer and David Ross, *Industrial Market Structure and Economic Performance*, 3rd ed. (Boston: Houghton Mifflin, 1990).

Eugene Singer, *Antitrust Economics* (Englewood Cliffs, N.J.: Prentice-Hall, 1968).

Don E. Waldman, ed., *The Economics of Antitrust* (Boston: Little, Brown, 1986).

Leonard Weiss and Michael Klass, eds., *Regulatory Reform: What Actually Happened* (Boston: Little, Brown, 1986).

Clifford Winston, "Economic Deregulation: Days of Reckoning for Microeconomists," *Journal of Economic Literature*, 31, 3 (September 1993), 1263–1289.

Richard L. Worsnop, "Privatization," *Congressional Quarterly Researcher* (November 13, 1992), 979–999.

9

Variants of Capitalism: Mature Economies

This chapter looks at five major variants of the market capitalist model—France, Great Britain, Germany, Japan, and Sweden. These countries exhibit certain distinguishing features that make them especially interesting to comparative economists. This chapter discusses these features and presents background material about these countries so that their special characteristics can be placed in proper historical and analytical context. The structural features of these countries are presented in Table 9.1.

All of these countries are market capitalist systems in which the market is the primary mechanism for resource allocation, private ownership is the dominant form of property holding, and material incentives are used to motivate people. Moreover, all are mature capitalist economies, and the state plays important but varying roles.

If the economies of these countries are broadly similar, what are their distinguishing characteristics? France's is a market capitalist system in which a national economic plan has been used to influence resource allocation. The French plan is a form of noncoercive or **indicative planning**. French indicative planning is an attempt to combine market and plan in a capitalist economic system.

Great Britain is an example of **mature capitalism**. The industrial revolution began in Great Britain in the eighteenth century, so the nation has had almost 300 years of experience as an industrialized capitalist country. Great Britain has experimented with state ownership of basic industries, with redistribution of income through the tax system, with the provision of public services by the state, and with income policies to stabilize the economy. British politics is characterized by strong differences in economic policy between the two dominant political parties that have held power alternately over recent decades. Labour Party governments have favored public ownership and an aggressive government role in income redistribution. Conservative governments have favored privatization, deregulation, and a nonaggressive state role in redistributing income.

Germany, which describes itself as a **social market economy**, is of interest because of its attempts to combine market allocation with worker participation and government intervention to achieve social goals. The strong performance of the postwar German economy makes the social market economy model especially

TABLE 9.1   Selected Structural Features of Developed Capitalist Variants

Feature	France	Great Britain	Germany[a]	Japan	Sweden	U.S.A.
Per capita GNP, 1991, in U.S. $	20,380	16,550	23,650	26,930	25,110	22,240
Percent of population urban, 1991	74	89	86	77	84	75
Percent of GDP derived from industry, 1991	37	44	39	42	34	35
Government expenditure as a percent of GNP, 1988	43.7	38.2	32.5	15.8	44.2	25.3
Gross domestic investment as a percent of GDP, 1991	21	16	21	32	17	15
Average annual rate of inflation, 1980–91	5.7	5.8	2.8	1.5	7.4	4.2
Defense expenditure as a percent of total central government expenditure, 1991	6.3	11.1	8.3	—	6.3	21.6

[a]West Germany prior to unification

Source: All data are from World Bank, *World Development Report 1993* (New York: Oxford University Press, 1990), Tables 1–32.

interesting. Moreover, the merger of the former East and West Germanys presents important new challenges to the united Germany.

The Japanese economy has achieved the highest growth rate among the major industrialized capitalist countries. Japan's strong economic performance has made it one of the most important industrialized economies in the world. In considering the sources of Japanese economic success, we look at the role of Japanese lifetime-employment policy, state industrial policy in promoting new industries, and government capital formation programs.

The Swedish economy is a prominent example of what is generally termed the **welfare state**. Sweden appears to combine efficiency with an egalitarian distribution of income and benefits typical of socialist ideology. However, there have been important changes in Sweden over the past decade.

This discussion of those different economies and their economic systems places special emphasis on the differing systemic and policy features that have interested Western observers. Although an understanding of overall economic performance is important, this chapter does not dwell on the details of yearly shifts.

France: Indicative Planning in a Market Economy

The post-World War II French economic system is viewed as a significant test of whether national economic planning and a democratic capitalist society can be effectively and harmoniously combined.[1] For those who believe that some or all of the ills of capitalism require some form of state intervention, the French example has been cited on both practical and theoretical grounds.[2] French planning uses noncoercive intervention while preserving the market economy. Moreover, the French planning mechanism has remained modest in size, an important issue raised by Hayek and others in the socialist controversy.

It is ironic that our primary interest in the French economy centers on its indicative planning, for there has been a significant decline in French involvement in planning since the late 1960s. Nevertheless, during the period when the French planning system was being structured and restructured (1949–1969), the economy grew at an average annual rate of 4.7 percent, a very good performance by international standards.[3] Did the French economy achieve this substantial economic progress after the war because or in spite of national economic planning? What is the nature of French indicative planning in the 1990s?

France: The Setting

Countries, as representatives of economic systems, possess features, such as location, size, and cultural and historical characteristics, that influence the economic system. Although such features frequently cannot be isolated and measured, they may be of great importance in molding the course of events. France, a country whose history and traditions bore heavily on its acceptance of national economic planning, is certainly a case in point.

France is a major world power with a long, rich, and varied history. It has a population of roughly 55 million people residing predominantly in urban areas and has a total land area slightly larger than twice the size of the state of Colorado. Although France enjoys excellent agricultural conditions, agriculture represents a relatively small proportion of gross domestic product (as is the case in most developed countries). By international standards, France is a developed country with a high standard of living and a record of relatively high economic growth.

To understand the French economic system, one must understand the French political system. France is a republic whose president is elected to serve for a term of seven years. The president in turn appoints the prime minister. The National Assembly or Parliament is elected.

Although one might look to earlier times to discover the roots of French thought on the appropriate economic role of the state, it is worth emphasizing that during the Fifth Republic, under the leadership of Charles De Gaulle (1958–1969), the power of the French presidency was substantially enhanced.[4] This power has been retained during the post–De Gaulle era.

During the 1970s, with growing concern for inflation, unemployment, and balance-of-payments problems, austerity was imposed under the leadership of Georges Pompidou and Valéry Giscard d'Estaing. This was a period of declining interest in planning as a mechanism to guide recovery. France became less and less interesting as a case of indicative planning.[5]

In the spring of 1981 François Mitterrand, a socialist, was elected to the French presidency, and a socialist majority was sent to the French National Assembly. Mitterrand was reelected in 1988. Although one might have expected a socialist government to be more sympathetic to planning, it is not clear that this has been the case. Nevertheless, planning is still evident in France, the tenth plan terminated in 1992, the proposed year of unification of the European market.

France and Indicative Planning: The Background

France has a long history of a strong state and acceptance of a strong role for the state in management of the nation's economic affairs.[6] This historical experience contrasts sharply with that of the United States, Canada, and Great Britain, where it is an article of faith, at least in most business circles, that the least government is the best government.[7] French history was an important element in the widespread postwar acceptance of planning. Indeed, the early development of the plan by M. Jean Monnet (the founder of the European Common Market) was predicated on acceptance of planning by influential business leaders.

The French tended to view their economy in a rather long-term perspective, emphasizing the primary importance of balanced economic growth and development.[8] Faith in the ability of the unfettered market mechanism to produce economic harmony is not strong. Even within the framework of national economic planning, the French have been willing to utilize mechanisms that are often viewed with skepticism in other countries. For example, the mixed enterprise in which the state and the private sector combine their entrepreneurship and managerial skills has a long history in France. The pattern of interchanging executives between the public and the private sector has facilitated a better understanding of the problems in each sector.[9] The recruitment of top executives for the public sector from the upper echelons of management creates a managerial style very different from that found in Britain.[10]

Although those characteristics of the French economy facilitated the introduction and operation of a planning mechanism, such a step represents both practical and theoretical problems for the market economy. Witness, for example, the widespread discussion generated by proposals to introduce mild forms of planning in the United States.[11] Although the U.S. case may be exceptional, the path to national economic planning in capitalist economic systems has generally been slow and unsure. Moreover, it has proved difficult to test the extent to which planning has in fact influenced economic outcomes.

The basic case for indicative planning—the theoretical underpinning of the French system—rests on the manner in which information guides the economic system in the face of uncertainty.[12] Specifically, it has been argued that decision making can be improved if some agency (a "planning" agency) collects, processes, and disseminates information to any and all decision makers. The mechanisms for plan implementation are also important. Indicative planning is nonauthoritarian in the sense that no directive targets are issued and that economic agents are encouraged to pursue plan objectives via indirect incentives. The nonauthoritarian nature of indicative planning has been viewed as a major positive feature.

French planning began immediately after World War II, when countries such as England and West Germany were dismantling the controls and planning of the war years. As in other countries that began to experiment with planning at that time, the planning experiment in France subsequently underwent significant change, especially as the economy moved away from the immediate postwar problems toward a period of more "normal" operation. The first plan, begun in 1946 and subsequently extended to 1952, was a transitional plan and was closely associated with the name of Jean Monnet.[13] Monnet headed the General Planning Commissariat, working closely with the Marshall Plan, and utilized direct controls to manipulate economic activity.

French planning has changed significantly over the years, largely in response to the changing needs of the French economy. The changes, however, have been mostly in terms of *goals* and the *means* to achieve these goals rather than in the administrative machinery of the plan. Each plan on a five-year horizon has had a theme. The first plan focused on the development of key sectors: transportation, agricultural machinery, steel, electricity, coal, and cement. The second five-year plan emphasized the improvement of productivity. The third was devoted to economic growth and the foreign sector. The plans thereafter departed from the traditional sectoral emphasis and focused instead on improved economic performance in general. They also placed strong emphasis on social goals: lessening income differentials, redressing regional economic imbalances, and so on.

Vera Lutz, a critic of French planning, argues that one should really distinguish between the Monnet and the post-Monnet plans. The former, she argues, were expedient at the time and were based on direct controls. The latter, on the other hand, relied on the indirect mechanisms for implementation that ultimately became the hallmark of French planning.[14]

The Plan Mechanism

The organizational arrangements of French planning remained relatively unchanged from after World War II until the early 1980s, at which time substantial modifications were made. Because the pre-1980s arrangements are important to any assessment of the planning system, they shall be discussed before recent changes are noted.

Historically, French planning relied on an unpretentious institutional structure to forge a social consensus among various interest groups, such as business, trade unions, and regions. The main planning organ was the General Planning Commissariat, a small and relatively modest operation. Under the General Planning Commissariat, some thirty "vertical" and "horizontal" **modernization commissions** were responsible for sectoral projections. The "vertical" commissions dealt with various sectors of the economy, whereas the "horizontal" commissions dealt with economy-wide matters such as finance. Consultation, a major feature of the French system, was achieved through the work of the Economic and Social Council.

The plan itself was based on a series of alternative projected growth paths for the French economy, including major state priorities, which were formulated by the Planning Commissariat. Subsequent elaboration was developed by the modernization commissions with help from various state agencies. In essence, the French plan consisted of broad sectoral growth targets related to input, output, investment, and productivity. These targets were derived from macroeconomic projections for the aggregate economy and included state objectives, but they also recognized important constraints, such as the foreign sector.

Characteristics of Indicative Planning

The traditional French plan, unlike its Soviet counterpart, does not order firms to do things. The plan is indicative; it offers suggested targets at a fairly high level of aggregation. The plan projections are a source of information that firms can use, along with traditional market signals, to make decisions. Why would a firm be guided by the plan if it is not compulsory? The mechanisms for plan implementation, both direct and indirect, are another distinctive feature of French planning.[15]

The state has two major vehicles for influencing economic outcomes: the budget and public ownership. Not all forms of investment that flow through the state are governed by the national economic plan. Furthermore, the degree of control the plan agencies exert over state investment is not uniform.[16] Plan control over investment in large public enterprises is considerable, but such control is limited in the case of local government investments.

It is difficult to untangle the budgetary process to measure the impact of the state on investment, especially in light of various changes over the years.[17] Investment by the state (not including public enterprises) has averaged roughly 12 percent of aggregate investment (compared with 20 to 23 percent in Great Britain). French public investment, moreover, has been concentrated in key sectors such as housing.

Like state investments, public ownership in France is concentrated in key sectors such as banking, coal, gas and electricity, transportation, and auto and aircraft production. As a producer, consumer, and financier, the state sector has influenced economic activity in both the public sector and the private sector through its control over the availability of credit and of crucial inputs such as electricity, the regional distribution of resources, and tax incentives.

Plan fulfillment depends on whether firms follow the plan. The logic of the plan suggests that the plan is designed to achieve the best possible economic performance that is consistent with intersectoral balance. Thus a firm, especially a large firm, operating in accordance with plan directives should be able to do *its* best and to avoid unpredictable constraints. This, if true, is an attractive feature of French planning: the creation of a predictable and harmonious business environment.[18] Evidence suggests that French firms in fact paid attention to the plans, especially firms important enough to know that the plan may influence their operation.

Monnet argued that a plan is likely to be carried out if those who will be implementing it have a voice in its creation.[19] This aspect of the French system is exemplified by the administrative structure of planning, especially the modernization commissions where the diverse interests of labor, the state, and business come together to forge a consensus. The relationship between business and the state in France has fostered an interchange of ideas and understanding where there would otherwise be antagonism.

Events of the 1970s (especially external shocks to the economy) resulted in a loss of interest in planning. The election of a socialist president in 1981 presented an opportunity for renewed planning activity. Although domestic economic problems and external events continued to keep planning on a back burner throughout the 1980s, interest in planning reappeared.[20]

In the early 1980s, a special commission was set up to assess the French planning system. While this assessment was in progress, external economic conditions resulted in terminating the eighth five-year plan (1981–1985) and replacing it with an interim plan (1982–1983). (Ultimately there was a new, ninth, five-year plan for the years 1984 to 1988.) Although the interim plan reflected the socialist government's policy of expanding the role of the public sector, conditions created by the worldwide recession took priority. French economic policies, therefore, were designed primarily to address the realities of weak foreign markets, inflation, and unemployment. These issues, along with the matter of European integration, remained important in the tenth plan (1988–1992).

The socialist government created a Ministry for Economic Planning and Regional Policy in 1981. Next, a National Planning Commission was established to bring together, in addition to the Minister of Planning, interest groups such as trade unions, regions, and employers for the purpose of spelling out plan priorities and methods of plan fulfillment. Along with these organizational changes, procedural changes were introduced. The new planning process distinguishes between identification of plan objectives and designation of the methods by which plan objectives will be achieved. The first phase places new emphasis on realistic macroeconomic projections; the second is concerned with such mechanisms as regional development, technological advancement, and so forth.

Another change of the 1980s was that regional plans were developed and incorporated into the national plan. In addition, contracts became an important mechanism for achieving plan fulfillment. One might argue that the recent changes were more an attempt to revitalize planning than to change its basic nature. However, the organizational framework of French planning clearly had undergone change. The notion of achieving objectives that are spelled out in a national consensus was given new force through the use of contractual arrangements. Moreover, in addition to emphasizing better planning in a number of dimensions, the arrangements of the 1980s harmonized regional and national objectives.

Has French Planning Worked?

The features that have made French planning attractive to many, especially its apparent consistency with the values of a Western pluralistic society, would be of little value if the plan did not work. Most observers of the post–World War II French economy would argue that in spite of some problems, the French economic record has generally been very good. Did indicative planning contribute to that performance?

There are many reasons why it is difficult to assess the impact of the French planning system on economic performance. However, three major issues stand out.

First, the planning system has changed in many ways. In the 1950s planners were concerned with sectoral goals in what was almost a developmental context. During the 1960s the plan grew more sophisticated and plan objectives broadened. By the 1970s, especially under conservative leadership, interest in planning waned. During that period traditional economic difficulties such as inflation, unemployment, and trade deficits were countered largely via traditional monetary and fiscal policy.[21] Market allocation was strengthened through the reduction of controls, less emphasis on the public sector, and more attention to the development of efficient capital markets. The 1970s was an era of reduced state intervention and of movement toward an **industrial policy**.

Although considerable attention was paid to changing the planning arrangements in the 1980s, the need to resolve macroeconomic problems overshadowed improvement of the planning system.

A second and closely related issue is the effectiveness of planning. Some observers argue that French planning has been of limited importance, especially in recent years, because planning is poorly done.[22] Only limited amounts of information are used to generate the plan, and plan objectives (consisting of single projections) are much too simplistic. Furthermore, this sort of information has been of little value to industrial firms, even state-owned firms, operating independently of state control. Finally, the 1970s witnessed declining coordination in the business sector, further reducing the potential usefulness of the plan to decision makers.

The 1980s saw renewed emphasis on plan execution. Procedures were established to monitor plan performance. In addition, both public and private sectors became more involved in monitoring plan performance and received more information. Even so, available evidence suggests that these changes have done little to enhance the importance of planning.

Third, in a mixed economy like that of France, what indicators can we use to judge the effectiveness of the plan? When specific results are examined—for example, sectoral growth targets in the 1950s—there tends to be considerable difference between plan and actual achievement. On this basis, plan performance is rather poor. Other observers, however, focus on more general outcomes, such as the rate of growth of output, arguing that the plan must have had something to do with improved growth.

One way to look at the impact of the plan is to ask business firms, both public and private, to what extent their decision making has been influenced by plan directives. Hans Schollhammer found that, on balance, French firms did consider the plan important, especially in providing useful information and creating a dynamic business environment.[23] The firms that paid attention to the plan were for the most part large, capital-intensive, and domestically owned. One could argue that this evidence, in combination with good economic performance in the postwar years, presents a circumstantial case in favor of the French planning system.

Another test is to examine the record of plan fulfillment. Have the mechanisms of plan implementation been so strong and the targets so realistic that plan fulfillment has generally been achieved?

In a study of plan fulfillment, Vera Lutz, a critic of French planning, argues that, on balance, the achievement record of French planning has been dismal.[24] In fact, Lutz argues, the French system of planning is not central planning at all. It is little more than "collective forecasting." Lutz's examination of the plan target and achievement data suggests that the degree to which targets were achieved has varied widely from one target to another and, overall, has probably not improved over time.

In another major study of French planning, John J. McArthur and Bruce R. Scott argue that "the national planning process did have some influence on the *general* measures and macroeconomic programs used by the state to shape the economic environment in which companies and industries worked."[25] McArthur and Scott contend that the plan mechanism has influenced economic outcomes through its *indirect* use of state influence. They suggest that the plan has had very little direct influence on corporate decision making, nor, they claim, has it had indirect influence through the state's manipulation of selective means of control. They argue that this lack of influence can be explained at least in part by the inability of the planning mechanism to adapt to the changing needs and circumstances of the French economy.

A survey by J. R. Hough suggests that the planning system may have been a factor creating a favorable climate for the good economic growth that France has achieved, at least prior to the energy crisis of the 1970s.[26]

In a survey of the literature on indicative planning and its relationship to the French experience, Saul Estrin and Peter Holmes argue that in spite of its theoretical basis, planning in France "lost practically all practical relevance after 1965."[27] Thus Estrin and Holmes emphasize the growing lack of interest in planning, poor planning, and inadequate mechanisms to implement plans.

A useful consensus on the French experience is provided in a study by Stephen S. Cohen.[28] Cohen points out that when economic progress is rapid, it is easy to be generous in interpreting the economic impact of planning. Although we have stressed improved French economic performance, that record changed for the worse after the 1970s. It may be that the plan mechanism did not adapt from its original objective of postwar recovery to the needs of what Cohen describes as "general resource allocation planning." With adverse macroeconomic conditions, the French government turned to traditional techniques for manipulating economic activity. Failure of those economic policies, combined with growing lack of interest in planning, resulted in a virtual halt in plan adaptation.[29]

Have the reforms of the 1980s changed the importance of planning in the French economy? Martin Cave suggests that pessimism is appropriate.[30] Cave notes that many of the reforms of the 1980s (for example, the National Planning Commission) have simply not worked. Moreover, the Mitterrand government, preferring traditional macroeconomic tools, has not placed confidence in the plan.

Although indicative planning has maintained a low profile in the 1990s, contemporary interest does remain. But the difficulties of assessing the impact of indicative planning also remain, complicated by a growing need to understand both the political and economic forces in open economies.

During the 1970s, there was a marked slowdown in the growth performance of the French economy.[31] Moreover, unemployment rates roughly tripled between the early 1970s and the early 1990s.[32] The 1990s witnessed increased unemployment, reduced consumption and efforts to reduce imports and expand exports.

The initial years of the Mitterrand government witnessed a substantial increase in the role of government in the French economy. Beginning in late 1981 and early 1982, a policy of nationalization was announced, especially in relation to the large industrial trusts where state involvement was already substantial. Substantial nationalization took place in the banking sector as well.[33]

In a study of the early years of the Mitterrand government, Bela Balassa notes that the public sector share "has risen from zero to 71 percent in iron ore, from 1 to 79 percent in iron and steel, from 16 to 66 percent in other metals, from 16 to 52 percent in basic chemicals, and from zero to 75 percent in synthetic fibers."[34] This certainly constitutes a trend toward greater government involvement in the French economy, evident even in the 1970s. For example, total government expenditure as a proportion of gross domestic product grew from 36.7 percent in 1960–1962 to 45.6 percent in 1977–1979. This growth in government share is comparable to that experienced by Great Britain over the same period but is well below that of the United States, where the government share grew from 28.5 percent to 33.9 percent. During the period from 1960–1962 to 1977–1970, real public expenditure in France grew at an average annual rate of 6.22 percent.[35]

Great Britain: Maturity, Instability, and Income Policy

Rightly or wrongly, the postwar French economy has carried an image of success, at least as compared with its historical performance. In contrast, Britain projected an image of poor economic performance, called the "British disease." Britain's classification as a capitalist welfare state derives from general acceptance of the public provision of services such as medical care, highly progressive taxes, and the nationalization of important sectors of the British economy.[36] Postwar British economic performance was poor until the 1980s.[37]

The election of a Conservative government under the leadership of Margaret Thatcher in 1979 was a pivotal point in contemporary British economic history. British economic performance improved in the 1980s under a package of Conservative economic reforms focusing on deregulation, privatization, incentives, and a redefined role for trade unions. In effect, these reforms were designed to undo the welfare state. It is difficult to separate the effects of these policies from those of other events, such as the discovery and exploitation of North Sea oil and gas. It is unclear whether the replacement of Margaret Thatcher by John Major in the early 1990s will lead to significant changes in "Thatcherism."

Britain is neither a planned economy nor a socialist system, according to our definition. The role of the state is significant but not exceptional by European standards (see Table 9.1). Britain is a mature economy—the first to experience industrialization in the eighteenth century. It remains at a high level of development in terms of the structure of production, urbanization ratios, and demographic characteristics.[38] Other economies in Western Europe and North America have well surpassed Great Britain in terms of per capita income. Thus *maturity* refers to Britain's longer experience with economic development.

Comparative analysts who look at the British economy often do so for the wrong reasons—to study nationalization, public services, and sharply progressive taxes. These features are important components of the British economy, but they are not unique. Other economies resemble Britain in terms of nationalization, public services, and progressive taxes. We consider broader questions: In the long run, are maturity and stagnation an inevitable combination? Can a particular combination of economic and political forces account for Britain's inability to deal with maturity? (Although a full assessment of the 1980s and the 1990s may eventually change this focus on stagnation.)

Great Britain: The Setting

Great Britain is an island economy; its land area is slightly greater than Minnesota's. Britain's history of achievement and its rise to world power have not been matched by good economic performance in contemporary times. Much of the literature on the British economy focuses on the reasons for its relative decline in the postwar era relative to its West European neighbors.

Great Britain has a population of more than 57 million persons, roughly 89 percent of whom live in urban areas. Although Great Britain was the home of the Industrial Revolution and the source of much innovative industrial activity, the resource base of the economy is quite limited. Thus it is not surprising that in modern times, the fate of the British economy is very closely tied to performance in the foreign sector. The British economy is dominated by the service and industrial sectors. The agricultural sector contributes only a very small fraction of gross domestic product.

Great Britain has limited amounts of good agricultural land, and given its relatively large population, intensive land use is essential. Although Great Britain has substantial deposits of coal and iron ore, these deposits have been heavily exploited and are not of high quality. From the 1960s through the 1990s, attention has focused on the discovery of substantial reserves of oil and natural gas in the North Sea and on the extent to which these reserves can be utilized to sustain and improve British economic performance.

Background of the British Economy

Great Britain is an open economy, particularly vulnerable to external shifts over which it has no control. Problems in the foreign sector have been a key theme of the postwar period. As an indicator of the importance of the foreign sector to the British economy, the sum of merchandise imports and exports accounts for half of British gross domestic product, whereas the comparable figure for the United States is 15 percent.

The British concept of the state's role in economic affairs is very different from that prevailing in France.[39] France had experienced economic difficulties in the prewar years and was acutely aware of the need for economic recovery. Whatever the motivating force, the state would play an important role in the direction of the French economy, and planning was viewed as the appropriate mechanism. In Britain, however, in spite of substantial war damage, the immediate postwar emphasis was on preserving the independence of small business and on intervening in the economy only through fiscal and monetary policy. The Keynesian revolution convinced the British of the superiority of "demand management" over central economic planning. Though impossible to quantify, this attitude about the role of the state has been a factor in the divergent economic paths taken by France and Britain.

Britain has suffered from rather significant regional inequalities.[40] Regional inequalities always existed. Modernization has fostered urbanization, and the increased mobility of labor brought the problems of regional differences to the attention of policymakers and the public.

The British political structure is based on strong conservative and labor parties, both of which have a role in the parliamentary structure, thus providing a testing ground for the capitalist and socialist ideologies. Labor policy has been basically socialist, particularly on questions of nationalization and income distribution. But there is an erroneous tendency to associate socialism with planning, and that is completely contrary to the British socialist tradition. As Andrew Schonfield points out, "By 1948, the basic elements of modern planning were present in Britain as in no other major Western country."[41] But there it ended until the limited introduction of planning in the 1960s. The basic elements of planning to which Schonfield refers are the Development Councils set up in the late 1940s to exert state control over the private sector, the nationalized sectors, state ownership of the Bank of England, and the wartime experience with planning.[42] All could have been important elements in a comprehensive planning system, but with the advent of a Conservative government in 1951, national economic planning was not seriously discussed for more than a decade.

Probably the most important reason for the disinterest in planning was the British Labour Party's view of socialism, which was based on old-style ideological convictions that had no connection to modern economic planning. Furthermore, wartime planning was short-term crisis planning that had little to do with long-term planning of the entire economy. After the war, wartime controls were phased out, though the nationalized industries remained. However, nationalization did not mean planning. In postwar Britain the mechanism to coordinate economic activity was predominantly the market.

War damage in Britain (as in France, Germany, and Japan) was extensive. The war years called for special means to direct British economic activity toward the single purpose of military victory. During the transition to peace, wartime controls were largely replaced by market allocation, but there was growing concern for the health of the economy. In the middle and late 1950s, this concern became an obsession with poor economic performance.[43]

The British experience is, like that of France, a special case. It is a case for which the theoretical underpinning—the economics of maturity—is limited.[44] It is, however, interesting because it is a case that may ultimately be relevant for other mature economic systems.

The British Economy: The Early Postwar Era

When a market economy has been operating for some time under controls, release from those controls can create adjustment difficulties. Such was the case in the immediate postwar British economy. Although British economic performance was relatively good in the late 1940s and early 1950s, the roots of subsequent inadequate economic performance were evident even in these early years. Policy measures taken to offset the subsequent malaise were at best useless and at worst harmful.[45] What were the roots and the dimensions of the impending economic problems?

British economic problems of the 1950s and 1960s are now familiar. The most visible was a growing balance-of-payments deficit produced in large part by Britain's declining ability to compete in export markets and by its overextended aid program. This problem was combined with growing home demand for imports, a slackening though respectable rate of economic growth, and increasing regional inequalities surfacing through inadequate mobility of labor and growing unemployment. Rather than treat underlying causes, the British government chose to stimulate and stabilize economic growth through the macroeconomic policy of **demand management**. Subsequent evidence suggests that the experience was destabilizing—and sufficiently so for it to be described as a period of **"stop-go" policies**.[46] In a sense, however, it was a continuation of the immediate postwar concern for the short run and a neglect of long-run policy remedies.

The main explanations for the poor performance of the British economy in the first decade and a half after the war were inflexible supplies of labor, inadequate investment, poor distribution of investment in non–growth-producing areas, inability to move ahead technologically, the burden of progressive taxation, and a heavy defense burden. In addition, demand management was inept and contributed to poor performance. Attention has focused on the foreign sector, notably the growing pressure of imports, worsened by the declining role of sterling as a key world currency and the inability of Britain to maintain a strong competitive position in world export markets.

Many would consider these features symptoms rather than causes. True, the inability of exports to keep up with the growth of imports was obviously a factor in the balance-of-payments problems, but why this backsliding in the growth of exports? Above all, why was the British economy in the early postwar years unable to adapt to change? The British managerial structure in industry and the civil service power structure were both molded by tradition, which for years served in place of expertise. Trade unions, on balance, probably tended to be skeptical of technological change, seeing it as leading to unemployment. In short, the British economy proved incapable of adapting to its new role in the world economic community and to the new role of the British consumer, whose expectations were high in the 1950s.

The British Economy: Planning in the 1960s

Although the main elements of national economic planning were present in the immediate postwar British economy, the subject received no attention after the election of a Conservative government in 1951 and languished until 1961, when the Conservative government itself introduced a measure of planning into the British economy. Alarm over economic difficulties caused this policy shift, though the instigation of planning meant very little under Conservative guidance and continued to mean little under subsequent Labour leadership.

In a period of generally poor economic performance, a balance-of-payments crisis in 1961, and concern for the shape of future relations with the emerging European Economic Community, the Conservative government in 1962 established the National Economic Development Council.[47] Both labor and industry supported the idea of planning, though each had a different concept of what planning was. Both also shared a rather peculiar view that there must be an "arm's-length" relationship between the state and the plan. In addition to creation of the main plan organization, a professional staff was organized in the newly created National Economic Development Office. Economic development committees (initially about 30) were created to serve as a forum for planning discussions by leaders of labor, business, and government.

There were really two economic plans prepared for the 1960s. One, begun in 1962, was to govern the growth of the economy through 1966. The second plan, introduced in 1965 and abandoned in 1966, was to govern the growth of the economy through 1970. Both plans were essentially sectoral elaborations on a projected aggregate growth rate. Both were based on inadequate information and had no means of implementation. Both failed.

As Werner Z. Hirsch observes, the years that followed were not really years of economic planning. They were, at least until the mid-1970s, merely a continuation of the British government's effort to develop macroeconomic forecasting and use it to manipulate economic outcomes.[48] The culmination of this exercise was the passage, under a Labour government, of the Industry Act of 1975, which created the National Enterprise Board and Planning Agreements. The National Enterprise Board was provided with funds to assist private industry and also to extend the scope of the public sector. The Planning Agreements were designed to increase collaboration between the private sector and government and to coordinate government assistance.

The British experience with national economic planning was a failure. It did not alter economic outcomes in desired ways. However, as Hirsch points out, it might be more appropriate to consider the experience as one designed to improve communication, information flows, and decision making, not as an exercise in planning per se. What were some of the more general problems of this experience?

First, any planning system must have accurate and up-to-date information. Furthermore, the planners must be privy to state decision making and especially to the state budget, which is a crucial element in both plan formulation and execution in a pluralistic society. During the early years of planning, there was no close relationship between the planning body and those making the important decisions in government, especially the treasury. Planners were not even informed of government financial and budgetary decisions.

Second, there was a continuous struggle over how various interest groups—unions, corporations, and the state—would be represented. Even if one is skeptical about French claims of harmony, the contrast between the British and the French experiences is striking. In Britain, instead of a state plan formulated with the inputs of interest groups and with built-in incentives for fulfillment, the planning structure proved to be a bargaining arrangement with an arm's-length relationship between the state and the planners. Schonfield notes that "the crucial issue in modern capitalist planning, which is the relationship between public power and private enterprise, remains open and undecided in the British case."[49]

Third, powerful tools used for plan implementation in France—bank control over investment, tax incentives, and others—were not brought to bear in Britain. In the British case, the state did have a substantial degree of control over state spending and over investment, but both were directed within a traditional framework of monetary and fiscal policy, and neither had much to do with the plan.

Fourth, organizational change was a frequent and destabilizing element, especially with the shifts between Labour and Conservative governments. Throughout the 1960s traditional policy measures continued to be used. Discussion focused more on the necessity for formulating an incomes policy. Personal income rose much more rapidly than gross domestic product.[50] To bring the two in line and to stabilize economic activity, fiscal and monetary policy were used, along with efforts to reach agreements with labor and management concerning wage and price increases. Such policies were described as "stop-go" policies in the 1950s, as "income policies" in the 1960s, and as "demand management" thereafter.

The "British Disease"

Observers of the British economy have identified a number of specific problem areas—investment levels and patterns, a noncompetitive position in export markets, a high burden of taxation, problems in the allocation of labor, and the defense burden—as manifestations or causes of Britain's economic difficulties of the post-war era.

Investment was between 16 and 20 percent of gross domestic product, rising somewhat during the 1950s and 1960s. This ratio was well below that of France and West Germany. Furthermore, although government and public enterprises accounted for over 40 percent of domestic capital formation, there is little evidence that the government played any useful role in directing investment activity toward growth-producing sectors or regions. Moreover, the British capital stock per worker was below that of other countries.[51]

The British tax system has also been singled out as a cause of economic problems. Is the tax burden of the British economy unusually high? The answer to this question is probably yes. The progressive tax on personal income has been higher in Great Britain than in the United States, but it has been significantly lower in Britain than in the United States for corporations. Furthermore, the disparity between the British personal and corporate tax widened between the 1950s and the 1960s, a change that depressed personal incentives. The loss of skilled professionals (physicians, engineers, and so forth) to other countries during this period is certainly consistent with this interpretation. The outcome of steeply progressive taxation—namely, a lessening of income differentials—can be seen. Data for the mid-1960s suggest that the income distribution in Britain was narrower than that in West Germany, France, or even Yugoslavia.[52]

Compared with countries such as France, Germany, and Italy, the British economy did not do well in obtaining economic growth from increases in the quality and quantity of the labor force. At the same time, the process of collective bargaining in Britain contributed to low industrial productivity. Contrary to the popular concept that Britain was plagued by strikes, for the period 1955–1964 far fewer days (as a proportion of employment in key sectors) were lost to strikes in Britain than in France, West Germany, Italy, or the United States.[53] However, this statistic may simply indicate a greater willingness on the part of private and public management to accede to wage and work-rule demands.

The share of gross domestic product devoted to defense in Great Britain has been smaller than that in the United States but considerably larger than that in West Germany, France, or Italy. Although defense spending shifts resources away from other potential uses, it is not clear that this process depressed Britain's economic growth.

Nationalization and the Market

Britain, at least prior to the long Conservative rule, was frequently described as a socialist economic system.[54] This identification is based on the state's playing a substantial role through the budgetary process, nationalized firms in key sectors, and (to a lesser degree) the existence of national economic planning. Although there is no single indicator of the state's role in an economic system, most available evidence supports the view that the role of the state in the British economy has been smaller than generally perceived and does not justify classification of the system as socialist.

A study by Frank Gould of public expenditure patterns in a number of Western industrialized countries sheds light on the growth of government spending.[55] General government spending as a proportion of gross domestic product in the early 1960s was 37 percent for France, 33 percent for the United Kingdom, and 28.5 percent for the United States. By the late 1970s, these shares had risen to 46 percent, 45 percent, and 34 percent, respectively. During that period, real general government expenditures grew at an average annual rate of 6 percent in France, 4 percent in the United Kingdom, and almost 5 percent in the United States. Gould concludes that although state and local government spending assumed greater importance, the major explanation for the rise in general government spending can be found in the growth of government transfers. As a proportion of general government spending, government transfers during the late 1970s represented 60 percent in France, 47 percent in the United Kingdom, and 41 percent in the United States. Public expenditure patterns in the United Kingdom did not appear different from those of other industrialized countries at the aggregate level.

The public sector in Britain has played a substantial role in both savings and investment. Public saving as a proportion of aggregate saving in the economy fluctuated from a low of 21 percent (1960) to a high of 46 percent (1950) over the period 1950–1966. For the same years, public investment as a proportion of total investment fluctuated from a low of 31 percent (1950) to a high of 56 percent (1952) and in recent years has been just over 40 percent. Over those years, public savings has averaged 31 percent of total savings, while public investment has averaged 42 percent of total investment. Judged by the experience of other industrialized countries, these ratios are average or, at best, slightly above average.[56] Thus while the public sector is important in the British economy, the system remains essentially a decentralized market-type economy.

Although public enterprise is highly visible in some sectors of the British economy, its overall contribution is really not large.[57] Although the share of public corporations in the capital formation of the public sector has grown (largely at the expense of capital formation by the central government), the contribution of public enterprises to output remains small. In 1950, for example, the net output of the public enterprise sector in Britain accounted for just over 8 percent of British gross domestic product; the equivalent figure for 1967 was just over 7 percent.[58]

It is difficult to judge the overall success of the **nationalization** experience, because in most cases nationalization came about as a result of problems in the particular sectors involved. However, in spite of a continuing conflict among objectives —that is, between financial health and some interpretation of public service or benefit—it is not clear that the nationalized industries have been especially important in carrying out government economic policies.

The British Economy in the 1990s: An End to Stagnation?

Some have argued that the problems plaguing the British economy are unique to that system: the "British disease."[59] Others have argued that the British economy is in a phase of deindustrialization brought on by a decline in importance of manufacturing.[60]

Prior to the 1980s, Britain's economic performance was inferior to that of other industrialized European economies. This performance gap arguably stemmed from a poor labor–management system, poor work attitudes, the welfare state, and a management system incapable of growth and change. Those deeply ingrained forces resulted in low growth of productivity, an inability to compete in export markets, and a growing domestic demand for imports.

The assessment of British economic performance depends on the standards chosen for judgment. For example, the rate of growth of output in Britain in the 1960s was modest compared with other European economies. However, the same can be said for the United States. While most economies experienced problems in the 1970s, British performance was inferior relative to its European neighbors.[61]

Real gross domestic product per person grew by 2.4 percent per annum in Britain in the 1960s and by 1.9 percent in the 1970s. Comparable figures for the United States were 2.9 percent and 1.8 percent; for Japan they were 15.9 and 4.8 percent, respectively.[62] In the 1970s Britain lost ground. For example, in 1967, per capita gross domestic product of Great Britain was 86 percent of the OECD (Organization for Economic Cooperation, and Development) average; by 1978, the comparable figure was 72 percent.[63] Most countries experienced rapid inflation in the 1970s. However, the British rate of inflation generally exceeded the average in all OECD countries.

Turning to the question of labor–market performance, unemployment increased substantially in the 1970s, though not always to levels experienced in other countries. At the same time, wages increased without concomitant rises in labor productivity. The increasing unit labor costs made British exports less competitive abroad. This latter trend was partially offset by the declining value of the pound sterling. Between 1966 and 1977, the average annual increase in unit labor costs in Britain was 11.5 percent, while the comparable figures for Japan, France, and the United States were 8.1 percent, 7.7 percent, and 4.4 percent, respectively.[64] Britain's share in the world export of manufactures declined between 1951–1955 and 1973–1977 by 11.4 percent. While the United States experienced a comparable decline of 7 percent, West Germany's share grew by 8 percent, Japan's by 9.8 percent, and France's by 0.3 percent.[65]

What are we to conclude from such numbers? In a study of British economic performance in the 1970s, W. B. Reddaway concluded that the "disease" view is one-sided, saying that while other economies had done better, "Even in the less-satisfactory 1970s the economy made faster progress, in real terms, than in any pre-war decade, and the two previous decades might be regarded as a golden age."[66] At the same time, a Brookings study argued that in the decade between 1967 and 1978, Britain lost ground among OECD countries, markedly so after 1973. The authors conclude: "Britain's economic malaise stems largely from its productivity problem, whose origins lie deep in the social system."[67]

The discovery of North Sea oil in the late 1970s and early 1980s was an important factor limiting the bad economic news for Britain. This positive input has a finite life span, however, and continuing improvement must rest on more fundamental changes in the British economy.[68]

British economic policies of the 1980s clearly represented a significant departure from those of earlier years. Such a departure is difficult to evaluate in the short run, although the volume of literature on the subject is already large.[69]

It is not surprising that the conservative Thatcher government placed the blame for past failures squarely on past economic policies, especially the ambitious role of the government in the British economy. Accordingly, economic polices in the 1980s were designed to reduce the role of government—and to do so in four important areas.[70]

First, to improve market stability, a monetary policy designed to reduce the rate of inflation was instituted. A reduction in the rate of growth of the money supply was combined with less public-sector borrowing and less use of fiscal policy. This aspect of the Thatcher economic policy became known as a monetarist macroeconomic policy and has been compared with policies of the Reagan administration in the United States. It became known officially as the "Medium Term Financial Strategy."

Second, to reinstitute a competitive market economy, government controls and regulations were reduced. This policy, designed to stimulate private market initiative, applied to both the domestic and the international economy.

A third area of focus, related to the issue of a competitive market economy, involved "privatization," or the return of the public sector (especially nationalized industries) to private ownership and operation.

Finally, steps were taken to reduce the powers of trade unions and make them more responsive to their members.

The implementation of these policy measures in the 1980s and 1990s generated a discussion of great importance. Obviously, the Thatcher government found implementation difficult. At the same time, British economic performance improved, though critics suggest that the improvement will be short-lived.[71]

Have **deregulation** and the **privatization** of the British economy succeeded? To the extent that the British effort to deregulate can be described as an industrial policy, it has been selective and difficult to evaluate. As one author has noted, British policy is based in large part on the notion that private ownership is in itself sufficient to generate efficient markets; at the same time, however, selective government support has increased.[72] For example, the British government has attempted to invigorate regional policy, stimulate industries where advanced technology is important, and boost the quality of investment. There has also been substantial privatization of firms, ranging from British Petroleum in the early 1980s to British Airports, British Airways, and automobile producers in the mid- and late 1980s.

Traditionally, little empirical evidence has been available for assessing the impact of privatization. However, a recent study of a large number of newly privatized firms (including the British case) has revealed significant benefits. Specifically, those documented include important performance improvements (sales, profitability, and the like) and sustained employment.[73]

Cure of the British Disease?

When Margaret Thatcher took office in 1980, she promised to cure the British disease. Have her programs of privatization, welfare-state reduction, and monetary stability[74] had the desired effect?[75]

Table 9.2 summarizes the economic performance of Great Britain before and after Thatcher. From the 1950s throughout the 1970s, Great Britain has indeed had the sickest economy of Europe. The English malady, as the figures show, resulted from a lack of participation in Europe's phenomenal economic performance between 1950 and 1970. The British economy during this period was much like that of the United States.[76]

The 1970s and 1980s witnessed a decline in the European economy, which experienced a rise in unemployment and a slowdown in economic growth. In fact, the 1980s narrowed the differences among the economies so that Great Britain's rates of growth and unemployment matched those of Europe and the United States.

Germany: The Social Market Economy[77]

The economy of Germany, the Federal Republic of Germany, belongs in a discussion of the variants of capitalism for three reasons. The first is that the economic performance of the German economy is generally perceived to be the strongest of the major European countries throughout the postwar era. Germany emerged as the economic leader of Europe. The second reason is Germany's combination of free market forces with significant state intervention to achieve desired social goals. The Germans label this combination the **social market economy** *(soziale Marktwirtschaft)*.[78] The combination of good economic performance with some of the ideals of a welfare state make Germany an interesting case study. Third, unification of East and West Germany provides a unique historical example of the integration of a planned socialist economy into a market economy.

TABLE 9.2   Great Britain: Before and After Thatcher

	1950–1960	1960–1970	1970–1980	1980–1990
Growth of real GDP				
Great Britain	2.8	2.9	1.9	2.6
European Community	5.3	4.8	3.0	2.3
U.S.	3.3	4.2	2.8	2.6
Unemployment rate (end of decade)				
Great Britain	2.3	9.2	13.3	6.9
European Community	2.6	2.3	5.2	7.0
U.S.	5.5	8.2	8.1	5.2

Source: *World Tables 1976, Handbook of Economic Statistics,* various years.

Background

The Federal Republic of Germany *(Bundesrepublik Deutschland)* came into existence as a federal republic in the late 1940s as the three allied occupation forces (the United States, England, and France) converted their occupation zones into a unified economic area *(Vereinigtes Wirtschaftsgebiet)* in 1947. A 1948 currency reform established the three occupation zones as a single currency area; Soviet authorities kept the Soviet occupation zone out of this currency union. This event signaled the splitting of Germany into two Germanys. The Basic Law for the Federal Republic of Germany was passed on June 23, 1949. It established West Germany as a federal republic consisting of a federal government (with two legislative houses and a federal bureaucracy of ministries), the states *(Länder)*, and the local governments *(Gemeinden)*. The Federal Republic is a democracy with two major parties, the Christian Democratic Union (CDU) and the Socialist party (SPD), that have dominated the political scene throughout the postwar era. Along with governmental bodies and agencies, a number of quasi-state organizations such as labor unions, employer organizations, and chambers of commerce are active in economic affairs.

The collapse of the communist governments of Eastern Europe took place in 1989 and 1990 as it became clear that the Soviet Union under Gorbachev would not use military force to prop up unpopular communist regimes in the region. On May 18, 1990, the West German chancellor and the East German prime minister signed the State Treaty on the establishment of a monetary, economic, and social union between East and West Germany. East Germany became part of the Federal Republic, accepting the constitution and laws of the Federal Republic. The monetary union between East and West Germany included the East in the German mark currency area, and East German citizens were allowed to exchange their East German marks for German marks at generous exchange rates. East German citizens were given all voting rights, and the former East German states were represented in the German parliament, according to the same rules and requirements as the West German states.

The integration of the former German Democratic Republic into the Federal Republic of Germany created a large nation by European standards. These formerly distinct nations now occupy a land area of approximately 350,000 square kilometers and had, in 1990, a total population of 78 million. This means that Germany now has a land area roughly two-thirds that of France and a population some 22 million greater.

From an ethnic perspective, the population is almost entirely German; religious affiliation is split between Roman Catholic and Protestant.

Origins of the Social Market Economy

The social market economy originated in the immediate postwar years. Its intellectual heritage can be traced to the so-called Freiburg school of neoliberalism, headed by Walter Eucken and Alfred Muller-Armack.[79] The Freiburg school believed that the state should play an active role in ensuring the workability of the competitive market system and that the market system should serve as the major instrument for allocating resources. The state should be prepared to intervene, however, to achieve important social goals. Intervention should be compatible with the underlying market order; thus policies that disrupt the working of the market, such as direct orders and price freezes should be avoided.

The political background of the social market economy can be traced to the immediate postwar years of Allied occupation. The initial Allied policy was to continue the wartime controls. Until 1947 its objective was to enforce payment of reparations and to destroy the German military industry potential. When the emphasis turned to rehabilitation and recovery, direct controls were dismantled and the running of the country's economy was gradually returned to German hands. Ludwig Erhard, the minister of economics during the Adenauer years, was a strong proponent of the teachings of the Freiburg school. He strongly favored decontrol, deregulation, and the turning of economic decisions over to the impersonal hands of the market.[80] The choice of market versus plan was heatedly debated, with the social democrats favoring strong state planning. Memories of the chaos of the inflationary 1920s and the depression of the 1930s convinced many German politicians of the dangers of a market economy. Two major political events signaled the return to market resource allocation: the Currency Reform and Price Reform of June 1948 and the passage of the Basic Law (Grundgesetz) of the Federal Republic in May 1949, the latter serving as the German constitution. Those events established the principle of the sanctity of private property, which was to serve as the foundation of economic policy in the postwar era.

Unlike the United States, where national economic goals (with the exception of full employment) are unwritten, the economic goals of the Federal Republic have been written into law. These goals are price stability, a stable currency; full employment; balance-of-payments equilibrium; and stable economic growth. Three social goals, closely associated with the notion of the social market economy, are also identified: social equity, social security, and social progress. The social goals provided much of the basis for state intervention in economic affairs in the Federal Republic.[81]

Characteristics of the Social Market Economy

The principal features of the social market economy have evolved over the years. The first principle remains the sanctity of private property. The second is that resource allocation should follow the dictates of the market unless there is a serious conflict with national social objectives. There is no significant planning apparatus in Germany, and the macroplanning that does exist works through traditional monetary and fiscal policy, with principal emphasis on monetary policy as carried out by the central bank (the *Bundesbank*).[82] German fiscal policy coordinates the budgets of the different levels of government. Unlike the United States, where fiscal policy is the responsibility of the federal government, the German "stability law" sets up a Business Cycle Commission *(Konjunkturrat)* and Finance Planning Commission *(Finanzplanungsrat)* to coordinate the federal, state, and local budgets for fiscal policy goals. In the area of monetary policy, German policymakers were never strongly caught up in the Keynesian revolution. The Bundesbank is more politically independent than the American Federal Reserve, and a country that has experienced hyperinflation is more likely to see inflation as a monetary phenomenon. Monetarism has been a long-run feature of German macropolicy. The economic forecasting of macroeconomic variables is a relatively recent phenomenon and is done by semi-independent research institutes, which serve as consultants for the federal government. In fact, a striking characteristic of Germany is the virtual absence of planning machinery at the federal level.

In view of the emphasis the Freiburg school placed on the state's responsibility to ensure the workability of competition, it is informative to see what procompetition arrangements emerged. Government policies in favor of competition are based on the anticartel law of 1957.

The Law Against Limitations on Competition *(Gesetz gegen Wettbewerbsbeschränkungen)* differs from American antitrust legislation. First, the German law is quite specific, and the courts have played a relatively minor role in interpreting the law. Second, the German law singles out labor unions as a clear exception to the anticartel rule. Labor is recognized as being unlike other commodities, and labor's right to form unions is clearly affirmed. Third, the German law uses both the *Verbotsprinzip* (outright prohibition) and the option to correct market abuses. Horizontal cartel contracts and agreements are illegal outright, whereas firms that occupy market-dominating positions are merely subject to the control and scrutiny of the cartel authorities. The law provides detailed definitions of "market-dominating" firms based on market shares (33 percent single-firm concentration ratio), financial power, and barriers to entry. Cartel authorities are supposed to disallow mergers if the merger produces a market-dominating firm.

The Law Against Limitations on Competition allows exceptions and exemptions that appear to contradict the basic principles of the social market economy. Agricultural, credit, insurance, transportation, rebate, "structural crisis," and "rationalization" cartels are exempted from the cartel laws. A "structural crisis" cartel is permitted when there has been a long-term decline in demand that requires the creation of a cartel to salvage an industry. A "rationalization" cartel can be formed when a cartel is deemed necessary to introduce new technologies into the industry. Critics point out that cartel authorities are placed in the position of having to judge whether a structural crisis exists or whether a new technology will be introduced only if a cartel is formed. This practice tends to lessen competition during economic downturns.[83]

The state actively limits competition in a number of areas based on its social responsibilities to the public. Examples of such interventions are strict state regulation of business hours, state support of minimum price legislation for brand-name articles, rent controls, laws that give renters virtual property rights, and government rules on the firing of employees, none of which is very unusual by European standards.

One type of state activity should be singled out—the extensive role played by state *(Länder)* governments in managing the occupational training of young workers. The chambers of commerce allocate young people into apprenticeships in industry and establish rules whereby local industries are responsible for the training of young workers, at the expense of these industries.

Social Correctives of the Market Economy

In the Federal Republic, social correctives of market resource allocations are actively pursued in cases of conflict between private economic decision making and national social objectives. Such social correctives occur in five major areas: (1) the security of employment, (2) the protection of employees, (3) insurance against the risks of workers, (4) improvement of the distribution of income, and (5) other measures that have a significant impact on social policy.

The first three instances are typical of most industrialized capitalist countries and involve programs of employment services; protection against dangerous employment conditions and protection of teen-age workers; unemployment, hospitalization, and accident insurance; and so on. The unusual aspects of the German case are that such programs were instituted so early (under Bismarck in 1881) and that they are so comprehensive in contemporary terms.

The German welfare state is highly developed and rapidly expanding. State expenditures as a share of GNP rose from 32.5 percent in 1960 to about 50 percent in the 1990s. The share of social expenditures of GNP rose in the same time period from 21 percent to about one-third. Between 1960 and the 1990s, expenditures for the state health insurance system rose by a factor of 10. Critics of the rising share of government expenditures point to the inefficiencies that such government programs eventually produce.

Correctives aimed at improving the distribution of income are more unusual. In Germany, progressive income taxes are not the principal vehicle for making the market-determined distribution of income more equal. Rather, the objective has been to use other instruments—the promotion of asset formation among lower-income groups, direct transfer payments (examples are child allowances and subsidization of rental payments), and direct state intervention (government funding of public housing and obligatory health insurance). Finally, the state has supported programs to allow workers to share in the profits of their enterprises as well as to have a say in the conduct of enterprise affairs (codetermination), all of which may affect the real distribution of income.

Let us first consider state policies to promote capital formation in general and savings of lower-income groups in particular. In some instances, the state supplements the savings of low-income families through a schedule of premiums, especially for savings, that cannot be withdrawn for seven or more years. Savings for home purchases receive similar treatment, and employer contributions to employee life insurance or other savings programs receive favorable tax treatment. These two features, in addition to government programs to ensure workers' access to the distribution of enterprise profits, seek to render even the lower-paid workers less dependent on their wage income. Earnings from assets should serve as income supplements. A side benefit of such pro–capital-accumulation (and anticonsumption) policies is to encourage a high domestic savings rate and a higher domestic growth rate.

In addition to these policies to promote capital formation even among working families, the income distribution is made more nearly equal by direct government interventions. A prime example is the fact that most apartment construction in contemporary Germany is funded (or sponsored) by state organizations for the purpose of making low-cost housing available to lower income groups.

Codetermination and Labor Unions

An important aspect of government social policy is codetermination *(Mitbestimmung)*. **Codetermination** means having worker representatives on the boards of directors of corporations. The objective of this policy is "industrial democracy," or forcing management to take workers' interests into consideration when making policy. Initially applied only to selected industries, codetermination has applied to almost all industry since German law was revised in 1976.[84] Firms with two thousand or more employees fall under the codetermination legislation. A separate codetermination law applies to the coal, iron, and steel industries.

According to the law, stockholders and workers should have an equal number of representatives on the board of directors. For example, if the board consists of twelve members, six should represent the stockholders and six, the employees. Of the latter, two must be representatives of the labor union, and at least one must be a "leading employee" (such as a foreman). The codetermination law requires the election of a chairman *(Vorsitzender)* of the board of directors. In the absence of a majority, the chairman is elected by the representatives of the stockholders. In this way, the codetermination law seeks to avoid a stalemate by giving the chairman the deciding vote in the case of an evenly split board. Although labor and stockholders appear to have parity on the board of directors, the stockholders actually have the advantage because of the way the chairman is selected and because "leading employees" often side with the stockholders.

The 1976 regulations are still being tested in the German courts. Because co-determination rules call for a nearly equal labor voice, they call into question the protection of private property guaranteed in the German constitution. Another objection raised to the codetermination legislation is that it puts labor representatives on both sides of the collective bargaining table and thus gives labor an unfair advantage. In steel industry negotiations, however, labor representatives on the management boards have sided with management against the steel workers' demand for a 35-hour workweek. It is not obvious, therefore, how labor representatives will behave when they in fact join management.

The codetermination law gives labor a voice in major policy decisions, but the board of directors rarely deals with shop-level issues. The Enterprise Constitution Law *(Betriebsverfassungsgesetz,* or BVG) of 1972 gives labor a voice in shop-floor decisions. The BVG requires the election of an enterprise council in enterprises employing five or more workers; "leading employees" are not eligible for election to that council. The enterprise council has codetermination responsibilities in the following areas: wages, length of the working day, firings, and layoffs. The influence of the enterprise council is strongest in personnel areas; every termination requires the approval of the enterprise council.

The BVG law of 1972, on paper at least, substantially constrains management in the area of personnel decisions. How the law works in practice remains to be fully researched. It is not yet known whether most enterprises actually follow the letter of the BVG law. Also, its effect on productivity remains to be measured. On the positive side, worker participation may raise worker loyalty and enthusiasm and reduce turnover; on the negative side, worker participation may prevent management from making necessary personnel changes.

Labor and Collective Bargaining

The right of workers to join together to form trade unions is recognized in the German constitution and the cartel laws. Workers have the freedom to contract with management or management organizations through collective bargaining. The "closed shop" (wherein all workers must belong to the union) is not allowed in Germany. The percentage of the labor force belonging to unions in Germany is more than 40 percent, much higher than the current American ratio of less than one in five. German unions are organized on an industry basis to prevent competition among individual unions for members. German unions are grouped into federations, the most important being the German Federation of Unions *(Deutscher Gewerk-schaftsbund),* which accounts for 84 percent of all union membership.

Collective bargaining between unions and management generally proceeds at a relatively high level. Unions have the right to strike, and management has the right to lock workers out *(Aussperrungen),* or close down firms in which workers are striking. The volume of strikes is relatively low in Germany (58 days per 1000 workers per year for the period 1970 to 1979), but management has been willing to respond to strikes with lockouts. For example, 1971 and 1978 were years of relatively high strike activity in Germany. In both years, the number of workdays lost through lockouts was about two-thirds of the number of workdays lost through strikes. German labor laws do not require compulsory arbitration, but it is commonly used to settle stalemates. Once unions and management agree to arbitration, they must hold their peace. Arbitration proposals are not binding, but they impose strong psychological pressure on the parties to agree.

The low frequency of strikes in Germany and the relatively low nominal wage increases agreed to by unions in the postwar period point to comparatively successful labor–management relations in postwar Germany. Many factors could contribute to this success: the codetermination laws, the role of the enterprise council, and the traditional German fear of inflation.

An interesting feature of German social policy is the notion that problems of income distribution should not be solved by collective bargaining for higher wages by unions and management. Although German workers are organized into powerful unions and the German social democratic party is strongly influenced by organized labor, collective bargaining in Germany has been more quiescent than in other European countries. Whether the government's social policies can be credited for this fact or whether fear of inflation is at the root, we cannot determine; but the failure of German unions to be more demanding has probably been an important factor in the lower rates of inflation in Germany.

Public Enterprise

The role of public enterprise is greater in Germany than in the United States. Not only do state enterprises dominate transportation and communication and the construction of apartment dwellings, but there is significant state participation in mining and metallurgy.[85] In some cases, government participation is indirect (as in the recent case of the Krupp industries); in others it is carried out through holding companies. Nevertheless, one cannot cite government enterprises as a unique feature of the German social and market economy, for it is quite typical of Europe in general.

In fact, at least prior to the 1980s, the German experience with nationalization has been the reverse of the British experience. In Germany, the emphasis has been on denationalization *(Privatisierung)*. The Federal Treasury Ministry *(Bundesschatzministerium)* was established in 1957 to deal with public enterprises. It was set up not as an instrument of central management but rather to lay the foundations for denationalization. The management of public enterprises has typically been decentralized to the enterprise itself. Two methods of denationalization have been used: (1) the sale of formerly public enterprises to private persons or private groups and (2) social **denationalization**, which is achieved by establishing a new type of equity, the so-called popular share, to be sold to low-income citizens on a preferential basis. The main denationalizations were those carried out at Volkswagen and Veba.

Union-owned and -organized enterprises represent a mix of public and private enterprise. For example, the union-owned *Gruppe Neue Heimat* was once the largest European apartment construction firm, the *Bank für Gemeinwirtschaft* is the fourth-largest German interregional bank, and the *Coop-Unternehmen* forms the second-largest retail trade organization in Germany. Officially, these firms were founded to serve the common good, not to maximize profits.

Performance

The annual growth rate of the West German economy averaged 4.5 percent between 1950 and 1990. Its most rapid growth came in the immediate postwar era, with a 1950–1960 growth rate of 8.5 percent. The West German investment rate has remained consistently around 25 percent of GNP—one of the highest among industrialized countries. A relatively low unemployment rate accompanied this rapid growth. In the 1950s and 1960s, unemployment rates at or below 1 percent were common. The German unemployment rate has increased since the mid-1970s, ranging from 5 to 7 percent in the late 1980s. Consumer prices increased at remarkably low rates for such rapid growth and low unemployment. In the 1950s consumer prices increased at a 2.6 percent rate. In the inflationary 1970s, the German inflation rate was a relatively low 5 percent per annum. In the 1980s, German inflation was under 1 percent per annum. Relative price stability led to a stable and generally rising exchange rate and a positive trade balance. The outstanding performance of the West German economy, especially during the late 1940s and 1950s, has caused analysts to speak of the German "economic miracle" *(Wirtschaftswunder).*

Unquestionably, the postwar performance of the German economy has been good. To what extent this performance is related to the economic system is, as always, difficult to know. However, certain aspects of the German system have arguably been important in influencing economic outcomes.

One unusual feature of the German system has been the rather intense effort on the part of state policy to promote capital formation, even among lower-income groups, while avoiding a steeply progressive income tax. Germany today has (along with Japan) one of the highest national savings rates of the industrialized countries, and this is at least a partial consequence of state policy. The concerted effort to promote investment while restraining consumption seems to have paid off in terms of economic growth and price stability, two of the hallmarks of the German Wirtschaftswunder.

Moreover, German state policy has sought to prevent discord between worker and employer, principally by ensuring the social security of the German worker. Contemporary developments in the area of codetermination can be viewed as a continuation of social reforms begun in the Bismarck era. These policies, combined with the traditional German fear of hyperinflation, have perhaps served to limit the wage demands of German unions, despite their enormous economic and political power. If interest had centered on the good economic performance of Germany's social market economy, the picture in the 1990s has changed.

First, contemporary Germany faces problems of inflation and unemployment, both in a new European setting. Second, and possibly more important, the costs of integrating the former East Germany into West Germany have been significant and may, in the 1990s, prove to be a burden greater than previously anticipated. The important issue of unification bears further examination.

Germany: Unification

The **unification** of the German Democratic Republic (GDR) with the Federal Republic of Germany (FRG) took place in 1990 and was an event of major political and economic significance. Prior to unification, examinations of the two countries focused on the GDR as a centrally planned socialist economic system and on the FRG as a market capitalist economic system. Although understanding these earlier arrangements is important from an historical perspective, contemporary interest centers on the political and economic reality of a new German economy, an economy formed through the unification of what were two very different economic systems. However, to understand the problems of unification, it is necessary to look at the arrangements that existed before it took place.[86]

This section examines three themes and offers a brief analysis of the systemic arrangements of the former GDR. It also discusses the state of the two economies on the eve of unification and examines the process of unification and the problems of integrating the former GDR into the market economic system of the FRG.

The GDR as a Planned Socialist Economic System   The economies of the FRG and the GDR prior to unification provide a case study of the differences between capitalism and socialism. This was especially fruitful because the two countries were similar in many dimensions *except* the economic system and economic policies. Though not all other things were equal, the *ceteris paribus* assumption was justified for a variety of reasons.

1. Although there were notable differences in population dynamics in the period following World War II, the two economies had, at the end of the war, a very similar stock of human capital and an essentially homogeneous population.
2. The presence of shared traditions, culture, and tastes was a second common factor present on the eve of the introduction of a very different economic system into GDR.
3. At the outbreak of World War II, Germany was among the most modern industrial economies, and the FRG and the GDR were roughly equivalent in per capita income and per capita industrial output. Moreover, the structures of the capital stocks were similar, and foreign trade patterns were typical of an advanced economy.

If there were similarities, there were also differences, some of which affected economic outcomes in the postwar period.

1. The GDR was a much smaller economy (the population of the GDR was roughly 25 percent that of the FRG) at the end of the war. And this proportion was to decline further, in part because of different population policies in the GDR and in part because of the "republic flight" (the ongoing loss of population from the GDR to the FRG, between 1945 and 1961, which varied annually from 144,000 to 365,000).
2. The resource base of the GDR was inferior to that of the FRG. Nevertheless, lignite coal was relatively abundant for fuel and for generation of electricity.

Moreover, one could argue that with a smaller population, the GDR had a more favorable ratio of population to land.

3. The war and its aftermath treated the GDR and the FRG differently. Approximately 50 percent of the GDR's industrial capacity was destroyed by the end of the war, compared with 25 percent of the FRG's. And whereas the GDR was making reparation payments in the early postwar period, the FRG benefited from assistance under the Marshall Plan. (At the same time, the FRG eventually paid out to the FRG some 33 billion marks in *Wiedergutmaching* payments, a sum double the amount of Marshall Plan aid.)

Thus both similarities and differences existed in nonsystem characteristics, but the economic systems themselves certainly were different in the postwar years. The Soviet model was introduced into the GDR after the war, and by the end of the 1940s, virtually all industry, banking, and transportation had been nationalized and were functioning under a system of central planning. The process of collectivization in agriculture began seriously in the early 1950s and was completed by the end of the decade. The only private ownership was found in some retail trade and in handicrafts.

The model of planning and management introduced into the GDR after the war was basically the same as the Soviet administrative command model. The Communist party dictated priorities to a state planning commission, which, in conjunction with ministries, established binding plans to govern enterprise operations. As in the Soviet Union, the system of balances was used for planning.

Beginning in the early 1960s, the GDR introduced the **New Economic System**, to decentralize some decision making to groups of state enterprises (formally Unions of State Enterprises or VVBs). As with early Soviet reform attempts, the objective was to improve lagging economic performance through limited devolution of planning authority, the latter to be coordinated through semi-decentralized contracts among economic units.

The New Economic System was abandoned in the early 1970s. In large part, this was a result of the recentralization of decision making and the continued use of gross output targeting. The drive for improved efficiency to sustain rapid economic growth was channeled, in the 1970s and 1980s, in a different direction. The thrust was the creation of new intermediate planning organizations known as combines (*Kombinat*) that differed from the earlier VVBs but were similar to those in the Soviet Union (*obedinenie*). The combines were formed to exploit economies of scale, to establish more effective supply relationships, and to provide better investment allocation. In effect, this system was designed to replace the three-level system (enterprise, intermediate authority, central authority) with a two-level system (combine, central authority). The combine would manage and coordinate its member enterprises. What powers the central authority was to have over the combine was a major and largely unresolved issue of this reform.

The described economic system closely resembled the Soviet administrative command model, and important policy positions were also very similar. The emphasis was on economic growth through high investment in industry. Moreover, policies in agriculture were similar to those in the Soviet Union, and the mechanisms and directions of foreign trade came to resemble those of the Soviet Union as the GDR was integrated into the Eastern COMECON system. Incentive arrangements were typical of the planned socialist system: reduction of income differentials, reliance on public goods, and the moral suasion of the socialist model.

If the economic system of the GDR closely mirrored the Soviet administrative command model, so too did its economic outcomes. These outcomes are especially important because they bear on both the costs and the benefits of unification. What was the state of the economy of the GDR on the eve of unification, and how did this economy compare to that of the FRG?

The FRG and the GDR on the Eve of Unification   The political changes of the late 1980s have undoubtedly permitted—and even necessitated—significant reassessment of economic performance of the GDR. Traditional views must therefore be interpreted with some caution. Table 9.3 presents a summary statistical picture of the FRG and the GDR on the eve of unification.

The FRG outperformed the GDR in growth, but not by large amounts and not in per capita terms. At the same time, and unlike other planned socialist economic systems, many of the increases in output in the GDR were attributable to intensive growth. After the 1960s, however, the GDR was unable to sustain its rate of economic growth, and a growing gap in living standards between the GDR and the FRG emerged. This gap played a part in promoting various reform attempts. Moreover, given that these two similar societies existed side by side, it was difficult for the GDR to tolerate a growing differential in living standards.

In terms of other criteria, the performance record of the GDR was mixed. Although the GDR seemed to enjoy greater stability and a more even distribution of income than the FRG in the 1970s and into the 1980s, performance problems and a worsening of the relative position of the GDR were seen as signs of trouble in that economy.

Unification and the Era of Transition   West German laws were transferred east by treaty, and in 1990, the Deutschmark replaced the East German Ostmark, prices were freed, and trading arrangements were relaxed. The *Treuhandanstalt* (**Federal Privatizing Trust**) held all the shares of East German firms (which were converted into joint-stock companies) and became the major mechanism through which privatization would take place. Much of the transition process in the former GDR has necessarily focused on the issue of privatization.

The "Treuhand" has been much more than simply a mechanism to hold the shares of the formerly state-owned firms in the GDR. The Treuhand was set up to be responsible for assembling the talent necessary to value and to liquidate these firms. Valuation has been very difficult. The most attractive firms found immediate buyers, but less attractive firms were faced with either liquidation or the need for interim support—another function of the Treuhand. There were cases where financial discipline simply could not be imposed. The loss of markets combined with the fact that wages in the former GDR had been sustained at inappropriately high levels,

TABLE 9.3   The Federal Republic of Germany and the German Democratic Republic: Selected Social and Economic Indicators, 1988

	Federal Republic of Germany	German Democratic Republic
Area and population		
Area (*in 1,000 square kilometers*)	249	108
Population (*millions*)	61.4	16.7
(*in percent of population*)		
Of working age	67.0[a]	65.0
Pensioners	18.5[a]	16.0
Employment		
Total employed (*in millions*)	27.4	9.0
(*in percent of population*)	44.5	53.9
Female employment (*in percent of total employment*)	38.1[a]	48.6
Employment by sector		
(*in percent of total*)		
Agriculture and forestry	4.0	10.8
Mining, manufacturing, and construction	39.8	47.1
Other sectors	56.2	42.1
Household income, consumption, and saving		
Average monthly gross earnings (*DM/M*)	3,850	1,270
Household saving (*in percent of disposable income*)	12.8	7.1
Households with:		
(*in percent of total*)		
Automobiles	97	52
Color television	94	52
Telephone	98	7[b]
Production, investment, and prices		
(*Annual real growth rate, 1980–88*)		
GNP/NMP	1.7	4.2
Gross fixed investment	0.7	2.0
Of which: Machinery and equipment	2.4	5.0
Consumer prices (*annual percent rate of change, 1980–88*)	2.9	—
External trade in goods		
(*in percent of total exports*)		
Exports to state-trading countries	4.4	69.5
Imports from state-trading countries	4.7	68.7
Trade balance		
(*in percent of GNP/NMP*)	6.0	1.0
Of which: State-trading countries	0.2	1.0
Monetary accounts of households		
Household financial assets[c] (*billions DM/M*)	1,196.6	167.2
Velocity of money[d]	1.11	0.97

[a] 1987.
[b] 1985.
[c] Currency and bank deposits. Year-end for the FRG and year average for the GDR.
[d] Private disposable income divided by household financial assets.

Sources: Statistisches Bundesamt, *Statistisches Jahrbuch der Bundesrepublik Deutschland,* 1989; Staatliche Zentralverwaltung für Statistik der DDR, *Statistisches Jahrbuch der DDR, 1989;* and Deutsche Bundesbank.

led to a surge in unemployment. Unemployment grew from roughly 1.6 percent in June of 1990 to almost 9 percent by February of 1991, a major cost to be borne by the new unified German economy.[87]

Although a number of firms in the GDR were attractive to potential buyers, the technological level of the GDR, once viewed as the leading economy in the CMEA (Council for Mutual Economic Assistance) bloc, turned out to be very low, necessitating fundamental change in the industrial base. Such changes have focused on several issues.

1. The privatization process had to deal with the issue of *claims* from past confiscation of property. Accordingly, the privatization process has been slower and substantially more complex.
2. If productivity levels in industry are to reach or even approach Western levels, major new investments will be necessary. But in addition to investment, the appropriate management skills are required to modernize outmoded industrial capacity. Indeed, the technological state of industry in the former GDR (and in other East European countries) has generally proved to be far lower than anticipated. By the middle of 1991, a number of firms had in fact been liquidated.
3. In the former GDR, there was substantial concentration in the existing industrial structure. Moreover, to the extent that it is the larger firms that are attractive and are bought by large Western firms, the level of industrial concentration is maintained if not actually increased. Such has indeed been the case, the major Western purchasers being companies such as Volkswagen, Daimler-Benz, and IBM Germany.
4. The social costs of privatization have risen and are bound to continue to rise. In addition to the need for direct financial support of the transition, the issues of unemployment, retraining, inflation, and the like will make defining a new social contract difficult.

The German Economy in the 1990s

The unification of Germany has had profound and unexpected effects on the German economy. Although Germans were told that the costs of unification would be low, the costs have actually been high and have had a temporarily negative effect on German economic performance.

The political decision to convert the monetary holdings of East Germans at a rate of approximately one German mark equaling one East mark resulted in a substantial increase in the German money supply. That increase, combined with the sharp reduction in output in the former Eastern states, created inflationary pressures in a country that fights inflation seriously. The German central bank fought those inflationary pressures by increasing interest rates, which were thought to contribute to the German recession of the mid-1990s.

With the need to upgrade East Germany's infrastructure, to correct environmental damage, and to prevent unemployment from reaching catastrophic proportions, the German government had to embark on a massive program of subsidies for the former East Germany. The public financial transfers to handle these problems comprised between 5.5 and 6.5 percent of German GNP in the early 1990s.

It was initially thought that the selling of East German enterprises would cover the costs of German reunification; however, this has not been the case. The cost of upgrading the technological state of those enterprises so they could be sold exceeded the revenue they generated. In many cases, subsidies were promised to new owners for correcting environmental damage and for retaining labor.

The combination of low technological level and relatively high East German wages, which were imposed as a political decision, has limited the flow of private capital from West to East. In West Germany, the ratio of private to public investment is four to one; in the eastern part, the ratio is the reverse.

By the mid-1990s, the major costs of the transition appear to have been paid. Production in the former East Germany had been stabilized and the eastern states were growing even more rapidly than those in the west. Although Germany paid dearly in terms of lost output, price stability, and unemployment, the transition has apparently been successfully completed.

Although costly, the integration of the two economies has proceeded under much more favorable circumstances than can be expected elsewhere. First, the East German transition occurred within the framework of West Germany's stable laws. Second, East Germany became part of the most stable currency union—the German mark union—that is managed by a strong, independent central bank. Third, the transformation took place in the strongest country economically in Europe, a country that could survive a transfer of resources that accounted for, at times, more than 6 percent of its GNP.

Japan: Growth Through the Market

Japan is a capitalist economy with a record of exceptional economic performance. Japan's postwar rate of economic growth is the highest among the major industrialized countries. For the admirer of high rates of economic growth, thought to be a hallmark of the early years of planned socialist systems, Japan is cited as a capitalist alternative to the Soviet model for the developing nations. However, in Japan as in other countries, growth rates have slowed. In the 1980s attention focused on how, and how well, the Japanese economy could adjust to external shocks from the world economy. Indeed, by the early 1990s, there was considerable pessimism about the performance of the Japanese economy.

This discussion of Japan stresses three areas: the historical traditions and special circumstances of Japan, its economic performance, and various observers' explanations of Japan's impressive growth record. It concludes with observations on contemporary performance issues.

Background of the Japanese Economy

Japan is a small country with adequate labor but generally limited supplies of natural resources and land. Prior to the Meiji restoration, which began in 1868, Japan was "a fossilized and closed society."[88] Therefore, interest in Japanese economic performance centers on the period since 1868, though the roots of modern development may be found in the Tokugawa period prior to the Meiji restoration.[89]

Japan, like Great Britain, is an island economy. With a population of approximately 123 million, 77 percent of whom live in urban areas, and a land area slightly smaller than that of the state of California, Japan is densely populated. Japan is a developed economy dominated by the service sector, the industrial sector, and a small agricultural sector.

Japan has a long, varied, and controversial history. Since its defeat in World War II, Japan has been governed under a democratic political system established by the Allied occupation forces. The Japanese parliament *(Diet)* is elected by the people; it chooses the prime minister, who is the leader of the country.

The Japanese have achieved rapid growth in a country whose natural resource base is minimal. Japan is not well endowed with minerals or fertile agricultural land. Thus Japanese performance must be explained by its economic system, its organizational arrangements, and the people who operate within this system.[90] Between the late 1860s and the early 1900s, Japan developed policy measures for economic growth based on special features of the Japanese system.

First of all, there was (and still is) among the Japanese population a unity of purpose fostered by the state and facilitated by Japanese cultural traditions and history. There are a discipline and devotion to work on the part of the laborers and a degree of paternalism on the part of employers seldom seen in other countries. Although it is difficult to pinpoint the sources of this unity, one observer has suggested that a long period of development of the labor market, based on the discipline of the home production process, and the generation of information for an efficient market combined to create an efficient and disciplined worker.[91]

Second, the state has performed important functions. The figures in Table 9.1 (with the possible exception of those on state ownership) suggest a rather modest role for the state in the Japanese economy. Such statistics may understate the role of the state in postwar Japan. For example, in the crucial area of capital formation, the government has played a key role, not only in promoting savings and investment, but also in encouraging the influx of foreign capital, which was important in the early years of Japanese development.

Although the rate of capital formation in postwar Japan has been much higher than in other capitalist economies, the *direct* state role has been smaller than in other nations. Government purchases have also been smaller proportionally than in any of these countries. The state's role, then, has been to stimulate *private* investment through strong incentives such as low tax rates, proinvestment state financial policy, and the limited provision of social services.

The role of the Japanese state as a purchaser was important in earlier times, especially in its capacity as an entrepreneur—a role that carries over to present-day

Japan. This state function has been important not only in getting industry started but also in focusing investment in growth sectors, at the best scale of operation, and utilizing the best available technology.

Third, historical experience is crucial to understanding modern economic growth in Japan. During the Meiji restoration, the Japanese economy was opened up to Western technology. Enrollment in formal educational programs increased rapidly, as did participation in the labor force, and a "dual economy" developed. The dual economy consisted of a large, increasingly modern industrial sector requiring skilled labor, existing alongside relatively primitive industrial operations where labor with minimal skills was utilized.

Agricultural development accelerated during this period, and technological progress and the expansion of conventional inputs (labor and fertilizer) were important to creating an agricultural surplus. Agriculture's role in Japanese development—in particular, the use of high taxation to extract the surplus—remains a matter of controversy.[92]

Fourth, military activity has been an important factor. The rapid pace of development after the 1860s through World War I was fostered in part by military spending. Thereafter, at least until 1946, war was a dominant theme. World War II warped the structure of production and led to an economy governed by controls and, later, manipulated by the American occupation forces. American occupation policies were primary land reform (large holdings were broken up), deconcentration of industrial ownership, the introduction of trade unionism, and an end to the military commitment.[93] All had important implications for Japan's development in the postwar period. No simple set of features can explain Japanese growth.

Japanese Economic Growth

Although the Japanese economy has been growing rapidly for a long time, the interesting facet of this record, as Kazushi Ohkawa and Henry Rosovsky emphasize, is the accelerating trend of economic growth at a particularly high level. The rate of growth of output of the Japanese economy in the postwar years has been exceptionally high by international standards, averaging close to 10 percent annually. This rate meets or exceeds even those of such rapidly growing countries as Germany and earlier the Soviet Union. Growth rates through the 1980s have been much slower, though they are certainly respectable by international standards.

The Japanese economy is a capitalist market economy in which national economic planning has played only a marginal role. One cannot look to extra-market mechanisms, such as planning, to explain Japanese growth. What, then, has led to this impressive economic performance? It is very difficult to isolate the key features that have influenced any economic system's performance. However, the pathbreaking work of Ohkawa and Rosovsky identifies two general influences: those that are narrowly economic and those of a broader nature.[94] Let us examine each in turn.

The economic explanations for postwar (and earlier) Japanese economic development, according to Ohkawa and Rosovsky, were a technology gap, a high rate of capital formation, and the availability of appropriate labor supplies. Being a closed economy, Japan had a technology gap and thus could benefit in a major way from the absorption of Western technology. Technology assimilation was facilitated by sharp increases in the size of the capital stock (through imports of capital, a high propensity to save, and the state's promotion of capital formation) and by elastic supplies of labor. Furthermore, the dual labor market permitted the shift of labor from the primitive to the modern sector at a rate dictated by the needs of the advanced sector, and wage increases lagged behind advances in productivity.[95]

At the same time, the Japanese economy was able to promote a growing role in foreign markets. During the early stages of development, while modern industry was growing, exports were derived primarily from traditional industries such as textiles. As modern technology was assimilated, Japanese exports shifted away from the traditional products toward the high-technology products that Japan, owing to its productive but relatively inexpensive labor, could produce with comparative advantage. In part, industrial development at home was enhanced by the state's policy of starting import-competing industries. These factors, combined with reparations from China and an aggressive external posture, made the foreign sector an important contributor to Japan's growth.

The factors emphasized by Ohkawa and Rosovsky are familiar—technology, capital creation, development of the labor force. The difference may be Japan's ability to assemble these features in a harmonious way. Ohkawa and Rosovsky place great emphasis on the noneconomic or special features of the Japanese nation. What are the important noneconomic features of the Japanese development experience?

First, we must again emphasize the important and multidimensional role of the state. The state gave impetus and direction to the drive for economic growth. The state intervened selectively and has been an important catalyst for ensuring not only a high rate of investment but also its proper distribution. For example, beyond the approval of general economic policies by the Diet, government is also more directly involved in business. Government offices *(genkyoku)* supervise individual industries, and ministries supervise sectors of the economy. Also, there are ministries (such as the Ministry of Finance) the interests of which cross specific industrial borders. Finally, the government is directly involved in a wide range of economic matters: the encouragement of designated industrial projects through low-interest loans from the Japan Development Bank, regulation of antitrust matters by the Fair Trade Commission, and so on.[96]

The role of the state in the Japanese economy is difficult to classify. It remains one of the intriguing aspects of the Japanese economic system. In terms of readily quantifiable indicators of state economic activity such as revenue and expenditure, the role of the state is small relative to most other industrialized capitalist systems. At the same time, the state has been very important as a facilitator of the market process, as the creator of a harmonious business environment, and as an entrepreneur and overseer of the development process.

Second, what Ohkawa and Rosovsky describe as the "human element" has been a very important factor in the Japanese story. In Japan, labor has a peculiar and growth-conducive attitude toward industry—the "permanent employment" system and the submissive attitude of labor toward the industrial establishment.[97] In addition, rising family incomes have produced unusually high levels of savings, most appropriate for rapid growth but hard to explain on other than traditional and cultural grounds.

Prior to World War II, the government suppressed the growth of the trade union movement, although it did grow to some degree along with the development of government regulations concerning the labor market. Having gained recognition in the postwar period, trade unions have a voice in wages, supplemental benefits, and working conditions. They are constrained, however, in that they are enterprise unions, enrolling long-term employees. Their primary strength is in the largest industrial enterprises.[98]

Third, one could cite a number of other factors—some narrowly economic, others less so—that have been important: favorable population growth and hence labor supplies, the end to military expenditure, and the limiting of low-growth sectors (such as housing).

Industrial Organization

An economy's industrial organization can affect its performance, and most capitalist theories associate competition with "good" economic performance. The Japanese economy presents a test case, for it appears to have combined an industrial structure dominated by giant vertical and horizontal trusts with rapid economic growth.

Prior to World War II, Japanese industry was dominated by giant holding companies called *zaibatsu*, which represented a complex maze of interlocking directorships, banking relationships, and family ties.[99] At the end of the war, this concentration of ownership had proceeded to the point where fewer than four thousand zaibatsu-connected families owned almost 50 percent of total outstanding shares. The American occupation forces sought to eliminate zaibatsu dominance by outlawing holding companies, breaking up monopolies, and making mutual shareholdings among zaibatsu firms illegal.

In the postwar era, shareholding in industry and banking has become more evenly distributed among the population. New industrial groupings called *kieretsu* have replaced the old zaibatsu organizations. Kieretsu can be either vertical or horizontal, either a large firm in charge of smaller ("children") firms or a horizontal association of interest groups. These new groups are less powerful than the old zaibatsu, and it is possible for a firm within a grouping to place its own interests above those of the group, an action inconceivable before the war.

One enduring feature of the large Japanese company is its emphasis on industrial paternalism. Established employees of large companies are, in effect, guaranteed lifetime employment. They are taught to think of the company as their family, and they believe that if they work hard for the company, the company will take care of them. John M. Montias singled out this characteristic of the Japanese enterprise for study and found that this "permanent employment" constraint on Japanese management is likely to alter resource allocation patterns, at least in theory.[100]

Clearly, arrangements for the allocation of labor in the Japanese economy differ from those familiar to Western students. Indeed, the Japanese economy has been characterized as a **share economy**, based on a framework suggested by Martin Weitzman.[101] The evidence for this characterization—the bonus system in Japan—is not strong, though differences in the allocation system make Japanese labor markets of great interest to the comparative analyst.[102]

The concepts of industrial paternalism and lifetime employment have received a great deal of attention, in large part because the system seems so different from other capitalist countries. How can labor be allocated in a rapidly changing environment if it is not mobile?

The answer to this question lies largely in the difference between appearance and substance. In fact, a number of forces at work in the Japanese economy limit the impact of guaranteed employment.[103] First, not all members of the Japanese labor force are covered by guaranteed employment. One study suggests that roughly 30 percent of the industrial labor force is covered by some form of guaranteed employment.[104] Second, Japanese firms have ways to create flexibility in employment. For example, a temporary labor force can be utilized, and the payment system, where bonuses can be important, serves as an inducement for employees to work hard. Third, Japanese firms can rely on subcontracting for industrial parts, thus lessening the need to hire the labor force necessary to produce these parts on a sustained basis. Finally, guaranteed employment does not mean that inefficient firms are in some way maintained. On the contrary, both the pressures of the market and the role played by government agencies encourage the productive sectors and discourage the unproductive sectors. All these factors substantially mitigate what would otherwise appear to be a starkly different system of labor–management relations.

Japanese Planning

Economic planning has not been an important element in the Japanese economy. Japan has had a planning agency since the late 1940s and has assembled numerous plans. Japanese plans have been highly pragmatic, with frequently shifting goals. They have been highly aggregative and are based on a simple extension of the national accounts. The plan targets (in addition to being highly aggregative) have been projected only to terminal years of the five-year planning period, making them of minimal value to private firms even when those firms want to be integrated into the plan projections.

One measure of the value of a plan is how closely it is fulfilled. Japanese economic performance has typically been better than that called for by the plan. Plan targets have typically been exceeded, sometimes by very large amounts. This sort of inaccuracy renders the plan targets of little use for purposes of coordination and leads to skepticism about the plan and the necessity for continued corrections by individual firms.

Although the discipline of Japanese firms and their management would make them look at and consider the plan, the real force of intervention in the life of the economy has been the state, not the planning agency.[105] Although we have emphasized this fact, it is worth noting again that discussion of intervention in the Japanese economy focuses not on the Economic Planning Agency but on the Ministry of International Trade and Industry, where the real power lies. In this sense, the state, its agencies, and its budget are the focus of attention. Thus whether we describe the mechanisms of the Japanese economy as planning or as something less, the state arguably plays an important role in directing the path of Japanese economic growth and development.

In a recent study of Japanese economic planning, Kazuo Sato describes the Japanese system as indicative planning but emphasizes the sectoral impact of planning and the role of the government through the Ministry of International Trade and Industry, rather than through traditional macroeconomic channels.

Japan: Industrial Policy?

Thus far we have traced the development of the Japanese economy by focusing on features that are thought to have contributed to rapid economic growth. It has been difficult, if not impossible, to render any substantive judgment on the role of government in the Japanese economy. Let us examine this question further.

First, Japanese social structure differs markedly from that in the United States. Above all, Japan is a country dominated by both vertical and horizontal organization, where group allegiance, formal and informal, is very important. Japanese society might be likened to a family, where the role of each member contrasts markedly with the sort of individualism familiar to us in the United States.

Second, government does play an important role in the Japanese economy, yet its role is difficult to measure.[106] The Japanese ministerial structure has a substantial impact on the economy, not only through direct participation in key aspects of economic life, but also through its indirect influence. For example, the Ministry of Finance, along with the Bank of Japan, is responsible for the traditional functions of monetary control. In the outside world, however, it is the **Ministry of International Trade and Industry (MITI)** that receives most attention.[107]

MITI has an impressive formal role, being responsible for international trade, domestic production, and domestic industrial structure. Whether formal or informal, though, MITI is frequently viewed as the purveyor of an "industrial policy" geared to promoting rapid economic growth.[108] MITI is responsible for guiding and influencing economic decisions by promoting key sectors of the economy and carefully phasing out other, low-productivity sectors. MITI uses public funds for research and development and provides assistance for organizational change, such as mergers. Although MITI is an important vehicle for transmitting information in the Japanese economy, few describe this function as planning.

Beyond the ministerial system, there is considerable government involvement in the economy. This activity ranges from the traditional provision of "public goods" to activities in less traditional areas. For example, special financial institutions provide supplementary services to the private industrial sector.

Traditional measures of government involvement in an economic system probably don't capture the essence of the Japanese system. In the absence of a major formal role for government and planning, the government is nevertheless able to influence both short- and long-term decision making. Rather than formal and powerful involvement in a few traditional and noticeable areas, the government exerts its influence through a myriad of arrangements that guide economic growth. Enthusiasts of an industrial policy cite the Japanese experience.

During the 1970s, American admiration for the Japanese economic system grew. In a time of general economic turmoil, the Japanese were perceived to have found the keys to sustained economic growth. Many writers attempted to discover the precise identity of the growth forces—whether industrial policy, a special role for the government, the managerial system, the labor–management arrangements, or the nature of Japanese society and the Japanese work force. This admiration has been limited only by our apparent inability to transplant these growth forces and by continuing friction in Japanese–American trade relations.

The 1970s, however, were not a tranquil decade for the Japanese economy. The early 1970s brought Japan two major shocks. The first was the move by the Nixon administration to end the long-fixed exchange rate between the American dollar and the Japanese yen and move toward a flexible exchange rate.[109] The second event was the initial impact of the energy crisis in 1973. The average annual rate of growth of real GNP declined from above 10 percent in the late 1960s to generally lower rates in the mid 1970s. The average annual rate of inflation reached almost 25 percent in 1974. Other performance indicators showed similar trends. Productivity (output per man-hour) in manufacturing declined, and manufacturing unit costs increased dramatically.

The late 1970s brought on a second, less severe energy crisis and (possibly more important) a sharply increasing positive balance on the current account. Once again, the problem of balancing Japanese–American trade became a major issue.

Nevertheless, the condition of the Japanese economy was generally positive: Although the rate of economic growth declined in the 1980s, performance was still impressive. Between 1965 and 1980, gross domestic product grew at an average annual rate of 6.3 percent, and from 1980 to 1987, 3.7 percent. For the same periods, the average annual rate of inflation declined from 7.5 to 1.5 percent.[110] Policies of restraint, intended to bring inflation under control and to restore economic growth and balance-of-payments equilibrium, were largely successful.

From the late 1980s through the mid-1990s, two themes have dominated discussions about Japan.[111] First, after a period of strong economic performance, negative changes have increased pessimism and concern among the people of Japan. This had led many in the West to question the economic strength and seeming invincibility of the Japanese economic system. Second, the Japanese trade surplus, especially its large imbalance with the United States, remains a point of contention for many and has been a dominant theme of U.S.–Japanese relations during the Clinton administration.[112] Both situations are interrelated and will undoubtedly be important issues throughout the decade.

A slower rate of economic growth for Japan in the 1990s, along with the end of a lengthy tenure for the Liberal Democratic Party, have changed the Japanese domestic economic scene. Increasing unemployment has fueled discussion about the future of the Japanese economy, especially regarding its position in research and development and the nature of such systemic arrangements and policies as employment.

Although the United States could take steps to reduce the large trade deficit with Japan, free trade implies a Japanese economy capable of sustaining growth of imports, and fewer "structural mechanisms" that inhibit the growth of imports, such as domestic regulations and business practices. These tend to limit the potential of foreign competitors in Japanese domestic markets.[113]

The Japanese economy of the 1990s sustains many of the basic systemic elements of earlier times, yet lagging economic performance has led to the questioning of macroeconomic and microeconomic policies that could lead to important changes in the Japanese economy and its interaction with the U.S. economy in particular and the world economy in general.

Sweden: The Welfare State in a Market Capitalist Setting

The Swedish economic system and its performance are of interest to many for a single but vitally important reason. Sweden is viewed as a system that has been able, over an extended period of time, to sustain economic progress through the efficiency of the market while at the same time implementing an egalitarian distribution of income more typical of a welfare state. Although the past two decades of the 1970s were a challenge to Sweden, nevertheless the Swedish system has been admired by many and has become a centerpiece of attention as a "middle way" to economic reform and change. This focus remains important, though in recent years, some have questioned the long-term viability of Swedish arrangements. Indeed, recession and important accompanying changes have altered substantially the Swedish economic system in the 1990s.

As with other system variants, it is useful to examine the nature of economic outcomes in the Swedish case and the forces influencing these outcomes, specifically the environmental setting, the systemic or organizational arrangements of the Swedish economy, and Swedish economic policies.[114]

Sweden: The Setting

Sweden is a relatively small but highly industrialized country. It has a total area of roughly 450,000 square kilometers (somewhat larger than the state of California), and it had a population of just over 8.5 million in 1990. As of 1988, Sweden had a per capita gross national product of almost $20,000 measured in U.S. dollars, the third highest in the world (behind Switzerland and Japan).[115] The bulk of this income is derived from industry and services; agriculture plays a very small role.

Since World War II, Sweden has experienced a long period of economic progress based on the development of its resources (timber, hydroelectric energy, and iron ore) with major reliance on a market economy and participation in foreign trade. During the 1960s, the growth of real gross domestic product in Sweden was over 4 percent annually. Although this rate was cut in half in the decade to follow, Sweden nevertheless sustained reasonable real growth rates of over 2 percent annually in the 1980s. Foreign trade is of vital importance to Sweden. In recent years, foreign trade turnover (exports plus imports) has accounted for more than 70 percent of gross national product, a very high proportion by international standards. As we examine the Swedish record and the difficulties Sweden had in coping with the decade of the 1970s, these facts will be of major importance.

Sweden is the prototype of a developed industrial society that has a significant involvement in foreign trade and a high standard of living based on an educated labor force functioning largely in an urban, industrial setting. It is a system, however, that has combined market efficiency with an egalitarian distribution of income in a democratic political setting. These arrangements are of major interest to comparative economists.

Sweden: The Welfare State?

Thus far we have emphasized that the Swedish economy has achieved a high level of output based on a good growth record. This type of economic performance facilitated the growth of consumption. However, although productivity growth was substantial in the 1960s, the decade of the 1970s brought this rapid growth in productivity to an end and presented a challenge to be faced in the 1980s. This challenge was serious: A system with declining economic performance simply could not support the pace at which the standard of living had been growing. Moreover, many began to question whether Sweden had really achieved compatibility between efficiency and equity.

Although the role of the state in influencing distribution can be measured in a variety of ways, a few basic numbers will serve to illustrate the Swedish case. The Swedish economy is predominantly a private enterprise economy in production, but a very different picture emerges when we examine the distribution of the product. For example, in the late 1980s fully 26 percent of aggregate demand was that of government, compared to 20 percent in the United States and 9 percent in Japan. For the same year, total government expenditure in Sweden accounted for 40.8 percent of gross national product; the comparable figure for the United States was 22.9 percent.[116]

Who receives the benefits of Swedish government spending? Not surprisingly, housing, amenities, social security, and welfare accounted for fully 54.2 percent of government spending in 1988—more than 20 percentage points greater than the proportion allotted to the equivalent sort of spending in the United States. Education also commands a much greater share of government spending in Sweden than in the United States, though of course the Swedish share of defense spending is much lower. Surprisingly, health accounted for a modest 1.1 percent of central government spending in 1988, compared to 12.5 percent in the United States.

As one might expect, major government programs in Sweden are financed by major taxes. In 1988, total central government revenue in Sweden accounted for 42.9 percent of gross national product; the comparable figure for the United States was 19.7 percent, and for the United Kingdom 36.4 percent. In addition to this much larger role for the state in Sweden, the sources of government revenue also differ significantly. In 1988, taxes on income, profits, and capital gains accounted for only 17.8 percent of Swedish central government revenue; the comparable figure for the United States was a whopping 51.5 percent. Social security contributions claim a high and similar share in both countries, but Sweden relies heavily on taxes on goods and services. This category accounts for 29.0 percent of central government revenue in Sweden, compared to a paltry 3.6 percent in the United States.

Possibly the ultimate test of state policies designed to redistribute income is examination of actual distribution outcomes. Unfortunately, many problems plague the measurement of income distribution, and estimates must be interpreted with some skepticism. However, the impact of the welfare state does show up in the Swedish case. For example, on the basis of household income for the mid-1980s, the lowest-earning 20 percent of households in Sweden received 8 percent of all household income, whereas the top-earning 20 percent of households received 26.9 percent of income. Comparable figures for the United States are 4.7 and 41.9 percent, respectively.[117]

Sweden: The Economic System

So far we have characterized the Swedish economy as a market economy based largely on private ownership but wherein the state plays a major role as an agent of income redistribution. Although there have been important changes, the nature of the Swedish economic system is more complex and deserves additional attention.

1. From an environmental perspective, the nature of Sweden dictates to a large measure the sorts of outcomes that one expects to observe. For example, it is obvious that Sweden, as a small country that needs to import fossil fuels, will be a major player in world markets and will be influenced by those markets in turn. Moreover, with a highly educated labor force, one would expect a production structure and economic policies appropriate to the available factor mix.
2. The essence of the Swedish model is the setting of social democracy, a system where, as one observer put it, a complementary rather than a competitive relationship exists between the competitive and the cooperative aspects of social existence.[118] Thus in terms of goals and the means through which goals will be achieved, the views of the population are articulated through participation in a variety of groups such as unions, clubs, and the like.
3. Within the framework of social democracy, important market information is shared in such a way that the process is viewed as contributing to social gain for most if not all of the population. Thus in the sphere of labor allocation, the Swedish economy is viewed as having a very active labor market in which labor mobility is critical to the effective allocation of labor. At the same time, the existence of industry-wide collective agreements preserves a measure of control over wage increases that is designed to promote both economic growth and stability.

4. Employees can participate in enterprise management, at least on an advisory basis, through worker councils. In addition, workers can participate in ownership through employee investment funds—a mechanism to, in effect, convert profits into employee ownership. Employee ownership is controversial, but its basic thrust is to create harmony between the interests of worker and enterprise.

5. The Swedish state is an active participant in the economy through the use of traditional tools of monetary and fiscal policy, which is especially important in an open economy. As we shall see, the state's role in this sphere has been controversial.

6. Sweden maintains an egalitarian distribution of income largely through transfers of various types, providing generous benefits for retirement, medical care, education, and the like. These programs, and Sweden's continuing commitment to full employment, create an environment of substantial economic security.

Performance: An End to the Swedish Model?

A key theme in this book has been how various systems responded to the economic challenges of the 1970s and early 1980s—and in particular to the energy crisis of the earlier decade. We have emphasized that most systems experienced difficulty during these troubled times.

The Swedish economy was no exception. Indeed, the problems of the 1970s and 1980s led many to ask whether the Swedish model had outlived its usefulness. Simply put, the energy shocks of the 1970s increased domestic costs, which, along with poor productivity performance, led to an erosion of the Swedish position in external markets. But the government followed a policy of expanding the deficit, which in turn stimulated inflation. Although it was more complex than this simple description suggests, the situation appeared to many a case where planners failed to find the appropriate policy mix, rather than evidence of any fundamental problems in the Swedish system. Some, however, argued that more basic changes were at work.

In a major survey of the Swedish model published in 1985, Erik Lundberg noted that in addition to failures of stabilization policies, support for the social democrats became more fragmented, and policy objectives were contradictory.[119] A theme noted by Lundberg and other observers was the conflict between existing wage-setting arrangements and the continued drive for an egalitarian distribution of income—a conflict that squeezed profits and limited the attractiveness of investment, while at the same time generating low levels of unemployment in largely artificial and noncompetitive ways. Finally, Lundberg emphasized the changing nature of the international economy, a setting where Sweden faced increasingly limited policy options and a greater need to conform to policies of other major countries. In essence, the problems were more than simply policy mistakes incorporating basic elements of the Swedish system.

From the vantage point of the mid-1990s, it is evident that the early and mid-1980s marked a major turning point for the Swedish economy. During that time, the Swedish economy fundamentally changed course, partly in response to a severe

TABLE 9.4   Sweden: Contemporary Performance

	1980–1991	1991	1992	1993	1994	1995
GDP (% change)	2.0[a]	−1.7	−1.7	−2.8	1.2	2.5
Unemployment (%)	—	2.9	5.3	8.0	8.7	8.6
Consumer Price Index (% change)	7.4[b]	9.4[c]	2.3	4.6	1.9	2.7
Current Account Deficit	—	20.3	29.9	—	36.7	59.5

[a] average annual
[b] average annual rate of inflation
[c] year to year

Sources: Data for 1980–1991 from World Bank, *World Development Report 1993* (New York: Oxford University Press, 1993), various tables; remaining data from *The Swedish Economy Autumn 1993* (Stockholm: National Institute of Economic Research, 1993), 6.

recession, but also because of the basic changes in Swedish society and its long pursuit of the welfare state.[120]

The evidence presented in Table 9.4, including projections through the middle of this decade, illustrates the direction of change in the economy. In the past, the Swedish economy experienced modest growth, low levels of unemployment, high rates of inflation, and a sustained negative current account balance. The system relied on fiscal and monetary controls and an income policy that provided a close relationship between wage increases and productivity growth.

Since the late 1980s, the economy shifted away from a high-inflation–low-unemployment posture to a more traditional monetarist perspective that relied increasingly on market mechanisms to allocate resources. Controls were reduced, real interest rates were allowed to rise significantly, which has resulted in a growing government budget deficit, a redistribution of income in favor of wealthier families, and a shrinking of domestic demand. In addition, changes were introduced to shift the economy away from public consumption, especially at the local government level, through changes in the social insurance system.

During the latter years of increasingly serious economic reform in the planned socialist economic systems, the Swedish model was often cited as a potentially attractive model that seemed to combine efficiency with a socialist view of equity. Contemporary changes now imply that this model has become as vulnerable as the planned socialist model and that markets have become the future path for both in the 1990s.

Summary

This chapter examined five mature capitalist economies that are interesting because of the significant differences in their system arrangements and economic policies. Although short-term changes were downplayed in economic performance, it is important to emphasize that characterization of the recent past can be useful in an attempt to isolate the impact of the economic system.

For most of those systems, the 1950s and 1960s were relatively tranquil. The 1970s and early 1980s were anything but tranquil, providing the opportunity to examine those systems under such shocks as the energy crisis.

If generalization is reasonable, then the past decade has had an effect on the basic indicators of performance: economic growth, productivity, unemployment, and the emergence of new trade patterns in the global economy of the 1990s. In addition to those effects, the demise of the major planned socialist economic systems placed a new emphasis on the subtle yet possibly important system differences such as the relevance of differing degrees of government intervention in the French and Japanese economies, for example.

The economy of France is of interest because it is a mature market capitalist economy that uses indicative planning. That planning system has been sustained despite the change in the French attitude toward planning arrangements. There is, however, relatively little agreement on whether the French plan explains the performance of the French economy. This disagreement reflects both methodological issues and the basic difficulties of associating performance differences with system differences.

The British economy is of interest as a mature economy in which the role of the state is important, not through a process of economic planning but rather through public ownership and the budgetary process. Although in the past, economic performance in Britain has been modest, the conservative government of Margaret Thatcher significantly changed economic policy and improved performance. Thatcher's approach was based on the issue of monetary policy, incentives, competitive markets, and privatization. Although critics question the costs associated with improved economic performance (for example, the persistent problem of unemployment), enterprise-level analysis of privatization is generally positive. But in the 1990s, the political power of Margaret Thatcher's successor—John Major—is in question, and concern lingers for the eventual decline of importance of North Sea Oil in the British economic equation.

Germany is described as a social market economy because of the strong combination of government intervention and worker participation in a market economy. Traditionally, the German economy has been viewed as an economic miracle, through recent problems of inflation and unemployment have tarnished that image. In the 1990s, the German economy needs to respond to the new European economic arrangements, but most importantly it must cope with the large costs of unification.

The economy of Japan is unique in that it combines unusual organizational arrangements with special social and cultural values that facilitate an important role for the state. Traditionally, the Japanese economy has been interesting because of its outstanding growth performance. In contemporary times, organizational arrangements, especially those involving the role of the state through organizations such as MITI, have captured our attention along with performance problems and related adjustments in the 1990s.

For many observes, Sweden is the classic example of a welfare state in which an egalitarian distribution of benefits is achieved with a major role for the state but with the efficiency of market arrangements. In the 1990s, this model has provoked growing disillusion as weakening performance has led to increased questioning of the dominant role of government in the economy. At the same time, former socialist systems that are undergoing transition have been looking to the Swedish model as a possible alternative.

Key Terms

indicative planning
mature capitalism
social market economy
welfare state
modernization commissions
industrial policy
income policy
demand management
"stop-go" policies
nationalization

deregulation
privatization
codetermination
denationalization
unification
New Economic System
Federal Privatizing Trust
share economy
Ministry of International Trade
  and Industry (MITI)

Notes

France

1. There is a large body of literature on the French economy. For an overview, see J. R. Hough, *The French Economy* (New York: Holmes & Meier, 1982); Stephen S. Cohen, *Modern Capitalist Planning: The French Model* (Berkeley: University of California Press, 1977); and Stephen S. Cohen and Peter A. Gourevitch, eds., *France in a Troubled World Economy* (Boston: Butterworth, 1982). For a discussion of the French economy and survey of the literature on indicative planning, see Saul Estrin and Peter Holmes, *French Planning in Theory and Practice* (Boston: Allen and Unwin, 1983); for a survey of this period, see Bela Balassa, *The First Year of Socialist Government in France* (Washington, D.C.: American Enterprise Institute, 1982). For a discussion of planning institutions, see John and Anne Marie Hackett, *Economic Planning in France* (Cambridge, Mass.: Harvard University Press, 1963). For an examination of the effectiveness of French planning, see John H. McArthur and Bruce R. Scott, *Industrial Planning in France* (Boston: Graduate School of Business Administration, Harvard University, 1969). For a critical view, see Vera Lutz, *Central Planning for the Market Economy: An Analysis of the French Theory and Experience* (London: Longmans Green, 1969). For an in-depth treatment of French economic performance, see J.-J. Carre, P. Dubois, and E. Malinvaud, *French Economic Growth* (Stanford, Calif.: Stanford University Press, 1975); for an historical survey, see Richard F. Kuisel, *Capitalism and the State of Modern France* (New York: Cambridge University Press, 1981); for a recent discussion, see Bernard Cazes, "Indicative Planning in France,"

Journal of Comparative Economics 14, 4 (December 1990), 607–620; Klaus-Walter Riechel, "Indicative Planning in France: Discussion," *Journal of Comparative Economics*, 14, 4 (December 1990), 621–624.

2. In market economic systems where planning has been introduced, or in planned economies where economic reform has meant the introduction of market forces, there have tended to be difficulties bringing the two different sorts of instruments together. This case has been argued in David Granick, "An Organizational Model of Soviet Industrial Planning," *Journal of Political Economy*, 67 (1959), 123–124; for an analysis, see Benjamin N. Ward, *The Socialist Economy: A Study of Organizational Alternatives* (New York: Random House, 1967), pp. 178–181.

3. Carre, Dubois, and Malinvaud, *French Economic Growth*, p. 21.

4. For background, see Richard F. Kuisel, *Capitalism and the State in Modern France*; and Andrew Schonfield, *Modern Capitalism: The Changing Balance of Public and Private Power* (New York: Oxford University Press, 1965).

5. See for example the discussion in Saul Estrin and Peter Holmes, *French Planning in Theory and Practice*, Ch. 8.

6. This case is argued in Andrew Schonfield, *Modern Capitalism: The Changing Balance of Public and Private Power*, Ch. 5.

7. For a detailed examination of the growth of the public sector in different countries, see Frederic L. Pryor, *Public Expenditures in Communist and Capitalist Nations* (London: Allen and Unwin, 1968); D. Cameron, "The Expansion of the Public Economy: A Comparative Analysis," *American Political Science Review*, 92 (1978), 1243–1261; and Frank Gould, "The Development of Public Expenditures in Western Industrialized Countries: A Comparative Analysis," *Public Finance*, 38, 1 (1983), 38–69.

8. Schonfield, *Modern Capitalism*, pp. 156–157.

9. The importance of technical planning experts in different planning efforts has been emphasized: a major role in the French case, a minimal role in the British case. For a comparison, see ibid., pp. 155–156.

10. The differing national styles of executive development have been examined in David Granick, *The European Executive* (New York: Doubleday, 1962). For a recent comparative analysis, see David Granick, *Managerial Comparisons of Four Developed Countries: France, Britain, United States and Russia* (Cambridge, Mass.: M.I.T. Press, 1972).

11. For a survey of views on planning in the United States, see Zoltan Kenessey, *The Process of Economic Planning* (New York: Columbia University Press, 1977). For a comparative viewpoint, see Morris Bornstein, ed., *Economic Planning, East and West* (Cambridge, Mass.: Ballinger, 1975). On the relevance of the French planning experience to the United States, see Stephen S. Cohen, *Recent Developments in French Planning: Some Lessons for the United States* (Washington, D.C.: U.S. Government Printing Office, 1977).

12. For an excellent survey of views, see Estrin and Holmes, *French Planning in Theory and Practice*, Chs. 1–2.

13. See Schonfield, *Modern Capitalism*, Ch. 7.

14. Lutz, *Central Planning for the Market Economy*, Ch. 6.

15. Any discussion of the French planning system invariably devotes a great deal of attention to the mystique of the planning system, the ability of the state and the planners to get things done in the absence of coercive power, flexibility and strength, democracy, and direction. For a generally balanced treatment of these features of French planning, see Schonfield, *Modern Capitalism*, Ch. 7; for a critical view, see Lutz,

Central Planning for the Market Economy; for a brief but useful discussion of pro and con views and references to the literature, see Hough, *The French Economy*, Ch. 5; for a recent view, see Bernard Cazes, "Indicative Planning in France," *Journal of Comparative Economics*, 14, 4 (December 1990), 607–620.

16. See Hans Schollhammer, "National Economic Planning and Business Decision Making: The French Experience," in Morris Bornstein, ed., *Comparative Economic Systems: Models and Cases*, 3rd ed. (Homewood, Ill.: Irwin, 1974), pp. 52–76.

17. For a useful discussion of the relationship among the state, the sources of investment funds, and the plan, see Carre, Dubois, and Malinvaud, *French Economic Growth*, Ch. 10.

18. Changing the nature of the business environment and the extent to which planning (as opposed to simple forecasting) is useful has been controversial. For a discussion of information flows and the French planning system, see ibid., Ch. 14; for a discussion of the theoretical question of reducing uncertainty through planning, see J. E. Meade, *The Theory of Indicative Planning* (Manchester, England: Manchester University Press, 1970); see also Estrin and Holmes, *French Planning in Theory and Practice*, Ch. 1–2; see also Joseph Brada and Saul Estrin (eds.), "Advances in Indicative Planning," *Journal of Comparative Economics*, 14, 4 (December 1990), 523–812.

19. Lutz, *Central Planning for the Market Economy*.

20. For a discussion of changes in the French planning system, see Martin Cave, "Decentralized Planning in Britain: Comment," *Economics of Planning* 19, 3 (1985), 141–144; Martin Cave, "French Planning Reforms, 1981–1984," *The ACES Bulletin* 26, 2–3 (1984), 29–38; Saul Estrin, "Decentralized Economic Planning: Some Issues," *Economics of Planning*, 19, 3 (1985), 150–156.

21. Robert Eisner argues that obsession with trade deficits has been a major focus of policy in the early 1980s. See his article "Which Way for France?" *Challenge*, 20 (July/August 1983), 34–41.

22. Such a case is made in Estrin and Holmes, *French Planning in Theory and Practice*.

23. See Schollhammer, "National Economic Planning and Business Decision Making," pp. 52–76.

24. Lutz, *Central Planning for the Market Economy*.

25. McArthur and Scott, *Industrial Planning in France*, pp. 26–27.

26. Hough, *The French Economy*.

27. Estrin and Holmes, "Preface," *French Planning in Theory and Practice*, p. vii.

28. Cohen, *Modern Capitalist Planning*.

29. Ibid., pp. 238–279.

30. Martin Cave, "French Planning Reforms."

31. Eisner, "Which Way for France?" pp. 35–37.

32. Ibid.

33. A. Dupont-Fauville, "Nationalisation of the Banks in France: A Preliminary Evaluation," *The Three Banks Review*, 139 (September 1983), 32–41.

34. Balassa, *The First Year of Socialist Government in France*, pp. 2–5.

35. Measures of government involvement are from Gould, "The Development of Public Expenditures in Western Industrialized Countries: A Comparative Analysis," pp. 42–43.

Great Britain

36. For a discussion of the British economy in the socialist mold, see Allan G. Gruchy, *Comparative Economic Systems*, 2nd ed. (Boston: Houghton Mifflin, 1977), Ch. 11.

For a more recent statement, see Michael Meacher, *Socialism with a Human Face* (London: Allen and Unwin, 1982).

37. The following are useful sources: John and Anne Marie Hackett, *The British Economy: Problems and Prospects* (London: Allen and Unwin, 1967); Richard E. Caves and Associates, *Britain's Economic Prospects* (Washington, D.C.: Brookings, 1968); Sir Alec Cairncross, ed., *Britain's Economic Prospects Reconsidered* (Albany: State University of New York Press, 1970); Richard E. Caves and Lawrence B. Krause, eds., *Britain's Economic Performance* (Washington, D.C.: Brookings, 1980); and W. P. J. Maunder, ed., *The British Economy in the 1970s* (London: Heinemann Educational Books, 1980); Sidney Pollard, *The Wasting of the British Economy* (New York: St. Martin's, 1982). A useful introductory survey is National Institute of Economic and Social Research, *The United Kingdom Economy* (London: Heinemann Educational Books, 1976); for a helpful update, see W. B. Reddaway, "Problems and Prospects for the U.K. Economy," *The Economic Record*, 59 (September 1983), 220–231.

38. For a statistical comparison of development patterns including Great Britain, see Hollis Chenery and Moises Syrquin, *Patterns of Development, 1950–1970* (New York: Oxford University Press, 1975).

39. Andrew Schonfield, *Modern Capitalism: The Changing Balance of Public and Private Power* (New York: Oxford University Press, 1965), Ch. 6.

40. On the regional question, see B. E. Coates and E. M. Rawstron, *Regional Variations in Britain* (London: Batsford, 1971).

41. Schonfield, *Modern Capitalism*, p. 88.

42. For an interesting discussion of a particular case of British wartime planning, see Ely Devons, *Planning in Practice* (Cambridge, England: Cambridge University Press, 1950).

43. In the period when British concern for poor economic performance, especially unemployment, was growing rapidly, actual performance was quite good, though possibly not on a par with that of the fast-growing nations of the period. For example, between 1959 and 1966, the average annual rate of unemployment was 2.6 percent in Britain, 5.4 percent in the United States, and 5.5 percent in Canada. For the period 1955–1964, per capita national income grew in Britain at an average annual rate of 2.1 percent, compared to 1.4 percent in the United States, 4.7 percent in Italy, and 4.3 percent in West Germany.

44. For a discussion, see Carlo M. Cipolla, ed., *The Economic Decline of Empires* (London: Methuen, 1970); see also Frank Blackaby, ed., *De-industrialisation* (London: Heinemann Educational Books, 1979).

45. We shall not discuss the details of British stabilization policy in this short survey. The interested reader should refer to the discussion in Hackett, *The British Economy*, Ch. 1; for a more recent brief survey, see G. D. N. Worswick, "Fiscal Policy and Stabilization in Britain," in Cairncross, *Britain's Economic Prospects Reconsidered*, pp. 36–60; for useful background, see Charles Feinstein, ed., *The Managed Economy* (Oxford, England: Oxford University Press, 1983). See also G. D. N. Worswick, "The End of Demand Management?" *Lloyd's Bank Review*, 123 (January 1977), 1–18.

46. Worswick, "Fiscal Policy and Stabilization in Britain."

47. For a brief but excellent survey of the British experience with national economic planning, see Werner Z. Hirsch, *Recent Experience with National Economic Planning in the United Kingdom* (Washington, D.C.: Government Printing Office, 1977).

48. Ibid., pp. 13–15.

49. Schonfield, *Modern Capitalism*, p. 173.

50. Hackett, *The British Economy*, p. 162.
51. Caves and Associates, *Britain's Economic Prospects*, pp. 271–274.
52. Chenery and Syrquin, *Patterns of Development*, table 5-4.
53. Caves and Associates, *Britain's Economic Prospects*, Ch. 8.
54. Meacher, *Socialism with a Human Face*.
55. The data presented here are from Frank Gould, "The Development of Public Expenditures in Western Industrialized Countries: A Comparative Analysis," *Public Finances*, 38, no. 1 (1983), 38–69.
56. See World Bank, *World Tables*, 2nd ed. (Baltimore: The Johns Hopkins University Press, 1980).
57. A great deal has been written about the nationalized industries in Great Britain. For a brief survey, see Richard Pryke, "Public Enterprise in Great Britain," in Morris Bornstein, ed., *Comparative Economic Systems: Models and Cases*, 3rd ed. (Homewood, Ill.: Irwin, 1974), pp. 77–92. For in-depth treatment, see R. Kelf-Cohen, *Twenty Years of Nationalisation* (London: Macmillan, 1969); R. Kelf-Cohen, *British Nationalisation, 1945–1973* (New York: St. Martin's, 1973); and Leonard Tivey, ed., *The Nationalized Industries Since 1960: A Book of Readings* (Toronto: University of Toronto Press, 1973). For a discussion of issues in the 1970s, see T. G. Weyman-Jones, "The Nationalised Industries: Changing Attitudes and Changing Roles," in W. P. J. Maunder, ed., *The British Economy in the 1970s*, Ch. 8.
58. Steel (denationalized in 1954 and nationalized again in 1965) is not included. See Pryke, "Public Enterprise in Great Britain," p. 82.
59. See, for example, the discussion in Reddaway, "Problems and Prospects for the U.K. Economy."
60. For a useful discussion, see Blackaby, *De-industrialisation*.
61. Poor performance after 1973 is emphasized in Caves and Krause, *Britain's Economic Performance*.
62. Reddaway, "Problems and Prospects for the U.K. Economy," table 1.
63. Computed from Caves and Krause, *Britain's Economic Performance*, table 2, p. 3.
64. Pollard, *The Wasting of the British Economy*, table 3.3, p. 53.
65. Ibid., table 1.2, p. 12.
66. Reddaway, "Problems and Prospects for the U.K. Economy," p. 225.
67. Caves and Krause, *Britain's Economic Performance*, p. 19.
68. For interesting background, see Bernard N. Nossiter, *Britain—A Future That Works* (Boston: Houghton Mifflin, 1978).
69. Useful sources include David S. Bell, ed., *The Conservative Government, 1979–84: An Interim Report* (London: Croom Helm, 1985); Paul Hare, *Planning the British Economy* (London: Macmillan, 1985); Grahame Thompson, *The Conservatives' Economic Policy* (London: Croom Helm, 1986); Alan Walters, *Britain's Economic Renaissance* (New York: Oxford University Press, 1986); and "Planning in Britain," *Journal of Comparative Economics* 19, 3 (1985).
70. Alan Walters, *Britain's Economic Renaissance*, pp. 4–5.
71. For a critical view, see David S. Bell, *The Conservative Government*.
72. Grahame Thompson, *The Conservatives' Economic Policy*, Ch. 7.
73. William L. Megginson, Robert C. Nash, and Mathias van Randenburgh, "The Financial and Operating Performance of Newly Privatized Firms: An International Empirical Analysis," *The Journal of Finance*, 44 (June 1994), 403–452.
74. See also John Vickers and George Yarrow, "Regulation of Privatized Firms in Britain," *European Economic Review*, 32 (1988) 465–472.

75. To the extend that systemic change is involved, assessment of the Thatcher years will require a much longer time horizon.

76. World Bank, *World Development Report 1987*, p. 223.

Germany

77. Our discussion of the early years is based on the following sources: Heinz Lampert, *Volkswirtschaftliche Institutionen* (Munich: Verlag Franz Vahlen, 1980); G. Gutman, W. Klein, S. Paraskewopolous, and H. Winter, *Die Wirtschafts-Verfassung der Bundesrepublik Deutschland*, 2nd ed. (Stuttgart: Fischer, 1979); Hannelore Hamel, ed., *Bundesrepublik Deutschland-DDR, Die Wirtschaftssysteme*, 4th ed. (Munich: C. H. Beck, 1983); and Gerhard Brinkman, *Okonomik der Arbeit*, Vol. I (Stuttgart: Ernst Klett Verlag, 1981).

78. This label is credited to A. Muller-Armack, "Soziale Marktwirtschaft," in *Handwörterbuch der Sozialwissenschaften*, Band IX (Stuttgart: Fischer, 1956), p. 390.

79. H. Jorg Thieme, *Soziale Marktwirtschaft: Konzeption und wirtschaftspolitische Gestaltung in der BRD* (Hanover: Berenberg, 1973), pp. 12–28; and Wolfram Engels, *Soziale Martwirtschaft: Verschmähte Zukunft* (Stuttgart: Seewald, 1973), pp. 40–45.

80. L. Erhard and A. Muller-Armack, *Soziale Marktwirtschaft* (Frankfurt am Main: Ullstein, 1972).

81. See Gutman, et al., *Wirtschaftsverfassung*, Ch. 8.

82. Thieme, *Soziale Marktwirtschaft*, pp. 83–87.

83. Lampert, *Institutionen*, pp. 31–49.

84. Martin Schnitzer and James Nordyke, *Comparative Economic Systems*, 2nd ed. (Cincinnati, Ohio: Southwestern, 1977), p. 328.

85. J. H. Kaiser, "Public Enterprise in Germany," in W. G. Friedman and J. F. Garner, *Government Enterprise: A Comparative Study* (New York: Columbia University Press, 1970).

86. For a discussion of the GDR and comparisons to the FRG, see Paul R. Gregory and Gert Leptin, "Similar Societies Under Differing Economic Systems: The Case of the Two Germanys," *Soviet Studies* 29 (October 1977), 519–541.

87. For recent comparative data, see Paul R. Gregory and Robert C. Stuart, *Comparative Economic Systems*, 3rd ed. (Boston: Houghton Mifflin, 1989), Ch. 13. Unemployment data are from George A. Akerlof, Andrew K. Rose, and Janet L. Yellen, "East Germany in from the Cold: The Economic Aftermath of Currency Union," paper presented at the Conference of the Brookings Panel on Economic Activity, Washington, D.C., April 4, 1991, p. 92. For recent analyses of the East German transition, see Helmut Wagner, "Reconstruction of the Financial System in East Germany," *Journal of Banking and Finance* 17 (1993), 1001–1029; Roy Vogt, "Transforming the Former GDR into a Market Economy," *Comparative Economic Studies*, 34 (Fall–Winter 1992), 68–80.

Japan

88. Angus Maddison, *Economic Growth in Japan and the USSR* (London: Allen and Unwin, 1969), Ch. 1.

89. For an excellent survey of the early years of Japanese economic development, see Kazushi Ohkawa and Henry Rosovsky, *Japanese Economic Growth* (Stanford, Calif.: Stanford University Press, 1973).

90. For an examination of the Japanese growth experience, see Lawrence Klein and Kazushi Ohkawa, eds., *Economic Growth: The Japanese Experience Since the Meiji Era* (Homewood, Ill.: Irwin, 1968); Japan Economic Research Center, *Economic Growth: The Japanese Experience Since the Meiji Era*, Vols. I and II (Tokyo: Japan Economic Research Center, 1973); and Hugh Patrick and Henry Rosovsky, eds., *Asia's New Giant: How the Japanese Economy Works* (Washington, D.C.: Brookings, 1976). For a discussion of Japanese economic planning, see Shuntaro Shishido, "Japanese Experience with Long-Term Economic Planning," and Tsunshiko Watanabe, "National Planning and Economic Growth in Japan," both in Bert G. Hickman, ed., *Quantitative Planning of Economic Policy* (Washington, D.C.: Brookings, 1965); and William Lockwood, ed., *The State and Economic Enterprise in Japan* (Princeton, N.J.: Princeton University Press, 1965). For an analysis of Japanese labor markets, see Koji Taira, *Economic Development and the Labor Market in Japan* (New York: Columbia University Press, 1970). For a discussion of Japanese multinationals, see Ozawa Terutomo, *Multinationalism Japanese Style* (Princeton, N.J.: Princeton University Press, 1979); Yoshi Tsurumi, *The Japanese Are Coming: A Multinational Interaction of Firms and Politics* (Cambridge, Mass.: Ballinger, 1976); and M. Y. Yoshino, *Japan's Multinational Enterprises* (Cambridge, Mass.: Harvard University Press, 1976). For a general discussion of the Japanese economic system, especially its organizational features, see G. C. Allen, *The Japanese Economy* (London: Weidenfeld and Nicolson, 1981).

91. Taira, *Economic Development*.

92. For a brief discussion, see Allen, *The Japanese Economy*, Ch. 5; for background, see I. J. Nakamura, *Agricultural Production and the Economic Development of Japan, 1873–1922* (Princeton, N.J.: Princeton University Press, 1966).

93. Maddison, *Economic Growth in Japan and the USSR*, Ch. 4.

94. For a survey of Japanese economic growth, see Ohkawa and Rosovsky, *Japanese Economic Growth*, Ch. 2.

95. Various aspects of the Japanese labor market are discussed in Allen, *The Japanese Economy*, Ch. 9; and Taira, *Economic Development*.

96. For a useful survey of organizational features of the Japanese economic system, see Kanji Haitani, *The Japanese Economic System* (Lexington, Mass.: Heath, 1976).

97. Ohkawa and Rosovsky, *Japanese Economic Growth*, Ch. 5.

98. In addition to Taira, *Economic Development*, see Robert E. Cole, *Japanese Blue-Collar: The Changing Tradition* (Berkeley: University of California Press, 1971); for a summary, see Robert E. Cole, "Industrial Relations in Japan" in Morris Bornstein, ed., *Comparative Economic Systems, Models and Cases*, 3rd ed. (Homewood, Ill.: Irwin, 1974), pp. 93–116.

99. Kozo Yamamura, "Entrepreneurship, Ownership and Management in Japan," in M. M. Postan et al., *Cambridge Economic History of Europe*, Vol. VII, pt. 2 (Cambridge, England: Cambridge University Press, 1978), pp. 215–264. See also Eleanor M. Hadley, *Antitrust in Japan* (Princeton, N.J.: Princeton University Press, 1970); Richard E. Caves and Masu Uekusa, *Industrial Organizations in Japan* (Washington, D.C.: Brookings, 1976); and Haitani, *The Japanese Economic System*.

100. John M. Montias, *The Structure of Economic Systems* (New Haven: Yale University Press, 1976), pt. 5.

101. Martin Weitzman, *The Share Economy* (Cambridge, Mass.: Harvard University Press, 1984).

102. Merton J. Peck, "Is Japan Really a Share Economy?" *Journal of Comparative Economics* 10 (1986), 427–432.

103. For a recent discussion, see Gregory B. Christainsen and Jan S. Hagendorn, "Japanese Productivity: Adapting to Changing Comparative Advantage in the Face of Lifetime Employment Commitments," *Quarterly Review of Business and Economics*, 23 (Summer 1983), 23–39. For a discussion of the labor–management issue in a growth context, see Harry Oshima, "Reinterpreting Japan's Postwar Growth," *Economic Development and Cultural Change*, 31 (October 1982), 1–43.

104. Christainsen and Hagendorn, "Japanese Productivity," p. 30.

105. The classic work on the Japanese factory is J. G. Abegglen, *The Japanese Factory* (Glencoe, Ill.: Free Press, 1958).

106. Assessing the role of government in the importance of the "public" sector in the Japanese economy is difficult for definitional reasons. For a discussion, see Chalmers Johnson, *Japan's Public Policy Companies* (Washington, D.C.: American Enterprise Institute, 1978).

107. Much has been written about MITI. For basics, see Haitani, *The Japanese Economic System*; for more detail, see Chalmers Johnson, *MITI and the Japanese Miracle* (Stanford, Calif.: Stanford University Press, 1982); and Christainsen and Hagendorn, "Japanese Productivity."

108. For a more restrained view of the role of MITI in the 1970s, see Kozo Yamamura, "Success That Soured: Administrative Guidance and Cartels in Japan," in Kozo Yamamura, ed., *Policy and Trade Issues of the Japanese Economy* (Seattle: University of Washington Press, 1982), pp. 77–112. On the role of the state in supporting key sectors, see also Gary R. Saxonhouse, "What Is All This About 'Industrial Targeting' in Japan?" *The World Economy*, 6 (September 1983), 253–273.

109. The movement from fixed to flexible exchange rates was, of course, much more an issue than U.S.–Japanese trade. See Patrick and Rosovsky, *Asia's New Giant*, Ch. 6. See also Takafusa Nakamura, *The Postwar Japanese Economy* (Tokyo: University of Tokyo Press, 1981), pt. 3; for specific references to the impact of oil shortages, see Yoichi Shinkai, "Oil Crises and Stagflation in Japan," in Yamamura, *Policy and Trade Issues of the Japanese Economy*, pp. 173–193.

110. Data are from World Bank, *World Development Report 1987* (New York: Oxford University Press, 1987), pp. 202–205.

111. Useful sources for analyzing contemporary adjustment policies include Ronald Dore, *Flexible Rigidities* (London: The Athlone Press, 1986); Chikara Higashi and G. Peter Lauter, *The Internationalization of the Japanese Economy* (Boston: Kluwer Academic Publishers, 1987); Edward J. Lincoln, *Japan: Facing Economic Maturity* (Washington, D.C.: Brookings, 1988); and Yoshio Suzuki, *Money, Finance, and Macroeconomic Performance in Japan* (New Haven: Yale University Press, 1986); Ryuzo Sato, "U.S.–Japan Relations Under the Clinton and Hosokawa Administrations," *Japan and the World Economy* 6, 1 (1994), 89–103; Gregory W. Noble, "Japan in 1993," *Asian Survey*, 34 (January 1994), 19–29.

112. See Ryuzo Sato, "U.S.–Japan Relations" and Gregory W. Noble, "Japan in 1993."

113. Ryuzo Sato, "U.S.–Japan Relations," 95.

Sweden

114. For a discussion of the Swedish Model, see Henry Milner, *Sweden: Social Democracy in Action* (New York: Oxford University Press, 1989); for background and a critique of the contemporary system, see Erik Lundberg, "The Rise and Fall of the Swedish Model," *Journal of Economic Literature* 23 (March 1985), 1–36; for an American

assessment, see Barry P. Bosworth and Alice M. Rivlin, eds., *The Swedish Economy* (Washington, D.C.: Brookings, 1987); Timothy A. Canova, "The Swedish Model Betrayed," *Challenge*, 37 (May–June 1994), 36–40; *The Swedish Economy Autumn 1993* (Stockholm: National Institute of Economic Research, 1993).

115. World Bank, *World Development Report 1990* (New York: Oxford University Press, 1990).
116. *World Development Report 1990*.
117. *World Development Report 1990*.
118. See Henry Milner, *Sweden: Social Democracy in Action*.
119. Erik Lundberg, "The Rise and Fall of the Swedish Model."
120. For a discussion of this point, see Assar Lindbeck, "Is the Welfare State in Trouble?" *Eastern Economic Journal* 13 (October–December 1987), 345–351; Timothy A. Canova, "The Swedish Model Betrayed."

Recommended Readings

France

Bela Balassa, *The First Year of Socialist Government in France* (Washington, D.C.: American Enterprise Institute, 1982).

Joseph Brada and Saul Estrin, eds., "Advances in Indicative Planning," *Journal of Comparative Economics*, 14 (December 1990), 523–812.

Bernard Cazes, "Indicative Planning in France," *Journal of Comparative Economics* 14 (December 1990), 607–619.

J.-J. Carre, P. Dubois, and E. Malinvaud, *French Economic Growth* (Stanford, Calif.: Stanford University Press, 1975).

Stephen S. Cohen, *Modern Capitalist Planning: The French Model* (Berkeley: University of California Press, 1977).

———, *Recent Developments in French Planning: Some Lessons for the United States* (Washington, D.C.: Government Printing Office, 1977).

Stephen S. Cohen and Peter A. Gourevitch, eds., *France in a Troubled World Economy* (Boston: Butterworth, 1982).

Saul Estrin and Peter Holmes, *French Planning in Theory and Practice* (Boston: Allen and Unwin, 1983).

John and Anne Marie Hackett, *Economic Planning in France* (Cambridge, Mass.: Harvard University Press, 1963).

Stanley Hottman and William Andrews, eds., *The Fifth Republic at Twenty* (New York: State University of New York Press, 1980).

J. R. Hough, *The French Economy* (New York: Holmes & Meier, 1982).

Richard F. Kuisel, *Capitalism and the State in Modern France* (New York: Cambridge University Press, 1981).

Vera Lutz, *Central Planning for the Market Economy: An Analysis of the French Theory and Experience* (London: Longmans Green, 1969).

John H. McArthur and Bruce R. Scott, *Industrial Planning in France* (Boston: Graduate School of Business Administration, Harvard University, 1969).

John Sheahan, *An Introduction to the French Economy* (Columbus, Ohio: Merrill, 1969).

W. Allen Spivey, *Economic Policies in France 1976–1981* (Ann Arbor: University of Michigan Graduate School of Business Administration, 1983).

Great Britain

David S. Bell, ed., *The Conservative Government, 1979–84: An Interim Report* (London: Croom Helm, 1985).

Frank Blackaby, ed., *De-industrialisation* (London: Heinemann Educational Books, 1979).

Richard E. Caves and Associates, *Britain's Economic Prospects* (Washington, D.C.: Brookings, 1968).

Richard E. Caves and Lawrence B. Krause, eds., *Britain's Economic Performance* (Washington, D.C.: Brookings, 1980).

Carlo M. Cipolla, ed., *The Economic Decline of Empires* (London: Methuen, 1970).

B. E. Coates and E. M. Rawstron, *Regional Variations in Britain* (London: Batsford, 1971).

Charles Feinstein, ed., *The Managed Economy* (Oxford, England: Oxford University Press, 1983).

John and Anne Marie Hackett, *The British Economy: Problems and Prospects* (London: Allen and Unwin, 1967).

Paul Hare, *Planning the British Economy* (London: Macmillan, 1985).

Werner Z. Hirsch, *Recent Experience with National Economic Planning in Great Britain* (Washington, D.C.: Government Printing Office, 1977).

R. Kelf-Cohen, *British Nationalization, 1945–1973* (New York: St. Martin's, 1973).

W. P. J. Maunder, ed., *The British Economy in the 1970's* (London: Heinemann Educational Books, 1980).

F. V. Meyer, D. C. Corner, and J. E. S. Parker, *Problems of a Mature Economy* (London: Macmillan, 1970).

National Institute of Economic and Social Research, *The United Kingdom Economy* (London: Heinemann Educational Books, 1976).

Sidney Pollard, *The Wasting of the British Economy* (New York: St. Martin's, 1982).

Grahame Thompson, *The Conservatives' Economic Policy* (London: Croom Helm, 1986).

Alan Walters, *Britain's Economic Renaissance* (New York: Oxford University Press, 1986).

Germany

George A. Akerlof, Andrew K. Rose, and Janet L. Yellen, "East Germany in from the Cold: The Economic Aftermath of Currency Union," paper presented at the Conference of the Brookings Panel on Economic Activity, Washington, D.C., April 4, 1991.

Gary R. Beling, "Selling Off the Family Silver? The Privatization of State Enterprises: The East German Case," unpublished paper, Princeton University, May 17, 1991.

Eduardo Borensztein and Manmohan S. Kumar, "Proposals for Privatization in Eastern Europe," Washington, D.C.: IMF Working Paper, April 1991.

Doris Cornelsen, "GDR: Current Issues," in NATO, *The Central and East European Economies in the 1990s: Perspectives and Constraints* (Brussels: NATO, 1990).

Irwin Collier, "The Estimation of Gross Domestic Product and Its Growth Rate for the German Democratic Republic" (Washington, D.C.: World Bank Staff Working Papers, #773, 1985).

Paul Gregory and Gert Leptin, "Similar Societies Under Differing Economic Systems: The Case of the Two Germanys," *Soviet Studies* 29, 4 (October 1977), 519–544.

Lutz Hoffmann, "Integrating the East German States into the German Economy: Opportunities, Burdens, and Options," paper presented at the American Institute for Contemporary German Studies, The Johns Hopkins University, Washington, D.C., November 13, 1990.

Barry W. Ickes, "What to Do Before the Capital Markets Arrive: The Transition Problem in Reforming Socialist Economies," paper presented at the Conference on the East European Transformation, Princeton University, May 3, 1991.

Henning Klodt, "Government Support for Restructuring the East German Economy," paper presented at the American Institute for Contemporary German Studies, The Johns Hopkins University, Washington, D.C., November 14, 1990.

Jack K. Knott, *Managing the German Economy* (Lexington, Mass.: Heath, 1981).

Oliver Letwin, *Privatizing the World* (London: Cassell, 1988).

Leslie Lipschitz and Donough McDonald, *German Unification: Economic Issues*, Washington, D.C., IMF, Occasional Paper #75, December 1990.

Philip L. Paarlberg, "Sectoral Adjustments in Eastern Germany Due to Market Forces," *Review of International Economics*, 2 (June 1994), 112–122.

Claus Schnabel, "Structural Adjustment and Privatization of the East German Economy," paper presented at the American Institute of Contemporary German Studies, The Johns Hopkins University, Washington, D.C., December 1990.

Martin Schnitzer, *East and West Germany: A Comparative Economic Analysis* (New York: Praeger, 1990).

———, *Income Distribution: A Comparative Study of the United States, Sweden, West Germany, East Germany, the United Kingdom, and Japan* (New York: Praeger, 1974).

Wolfgang Stolper, *The Structure of the East German Economy* (Cambridge, Mass.: Harvard University Press, 1960).

Helmut Wagner, "Reconstruction of the Financial System in East Germany," *Journal of Banking and Finance*, 17 (1993), 1001–1029.

Norbert Walter, "Beyond German Unification," *The International Economy*, (October/November, 1990).

Japan

J. G. Abegglen, *The Japanese Factory* (Glencoe, Ill.: Free Press, 1958).

G. C. Allen, *The Japanese Economy* (London: Weidenfeld and Nicolson, 1981).

Edward F. Denison and William K. Chung, *How Japan's Economy Grew So Fast: The Sources of Postwar Expansion* (Washington, D.C.: Brookings, 1976).

Ronald Dore, *Flexible Rigidities* (London: The Athlone Press, 1986).

Kanji Haitani, *The Japanese Economic System* (Lexington, Mass.: Heath, 1976).

Japanese Economic Research Center, *Economic Growth: The Japanese Experience Since the Meiji Era*, Vols. I and II (Tokyo: Japanese Economic Research Center, 1973).

Chalmers Johnson, *Japan's Public Policy Companies* (Washington, D.C.: American Enterprise Institute, 1978).

———, *MITI and the Japanese Miracle* (Stanford, Calif.: Stanford University Press, 1982).

Lawrence Klein and Kazushi Ohkawa, eds., *Economic Growth: The Japanese Experience Since the Meiji Era* (Homewood, Ill.: Irwin, 1968).

Edward J. Lincoln, *Japan: Facing Economic Maturity* (Washington, D.C.: Brookings, 1988).

William Lockwood, ed., *The State and Economic Enterprise in Japan* (Princeton, N.J.: Princeton University Press, 1965).

Angus Maddison, *Economic Growth in Japan and the USSR* (London: Allen and Unwin, 1969).

Ryoshin Minami, *The Economic Development of Japan* (London: Macmillan, 1986).

Takafusa Nakamura, *The Postwar Japanese Economy* (Tokyo: University of Tokyo Press, 1981).

Meiko Nishimizu and Charles R. Hulten, "The Sources of Japanese Economic Growth, 1955–71," *Review of Economics and Statistics*, 60 (August 1978), 351–361.

Kazushi Ohkawa and Henry Rosovsky, *Japanese Economic Growth* (Stanford, Calif.: Stanford University Press, 1973).

Kazushi Ohkawa and Hirohisa Kohama, *Lectures on Developing Economies: Japan's Experience and Its Relevance* (Tokyo: University of Tokyo Press, 1989).

Hugh Patrick and Henry Rosovsky, eds., *Asia's New Giant: How the Japanese Economy Works* (Washington, D.C.: Brookings, 1976).

M. M. Postan et el., eds., *Cambridge Economic History of Europe*, Vol. VII, pt. 2 (Cambridge, England: Cambridge University Press, 1978), Chs. 3–5 on Japan.

Ozawa Terutomo, *Multinationalism Japanese Style* (Princeton, N.J.: Princeton University Pres, 1979).

Ryuzo Sato, "U.S.–Japan Relation Under the Clinton and Hosokawa Administrations," *Japan and the World Economy*, 6, 1 (1994), 89–103.

Yoshio Suzuki, *Money, Finance, and Macroeconomic Performance in Japan* (New Haven: Yale University Press, 1986).

Yosho Tsurumi, *The Japanese Are Coming: A Multinational Interaction of Firms and Politics* (Cambridge, Mass.: Ballinger, 1976).

Kozo Yamamura, ed., *Policy and Trade Issues of the Japanese Economy* (Seattle: University of Washington Press, 1982).

M. Y. Yoshino, *Japan's Multinational Enterprises* (Cambridge, Mass.: Harvard University Press, 1976).

Sweden

Barry P. Bosworth and Alice M. Rivlin, eds., *The Swedish Economy* (Washington, D.C.: Brookings, 1987).

Timothy A. Canova, "The Swedish Model Betrayed," *Challenge* 37 (May–June, 1994), 36–40.

Peter Lawrence and Tony Spybey, *Management and Society in Sweden* (London: Routledge and Kegan Paul, 1986).

Erik Lundberg, "The Rise and Fall of the Swedish Model," *Journal of Economic Literature* 23 (March 1985), 1–36.

Michael Maccoby, ed., *Sweden at the Edge* (Philadelphia: University of Pennsylvania Press, 1991).

Per-Martin Meyerson, *The Welfare State in Crisis—The Case of Sweden* (Stockholm: The Federation of Swedish Industries, 1982).

Henry Milner, *Sweden: Social Democracy in Action* (New York: Oxford University Press, 1989).

Bengt Ryden and Villy Bergstrom, eds., *Sweden: Choices for Economic and Social Policy in the 1980s* (London: Allen and Unwin, 1982).

The Swedish Economy Autumn 1993 (Stockholm: National Institute of Economic Research, 1993).

10

Variants of Capitalism: Developing Nations

Mature capitalist economies, such as those discussed in the previous chapter, have achieved a high level of economic development. Per capita incomes in those economies yield high standards of living. The task of those economies is no longer to achieve economic development but to use available resources efficiently and to create new and better technologies to support continued economic growth. As the contrasting examples of Great Britain and Japan show, a fast-growing economy can overtake one that is slow-growing and that fails to generate sufficient economic growth. Economic maturity, however, does not mean that a country can rest on its laurels.

Almost 80 percent of the world's population lives in countries that have yet to achieve a reasonably high standard of living. Poverty is more prevalent than affluence in today's world. Most peoples of Asia, Africa, and Latin America live in underdeveloped economies. Figure 10.1 shows that more than 75 percent of the world's population lives in less developed countries, which account for 30 percent of world GDP. On the other hand, fewer than 17 percent of the world's population lives in developed countries, which produce 60 percent of world GDP. This means that, on average, a resident of a developed country has a per capita income ten times greater than a resident of an underdeveloped country.

The task of the underdeveloped countries, therefore, is simply to increase economic development. But if the solutions to the problem of underdevelopment were easy, then few countries would remain underdeveloped. In fact, one of the mysteries of economic history is why economic development has been limited to such a small group of countries.

This chapter examines two models of economic development—one unsuccessful, the other successful. India, the unsuccessful model, is one of the world's largest countries that uses heavy state intervention to promote economic development. Taiwan, South Korea, Hong Kong, and Singapore—called the Four Tigers—comprise the successful model. These four East Asian countries have experienced extremely rapid economic development over the past two decades. They have relied more on market forces and on free trade than on the state to promote their economic development. Thus, this chapter focuses on capitalism and the policy combinations appropriate for promoting economic growth and development in different natural settings.

FIGURE 10.1 World Gross Domestic Product and Population, 1991

Percent

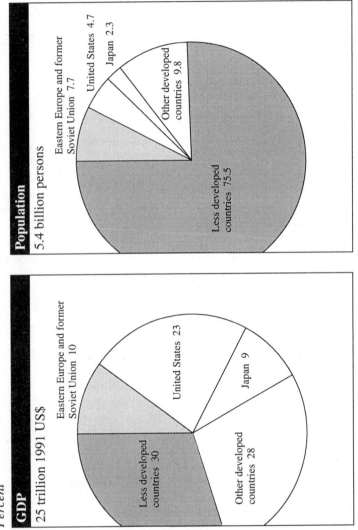

GDP

25 trillion 1991 US$

Eastern Europe and former
Soviet Union 10

United States 23

Japan 9

Other developed
countries 28

Less developed
countries 30

Population

5.4 billion persons

Eastern Europe and former
Soviet Union 7.7

United States 4.7

Japan 2.3

Other developed
countries 9.8

Less developed
countries 75.5

Source: *Handbook of International Economic Statistics 1992*, p. 14.

The State and Economic Development

Economists have had differing views of the role of the state in promoting economic development. In the 1950s and 1960s, development economists believed market failure caused underdevelopment. Private markets were unable to promote economic development because of external factors and a lack of information. Those economists argued that underdeveloped countries had insufficient market demand; hence, the state might need to artificially promote one leading sector to create demands for the products of other sectors. Underdeveloped economies might not produce proper market signals on profit opportunities; so that state might have to develop a national economic plan to move economic activity in the right direction. Externalities might be more prominent in underdeveloped countries; the return from private education or from innovation may be too low. Accordingly, the state had the responsibility of intervening. Low domestic savings in underdeveloped countries would force the state to create nonmarket institutions that promote capital formation. Another belief was that domestic markets must be protected from import competition—the infant industry argument—in order to develop domestic industries.[1]

The 1980s and 1990s witnessed a change in economists' attitudes toward the state and economic development. The state came to be regarded as an obstacle to economic development because of government's tendency to promote **monopoly rent seeking.** Monopoly rent seeking occurs when private parties expend resources to gain monopoly rights from government to use for their private benefit. Examples might include private groups obtaining tariff protection from government to create monopoly profits for domestic producers or bribing government officials to obtain franchises. Monopoly rent seeking reduces competition, raises prices, and creates welfare losses by lowering production and raising prices. Examples would be the over 200 percent effective rates of protection of certain Turkish industries and Indian industry with an effective tariff rate of 3,354 percent.[2]

While the literature of the 1950s and 1960s viewed the state as a positive force toward promoting economic development, economists of the 1980s and 1990s emphasized the predatory role of the state that could retard economic development. Examples of that predatory state include Haiti under "Papa Doc" and "Baby Doc" Duvalier, the Philipines under Ferdinand Marcos, and Nicaragua under Anastasio Somoza.[3]

The modern literature on public choice also questions the role of the state in economic development. Majority-rule political systems are characterized by logrolling, vote trading, and special-interest legislation that could harm development. If logrolling and vote trading dominate an underdeveloped country's political system, the result will be special interest legislation, protection of domestic industries from competition, and restrictions on developing new industries. Such an environment discourages entrepreneurship and innovation. Experience has shown that majority-rule voting is especially inimical to free trade, insofar as the beneficiaries of free trade are widely dispersed and poorly organized while the beneficiaries of protection are concentrated and well organized. Now consider India and the Four Tigers in light of these comments.

India is an important example of capitalism in a large and poor country. Unlike China, India has chosen an economic system that is basically capitalist in character, but it combines this system with a significant degree of state influence, the latter implemented through various types of controls and a state planning system. Economic growth and economic development are important goals of Indian economic policy. Thus, because we seek examples of the early stages of economic growth and economic development in large and relatively poor countries, it makes more sense to compare India and China than, for example, China and the United States. Moreover, India is a country with economic policies that have been redirected in the 1990s, away from the socialist path toward greater reliance on workers. It is, therefore, an interesting test of how poor countries respond to the decline of the Soviet model as a path to economic development.

India: The Quest for Economic Development

Early on, this book posed a question: Does any one economic system appear better suited than others to solving the development problems of low-income countries? It is therefore incumbent on us to include a low-income country among our capitalist variants. There are more poor countries than affluent ones. In fact, affluence is limited to a very small proportion of the world's population. The difficulty is that there is more diversity among the **less developed countries** (the **LDCs**) than among the industrialized economies. Some LDCs are only a step removed from the economic arrangements they have exhibited for centuries; others appear to be on their way to transforming themselves into developed countries. Moreover, the LDCs have diverse political and social institutions. In some LDCs, tribal or traditional authority still prevails; others have adopted Western democratic political institutions; and still others are controlled by dictatorships of one kind or another.

What common features can be extracted from this diversity? LDCs possess the characteristics generally associated with low levels of income: the dominant role of agriculture, high fertility and mortality rates, limited use of advanced technology, and lower saving rates. In addition to these features, LDCs share other characteristics: concentration of the ownership of wealth, reliance on indirect taxes, extensive government control of international transactions, poorly developed capital markets, and monopoly power in the limited industrial sector.[4]

It is also important, from a systems perspective, to appreciate the fact that poor countries have generally admired what has been viewed as the rapid economic progress of planned socialist systems. This admiration is reflected in such features as cooperative arrangements in agriculture and a major role for the state in economic development, not to mention the appeal of policies to influence the distribution of income. Will recent developments in the Soviet Union and Eastern Europe alter these views, and if so, what will be the results?

Rather than attempt to deal with the LDCs as a group, we have selected one, India. We believe that the Indian economy is reasonably representative of the operation of the capitalist economic system at low levels of economic development.

Moreover, this populous and strategically important country is the closest capitalist counterpart to China, the planned socialist LDC discussed in Chapter 17.[5]

Basic Characteristics[6]

Table 10.1 shows summary statistics for India, with appropriate comparisons to China and the United States. India is the world's second most populous country (almost 850 million in 1990), with approximately 15 percent of the world's population. On the other hand, India accounts for under 2 percent of world GNP. These two facts highlight India's very low per capita income (roughly $300–$400 in U.S. dollars). Approximately 31 percent of India's GNP originates in agriculture, and only 1 in 4 persons lives in urban areas. Some 70 percent of the labor force works in agriculture. Population has tended to grow at a rate of over 2 percent per annum (compared with about 0.5 percent in the industrialized countries), and life expectancy is under 50 years. Only 1 in every 3 adults is literate.

Although India is a large country, natural conditions are less than ideal both from a climatic perspective and in terms of environmental decay, for example, resulting from industrial pollution and land use arrangements. India has substantial mineral deposits and large reserves of coal.

India has been called the world's largest democracy. Its government is patterned on the English parliamentary system, and over the years Indian politics has been dominated by the Congress Party. India comprises a multiplicity of ethnic groups, who speak different languages, and has suffered over the years from ethnic and regional strife. Indeed, this strife remains important in the 1990s.

TABLE 10.1 Selected Structural Features of Less-Developed Capitalist Variants

Feature	India	China	U.S.A.
Per capita GNP, 1991, in U.S. $	330	370	22,240
Percent of population urban, 1991	27	60	75
Percent of GDP derived from industry, 1991	27	42	33[a]
Government expenditure as a percent of GNP, 1991	17.5	n.a.	25.3
Gross domestic investment as a percent of GDP, 1991	20	36	15
Average annual rate of inflation, 1980–91	8.2	5.8	4.2
Defense expenditures as a percent of total central government expenditure, 1991	17.0	n.a.	21.6

[a] 1988

Source: All data are from World Bank, *World Development Report 1993* (New York: Oxford University Press, 1993), Tables 1–32.

The Indian Economy: Historical Background[7]

The Indian economy prior to independence from Britain in 1947 makes an ideal case study of a traditional society with a long history of colonial domination. Prior to British rule (first under the British East India Company and then under the Crown), the Indian moghul economy (so called because a Moslem minority was the ruling elite) operated according to long-standing traditional rules. Society was divided into castes: the religious leaders, warlords, and their retainers were at the top, and the small peasant and untouchable castes were at the bottom. In this hierarchical system, one's place in society, as well as one's occupation, was determined at birth. Occupations were not distributed according to the skills, qualifications, and wishes of individuals or according to the needs of society. Moreover, work was considered beneath the dignity of the upper castes; physical labor could be engaged in only by the lower castes.

In contrast to other feudal societies, the ruling class itself generally did not own the means of agricultural production and was not involved in its management. Instead, the actual land cultivators paid taxes (tribute, often 50 percent of the harvest) to the ruling classes according to custom and in return for protection, which was necessary in an area torn by regional factionalism, warlordism, and civil strife. Agricultural taxes were levied not only to meet the needs of general government but also to support the high living standards of the upper castes. In the village community, the ruling class controlled the land, but because property rights were poorly defined, the farm family (and the landlords) had little incentive to undertake land improvements. In the farm family, an extended family system prevailed whereby income was shared among brothers, cousins, uncles, and so on.

The wealthy classes were not motivated to make productive investments; instead, their savings were devoted to acquiring precious metals, and little social overhead investment (such as irrigation) was undertaken. Foreign trade was conducted primarily by foreigners, who traded Indian spices and handicrafts for gold and silver. The limited education that did exist was purely religious in character, and the education of women was proscribed.

Economic progress under the moghul economy was limited. Population did not increase for two thousand years. It is likely that in the sixteenth century, per capita income in India was on a par with that of Western Europe, and contemporary European visitors even felt that average living standards were higher in India than at home. By the time of British rule, however, per capita income in India was very low compared with that of Western Europe. Thus during the era when Europe was preparing for its initial industrialization and population expansion, the Indian moghul economy was becoming relatively backward. The reasons for this declining economic position are not hard to identify: the rigid caste system, religious restrictions, uncertain property rights, barriers against productive investment, and civil strife. It was this last, particularly the enmity between the majority Hindu population and their Moslem rules (as well as regional factionalism), that allowed the British to turn India easily into a colonial dominion.

The Indian economy under British rule was not dramatically different, but the British did remove the old moghul warlord aristocracy, replacing it with a new indigenous ruling elite (supportive of the British) and a professional British bureaucracy, both designed to preserve law and order. Britain's objective was not to promote the economic development of India but to use India as a guaranteed market for British products. Tariff barriers were erected against Indian textiles abroad, and the removal of the moghul princes reduced the demand in India for the traditional luxury products of Indian handicraft. The British accepted and even intensified the caste system by establishing themselves as a separate ruling class. After 1930, native Indians gradually infiltrated the bureaucracy. This native bureaucracy became a wellspring of nationalism and was instrumental in achieving independence for India in 1947.

During British rule, the population of India began to grow for the first time over an extended period, and the economy grew along with it. Nevertheless, per capita income failed to increase perceptibly. Although British colonial rule did establish conditions for the growth of output and population, it did not allow output growth to exceed population growth. The positive economic features of the colonial period were the creation of a professional bureaucracy, the introduction of a secular education system to replace the system of religious education, a reduction of the tax burden on agriculture, and the creation of some property rights in agriculture (for the new ruling class). Under British rule, the proportion of national income going to the nonvillage economy declined somewhat with elimination of the moghul elite, and a lower proportion of national income went to the new ruling elite (British officials, native princes, and their retainers). However, the share of income received by those at the bottom of the ladder did not increase.

The Modern "Socialist" Indian Economy

The modern Indian economy is the creation of the Congress party and its leaders, Mahatma Gandhi and Jawaharlal Nehru, who referred to India as a "socialist" economy, though they differed on the appropriate course of **Indian socialism**. Gandhi extolled the traditional village community as the ideal economic organization and downgraded industrialization and the profit motive. Nehru favored industrialization and emphasized heavy industry as the appropriate path for Indian socialism. According to our definition, *socialism* is largely a misnomer in the case of India, except for government ownership in industry and commerce. Indian leadership has not pursued a socialist distribution of income. India is still primarily an agricultural country, and the distribution of income depends mainly on the distribution of agricultural property. Since independence, only limited progress has been made in land reform. Although there have been some efforts to distribute land to the poor peasants, land remains unequally distributed, and there is no evidence that the range of income inequality has been reduced.[8] It is true that the pensioning off of the native princes and limitations on landholdings have reduced the number of enormous estates, but the land-limiting legislation has been circumvented, and many Indian states have not been able (or willing) to push land reform because of the strength of vested landed interests. The tax system continues to be regressive, direct taxes are rarely levied on land, and the nominally high urban income taxes are ameliorated by evasion and through numerous exemptions.

The pretax income distribution figures sum up the failure to establish a more equitable distribution of income. In 1960, the bottom 10 percent of families accounted for less than 1 percent of all income, while the top 10 percent accounted for more than one-third. This income distribution is less equitable than in the industrialized capitalist countries (a less equitable distribution is characteristic of less-developed countries).[9] The after-tax distribution is not significantly different from this pretax distribution because of the predominance of regressive indirect taxes. A native Indian elite of civil servants, the military, and capitalists has replaced the British and the native princes at the top of the income distribution. Landless agricultural laborers, small landholders, and the urban poor remain at the bottom.

Rather than seeking to achieve "socialist" objectives through income redistribution, the architects of the modern Indian economy emphasized state ownership in industry. The feeling was that socialism could be achieved through state control of industry, which would serve as a surrogate for social change. State promotion of heavy industry (through ownership and government controls) was to lead to economic development and limit the concentration of wealth in private hands, and it was assumed that economic development would inevitably bring about necessary social change. In the early postwar period, the Indians adopted one basic feature of the Soviet development model (discussed in Chapter 11): the priority of heavy industry over light industry and agriculture. It was argued that the creation of a domestic heavy-industry base would lead to more rapid development, would promote domestic savings, and would make India less dependent on the outside world (freeing India to pursue an independent political course).[10]

India's heavy-industry strategy was reflected in the public ownership of heavy industries and banking. Steel, heavy machinery, chemicals, power, fuel, communication, transportation, and life insurance were nationalized in the early 1950s. In the 1970s the state moved to enlarge the public sector by nationalizing the large banks, the copper industry, the wholesale grain and jute trade, and a number of coal mines and textile mills. In some instances, the Indians followed the British pattern of nationalization to rescue failing private companies. In others (such as the wholesale grain trade), nationalization was undertaken to expand state control over the private economy. Nationalization was usually accomplished by compensation of previous owners (rather than expropriation), and an increasing "Indianization" of industrial ownership has evolved as foreign owners have been displaced.

Despite substantial nationalization, the scope of the public sector remains limited. Private enterprise still accounts for some 90 percent of industrial output.[11] The public sector (general government and public enterprises) accounts for approximately 15 percent of national output.[12] The government's share of savings is 13 percent.[13] These figures indicate that the role of the public sector in India is below average or small compared to that in the industrialized countries.[14] Thus the strategy of pursuing socialism through public ownership has had only a limited effect on the aggregate economy. However, one must bear in mind that the Indian economy is still highly underdeveloped and that most of the labor force remains concentrated in agriculture and personal services. This means that the share of the heavy-industry sector (the focal point of nationalization) must necessarily be limited. Moreover, the impact of public policy on economic affairs may be greater than the figures indicate because of a pervasive system of indirect controls and planning.

The organization of the private industrial sector is quite concentrated in India, and the objective of limiting industrial wealth holdings has not been achieved. At the end of the 1950s, the twenty largest industrial groups owned one-third of the share capital of the private corporate sector.[15] Although measures have been introduced since then to reduce this concentration of private wealth and power (the most significant being the nationalization of large banking interests), large private interests are probably promoted by the existing system of economic control. In addition, major industrialists are key figures in the Congress party.

Economic Planning in India[16]

Economic planning in India has attracted considerable attention because India is one of the few LDCs to have well-organized and sophisticated planning machinery. The planning apparatus in a typical LDC is as underdeveloped as the economy, so the Indian example serves as a useful test case of the potential contribution of the planning in an LDC.

According to the definitions developed in Chapters 2 and 6, **Indian planning** would be classified as indicative, even though its heritage is the Soviet experience. It is a noncompulsory form of planning, in keeping with the Indian philosophy that the use of force is contrary to Indian democracy. This is not to suggest that Indian plan directives have not been implemented. In the industrial sector a wide range of enforcement mechanisms have been available. Much heavy industry is directly owned by the state and can be expected to follow plan guidelines; industrial credit is largely state-controlled; import licenses are also granted by the state. The fact that the Indian economy has developed a relatively large heavy-industry sector for an LDC demonstrates better than anything else that planning has mattered. Nevertheless, India continues to be an agricultural country, and agriculture, which cannot be planned in any effective way, remains largely out of the control of planners.

India has concentrated on long-term plans, typically of five years' duration. Attempts to devise annual operational plans have not been successful. Planning goals and planning methods have changed over the years, although the general objectives (raising the rate of economic growth and the investment ratio, reducing inequalities, and stimulating employment) are familiar to observers of national economic planning. The first plan was based on simple Keynesian growth models. The second plan (1956–1961) emphasized the priority of heavy industry. Later plans have concentrated on multisectoral balances and have to some extent moved away from the emphasis on heavy industry.

Balances for the major industrial sectors have been constructed (via either rudimentary methods or input–output tables) to determine the consistency of the plan. A crucial component of the plan is the investment subplan, which indicates the growth rates of investment in the public and private sectors. The investment plan, which determines the basic direction of the economy, is most amenable to enforcement because of the state's control of public enterprises, raw-material allocations, investment credit, and imports.

Economic planning in India is carried out on an aggregated level; specific output directives are not normally issued to the private industrial sector. In the public sector, an industry often consists of a small number of publicly owned enterprises, so the aggregate directives can be converted into actual production and investment targets. On the surface, it would appear that Indian planners are in a better position to influence the behavior of industry with the arsenal of controls at their disposal, but it is difficult to establish what degree of control they actually exercise over the private sector.

Recent studies of Indian planning reveal a system that has had both successes and failures. On balance, however, the Indian planning system did not always achieve its objectives, and it failed to adapt to change in an economy in which private ownership and markets have been important.

Economic Controls[17]

Governmental controls over resource allocation are more extensive in India than in the industrialized capitalist countries. In addition to the planning apparatus, a whole range of extramarket controls are utilized. The rationale for these controls is the widespread belief that the free market cannot be trusted to allocate resources in a low-income country.

The basic instrument for control of private industry was the Industries Act of 1951, which covered almost all manufacturing, mining, and power. It gave the government authority to grant licenses for expanding capacity and to control the allocation and prices of raw materials and, in some instances, the prices of finished products. The prices of basic agricultural products are controlled by the state, and a complex zonal pricing system exists to regulate the flow of agricultural products from regions of surplus to regions of deficit. Moreover, the state disburses food products received under foreign aid programs and in this way exerts further influence over agricultural prices.

A most important instrument of state control is state regulation of foreign exchange and imports. Since the mid-1950s, India has been on a strict import and exchange control system. Imported capital equipment, crucial to industrial expansion, has been regulated by industrial licensing, and input and raw-material licenses have regulated the disbursement of imported materials to industrial users. The import control system has operated on the principles of essentiality and indigenous nonavailability. In order to justify an import, the domestic user has to demonstrate that the commodity is essential and that it cannot be purchased at home. Import restrictions, when strictly applied, have given automatic protection to domestic industry and, according to many economists,[18] have reduced the efficiency of the Indian economy.

In the late 1960s, the Indian system of **economic controls** was reexamined, and an attempt was made to limit controls (except for agricultural pricing) to large firms. The retention of controls, despite the growing recognition of their inefficiency, can be attributed to three factors.[19] The first is that many large firms actually like controls because they reduce risk and guarantee profits. Second, controls enhance the power and positions of bureaucrats. Third, distrust of the market is ingrained in the Indian bureaucracy.

It is difficult to quantify the effect of government controls on Indian resource allocation because one cannot know to what extent they are circumvented. What one can say is that the system of state controls is more comprehensive than that in the advanced capitalist countries.

Growth Performance

The growth of the Indian economy after 1947 represents a marked improvement over its historical performance. As we have already noted, the moghul economy was stagnant for centuries, and per capita income failed to grow during British colonial rule; therefore any growth of per capita income is an improvement over historical standards. The difficulty in evaluating Indian growth performance is that the world economy experienced accelerated growth after World War II, and India would be expected to participate in this acceleration.

India's per capita GNP averaged a 1.7 percent growth for the period 1965–1985. According to Angus Maddison, the reasons for this per capita growth rate are the expansion of government services (education and credit assistance), a high investment rate, the increase in both public and private investment, foreign aid, and the importation of advanced technology. Although inflation averaged about 7 percent annually in the 1980s, growth in real output has been sustained largely as a result of growth in the industrial sector.

On the positive side of the ledger is the steady but unspectacular rise in per capita income despite substantial population pressures. In the crucial agricultural area, output has expanded slightly more rapidly than population (at a per capita rate of about one-half of 1 percent per year). India's dependence on imported grains has declined over the years, and now India is largely self-sufficient in basic food grains. On the negative side, India's per capita income growth has been slow relative to the performance of other developing countries (whose per capita growth tended to be around 2 to 3 percent per year). India's growth performance has been well below that of China, although China and India began their postcolonial development from an equivalent point. Because of lower growth, India's per capita income today is only three-quarters that of China.[20] Additional negative features include persistent high unemployment (and underemployment), rapid inflation, and susceptibility to external shocks (such as the oil price explosion of the 1970s).

Maddison and Malenbaum argue that Indian growth has been substandard for the LDCs in the postwar era, and Maddison calculates that the Indian growth rate has been 25 percent below its potential.[21] The reasons for this underutilization of growth potential are India's extremely low per capita income, its relatively small per

capita receipts of foreign capital, its poor natural resources, the drain of a large
military, the retention of institutional constraints (caste restrictions, maldistribution
of agricultural land, taboo on slaughter of livestock), and the inefficiency of public
enterprise, which has been operated at a loss throughout most of the postwar era.

Capitalism in India

Notwithstanding the large share of government ownership of heavy industry and
finance, India is a capitalist economy. The public enterprise sector is a small part
of the total economy, and private ownership prevails throughout the rest of the
economy. The dominant sector, agriculture, is characterized by private ownership
of land. There has been no significant change in the distribution of income, and the
inequality of income distribution is greater in India than in the advanced capitalist
countries, whether calculated on a pretax or a posttax basis. Economic planning is
primarily indicative, although planning of the public enterprise sector may carry
with it some compulsory elements. Nevertheless, noncoercion remains the foundation of Indian planning.

Government intervention in private economic decision making is probably more
extensive in India than in the advanced capitalist countries, although the actual
degree of compliance is difficult to establish. Government controls have been placed
on prices, imports, foreign exchange, raw materials, and capacity expansion. One
reason for these controls is a rather deep-seated distrust of market resource allocation. On the other hand, controls seem to be a characteristic feature of capitalism
under conditions of underdevelopment, so in this sense, India conforms to the general pattern of underdevelopment.

Problems and Prospects

The basic challenge facing India over the coming decades is to improve the utilization of its abundant resource, labor. Endemically high rates of unemployment and
underemployment attest to labor's underutilization, but the best means of correcting
the situation remains a heatedly debated issue. Should there be more or less planning? Should government intervention and controls be increased or reduced? Can
ways be found to remove the remaining vestiges of feudalism and the caste system?
Can centuries-old regional and ethnic factionalism be removed? Can there be any
narrowing in income inequality? In a sense, the biggest decision facing India appears to be whether to choose more market or more plan. Should resource allocation
be more fully entrusted to the market, with government acting on the sidelines to
protect property rights and promote competition? Or is it dangerous to trust market
guidance in a developing country?

The Indian Economy in the 1990s

The past Soviet experience with national economic planning, especially, has had a
significant impact on the policies and on the systemic arrangements of the Indian

economy. At the same time, performance problems with sectoral difficulties, in particular, led to an ongoing reassessment of the planning system in the 1980s. The result reduced the extent to which government controls intervened in the private sector, though the actual magnitude of change at this time has been the subject of debate.[22]

By the summer of 1991, however, India was moving toward the implementation of market strategies using traditional macroeconomic tools to handle budgetary deficits, inflation, and balance of payments. There has also been a move toward deregulation in the private sector and decentralization of decision making in the public sector. It has been argued that these changes do, in fact, represent an important shift in the arrangements of the Indian economic system.[23]

India is a large, poor country pursuing industrialization and economic development with differing policies and systemic arrangements. While that mix has been changing, prospects for the long term are likely to include a continuing reduction in the use of Soviet-type planning and control arrangements and greater reliance on decentralized market forces.

Asian Systems: South Korea, Singapore, Taiwan, and Hong Kong

The **Four Tigers**—South Korea, Singapore, Taiwan, and Hong Kong—are frequently characterized as the newly industrialized countries of Asia.[24] These countries are the object of considerable interest in a region of the world where contemporary economic progress has been great but uneven. Moreover, these are all systems that have achieved significant rates of economic growth, judged by world historical standards, and have made progress through the market mechanism and a strategy of export-led industrialization. Although there are important differences among these countries, it is their similarities, and their economic progress via similar mechanisms and policies, that stand out. These Asian success stories deserve our attention.

Background

The Four Tigers vary considerably in size and natural endowment. In terms of population, the smallest country is Singapore (6 million) and the largest is South Korea (43 million). None is particularly well endowed with natural resources. For example, Singapore is a wholly urban society with a strong manufacturing base, an active service sector, and virtually no agriculture. At the other end of the spectrum, South Korea is an industrialized country with a substantial agricultural sector, an urbanization level of roughly 70 percent at the end of the 1980s, and limited amounts of such resources as coal. Taiwan has an important agricultural sector, but its natural and climatic conditions are less than ideal and minerals are in short supply. Agriculture is relatively unimportant in Hong Kong.

Performance: System and Policy

The evidence presented in Table 10.2 summarizes, in a few simple numbers, an economic success story. All these countries have experienced very rapid economic growth and limited inflation, resulting in significant levels of per capita product. Moreover, with variations, foreign trade has been a dominant mechanism. And though this dimension is difficult to measure accurately, the Four Tigers seem to have achieved these gains with little if any increases in inequality. They are, therefore, systems generating both efficiency and equity.

Economic growth has been driven by export-led industrialization. Exports have been largely manufactures, but in recent years a somewhat more diversified export pattern has emerged (for example, financial services in the case of Singapore).[25] Growth has been achieved with a traditional mix of inputs. Although external capital played a role in earlier years, rates of domestic saving have increased rapidly, as have rates of investment, the latter largely supported by domestic sources.

For example, in the case of South Korea, gross domestic savings accounted for 8 percent of gross domestic product in 1965 and for 38 percent in 1988. Between the same two years, gross domestic investment as a share of gross domestic product increased from 15 to 30 percent.[26] Similar changes occurred in Singapore; in Hong Kong, the ratios were high for both years but fell somewhat in the latter period.

Most of these countries have had modest and declining rates of population growth, though the transformation of agriculture has resulted in substantial growth of the labor force to support the industrialization process, most notably in South Korea and Taiwan. Structural change has been typical and quite rapid.

TABLE 10.2   Selected Characteristics of the Four Tigers

	South Korea	Singapore	Taiwan	Hong Kong
Population, 1991, in millions	43.3	2.8	20	5.8
Per capita GNP, 1991, U.S. $	6,330	14,210	6000[b]	13,430[a]
Growth: PCGNP Average annual, 1980–1991	8.7	5.3	6.6[c]	5.6
Industry: share of domestic production, 1991	45	38	n.a.	25
Exports + imports/GNP 1988, U.S. $	—	347	97	—

[a] GDP
[b] 1989
[c] 1970–1985

Sources: World Bank, *World Development Report 1990* (New York: Oxford University Press, 1990); and Miyohei Shinohara and Fu-chen Lo, *Global Adjustment and the Future of the Asian-Pacific Economy* (Tokyo and Kuala Lumpur: Institute of Developing Economies and Asian and Pacific Development Centre, 1989).

The State and Economic Development

The setting of economic activity is predominantly a market economy with private ownership, but the role of the government has been important in varying ways. Although the arrangements for labor–management negotiations differ from one case to another, certain generalizations are possible. Through a strong government role and social consensus about that role, wage increases have been constrained such that labor costs in the manufacturing sector have not risen rapidly, as they often do during a period of rapid industrialization. Measures of government spending as a proportion of total product can be both difficult to compute and misleading. However, the evidence suggests a strong and growing role for the government sector in Singapore and Hong Kong, though less so in South Korea.

Each of the Four Tigers has a different political system. The governments of South Korea and Singapore have been more repressive than that of Hong Kong, which has not suppressed labor unions. Singapore, however, is strongly opposed to trade unionism and has invoked economic arguments against unionism. In South Korea, an active and noisy form of trade unionism has developed.

The common feature of state policy in this region has been the consistent support of the policy of *export promotion* over *import substitution*. Export promotion refers to state policies to promote exports. Such policies can range from subsidies of export industries to free-trade practices for the economy as a whole. Import-substitution policies are those that protect domestic industries from foreign competition by tariffs or other barriers against foreign products. Industrial policies in some developing nations may be directed toward planning and protectionism. Industrial policy in the Four Tigers aims to promote the export of industries in the context of generally free trade.

The World Bank provides evidence of the success of the free-trade orientation of the Four Tigers. The World Bank has classified Hong Kong, Singapore, and South Korea as the world's most strongly outward-oriented economies among the developing countries during the periods 1963–1973 and 1973–1985. Notable, the same study classified India as among the most strongly inward-oriented economy of the developing economies.[27] More general statistical studies, while plagued by conceptual and empirical difficulties, generally conclude that the relationship between export orientation and economic growth is positive.[28]

Asia: The Future

The Asian success stories are important not only for what they tell us about the sources of successful economic growth and development, but also as models for those countries in Asia and elsewhere in which economic progress has not been achieved. We have noted that in spite of considerable differences in natural endowment, the Four Tigers have promoted rapid industrialization through strikingly similar policies focusing on the export sectors. Can these achievements continue through the decade of the 1990s?

If the past is any guide, the answer is likely to be yes. These systems have been surprisingly resilient in the face of cyclical downturns. Although examination of year-to-year growth rates in the 1980s indicates some slowing, projections suggest slower but very substantial rates of economic growth through the end of the century.

These systems have also been resilient in the face of a need to adapt. For example, South Korea has developed its heavy-industrial capacity as a basic strength of the economy.

Finally, a great deal of uncertainty exists about the future economic prospects of Hong Kong, which reverts to the People's Republic of China in 1997.[29] Although the Chinese have indicated that they will leave the market economy of Hong Kong intact, sustaining two economic systems may be difficult, especially inasmuch as foreign participation in the domestic economy of Hong Kong remains important. Moreover, the departure of talented people from Hong Kong will present a serious labor problem similar to that which occurred in cases such as the former German Democratic Republic.

Another factor in Asian economic growth has been the presence of a strong entrepreneurial class (sometimes from abroad) working with a population and labor force said to have a strong work ethic. Though more difficult to quantify than, say, investment, these factors may have been very important.

Summary

The Indian economy has always interested economists because it is a large, poor country pursuing economic growth and economic development with private ownership and market mechanisms but with a socialist overlay in a number of dimensions influenced by the experience of the former Soviet Union. Thus India has promoted economic growth through a policy of investment expansion guided in part by substantial state controls and a system of economic planning.

The comparison of India with China has always been of interest for both the similarities and the differences between these two large and poor countries. This comparison has remained of interest in the 1990s because China has pursued major economic reforms and, beginning in the early 1990s, India has begun to abandon the use of controls for an emphasis on markets and market-oriented macroeconomic and microeconomic policies.

The Four Tigers (South Korea, Singapore, Taiwan, and Hong Kong) have captured our attention in recent years for both their diversities and their similarities. Though the four countries are very different in a number of basic dimensions (such as size and resource endowment), these countries have all experienced rapid and sustained economic growth through heavy reliance on the export of manufactures. This strategy of export-led industrialization is often viewed as a model capable of being transplanted to other settings.

Those countries represent important examples of the pursuit of economic development in very different natural settings and differing economic systems and policies. It is important to note that in the mid-1990s, after the collapse of the Soviet and Eastern European economic and political systems, it remains difficult to isolate the key features that have contributed to economic growth and development and to assess the transferability of those features to other contexts. These and other cases provide evidence that the 1990s is becoming the decade of the market, though it would be premature to suggest that controls, in various degrees, will not sustain in a variety of settings.

Key Terms

monopoly rent seeking
LDC (less developed country)
Indian socialism
Indian planning

economic controls
Four Tigers
economic growth
export-led industrialization

Notes

India

1. A survey of these views of the positive role that the state must play is found in Hla Myint, *The Economics of the Developing Countries* (New York: Praeger, 1968).
2. Anne O. Krueger, "Government Failures in Development," *Journal of Economic Perspectives*, vol. 4 (Summer 1990), 14.
3. Pranab Bardhan, "Symposium on the State and Economic Development," *Journal of Economic Perspectives*, vol. 4 (Summer 1990), 3–7.
4. The literature on the economic characteristics of LDCs is summarized in Marvin Miracle, "Comparative Market Structures in Developing Countries" (Association for Comparative Economics, Proceedings in Conjunction with the Midwest Economic Association, Detroit, April 1970). Also see John Due, *Indirect Taxes in Developing Countries* (Baltimore: The Johns Hopkins University Press, 1970).
5. Indian and Chinese economic growth are compared in Subramanian Swamy, "Economic Growth in China and India, 1952–1970: A Comparative Appraisal," *Economic Development and Cultural Change*, 21 (July 1973), 1–84; and Wilfred Malenbaum, "Modern Economic Growth in India and China: The Comparisons Revisited," *Economic Development and Cultural Change*, 3 (October 1982), 45–84.
6. Data here are compiled from World Bank, *World Development Report 1990* (New York: Oxford University Press, 1990), Tables 1–32.
7. This discussion is based principally in Angus Maddison, *Class Structure and Economic Growth: India and Pakistan Since the Moghuls* (New York: Norton, 1971), Chs. 2–4.
8. Raj Krishna and G. S. Raychaudhuri, "Trends in Rural Savings and Capital Formation in India, 1950–51 to 1973–74," *Economic Development and Cultural Change*, 30 (January 1982), 289–294.
9. Maddison, *Class Structure and Economic Growth*, Ch. 6.
10. For a discussion of the Indian controversy over planning priorities, see Jagdish Bhagwati and Sukhamoy Chakravaty, "Contributions to Indian Economic Analysis: A Survey," *American Economic Growth*, 59 (September 1969), 4–29; and V. V. Bhatt, "Development Problem, Strategy, and Technology of Choice: Sarvadaya and Socialist Approaches in India," *Economic Development and Cultural Change*, 21 (October 1982), 85–100.

11. Maddison, *Class Structure and Economic Growth*, p. 119.
12. Allan G. Gruchy, *Comparative Economic Systems*, 2nd ed. (Boston: Houghton Mifflin, 1977), p. 638.
13. World Bank, *World Tables, 1976*, p. 428.
14. Ibid., summary tables.
15. Maddison, *Class Structure and Economic Growth*, p. 127.
16. Our discussion of Indian planning is based on Gruchy, *Comparative Economic Systems*, pp. 639–653; and Bhagwati and Chakravaty, "Contributions to Indian Economic Analysis," pp. 2–73; for a contemporary discussion, see Rakesh Mohan and Vandana Aggarwal, "Commands and Controls: Planning for Indian Industrial Development, 1951–1990," *Journal of Comparative Economics*, 14 (December 1990), 681–712; William A. Byrd, "Planning in India: Lessons from Four Decades of Development Experience," *Journal of Comparative Economics*, 14 (December 1990), 713–735.; Arvind Panagariya, "Indicative Planning in India: Discussion," *Journal of Comparative Economics* 14 (December 1990), 736–742; E. Wayne Nafziger, *The Economics of Developing Countries*, 2nd ed. (Englewood Cliffs, N.J.: Prentice-Hall, 1990), Ch. 19.
17. This discussion is based on Maddison, *Class Structure and Economic Growth* pp. 120–125.
18. Bhagwati and Chakravaty, "Contributions to Indian Economic Analysis," pp. 60–66.
19. Maddison, *Class Structure and Economic Growth*, pp. 122–124.
20. Malenbaum, "Modern Economic Growth in India and China," pp. 45–84; World Bank, *World Tables, 1980*, pp. 372–375.
21. Maddison, *Class Structure and Economic Growth*, p. 81.
22. See for example Rakesh Mohan and Vandana Aggarwal, "Commands and Controls."
23. J. S. Uppal, "India's New Economic Policy," *Journal of Economic Development*, 18 (December 1993), 33–61.

South Korea, Singapore, Taiwan, Hong Kong

24. There is a large literature on these economies. See, for example, Edward K. Y. Chen, *Hyper-Growth in Asian Economies* (London and Basingstoke, England: The Macmillan Press Ltd., 1979); Eddy Lee, ed., *Export-Led Industrialization and Development* (Geneva: ILO, 1981); Roy A. Matthews, *Canada and the Little Dragons* (Montreal: The Institute for Research on Public Policy, 1983); Miron Mushkat, *The Economic Future of Hong Kong* (Boulder, Colo., and London, England: Hong Kong University Press, 1990); Miyohei Shinohara and Fu-chen Lo, *Global Adjustment and the Future of Asian-Pacific Economy* (Tokyo and Kuala Lumpur: Institute of Developing Economies and Asian and Pacific Development Centre, 1989); Julian Weiss, *The Asian Century* (New York: Facts on File, 1989); and Jon Woronoff, *Asia's "Miracle" Economies* (Armonk, N.Y.: M. E. Sharpe, 1986).
25. Eddy Lee, ed., *Export-Led Industrialization and Development* (Geneva: ILO, 1981); Robert A. Scalapino, Seizaburo Sato, and Jusuf Wanandi, eds., *Asian Economic Development—Present and Future* (Berkeley: University of California Press, 1985).
26. World Bank, *World Development Bank 1990* (New York: Oxford University Press, 1990).
27. World Bank, *World Development Report 1987* (Oxford: Oxford University Press, 1987).
28. Sebastian Edwards, "Openness, Trade Liberalization and Growth in Developing Countries," *Journal of Economic Literature*, 31 (September 1993), 1387.
29. See Miron Mushkat, *The Economic Future of Hong Kong*.

Recommended Readings

India

A. N. Agrawal, *Indian Economy*, 2nd ed. (New Delhi: Vikas Publishing House, 1976).

Jagdish Bhagwati and Sukhamoy Chakravaty, "Contributions to Indian Economic Analysis: A Survey," *American Economic Review*, 59 (September 1969), 4–29.

William A. Byrd, "Planning in India: Lessons from Four Decades of Development Experience," *Journal of Comparative Economics*, 14 (December 1990), 713–736.

Pramit Chaudhuri, ed., *Aspects of Indian Economic Development* (London: Allen and Unwin, 1971).

Francine R. Frankel, *India's Green Revolution* (Princeton, N.J.: Princeton University Press, 1971).

———, *India's Political Economy, 1947–1977* (Princeton, N.J.: Princeton University Press, 1978).

Raj Krishna and G. S. Raychaudhuri, "Trends in Rural Savings and Capital Formation in India, 1950–1951 to 1973–1974," *Economic Development and Cultural Change*, 30 (January 1982), 271–298.

William A. Long and K. K. Seo, *Management in Japan and India* (New York: Praeger, 1977).

Angus Maddison, *Class Structure and Economic Growth: India and Pakistan Since the Moghuls* (New York: Norton, 1971).

Wilfred Malenbaum, "Modern Economic Growth in India and China: The Comparison Revisited, 1950–1980," *Economic Development and Cultural Change*, 31 (October 1982), 45–84.

Rakesh Mohan and Vandana Aggarwal, "Commands and Controls: Planning for Indian Industrial Development, 1951–1990," *Journal of Comparative Economics*, 14 (December 1990), 681–712.

Arvind Panagariya, "Indicative Planning in India: Discussion," *Journal of Comparative Economics*, 14 (December 1990), 736–742.

C. H. Shah and C. N. Vakil, eds., *Agricultural Development of India: Policy and Problems* (New Delhi: Orient Longman, 1979).

Subramanian Swamy, "Economic Growth in China and India, 1952–1970: A Comparative Appraisal," *Economic Development and Cultural Change*, 21 (July 1973), 1–84.

South Korea, Singapore, Taiwan, Hong Kong

Edward K. Y. Chen, *Hyper-Growth in Asian Economies* (London and Basingstoke, England: The Macmillan Press Ltd., 1979).

Shirley W. Y. Kao, Gustav Ranis, and John C. H. Fei, *The Taiwan Success Story: Rapid Growth with Improved Distribution in the Republic of China, 1952–1979* (Boulder, Colo.: Westview, 1981).

Paul Kuzner, "Indicative Planning in Korea," *Journal of Comparative Economics*, 14 (December 1990), 657–676.

Eddy Lee, ed., *Export-Led Industrialization and Development* (Geneva: ILO, 1981).

Roy A. Matthews, *Canada and the Little Dragons* (Montreal: The Institute for Research on Public Policy, 1983).

Miron Mushkat, *The Economic Future of Hong Kong* (Boulder, Colo., and London, England: Hong Kong University Press, 1990).

Gavin Peebles, *Hong Kong's Economy: An Introductory Macroeconomic Analysis* (New York: Oxford University Press, 1988).

J. L. Saking, "Indicative Planning in Korea: Discussion," *Journal of Comparative Economics*, 14, 1 (December, 1990), 677–680.

Robert A. Scalapino, Seizaburo Sato, and Jusuf Wanandi, eds., *Asian Economic Development—Present and Future* (Berkeley: University of California Press, 1985).

Miyohei Shinohara and Fu-chen Lo, *Global Adjustment and the Future of the Asian-Pacific Economy* (Tokyo and Kuala Lumpur: Institute of Developing Economies and Asian and Pacific Development Centre, 1989).

Julian Weiss, *The Asian Century* (New York: Facts on File, 1989).

Jon Woronoff, *Asia's "Miracle" Economies* (Armonk, N.Y.: M. E. Sharpe, 1986).

11

The Soviet Economy: The Command Experience

This book attempts to compare real-world economic systems with their theoretical underpinnings. Although the organization of the Soviet economy varied during the years following the 1917 **Bolshevik revolution**, state ownership, national economic planning, and the collectivization of agriculture were all introduced in the late 1920s and lasted through 1991, which marked the demise of the Soviet Union as a country.

Thus the **administrative command economy** was the primary mechanism for resource allocation in the former Soviet Union for more than sixty years. The Soviet experience of centrally planned socialism remains the main example of an attempt to remake the society and to forge rapid economic development without the use of market mechanisms.

Although the concept of economic reform received a great deal of attention in the Soviet Union since the mid-1950s, reform did little to change the fundamentals of the system. Thus from 1928 through 1985, when Mikhail Gorbachev introduced Perestroika, there is a long period in which to examine the nature and operation of the Soviet economic system.

The demise of the political and economic systems of the former Soviet Union (and other similar systems in Eastern Europe) has necessarily focused attention on issues of performance. Part IV examines the performance of these systems in an effort to understand the reasons both for their demise and for the legacy from which transition has thus far proceeded in the 1990s.

Historical Perspectives

Our examination of American capitalism was not cast in historical perspective. The American economy is, after all, an open economy undergoing change all the time. The Soviet experience was different. Just as the Gorbachev era represented a sharp break with the Soviet past, the Bolshevik revolution of 1917 represented a sharp break with the preceding **czarist era**.[1] Indeed, Soviet experimentation between 1917 and 1928 provide important insights into the roots of the administrative command system and the difficulties that arose in reforming that system.

269

The era of the czars came to a close and the era of the Soviets began with the Bolshevik revolution of 1917. Although the Soviet economic system of the plan era dates from 1928, analysis of the Soviet era must begin with the *level* **and** *rate* **of economic development** at the end of the czarist era.

Economic development as of 1917 was at a relatively low level, judged by indicators such as per capita gross national product. However, there had been considerable increase in rate of growth, especially industrial growth, during the last three decades of czarist rule, and the Soviets could therefore build on an attractive base (transportation, industrial capacity, minerals, and so forth).

At the end of the 1920s the Soviet leader, Joseph Stalin, made two important decisions. First, a comprehensive system of central economic planning based on compulsory state and party directives was established. An abrupt end to the prevailing system of market relations in industry ensued, and there was a sudden shift in industrial production away from consumer goods and toward producer goods. Second, the agricultural sector was collectivized. A vast network of **collective farms** (*kolkhozy*) was created, in which more than 90 percent of Soviet peasant households were living by the mid-1930s.[2] These two major decisions, though sudden at the time, did not arise out of a vacuum.

Two economic "experiments" were conducted in the period following the revolution of 1917: **war communism** (1917–1920) and the New Economic Policy (1921–1928).[3] Both responded to the need to consolidate power and at the same time to marshal economic resources in a time of crisis.[4]

War communism, implemented by Lenin during the Russian Civil War, saw the introduction of substantial state ownership (nationalization), an attempt to eliminate market relationships in industry and trade, and the gathering of agricultural products from the peasants by forced requisitioning. In a sense, it seemed that Lenin was attempting to by-pass socialism and move directly from a capitalist to a communist system. Whatever the intent, the economic consequences were a disaster by the end of the civil war; the economy was in ruin.[5]

In an attempt to instill economic recovery, Lenin introduced the **New Economic Policy (NEP)** in 1921. NEP signaled a partial return to private ownership (the so-called commanding heights of industry remained nationalized), reintroduction of the market as a primary mechanism for resource allocation, and implementation of a more viable tax system on agriculture. By 1927, the Soviet economy had recovered from the losses of war communism and was at, and in some cases above, the prewar level.[6]

The period of Soviet history from 1917 to 1928 provided some important lessons—lessons that permeated Soviet thinking. First, it became apparent that if the market were to be eliminated, some mechanism for coordination had to take its place. During war communism Lenin nationalized industries and eliminated the market, but he did not replace the market with a plan or some other substitute mechanism. Second, partly as a result of inept state policies, the peasants came to be viewed as holding considerable power over the pace of industrialization.[7] After all, the economy was largely agricultural, so resources would have to come primarily from the rural sector. Third, the response to Lenin's attempt to introduce payment in kind and to downgrade the importance of money during war communism made it obvious that, whatever the system, **material incentives** would be crucial to motivate labor.

In addition to the experience of war communism and NEP, the 1920s witnessed open and important discussions, the "great industrialization debate" and the beginnings of the theory of planning.[8] The debate on industrialization focused on modes of industrialization and, in particular, on differing roles for the agricultural and industrial sectors. All participants agreed that industrialization was essential and that the peasants would play a key role. The end result, however, was not readily foreseen by the debate's participants.

The economic system that Stalin put in place in the late 1920s and early 1930s was radically different from then-existing systems. Although the economic system evolved through time, and a variety of reform attempts were made beginning in the late 1950s, the system Mikhail Gorbachev inherited in the mid-1980s looked surprisingly similar to that of earlier years.

The Setting

Before we examine the Soviet command economy, we should briefly discuss its natural setting. By almost any measure, the Soviet Union was a very large country, a fact important to its economic development. The Soviet Union occupied 8.6 million square miles, an area more than twice that of the United States. In terms of population, the Soviet Union entered the 1990s with approximately 290 million persons, some 15 percent more than the population of the United States. The majority of the Soviet population (roughly 65 percent) lived in urban areas, and approximately 80 percent of the labor force was in industry and related nonagricultural occupations. Urbanization characterized the Soviet experience, along with the traditional shift of the labor force away from rural/agricultural pursuits.

Equally significant, the Soviet Union was a very diverse nation consisting of 15 union republics. The largest of these, the Russian Republic, accounted for just over 50 percent of the Soviet population. The remainder of the population comprised the Latvians, Lithuanians, and Estonians (the Baltic region); the Ukrainians; the peoples of Central Asia, including Uzbekistan, Kirgizstan, Tadzhikistan, and Turkmenistan; and those of the Caucasus, including Georgia, Azerbaidzhan, and Armenia. These and other peoples of the Soviet Union infused it with vast ethnic, cultural, and historical diversity. Ethnic and regional differences have remained important in the post-Soviet era.

Sharp differences also existed in the Soviet Union's natural environment. The climate ranged from the hot, dry areas of Central Asia to the cold expanses of Siberia and the cool, wet plains of the west. Needless to say, significant regional differences in climate dictated major variations in resource usage, especially in agriculture.

Finally, the Soviet Union had an extraordinarily rich resource base. In addition to being a major producer of fish and forest products, the Soviet Union was amply endowed with minerals and was the world's largest producer of petroleum, coal, and iron ore. Indeed, there are very few minerals for which the Soviet Union had inadequate domestic reserves.

The Soviet Economy: A Framework for Analysis

Differences in outcomes can be related to differences in economic systems. As we have noted before, system differences fall into four basic and important categories: **decision-making** *levels*, mechanisms of information (*market* and *plan*), **property rights** (*public* versus *private*), and the nature of incentives (*material* versus *moral*).

As we examine the Soviet command economy and its organizational arrangements, it is important to ask two questions: How did this system differ from the ideal of planned socialism? How can the actual command system be categorized according to our four criteria?

In terms of the decision-making arrangements, the Soviet economy was organized in a vertical hierarchical fashion of the sort described in Figure 2.4 (Panel B). The Soviet state, operating through government ministries, and the **Communist party**, operating through groups and cells in organizations, shared authority and responsibility. There were several decision-making layers, including the state and party structure at the top, the ministries and regional authorities (and sometimes trust organizations) in the middle, and the basic production units (enterprises and farms), at the lower level.

From the perspective of resource allocation, the Soviet system was a centralized economic system. Moreover, the dominant mechanism for generating and using information was the national economic plan and its subcomponents. The state and party organizations made key decisions on production, distribution, and accumulation that were spelled out in the long- and short-term plans. While planning was the dominant mechanism for resource allocation, there were instances in which market forces and influences affected that process, for example, in the allocation of labor and in the second, or underground, economy.

The most striking difference between the Soviet economy and a market capitalist economy was in the area of property rights. The Soviet state as the primary property owner controlled virtually all aspects of property utilization. Although collective farms, for example, were exceptions to full state ownership of property, in fact such distinctions were not particularly important.

Significantly, state ownership of property meant that there were no capital or land markets and no formal system of rewards to these inputs. Rather, income generated from their use accrued directly to the state with **wage income** being the method of payment to workers. Beyond **material incentives**, however, the Communist party placed considerable emphasis on developing **moral incentives**, an important characteristic of socialist systems.

When examining the Soviet economy, it is important to be aware that this treatment of that system as a centrally planned socialist system is not at the expense of alternative paradigms. Thus ideology was an important determinant of system objectives. Moreover, it is interesting to cast the Soviet experience in the mold of the more general process of economic development.

Organizational Features of the Command Model

Since the beginning of the plan era in 1928, organizational change occurred frequently in the Soviet Union. At the same time, there was continuity in the basic arrangements, a stylized picture of which is presented in Figure 11.1. Under these arrangements, the Soviet Union was nominally governed by an elected government, the operative organ of which was the Council of Ministers at the federal (all-Union) and republican levels. A parallel structure, the Communist Party of the Soviet Union (CPSU), was the principal organ of control and supervision. It operated through a complex centralized structure beginning at the national level and terminating with individual party cells in each industrial enterprise, farm, and organization.[9] Regional party organizations were important agents for controlling the allocation of resources at the local level.

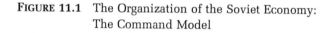

FIGURE 11.1   The Organization of the Soviet Economy:
                The Command Model

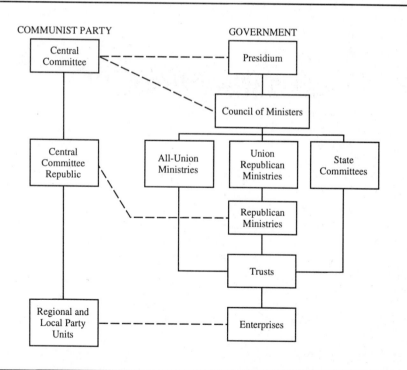

In this system, the means of production were, with only limited exceptions, owned by the state; firms and other organizations operated under the control of the state and party apparatus.[10] The agricultural sector was organized into state farms, collective farms, and a private sector, the latter governed by strict regulations. Both vertical and horizontal integration characterized the contemporary agricultural scene, as farms and industrial processing were linked in agro-industrial combines.

The major decisions about resource allocation were made by **Gosplan**, the state planning agency. Traditionally, the communist party developed the general directives on resource allocation. Gosplan then converted those directives into operative plans, with the aid of the ministerial structure and the individual enterprises. Finally, it was the responsibility of the individual enterprises to carry out the plan directives.

Over the years, the organizational arrangements and the policy directives of the Soviet economic system changed, and yet there was remarkable stability. The administrative command system was a hierarchical command system in which public ownership was combined with material incentives aimed at encouraging the carrying out of state and party directives. In this system, information flowed from top to bottom and vice versa, intra-enterprise activities were plan-coordinated, and money and markets played only a limited role.

From an economic standpoint, two properties of the command system deserve emphasis. First, the major organization around which the industrial activity of enterprises and the agricultural activities of farms were organized was the **ministry**. Ministries were hierarchically organized by type of production—steel, agriculture, and so on. The ministerial structure was shifted to organization on a *regional* basis in 1957 under the leadership of Nikita Khrushchev. The purpose, apparently, was to break down the tendency of ministries to become self-sufficient and to ignore interactions with other ministries. The reform did not work and was abandoned when Khrushchev fell from power in 1964. Ministries differed in importance, depending on their function. The most important branches of industry were governed by all-union ministries. Important decisions concerning, for example, steel production facilities were made at the center. Union republican ministries dispersed a measure of decision-making authority to the level of the 15 republics. The ministries, then, were the organizational superiors of the industrial and agricultural enterprises. Organizational reforms experimented with combining enterprises into trusts, intended to serve as an intermediary between the enterprise and the ministry.

Second, planning was done by Gosplan, the state planning agency. Gosplan was responsible for converting general directives of the Communist party into operative plans, with the help of the ministries and individual enterprises. Although planning, in the sense of making all economic decisions, is virtually impossible, in practice the Soviet command system utilized a variety of means to simplify the planning task.

Planning in Practice

The allocation of resources in the Soviet Union was conducted primarily through the plan. There were short-term (1-year), longer-term (5- or 7-year), and even

20-year "perspective" plans. The annual plans, which directed economic activity, are of central interest.

The essence of plan formulation was the material balance technique, the theoretical basis of which was examined in Chapter 6.[11] The plan was formulated in the following manner. General directives on the economy were provided by the CPSU and converted into control figures by Gosplan. The control figures, or tentative production targets, were transmitted through the ministries down to the level of individual enterprises, with comment and informational input being sought from each level in the hierarchy. The control figures then moved back up through the hierarchy and at the Gosplan level were "balanced"; that is, for major items in the plan, supply and demand must balance. Once balance was achieved, the plan was disaggregated and the targets once again disseminated down through the ministries to the individual enterprises. The final result, the **techpromfinplan** (technical-industrial-financial plan), was legally binding and contained detailed directives for enterprise operations during the forthcoming year.

In practice, the formulation of this plan was time consuming and complex, and clearly could not approach the theoretical ideals posed in Chapter 6. This brief description cannot do justice to the bargaining, haggling, interplay among the various units, and delays that were integral parts of Soviet planning. Frequently the new plan was late in arriving, so the enterprise would continue to operate under the guidance of the old plan. The **material balance system** worked in large part because it had built-in flexibility. The planning process did not start from scratch each year. The plan for year *t* was, in effect, little more than a revision and update of the plan for year *t* − 1. This practice was described as "planning from the achieved level." Although it simplified the planning process, it built in considerable inflexibility. In addition, Soviet planners did not plan all items produced by the economy and planned at the center only a relatively small number of items. Major commodities such as steel and machinery were called **funded commodities** or **limited commodities** and were planned at the center. Their number varied over time from a few hundred to a few thousand. Other commodities were planned at progressively lower and lower levels, depending on the importance of the commodities in the economy. This simplified the planning process, but left much to be done at the lower levels— for example, in the various republics.

In constructing balances for major materials, planners faced a dilemma. On the one hand, they wanted the **balance** to be achieved at the highest possible level; on the other hand, they knew that the more *taut* the **plan**—that is, the closer the targets were to maximum capacity—the more likely errors and supply imbalances would occur.[12] The approach was, in practice, to attempt to find a balance at a reasonably high level through adjusting input usage, manipulating final demand, adjusting stocks, and/or seeking foreign supplies. All these stratagems were devices for ensuring that the plan was demanding yet at the same time in balance. Soviet planners did not employ sophisticated planning techniques to "balance" supplies and demands. In fact, ad hoc tallies of sources and material requirements were maintained, and past experience was the principal guide. Accordingly, Soviet planners were usually satisfied if they were able to come up with a *consistent* **plan**, but they did not have the luxury of seeking out the *optimal* **plan** from among all possible consistent plans.

In addition to these formal mechanisms to adjust supply and demand, informal patterns of managerial response also served to manipulate plan patterns, sometimes in undesirable directions. **Buffer sectors**, typically consumer goods, were also used to absorb shortages as they arose.

This picture of traditional Soviet planning is a distortion of reality, for it suggests an economy that was rigidly planned and controlled by central authorities. In relative terms this view is correct. All economies combine some mix of market and plan, and the Soviet economy leaned most heavily in the direction of planning by directive. Most facets of the Soviet economy were planned, and there was almost total public ownership of the means of production. But beneath the façade of rigid centralized planning, numerous informal and some quasi-market mechanisms affected resource allocation. Little is known about the scope and workings of those informal mechanisms, although our knowledge has expanded in the post-Soviet era.

We know that the formal plan was really only the initial blueprint for economic activity both at the economy-wide and at the enterprise levels. The manner in which the plan was revised in the course of plan fulfillment was probably as important as the initial plan itself. In fact, the changes and revisions that took place after the plan was finalized were so great that some analysts question whether it is appropriate to call the Soviet economy a planned economy. We also know that a variety of unofficial markets existed and were important, yet they had little to do with the formal planning process.[13] Most products, in fact, were planned at regional or local levels or were not planned at all. In some instances, indirect signals (for example, prices) played a role in resource allocation, especially at the managerial level.

It is not possible to characterize precisely the balance between the formal and informal forces that affected resource allocation in the Soviet Union. We know that compared to market economies, the balance was strongly in favor of centralized administrative allocation, but the role of informal forces was also recognized.[14]

The previous discussion of the theory of planning emphasized three important stages in the planning process: plan development, implementation, and feedback. Thus far, this book has concentrated on organizational arrangements and on formulation of the plan. But plan implementation was in large part the responsibility of the individual firm or agricultural enterprise. What sort of rules were needed to ensure that each enterprise was in fact motivated to follow plan directives and thus fulfill the wishes of the central planners? What happened when mistakes in planning were made or when allocation decisions were omitted from plan directives?

The Soviet Enterprise

In the planned economy, all enterprises have a plan, which is usually specified in annual terms but broken down into monthly (and even shorter) periods. The plan is a comprehensive document covering many facets of the firm's operations, and it carries the force of law. The plan specifies both inputs and outputs in physical and financial terms; it specifies the sources and the distribution of funds for the firm; and so on. However, it would be erroneous to think that the Soviet manager was fully regimented, mechanically followed instructions, and had little freedom of action. In fact, quite a lot of managerial freedom existed. To understand Soviet management and plan fulfillment, one must understand how managers responded in this environment and what impact they had on the plan and its fulfillment.

Much of the traditional Soviet managerial milieu can be summed up as "the managerial success indicator problem." Soviet managers were offered substantial rewards for achieving a number of planned objectives, but those objectives were fuzzy and often led to dysfunctional managerial behavior.[15] This was a classic principal–agent problem.

Historically, **gross value of output** was the most important target from the manager's viewpoint. The manager's performance was judged on the basis of fulfillment of that target. But even if prices accurately reflected relative scarcities, it would be difficult for planners to specify output objectives unequivocally. For example, if managers were told to maximize the gross value of output, they would ignore items that made a small contribution, relative to their claim on scarce resources, to gross value and would overproduce items that made a large contribution. The *mix* or **assortment of goods** within the plan would be ignored, if ignoring it was necessary to meet the gross output target. Within the patterns of Soviet managerial bonuses, such behavior, though potentially disruptive, was rewarding to the manager and the enterprise. The bonus system typically paid little or nothing until the output plan was 100 percent fulfilled. Then rewards were paid for production over this level, resulting in an average managerial bonus of 25 or 35 percent of base salary.[16] Top managers received bonuses in excess of 50 percent. Moreover, managerial perks and job tenure depended on fulfillment of the gross output target. Generally taut targets and uncertain supply (especially for "limited" goods) were combined with substantial rewards for fulfillment of planned output targets. The result was informal and dysfunctional managerial behavior—a problem not anticipated by the socialist economic theorists, who assumed that managers would obey all rules handed down by superior authorities.

How did Soviet managers protect themselves and prosper in such an environment? First, managers, during the plan formulation stage, attempted to secure "easy" targets—that is, targets that were low vis-à-vis the actual capacity of the enterprise. This is a problem of any system in which participants can manipulate the objectives against which they will be measured. And it is why the reward system is so important in a planned economy.

Second, managers could emphasize what was important in terms of their rewards and neglect other areas. Thus cost-saving targets, along with assortment targets, could be sacrificed for the sake of ensuring fulfillment of gross output targets. This was a major explanation for the shortage of spare parts in Soviet industry: Their manufacture disrupted production lines and did not contribute sufficiently to rewards. Third, managers could seek "safety" in various other practices. They could stockpile materials that were expected to be in short supply; they could avoid innovation; and they could establish informal or "family" connections to ensure a supply of crucial inputs.

Many features of the informal Soviet managerial milieu were disruptive and shifted the results of production away from those envisaged by the planners. Others were necessary to correct for errors made by planning authorities and for break-downs in the supply system. Plan execution, therefore, was subject to a substantial measure of flexibility and variation not envisaged in the theoretical models: People simply did not do what they were told. But the state did not stand idle; it exercised control over enterprise management.

Planners monitored enterprise performance, though this was not a simple task in an economy the size of the Soviet Union. The CPSU was an important control institution. Most organizations contained party cells, and enterprise managers were almost always party members. They were therefore aware of party priorities. Never-theless, at almost all levels of the Soviet economy there was a bias in favor of reporting successful results. If local enterprises performed well, the careers of local party officials were advanced, and so on up the hierarchy. Another monitoring de-vice was the state bank (Gosbank).[17] Most Soviet enterprises were budget-financed, which meant that funds both to and from enterprises flowed through the state bank into and out of the state budget. The state budget was the a major source of enter-prise investment funds or, for an enterprise that lost money, of subsidy funds. Profits, too, were channeled through the state bank, and profit taxes were the major source of Soviet budgetary revenue. Each enterprise was required to hold accounts with the state bank where all transactions were recorded. Not only were the firm's labor requirements specified in the plan, but the fund used to pay for the labor was held and monitored by the state bank.

Second, managerial behavior was manipulated by the reward system.[18] Soviet managers earned substantial monetary bonuses for meeting targets. There were other rewards, such as housing, vacations, automobiles, and promotions. On the negative side, managers who did not perform were dismissed, a sanction that was widely used in the early days of Soviet planning.[19]

Soviet plans existed in both physical and monetary variants. The financial plans were derived from the physical plans. Beginning in the reform era of the late 1950s, increasing attention was paid to financial variables and hence to the nature and rationality of the Soviet price system. In market economic systems, prices clearly influence resource allocation. Indeed, as financial variables grew more important in the command economy, the issue of price formation grew in importance.

Prices and the Allocation of Land, Labor, and Capital in the Command System

Soviet Prices: General Features

With some exceptions, Soviet prices were set by administrative authorities.[20] In the case of the collective farm markets, and in services provided by moonlighting workers, prices resulted from supply and demand. Soviet industrial prices were set to equal the average cost by the industrial branch plus a small profit markup. **Branch average cost** generally excluded rental and interest charges, and its use as a standard resulted in enterprises making both planned profits and planned losses within the same branch. Pricing authorities sought, through periodic price "reforms," to raise prices enough to make the average branch enterprise profitable. This meant that when the price reform was introduced, the average enterprise broke even and others made substantial profits. The administrative difficulty of making frequent price reforms meant that historically prices lagged behind cost increases, and the majority of enterprises in particular branches made planned losses. During the last quarter-century of the Soviet system, major price reforms were rare. Wholesale prices established in 1955 remained generally in effect until 1966. The 1966–1967 price reform remained in effect until the general price reform of 1982. Prices had limited use, because they were unrelated to relative scarcities.

As far as inter-enterprise relations were concerned, wholesale prices played primarily an accounting role, for supplies and demands were administratively planned and were not functions of prices. However, when a product left the wholesale level to be sold at the retail level, the matter was not so simple. Figure 11.2 illustrates retail price formation.

FIGURE 11.2   Soviet Turnover Tax

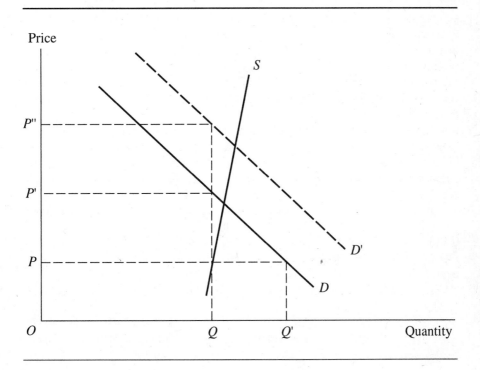

The supply of consumer goods at the retail level was determined largely by the planners, although producers, if they had a choice in output mix, might choose to produce a product with a higher relative price. Thus we draw the supply curve (*S*) with a steep upward slope. The demand curve (*D*) is a function of relative prices, incomes, and tastes and could not be controlled by the planners. How could the planners ensure that supply and demand would balance at the retail level? Typically, the retail price was established at or near a market-clearing level by adding either a **turnover tax** or a subsidy (if the wholesale price was above the clearing level). If the retail price were set at the wholesale (cost-based) price (*P* in Figure 11.2), there would be an excess demand of $Q'Q$, for OQ would be produced and OQ' demanded. Some form of rationing would be required.

In addition to administrative rationing and rationing of goods through long lines, Soviet authorities relied on the turnover tax to balance supply and demand. If the authorities chose to ration via price, the retail price would be set at OP' and approximate equilibrium would prevail. It is important to note that raising the retail price *did not* raise the quantity supplied above OQ, because the enterprise continued to receive the wholesale price OP for the product. The difference between the retail and wholesale prices was the turnover tax.

The turnover tax, in this case PP', was an important component of Soviet budgetary revenue. Unlike Western sales taxes, its proportion differed widely from one product to another, and it was included in the price rather than being added on at the time of sale. Its share of retail prices declined over time, as planners increased supplies of consumer products and raised the wholesale prices of farm products.

Although prices approached equilibrium at the retail level, this mechanism was different from that prevailing in the capitalist market economy. What we saw in the Soviet case as a tax would in effect be a profit accruing to the capitalist producer, which signaled to existing producers to expand supply and to new producers to enter the market. There was no such signal in the Soviet case, because what would be profit in the capitalist context accrued as tax revenue to the state. The producer at the wholesale level was unaware of and largely uninterested in retail prices. The link between consumer demand and the producer was broken. Say demand increases from *D* to *D'*. As the producer continues to receive the wholesale price OP, the quantity produced remains at OQ. But at the old retail price OP', there is now an excess of demand over supply. The state reacts eventually by raising the turnover tax by $P'P''$.

In the Soviet case the mix of consumer goods was determined by **planners' preferences**, not by **consumer demand**, although in the long run, planners may well have considered consumer signals when establishing plan targets. Thus prices played only a very limited **allocative** role and were used primarily for measurement, control, and manipulation of the distribution of income.

Soviet price policy emphasized the desirability of pricing some goods and services relatively "low" and others relatively "high." This policy reflected a very different socialist attitude toward the "equitable" distribution of income and toward determining what was a necessity and what was a luxury. Thus the prices of books, housing, medical care, and transportation were very low, and the prices of automobiles and vodka were very high. Price policy affected the distribution of real incomes in accordance with state objectives.

The issues surrounding prices and pricing policies in the command economy are complex. In the pre-Gorbachev era, Soviet price reform was generally aimed at making prices more realistic in the sense of accurately reflecting production costs; thus they should promote greater efficiency in the use of inputs. However, despite numerous reform attempts, Soviet prices remained, throughout the plan era, largely ineffective in promoting the rational allocation of resources. Given the indispensable role of prices in a market system, one can readily appreciate the difficulty of replacing plan by market under these conditions.

Input Prices: Land and Labor

In the Soviet economy, the prices of inputs—land, labor, and capital—reflected a peculiar combination of Marxian orthodoxy, pragmatism, and allocative necessity. There was, for the most part, no rental price for agricultural land. Land was allocated to collective and state farms administratively. Planners determined land utilization within the framework of the plan, taking into account technical and local conditions. The absence of land charges made farm accounting a questionable exercise, the result of which was an endless debate over the role of land rent under socialism. Despite some interest in land valuation, the Soviet Union never formalized a system of land valuation. Historically, however, Soviet planners attempted to extract a rent from the Soviet countryside by using regionally differentiated procurement prices and differential charges for machine services provided by the state.

The allocation of labor in the Soviet Union was a very different case, for there was a price for labor in the form of a wage rate. How were wages set in the Soviet Union, and what role did wages have in allocating labor among that country's various occupations, uses, and regions?[21]

Historically, wage differentials were one of several mechanisms utilized to allocate labor in the Soviet Union. The demand for labor was primarily plan-determined. Once output targets were established, labor requirements were determined by applying technical coefficients that represent the amount of labor required per unit of output under existing technology. On the supply side, however, households were substantially free to make occupational choices and to decide between labor and leisure. The state set wage differentials—for example, by occupation and by region—in an attempt to induce appropriate supplies to meet planned demands.

The Soviet wage-setting procedure was straightforward. For an industrial branch, a base rate was established. This rate determined the wage level for that branch relative to other branches. A schedule gave all rates above this level as a percentage of the base and established the pattern of wage differentials within the branch. Thus the level and differential could be adjusted by manipulating the base or the schedule. Soviet trade unions and individual workers played virtually no role in setting wages; wages were set by administrative authorities. But unlike many other areas in the Soviet economy, planners were willing to *use* these differentials to manipulate labor supply. There was a substantial degree of market influence on the structure of Soviet wages.[22]

In addition to wage differentials, other devices were used to manipulate labor supply. Higher- and technical-education institutions expanded in direct relation to the desired composition of the labor force, and this was a matter under state control. In addition, nonmonetary rewards, adulation in the press, social benefits, and other such moral incentives were used to affect the supply of labor. **Organized recruitment** by special organizations and the party were important in the past but declined in contemporary times with the exception of the seasonal needs of agricultural production.[23] The Soviet system, therefore, combined both material and moral rewards, with the emphasis on the former.

Soviet labor policies, including the forced-labor campaigns of the 1930s, ensured a very high rate of labor force participation to provide rapid economic development. In more recent years, the participation rate, defined as the civilian labor force as a proportion of the able-bodied population, generally exceeded 90 percent. On the other hand, structural problems grew more serious and became a major test of the ability of central planning to allocate labor. For example, the rapid rate of urbanization left shortages in some areas, surpluses in others. Those imbalances were especially true for the regional distribution of labor, where Soviet authorities were unable to meet the labor needs of Siberia and the Far North. In addition, the restrictive role of Soviet trade unions and the policy of "full employment" have resulted in overemployment—artificially high levels of staffing at the enterprise level. It was quite difficult to lay off workers even if they were redundant. This problem prompted the state to experiment with programs to encourage the firing of unproductive workers. The Soviet economy did not solve the problems of **overfull employment policies** and the resulting allocative inefficiencies.

Capital Allocation

Capital is not a value-creating input in the Marxian scheme.[24] Why then should the use of capital generate a reward in the form of an interest charge? Even if capital has no value-creating capacity, less is available than is demanded. Some means must be devised for its allocation. Furthermore, even if a "price" is used in this allocation function, it will perform *only* this function. Where all capital is owned by the state, the "income" from capital accrues directly to the state, not to individuals.

In the Soviet case, investment was largely controlled by central planning authorities and the ministries. In drawing up the output plan, planners used technical coefficients to determine the amounts of capital investment necessary to produce the planned output, and investment funds were authorized. Some funds were available from internal enterprise sources, but even those funds remained under control of the banking system. The aggregate supply of investment funds was largely under the control of planners. It is not surprising, therefore, that the ratio of saving to gross national product was very high in the Soviet Union—much higher than in the United States. Indeed, this illustrates a basic feature of planners' preferences. In a market capitalist economy, saving is influenced by government but is largely determined by individuals and businesses as they choose between consumption in the present and greater consumption in the future. In the Soviet context, the state controlled saving (primarily by the state and by enterprises). In a capitalist economy, saving arises as undistributed profits in enterprises and as income that is not consumed in households. Both *types* of saving existed in the Soviet case, but because wages and prices were set by the state, the state itself could accumulate savings at whatever rate it chose without recourse to the indirect method of taxation. This ability to control saving and investment was a powerful mechanism to promote a more rapid rate of capital accumulation than would probably be tolerated in an economy directed by consumer sovereignty.

After the late 1960s, Soviet enterprises paid an interest charge for the use of capital. This charge was typically low and was designed to cover the administrative costs of making the capital funds available to the enterprise.

At the enterprise level, Soviet authorities devised rules for choosing among investment projects. Suppose there was a directive to raise the capacity to generate a certain volume of electric power. Will the capacity be hydroelectric, nuclear, coal-fueled, or what? How can one compare the capital-intensive variant that has low operating costs with the variant that requires less capital initially but has high annual operating costs? Although quasi-market techniques for making this sort of decision were rejected by Stalin in the 1930s in favor of planners' wisdom, those methods surfaced again in the late 1950s and were used widely thereafter.

Soviet planners accepted the principle that the selection among competing projects should be based on cost-minimizing procedures. A general formula, called the **coefficient of relative effectiveness**, was used to compare projects:

$$C_i + E_n K_i = \text{Minimum}$$

where

C_i = current expenditures of the ith investment project
K_i = the capital cost of the ith investment project
E_n = the normative coefficient

This formula was used to weigh the tradeoff between higher capital outlays (K_i) and lower operating costs (C_i). The principle was that that project variant should be selected that yields the minimum full cost, where an imputed capital charge is included in the cost of calculation. The capital cost was calculated by applying a "normative coefficient" (E_n) to the projected capital outlay.

For example, assume that a choice must be made between two projects, the first having an annual operating cost (C) of 10 million rubles and a capital cost (K) of 30 million rubles, the second having a C of 7 million rubles and a K of 50 million rubles. Applying a normative coefficient of 10 percent yields a full cost of 13 million rubles for the first project and 12 million rubles for the second. The second project should be chosen, because it is the minimum-cost variant. However, suppose a normative coefficient of 20 percent is applied. In this case, the full cost of the first variant is 16 and that of the second variant is 17. In this case—and all that has changed is the normative coefficient—the first variant should be chosen.

An important feature of this formula should be noted. The higher the normative coefficient, the higher the imputed capital cost, and the *less* likely that capital-intensive variants will be selected. Between 1958 and 1969, a system of differentiated normative coefficients was used that gave priority to heavy industry by applying low E_ns to heavy-industrial branches and high E_ns to light industry. In 1969, a new **Standard Methodology**[25] replaced the earlier differentiated system with a standard normative coefficient of 12 percent. It was supposed to be applied equally to all branches of the economy.

The principle that capital should be allocated among projects on the basis of such rate-of-return calculations should not obscure the fact that the basic allocation of capital still proceeded through an administrative investment plan, which itself was a derivative of the output plan. The rate-of-return calculations were used only to select among projects that followed planners' preferences in the first place. Thus they were used to decide what type of plant should be used to generate electricity, not whether the investment should be in the generation of electricity or, for example, in steel production. In fact, the standardized coefficient introduced in 1969 was watered down thereafter by numerous exceptions for particular branches of heavy industry and for various regions.

Financial Planning

The Soviet economy was run by largely administrative rules and instructions. Although value categories (prices, costs, profits, and so on) always existed, they played only a limited role in allocating resources. Even in a centralized economy where few decisions were made at local levels, households made decisions about how much members would work and what they would buy. How could planners ensure that there will be a macroeconomic balance of consumer goods? Aggregate consumer demand and supply can be illustrated in the following framework:

$$D = WL - R \qquad\qquad\qquad (11.1)$$

$$S = P_1 Q_1 \qquad\qquad\qquad (11.2)$$

where

D = aggregate demand
S = aggregate supply
W = the average annual wage
L = the number of worker-years of labor used in the economy
R = the amount of income not spent on consumer goods
  (equal to the sum of direct taxes and savings)
Q_1 = the real quantity of consumer goods produced
P_1 = the price level of consumer goods

The problem here is conceptually quite simple. As the Soviet socialist economy developed rapidly in the early plan years, it paid labor increasingly large salaries to motivate higher participation and greater effort, but the state wanted that labor to produce producer goods, not consumer goods (Q_1). Thus the state permitted wages (W) to rise rapidly in order to encourage labor inputs (L) to rise. In the absence of sharp increases in Q_1, however, it was necessary to pursue alternative steps to achieve a balance between S and D—notably to let P_1 rise along with R (the latter through forced bond purchases). However, prices were not allowed to rise fast enough to absorb the full increase in demand; an imbalance between aggregate supply and demand was allowed to develop. This technique, typical for any less developed economy during the early stages of development, is known as **repressed inflation** and was used widely in the Soviet Union.[26]

During the years following World War II, the quantity of consumer goods increased, although simultaneous increases in purchasing power made it difficult to determine to what degree excess demand was reduced. Indeed, as noted earlier, Janos Kornai developed a general model of the socialist economy suggesting that such systems can in fact be shortage-based systems, even when expansion in the production of consumer goods is taking place.

At the end of the Soviet era, the focus of discussion for the Soviet Union and other formerly planned socialist systems was on repressed inflation.[27] In a system where excess demand is unlikely to result in price increases, **disequilibrium analysis** (see Appendix 11A) was shown to be an effective tool. Western research focused on Soviet savings as evidence of repressed inflation, arguing that people save because there is nothing to buy at prevailing prices. Moreover, much research effort was focused on the direct modeling of consumer goods markets.

Market Forces in the Command Economy

The American economy is a market economy in which the state plays a growing and frequently controversial role. The Soviet economy, at least until the era of *Perestroika*, was a planned economy in which market forces were of only moderate and secondary importance. Thus, although the role of markets in the traditional Soviet economy is a matter of some controversy, their role in resource allocation has generally been viewed as an exception to the plan. The issue of markets in what is usually described as a planned economy deserves additional attention.

In an economic system, ownership and control are closely related. The Soviet state, as the primary owner of the means of production, exercised control over the direction of economic activity through the national economic plan.

Paul Craig Roberts argued that the Soviet economy was a **"polycentric" system** in which control was diversified.[28] He maintained that the interaction of enterprises at the local level, their informal interrelationships, and the generation of local information flows, not the plan, were the main forces determining economic activity. Eugene Zaleski concluded from his analysis of plan fulfillment that administrative adjustments made after the plan was finalized had a stronger bearing on resource allocation than the plans themselves. Zaleski refers to the Soviet economy as an administratively managed (not a planned) economy.[29]

A number of other Western analysts have come to question whether the Soviet economy was a "planned" economy. John H. Wilhelm argued that the original plan typically was not workable, was continuously changed in the course of plan fulfillment, and in the end was revised to correspond to expected fulfillment. Under these circumstances, Wilhelm argues, it is inappropriate to call the Soviet economy a planned economy.[30] Available evidence does not allow us to draw a firm conclusion, but we would reject the argument that the plan was not a critical determinant of economic activity. Rather, the relevant issue is whether, and how much, additional forces affected economic outcomes.

Western economists have long argued that in some areas of the Soviet economy —for example, labor allocation—planners used market-type mechanisms to influence observed outcomes. Thus wage differentials were used to influence the distribution of labor by region, by season, and by profession; and retail prices, to allocate available consumer goods. The fact that wages and retail prices were set by planners does not rule out market forces. In such instances, planners were actually acting as market intermediaries.

A third role for market forces was the **second economy**. The second economy has been analyzed extensively by Gregory Grossman, Dimitri Simes, Vladimir Treml, Michael V. Alexeev, Aron Katsenelinboigen, and others.[31] It consisted of a number of market-type activities of varying importance and degrees of legality, all facilitating "unplanned" exchange among consumers and producers. According to Grossman, second-economy activities must meet at least one of the following two criteria: (1) the activity is engaged in for private gain; (2) the person engaging in the activity knowingly contravenes existing law.

Examples of second-economy activities abound. Indeed, since the advent of Glasnost and the ultimate demise of the Soviet Union, a good deal more has been learned about the second economy. A physician might treat private patients for higher fees. A salesperson might set aside quality merchandise for customers who offer large tips. The manager of a textile firm might reserve goods for sale in unofficial supply channels. A collective farmer may divert collective farm land and supplies to his private plot. Black marketeers in port cities may deal in contraband merchandise. Owners of private cars may transport second-economy merchandise. In some cases, official and second-economy transactions were intertwined. A manager may divert some production into second-economy transactions to raise cash to purchase unofficially supplies needed to meet the plan. The official activities of an enterprise may serve as a front for a prospering second-economy undertaking.

Second-economy activities were concentrated in collective farms and in the transportation network. Apparently, the supervision of collective farms was more lax; they therefore served as better fronts for the second economy. Transportation enterprises were critical to the second economy, for its merchandise must somehow be moved. The increase in private ownership of automobiles apparently enhanced the operation of the second economy.

How important was the second economy? Unfortunately, it is difficult to estimate accurately the magnitude of second-economy activity. In a survey of Soviet émigrés conducted by Gur Ofer and Aron Vinokur, during the early 1970s earnings derived from activity other than that at the main place of employment were found to account for approximately 10 percent of earnings.[32] A study of Soviet alcohol production and consumption, conducted by Vladimir Treml in the mid-1980s, found that between 20 and 25 percent of transactions were illegal. Although the second economy was important in the overall command economy, there were substantial variations from one sector to another. It was not surprising for secondary activities to arise in a setting of rising incomes and limited resources devoted to the service sector. Moreover, the growth of a second economy might be viewed as in some ways helpful to those attempting to control the economy through planning arrangements.

The second economy had its advantages and disadvantages as far as the planners were concerned. It helped to preserve incentives, because higher wages and bonus payments could be spent in the second economy. Moreover, the second economy served to reduce inflationary pressures on the official economy. On the negative side, the second economy diverted people from planned tasks and loosened planners' control. Soviet authorities long tolerated the second economy. Reforms of the late 1980s moved to legalize a number of second-economy activities that did not involve the use of hired labor.

A fourth area of market influence was the private sector of Soviet agriculture. Under certain restrictions, the farm family could use a plot of land, hold animals, and raise crops. The resulting products were sold in the kolkhoz market and tolerated by the authorities. Prices freely established by supply and demand provided a substantial portion of the farm family's income. It was not by accident that the private plots produced farm products that were poorly suited to planning, such as fruits, vegetables, and dairy products—all of which required much personal care and motivation.

The existence of second-economy activity in the administrative command economy is of more than passing interest. Although it is now difficult to quantify this second economy with precision, it is nevertheless viewed as an important—if unevenly distributed—part of the overall economic system. It is of theoretical interest that such a mechanism arises in the command economy beyond the purview of the planners. Moreover, if we find that its magnitude increased over time, we may have discovered a crude indicator of the divergence between plan targets and achievements and consumer demands in the economy.

Agriculture in the Command Economy

Our discussion of the American economic system did not include any specific treatment of agriculture. In an advanced economy such as the United States, agriculture plays a relatively much more modest role than it did in the developing Soviet economy. Even at the beginning of the Gorbachev era in the mid-1980s, agriculture accounted for 20 to 25 percent of Soviet gross national product and absorbed a great deal of the Soviet labor force. However, there is a second reason for looking more closely at Soviet agriculture: It exhibited unique organizational arrangements, and the results achieved were modest in spite of continuing attention from Soviet policy makers.

During war communism and the New Economic Policy, various forms of organization existed, but private peasant agriculture dominated.[33] The rural sector was seen as crucial to any Soviet development effort, because industrialization would depend on agricultural deliveries. Whether or not the perception of agriculture in the 1920s as the key to industrialization was correct, it was the rationale for Stalin's decision to collectivize in 1929.[34]

Two major institutions were dominant in Soviet agriculture since 1928. The collective farms (**kolkhozy**) were to operate like cooperatives; the **state farms** (**sovkhozy**), in which the farmers would be paid like industrial workers, would be a "factory in the fields." The sovkhoz was a state enterprise with state-appointed management.[35] The kolkhoz was, in theory, a cooperative with elected management. Sovkhoz workers were state employees and received fixed wages like other state employees. Kolkhoz peasants, on the other hand, received a dividend instead of a wage. Because this unique payment system was the cornerstone of Stalin's attempt to extract a surplus from the countryside, dwelling on it for a moment is worthwhile, even though it was abandoned in 1966.[36]

Before 1966, payment for peasants in the kolkhoz was established in the following fashion. For a particular task assigned to a peasant by, say, a brigade leader, a certain number of labor days would be "paid" and recorded in the peasant's work book. The **labor day** was not necessarily a measure of time or effort, but rather an often arbitrary measure of work input. At the end of the year, the *value* of one labor day would be determined by the following formula:

Value of one labor day = farm income after required deliveries and
other expenses ÷ total number of labor days
for entire kolkhoz

The value of a labor day having been determined, it would then be possible to pay each individual a "dividend" by multiplying the number of labor days accumulated by the value of one labor day.

This system of payment was highly arbitrary. The work demanded for one labor day could and did vary regionally, seasonally, and from farm to farm. Furthermore, contrary to the principles of any good incentive system, the peasant had little idea in advance what she or he would earn per labor day. The labor day system was finally abandoned in 1966 and was replaced by a guaranteed wage.

Differences Between Collective Farms and State Farms

Most input and output determinations in the kolkhoz and the sovkhoz were planned in a fashion similar to that used in an industrial enterprise. There were, however, some noteworthy differences. First, the method of payment for labor in the kolkhoz was, until 1966, very different from that in the sovkhoz. Second, the manner in which capital investment was provided was different: Kolkhoz investments were largely self-financed; sovkhoz investment funds came directly from the state budget.[37] Third, until the late 1950s, machinery and equipment were maintained in the Machine Tractor Stations and were provided to the collective farms for a payment.[38] This mechanism served as an important external control over the management of the kolkhozy. Fourth, the method of distribution of output was different. The sovkhoz, as a state enterprise, distributed the bulk of its output through the normal state trade channels, as an industrial enterprise might do. The kolkhoz, in contrast, was required to make compulsory deliveries to the state, often at very low fixed prices; but the remainder of its output was free for sale either to the state at higher prices or on the collective farm markets. This two-tier pricing arrangement allowed the state to extract the product from the kolkhoz.

In both the kolkhoz and the sovkhoz, families were entitled to small plots of land (typically about half an acre) for their private use.[39] The produce from this land, important in the case of some products (typically truckgarden products), could be consumed on the farm, sold to the state, or sold by the peasants in the collective farm markets. To give some idea of the importance of the private sector, we note that in the 1960s, the private sector accounted for roughly 60 percent of total potato output, 70 percent of total vegetable output, and 30 percent of total milk output. In the postwar period, the private sector accounted for approximately 40 percent of family income on collective farms. Peasants were also entitled to hold some animals, although the permitted number of each type varied over time. For example, roughly 40 percent of all cows were owned privately in the 1960s.

Changes in Soviet Agriculture

Organizational arrangements in agriculture changed substantially after the 1930s, although the kolkhoz, the sovkhoz, and the private sector remained at least in name through 1991. We note the main trends of change.[40]

First, since the 1940s, a program of merger and consolidation sharply reduced the number and importance of kolkhozy; at the same time, the number of sovkhozy increased, and their average size became greater. In 1940, there were 237,000 kolkhozy in the Soviet Union with an average sown area of 1235 acres. By the mid-1980s, the number of kolkhozy had been reduced to just over 26,000, and each kolkhoz had an average sown area of just over 8600 acres. As for sovkhozy, in 1940 there were 4200, averaging just over 6900 acres of sown area on each farm. By the mid-1980s, the number of sovkhozy had increased to almost 22,700, with an average sown area of almost 12,000 acres per farm.[41] In 1940, roughly 78 percent of all sown area was accounted for by kolkhozy; this was reduced to 44 percent by the mid-1980s.

Possibly the most important organizational change in contemporary Soviet agriculture was the introduction of **agro-industrial integration** on a major scale.[42] Begun with renewed emphasis in the 1970s, agro-industrial integration brought both kolkhozy and sovkhozy together with industrial-type activity (for example, processing) into integrated production units with centralized management. These changes, along with organizational changes on the regional level introduced with the Brezhnev "Food Program" of 1982, set the scene for further changes to occur with Perestroika under Gorbachev.

Second, there were changes in planning and supervisory organs and in the farm managerial system. The **Machine Tractor Stations** were abolished in 1958, and their equipment was sold to the farms, a move that gave farm managers enhanced control over farm equipment. In addition, the quality of managerial personnel improved dramatically thereafter.

Third, rural incomes increased sharply after the 1950s, generally more rapidly than industrial incomes. In addition, a pension system introduced in the 1960s substantially improved the welfare of rural workers and peasants and reduced the rural–urban income differential.[43] However, expanded production costs at the farm level and unwillingness to raise retail food prices significantly resulted in a very large subsidy to the agricultural sector.[44]

Fourth, after a period of extensive campaigns by Nikita Khrushchev in the 1950s (the Virgin Land Campaign, the corn program, and so on) designed to expand inputs, the emphasis in the 1960s and 1970s shifted to improvement of productivity, in part through significant increases in the volume of investment provided by the state.

Fifth, there was an ongoing program to examine seriously the problems of agriculture in an urban industrial economy. For example, Soviet planners devoted (though not always successfully) considerable attention to the problems of supplying large cities with vegetables. Also, efforts were made to stem the continuing rapid flow of young males from the rural areas and hence to alleviate the problem of labor shortages and imbalances.

Soviet agriculture has been of more than passing interest to Western observers. Catastrophic crop failures, minimal supplies of meat, and the virtual absence of produce in Soviet cities in winter were always puzzling in a heavily industrialized nation. Many observers laid the blame for uneven Soviet agricultural performance on unique Soviet organizational arrangements or on limited investment in agriculture.

We must ask whether the agricultural sector of the Soviet economy was neglected in some sense and what sorts of policies were developed in the 1970s and early 1980s. The Brezhnev years saw important developments in Soviet agriculture, though change was implemented less flamboyantly than it had been under his predecessor. Capital investment increased from roughly 15 percent of aggregate investment to almost 27 percent—a substantial increment by any standard. At the same time, agricultural productivity remained a problem, imports became very important, and Gorbachev criticized agricultural performance. Clearly, productivity had to be improved but, possibly more important, the infrastructure of Soviet agriculture was primitive, especially food processing, storage, and distribution arrangements.

In sum, it is difficult to study the Soviet development experience—and especially the implementation of the administrative command economy—without paying close attention to agriculture. As we have seen, agricultural policy was a focal point of controversy from the beginning, and it remained so in those East European nations where the Soviet model was imposed after World War II. During the postwar era, there was probably no sector in the Soviet economy to which so much attention was devoted. Even so, poor performance and sharply rising costs far exceeded what might reasonably be expected under less than ideal natural conditions. Agriculture remains a major challenge for the leaders of the "post-command" era.

International Trade in the Command Economy

No discussion of the Soviet command model would be complete if it failed to address the role of international trade in this model.[45] Foreign trade played a major role in the Soviet development experience. Moreover, the organizational arrangements used differed significantly from those generally found in market economic systems. The policies and the systemic arrangements of foreign trade in the command model differed widely from market economies.

Decision making—in terms of what will be traded, with whom, and on what terms—was relatively centralized in three major institutions: the Ministry of Foreign Trade (MFT), the *Vneshtorgbank* or **Bank for Foreign Trade** (BFT), and the various **foreign trade organizations** (FTOs). The formal organization of Soviet foreign trade is represented in Figure 11.3. The **Ministry of Foreign Trade**, like other Soviet ministries, was a relatively centralized body concerned with issues of foreign trade planning—the development of import/export plans, material supply plans, and balance-of-payments plans—all of which were an integral part of the Soviet material balance planning system.

FIGURE 11.3   The Organization of Soviet Foreign Trade: The Command Model

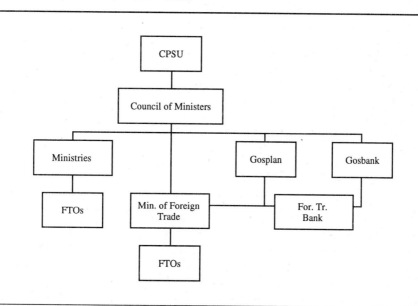

Individual Soviet enterprises generally did not deal with the external world, although reforms proposed by Gorbachev in 1987 changed this posture. Rather, for both imports and exports, enterprises dealt with the FTOs in domestic currency at domestic prices, and the FTOs dealt with the external world via financial arrangements handled by the Ministry of Foreign Trade and the BFT. In the Soviet case, a monopoly in the hands of the Soviet government conducted foreign trade. The domestic users or producers of goods entering the foreign market were substantially isolated from foreign markets by this foreign trade monopoly. As viewed by Western economists, Soviet foreign trade operated according to formal rules: Export what is available to be exported to pay for necessary imports, and limit the overall volume of trade to control the influence of market forces on the Soviet economy.

Traditionally, most Soviet trade, even with other socialist countries, was bilateral—that is, directly negotiated for each trade deal with each trading partner. Bilateral trade means that Soviet exports and imports were handled largely on a barter basis. The difficulties of operating according to offsetting barter deals hampered Soviet trade turnover through the years. In part, bilateral trading arrangements arose from and contributed to the nonconvertibility of the Soviet ruble, which was not accepted as a medium of exchange in world financial markets.

Soviet organizational arrangements were not conducive to maintaining an expanding and competitive position in world markets, but Western economists generally argued that the Soviet Union followed a policy of deliberate **trade aversion.**[46] What are the justifications for trade aversion? Dating from the late 1920s and early 1930s, Soviet trade ratios (that is, the ratio of imports and exports to gross national product) generally declined. For many years they remained low by world standards. This pattern may have resulted from the Soviet Union's adverse position in world markets at that time, or it may have been in part a deliberate policy response. In any event, for the trade that *was* conducted, a very successful effort was made to redirect Soviet imports away from consumer goods and toward producer goods, an outcome that contributed to the development effort.

The latter years of the Soviet era witnessed changes in Soviet foreign trade. First, Soviet trade ratios increased, signaling a growing participation in the world economy. The extent of this rise has been difficult to estimate because of the peculiarities of Soviet foreign trade accounting,[47] but there is little doubt that Soviet participation in foreign trade in the 1980s was well above the rates of the 1950s and 1960s.

Second, the 1960s and 1970s saw organizational changes. One major example was the continuing discussion in the Soviet Union about the need to make its enterprises more responsive to world markets and to streamline the FTOs as the mechanism through which enterprise contacts with world markets were channeled. These themes became important components of reform in the Gorbachev era.

Third, there was a revolution in Soviet attitudes toward foreign trade. There was renewed interest in Western, or neoclassical, trade theory and, most important, in the development and application of useful criteria on which to base trade decisions.

Fourth, the Soviet Union, though fundamentally conservative throughout the command era when compared to most of its East European neighbors, nevertheless displayed increasing interest in participating in world trade arrangements and organizations. Thus Soviet attitudes toward the external world changed even before the Gorbachev era.

Foreign trade played a key role in the Soviet development experience. However, in spite of changes in Soviet trading mechanisms through the mid-1980s, it was also evident that both the organizational arrangements and the policies of the Soviet command model inhibited the effective utilization of foreign trade. In the face of dramatically changing world trading arrangements, and given the critical Soviet need for productivity growth, the stage was set for change as Gorbachev introduced Perestroika in the mid-1980s.

The Soviet Economy: A Postscript

From the perspective of differing economic systems, the Soviet command era has provided a unique opportunity to understand a major and long-term effort to build a new society and a new economy as a world power. Although the Soviet Union and its political and economic systems ended in 1991, interest in this experiment has sustained for a variety of reasons.

First, a number of economies are currently using some or all of the components familiar to the Soviet analyst, such as state ownership, socialized agriculture, and macroeconomic planning. For example, the Chinese economy, as described in Chapter 17, has similar basics, but has chosen a different reform path.

Second, from many differing perspectives, it is impossible to ignore the long period of Soviet rule while looking at the contemporary economic systems now emerging in the territories of the former Soviet Union. Soviet society clearly left a substantial legacy for its population, a legacy that remains an important factor conditioning the nature and the pace of transition in the now independent countries. Indeed from an economic standpoint, the transition had to begin from the structure left after sixty years of the administrative command experience, an issue that Chapter 12 pursues in greater depth.

Third, the performance of the Soviet economy has always created a great deal of interest. This interest sustains, but with a different focus: What were the defining characteristics of economic decline in the former Soviet Union? Why did the system ultimately fail, and to what degree can blame be placed upon the economic as opposed to political, social, and other arrangements? Chapter 12 pursues those issues and examines the general issue of comparative economic performance across differing economic systems.

Finally, while seeking to understand the meaning of the Soviet past, an interesting question emerges: Does the collapse of the Soviet era and the restrictions that it imposed on scientific investigation mean that significantly better information will be available for pursuing some of the issues previously discussed? The answer to this question is not clear; however, the fading of the Soviet era will inevitably focus research on such contemporary problems as those found in Russia, Ukraine, or Uzbekistan. At the same time, it will be possible to investigate issues largely outside the purview available during the Soviet era, such examples include the microeconomics of enterprise behavior or the role of money and budgets in the Soviet system. Those possibilities will undoubtedly provide a better picture of the command economy, or at least the Soviet version of that economy, and also lead to a better understanding of the characteristics of different economic systems. Contemporary developments in neoclassical economic theory will be important in developing these new understandings.

Summary

What became known as the administrative command model is the economic system that dominated resource allocation in the Soviet Union for almost sixty years. Although Mikhail Gorbachev began a serious attempt to dismantle key features of this system, it remains as a very significant example of economic development in a largely nonmarket context. The main features of this system were as follows:

1. The administrative command system was put in place in 1928 with nationalization of the means of production, a system of national economic planning, and the collectivization of agriculture. Although there were numerous changes in this system over the years, its fundamental aspects remained remarkably stable.
2. The Soviet system was a relatively centralized economic system. The broad objectives of the Communist party were implemented through the state planning agency (Gosplan), the ministries, and individual firms and agricultural units.
3. The essence of Soviet planning was the material balance system, in which balances were developed to equate the demand and supply of key industrial commodities, labor inputs, and the like. The balance approach stressed consistency but not optimality, and there was only minimal reliance on money and prices for the allocation of resources.
4. Soviet enterprises were responsible for fulfilling plan targets, and managers were motivated within an incentive framework. In the absence of a price system reflecting relative scarcities and thus enabling managers to make rational decisions, dysfunctional behavior was a major problem.
5. Prices were cost-based, and the demand side had little or no influence. Prices served primarily an accounting and control function. Retail markets and the allocation of labor were exceptions; here the allocative role of prices was greater. Although capital was allocated in accordance with rules that resembled rates of return, capital allocation was largely accomplished by administrative decree.
6. Market-type influence existed in the allocation of labor. At the same time, market forces were prevalent in the second economy, which, though it varied in importance from one sector to another, dominated in the service sector. Market mechanisms also played an important role in the private sector of Soviet agriculture.
7. Soviet agriculture was traditionally dominated by the collective farms, the state farms, and the private sector. The latter was an important source of food products in spite of its relatively small size in terms of land area. In recent years,

agro-industrial integration became an important mechanism for combining farm activity with industrial processing.

8. Soviet foreign trade was a state monopoly. Soviet domestic enterprises were largely isolated from world markets through the intermediary function of the Foreign Trade Organization and the **nonconvertible ruble**.

Key Terms

incentives
Bolshevik revolution
administrative command economy
czarist era
level and rate of economic development
collective farms (kolkhozy)
war communism
New Economic Policy (NEP)
material incentives
decision-making levels
market
planning
public property rights
private property rights
Communist party
wage income
material incentives
moral incentives
Gosplan
ministry
techpromfinplan
material balance system
funded commodities
limited commodities
balanced plan
taut plan
consistent plan
optimal plan

buffer sectors
gross value of output
mix or assortment of goods
branch average cost
turnover tax
planners' preferences
consumer demand
organized recruitment
overfull employment policy
coefficient of relative effectiveness
Standard Methodology
repressed inflation
Perestroika
disequilibrium analysis
polycentric system
second economy
state farms (sovkhozy)
labor day
agro-industrial integration
Machine Tractor Stations
Bank for Foreign Trade
foreign trade organizations (FTOs)
Ministry of Foreign Trade
trade aversion
nonconvertible ruble
incentives
success indicators
barter trade

Notes

1. For a general treatment of the Soviet economy and references to the specialized literature, see Paul R. Gregory and Robert C. Stuart, *Soviet and Post-Soviet Economic Structure and Performance*, 5th ed. (New York: HarperCollins, 1994); Alec Nove, *The Soviet Economic System*, 3rd ed. (New York: Unwin Hyman, 1986); and Michael Ellman, *Socialist Planning* (New York: Cambridge University Press, 1989). For useful

background papers, see U.S. Congress, Joint Economic Committee, *Soviet Economy in the 1980s: Problems and Prospects*, Parts 1 and 2 (Washington, D.C.: Government Printing Office, 1982). For a briefer treatment of the Soviet economy, see Franklyn D. Holzman, *The Soviet Economy: Past, Present, and Future* (New York: Foreign Policy Association, 1982); and James R. Millar, *The ABC's of Soviet Socialism* (Urbana: University of Illinois Press, 1981).

2. For a discussion of these years, see M. Lewin, *Russian Peasants and Soviet Power* (London: Allen and Unwin, 1968); for a brief survey, see Gregory and Stuart, *Soviet and Post-Soviet Economic Structure and Performance*, Ch. 5.

3. A considerable amount has been written about the Soviet economy during these early years. See, for example, Alec Nove, *An Economic History of the U.S.S.R.*, rev. ed. (London: Penguin Books, 1982); Eugene Zaleski, *Planning for Economic Growth in the Soviet Union, 1928–1932* (Chapel Hill: University of North Carolina Press, 1971); Maurice Dobb, *Soviet Economic Development Since 1917*, 5th ed. (London: Routledge and Kegan Paul, 1960); E. H. Carr and R. W. Davies, *Foundations of a Planned Economy, 1926–1929*, Vol. I, Pt. 2 (New York: Macmillan, 1969); Roger Munting, *The Economic Development of the USSR* (London: Croom Helm, 1982); R. W. Davies, *The Socialist Offensive, the Collectivization of Soviet Agriculture 1929–30* (London: Macmillan, 1980); and Thomas F. Remington, "Varga and the Foundation of Soviet Planning," *Soviet Studies*, 34 (October 1982), 585–600.

4. There is considerable debate about the *level* of economic development in the Soviet Union in 1917 and hence the readiness of that country, in the Marxian schema, for the introduction of socialism. For a discussion of this issue, see Gregory and Stuart, *Soviet and Post-Soviet Economic Structure and Performance*, Ch. 2; for more detail, see Paul R. Gregory, "Economic Growth and Structural Change in Tsarist Russia: A Case of Modern Economic Growth?" *Soviet Studies*, 23 (January 1972), 418–434; Paul R. Gregory, *Russian National Income 1885–1913* (New York: Cambridge University Press, 1983); and R. W. Davies, ed., *From Tsarism to the New Economic Policy* (Basingstoke, England: Macmillan, 1990).

5. By 1920 the index of industrial production (1913 = 100) had fallen to 20, the index of agricultural production had fallen to 64, and the index of transportation had fallen to 22. See Gregory and Stuart, *Soviet and Post-Soviet Economic Structure and Performance*, p. 58.

6. By 1928 the index of industrial production (1923 = 100) had risen to 102, the index of agricultural production had risen to 118, and the index of transportation had risen to 106. See ibid., p. 56.

7. For a discussion of the policy issues of this period, see Jerzy F. Karcz, "From Stalin to Brezhnev: Soviet Agricultural Policy in Historical Perspective," in James R. Millar, ed., *The Soviet Rural Community* (Urbana: University of Illinois Press, 1971), pp. 36–70; and Davies, *The Socialist Offensive*.

8. The classic work is Alexander Erlich, *The Soviet Industrialization Debate, 1924–1928* (Cambridge, Mass.: Harvard University Press, 1960). For a translation of original contributions to the debate, see Nicolas Spulber, *Foundations of Soviet Strategy for Economic Growth* (Bloomington: Indiana University Press, 1964).

9. There was, however, only a single candidate for each position, although Gorbachev later proposed changes. For a comprehensive discussion of the Soviet government and party structure, see Jerry F. Hough and Merle Fainsod, *How the Soviet Union Is Governed* (Cambridge, Mass.: Harvard University Press, 1979). T. H. Rigby, *Political Elites in the USSR* (Brookfield, Vt.: Edward Elgar, 1990).

10. For a study of the Communist party of the Soviet Union, see Leonard Shapiro, *The Communist Party of the Soviet Union* (New York: Random House, 1971); and Hough and Fainsod, *How the Soviet Union Is Governed.* For a statistical survey of party membership, see T. H. Rigby, *Communist Party Membership in the U.S.S.R., 1917–1967* (Princeton, N.J.: Princeton University Press, 1968). For further evidence, see T. H. Rigby, "Soviet Communist Party Membership Under Brezhnev," *Soviet Studies*, 28 (July 1976), 317–337; and Jan Adams, *Citizen Inspectors in the Soviet Union: The People's Control Committee* (New York: Praeger, 1977).

11. The material balance technique has been analyzed in some detail. The classic article is J. M. Montias, "Planning with Material Balances in Soviet-Type Economies," *American Economic Review*, 49 (December 1959), 963–985; for a summary, see Gregory and Stuart, *Soviet and Post-Soviet Economic Structure and Performance*, p. 163 ff. For a theoretical discussion, see Raymond P. Powell, "Plan Execution and the Workability of Soviet Planning," *Journal of Comparative Economics*, 1 (March 1979), 51–76.

12. This important point represents a sharp difference between the functioning of a planned economy and that of a market economy. In the market economy, the producing enterprise normally has supply contracts for required inputs. However, the firm can, with limitations, enter the market either to secure better contractual arrangements or to find a replacement if existing arrangements are interrupted for some reason. In the planned economy, the producing enterprise relies on an inter-enterprise delivery specified in the annual plan. If this delivery is interrupted for any reason, the producing enterprise has no market to which it may turn. In such cases production is typically interrupted. Unless formal or informal stopgap measures can be taken, the imbalances tend to accumulate throughout the economy.

13. See, for example, A. Katsenelinboigen, "Coloured Markets in the Soviet Union," *Soviet Studies*, 29 (January 1977), 62–85; Vladimir G. Treml, "Alcohol in the USSR: A Fiscal Dilemma," *Soviet Studies*, 27 (April 1975), 161–177; and Boris Rumer, "The 'Second' Agriculture in the USSR," *Soviet Studies*, 33 (October 1981), 560–572.

14. The role of the Soviet second economy was the focus of a major research effort undertaken by Gregory Grossman and Vladimir Treml. The Grossman–Treml project involved interviews with Soviet émigrés concerning their personal experiences in the second economy. Gur Ofer and Aaron Vinokur have conducted studies of second-economy earnings among Soviet émigrés to Israel, and the Soviet Interview Project has studied second-economy earnings among Soviet emigrants to the United States. For initial results from these surveys, see J. R. Millar, ed., *Politics, Work, and Daily Life in the USSR* (New York: Cambridge University Press, 1987).

15. There is a substantial body of literature on the problems of Soviet enterprise management. See Joseph Berliner, *Factory and Manager in the USSR* (Cambridge, Mass.: Harvard University Press, 1957); David Granick, *The Red Executive* (New York: Doubleday, 1960); David Granick, *Managerial Comparisons of Four Developed Countries: France, Britain, United States and Russia* (Cambridge, Mass.: M.I.T. Press, 1972); William J. Conyngham, *The Modernization of Soviet Industrial Management* (New York: Cambridge University Press, 1982); and Jan Adams, "The Present Soviet Incentive System," *Soviet Studies*, 32 (July 1980), 360.

16. Gregory and Stuart, *Soviet and Post-Soviet Economic Structure and Performance*, pp. 215–216.

17. Unfortunately, relatively little research has been done on the structure and functions of the Soviet state bank. For a survey, see Paul Gekker, "The Banking System of the USSR," *Journal of the Institute of Bankers*, 84 (June 1963), 189–197; and Christine

Netishen Wollan, "The Financial Policy of the Soviet State Bank, 1932–1970" (Ph.D. dissertation, University of Illinois, Urbana, 1972).

18. Incentives—how to make enterprises do what the center wants—have been the subject of a considerable amount of research. See David Conn, special ed., *The Theory of Incentives*, published as Vol. 3, no. 3, *Journal of Comparative Economics* (September 1979); and J. Michael Martin, "Economic Reform and Maximizing Behavior of the Soviet Firm," in Judith Thornton, ed., *Economic Analysis of the Soviet-Type System* (New York: Cambridge University Press, 1976).

19. In contemporary times, the rate of turnover of Soviet industrial managers declined.

20. For a basic survey of Soviet price policy and citation of the important literature, see Gregory and Stuart, *Soviet and Post-Soviet Economic Structure and Performance*, Ch. 8. For an update, see Morris Bornstein, "Soviet Price Policy in the 1970s," in U.S. Congress, Joint Economic Committee, *Soviet Economy in a New Perspective* (Washington, D.C.: Government Printing Office, 1976), pp. 17–66; Morris Bornstein, "The Administration of the Soviet Price System," *Soviet Studies*, 30 (October 1978), 466–490; and Morris Bornstein, "Soviet Price Policies," *Soviet Economy*, 3, 2 (1987), 96–134.

21. For a discussion of Soviet wage-setting procedures, see Leonard J. Kirsch, *Soviet Wages: Changes in Structure and Administration Since 1956* (Cambridge, Mass.: M.I.T. Press, 1972); B. Arnot, *Controlling Soviet Labour* (London: Macmillan, 1988); D. Granick, *Job Rights in the Soviet Union: Their Consequences* (New York: Cambridge University Press, 1987); and Silvana Malle, *Employment Planning in the Soviet Union* (Basingstoke, England: Macmillan, 1990).

22. See Abram Bergson, *The Economics of Soviet Planning* (New Haven: Yale University Press, 1964), Ch. 6.

23. The provision of appropriate manpower to the Soviet economy was a matter of both interest and complexity because it involved analysis of Soviet demographic trends. For a summary of statistical trends, see Murray Feshbach and Stephen Rapawy, "Soviet Population and Manpower Trends and Policies," in Joint Economic Committee, *Soviet Economy in a New Perspective*, 113–154. For the specific case of agriculture, see Karl-Eugen Wadekin, "Manpower in Soviet Agriculture—Some Post-Khrushchev Developments and Problems," *Soviet Studies*, 20 (January 1969), 281–305. Contemporary evidence is presented in Murray Feshbach, "Population and Labor Force," in Abram Bergson and Herbert S. Levine, eds., *The Soviet Economy: Towards the Year 2000* (Winchester, Mass.: Allen and Unwin, 1983), pp. 79–111; Jan Adams, ed., *Employment Policies in the Soviet Union and Eastern Europe*, 2nd ed. (New York: St. Martin's, 1987); and P. R. Gregory and I. L. Collier, "Unemployment in the Soviet Union: Evidence from the Soviet Interview Project," *The American Economic Review*, 78 (September 1988), 613–632.

24. For a brief summary of the socialist attitude toward an interest charge for capital, see A. C. Pigou, *Socialism Versus Capitalism* (London: Macmillan, 1937), Ch. 8. For a discussion of Soviet investment planning, see Gregory and Stuart, *Soviet and Post-Soviet Economic Structure and Performance*, Ch. 7. For details, see David A. Dyker, *The Process of Investment in the Soviet Union* (Cambridge, England: Cambridge University Press, 1983).

25. For a discussion of the rules, see Alan Abouchar, "The New Soviet Standard Methodology for Investment Allocation," *Soviet Studies*, 24 (January 1973), 402–410; P. Gregory, B. Fiedlitz, and T. Curtis, "The New Soviet Investment Rules: A Guide to Rational Investment Planning?" *Southern Economic Journal*, 41 (January 1974), 500–504; Frank

A. Durgin, "The Soviet 1969 Standard Methodology for Investment Allocation Versus 'Universally Correct' Methods," *The ACES Bulletin*, 19 (Summer 1977), 29–53; Frank A. Durgin, Jr., "The Third Soviet Standard Methodology for Determining the Effectiveness of Capital Investment (SM-80, Provisional)," *The ACES Bulletin*, 24 (Fall 1982), 45–61; and Janice Giffen, "The Allocation of Investment in the Soviet Union: Criteria for the Efficiency of Investment," *Soviet Studies*, 33 (October 1981), 593–609. For a useful summary, see David Dyker, *The Process of Investment in the Soviet Union* (New York: Cambridge University Press, 1981).

26. Since the mid-1970s, there has been a debate over the extent of repressed inflation in the former Soviet Union. See D. H. Howard, "The Disequilibrium Model in a Controlled Economy: An Empirical Test of The Barro-Grossman Model," *American Economic Review*, 66 (December 1976), 871–879; Richard Portes, "The Control of Inflation: Lessons from East European Experience," *Economics*, 44 (May 1977), 109–130; Richard Portes and David Winter, "A Planners' Supply Function for Consumption Goods in Centrally Planned Economies," *Journal of Comparative Economics*, 1 (December 1977), 351–365; and Richard Portes and David Winter, "The Demand for Money and for Consumption Goods in Centrally Planned Economies," *Review of Economics and Statistics*, 60 (February 1978), 8–18.

27. Joyce Pickersgill and Gur Ofer conducted early empirical studies of Soviet saving behavior and concluded that Soviet citizens appear to save for the same reasons Westerners do. On this, see Gur Ofer and Joyce Pickersgill, "Soviet Household Saving: A Cross-Section Study of Soviet Emigrant Families," *Quarterly Journal of Economics*, 95 (August 1980), 121–144; and Joyce Pickersgill, "Soviet Household Saving Behavior," *Review of Economics and Statistics*, 58 (May 1976), 139–147. Other scholars see increases in excess demand as the cause of increases in saving. On this, see D. W. Bronson and Barbara S. Severin, "Recent Trends in Consumption and Disposable Money Income in the USSR," U.S. Congress, Joint Economic Committee, *New Directions in the Soviet Economy*, Part II-B (Washington, D.C.: Government Printing Office, 1966); and Igor Birman, *Secret Income and the Soviet State Budget* (Boston: Kluwer, 1981).

28. Paul Craig Roberts, "The Polycentric Soviet Economy," *Journal of Law and Economics*, 12 (April 1969), 163–181.

29. Eugene Zaleski, *Stalinist Planning for Economic Growth, 1932–1952* (Chapel Hill: University of North Carolina Press, 1980).

30. John Wilhelm, "Does the Soviet Union Have a Planned Economy?" *Soviet Studies*, 31 (April 1979), 268–274.

31. Gregory Grossman, "The 'Second Economy' of the USSR," *Problems of Communism*, 26 (September–October 1977), 25–40; Aron Katsenelinboigen, "Coloured Markets in the Soviet Union," *Soviet Studies*, 29 (January 1977), 62–85; Dimitri Simes, "The Soviet Parallel Market," *Survey*, 21 (Summer 1975), 42–52; and *Studies on the Soviet Second Economy* (Durham, N.C.: Berkeley-Duke Occasional Papers on the Second Economy in the USSR, December 1987).

32. Vladimir Treml, "Alcohol in the USSR: A Fiscal Dilemma," *Soviet Studies*, 41 (October 1973), 161–177; Dennis O'Hearn, "The Consumer Second Economy: Size and Effects," *Soviet Studies*, 32 (April 1980), 221; and Vladimir G. Treml, *Purchase of Food from Private Sources in Soviet Urban Areas* (Durham, N.C.: Berkeley-Duke Occasional Papers on the Second Economy in the USSR, September 1985).

33. For a discussion of the various forms of agricultural organization, see D. J. Male, *Russian Peasant Organization Before Collectivization* (Cambridge, England: Cambridge

University Press, 1971); and Robert G. Wesson, *Soviet Communes* (New Brunswick, N.J.: Rutgers University Press, 1963).

34. For a survey of thinking on this issue, see Karcz, "From Stalin to Brezhnev."
35. Because the sovkhoz was a relatively straightforward state enterprise operating under the same general principles as the industrial enterprise, relatively little attention had been paid to its structure and operation. It is important to note, however, that whereas the sovkhoz was state-owned property, the kolkhoz was an ideologically inferior form of property holding known as kolkhoz-cooperative property. Many of the changes in the kolkhoz could be explained by the implementation of state policy designed to "improve" the kolkhoz and raise it to the same level as the sovkhoz.
36. For a detailed discussion of the kolkhoz and the labor day mechanism, see Robert C. Stuart, *The Collective Farm in Soviet Agriculture* (Lexington, Mass.: Heath, 1972) and R. W. Davies, *The Industrialization of Russia*, Vols. 1 and 2 (Cambridge, Mass.: Harvard University Press, 1980). Research has supported the view that during the introduction of the collectives there was no increase in the net surplus generated by agriculture. For a discussion of this question, see James R. Millar, "Soviet Rapid Development and the Agricultural Surplus Hypothesis," *Soviet Studies*, 22 (July 1970), 77–93; and M. J. Ellman, "Did the Russian Agricultural Surplus Provide the Resources for the Increase in Investment in the USSR During the First Five-Year Plan?" *Economic Journal*, 85 (December 1975), 844–863. For a summary, see Gregory and Stuart, *Soviet and Post-Soviet Economic Structure and Performance*, Ch. 5. For a critical view, see David Morrison, "A Critical Examination of A. A. Barsov's Empirical Work on the Value of Balance Exchanges Between the Town and the Country," *Soviet Studies* 34 (October 1985), 570–584.
37. For a discussion of the financing of the kolkhozy, see James R. Millar, "Financing the Modernization of Kolkhozy," in Millar, *The Soviet Rural Economy*, pp. 276–303.
38. The standard work on the Machine Tractor Stations is Robert F. Miller, *One Hundred Thousand Tractors* (Cambridge, Mass.: Harvard University Press, 1970).
39. For an in-depth discussion of the private sector in Soviet agriculture, see Karl-Eugen Wadekin, *The Private Sector in Soviet Agriculture* (Berkeley: University of California Press, 1973); and A. Lane, "U.S.S.R.: Private Agriculture on Center Stage," in U.S. Congress, Joint Economic Committee, *Soviet Economy in the 1980s: Problems and Prospects*, Pt. 2 (Washington, D.C.: U.S. Government Printing Office, 1982), pp. 23–40.
40. For a survey of postwar developments in Soviet agriculture and references to the specialized literature, see Gregory and Stuart, *Soviet and Post-Soviet Economic Structure and Performance*, Ch. 6.
41. Robert C. Stuart, "The Changing Role of the Collective Farm in Soviet Agriculture," *Canadian Slavonic Papers*, 26 (Summer 1974), 145–159.
42. For a survey, see K.-E. Wadekin, *Agrarian Policies in Communist Europe: An Introduction* (Totowa, N.J.: Allanheld and Osmun, 1982), Ch. 12.
43. Rural income levels are discussed in David W. Bronson and Constance B. Krueger, "The Revolution in Soviet Farm Household Income, 1953–1967," in Millar, *The Soviet Rural Economy*, pp. 214–257; and in more general terms in Gertrude E. Schroeder and Barbara S. Severin, "Soviet Consumption and Income Policies in Perspective," in Joint Economic Committee, *Soviet Economy in a New Perspective*, pp. 620–660.
44. For a discussion of subsidies, see W. G. Treml, "Subsidies in Soviet Agriculture: Record and Prospects," in U.S. Congress, Joint Economic Committee, *Soviet Economy in the 1980s: Problems and Prospects* (Washington, D.C.: U.S. Government Printing Office, 1982), pp. 171–186.

45. For a survey of Soviet foreign trade and references to the literature, see Gregory and Stuart, *Soviet and Post-Soviet Economic Structure and Performance*, Ch. 9.
46. For a different view, see Steven Rosefielde, "Comparative Advantage and the Evolving Pattern of Soviet International Commodity Specialization, 1950–1973," in Steven Rosefielde, ed., *Economic Welfare and the Economics of Soviet Socialism* (New York: Cambridge University Press, 1981), pp. 185–220.
47. See Vladimir Treml and Barry Kostinsky, *Domestic Value of Soviet Foreign Trade: Exports and Imports in the 1972 Input-Output Table*, Foreign Economic Report No. 20, U.S. Department of Commerce, October 1982.

Recommended Readings

General Works

Robert W. Campbell, *The Soviet-Type Economies: Performance and Evolution*, 3rd ed. (Boston: Houghton Mifflin, 1981).

R. W. Davies, ed., *The Soviet Union* (Winchester, Mass.: Unwin Hyman, 1989).

David A. Dyker, *The Future of the Soviet Planning System* (Armonk, N.Y.: M. E. Sharpe, 1985).

Paul R. Gregory and Robert C. Stuart, *Soviet and Post-Soviet Economic Structure and Performance*, 5th ed. (New York: HarperCollins, 1994).

Franklyn D. Holzman, *The Soviet Economy: Past, Present, and Future* (New York: Foreign Policy Association, 1982).

Tania Konn (ed.), *Soviet Studies Guide* (London: Bowker–Saur, 1992).

James R. Millar, *The ABC's of Soviet Socialism* (Urbana: University of Illinois Press, 1981).

Alec Nove, *The Soviet Economic System*, 2nd ed. (London: Unwin Hyman, 1981).

United States Congress, Joint Economic Committee, *Gorbachev's Economic Plans*, Vols. I and II (Washington, D.C.: U.S. Government Printing Office, 1987).

Soviet Economic History

E. H. Carr and R. W. Davies, *Foundations of a Planned Economy, 1926–1929*, Vol. 1, pts. 1 and 2 (New York: Macmillan, 1969).

R. W. Davies, *The Industrialization of Soviet Russia*, Vols. I and II (Cambridge, Mass.: Harvard University Press, 1980).

R. W. Davies, Mark Harrison, and S. G. Wheatcroft, eds., *The Economic Transformation of the Soviet Union 1913–1945* (Cambridge: Cambridge University Press, 1994).

Maurice Dobb, *Soviet Economic Development Since 1917*, 5th ed. (London: Routledge and Kegan Paul, 1960).

Alexander Erlich, *The Soviet Industrialization Debate, 1924–1928* (Cambridge, Mass.: Harvard University Press, 1969).

Paul R. Gregory, *Russian National Income, 1885–1913* (New York: Cambridge University Press, 1983).

Gregory Guroff and Fred V. Carstensen, *Entrepreneurship in Imperial Russia and the Soviet Union* (Princeton, N.J.: Princeton University Press, 1983).

Moshe Lewin, *Political Undercurrents in Soviet Economic Debates: From Bukharin to the Modern Reformers* (Princeton, N.J.: Princeton University Press, 1974).

Roger Munting, *The Economic Development of the USSR* (London: Croom Helm, 1982).

Alec Nove, *An Economic History of the U.S.S.R.*, rev. ed. (London: Penguin Books, 1982).
Nicolas Spulber, *Soviet Strategy for Economic Growth* (Bloomington: Indiana University Press, 1964).

The Communist Party and the Manager

Donald D. Barry and Carol Barner-Barry, *Contemporary Soviet Politics: An Introduction*, 2nd ed. (Englewood Cliffs, N.J.: Prentice-Hall, 1982).
William J. Conyngham, *The Modernization of Soviet Industrial Management* (New York: Cambridge University Press, 1982).
Andrew Freiis, *The Soviet Industrial Enterprise* (New York: St. Martin's Press, 1974).
David Granick, *Managerial Comparisons of Four Developed Countries: France, Britain, United States, and Russia* (Cambridge, Mass.: M.I.T. Press, 1972).
Leslie Holmes, *The Policy Process in Communist States* (Beverly Hills: Sage Publications, 1981).
Jerry F. Hough and Merle Fainsod, *How the Soviet Union Is Governed* (Cambridge, Mass.: Harvard University Press, 1979).
David Lane, *Politics and Society in the USSR*, 2nd ed. (London: Martin Robertson, 1978).
Nathan Leites, *Soviet Style in Management* (New York: Crane Russak, 1985).
Leonard Shapiro, *The Government and Politics of the Soviet Union*, 6th ed. (Essex, England: Hutchinson Publishing Group, 1978).

Selected Aspects of the Soviet Economy

R. Amann and J. M. Cooper, eds., *Industrial Innovation in the Soviet Union* (New Haven: Yale University Press, 1982).
Joseph S. Berliner, *The Innovation Decision in Soviet Industry* (Cambridge, England: Cambridge University Press, 1983).
Morris Bornstein, ed., *The Soviet Economy: Continuity and Change* (Boulder, Colo.: Westview Press, 1981).
Robert W. Campbell, *Soviet Energy Technologies* (Bloomington: Indiana University Press, 1980).
David A. Dyker, *The Process of Investment in the Soviet Union* (Cambridge, England: Cambridge University Press, 1983).
Franklyn D. Holzman, *International Trade Under Communism* (New York: Basic Books, 1976).
Alastair McAuley, *Women's Work and Wages in the Soviet Union* (London: Unwin Hyman, 1981).
Mervyn Matthews, *Education in the Soviet Union* (London: Allen and Unwin, 1982).
————, *Poverty in the Soviet Union* (New York: Cambridge University Press, 1987).
James R. Millar, *Politics, Work, and Daily Life in the USSR* (New York: Cambridge University Press, 1987).
Henry W. Morton and Robert C. Stuart, eds., *The Contemporary Soviet City* (Armonk, N.Y.: M. E. Sharpe, 1984).
Robert C. Stuart, ed., *The Soviet Rural Economy* (Totowa, N.J.: Roman and Allenheld, 1983).
Murray Yanowitch, *Social and Economic Inequality in the Soviet Union* (London: Martin Robertson, 1977).
Eugene Zaleski, *Planning Reforms in the Soviet Union, 1962–1966* (Chapel Hill: University of North Carolina Press, 1967).

For the Advanced Reader

Alan Abouchar, ed., *The Socialist Price Mechanism* (Durham, N.C.: Duke University Press, 1977).

Edward Ames, *Soviet Economic Processes* (Homewood, Ill.: Irwin, 1965).

Abram Bergson and Herbert S. Levine, eds., *The Soviet Economy: Towards the Year 2000* (London: Allen and Unwin, 1983).

Martin Cave, Alastair McAuley, and Judith Thornton, eds., *New Trends in Soviet Economics* (Armonk, N.Y.: M. E. Sharpe, 1982).

Michael Ellman, *Soviet Planning Today: Proposals for an Optimally Functioning Economic System* (Cambridge, England: Cambridge University Press, 1971).

David Granick, *Job Rights in the Soviet Union: Their Consequences* (New York: Cambridge University Press, 1987).

Kenneth R. Gray, ed., *Soviet Agriculture* (Ames: Iowa State University Press, 1990).

Donald W. Green and Christopher I. Higgins, *SOVMOD I: A Macroeconometric Model of the Soviet Economy* (New York: Academic, 1977).

Paul R. Gregory, *The Soviet Economic Bureaucracy* (Cambridge, England: Cambridge University Press, 1990).

John Hardt et al., *Mathematics and Computers in Soviet Planning* (New Haven: Yale University Press, 1977).

Peter Murrell, *The Nature of Socialist Economies: Lessons from Eastern European Foreign Trade* (Princeton, N.J.: Princeton University Press, 1990).

Steven Rosefielde, ed., *Economic Welfare and the Economics of Soviet Socialism* (New York: Cambridge University Press, 1981).

Robert C. Stuart, ed., *The Soviet Rural Economy* (Totowa, N.J.: Roman and Allenheld, 1983).

Judith Thornton, ed., *Economic Analysis of the Soviet-Type System* (New York: Cambridge University Press, 1976).

Alfred Zauberman, *Mathematical Theory in Soviet Planning* (Oxford, England: Oxford University Press, 1976).

Appendix 11A: Measuring Outcomes in the Command Economy

Throughout, this book has emphasized both the importance and the difficulty of relating varying outcomes to different systemic arrangements. Although it is critical to understand how systems and outcomes are related, there are a variety of problems of both a general and a specific nature.

For example, to assess the Soviet economic experience, a variety of general paradigms may be used. This experience might be assessed by examining it in terms of the Marxist–Leninist vision of economic history, or by using the more general concepts of economic development.

Suppose, however, a more specific issue demands examination, such as the common conception that the Soviet Union had persistent excess demand for consumer goods—what is generally called repressed inflation. An anecdotal approach could be pursued by looking at the media and reports that attempt to gather information on consumer complaints, the existence of waiting lines, and the like. That approach might be necessary in the absence of appropriate data, although not be fully satisfactory.

If the question of excess demand occurred in a market economy, sophisticated techniques would be available first to develop a theory or model of the particular market and then to test the model using empirical evidence. But can such techniques, based on contemporary neoclassical economic theory and relevant econometric methods, be used in a setting as different as that which existed in the former Soviet Union. Although the immediate goal is to examine a particular issue in the Soviet context, broader methodological issues are involved.

The Market Context

If we wish to examine outcomes of the supply of and demand for, say, consumer goods in the market context, a familiar approach is to specify estimate demand and supply equations representing the particular market. Equations 11A.1 and 11A.2 illustrate the demand and supply equations, respectively.

$$Q_d = a + bP + cY + u \tag{11A.1}$$

$$Q_s = d + eP + fC + u' \tag{11A.2}$$

This model, designed only for illustrative purposes, would allow us to give empirical content to the demand and supply relationships, where demand is viewed as a function of prices (P) and incomes (Y), and supply is a function of prices (P) and some measure of production capacity (C). Familiar techniques are available for the estimation of this sort of model.[1]

This sort of model is generally not discussed in an introductory text in economics, but an important proposition underlying the model *is* generally discussed—namely, the identification problem. As most discussions of supply and demand emphasize, when we observe prices and quantities in the real world, let us say over time, we are in fact observing a series of equilibrium positions, or intersections of supply curves and demand curves. To take a simple case in which demand is unchanged but supply is increasing through time, the price–quantity combinations that we would observe are those represented by the letters *A, B,* and *C* in Figure 11.4.

It is important to note that in this approach, the market clears; at each point in time, equilibrium prevails. Suppose, however, that the market does not clear. Let us consider the disequilibrium case.

The Disequilibrium Context

In recent theoretical and empirical work, it has been argued that the equilibrium approach may be inappropriate in the presence of persistent excess demand.[2] For example, if we consider a simple static case where the price is set by state authorities, the outcome could be represented by Figure 11.5, where the magnitude of excess demand is given by the distance $Q_s Q_d$, and the prevailing price is set by the state at OP'.

FIGURE 11.4   Supply and Demand: Equilibrium

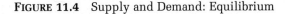

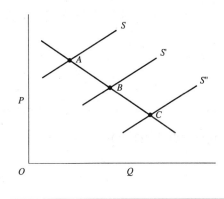

It is quite obvious that in this case we would not, in the real world, observe the intersection of the supply and demand curves when we examined combinations of price and quantity. Under the conditions specified in Figure 11.5, we would observe the state-set price of OP', some rationing device (about which we may or may not have information), and a resulting quantity actually sold, probably Q_s. If we move from this simple case to a more realistic case with persistent excess demand through time, it is clearly possible that the magnitude of the excess demand may change. Could we capture the increased complexity of this disequilibrium case in a formal model? One approach that has been suggested can be represented as follows:

$$Q_d = a + bP + cY + u \tag{11A.3}$$

$$Q_s = d + eP + fC + u' \tag{11A.4}$$

$$Q = \min(D,S) \tag{11A.5}$$

In this particular case, equation 11A.5 is introduced to provide a rule by which the suspected shortage will be handled. Once again, various methods of estimation are available, with price (P) assumed to be exogenous. In this approach, interest centers on the appropriate specification, on alternative methods of estimation, and, finally, on empirical verification of whether in fact a disequilibrium specification is appropriate.[3]

A more sophisticated variant would include the possibility that if there is excess demand in a particular market at a particular time, planners may (1) have some knowledge about this excess demand and (2) take some steps to lessen its magnitude through time. A number of attempts have been made to construct macroeconometric models of planned socialist economic systems. It is particularly appealing on a number of grounds to consider a model in which planners have available and utilize various policy controls for manipulation of the economic system through time. Although one can imagine a wide array of possible controls, let us, for the

FIGURE 11.5 Supply and Demand: Disequilibrium

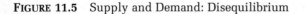

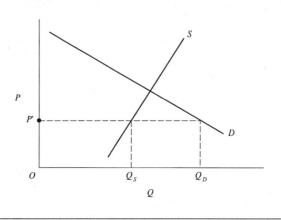

sake of illustration, consider a basic approach suggested by Richard Quandt.[4] Thus, to consider the response of planners over time, we specify a more complex model:

$$Q_t^d = a + bP_t + cY_t + u \tag{11A.6}$$

$$Q_t^s = d + eP_t + fC_t + u' \tag{11A.7}$$

$$Q_t = \min(D_t, S_t) \tag{11A.8}$$

$$P_t - P_{t-1} = g(D_t - S_t) + u'' \tag{11A.9}$$

In the model presented in equations 11A.6 through 11A.9, price (P) is again exogenous and is assumed to be the mechanism through which planners make adjustments. Specifically, planners vary price through time, depending on the magnitude of the excess demand. Other approaches could be considered, but this particular model captures the essence of the Lange adjustment and is thus of more than passing interest.

The disequilibrium approach is, of course, a competing hypothesis to the equilibrium approach and is not, therefore, necessarily limited to application in the case of the command economy. The approach is, however, relatively recent in origin. There is now a substantial literature applying this approach to the Soviet case, especially in the examination of consumer markets. The approach remains controversial, and methodological difficulties complicate both specification and estimation of the model.

Notes

1. See William H. Greene, *Econometric Analysis*, 2nd ed. (New York: Macmillan, 1993). For a discussion of disequilibrium models that provides extensive references to the literature, see Richard E. Quandt, *The Econometrics of Disequilibrium* (New York: Basil Blackwell, 1988).

2. For example, Western interpretations of the Soviet consumer goods market have generally suggested that although there is excess demand, the turnover tax has been used to bring prices close to the point of equilibrium. One could argue, however, that if prices are in fact "close" to equilibrium, planners would have sufficient knowledge and power to raise prices *to* equilibrium, thus eliminating the persistent complaints about shortages. The possibility of persistent excess demand deserves our attention, especially because it is a basic underpinning of the work of Kornai described in Chapter 7.

3. See, for example, Richard E. Quandt, "Tests of the Equilibrium vs. Disequilibrium Hypotheses," *International Economic Review*, 19 (June 1978), 435–452.

4. Ibid.

Recommended Readings

R. J. Barro and H. I. Grossman, "A General Disequilibrium Model of Income and Employment," *American Economic Review*, 61 (March 1971), 82–93.

W. Charemza and M. Gronicki, *Plans and Disequilibria in Centrally Planned Economies* (Amsterdam: North-Holland, 1988).

Christopher M. Davis, "The Second Economy in Disequilibrium and Shortage Models of Centrally Planned Economies," *Berkeley-Duke Occasional Papers on The Second Economy in The USSR* (July 1988).

S. M. Goldfeld and R. E. Quandt, "Estimation in a Disequilibrium Model and the Value of Information," *Journal of Econometrics*, 3 (November 1975), 325–348.

———, "Single-Market Disequilibrium Models: Estimation and Testing," *The Economic Studies Quarterly*, 32 (April 1981), 12–28.

———, "Some Properties of the Simple Disequilibrium Model with Covariance," *Economics Letters*, 1, 4 (1978) 343–346.

David H. Howard, *The Disequilibrium Model in a Controlled Economy* (Lexington, Mass.: Lexington Books, 1979).

———, "The Disequilibrium Model in a Controlled Economy: An Empirical Test of The Barro–Grossman Model," *American Economic Review*, 66 (December 1976), 871–879.

Richard Portes and David Winter, "The Demand for Money and for Consumption Goods in Centrally Planned Economies," *Review of Economics and Statistics*, 60 (February 1978), 8–18.

———, "The Supply of Consumption Goods in Centrally Planned Economies," *Journal of Comparative Economics*, 1 (December 1977), 351–363.

Richard E. Quandt, *The Econometrics of Disequilibrium* (New York: Basil Blackwell, 1988).

———, "Tests of the Equilibrium vs. Disequilibrium Hypotheses," *International Economic Review*, 19 (June 1978), 435–452.

H. S. Rosen and R. E. Quandt, "Estimation of a Disequilibrium Aggregate Labor Market," *Review of Economics and Statistics*, 60 (1978), 371–379.

12

The Command Economies: Performance and Decline

Probably no issue in the field of comparative economic systems is of greater relevance than comparative performance. The early chapters of this book emphasized the fact that systems differ and that performance differences could be related to system differences to assess the merits of various different economic systems.

This chapter compares economic performance across real-world variants of economic systems to form judgments about their comparative performance. In light of the demise of most planned socialist economic systems, we attempt to relate economic performance problems to systemic arrangements in these cases.

Problems of Evaluation

System objectives differ from one case to another. Socialist systems have typically pursued objectives different from those of capitalist systems. The pursuit of each objective presents a cost in terms of resources used, and thus, in any system, difficult choices must be made. Unless different systems pursue the same goals and place the same weights on each goal, it is difficult to evaluate the overall performance of the different economic systems. There is no single or dominant goal, and thus in the end, we must make subjective judgments about which goals are the most important for making accurate performance comparisons.

Evaluating economic performance is not easy, even if it were possible to identify a single dominant objective, for example, economic growth. To compare, say, the growth experience of socialist with capitalist economic systems. Assuming that we can agree on basic system definitions, how will we select the economies to be evaluated, and over what time frame will the evaluation be performed? Some criterion for selection must be used. For example, if **representative economic systems** were chosen, how would the approach be defined? Using a sampling approach may cause serious problems because of the relatively small number of planned socialist economies in that particular population.

Another aspect of country selection is that of controlling for nonsystem characteristics. For example, if economic growth is influenced by both system and nonsystem factors, we must be able to control for the latter. Thus as socialist and capitalist economies are observed, very different levels of economic development become apparent as does the fact that rates of economic growth are systematically related to different levels of economic development.

For performance comparisons to be valid, the *ceteris paribus* assumption must hold. The economies compared should be alike *in all respects* except their economic systems. In Chapter 3, the *ceteris paribus* problem was described as follows: Outcomes (O) are a function of a variety of environmental factors (ENV; for example, natural and human resource endowments and level of development), economic policy (POL), and the economic system (ES).

$$O = f(\text{ENV, POL, ES}) \tag{12.1}$$

Because ENV and POL differ by country, one cannot make a statement about the impact of ES on outcomes without a clear understanding of the role of the ENV and POL factors.

Labor productivity in the Soviet Union was always low, relative to that in the United States and industrialized Western Europe.[1] The question, however, is whether this was a consequence of the *system* or a product of the other (ENV, POL) factors. The level of economic development of the Soviet Union always lagged behind that of the United States and Western Europe, and productivity is positively associated with economic development. Can the Soviet productivity gap be accounted for entirely by these other factors, or was the economic system itself to blame? *Long-term* economic growth in the Soviet Union outpaced the United States and Western Europe through the 1970s.[2] Was this a consequence of the economic system or of other factors?

Two related approaches can be used to deal with this problem. The first is to compare economies that are alike in all respects other than economic system. In terms of equation 12.1, this means making performance comparisons only in instances where ENV and POL are equal so that performance differences can be attributed to the system. The nearest (yet imperfect) example would be the comparison of previously unified countries that belonged to different economic blocs (East and West Germany or North and South Korea, for example), but such examples are rare.[3] The basic drawback is that real-world cases where all factors other than the economic system are constant do not exist.

The econometric approach to the *ceteris paribus* problem requires estimation of the impact of the ENV and POL factors on O. Once known, these factors can be held constant, revealing the impact of the economic system on performance. This approach requires the investigation of *groups* of capitalist and socialist economies that differ according to ENV and POL characteristics, so that their impact can be isolated and held constant.[4]

Because economic systems are multidimensional, their attributes are difficult to measure, and we cannot formulate an *objective* and *quantitative* measure of ES that differentiates economies according to the degree of capitalism or planned or market socialism. We cannot determine whether the Soviet economy was more "planned socialist" than the East German economy was or whether the U.S. economy is more "capitalist" than the British economy. Therefore, we must bunch real-world economies into political–economic groupings without being able to hold constant the effect of variations in ES *within* a particular group.

Real-world economies are grouped into two categories: capitalism and planned socialism. This requires combining economies that differ in important respects. In the comparisons that follow, intermediate- and low-income countries such as Greece, Spain, Turkey, and India are included in the "capitalist" group, despite their substantial differences from industrialized capitalist countries. There was much greater homogeneity within the planned socialist group prior to the reforms of the late 1980s. Yet even they had differences (ownership and control arrangements in agriculture), so the planned socialist economies were by no means uniform.[5]

How well the representatives of economic systems have actually performed is the appropriate standard for evaluating the performance of economic systems. What counts is not how an economic system would conceivably perform under ideal circumstances, but how well it performs in the real-world.

The Performance of Systems

Recognizing the difficulties inherent in evaluating economic systems, the most important performance indicators—economic growth, economic efficiency, the "fairness" of the distribution of income, and economic stability—are used to determine how well selected representatives of capitalism and socialism have performed. The available empirical evidence is updated with new evidence, where it exists.

The Choice of Countries

The selection of representatives of capitalism and socialism is dictated by the availability of data. Data limitations dictate the principal emphasis on comparisons of the former Soviet Union and East European nations with the industrialized and near-industrialized capitalist nations.[6] The data for the smaller Asian communist countries (North Korea, Vietnam, Cambodia, and Mongolia) are too meager to support meaningful comparisons.[7]

How about the performance of China vis-à-vis its non-communist Asian counterparts? China may be representative of planned socialism in a large and backward economy. Chinese economic performance has been significantly affected by political upheavals. There is the further difficulty of finding appropriate counterparts against which to gauge China's economic performance. Should China be measured against Japan (an immediate Asian neighbor), against India[8] (another Asian neighbor, almost equally populous), or against the large and small non-communist Asian nations combined? If the yardstick is Japan, then Chinese performance will not be impressive; if it is Bangladesh, it will appear more impressive. Moreover, in the era since the late 1970s, major reforms in China (examined in Chapter 17) have significantly altered the nature of the Chinese economic system.

Data: Concepts and Reliability

Economic aggregates, such as GNP, industrial production, and per capita consumption, were not compiled uniformly by the statistical agencies in Eastern and Western countries.[9] The planned socialist nations excluded from final output "nonproductive" services, which did not directly support material production. The aggregate figures used in this chapter are recalculations that make the planned socialist figures conform as closely as possible to Western national accounting practices.[10] Western recalculations of Soviet and East European national accounts made adjustments for omitted costs and for omitted product categories (such as services). They all used the **adjusted factor cost concept** pioneered by Abram Bergson.[11] Western economists were not in a position to recalculate the output of planned socialist economies on the basis of utility values. If planners dictated the production of goods and services that did not raise welfare (such as excessively heavy reinforced concrete, inferior shoes, or the collected works of Leonid Brezhnev), we have no choice but to value those goods and services at the cost of supplying them. A market economy might reject these goods and services (by setting zero prices), but a planned socialist economy dictated by planners' preferences would continue to order their production.

The *Glasnost* movement that swept through the Soviet Union and Eastern Europe in the second half of the 1980s raised serious questions about statistical reliability.[12] For example, Romanian statistical authorities subsequently revealed that their statistics contained wild exaggerations of economic performance. Independent estimates by Soviet economists and journalists claim that official Soviet statistics overstated growth by a factor of more than 2.[13]

The demise of the Soviet Union and the other planned socialist economies of Eastern Europe has made the matter of accessing accurate and meaningful statistical information complex. Although the situation may appear dramatically better, that is not necessarily the case. First, the former planned socialist systems generally began the conversion to western accounting practices at or just prior to the end of the plan era, new series for earlier years (for example, relating to the components of national income) were not necessarily generated. Second, new empirical evidence that has become available is highly variable. Finally, the availability of new data does not necessarily mean that new analysis has been done.

An Economic Profile: Structural Characteristics of East and West

Table 12.1 provides an economic profile of the planned socialist countries and selected capitalist countries. This profile shows what factors should be held constant in performance comparisons, and it provides insights into the socialist model of industrialization.[14] We focus on the mid-1980s as a period of relative "normalcy" in Eastern Europe prior to the dramatic changes of the late 1980s.

TABLE 12.1 An Economic Profile of Socialist and Capitalist Countries in the 1980s

	(1) Per Capita GNP, 1985 (U.S. $)	(2) Population 1985 (Millions)	(3a) Share of Industry and Construction in GNP (1982)	(3b) Agriculture	(3c) Services	(4) Proportion of Labor in Agriculture (1985)	(5) Gross Investment as a Percentage of GNP (1982)
			A. Planned Socialism				
East Germany	10,440	16.7	51	13	36	10	24
Czechoslovakia	8,750	15.5	49	15	36	13	25
Hungary	7,560	10.6	38	26	36	18	29
Soviet Union	7,400	278.9	42	19	39	19	30
Poland	6,470	37.2	37	27	36	29	27
Bulgaria	6,420	9.0	46	23	31	20	28
Romania	5,450	22.7	46	26	28	29	38
China	340	1,042.4	45	35	20	68	28

B. Capitalism

	(1) Per Capita GNP, 1985 (U.S. $)	(2) Population 1985 (Millions)	(3a) Share of Industry and Construction in GNP (1982)	(3b) Agriculture	(3c) Services	(4) Proportion of Labor in Agriculture (1985)	(5) Gross Investment as a Percentage of GNP (1982)
Norway	16,719	4.2	41	5	54	9	26
United States	16,710	238.6	34	3	63	3	19
Canada	16,538	25.4	32	4	64	5	25
Denmark	14,603	5.1	22	5	73	7	16
West Germany	14,432	61.0	53	3	44	6	23
France	13,755	55.0	41	4	55	9	21
Japan	13,312	120.7	40	5	55	10	31
Belgium	13,219	9.9	42	4	54	3	18
Netherlands	12,741	14.5	33	4	63	5	18
Austria	12,343	7.6	39	4	57	9	26
United Kingdom	12,042	56.4	33	2	65	3	17
Italy	10,928	57.1	41	6	53	13	21
Spain	9,008	39.1	34	6	60	18	20
Greece	6,854	10.0	31	17	52	31	25
Turkey	2,135	45.1	31	22	47	60	25
India	250	767.7	26	36	38	70	25

Sources: U.S. Department of Commerce, *Statistical Abstract of the United States, 1981* (Washington, D.C.: Government Printing Office, 1981), pp. 876–879; National Foreign Assessment Center, *Handbook of Economic Statistics 1986* (Washington, D.C.: Central Intelligence Agency, 1986); World Bank, *World Tables*, 3rd ed. (Baltimore: The Johns Hopkins University Press, 1984); OECD, *Historical Statistics, 1960–1985* (Paris, OECD, 1987); Thad Alton, "East European GNPs," Joint Economic Committee, *East European Economics: Slow Growth in the 1980s, Vol. 1* (Washington, D.C.: Government Printing Office, 1985), pp. 81–132. The East European investment rates are calculated by subtracting the rates of defense spending and the GNP from Alton's residual expenditure category (p. 95).

In terms of per capita income, the Soviet Union and Eastern Europe were well behind the advanced capitalist countries in the mid-1980s. The per capita incomes in the more advanced planned socialist economies (Czechoslovakia, East Germany, the Soviet Union) were well below those in Japan and the United Kingdom and between those in Italy and Spain. Poland, Romania, and Hungary and the less-advanced Bulgaria were well below Italy and Spain but close to Greece. The planned socialist countries as a group were less advanced than the industrialized Western countries with which they were most often compared.

Despite relatively low per capita income, the share of industry and construction in GNP in the socialist countries was roughly equal to that of the capitalist countries in the mid 1980s. In fact, the socialist industry share averaged 43 percent; the average of capitalist countries (United States to Italy) was 36 percent. One would have to conclude that, if per capita income were held constant, the planned socialist industry share was high relative to capitalism. The socialist shares of agriculture and services were even more different from their Western counterparts. Agriculture's share of both GNP and labor force was quite high in the planned socialist countries once per capita income was held constant, but the share of the service sector was well below that of capitalist countries at similar levels of development. The data on investment rates do not yield a clear trend. The socialist countries tended to have investment rates in the high ranges of 24 to 38 percent, but one can find similarly high investment rates among the capitalist countries. The East German investment rate, on the other hand, was relatively low.

Other differences, not recorded in Table 12.1, can also be noted. If one breaks down the industry sector into heavy and light industry, the planned socialist shares of heavy industry were well *above* those of a capitalist country at a similar level of development. The shares of the urban population of the socialist countries were well *below* those of a capitalist country at a similar stage of economic development.

All of these features constitute the distinguishing characteristics of the socialist industrialization model. What was the logic behind the socialist model? It aimed at "building socialism" as quickly as possible. In order to do so, industrialization had to be accorded priority. Activities that did not contribute to material production, such as services, would be limited, and, within industry, priority had to be granted to heavy industry, which laid the foundation for socialism. Urbanization should be retarded to limit the flow of scarce investment resources into social overhead capital, a form of capital that does not lead immediately to expanded industrial capacity. Extra resources were devoted to agriculture to promote self-sufficiency, even if this worked against comparative advantage. Resources were allocated away from consumption into investment in order to achieve a high investment rate.

The socialist industrialization model is of interest for several reasons. First, it has been of great interest in Third-World countries, for example India, where socialist economic policies and economic planning were borrowed from the past Soviet experience. Second, examining the socialist growth record will reveal that these countries were not indifferent to what was being produced. Thus, while growth has been emphasized in these systems, that emphasis has been directed toward particular sectors, such as heavy industry, while others, such as services, have been neglected.

It is important to note that when looking at efficiency measures, inputs are related to all output, not just the output of priority sectors.

Economic Growth

Table 12.2 and Figure 12.1 supply data on GNP growth rates for the postwar period in socialist and capitalist countries. One should be cautious about attaching importance to small differences in growth rates, for there is measurement error in such calculations. Moreover, the measured growth rate of economies experiencing substantial structural changes can be ambiguous—the problem of index number relativity.[15] Growth rates must be regarded as approximate and often ambiguous measures of the expansion of real goods and services. This is especially true of East–West comparisons, where substantial adjustments must be made to render the past GNP data comparable.

In Table 12.2, we have assembled growth rates of real GNP and of real GNP per capita for the entire postwar period. In panel A we supply growth rates for the Soviet Union, Eastern Europe, and China. We also supply growth rates for a number of capitalist countries at various stages of economic development (panel B). We include comparative growth data for China and India, two poor and populous Asian giants, one a planned socialist economy, the other a basically capitalist economy.

Are there systemic differences in growth rates? Was economic growth more rapid in the planned socialist economies? Table 12.2 examines postwar economic growth from the heady growth of the 1950s and 1960s to the generally slower growth of the mid-1970s and 1980s. It illustrates the dangers of using a pair of countries (such as the United States and the Soviet Union) to judge the growth performance of capitalism and socialism. One can find capitalist countries (such as Japan) that have grown much more rapidly than most socialist countries, and one can find socialist countries (such as Bulgaria or China) that grew more rapidly than most capitalist countries. Moreover, some countries grew rapidly in one period (Bulgaria in the 1950s and 1960s) and then grew slowly in another period (Bulgaria in the period 1975 to 1980).

It is difficult to reach firm conclusions about the growth performance of capitalism and socialism on the basis of these data. If one simply takes unweighted averages of the eight planned socialist and sixteen capitalist countries, the socialist group grew slightly more rapidly in the 1950s (5.7 percent per year versus 5.0 percent for the capitalist group). The capitalist group grew more rapidly in the 1960s (5.5 percent versus 4.4 percent in the first half and 5.5 percent versus 4.3 percent in the second half). The capitalist group experienced severe growth recessions in the mid-1970s, whereas the socialist group enjoyed a noticeable growth advantage for the first half of the 1970s (4.8 percent versus 3.9 percent). The growth of the capitalist group continued to lag during the second half of the 1970s (at 3.4 percent), but the slowdown of growth was even more severe in the socialist group (falling to below 3 percent). For the period 1980 to 1985, the average socialist growth rate exceeded the average capitalist rate. The marked slowdown of socialist growth in

TABLE 12.2 Average Annual Growth of GNP and GNP Per Capita in Socialist and Capitalist Countries, 1950–1990 (Per Capita Figures in Parentheses)

	1950–1960	1960–1965	1965–1970	1970–1975	1975–1980	1980–1985	1985–1990
A. Planned Socialist Countries							
Czechoslovakia	4.8 (3.9)	2.3 (1.6)	3.4 (3.2)	3.4 (2.7)	2.2 (1.5)	1.5 (1.2)	1.2 (1.2)
East Germany	5.7 (6.7)	2.7 (3.0)	3.0 (3.1)	3.4 (3.8)	2.3 (2.5)	1.8 (1.9)	1.6 (1.6)
Soviet Union	5.7 (3.9)	5.0 (3.5)	5.2 (4.2)	3.7 (2.7)	2.7 (1.8)	2.0 (1.1)	1.8 (1.1)
Poland	4.6 (2.75)	4.4 (3.2)	4.1 (3.4)	6.4 (5.4)	.7 (0)	.7 (−.1)	.2 (.2)
Hungary	4.6 (4.0)	4.2 (3.9)	3.0 (2.7)	3.4 (2.9)	2.0 (1.9)	1.7 (1.7)	.7 (.7)
Romania	5.8 (4.55)	6.0 (5.3)	4.9 (3.7)	6.7 (5.8)	3.9 (3.0)	1.0 (.8)	.6 (.6)
Bulgaria	6.7 (5.9)	6.7 (5.7)	5.1 (4.2)	4.6 (4.2)	.9 (.9)	1.2 (1.0)	.4 (.4)
China	7.9 (5.6)	4.0 (2.5)	7.1 (4.0)	7.0 (4.5)	6.2 (4.6)	9.3 (8.0)	8.6 (7.2)
Unweighted average	5.7 (4.7)	4.4 (3.6)	4.3 (3.6)	4.8 (4.0)	2.6 (2.0)	2.4 (2.0)	1.9 (1.5)
Without China	5.4 (4.5)	4.5 (3.7)	4.1 (3.5)	4.5 (3.9)	2.1 (1.7)	1.4 (1.1)	.9 (.8)
B. Capitalist Countries							
United States	3.3 (1.5)	4.6 (3.2)	3.1 (2.1)	2.3 (1.6)	3.7 (2.6)	2.4 (1.4)	3.1 (2.1)
Canada	4.6 (1.3)	5.7 (3.8)	4.8 (3.0)	5.0 (3.6)	2.9 (1.9)	2.2 (.9)	3.3 (2.3)

	1950–1960	1960–1965	1965–1970	1970–1975	1975–1980	1980–1985	1985–1990
West Germany	7.9 (6.3)	5.0 (3.5)	4.4 (3.9)	2.1 (1.7)	3.6 (3.7)	1.1 (1.4)	2.8 (2.4)
Denmark	3.6 (2.9)	5.1 (4.3)	4.5 (3.7)	2.8 (2.4)	2.7 (2.4)	2.3 (2.3)	2.4 (2.4)
Norway	3.6 (2.5)	4.8 (4.3)	4.8 (3.9)	4.6 (4.0)	4.6 (4.2)	3.0 (2.8)	3.3 (3.3)
Belgium	3.0 (2.5)	5.2 (4.5)	4.8 (4.4)	3.9 (3.5)	2.5 (2.3)	.4 (.4)	2.7 (2.7)
France	4.4 (3.8)	5.8 (4.5)	5.4 (4.5)	4.0 (3.2)	3.2 (2.9)	1.2 (.7)	2.7 (2.2)
Netherlands	5.0 (3.3)	4.8 (3.5)	5.5 (4.4)	3.2 (2.0)	2.6 (1.9)	.5 (.1)	2.1 (1.6)
Japan	7.9 (6.6)	10.0 (9.0)	12.2 (11.2)	5.0 (3.8)	5.1 (4.2)	3.9 (3.2)	3.8 (3.4)
Austria	5.6 (5.4)	4.3 (3.7)	5.1 (4.6)	3.9 (3.5)	4.0 (4.0)	2.8 (2.8)	2.2 (2.2)
United Kingdom	3.3 (2.3)	3.1 (2.4)	2.5 (2.2)	2.0 (1.4)	1.6 (1.6)	1.7 (1.3)	3.1 (2.9)
Italy	5.6 (4.8)	5.2 (4.3)	6.2 (5.4)	2.4 (1.5)	3.9 (3.4)	.8 (.5)	2.9 (2.7)
Spain	6.2 (5.3)	8.5 (7.5)	6.2 (5.2)	5.5 (4.6)	2.3 (1.3)	1.4 (.8)	4.1 (3.7)
Greece	6.0 (5.0)	7.7 (7.2)	7.2 (6.6)	5.0 (4.5)	4.4 (3.2)	1.0 (.4)	1.8 (1.8)
Turkey	6.4 (3.4)	4.8 (2.8)	6.6 (3.7)	7.5 (5.0)	3.1 (.6)	4.9 (2.7)	5.1 (2.7)
India	3.8 (1.9)	4.0 (1.7)	5.0 (2.6)	3.0 (1.0)	3.4 (1.6)	4.1 (1.9)	6.0 (3.9)
Unweighted average	5.0 (3.7)	5.5 (4.4)	5.5 (4.5)	3.9 (2.95)	3.4 (2.6)	2.0 (1.5)	3.2 (2.7)

Sources: Thad Alton, "Economic Structure and Growth in Eastern Europe," in U.S. Congress, Joint Economic Committee, *Economic Developments in Countries of Eastern Europe* (Washington, D.C.: Government Printing Office, 1970), p. 49; Thad Alton, "Comparative Structure and Growth of Economic Activity in Eastern Europe," in U.S. Congress, Joint Economic Committee, *East European Economies Post Helsinki* (Washington, D.C.: Government Printing Office, 1977), p. 237; Thad Alton, "Production and Resource Allocation in Eastern Europe: Performance, Problems, and Prospects," in U.S. Congress, Joint Economic Committee, *East European Economic Assessment*, Part 2 (Washington, D.C.: Government Printing Office, 1981), p. 381; U.S. Congress, Joint Economic Committee, *USSR Measures of Economic Growth and Development, 1950–1980* (Washington, D.C.: Government Printing Office, 1982), pp. 15–21; *Statistical Abstract of the United States, 1981*, pp. 878–879; Wilfred Malenbaum, "Modern Economic Growth in India and China: The Comparison Revisited, 1950–1980," *Economic Development and Cultural Change*, 31 (October 1982), 53; *Handbook of Economic Statistics 1990*; Thad Alton et al. Occasional Papers Nos. 75–79 of the Research Project on National Income in East Central Europe (New York, 1983), pp. 7–12, 25; Rush Greenslade, "The Real Gross National Product of the USSR, 1950–75," in U.S. Congress, Joint Economic Committee, *Soviet Economy in a New Perspective* (Washington, D.C.: Government Printing Office, 1975), p. 271; World Bank, *World Tables*, 3rd ed. (Baltimore: The Johns Hopkins University Press, 1983); OECD, *National Accounts, 1960–1985* (Paris: OECD, 1987); "Eastern Europe: Long Road to Economic Well-Being," Tables C-1 to C-21.

FIGURE 12.1   Average GNP Growth Rates, Planned Socialist and Capitalist
Countries, 1950–1990 (Unweighted Annual Average Growth Rates)

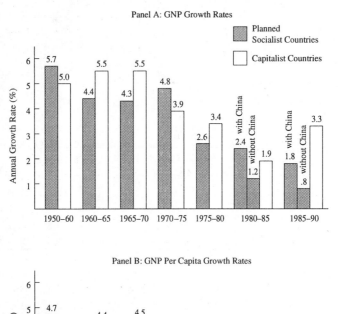

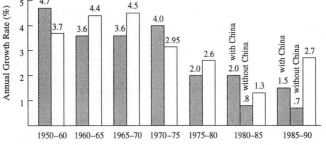

Source: Table 12.2.

the second half of the 1980s (coupled with the recovery of capitalist growth rates)
gives the clear advantage to the capitalist group. Trends in per capita GNP, given
in parentheses in Table 12.2, mirror these GNP growth trends.

Because only eight planned socialist countries are covered, growth of any one
has a strong effect on the averages of the group. As Table 12.2 shows, China's
growth up to the mid-1970s was not so different from that of the other socialist
countries. From 1975 onward, however, China's rapid growth stood in marked contrast to the slowing growth rates of the other socialist countries. If China is excluded
from the socialist group, their average growth rate sinks well below that of the
capitalist group from 1975 on. For example, for the period 1980 to 1985, the average

socialist growth rate without China was a meager 1.2 percent per annum, versus the capitalist rate of 1.9 percent per annum. In fact, if one omits the soaring Chinese growth rates of the mid-1970s and 1980s, the decline in socialist growth rates is very pronounced: from above 4 percent per annum, to 2 percent in the late 1970s, to 1 percent in the 1980s. From 1985 to 1990, the collapse of socialist growth is so pronounced that Western growth outstrips socialist growth by a large factor, whether China is included or not. This point is returned to later in this chapter.

One contrast between capitalism and planned socialism that holds over the entire postwar period is the lesser variability of socialist country growth rates. From 1950 to 1960, for example, the gap between the lowest and highest socialist growth rate was the difference between 4.6 and 7.9 percent; for the capitalist group, the difference was between 3.0 and 7.9 percent. The capitalist averages conceal more variation than do the socialist averages. This pattern was altered somewhat by the marked contrast in growth rates between China and the other socialist countries after 1975, but it persisted within the Soviet and East European group. The planned socialist economies avoided the extreme differences among capitalist countries.

Direct comparisons of planned socialist and capitalist average growth rates did not reveal significant growth differences. However, if one makes a rule-of-thumb adjustment for differences in per capita income by including only the capitalist countries that fall within the approximate per capita income range of the socialist sample —say $3000 to $6000—some striking findings emerge. The rationale for this adjustment is that growth rates in the postwar period have tended to vary inversely with the level of development. Countries with low per capita income have grown more rapidly as a group. There are four capitalist countries that fall within this income rate (Spain, Greece, Italy, and Venezuela), but comparing their average growth rates with those of the former Soviet Union and Eastern Europe is nevertheless informative. For the entire postwar period, the unweighted average annual growth rate of these four capitalist economies was almost 6 percent (4.25 percent on a per capita basis). Even when China is included, the planned socialist average was around 4.5 percent per annum (3.8 percent on a per capita basis). Among countries at a similar stage of development, the planned socialist economies experienced slower growth than their capitalist counterparts.[16]

Frederic Pryor examined the comparative growth rates of capitalist and socialist economies for the period 1950 to 1979, using econometric methods to hold factors other than the economic system constant. Pryor found that although the socialist-system effect was negative, the system coefficient was not statistically significant either for the growth of GNP or for the growth of GNP per capita.[17]

The pattern of decline of planned socialist growth rates goes a long way toward explaining the desire to convert from planned socialism to market resource allocation. Both East and West experienced relatively high rates of growth from 1950 through 1970. In the West, growth was well above long-term historical performance during this period. The growth rates of the planned socialist economies began their descent in the mid-1970s; lower growth rates were recorded in each successive half-decade. In the Soviet Union and Eastern Europe, economic growth had all but ceased by the latter half of the 1980s.

On the other hand, the West (after slow growth in the early 1980s) continued to grow at approximately its long-term historical rates. For the West, the first two decades after the war were periods of peak economic performance, after which it returned to its long-run historical pattern. The West, with two hundred years of recorded growth history, had demonstrated its ability to grow over the long run. The East, on the other hand, with a limited history of economic growth, feared that the planned socialist system had lost its ability to generate economic growth.

The Chinese and Indian comparisons shed light on the growth performance of capitalism and planned socialism in large and very poor countries. Although the Chinese data are fairly rough, most authorities agree that China has outperformed India in GNP growth and per capita GNP growth. It is likely that India and China entered the postwar era with similar levels of per capita income. China's current advantage in per capita income is the consequence of its more rapid growth.

The importance of China as a development model for poor, populous countries requires a further look at Chinese economic growth in an Asian context. Table 12.3 gives the annual growth rates of seven Asian countries for the period 1960–1985. It shows that Chinese economic growth has indeed been rapid even compared with that of other rapidly growing Asian economies, such as Japan, South Korea, and Taiwan. Chinese economic performance looks even better when compared with that of poor, populous Asian countries. Chinese growth has been more than double that of India and Pakistan.[18]

There is no evidence that the planned socialist countries as a group outgrew their capitalist counterparts. One would have to conclude, that the growth rates of capitalism and planned socialism were quite similar until the collapse of growth in the East after 1985.

The conclusion that economic growth was not more rapid in the planned socialist economies is a strong one in view of the priority of growth in these countries and the low weight attached to economic growth by many of the capitalist countries. If one makes a crude *ceteris paribus* adjustment for differences in per capita income, capitalist growth even emerges as more rapid.

TABLE 12.3   Annual GNP Growth Rates of Selected Asian Economies, 1960–1991

China	6.9
Taiwan	7.6
South Korea	7.9
Japan	5.7
Philippines	4.2
India	4.1
Pakistan	4.0

Source: National Foreign Assessment Center, *Handbook of International Economic Statistics 1992* (Washington, D.C.: Central Intelligence Agency, 1992), Table 8 and Table 12.2.

The Sources of Economic Growth

Socialist growth rates were in many ways comparable to those in capitalist systems, though differences in priorities, levels of economic development, and other such influences affect this conclusion. Toward the end of the planned socialist era in the Soviet Union and Eastern Europe, growth rates declined seriously. In the Soviet Union, the rate of growth of output became negative by 1990 as the collapse was imminent.

Why did rates of economic growth ultimately decline sharply in the planned socialist economic systems? Were declining rates of economic growth a symptom of more basic economic difficulties in these systems? To answer these questions, it is necessary to look closely at the sources of economic growth and especially at issues of efficiency.

Chapter 3 distinguished between extensive growth and intensive growth. Extensive growth is the growth of output from the expansion of inputs, land, labor, and capital. Intensive growth is the growth derived from increasing output per unit of factor input—that is, from the better use of available inputs.

The sources of economic growth are important for two reasons. First, historical experience shows that as economies grow and develop, the sources of growth tend to change. During the early stages of development, the task is to bring idle resources into production, a model where output expansion is achieved largely from using more inputs. As economic development proceeds, the tendency is to generate growth from the better use of inputs (and improvements in input quality). The distinction between intensive and extensive growth is important, for input expansion comes from sacrificing leisure time and increasing work time and from reducing current consumption with the hope of greater improvements in the future. Intensive growth, however, is derived largely from increased efficiency, for example, through improved managerial systems and technological change.

It is relevant to ask which economic system has done a better job in generating economic growth, where *better* is defined in terms of the relative weights of **intensive growth** versus **extensive growth**. Two such comparisons pertain. The first, **static efficiency**, takes a snapshot of planned socialist and capitalist countries at a particular point in time to determine how much output they are generating from a given amount of factor inputs. The second, **dynamic efficiency**, probes the question of efficiency performance over time—that is, the extent to which output expands more rapidly than inputs, the difference being the growth rate of factor productivity.[19]

Dynamic Efficiency

Table 12.4, supplies information on the dynamic efficiency of the planned socialist and the industrialized capitalist countries. Specifically, it provides the annual growth rates of aggregate employment ($\hat{L}$) and reproducible capital ($\hat{K}$), which we then compare with the growth rate of aggregate output ($\hat{Q}$). By subtracting the growth rates of employment and capital, respectively, from the growth rate of output, we obtain the growth rates of **labor productivity** $(\hat{Q} - \hat{L})$ and **capital productivity** $(\hat{Q} - \hat{K})$, respectively.

Because the productivity of labor or capital is affected by substitutions between the two factors, it is desirable to have a comprehensive measure of the growth rate of combined labor and capital productivity. One must first calculate the growth rates of labor and capital combined $(\hat{L} + \hat{K})$, or total factor input. This is typically done by taking a weighted average of the growth rates of labor and capital, where the weights represent each factor's share of national income. Thus **total factor productivity** is defined as $\hat{Q} - (\hat{K} + \hat{L})$. Here

$$\hat{K} + \hat{L} = \hat{K}W_K + \hat{L}W_L$$

where

$$W_K = \text{capital's share of income}$$
$$W_L = \text{labor's share of income}$$

We use rates of growth of labor and capital combined $(\hat{L} + \hat{K})$, calculated in this manner. Inasmuch as a return to capital was typically not included in prices in the planned socialist countries, "synthetic" factor shares must be used to calculate their $\hat{L} + \hat{K}$ growth rates.[20] Once the growth rate of combined factor inputs is calculated, it is then subtracted from the growth rate of output to obtain the growth rate of factor productivity $[\hat{Q} - (\hat{K} + \hat{L})]$. All of these figures are given in Table 12.4.

The approximative nature of these productivity calculations is worth emphasizing. Factors of production, especially labor, can expand in both quantitative and qualitative terms, yet our measure captures only its quantitative advance.[21] If comparable data were available, one could calculate a more comprehensive measure of labor's growth by adjusting for the growth in education, training, and composition of the labor force. Because we use employment rather than actual hours, we are not even capturing the quantitative growth of labor accurately. Moreover, the capitalist data do not adjust for unemployment (which rose over this period). We use the official capital stock estimates of the planned socialist economies, except for the Soviet Union. We have no way of knowing whether they are comparable to Western data or their reliability.[22]

What conclusions are to be drawn from Table 12.4? The first is that through the mid-1980s, the growth rates of capital and labor inputs were similar for capitalism and socialism. The planned socialist and capitalist averages suggest roughly equivalent rates of growth of employment and, although the socialist growth rate of capital was probably slightly lower during the 1950s and higher thereafter, for the entire period capital grew at an average rate of roughly 5 percent in each economic system. The stereotype, fostered by the rapid growth of both labor and capital in the Soviet Union, that the planned socialist system generates a more rapid rate of growth of inputs is not supported. The rates of growth of labor and capital combined round to 2 percent per annum for both capitalism and planned socialism.

Unlike GNP growth, the variability of factor-input growth by country appears to have been as great under planned socialism as under capitalism. Some planned

TABLE 12.4 Annual Growth of Inputs and Output per Unit of Inputs in Socialist and Capitalist Countries

		(1) Employment ($\hat{L}$)	(2) Fixed Capital ($\hat{K}$)	(3) Labor & Capital ($\hat{L} + \hat{K}$)	(4) Output ($\hat{Q}$)	(5) Labor Productivity ($\hat{Q} - \hat{L}$)	(6) Capital Productivity ($\hat{Q} - \hat{K}$)	(7) Total Factor Productivity $\hat{Q} - (\hat{L} + \hat{K})$
				A. Planned Socialist Countries				
Czechoslovakia	1950–60	.7	3.5	1.4	4.8	4.1	1.3	3.4
	1960–83	1.0	4.7	2.1	2.6	1.6	−2.1	.5
East Germany	1950–60	.0	2.0	.5	6.1	6.1	4.1	5.6
	1960–83	.3	4.0	1.4	2.8	2.5	−1.2	1.4
Soviet Union	1950–60	1.2	9.4	3.4	5.8	4.6	−3.6	2.4
	1960–85	1.3	7.3	2.8	3.6	2.3	−3.7	.8
Poland	1950–60	1.0	2.6	1.4	4.6	3.6	2.0	3.2
	1960–83	1.5	4.7	2.5	3.3	1.8	−1.4	.8
Hungary	1950–60	1.0	3.6	1.7	4.6	3.6	1.0	2.9
	1960–83	.3	5.0	1.7	2.9	2.6	−2.1	1.2
Romania	1950–60	1.1	—[a]	—	5.9	4.8	—	—
	1960–85	.4	—[a]	—	4.6	4.1	—	—
Bulgaria	1950–60	.2	—[a]	—	6.7	6.5	—	—
	1960–85	.5	—[a]	—	3.7	3.2	—	—
Unweighted average	1950–60	.8	4.2	1.7	5.5[b] (5.2)[c]	4.8	1.0	3.5
	1960–83(85)	.8	5.1	2.1	3.3[b] (3.0)[c]	2.5	−2.1	.9

TABLE 12.4 Annual Growth of Inputs and Output per Unit of Inputs in Socialist and Capitalist Countries (*Cont.*)

B. Capitalist Countries

	Period	(1) Employment ($\hat{L}$)	(2) Fixed Capital ($\hat{K}$)	(3) Labor & Capital ($\hat{L} + \hat{K}$)	(4) Output ($\hat{Q}$)	(5) Labor Productivity ($\hat{Q} - \hat{L}$)	(6) Capital Productivity ($\hat{Q} - \hat{K}$)	(7) Total Factor Productivity $\hat{Q} - (\hat{L} + \hat{K})$
United States	1950–60	1.4	3.6	1.8	3.1	1.7	-.5	1.3
	1960–85	2.0	3.3	2.4	3.1	1.1	-.2	.7
Canada	1960–85	2.7	4.7	3.3	4.2	1.5	-.5	.9
Belgium	1950–62	.6	2.3	1.0	3.2	2.6	.6	2.2
Denmark	1950–62	.9	5.1	1.8	3.5	2.6	-1.6	1.7
	1950–60[d]	.1	4.2	1.0	4.9	4.8	.7	3.9
	1960–85	.7	4.8	1.8	3.9	3.1	-.9	2.1
West Germany	1950–60[d]	2.0	6.4	3.1	7.3	5.3	.9	4.2
	1960–85	.0	4.8	1.2	3.1	3.1	-1.7	1.9
Italy	1950–62	.6	3.5	1.3	6.0	5.4	2.5	4.7
Finland	1960–85	.7	4.6	1.9	3.9	3.2	-.5	2.0
Sweden	1962–83	.6	3.5	1.5	2.8	2.2	-.7	1.3
Netherlands	1950–62	1.1	4.7	1.9	4.7	3.6	.0	2.8
Norway	1950–60[d]	.2	4.2	1.2	3.5	3.3	-.7	2.3
	1960–85	.5	3.6	1.4	4.2	3.7	.6	2.8
United Kingdom	1950–60[d]	.7	3.4	1.2	2.3	1.6	-1.1	1.1
	1960–85	.5	3.2	1.1	2.3	1.8	-.9	1.2

	(1) Employment ($\hat{L}$)	(2) Fixed Capital ($\hat{K}$)	(3) Labor & Capital ($\hat{L} + \hat{K}$)	(4) Output ($\hat{Q}$)	(5) Labor Productivity ($\hat{Q} - \hat{L}$)	(6) Capital Productivity ($\hat{Q} - \hat{K}$)	(7) Total Factor Productivity $\hat{Q} - (\hat{L} + \hat{K})$
Japan 1953–70	1.7	9.8	3.8	10.0	8.3	.2	6.2
1970–85	.9	8.2	2.3	4.4	3.5	-3.8	2.1
Greece 1960–85	.4	5.8	2.0	5.1	4.7	-.7	3.1
Unweighted average[e] 1950–60	.9	4.7	1.8	4.8	3.9	.1	3.0
Unweighted average 1960–85	.9	4.7	1.9	3.7	2.8	-1.0	1.8

Note: All figures are annual growth rates.

$\hat{L}$ = growth rate of employment

$\hat{K}$ = growth rate of reproducible capital

$\hat{Q}$ = growth rate of output

($\hat{L} + \hat{K}$) = growth rate of labor and capital combined

[a] The official Romanian and Bulgarian capital stock series are not cited because they are in current, not constant, prices.

[b] Average of all 7 countries.

[c] Average of first 5 countries.

[d] 1950–1962.

[e] Includes Japan, 1953–1970.

Sources: *Panel A: Employment:* Andrew Elias, "Magnitude and Distribution of the Labor Force in Eastern Europe," in U.S. Congress, Joint Economic Committee, *Economic Developments in Countries of Eastern Europe* (Washington, D.C.: Government Printing Office, 1970), pp. 208–214; Thad Alton, "Comparative Structure and Growth of Economic Activity in Eastern Europe," in U.S. Congress, Joint Economic Committee, *East European Economies Post Helsinki* (Washington, D.C.: Government Printing Office, 1977), p. 218; *Handbook of Economic Statistics 1980,* p. 47. *Capital Stock:* Official CMEA estimates of productive funds (*osnovnye fondy*) from *Statisticheski ezhegodnik stran-chlenov Soveta Ekonomicheskoi Vzaimopomoschi 1974* (Moscow: Statistika), p. 27; Alton, "Production and Resource Allocation in Eastern Europe," p. 372; *Handbook of Economic Statistics 1980,* p. 58; and Alton, "Comparative Structure and Growth," p. 223. *Output:* Table 10.1. *Panel B: Growth Rates of Employment, Reproducible Capital, and Output:* Edward Denison, *Why Growth Rates Differ* (Washington, D.C.: Brookings, 1967), pp. 42, 190, and Ch. 21; Edward Denison, *Accounting for United States Economic Growth, 1929–1969* (Washington, D.C.: Brookings, 1976), pp. 19, 31; OECD, Department of Economics and Statistics, *Flows and Stocks of Fixed Capital, 1960–1985* (OECD: Paris, 1987); and William Chung, *How Japan's Economy Grew So Fast* (Washington, D.C.: Brookings, 1976), pp. 32, 58; Edward Denison *Handbook of Economic Statistics 1986; World Table,* 3rd ed.

socialist countries (East Germany, for example) experienced low growth of both labor and capital, while others (the Soviet Union and Poland, for example) experienced rapid input growth. One finds similar variability among the capitalist countries, with some (notably Japan) experiencing quite rapid growth of both labor and capital inputs.

Both the socialist and the capitalist countries experienced a slowdown in productivity growth after the 1960s: The planned socialist growth rate of output declined after 1960 by about 40 percent; yet inputs, both labor and capital, grew more rapidly after 1960 (about one-quarter faster). Thus both labor and capital productivity and total factor productivity declined dramatically after 1960 in the planned socialist economies—labor productivity from an average of 4.8 to 2.5 percent, and total factor productivity from 3.5 to .9 percent. Efforts to stabilize the growth of output by raising the growth of inputs did not succeed; rather than becoming more intensive, the growth of the planned socialist economies became more extensive after 1960.

The greater extensivity of socialist growth after 1960 is apparent when we compare the growth rates of total factor productivity with the growth rates of output. Taking those five socialist countries for which capital data are available, the average GNP growth rate was 5.2 percent per annum between 1950 and 1960, while the growth of efficiency (factor productivity) was 3.5 percent. Thus 67 (3.5/5.2) percent of economic growth was accounted for by increasing output per unit of input. The corresponding figures for the 1960 to 1983 period are .9 percent and 3.0 percent. Thus from 1960 to 1983, only 30 percent of growth was accounted for by increasing inputs. The declining growth of productivity was felt by both labor and capital, but the decline in capital productivity from a positive rate to a negative rate of −2.1 percent per annum was especially prominent.

The capitalist group also experienced a slowdown in productivity growth after 1960. Average labor productivity growth fell from 3.9 to 2.8 percent; capital productivity growth fell from zero to −1.0 percent; and total factor productivity growth fell from 3.0 to 1.8 percent. In the 1950s, some 65 (3.0/4.8) percent of growth in the capitalist group was explained by the growth of efficiency; for the period 1960–1985, 49 (1.8/3.7) percent of growth was explained by efficiency gains.

Table 12.4 shows the planned socialist economies in a favorable light because it does not include the productivity collapse of the second half of the 1980s. During this period, all the planned socialist economies experienced negative productivity growth except the USSR, which experienced zero productivity growth.[23]

What are the overall conclusions concerning the growth of efficiency under capitalism and planned socialism? As in the case of economic growth, there appears to be no evidence to suggest a more rapid rate of growth of productivity under planned socialism (see Figure 12.2). Since 1960, at least, it appears that the productivity performance of planned socialism deteriorated seriously and that socialist growth became much more extensive in character. We must emphasize that these conclusions are based on approximate data with little evidence on the qualitative growth of inputs. We believe, however, that they would hold up even if more exhaustive data were available.

Consumption Costs of Growth

One cost of economic growth is the sacrifice in current consumption required to add to the nation's stock of capital. Although growth rates in the East and West have been similar, it is not true that this growth was achieved with a similar allocation of resources between consumption and investment. Information on resource-allocation

FIGURE 12.2   Productivity Growth in Socialist and Capitalist Countries, 1960–85

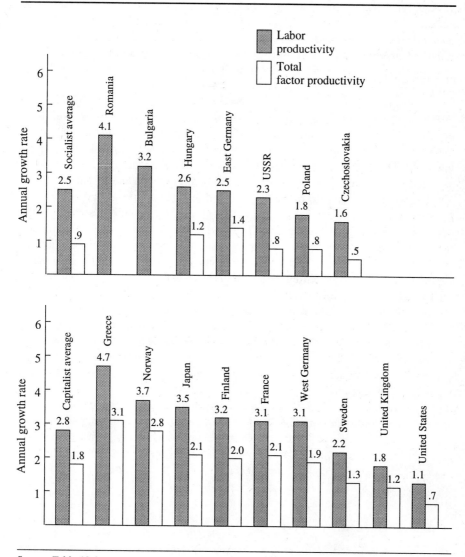

Source: Table 12.4

policies is summarized in Table 12.5.[24] Although the capitalist and socialist data cover slightly different time periods, they tell an interesting story. Again the GNP growth rates are quite similar, but personal consumption fared relatively better than investment under capitalism. In fact, while personal consumption grew on the average at a more rapid rate in the capitalist sample (4.7 percent versus 3.6 percent), gross investment grew faster under planned socialism (6.4 percent versus 5.6 percent).

More interestingly, if one takes the ratio of the growth rates of consumption and investment as a measure of resource allocation, a distinct pattern emerges. Although there seems to be a positive relationship between this ratio and per capita income, the socialist consumption–investment ratios appear to be well below those of capitalist countries at a similar stage of development. The achievement of similar rates of growth in East and West has required a greater sacrifice of current consumption under planned socialism. In fact, the resource allocation pattern of the socialist countries was remarkably uniform and closest to the pattern of the less-industrialized capitalist countries (such as Turkey and Spain).

Given the higher investment rates under planned socialism in the 1950s and 1960s, it follows that socialist per capita consumption was lower for a given level of per capita national income *ceteris paribus*. This is the other side of the coin—namely, the cost of maintaining economic growth through expansion of capital inputs.[25] The absolute level of per capita consumption depends on the economic potential of the country, and to argue that one country has outperformed the other simply because its standard of living is higher begs the question. The major issue is what standard of living is being supplied, given the economic resources at the nation's disposal. Such a comparison shows that the socialist living standards are low relative to per capita income. This reflects the decision of growth-oriented socialist planners to devote a relatively larger share of GNP to investment than under capitalism. However, the telling point is that this decision did not lead to a notably higher rate of growth for the planned socialist nations. The planners' consumption policies did not pay off in terms of more rapid growth.

These findings have negative implications concerning the viability of the planned socialist systems. While the reasons for the productivity problem have not yet been considered, the incentive impact on the socialist consumer must have been harmful to these economies. First, the systems, especially that of the former Soviet Union, emphasized a basic socialist postulate—sacrifice now through expanded savings and reduced consumption (such as that which took place in the 1930s) to enjoy significant gains in consumption in the future. But in general those gains did not materialize. When they did, the pace of improvement was slow, a fact that Soviet consumers could recognize as they watched other countries outperform their own system. Although these patterns are not easily quantifiable, the effort contributed by the Soviet worker must have suffered, especially in the 1970s and 1980s.

Static Efficiency

Static efficiency is a difficult concept to measure. To do so correctly requires first a notion of an economy's productive potential, as defined by its total resources, and

TABLE 12.5   Annual Rates of Growth of Personal Consumption, Investment, and GNP in Planned Socialist and Capitalist Countries

Country	(1) Personal Consumption	(2) Gross Investment	(3) GNP	(4) Consumption Growth as a Percentage of Investment Growth (1) ÷ (2)
A. Planned Socialist Countries				
Czechoslovakia (1950–67)	2.2	5.2	3.2	.42
East Germany (1960–75)	3.7	6.1	4.9	.61
Hungary (1950–67)	3.4	5.2	4.0	.65
Poland (1950–67)	4.2	7.9	5.1	.53
Soviet Union (1950–80)	4.3	7.7	4.7	.56
Unweighted average	3.6	6.4	4.4	.56
B. Capitalist Countries, 1950–1977				
United States	3.4	3.1	3.6	1.10
Canada	4.7	4.6	4.8	1.02
West Germany	4.7	5.0	4.8	.94
Denmark	3.5	4.9	3.8	.71
Norway	3.9	4.6	4.2	.85
Belgium	3.7	4.6	4.0	.81
France	5.0	6.1	5.0	.82
Netherlands	4.6	4.2	4.5	1.09
Japan	7.8	11.0	8.4	.71
Austria	5.4	5.1	4.9	1.06
United Kingdom	2.2	4.4	2.5	.50
Italy	4.6	5.0	4.8	.92
Greece	6.0	7.1	6.4	.85
Spain	5.2	6.7	5.6	.77
Turkey	6.1	8.2	6.3	.74
Unweighted average	4.7	5.6	4.9	.84

Sources: Thad Alton, "Economic Structure and Growth in Eastern Europe," in U.S. Congress, Joint Economic Committee, *Economic Developments in Countries of Eastern Europe* (Washington, D.C.: Government Printing Office, 1970), pp. 52–53; *Deutsches Institut fur Wirtschaftsforschung Wochenbericht*, 44 (June 1977), p. 199; Rush Greenslade, "The Real Gross National Product of the USSR, 1950–75," in U.S. Congress, Joint Economic Committee, *Soviet Economy in a New Perspective* (Washington, D.C.: Government Printing Office, 1975), p. 275; World Bank, *World Tables 1980* (Baltimore: The Johns Hopkins University Press, 1980), country tables; U.S. Congress, Joint Economic Committee, *USSR: Measures of Economic Growth and Development, 1950–80* (Washington, D.C.: Government Printing Office, 1982), pp. 65–67.

then a determination of how closely the economy comes to meeting that potential. This problem is explained in Figure 12.3. To show that the Soviet Union, for example, obtained half as much output as the United States from a given amount of conventional labor and capital inputs would not unambiguously prove the greater static efficiency of the American economy. The measurement of conventional inputs may fail to capture the full range of resources (in both qualitative and quantitative terms) at the disposal of each economy.

One way to illustrate the static efficiency measurement problem is to note the strong positive relationship between the level of economic development and output per unit of input. Any evaluation of the static efficiency of capitalism and planned socialism must distinguish between "normal" differences caused by unequal economic development and differences due to the economic system. What is missing is

FIGURE 12.3   Why It Is Difficult to Evaluate Static Efficiency: Different
Country Production Possibilities

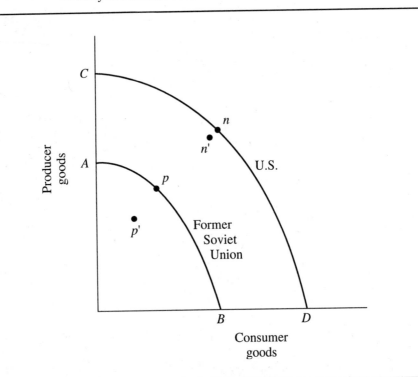

Explanation: CD represents the production possibilities frontier (PPF) of, say, the United States. AB is the PPF of, say, the former Soviet Union. The U.S. PPF is to the northeast of the Soviet PPF because of greater resources and better technology. The relevant measure of static efficiency is how closely each economy comes to operating on its PPF. If, for example, the United States operates very close to n at n' and the Soviet Union operates at p', which is very far from p, the United States is more efficient. In real-world measurement, all we observe is p' and n'. We have no way of knowing what p and n are.

information on what the economy should be able to produce at maximum efficiency from its resources.

Abram Bergson has made a careful study of comparative productivity under capitalism and socialism that sheds light on the issue of relative productivity performance.[26] Bergson's data for 1975 are reproduced in Table 12.6. They give per capita outputs and labor (adjusted for quality differences), capital, and land inputs of various capitalist and socialist countries (where the socialist group includes Yugoslavia) as a percentage of the U.S. per capita figures. Table 12.6 shows, for example, that Italy had a per capita output 61 percent that of the United States, a per capita employment 75 percent that of the United States, and a per capita capital stock 62 percent that of the United States. The Soviet Union had a per capita output 60 percent that of the United States, a per capita employment 104 percent that of the United States, and a per capita capital stock 73 percent that of the United States.

The issue is whether the socialist countries systematically obtained less output from their available inputs than the capitalist countries. In the data comparing Italy and the Soviet Union, Italy obtained more output from its available inputs. Italy and the Soviet Union had the same per capita output, when compared with the United States, yet the Soviet Union used more labor and capital per capita to produce that output.

Bergson demonstrates that there was a systematic tendency for the output per worker (labor productivity) in socialist economies to fall short of output per worker in capitalist countries, when inputs are held constant. According to Bergson's

TABLE 12.6 Per Capita Output, Employment, Capital, and Land, 1975 (United States = 100)

Country	Output per Capita	Employment per Capita Adjusted for Labor Quality	Reproducible Capital per Capita	Farm Land per Capita
United States	100.0	100.0	100.0	100.0
West Germany	90.0	84.0	107.3	14.8
France	92.2	88.3	83.0	40.1
Italy	61.3	75.2	61.6	24.9
United Kingdom	67.2	89.6	77.2	14.5
Japan	82.8	129.0	95.2	5.4
Spain	64.6	95.4	47.7	67.0
Soviet Union	60.0	104.1	73.2	103.5
Hungary	61.1	115.6	70.9	59.8
Poland	54.8	122.7	51.6	50.4
Yugoslavia	41.5	98.8	35.9	45.6

Source: Abram Bergson, "Comparative Productivity: The USSR, Eastern Europe, and the West," *American Economic Review*, 77 (June 1987), 347.

calculations, output per worker in the socialist group fell 25 to 34 percent short of output per worker in the capitalist group *ceteris paribus*.

Bergson's findings are important, though this sample is small. It will be a long time before a similar experiment on a larger number of countries can be performed. Meanwhile, we believe it is appropriate to conclude that socialist economies have relatively lower productivity, *ceteris paribus*, than industrialized capitalist countries.[27]

As previously shown, it is difficult to assess the comparative static efficiency of socialist and capitalist economic systems because determining how closely real-world economies operate to their production possibilities frontier is not possible. However, beginning with the work of Judith Thornton in 1971, a number of predictive studies inclusive of the early 1990s have attempted to examine **allocative efficiency** by estimating various production functions and by focusing on the allocation of inputs among industries in socialist economies.[28] These studies generally found that there was allocative inefficiency in that reallocation could raise the value added; that was increasingly so through the 1970s. Similar studies conducted in the 1980s resulted in similar conclusions, though the estimated magnitudes of inefficiency were generally not very large. While these types of studies generally supported the existence of allocative inefficiency, their results have sparked controversy, especially because of a variety of basic measurement problems that remain unresolved.

A number of studies of **enterprise (technical) efficiency** have looked at enterprises in socialist and capitalist systems and, in some cases, have made comparisons. Although generalizing across a wide variety of studies that differ in scope and approach is difficult, most studies have not shown unusually low levels of efficiency in enterprises of planned socialist economic systems. But, as with measures of allocative efficiency, these measures of technical efficiency are difficult to interpret because of basic underlying measurement problems.

In sum, these studies have led to a general presumption that efficiency was lower in the planned socialist systems than in market capitalist systems. The issue, however, remains controversial and undoubtedly will spur further analyses in the future.

Income Distribution

Another measure of the performance of economic systems is the distribution of income among the members of society. What constitutes a good distribution of income must be a subjective matter, but there would be agreement that a distribution in which the top 5 percent of the population receives 95 percent of all income is "unfair" and that a completely equal distribution is "unfair." Marx himself rejected the notion of an equal distribution of income during the transition from socialism to communism, arguing instead for a distribution that reflected the individual's contribution to the well-being of society.[29]

Another reason why most people reject a perfectly equal distribution of income is that rewards must be offered for differential effort and for scarce resources; otherwise, incentives will diminish and the economy will not produce its potential output.

The issue therefore is now to construct a distribution of income that both is "fair" and provides necessary incentives. Both socialism and capitalism must face this issue.

What differences would one expect in the distribution of incomes under capitalism and socialism? In capitalist societies, the two major sources of income inequality are the unequal distribution of property ownership (land and capital resources) and of human capital. Both forms of capital yield income—the first in the form of property income from rent, interest, dividends, and capital gains; the second from wages and salaries.

Under both planned and market socialism, property other than consumer durables and housing is owned by the state, and the return from this state-owned property is at the state's disposal. Under capitalism, the bulk of property is owned privately, and property income accrues to private individuals.

The distribution of human capital depends on the manner in which schooling and on-the-job training are provided. Free or subsidized public schooling is available in both types of societies, although there is a greater tendency for the state to pay for higher education in socialist societies. Nevertheless, the differences between the two systems would not be expected to be great.

The major distinction is the absence of private ownership of income-earning property under socialism. Unless offset by higher earnings differentials, the distribution of property plus labor income should be more nearly equal under socialism. The distribution of income after taxes depends on the extent to which the state uses redistributive taxes and transfers to equalize income distribution.

As to earnings differentials, planned socialist societies recognized that labor cannot be allocated administratively and must be allowed relative freedom of choice of occupation. Therefore, the distribution of wage and salary income under socialism should follow roughly the same principles as under capitalism.

Arguments can be made, however, that the distribution of labor incomes varies according to the economic system.[30] Some argue that labor income is more equally distributed under socialism because of the more nearly equal distribution of education and training and because the government can control the power of labor groups. Moreover, socialist governments have a greater doctrinal commitment to equality.

Frederic Pryor made an extensive econometric study of the distribution of labor income among workers for the late 1950s and early 1960s.[31] He found that the distribution of labor income was *more equal* under socialism, once per capita income and the size of the country were held constant. He also found that labor incomes were more unequal in the Soviet Union than in the other socialist countries; therefore, studies that generalize from the Soviet experience are likely to give a false impression.

More recent data on the distribution of earnings for full-time wage and salary earners confirm most of Pryor's findings for the 1950s and early 1960s.[32] Earnings were more nearly equally distributed in Eastern Europe, Yugoslavia, and the Soviet Union than in the United States in the 1970s. For the USSR, this was a relatively new phenomenon, for as late as 1957, Soviet earnings were more unequal than those in the United States.[33]

We now turn from the distribution of **labor income** to the distribution of **total income**. Table 12.7 gives data on the distribution of per capita income after income taxes in a limited number of planned socialist and capitalist countries for which data are available.[34] The socialist data generally excluded top income-earning families (party leaders, government officials, artists, and authors), including instead only families of workers and employees. Many second economy activities considered legal in capitalist societies (the provision of private repair and medical services, for example) were not recorded. Also, a relatively larger volume of resources (even excluding free educational and medical benefits) was provided in socialist societies on an extra-market basis—shopping privileges, official cars, vacations—and were not included in reported income.

Table 12.7 shows that income is distributed more unequally in the capitalist countries in which the state plays a relatively minor redistributive role either through progressive taxation or through the distribution of social services (the United States, Italy, and Canada). Yet even where the state played a major redistributive role (the United Kingdom and Sweden), the distribution of income appeared to be slightly more unequal than in the planned socialist countries (Hungary, Czechoslovakia, and Bulgaria). The Soviet Union in 1966 appeared to have had a less egalitarian distribution of income than its East European counterparts. The USSR distribution was scarcely distinguishable from the British and Swedish distributions (it may even have been more unequal). Table 12.8 reveals that Soviet income distribution was more nearly equal than that in Australia, Canada, and the United States but not much different from that in Norway and the United Kingdom.

The **Gini coefficient** is a convenient summary measure of income inequality. The higher the Gini coefficient, the more unequal the distribution of income. A Gini coefficient of zero denotes perfect equality; a Gini coefficient of 1 denotes perfect inequality. Gini coefficients for Great Britain and Sweden for the early 1970s are both around .25. The Czech, Hungarian, and Polish Gini coefficients for the same period are .21, .24, and .24, respectively—that is, very close to the British and Swedish coefficients. The Canadian and U.S. Gini coefficients, on the other hand, are .34 and .35, respectively, well above the socialist coefficients.[35]

Figure 12.4 provides Lorenz curves for Hungary, Sweden, West Germany, Spain, Mexico, and Yugoslavia. The reader will recall from Chapter 3 that the further the Lorenz curve departs from the line of perfect equality, the more unequal the distribution. These curves, which refer to the early 1970s, confirm the basic pattern shown in Table 12.7: Hungary was about the same as Sweden but was much more egalitarian than West Germany and Spain (two capitalist countries without considerable state income redistribution); Yugoslavia did not differ significantly from West Germany and Spain. However, there apparently was a narrowing of differentials in Yugoslavia between the early 1960s and early 1970s.

The Mexican Lorenz curve is included to make a general point about the Yugoslav (and Hungarian, Polish, Soviet, and Czech) distributions. As the Mexican curve shows, inequality tends to be negatively related to the level of development.[36] If one could adjust for lower per capita income, the socialist distributions would appear even more nearly equal than they do in direct comparisons.

TABLE 12.7 Distribution of Per Capita Income Among Families After Income Taxes in Planned Socialist and Capitalist Countries

	U.K. 1969	U.S. 1968	Italy 1969	Canada 1971	Sweden 1971	Hungary 1964	Czecho-slovakia 1965	Bulgaria 1963–65	USSR 1966
Per capita income of individual in 95th percentile ÷ that of individual in 5th percentile	5.0	12.7	11.2	12.0	5.5	4.0	4.3	3.8	5.7
Per capita income of individual in 90th percentile ÷ that of individual in 10th percentile	3.4	6.7	5.9	6.0	3.5	3.0	3.1	2.7	3.5
Per capita income of individual in 75th percentile ÷ that of individual in 25th percentile	1.9	2.6	2.5	2.4	1.9	1.8	1.8	1.7	2.0

Source: P. J. D. Wiles, *Economic Institutions Compared* (New York: Halsted Press, 1977), p. 443. By permission of Basil Blackwell, Oxford.

TABLE 12.8   An International Comparison of Income Shares of Selected
Percentile Groups, Distributions of Households by Per Capita
Household Income, and GDP Per Capita

Distribution, Country and Year	Percentage Income Share of			
	Lowest 10%	Lowest 20%	Highest 20%	Highest 10%
Nonfarm households (pretax) USSR, 1967	4.4	10.4	33.8	19.9
Urban households (post-tax) USSR, 1972–1974	3.4	8.7	38.5	24.1
All households (pretax) Australia, 1966–1967	3.5	8.3	41.0	25.6
Norway, 1970	3.5	8.2	39.0	23.5
U.K., 1973	3.5	8.3	39.9	23.9
France, 1970	2.0	5.8	47.2	31.8
Canada, 1969	2.2	6.2	43.6	27.8
U.S., 1972	1.8	5.5	44.4	28.6
All households (post-tax) Sweden, 1972	3.5	9.3	35.2	20.5

Source: Abram Bergson, "Income Inequality Under Soviet Socialism," *Journal of Economic Literature*, 22 (September 1984). ˙

In general, we conclude that the differences in distribution of income between the planned socialist economies and the capitalist welfare states have been relatively minor. This is a surprising conclusion. One would have expected the absence of private ownership of property to make more of a difference. Nevertheless, differences are apparent when one contrasts the socialist distributions with those of the capitalist nations in which the state does not play a major redistributive role. In this instance, the expected contrast emerges, although we must re-emphasize the difficulty of interpreting the socialist distributions because of the omitted income categories.

Economic Stability

A final indicator of economic performance is economic stability. By economic stability we mean the absence of excessive movements in prices, unemployment, and output. Stability also refers to the absence of persistent (as opposed to cyclical) high unemployment rates or inflation rates.

The postwar era witnessed several recessions in the major capitalist countries, the most severe occurring in the mid-1970s and at the start of the 1980s. Socialist countries experienced "growth recessions"—that is, periods when the growth rate

FIGURE 12.4   Lorenz Curves of the Distribution of Per Capita Income in
Hungary, Sweden, West Germany, Spain, Yugoslavia, and Mexico[a,b]

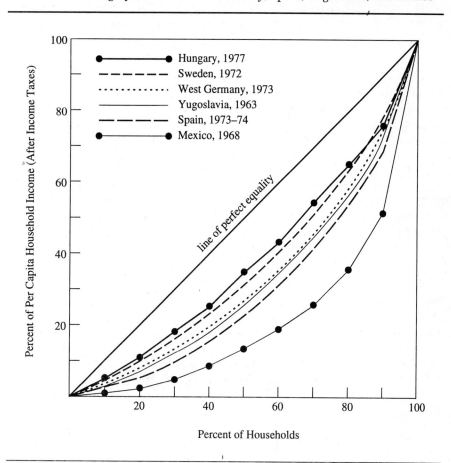

[a] For an explanation of the Lorenz curve see Chapter 3.
[b] Mexican data are prior to income taxes, but we doubt that their inclusion would move the Mexican Lorenz curve dramatically.

Sources: Malcolm Sawyer, *Income Distribution in OECD Countries* (Paris: OECD, 1976), p. 17; Jan Adams and Miloslav Nosal, "Earnings Differentials and Household-Income Differentials in Hungary —Policies and Practice," *Journal of Comparative Economics*, 6 (June 1982), 197; and Wouter van Ginneken, "Generating Internationally Comparable Income Distribution Data," *Review of Income and Wealth*, 28 (December 1982), 374.

declined but remained positive, but they largely avoided recessions before 1980. In the 1980s, however, the majority of the planned socialist countries experienced periods of negative growth.

The literature recognizes that cyclical fluctuations are present in planned socialist economies, but it was believed that socialist fluctuations were less pronounced. However, Frederic Pryor found that socialist fluctuations in GNP, industrial output, and investment are not statistically distinguishable from capitalist fluctuations. Moreover, socialist fluctuations in agricultural output were more pronounced than those in capitalist agriculture.[37]

The planned socialist economies claimed that socialist planning "liquidated" unemployment. No society can eliminate unemployment entirely, for at any given time some people are in the process of changing jobs. It does appear that the planned socialist economies reduced the rate of unemployment to small proportions relative to capitalist economies.[38] This was a consequence of deliberate full-employment planning. Enterprises were either unwilling or unable to release underemployed workers, creating such a problem that experiments were attempted to encourage the laying off of redundant workers. Generally, however, enterprises were given hiring quotas for new graduates, and the planning system served to provide employment for able-bodied individuals, whether in a necessary or an underemployed position.[39]

Moreover, the planned system avoided unemployment problems by not allowing enterprises to fail. Enterprises have typically been rewarded on the basis of output rather than sales, and the existence of the enterprise has been guaranteed regardless of its performance.

If one examines price inflation under capitalism and planned socialism, a striking contrast emerges from the official statistics (see Table 12.9). Between 1960 and 1980, for example, the capitalist countries experienced considerable inflation, which accelerated after 1970. According to official socialist indexes, on the other hand, consumer prices rose at a very modest pace over this period. The planned socialist economies' claims of virtual price stability for the 1960s and 1970s evoke skepticism about the official consumer price series.[40] First, the official price series ignored substantial price increases for "new" or "higher quality" products. Often an enterprise could obtain a higher price by claiming superficial or nonexistent quality improvements in its products. Second, the official series failed to capture the price increases of goods sold in legal and illegal free markets. Third, the official indexes did not include the costs of standing in line or of the bribes required to obtain goods. When these circumstances prevail, demand exceeds supply at the established official price, and **repressed inflation** results. Supplies offered at established state prices were rationed out by standing in line, special shopping privileges, or ration coupons.

There is evidence that the official price series understated actual inflation in the socialist countries. Recalculated price indexes (shown in parentheses in Table 12.9) suggest that prices rose more rapidly than official sources claim for the 1960 to 1980 period. The relatively stable state retail prices concealed an unknown degree of repressed inflation, which has had a serious destabilizing effect in some planned socialist economies, such as Poland. For political and other reasons, authorities were unwilling to raise official consumer prices to market-clearing levels. Price stability was achieved only at the cost of serious shortages, redirection of purchasing power into collective farm markets and black markets, and growing discontent.

The second column of Table 12.9 gives inflation rates for 1980 to 1989, a period that saw the partial liberalization of state price controls in the East. In the two countries that have converted most to market prices (Poland and Hungary), inflation well outpaced the West. Even in the Soviet Union, Bulgaria, and Romania,

TABLE 12.9   Indexes of Consumer Prices in 1980 and 1989
(Recalculated Socialist Indexes in Parentheses)

	1980 (1960 = 100)		1989 (1980 = 100)	
	A. Socialist Countries			
	official	recalculated	official	recalculated
Soviet Union	100	(140)	109	(—)
Bulgaria	130	(207)	113	(126)
Czechoslovakia	126	(173)	116	(115)
East Germany	98	(127)	110	(114)
Hungary	169	(210)	215	(220)
Poland	185	(254)	6515	(—)
Romania	120	(—)	130	(141)
Yugoslavia	1449		246560	
	B. Capitalist Countries			
United States	280		150	
Canada	287		170	
Belgium	261		150	
France	382		178	
Italy	546		236	
Japan	420		119	
Netherlands	295		124	
United Kingdom	547		172	
West Germany	213		126	

Sources: *Statistical Abstract of the United States, 1981*, p. 881; *Economic Report of the President, 1981*, p. 355; Martin Kohn, "Consumer Price Developments in Eastern Europe," in U.S. Congress, Joint Economic Committee, *Eastern European Economic Assessment*, Part 2 (Washington, D.C.: Government Printing Office, 1981), p. 3330; Thad Alton et al., *Official Alternative Consumer Price Indexes in Eastern Europe, 1960–1980*, OP-68, Research Project on National Income in East Central Europe (New York, 1981); Directorate of Intelligence, CIA, *Soviet Gross National Product in Current Prices, 1960–80*, SOV 83-10037 (March 1983), pp. 6, 22; *Handbook of Economic Statistics 1990*, p. 45; "Eastern Europe: Long Road Ahead to Economic Well-Being," 1990, Tables C-2 to C-21; and *Narodnoe Khoziaistvo SSSR 1988*, p. 125.

where prices remained state-controlled during this period (and where the official statistics probably understated inflation), inflation was about the same as in such low-inflation Western countries as Japan, Germany, and the Netherlands.

The rapid increase of prices in Poland and Hungary show the extent of repressed inflation on the eve of liberalization. The freeing of prices led to very high rates of inflation. In Poland, the result was a 65-fold increase in prices in 1989 as price controls were removed, after which prices stabilized. The apparent price stability of earlier periods (as reflected in the official statistics) has concealed churning inflationary forces. In fact, the pent-up inflationary forces present a serious obstacle to economic reform. The conversion to a market economy requires releasing inflationary pressures. In Eastern Europe, both the governments and the public have a strong fear of inflation—of its effect on output and on the distribution of income. This fear of inflation reduces public support for market reform.

Yugoslavia has experienced a more rapid rate of inflation than any capitalist country in our sample. After 1980, Yugoslavia experienced hyperinflation. Moreover, the Yugoslav unemployment rate was higher than that in the planned socialist countries.[41] Thus Yugoslavia does not appear to match the planned socialist record of stability but is more like a capitalist LDC in this regard. In fact, Yugoslavia's rates approximated those of Portugal and Turkey.

Performance Comparisons and Decline

At the beginning of this chapter two questions were examined: First, to what extent and in what ways did the performance of the former planned socialist economic systems differ from the performance of market capitalist systems? Second, to what extent and in what ways can the demise of many of these systems be blamed upon economic factors?

Economic Decline in the Planned Socialist Systems

Although empirical evidence suggests that some aspects of socialist performance were good in earlier years, noticeable declines in the growth rate of output and productivity were observed in the 1970s and 1980s. That declining performance attracted considerable attention as well as many explanations.

A popular approach to understanding the growth slowdown in the planned socialist economies focused on analysis of input and output growth (production function analysis).[42] Such analyses seemed to suggest that the growth of total factor productivity, while generally (though not always) positive, declined rather steadily during the 1970s and 1980s. Moreover, studies examining labor and capital productivity usually demonstrated a positive and declining labor productivity and an increasingly negative capital productivity. The simple conclusion was that overall diminishing returns and/or declining marginal product of capital occurred in a setting where capital was substituted for labor. This evidence was used to conclude that planned socialist systems rather than becoming more intensive were, in fact, achieving increasingly less growth from a given input expansion.

Analysis of these concepts required the use of production function analysis to relate inputs to outputs in a formal econometric model. Lack of technological progress has been a problem, but for some periods, diminishing returns to capital has also been an explanatory factor.

Beyond the statistical analysis of economic growth in the planned socialist economic systems, there have been a variety of other theories attempting to provide reasons for the observed slowdown. Many of these focus on problems with information and/or incentives.

The microeconomics of the planned socialist systems revealed various sources of inefficiency. In the absence of the pressures of competition and for cost minimization, socialist industrial and agricultural production units demonstrated little interest in efficiency, functioning in an environment of persistent, excess demand along with shortages and bottlenecks in the material supply system. Moreover, lack of innovative activity became understandable in a system where little if any rewards were reaped for either product or process innovation.[43]

Besides the microeconomic problems, a number of observations have been made about more general macroeconomic issues. For example, the evolutionary approach to change may have been a growth advantage for the early years of such systems, but in fact, became a disadvantage in later years.[44] Thus it has been argued that the devolution of the planned economies occurred because micro-units, responding to central directives, could be directed and controlled in the early years. But as time passed, those units learned how to collude, restricting and manipulating information flows, which limited the effectiveness and control the central planners had over the economy.

In addition, the growing complexity of the planned socialist systems could have contributed to the lagging performance.[45] There is, in fact, empirical evidence to suggest that as an economy grows, more units produce more products with increasingly varied inputs. As a result, the basic coordination function becomes increasingly difficult, especially when efforts have been made to avoid the decentralizing decision making to local levels where the necessary information is available.

A major problem in the planned socialist systems was the nature of incentives. Incentives arrangements may possibly provide the broadest indictment of the planned socialist systems. Although it is difficult to demonstrate empirically, some have argued that the lack of perceived improvements in standards of living and especially shortages of quality consumer goods caused the labor force to become increasingly unwilling to make the effort required to stimulate growth and efficiency.

Finally, a variety of issues relate to the general development patterns of socialist economic systems. In a variety of dimensions, especially structural ones, socialist development patterns were different from those observed in market capitalist systems. Sectoral expansion paths differed; for instance, the socialist system emphasized heavy industry at the expense of consumer and service sectors. Although attempts were made to offset the slow growth in private consumption, such as the expansion of social consumption, the bias against market patterns undoubtedly influenced the forces affecting economic growth. While structural issues were discussed in a growth context during the era of the planned socialist economic systems, as will be seen in this book's discussion of transition issues, those issues remain important as forces influencing the rate and pattern of adjustment in the 1990s.

Although there is no general and decisive explanation for the decline of the planned socialist economic systems, the so-called strengths at lower levels of economic development might have become weaknesses in subsequent years. These systems were largely incapable of institutional adaption. Put another way, traditional economic reform failed, and even last-minute efforts, such as the Soviet Union's attempts at perestroika, were too little and too late. Moreover, in places like Hungary, where change may have been more successful, it served mainly to make the ultimate transition to markets easier as the political support for the socialist regime collapsed.

Summary

This chapter focuses on two issues: comparisons of the performance of planned socialist systems with market capitalist systems, and the economic reasons for the decline and ultimate demise of many of the socialist systems.

Although performance comparisons are important for understanding different economic systems, meaningful comparisons and overall conclusions are difficult to make without using some subjective criteria, for example, whether economic growth is more or less important than, say, full employment. It is possible, however, to consider comparative economic performance by using a series of separate indicators to see how well different systems measure up.

Although cases of rapid economic growth in socialist systems do exist, these systems have generally not surpassed their capitalist counterparts despite the importance given to economic growth in socialist systems. Indeed, if one were to control for other factors, such as the level of economic development, rates of economic growth were highest in capitalist systems, even though there has been a capitalist slowdown in contemporary times. Socialist growth rates slowed markedly in the final years of the Soviet and East European experiences.

Structural differences between socialist and capitalist economic systems are also important. If one attempts to control for per capita income, a comparison of the two systems reveals that industry shares were high under socialism, service sector shares low, and urbanization underemphasized, all of which are characteristic of the socialist industrialization model.

To understand differences in economic growth, it is necessary to examine the sources of growth, especially the increased use of inputs (extensive growth) vis-à-vis the better use of inputs (intensive growth). The growth of inputs for the differing systems was broadly similar during the postwar years, though after 1980 factor inputs probably grew more rapidly under planned socialism, despite the declining rate of output growth in this era.

During the early postwar era, productivity growth was broadly similar in both systems. For example, during the 1950s, efficiency growth accounted for more than 60 percent of the growth in planned socialist systems, a figure close to the capitalist achievement during that same period. In the era after 1960, however, planned socialist economic growth became more extensive, a troubling sign because almost 80 percent of socialist growth was accounted for by the expansion of inputs.

The phenomenon of a more extensive growth pattern in the socialist systems was evident in both the levels and differential growth rates of consumption and investment, suggesting greater consumer sacrifices in the socialist systems, precisely the opposite of what socialist theory would suggest for advanced levels of economic development. Other inputs remaining constant, the planned socialist countries generally achieved less output per unit of labor input than did their capitalist counterparts.

Income distribution was always difficult to measure in the socialist systems because of the lack of meaningful data. However, past studies have generally argued that income is distributed more equally in those systems in which the state plays a major redistributive role. Thus the differences between the planned socialist systems and the capitalist welfare states are surprisingly small.

Conventional measures of stability suggest, for the most part, that the socialist systems were more stable than the capitalist systems. But common measures, such as inflation and unemployment, are difficult to interpret across systems because of the serious underemployment and repressed inflation in the socialist setting.

The apparent decline of rates of economic growth in the planned socialist systems has been analyzed largely by using production function analysis. Although evidence is mixed, the focus is on diminishing returns and/or declining productivity of capital due to substitution of capital for labor with lack of technological change.

In addition to an analysis of slowdowns in growth, a number of more general explanations have been given for the slowing economy, including the growing complexity and the devolution of the system and its general inability to adjust to changes over time.

Key Terms

system objectives	capital productivity
representative economic system	total factor productivity
net material product	income distribution
nonproductive services	Gini coefficient
adjusted factor cost concept	allocative efficiency
economic growth	enterprise (technical) efficiency
intensive growth	total income
extensive growth	labor income
static efficiency	repressed inflation
dynamic efficiency	underemployment
labor productivity	

Notes

1. Abram Bergson, *Planning and Productivity Under Soviet Socialism* (New York: Columbia University Press, 1968).
2. Paul R. Gregory and Robert C. Stuart, *Soviet Economic Structure and Performance*, 4th ed. (New York: HarperCollins, 1990), Ch. 12.

3. See Joseph Chung, "The Economies of North and South Korea" (Annual Meeting of the American Economic Association, Atlantic City, N.J., September 1976) and Paul Gregory and Gert Leptin, "Similar Societies Under Differing Economic Systems: The Case of the Two Germanys," *Soviet Studies*, 24 (October 1977), 519–542. Also see the papers on the panel: "Different Strategies, Similar Countries: The Consequences of Growth and Equity" (Annual Meeting of the American Economic Association, New York, December 1982).

4. Gur Ofer, "Industrial Structure, Urbanization, and the Growth Strategy of Socialist Countries," *Quarterly Journal of Economics*, 90 (May 1976), 219–243; Gur Ofer, *The Service Sector in Soviet Economic Development* (Cambridge, Mass.: Harvard University Press, 1973); Paul Gregory, *Socialist and Nonsocialist Industrialization Patterns* (New York: Praeger, 1970); Frederic L. Pryor, *Public Expenditures in Communist and Capitalist Nations* (Bloomington: Indiana University Press, 1973); and Frederic L. Pryor, *Property and Industrial Organization in Communist and Capitalist Nations* (Bloomington: Indiana University Press, 1973). For a discussion of the pure methodology of econometric performance evaluation, see Edward Hewett, "Alternative Econometric Approaches for Studying the Link Between Economic Systems and Economic Outcomes," *Journal of Comparative Economics*, 4 (September 1980), 274–294. For a discussion of the methodology of growth comparisons, see Gur Ofer, "Soviet Economic Growth, 1928–1985," *Journal of Economic Literature*, 25 (December 1987), 1767–1833.

5. For example, Gregor Lazarcik found that the centrally planned economies with more decentralized agriculture (such as Hungary and Poland) have performed better in terms of output and efficiency than those with centralized agriculture. On this, see Gregor Lazarcik, "Comparative Growth, Structure, and Levels of Agricultural Output, Inputs, and Productivity in Eastern Europe, 1965–79," in U.S. Congress, Joint Economic Committee, *East European Economic Assessment*, Part 2 (Washington, D.C.: Government Printing Office, 1981), pp. 587–634.

6. The major sources of data on the Soviet Union, Eastern Europe, and China are contained in various reports to the U.S. Congress prepared by the Joint Economic Committee. See, for example, *East European Economies: Slow Growth in the 1980s*, Vols. 1–3 (Washington, D.C.: Government Printing Office, 1986) and *Gorbachev's Economic Plans*, Vols. 1–2 (Washington, D.C.: Government Printing Office, 1987). Another useful statistical compendium is the Central Intelligence Agency, Directorate of Intelligence, *Handbook of Economic Statistics*. The most useful official East European source is the CMEA handbook: *Statisticheski ezhegodnik stran chlenov Sovet Ekonomicheskikh Vzaimopomoshichi*, various annual editions. For data on the Chinese economy, see U.S. Congress, Joint Economic Committee, *China: A Reassessment of the Economy* (Washington, D.C.: Government Printing Office, 1975); and Alexander Eckstein, ed., *Quantitative Measures of China's Economic Output* (Ann Arbor: University of Michigan Press, 1980).

7. Statistical comparisons of industrialized capitalism and planned socialism are Maurice Ernst, "Postwar Economic Growth in Eastern Europe," in U.S. Congress, Joint Economic Committee, *Economic Developments in Countries of Eastern Europe* (Washington, D.C.: Government Printing Office, 1970), pp. 41–67; and Thad Alton, "East European GNPs," Joint Economic Committee, *East European Economies: Slow Growth in the 1980s*, Vol. 1, pp. 81–132. Also see Andrew Stollar and G. R. Thompson, "Sectoral Employment Shares: A Comparative Systems Context," *Journal of Comparative Economics*, 11 (March 1987), 62–80; and Thad Alton, "Production and Resource Allocation in Eastern Europe: Performance, Problems, and Prospects," in Joint Economic Committee, *East European Economic Assessment*, Part 2, pp. 348–408.

8. See, for example, Subramanian Swamy, "Economic Growth in China and India, 1952–1970: A Comparative Appraisal," *Economic Development and Cultural Change*, 21 (July 1973), 1–84; and Wilfred Malenbaum, "Modern Economic Growth in India and China: The Comparison Revisited," *Economic Development and Cultural Change*, 31 (October 1982), 45–84.

9. For a discussion of CMEA statistical practices, see Thad Alton, "Economic Structure and Growth in Eastern Europe," in Joint Economic Committee, *Economic Developments in Countries of Eastern Europe*, pp. 43–45; and Alton, "Production and Resource Allocation in Eastern Europe," pp. 384–408.

10. The pioneering work on reconstructing planned socialist national income accounts was for the Soviet Union and was carried out by Abram Bergson and his associates. For an account of these efforts, see Abram Bergson, "Introduction," *Real National Income of Soviet Russia Since 1928* (Cambridge, Mass.: Harvard University Press, 1961).

11. *The Real National Income of Soviet Russia Since 1928*, Chs. 2 and 3.

12. On this, see Directorate of Intelligence, *Measuring Soviet GNP: Problems and Solutions: A Conference Report*, SOV 90–10038, September 1990; "Eastern Europe: Long Road Ahead to Economic Well-Being," A Paper by the Central Intelligence Agency Presented to the Subcommittee on Technology and National Security of the Joint Economic Committee, May 1990; and Directorate of Intelligence, *Revisiting Soviet Economic Performance Under Glasnost: Implications for CIA Estimates*, SOV 88–10068, September 1988.

13. *Measuring Soviet GNP: Problems and Solutions*, p. 187.

14. For discussions of the socialist industrialization model, see Gregory, *Socialist and Nonsocialist Industrialization Patterns*; Ofer, "Industrial Structure, Urbanization, and the Growth of Socialist Countries" and *The Service Sector in Soviet Economic Development*; and Gregory and Stuart, *Soviet Economic Structure and Performance*, Ch. 12.

15. For a discussion of index number relativity, see Bergson, *Real National Income of Soviet Russia Since 1928*, Ch. 3.

16. This result was noted first by Abram Bergson in "Development Under Two Systems: Comparative Productivity Growth Since 1950," *World Politics*, 20 (July 1971), 579–617.

17. Frederic Pryor, *A Guidebook to the Comparative Study of Economic Systems* (Englewood Cliffs, N.J.: Prentice-Hall, 1985), p. 78.

18. See, for example, Swamy, "Economic Growth in China and India," pp. 81–83; and Malenbaum, "Modern Economic Growth in India and China," pp. 45–84.

19. For a discussion of the measurement of static and dynamic efficiency, see Bergson, *Planning and Productivity Under Soviet Socialism*.

20. Edward Denison and William Chung, *How Japan's Economy Grew So Fast* (Washington, D.C.: Brookings, 1976), p. 30.

21. The classic treatment of the measurement of factor productivity is Edward Denison, *Why Growth Rates Differ* (Washington, D.C.: Brookings, 1967).

22. Apparently the Romanian and Bulgarian capital stock figures are in current prices. On this, see Alton, "Comparative Structure and Growth of Economic Activity in Eastern Europe," p. 223.

23. "Eastern Europe: Long Road Ahead to Economic Well-Being," Tables C-1 to C-21.

24. A considerable amount of research has gone into the subject of the relative growth of investment and consumption in Eastern Europe. Unfortunately, studies that cover the 1970s have not succeeded in calculating directly the real growth of investment. For a discussion of this point, see Alton, "Production and Resource Allocation in Eastern Europe," pp. 314–367. Also see Alton, "East European GNPs," pp. 94–98.

25. See the following studies of per capita consumption in the USSR and Eastern and Western Europe: Terence Byrne, "Levels of Consumption in Eastern Europe," in Joint Economic Committee, *Economic Developments in Countries of Eastern Europe*, pp. 297–315; and U.S. Congress, Joint Economic Committee, *Consumption in the USSR: An International Comparison* (Washington, D.C.: Government Printing Office, 1981).

26. Abram Bergson, "Comparative Productivity: The USSR, Eastern Europe, and the West," *American Economic Review*, 77 (June 1987), 342–357. For Bergson's earlier work on this subject, see his discussion of relative Soviet output per unit in Abram Bergson, *The Economics of Soviet Planning* (New Haven: Yale University Press, 1964), Ch. 14. Also see Bergson, *Production and the Social System: The USSR and the West* (Cambridge, Mass.: Harvard University Press, 1978).

27. This view is shared by Pryor, *Property and Industrial Organization in Communist and Capitalist Nations*, p. 80.

28. Padma Desai and Ricardo Martin, "Efficiency Loss from Resource Misallocation in Soviet Industry," *Quarterly Journal of Economics*, 98 (August 1983), 441–456. Also see Judith Thornton, "Differential Capital Charges and Resource Allocation in Soviet Industry," *Journal of Political Economy*, 79 (May/June 1971), 545–561. A useful summary of major studies can be found in Peter Murrell, "Can Neoclassical Economics Underpin the Reform of Centrally Planned Economies?" *Journal of Economic Perspectives*, 5 (Fall 1991), 59–76.

29. For comprehensive discussions of income distribution under capitalism and socialism, see P. J. D. Wiles, *Economic Institutions Compared* (New York: Halsted Press, 1977), Ch. 16; Martin Schnitzer, *Income Distribution: A Comparative Study of the United States, Sweden, West Germany, East Germany, the United Kingdom, and Japan* (New York: Praeger, 1974); and Abram Bergson, "Income Inequality Under Soviet Socialism," *Journal of Economic Literature*, 22 (September 1984); C. Morrison, "Income Distribution in East European and Western Countries," *Journal of Comparative Economics*, 8 (1984), 121–138. Anthony B. Atkinson and John Micklewright, *Economic Transformation in Eastern Europe and the Distribution of Income.* (Cambridge: Cambridge University Press, 1992).

30. See Pryor, *Property and Industrial Organization in Communist and Capitalist Nations*, pp. 74–75.

31. Ibid., pp. 74–89.

32. John R. Moroney, ed., *Income Inequality: Trends and International Compromise* (Lexington, Mass.: Heath, 1978), p. 5.

33. Janet Chapman, "Earnings Distribution in the USSR, 1968–1976," *Soviet Studies*, 35 (July 1983), 410–413.

34. See also a specialized study for the Soviet Union by Alastair McAuley, "The Distribution of Earnings and Income in the Soviet Union," *Soviet Studies*, 29 (April 1977), 214–237.

35. Harold Lydall, "Some Problems in Making International Comparisons of Income Inequality," in Moroney, *Income Inequality*, pp. 31–33. For recent analysis of the available evidence, see Anthony B. Atkinson and John Micklewright, *Economic Transformation in Eastern Europe and the Distribution of Income.*

36. Simon Kuznets, *Modern Economic Growth* (New Haven: Yale University Press, 1966).

37. For studies of socialist business and trade cycles, see C. W. Lawson, "An Empirical Analysis of the Structure and Stability of Communist Foreign Trade, 1960–68," *Soviet Studies*, 26 (April 1974), 224–238; G. J. Staller, "Patterns and Stability in Foreign Trade, OECD and COMECON," *American Economic Review* (September 1967); Josef Goldman,

"Fluctuations and Trends in the Rate of Economic Growth in Some Socialist Countries," *Economics of Planning*, 4, no. 2 (1964), 89–98; Oldrich Kyn, Wolfram Schrette, and Jiri Slama, "Growth Cycles in Centrally Planned Economies: An Empirical Test," Osteuropa Institute, Munich, *Working Papers*, No. 7 (August 1975); Gerard Roland, "Investment Growth Fluctuations in the Soviet Union: An Econometric Analysis," *Journal of Comparative Economics*, 11 (June 1987), 192–206. Pryor's results are in Pryor, *A Guidebook*, pp. 114–118.

38. P. J. D. Wiles, "A Note on Soviet Unemployment in U.S. Definitions," *Soviet Studies*, 23 (April 1972), 619–628. David Granick, *Job Rights in the Soviet Union: Their Consequences* (Cambridge, England: Cambridge University Press, 1987).

39. Morris Bornstein, "Unemployment in Capitalist Regulated Market Economies and Socialist Centrally Planned Economies," *American Economic Review, Papers and Proceedings*, 68 (May 1978), pp. 38–43; and Paul Gregory and Irwin Collier, Jr., "Unemployment in the Soviet Union: Evidence from the Soviet Interview Project," *American Economic Review*, 78 (September 1988), 613–632.

40. Authoritative discussion of official socialist price indexes and repressed inflation are found in Richard Portes, "The Control of Inflation: Lessons from East European Experience," *Economica*, 44 (May 1977), 109–129. For some empirical estimates, see Richard Portes and David Winter, "The Demand for Money and Consumption Goods in Centrally Planned Economies," *Review of Economics and Statistics*, 60 (February 1978), 8–18; and Martin J. Kohn, "Consumer Price Developments in Eastern Europe," in Joint Economic Committee, *East European Economic Assessment*, Part 2, pp. 328–347.

41. World Bank, *World Tables 1976* (Baltimore: The Johns Hopkins University Press, 1976).

42. For a summary of views, see "The Soviet Growth Slowdown: Three Views," *American Economic Review: Papers and Proceedings*, 76 (May 1986), 170–185.

43. See for example, Joseph S. Berliner, *The Innovation Decision in Soviet Industry* (Cambridge, Mass.: MIT Press, 1976).

44. Peter Murrell and Mancur Olson, "The Devolution of Centrally Planned Economies," *Journal of Comparative Economics*, 15 (June 1991), 239–265.

45. Abhijii V. Banerjee and Michael Spagat, "Productivity Paralysis and the Complexity Problem: Why Do Centrally Planned Economies Become Prematurely Gray?" *Journal of Comparative Economics*, 15 (December 1991), 646–660.

Recommended Readings

A. General References

Trevor Buck, *Comparative Industrial Systems* (New York: St. Martin's, 1982).

Irving B. Kravis, "Comparative Studies of National Incomes and Prices," *Journal of Economic Literature*, 22 (March 1984).

Irving B. Kravis, Allen Heston, and Robert Summers, "Real GDP Per Capita for More than One Hundred Countries," *Economic Journal*, 88 (June 1978).

Irving B. Kravis, *World Product and Income: International Comparisons of Real Gross Product* (Baltimore: Johns Hopkins University Press for the World Bank, 1982).

Frederic L. Pryor, *Property and Industrial Organization in Communist and Capitalist Nations* (Bloomington: Indiana University Press, 1973).

————, *A Guidebook to the Comparative Study of Economic Systems* (Englewood Cliffs, N.J.: Prentice-Hall, 1985).

B. Economic Growth

Thad P. Alton and associates, *Economic Growth in Eastern Europe 1970 and 1975–1985*, Research Project on National Income in East Central Europe (New York: L. W. International Financial Research, Inc., (occasional paper no. 90).

Abram Bergson, *Soviet Post-War Economic Development* (Stockholm: Almquist & Wicksell, 1974).

———, "The Soviet Economic Slowdown," *Challenge*, 21 (January–February 1978), 22–27.

Norman E. Cameron, "Economic Growth in the USSR, Hungary, and East and West Germany," *Journal of Comparative Economics*, 5 (March 1981), 24–42.

Stanley Cohn, "The Soviet Path to Economic Growth: A Comparative Analysis," *Review of Income and Wealth* (March 1976), 49–59.

Edward Denison, *Why Growth Rates Differ: Postwar Experience in Nine Western Countries* (Washington, D.C.: The Brookings Institution, 1967).

Padma Desai, *The Soviet Economy: Efficiency, Technical Change and Growth Retardation* (Oxford: Basil Blackwell, 1986).

———, "Soviet Growth Retardation," *American Economic Review Papers and Proceedings* 76 (May 1986), 175–179.

Stanislaw Gomulka, "Soviet Growth Slowdown: Duality, Maturity and Innovation," *American Economic Review Papers and Proceedings*, 76 (May 1986), 170–174.

Vladimir Kontorovich, "Soviet Growth Slowdown: Econometric vs. Direct Evidence," *American Economic Review Papers and Proceedings*, 76 (May 1986), 181–185.

Sima Lieberman, *The Growth of European Mixed Economies* (New York: Halstead Press, 1977).

Angus Maddison, *Economic Growth in Japan and USSR* (New York: Norton, 1969).

———, "Growth and Slowdown in Advanced Capitalist Economies," *Journal of Economic Literature*, 25 (June 1987), 649–698.

Wilfred Malenbaum, "Modern Economic Growth in India and China: The Comparison Revisited," *Economic Development and Cultural Change*, 31 (October 1982), 45–84.

C. Productivity

Abram Bergson, "Comparative Productivity: The USSR, Eastern Europe, and the West," *American Economic Review*, 77 (June 1987), 342–357.

———, *Planning and Productivity Under Soviet Socialism* (New York: Columbia University Press, 1967).

———, *Productivity and the Social System: The USSR and the West* (Cambridge, Mass.: Harvard University Press, 1978).

———, "Productivity under Two Systems: The USSR versus the West," in Jan Tinbergen et al., eds., *Optimum Social Welfare and Productivity: A Comparative View* (New York: New York University Press, 1972).

Padma Desai, "Total Factor Productivity in Postwar Soviet Industry and its Branches," *Journal of Comparative Economics*, 9 (March 1985), 1–23.

Padma Desai and Ricardo Martin, "Efficiency Loss from Resource Misallocation in Soviet Industry," *Quarterly Journal of Economics*, 98 (August 1983), 441–456.

Herbert S. Levine, "Possible Causes of the Deterioration of Soviet Productivity Growth in the Period 1976–80," in United States Congress, Joint Economic Committee, *Soviet*

Economy in the 1980s: Problems and Prospects, Part 1 (Washington, D.C.: United States Government Printing Office, 1982), 153–168.

Peter Murrell and Mancur Olson, "The Devolution of Centrally Planned Economies," *Journal of Comparative Economics*, 15 (June 1991), 239–265.

Gertrude Schroeder, "The Slowdown in Soviet Industry, 1976–1982" *Soviet Economy*, 1 (January–March 1985), 42–74.

Subramanian Swamy, "The Economic Growth in China and India, 1952–1970: A Comparative Appraisal," *Economic Development and Cultural Change*, 21 (July 1973), 1–84.

United States Congress, Joint Economic Committee, *USSR: Measures of Economic Growth and Development, 1950–1980* (Washington, D.C.: U.S. Government Printing Office, 1982).

———, *East European Economies: Slow Growth in the 1980s*, vols. 1–3 (Washington, D.C.: United States Government Printing Office, 1985).

Martin Weitzman, "Soviet Postwar Economic Growth and Capital–Labor Substitution," *American Economic Review*, 60 (December 1970), 676–692.

D. Technology

R. Amann and J. Cooper, eds., *Industrial Innovation in the Soviet Union* (New Haven: Yale University Press, 1982).

Abram Bergson, "Technological Progress," in Abram Bergson and Herbert S. Levine, eds., *The Soviet Economy Towards the Year 2000* (London: Allen & Unwin, 1983).

Joseph S. Berliner, *The Innovation Decision in Soviet Industry* (Cambridge, Mass.: MIT Press, 1976).

E. Income Inequality

Michael V. Alexeev and Clifford G. Gaddy, "Trends in Wage and Income Distribution under Gorbachev: Analysis of New Soviet Data," (Durham, N.C.: Berkeley–Duke Occasional Papers on the Second Economy in the USSR, # 25, 1991).

Anthony B. Atkinson and John Micklewright, *Economic Transformation in Eastern Europe and the Distribution of Income* (Cambridge: Cambridge University Press, 1992).

Abram Bergson, "Income Inequality under Soviet Socialism," *Journal of Economic Literature*, 22 (September 1984).

Janet Chapman, "Are Earnings More Equal Under Socialism: The Soviet Case, with Some United States Comparisons," in J. R. Moroney, ed., *Income Inequality: Trends and International Comparisons* (Lexington, Mass.: D. C. Heath, 1979).

———, Earnings Distribution in the USSR, 1968–1976," *Soviet Studies*, 35 (1983), 410–413.

———, "Income Distribution and Social Justice in the Soviet Union," *Comparative Economic Studies*, 31 (1989), 14–45.

John Moroney, *Income Inequality: Trends and International Comparisons* (Lexington, Mass.: D. C. Heath, 1978).

Martin Schnitzer, *Income Distribution: A Comparative Study of the United States, Sweden, West Germany, East Germany, the United Kingdom, and Japan* (New York: Praeger, 1974).

P. J. D. Wiles, *The Distribution of Income, East and West* (Amsterdam: North Holland, 1974).

F. Welfare Issues

Abram Bergson, "The USSR before the Fall: How Poor and Why?" *Journal of Economic Perspectives*, 5 (Fall 1991), 29–44.

M. Matthews, *Privilege in the Soviet Union* (London: Allen & Unwin, 1978).

Alastair McAuley, *Economic Welfare in the Soviet Union* (Madison: University of Wisconsin Press, 1979).

————, "The Welfare State in the USSR," in T. Wilson and D. Wilson, eds., *The State and Social Welfare* (London: Longmans, 1991).

G. Ofer and A. Vinokur, *The Soviet Household Under the Old Regime* (Cambridge: Cambridge University Press, 1992).

A. Vinokur and G. Ofer, "Inequality of Earnings, Household Income, and Wealth in the Soviet Union in the 1970s" in James R. Millar, ed., *Politics, Work, and Daily Life in the USSR* (Cambridge: Cambridge University Press, 1987).

Murray Yanowitch, *Social and Economic Inequality in the Soviet Union* (White Plains, N.Y.: M. E. Sharpe, 1977).

Appendix 12A:
The Index Number Problem in
International Comparisons

In this chapter we cited a large number of statistics comparing the level of GNP, output per worker, and so on, among capitalist and socialist countries.[1] For purposes of simplicity, we glossed over the fact that the price system that underlies the above valuations can have a substantial impact on the outcome. For example, for us to compare levels of GNP meaningfully, the GNPs of all countries being compared must be valued in some common currency (dollars, rubles, marks, pounds, whatever). These issues bear scrutiny since they are basic to international comparisons even in the 1990s as systems change.

Let us take the case of comparing the levels of GNP of the Soviet Union and the United States in 1980. To simplify the illustration, let us say that both countries produce only two goods, wheat and lathes. In the USSR, wheat is expensive relative to lathes; in the United States, wheat is cheap relative to lathes (as judged by Soviet prices). Production and domestic prices of these two commodities in each country are given in Table 15A.1.

From this information, we can make two types of calculations: We can calculate the GNPs of both countries using U.S. prices or we can calculate the GNPs of both countries using Soviet prices.

In U.S. prices, we get

$$\text{Soviet GNP} = (\$2 \times 10) + (\$2 \times 20) \quad \text{or} \quad \$60$$
$$\text{U.S. GNP} = (\$2 \times 30) + (\$2 \times 40) \quad \text{or} \quad \$140$$

Result: In U.S. prices, Soviet GNP is 60/140 = 43 percent of U.S. GNP.

In Soviet prices, we get

$$\text{Soviet GNP} = (5R \times 10) + (1R \times 20) \text{ or } 70R$$
$$\text{U.S. GNP} = (5R \times 30) + (1R \times 40) \text{ or } 190R$$

Result: In Soviet prices, Soviet GNP is only 70/190 = 37 percent of U.S. GNP.

The comparison is more favorable when the prices of the other country are used than when the country's own prices are used. Why is this typically the case? It is an empirical fact that the relative prices of any country tend to be inversely related to the relative quantities produced by that country. Products that can be produced relatively cheaply (because of abundant domestic resources) tend to be produced in abundance, and products that can be produced relatively expensively tend to be limited in production. Insofar as relative prices differ among countries (as a result of differences in human capital and natural resources), we find that each country emphasizes the production of relatively cheap commodities. Therefore, when the GNP of one country is valued using the different relative prices of another country, its total output appears relatively large.

To take a real-world example of this index number phenomenon, we can cite studies of Soviet per capita consumption as a percentage of U.S. consumption. In 1976, Soviet and U.S. consumption per capita were 1,116R and 4,039R, respectively, when valued in rubles. In other words, the Soviet Union stood at 28 percent of the U.S. level. Valued in dollars, Soviet and U.S. per capita consumption were $2,395 and $5,598, respectively; that is, Soviet consumption per capita was 43 percent of the U.S. level. Which figure (28 percent or 43 percent) is the correct one? There is no "true" value in such comparisons. One comparison is as real as the other, for each system of relative prices yields a different answer.

It should be noted that in the comparisons used in this chapter, we consistently use dollar valuations. Dollar valuations make Soviet and East European values look more favorable than they would have if, say, ruble prices had been used.

TABLE 12A.1

	Output		Price	
	Wheat	Lathes	Wheat	Lathes
Soviet Union, 1980	10	20	5R	1R
United States, 1980	30	40	$2	$2

Note

1. U.S. Congress, Joint Economic Committee, *Consumption in the USSR: An International Comparison* (Washington, D.C.: Government Printing Office, 1981), p. 6.

References

Trevor Buck, *Comparative Industrial Systems* (New York: St. Martin's, 1981), Ch. 5.

Irving B. Kravis et al., *A System of International Comparisons of Gross National Product and Purchasing Power* (Baltimore: The Johns Hopkins University Press, 1975).

Richard Moorsteen, "On Measuring Productive Potential and Relative Efficiency," *Quarterly Journal of Economics*, 75 (August 1981), 451–467.

PART IV

Economic Systems in Transition

13

Reform and Transition: The Basics

Chapter 4 examined general issues of systemic change including broad socioeconomic and historical perspectives. It also emphasized that neoclassical economic theory has traditionally paid little attention to change, especially the emergence and modification of institutions. Indeed for the field of comparative economic systems, attention to change was limited because the dichotomies of market capitalism and planned socialism seemed immutable. Although broad interpretations of the convergence hypothesis suggest that systems might become increasingly similar over time, limited systematic evidence supports this interpretation.[1] Moreover, it would seem that fundamental changes in, for example, the convergence of structures of different economies, did not in fact take place to any significant degree, despite the difficulties in measuring and assessing structural change.[2]

But the environment for examining economic systems has changed, necessitating a fundamental reconsideration of systemic change—a line of inquiry for which in the mid-1990s there is a growing body of practical experience with only limited theoretical underpinnings. Although it is possible to "learn by doing," as evidenced in the upcoming examination of Eastern Europe and the former Soviet Union, there are indeed broad similarities as well as important differences from case to case, for which we have only a relatively limited span of time for examination.

Economic Reform

Although we lack precision in the use of terminology, some basics deserve attention. The concept of **economic reform** traditionally refers to modifications of an existing system rather than the replacement of one economic system by another. Although boundaries between significant and insignificant past reforms are difficult to draw, classic examples of reform include the many attempts to change the planned socialist systems of the Soviet Union and Eastern Europe, such as the Kosygin reforms of 1965 in the Soviet Union and the New Economic Mechanism (NEM) introduced in Hungary in the late 1960s. Although these are only two examples, all such reforms have a number of common characteristics.[3]

The first similarity has to do with the manner in which the reforms arose and the forms they assumed. Western thought argues that in the planned socialist economic systems, reform programs were regime directed—that is, planners engineered reform on a relatively centralized basis within the existing political framework and constraints.[4] In that sense, reforms were indeed programs rather than ad hoc and ongoing modifications to systems and policies. Such modifications, it was argued, were more typical of change in market capitalist economic systems, though certainly in the capitalist case, the political leadership could bring forth major programs, for example, the great society programs of the Lyndon Johnson administration in the United States, the major thrust towards deregulation during Ronald Reagan's administration or the thrust towards privatization in Great Britain during Margaret Thatcher's era as prime minister.

Second, although the attempted reforms in the planned socialist systems might all be broadly described as reform programs, the content and origins of each differ considerably. For example, although orchestrated media campaigns are customary, the discussion of enterprise profitability in the Soviet media during the late 1950s and early 1960s revealed no perception of any mass involvement in change. In Eastern Europe, however, especially in Poland and Czechoslovakia, such involvement was more evident. Thus although there is a tendency to categorize reform in socialist versus capitalist economic systems, in fact significant differences within systems types did exist.

Third, many of the better-known reforms of the postwar era were all initiated because of lagging economic performance, and most were aimed at improving and encouraging decision making at the enterprise level. Both the Kosygin reforms in the Soviet Union and the NEM program in Hungary, though very different from each other, could nevertheless be characterized as a response to lagging economic performance. They both attempted to address what had long been broadly described as the "success indicator" problem in socialist enterprises.[5]

Socialist reform programs have a fourth common element, namely failure. But how is success judged? The success or failure of socialist reform programs was determined by whether the elements of the reform program were actually implemented, and whether the intended result—typically improved economic performance—could be observed. Unfortunately, from both perspectives, relating outcomes to programs proved to be very difficult for many statistical and methodological reasons. Although the data pertaining to reform implementation were never good, most observers argued that these reforms were in fact not implemented (although the controlled media typically argued the reverse) in the sense that prereform procedures and routines remained in place.

The Soviet Union of the 1960s, for example, attempted to decentralize investment down to the enterprise level because managers are best equipped to judge the amount and direction of investment that should take place within their enterprise. Subsequent evidence, however, showed that a decentralization of investment did not occur largely because the rules relating to investment were not changed and managers were unaccustomed to making such decisions in the setting of the administrative command system. To further confound the issue, the Soviet Union usually announced success with numbers that suggested that large shares of, say, industrial enterprises had switched to the "new system" when in fact little of substance had changed.

An examination of general performance indicators, such as the growth rate of output to judge the success of economic reform, also reveals methodological difficulties. If, for example, the rate of growth of output improved after a reform program was announced, how could we be sure that the reform program was in fact the cause of changed performance? We could look systematically at structural shifts in the economy, but for the most part, such shifts were modest, and it was difficult to relate these shifts to reforms. A close examination of economic trends in cases such as the Soviet Union in fact revealed little if any improvement following attempted reforms, which over time has led to the generally negative assessment of Soviet reform programs.

Despite such negative assessments, the Soviet economy clearly did change on a daily basis. In fact, during the era of Nikita Khrushchev, in the 1950s and early 1960s, many changes were attempted and some were successful. For example, fundamental changes were made in the organizational arrangements in agriculture, though Khrushchev's attempts to reorganize industrial planning from a sectoral to a regional basis did not survive after Leonid Brezhnev replaced him. But if the system changed to some degree over time, why did formal reform programs tend to fail?

Socialist Economic Reforms: Reasons for Failure

The failure of economic reform in the planned socialist systems are the result of a variety of forces, some of which remain relevant in the radically different 1990s. First, political factors were important. For example, the Soviet Union would not have permitted the reforms in Eastern Europe that were designed to move dramatically away from the planned socialist system. Moreover, even a country such as the Soviet Union had significant internal political differences that, though generally hidden from public view, nevertheless influenced the potential success of reform programs. Indeed, it has often been argued that the ouster of Khrushchev as Soviet leader in the early 1960s was directly related to a negative assessment of his penchant for change.[6]

Another reason for the failure of the reform programs is that they were often ill-conceived piecemeal efforts that would have likely been difficult to implement, even in the best of circumstances. The earlier example of the decentralization of investment is a case in point. While reformers might wish for such decentralization, there were no decentralized markets in which managers could directly and easily invest, let alone prices to serve as purveyors of useful information for decentralized decision making. Additionally, the incentive arrangements for managers precluded their interest in decentralized investment, because such a centralized system could quite likely disrupt, at least in the short run, the bonuses managers received for output increases.

Finally, attempts at reform failed because of the resistance to change. Such resistance might be very basic. For instance, as it was often argued, if the participants in the ministerial bureaucracy indeed did very well under the existing rules and systemic arrangements, why would they be interested in change? Managers have always been influenced by the prevailing incentive arrangements, a fact that unquestionably inhibits change, especially when that change is poorly thought out. For example, the lack of interest in technological change at the enterprise level could in part be explained by inappropriate incentive arrangements.[7] Thus if a manager were rewarded mainly for the expansion of output with little compensation for cost reduction or quality improvement, then a reform program that interrupts production would be rejected, even though the result might be a better product at a lower unit cost. In light of these characteristics of past reform attempts in the planned socialist economic systems, it is not surprising that a great deal of attention is given to the information about and incentive characteristics of such systems.

The changes to the former planned socialist systems in the 1990s have been dramatic and fundamentally different from those attempted earlier. Although the socialist systems generally performed poorly, many observers viewed their political control as substantial, providing a setting in which the prevailing economic system was not threatened. Conceivably, the convergence hypothesis—specifically the notion that socialist and market capitalist systems would become increasingly similar over time—might explain long-term modifications of planned socialist systems. And although these systems tended to be isolated from the structural adjustments dictated by world market forces, limited attention had been paid to the long-term implications of these facts. Indeed, there was a tendency to believe that if important systemic changes were to be made in an effort to face serious performance problems, they would probably be gradual, beginning largely within the agricultural sector to develop and to sustain popular support for change. As we now know, events of the 1990s have largely unfolded in different directions.

Transition

While past changes in planned socialist economic systems are generally considered **economic reform**, changes in the 1990s are seen as transition. The concept of **transition** refers to the replacement of one economic system with another. The contemporary example is of course the transition from plan to market in the former Soviet Union and the countries of Eastern Europe. The broad set of socioeconomic changes might be described as a general **transformation**. This definition must be inexact, in that a majority of system elements may be changed but without complete dismantling of old systemic elements. Moreover, because in most cases the transitions are in their relatively early stages of the transition process, the precise nature of these systems in, say, twenty years is as yet unclear. But as characterized by the system of classification developed in the early chapters of this book, the essence of transition is clear. Private property will replace public or state ownership, decision making will be decentralized from the upper levels of the state hierarchy to individual production units and instead of responding to planners decisions will increasingly be based on signals from markets and will be dominated by material incentives.

The contemporary literature on transition can be divided into several different but overlapping themes.[8] The **microeconomics of transition** typically focuses on privatization, the creation of markets, and the closely related issue of prices. The **macroeconomics of transition** generally refers to the role of the state and the guidance of the economy through the budget process and associated monetary and fiscal policies and more generally, the financial infrastructure. Both these topics are discussed in Chapter 14. Finally, two special topics, namely the issue of **international trade** and the development of a domestic **safety net**, which along with special sectoral issues such as agriculture, energy, and the military are the focus of attention in Chapter 15. The remainder of this chapter discusses general issues relation to the nature of transition.

Transition: Speed and Sequencing

The basic issues of transition can be conveniently divided in two—the **speed of transition** and the **sequencing of transition.** These aspects of transition are interrelated and therefore deserve attention.

In part because of Poland's experience with transition (which Chapter 18 examines in some detail), transition can either be identified as rapid, the so-called **big bang** approach, or slow, the so-called **gradualist** approach. In the absence of theoretical underpinnings to precisely isolate the costs and benefits of alternate paths of transition, much of the discussion of speed has focused on real-world variations. In fact, real-world events in the early 1990s have reduced the emphasis on a simpleminded dichotomy between the big bang and gradualist approaches and have turned the focus on degrees of variability in approaches and has varied the components of approaches in differing cases.[9]

The appropriate speed of transition seems to vary depending on a number of factors, most of which differ according to specific cases and natural (geographic) settings. First, one could argue that political instability provides an opening for change. If that opportunity is ignored, it will disappear. This argument seems appealing if one assumes that political instability is likely to be accompanied by poor economic performance and thus erosion of popular support for change. Certainly that was argued in the case of Russia where many felt that the end of the Yegor Gaidar era and the political turmoil surrounding Boris Yeltsin would cause retrenchment. At the same time, that argument assumes that a political authority is strong enough to enact retrenchment and to limit decentralized changes already in progress.

The starting point of a transition is another factor that affects its pace. The main issue here may be **stabilization**. Although the administrative command economies began their transition from a position of significant distortion, the nature, magnitude, and potential impact of this distortion is in fact a complex issue.

From contemporary experience, we know that transition can be characterized by the concept of the "J" curve.[10] Specifically, the collapse of the old economic system and its gradual replacement by new organizational arrangements and new policies has typically resulted in reductions of aggregate output and the decline of related indicators such as employment. More difficult to characterize, however, are the depth and length of the decline, the pattern of subsequent improvement, and the forces influencing these changes. In general, however, it has been argued that the transition is most difficult when the initial distortions are greatest.

For example, consider a case of structural distortion where the production of a particular industrial product is disproportionately large, or a case where factor proportions—the mix of capital and labor, for example—in production are out of tune with advanced world standards. In either situation, a transition can take a relatively long time. Production capacity can be converted, labor can be retrained, and restructuring can, in fact, take place, but such changes take time. On the other hand, consider a distortion characterized by significant macroeconomic imbalances.[11] Such as in the case of monetary overhang, in which, simply put, it was argued that prior to the collapse of the planned socialist systems, the population had excess purchasing power relative to the amounts of goods and services that could be purchased.[12] In that case, attention might initially be given to immediate stabilization rather than basic structural change. Thus to sustain a reasonable pace for the transition of an economy, it becomes important to immediately pursue short-term stabilization measures. It is not surprising that when prices are no longer controlled, price increases are initially large, while subsequent increases are less drastic. From the point of view of expectations and reaction to those expectations, the quick release of prices makes sense, even though the sudden readjustment creates difficulties for the population. Moreover, in most cases some price controls are sustained, such as in energy consumption.

Controlling inflation has been a serious problem in most transitions, with the possible exception of Hungary. After an initial burst of inflation, Hungary brought down price increases to reasonable levels and was also able to liberalize prices to change relative prices and thus shift resources from less effective to more effective uses.

If the case of inflation seems to support an element of the big bang for initial adjustment purposes, one could cite the collapse of the trading arrangements of the CMEA, the Socialist trading bloc, as an opposite case.[13] Clearly the quick collapse of the CMEA and the lack of an immediate replacement had an unfortunate and in some respects unnecessarily negative impact on the countries most directly involved. Thus the Soviet Union and the socialist systems of Eastern Europe collapsed along with the foreign trade arrangements of the Eastern bloc. The same can be said for the trading arrangements among the republics (now countries) of the former Soviet Union. As these countries began developing national and convertible currencies, initially trade among the former socialist countries was sharply reduced and reoriented toward the Western world. But to the extent that production in these former socialist countries was closely if artificially tied to trade among themselves, then a slower, more controlled pace of change would arguably have been more appropriate—that is, the impact of the collapse of trade on the decline of output could have been lessened.

The speed of transition may also be closely tied to the issue of **sequencing**. Sequencing is itself a complex issue. Fundamentally, if the ultimate goal is to connect price formation to market forces such that the resulting prices become meaningful indicators for resource allocation, does it make sense to free prices and allow them to fluctuate in the absence of markets and market institutions? If the answer if no, then privatization must proceed quickly along with the release of prices and the development of an appropriate market infrastructure including all of the legal and accounting mechanisms. Maybe the issue is even more complicated; possibly privatization must proceed such that the resulting industrial structure will be competitive! Clearly these demands of sequencing are unlikely to prevail in the real world, though simultaneously pursuing the beginnings of price liberalization and privatization is quite reasonable. The issue here is the nature of change, which is a separate and important issue.

Timing is another matter that can be related directly to a much more fundamental issue, namely the interpretation of how change actually takes place in the real world. Although Chapter 4 examined the broad perspectives of change, the issue here is quite focused: if the institutions of a market economy do, in fact, evolve slowly over time—that is, in an evolutionary manner—then it makes little sense to believe that the big bang can be anything more than an initial shock that may or may not be productive.

In fact, the dichotomy between the big bang and the gradualist approaches may be too simplistic. A big bang strategy may be quite appropriate for some part of the economy, or for various parts of the economy, for some limited period of time. However, fundamental change and the creation of new market institutions and infrastructures are much longer evolutionary processes, indeed, ones that may differ considerably from one economy to another. Moreover, as emphasized earlier in the discussion of change, a basic issue is whether the theoretical underpinning is appropriate for understanding change. Thus critics of neoclassical economic theory have argued that institutions and institutional change cannot be appropriately understood using this body of theory. Neoclassical economic theory postulates that rational maximizing agents achieve equilibria through time. An alternative paradigm, namely **evolutionary economics**, views institutions as complex arrangements developed by humans with inevitable limitations of knowledge and foresight.[14] Cast in the latter perspective, systemic change is much more likely to be understood as a continuing sequence of limited changes through which some end point (institutional structure) gradually emerges over time.

There is one final important issue related to both the timing and the sequencing of change. Consider this major reason for price liberalization. Price liberalization creates a set of market-type signals to which enterprise managers (among others) can respond when making decisions about resource allocation. Anyone familiar with the nature of enterprise management during the administrative command era knows that such a concept would be quite alien to managers. In that context, harmonizing change makes a great deal of sense. In fact, if economic agents are to respond to signals in the market economy, then a wide variety of preconditions and arrangements must exist. At minimum, the release of prices might be coordinated with privatization, restructuring, and the retraining of managers so they can respond appropriately to market-type signals.

Beyond Transition: Restructuring

Thus far some of the basic issues relating to the process of transition have been examined. However, transition is not simply the replacing of one set of institutions and policies with another. Thus, if an industrial enterprise once owned by the state is now owned privately, it may well be (especially in the short run) that no additionally changes other than equity arrangements have occurred. The concept of **restructuring** involves a myriad of associated changes that must take place after formal privatization has been completed and that will fundamentally alter the behavior of enterprises.[15] So defined, restructuring is critical to the success of transition efforts.

The transition cases of the early 1990s examined in this book have looked in part at privatization and the problems of carrying out privatization. The remainder of the decade will be about restructuring or the change of enterprise behavior. What sorts of behavioral change might be expected in the transition setting?

If property rights are appropriately defined through privatization, the entire managerial environment will change. Specifically, enterprise objectives will change and goal-achievement behavior will be formulated in response to decentralized market-type information signals. First, enterprise managers must increasingly face difficult budget constraints, and must make enterprise decisions based on myriad new financial variables. Second, enterprise financial analysis will be implicated by a new approach to factor markets, and especially factor substitution as costs and cost reduction become a critical management issue. Third, as managers respond to a new environment, the nature of existing products and more generally the product mix will likely change in response to information gathered from product markets.

In the long term, patterns of restructuring will be much more important than the short-term problems of changing equity arrangements, though the latter will obviously affect the former. But successful restructuring assumes the emergence of a new and appropriate managerial environment, responses to that new environment, and finally, a process of feedback to modify basic structures and policies.

Summary

This chapter has examined the concepts of economic reform and transition. Although these concepts are sometimes used interchangeably, it is useful to consider economic reform as modifications designed, for example, to improve the economic performance of that system. Transition, on the other hand, generally refers to the shift from one economic system to another, for example, the movement from plan to market in the former Soviet Union and the countries of Eastern Europe.

The concept of economic reform is used to describe the systemic and related changes attempted in the former planned socialist economic systems. These attempts at change, typically motivated by lagging economic performance (for example, the marked slowdown in economic growth), have been generally unsuccessful. Those failures can be attributed to the lack of political cohesion and motivation, faulty reform design, and the absence of population motivation to implement change that, in many cases, was not viewed as rewarding. Thus, while changes were made, systemic change was limited, economic performance continued to slip, and ultimately the systems collapsed.

Transition is a contemporary focus searching for a theoretical framework. Much interest centers on the speed of transition—should there be a rapid "big bang" approach or a slower "gradualist" approach? And how should the elements of transition be sequenced—must privatization first take place to develop markets to allow rational price formation, or can prices be freed with markets and the related market infrastructure developing later? Fundamentally, some have argued that neoclassical economic theory does not suitably explain systemic change. That suggests an alternative, evolutionary economics, focusing on the complexity of institutions and the limits of human capability for understanding and implementing change thereby considering evolutionary adjustment through time. The dichotomy of a big bang versus a gradualist approach therefore seems increasingly simplistic.

Ultimately the process of transition implies changes in basic system characteristics, while restructuring implies a set of more fundamental changes in which agents respond to new signals in different settings. As privatization is formally completed, a major component of successful transition in the future will be managers functioning in a new environment and responding to market signals, thus changing the nature of the enterprise and its operations.

Key Terms

economic reform

transition

transformation

microeconomics of transition

macroeconomics of transition

international trade

safety net

speed of transition

sequencing of transition

big bang

gradualist

stabilization

evolutionary economics

restructuring

sequencing

Notes

1. For a contemporary discussion of the convergence hypothesis, see Bruno Dallago, Horst Brezinski, and Wladimir Andreff, eds., *Convergence and System Change* (Brookefield, Vt.: Dartmouth Publishing, 1992).
2. Structural convergence refers to sectoral shares and their changes over time, for example, heavy industry, light industry, etc.

3. For a discussion of economic reform, see, for example, Paul R. Gregory and Robert C. Stuart, *Soviet and Post-Soviet Economic Structure and Performance*, 5th ed. (New York: HarperCollins, 1994), Chapter 12.

4. Ibid.

5. The expression "success indicator" derives from the long-standing difficulty of establishing unequivocally clear management incentive arrangements in traditional socialist enterprises, such as those of the former Soviet Union.

6. During the era of Nikita Khrushchev in the former Soviet Union a great many day-to-day changes took place in the economic system as well as in more formal and often grandiose reform programs. For a brief introduction to the Khrushchev era, see Paul R. Gregory and Robert C. Stuart, *Soviet and Post-Soviet Economic Structure and Change*, Chapter 6.

7. See, for example, Joseph S. Berliner, *The Innovation Decision in Soviet Industry* (Cambridge, Mass.: The MIT Press, 1976).

8. A useful source is Oliver Jean Blanchard, Kenneth A. Froot, and Jeffrey D. Sachs, eds., *The Transition in Eastern Europe*, vols. 1 and 2 (Chicago: University of Chicago Press, 1994).

9. See, for example, the discussion in Jozef M. van Brabant, "Lessons from the Wholesale Transformations in the East," *Journal of Comparative Economics*, 35 (Winter 1993), 73–102; Peter Murrell, "Evolution in Economics and in the Economic Reform of Centrally Planned Economies," in Christopher C. Clague and Gordon Rausser, eds., *Emerging Market Economies in Eastern Europe* (Cambridge, Mass.: Blackwell, 1992); Jim Leitzel, "Russian Economic Reform: Is Economics Helpful?" *Eastern Economic Journal*, 19 (Summer 1993), 365–378.

10. Josef C. Brada and Arthur E. King, "Is There a J-Curve in the Economic Transition from Socialism to Capitalism?" *The Economics of Planning*, 23 (1992), 37–52.

11. For a discussion of macroeconomic issues, see, for example, Ronald I. McKinnon, *Financial Control in the Transition from Classical Socialism to a Market Economy,"* *Journal of Economic Perspectives*, 5 (Fall 1991), 107–133; Roger H. Gordon, "Fiscal Policy During the Transition in Eastern Europe," in Oliver Jena Blanchard, Kenneth A. Froot, and Jeffrey D. Sachs, eds., *The Transitions in Eastern Europe*, vol, 2, pp. 37–70.

12. The issue of monetary overhang in the former planned socialist economies is a matter of considerable controversy. See, for example, I. Birman, "The Budget Gap, Excess Money, and Reform," *Communist Economies* (1990), 25–45; M. Alexeev, C. Gaddy, and J. Leitzel, "An Economic Analysis of the Ruble Overhang," *Communist Economies* (1991), 467–479; G. Ofer, "Budget Deficit, Market Disequilibrium and Soviet Economic Reforms," *Soviet Economy* (April–June 1989), 107–161.

13. See, for example, Jozef M. van Brabant, "Lessons From the Wholesale Transformation in the East," *Comparative Economic Studies*, 35 (Winter 1993), 73–102.

14. For a discussion of evolutionary economics as a framework for interpreting transition, see, for example, Peter Murrell, "Evolution in Economics and in the Reform of Centrally Planned Economies." The basic source is Richard R. Nelson and Sidney G. Winter, *An Evolutionary Theory of Economic Change* (Cambridge, Mass.: Harvard University Press, 1982).

15. See, for example, Oliver Jean Blanchard, Kenneth A. Froot, and Jeffrey D. Sachs, eds., *The Transition in Eastern Europe*, vol. 2; for a specific case, see, for example, Saul Estrin and Xavier Richet, "Industrial Restructuring and Microeconomic Adjustment in Poland: A Cross-Sectoral Approach," *Comparative Economic Studies*, 35 (Winter 1993), 1–20.

Recommend Readings

Jozef M. van Brabant, "Lessons From the Wholesale Transformations in the East," *Comparative Economic Studies*, 35 (Winter 1993), 73–102.

Josef C. Brada and Arthur E. King, "Is There a J-Curve for Economic Transition from Socialism to Capitalism?" *Economics of Planning*, 23 (1992), 37–51.

John Fender and Derek Laing, "A Macro Model of Queuing and Resale in a Transition Economy, *Comparative Economic Studies*, 35 (Summer 1993), 1–17.

Hans van Ees and Harry Garretsen, "The Theoretical Foundation of the Reforms in Eastern Europe: Big Bang versus Gradualism and the Limitations of Neo-Classical Theory," *Economic Systems*, 18 (March 1994), 1–13.

Norbert Funke, "Timing and Sequencing of Reforms: Competing Views and the Role of Credibility," *Kyklos*, 3 (1993), 337–362.

Paul G. Hare, "Economic Reform in Eastern Europe," *Journal of Economic Surveys*, 1 (1987), 25–58.

Janos Kornai, *The Road to a Free Economy* (New York: Norton, 1990).

Peter Murrell, "Can Neoclassical Economics Underpin the Reform of Centrally Planned Economies?" *Journal of Economic Perspectives*, 5 (Fall 1991), 59–76.

———, "Symposium on Economic Transition in the Soviet Union and Eastern Europe," *Journal of Economic Perspectives*, 5 (Fall 1991).

——— and Yijiang Wang, "When Privatization Should Be Delayed: The Effects of Communist Legacies on Organizational and Institutional Reforms," *Journal of Comparative Economics*, 17 (1993), 385–406.

A. Schipke and A. M. Taylor, eds., *The Economics of Transformation* (New York: Springer-Verlag, 1994).

Huizhong Zhou, "Behavior of State Enterprises in a Hybrid Economy with Imperfect Markets," *Economic Systems*, 18 (March 1994), 35–54.

14

Transition: Microeconomic and Macroeconomic Issues

Chapter 13 examined the broad issues of transition, relying on both theory and real-world situations to develop an understanding of relevant issues. This chapter turns to different aspects of transition, namely microeconomic and macroeconomic issues. Obviously there is considerable overlap between the two sets of issues. However, the distinction remains useful in order to isolate and understand the important components of transition.

The fundamental macroeconomic issue in transition is the stabilization of the economy as the old order collapses and new market-type institutions begin to emerge. Beyond the initial stages of stabilization, the focus is on a new role for the state and the associated development of new monetary and fiscal policies and institutions.

The fundamental microeconomic issue in transition is the development of markets, specifically factor markets, product markets, and financial markets. Although each type of market presents particular problems, proceeding with privatization, restructuring, the development of new institutional arrangements, and the legal infrastructure is necessary to guide and develop market mechanisms.

The Microeconomy: Privatization

The transition from plan to market implies that in the end, market forces, not central planners, will direct resource allocation. Although there is a lack of experience in the immediate creation of markets where none existed, it is widely argued that the most fundamental component of markets is the creation of **property rights** such that the basic elements of supply and demand, exchange, and therefore prices can emerge.

It is not surprising, therefore, that a major component of the literature on transition focuses on **privatization**. In the 1990s, however, it is important to bear in mind that privatization is a worldwide phenomenon, not a system change found only in those former command economies that are now creating markets.

Both **efficiency** and **equity** considerations drive privatization.[1] It is, moreover, based on differing perceptions of the appropriate role of government in the market economy. While **market failure** (for example the presence of externalities) is typically used to justify government intervention in the economy, one might argue that **government failure** would dictate a reduction of the role of government in the economy.

A major role of government in any economic system is redistribution based on equity considerations. However the redistribution patterns in a particular country may be characterized, efficiency considerations may lead to the production of merit goods, for example, by private enterprise.

Although the forces motivating privatization in different economic systems may be quite general, the privatization process itself differs in contemporary Western market economies and in the formerly planned socialist economies undergoing transition. In the case of market economies, privatization is pursued to achieve perceived benefits from a general reduction of public-sector activity, possibly a different pattern of redistribution, or a greater efficiency in the production of desired public-sector goods and services.[2]

Privatization in established market economies may involve changes in ownership, similar to the changes made in major sectors of the British economy during the Margaret Thatcher years.[3] But it may also involve changes in the way public goods and services are produced and financed or in the way the state intervenes in the market economy, such as the changes in the regulatory process that have occurred in the United States.[4]

Privatization in the formerly planned socialist systems implies primarily (though not exclusively) broad changes in equity or ownership arrangements: the transfer of property rights to enterprises, land, housing, and other assets from the state to individuals, and the subsequent management of those assets by individuals who are responding to market forces. In such cases, the fundamental motivation for privatization is to create a market economy and to gain efficiency from the better management of society's assets. However, beyond the obvious efficiency considerations are major considerations of equity in these broad privatization campaigns.

The mechanics of privatization in Western market economies are quite different from those in the contemporary transition cases. In the market economies, while there has been sale of state assets to the public, the more prevalent form of privatization in contemporary times is through some mechanism such as **contracting**. Such services might include trash collection or meals for the elderly.[5] In such instances of privatization, the state establishes specifications for those required services followed by some form of bidding and then the development of an appropriate contract with a private firm that will provide the appropriate services. The services may be funded by user charges, or they may be funded in traditional ways, through taxes or other state budgetary revenues.

In the formerly planned socialist economic systems, the process of establishing markets has generally been termed **mass privatization**.[6] In these systems, the problem has been the creation of private property rights in formerly state-held assets such as housing, industrial enterprises, land, and urban buildings. Since the state holds virtually all assets, the task of privatization is large and difficult.

In most transition cases, a state agency is created to determine the assets that will and will not be privatized. Thereafter, that agency generally oversees the privatization process, which can be carried out in a variety of ways.

Although assets can be distributed directly to the population (as apartments were in Russia), the more typical approach is to use **vouchers** and subsequently sell the asset either directly or through some form of **auction**.[7] The mechanics of the privatization process deserve additional attention.

If the legal basis of private property is established, the means of valuing assets are available, and the sources of capital are known, then changing ownership is not difficult. Unfortunately, in most contemporary transition cases, none of theses conditions are met. Although some of these conditions may be met for limited cases—for example, small businesses in the service sector—the privatization of large state enterprises is much more difficult but potentially very important. In light of these important sectoral differences, it is not surprising that much interest centers on the nature of privatization for large enterprises.

In the latter case, the state property fund identifies the enterprise(s) to be privatized. The next stage is **corporatization**, or the creation of a corporate structure with shares that can be sold to workers, managers, the general public, or external investors. In fact, the typical pattern in Russia has been the **employee buyout**, where those associated with the enterprise have access, through different purchasing variants, to the shares of the corporation.[8]

Individuals pay for the assets they wish to acquire either by directly purchasing them when the state property agency puts the particular asset up for sale, or by accumulating the appropriate amount of capital through some form of group arrangement. However, for many citizens in transition economies, access to these assets is more likely achieved through a voucher system. Voucher systems have differed considerably from one case to another, but fundamentally, citizens are given vouchers with a specified face value, for example, 10,000 Russian rubles in 1992.[9] These vouchers can then be used to gain ownership of, say, shares in an enterprise. The primary intent is that the vouchers will be traded for shares, either directly, through an auction, or indirectly, through an intermediary such as a mutual fund. In most cases, however, there is an active secondary market in vouchers, and some will sell them for cash, generally at a discount. In addition to facilitating mass privatization at a rapid pace, vouchers have a major political component because they provide access to state property for those who would otherwise not have the means to participate.[10]

Although one can find most varieties of privatization taking place in the transition economies with varying degrees of success, there are a number of difficulties that must be resolved.

First, in the transition from socialism, concerns about equity have created delays in the privatization process, especially in Eastern Europe.[11] Should those owners who held property prior to nationalization in the 1940s be able to exercise claims, and if so, how should this process proceed? Not only is it difficult to identify former owners in some cases, but there are also complex issues surrounding the changes made since nationalization. Voucher schemes may broaden the base of ownership, but they do not resolve that issue.

Second, the matter of valuation is complex. Even in a market economy, determining the value of an enterprise can be a difficult task. Yet in a market setting, using reasonable accounting procedures, the process is not impossible. In socialist enterprise, in the absence of markets and with accounting procedures providing little if any guidance, how are asset values determined?

Third, in countries where the level of per capita income is modest at best, how will buyers be found, especially in cases where capital markets don't exist? This is partially a sequencing issue in which it may be appropriate to create a minimal degree of infrastructure prior to privatization. But it is also an equity issue because many fear that those on the "inside" will gain access to valuable assets at prices well below their potential worth, in spite of the voucher mechanisms.

Fourth, as noted earlier, the process of privatization is very different in various sectors of the economy. For example, while privatization in the small-business sector has generally been quite rapid, the privatization of land and large state enterprises is more complicated and therefore much slower.

Finally, the process of privatization will of necessity proceed through a series of stages. The initial distribution of state property, however it takes place, may not conform with existing views of equity or efficiency. For example, it is evident that the holding of assets will be quite uneven, that resulting industrial structures may be far from competitive, and that criminal elements may be heavily involved. Moreover, the surrender of vouchers in exchange for shares of a corporate entity provides no funds for the corporation. Possibly most important, in an enterprise that proceeds through corporatization, merely changing ownership may not guarantee a change in the way the assets are managed in the absence of **restructuring**. Privatization changes the ownership arrangements for the assets of a firm, while restructuring changes the manner in which those assets are managed in the postprivatization era. Ultimately, transition will be judged by the success of restructuring.

In a new setting, managerial talent must be found and the internal guidance arrangements for enterprises must function in an economic system only partially transformed from plan to market arrangements. Following privatization, the goal is to change the working arrangements to reflect the influence of market forces, which will hopefully raise the level of efficiency.

The legal infrastructure so necessary for the effective functioning of an enterprise will likely be primitive. Also, there is no simple relationship between the nature of the privatization process and the resulting market structure. It may well be that substantial and inappropriate degrees of industrial concentration will occur in a setting where little or no regulatory intervention can be envisioned, at least in the short run.

The outcome of privatization in the formerly planned socialist economies is difficult to determine. It will be many years before substantive evaluations can be provided, and yet the preliminary evidence in Poland, the Czech Republic, and Russia can be instructive.[12] While Chapters 17 and 18 examine the details of these cases, some generalizations are relevant here.

The pattern and pace of transition have been uneven, though probably more rapid than might have been expected considering the difficulties faced. Familiar factors have influenced the pace of privatization, such as the nature of the industrial structure, the policies pursued, and the privatization mechanisms. Moreover, small-scale activities have generally been easier to privatize than large-scale enterprises. Although the percentage of economic activity that has been privatized in a sector of a particular economy can be identified generally, such data ought to be interpreted with caution, since they may only represent formal changes and may disregard resource allocation in a particular sector. However, with this caveat in mind, it is reasonable to generalize that privatization has moved unevenly but quickly, occurring most rapidly in the small-scale service sector and much more slowly in the industrial and agricultural sectors.

Initial studies seem to confirm the widely held view that while privatization is necessary and ongoing, in many cases restructuring has been slow, uneven, and much more difficult. Thus it is not unusual to find relatively large enterprises that have been corporatized and subsequently privatized but that have had only limited changes in their operational characteristics. That initial pattern in the transition cases seems to be quite different from the results of privatization elsewhere.

The Microeconomy: Prices and Price Liberalization

The major characteristics of the administrative command economy are that planning authorities in those systems set prices typically on some variant of an average cost basis. Such prices bore little or no relation to relative scarcities and were of limited or no use in the effective allocation of resources, though they did perform other functions such as accounting and control. Moreover, in such cases as wage setting, it was argued that market-type forces had some influence. In light of the substantial distortions of prices of almost all types, it is not surprising that an immediate focus of transition has been the **price liberalization**. The main initial problem in transition cases has been the need to liberalize prices, but in a setting where markets for the most part don't exist, a case where both equity and efficiency issues are at the forefront.

In most cases, prices were liberalized quickly although usually with a variety of controls sustained, for example in major sectors such as energy and for inputs such as labor where controls may be used to limit the growth of money wages. The inevitable result has been a sudden and sharp increase in prices, but with a subsequent slackening of the inflationary impact.

The Macroeconomy

One of the most fundamental differences between contemporary industrialized market economies and the former administrative command economies is found in the macroeconomic sphere. As previously emphasized, the planned economies functioned through direct plan commands, not through decentralized responses to market forces. In that setting, the typical components of a money–macro system were missing. The banking system was state owned and did not provide the services that would be expected in a market setting. The state controlled the money supply, and, in the absence of financial markets, the state budget, not macropolicy variables, controlled the behavior of state enterprises.

In such a setting, it is not surprising that the development of basic macroeconomic mechanisms would be a major challenge.[13] But there were additional problems. As the old order collapsed, the command economies increasingly lacked guidance because new arrangements were not in place. Moreover, most of these systems entered transition from positions of considerable distortion—for example, with significant misallocation of resources by sector—such that initial transition policies would have to focus on **stabilization**, not the more fundamental issues of economic growth and long-term stability. The extent of the distortions at the start influenced the sorts of policies instituted, the tools that might be developed and used, and the speed with which adjustments could be made.

In the long term, the former command economies must define a new and appropriate role for the state, a role that will probably differ considerably from country to country. In the short term, however, the budget and the banking structure are of immediate importance.

During the early phase of transition, the story is familiar. Traditional budget revenues derived directly through state-owned enterprises decline or disappear, necessitating the introduction of a set of appropriate taxes. Without such taxes and with major compliance problems where taxes are introduced, budget revenues shrink; however, the demands placed on the budget generally do not shrink. For example, there has been a general lack of willingness to end the **subsidization** of major sectors of the economy, while new demands, such as safety-net provisions in a shrinking economy, emerge. The imbalance between revenues and expenditures has generally been met by the excessive expansion of the money supply. The inevitable result is rapid inflation with severe distributional consequences, and a declining faith in the national currency. In this setting, the need is for a new tax system, expenditure control and the introduction of a "hard budget constraint" in industrial and other enterprises. One could expect these measures to be different from those taken in the long term as economic growth and stability become the priorities of **monetary** and **fiscal policies**.

In addition to fiscal changes in the economy, is the development of a banking system that is appropriate for the needs of a market economy. Rather than the monobank of the administrative command era, a system of banks will need to be developed to serve the emerging market economy. There are, however, several major problems. First, in the initial stages of transition, the banks themselves do not exist. Second, as banks emerge, they are frequently owned by enterprises (such as those in Russia), they are small (there were more than 1,600 banks in Russia in 1992), and their capitalization is typically inadequate. Third, steps must be taken to handle the large volume of existing enterprise debt and the use of directed credit. Finally, the infrastructure and the policies must be developed such that banks behave as banks do in a market environment, for example, extending credit based on economic rather than political considerations. What should be done?

A study in 1993 by the World Bank revealed that a core of well-managed banks should be created based on the International Standard Bank (ISB) program and with the necessary associated financial infrastructure, legal framework, generally accepted accounting and auditing standards, and an overhaul of the Russian payments system.[14] Most importantly, these recommendations focused on establishing basic banking practices, especially the use of directed credit as a component of monetary policy and as a device to provide liquidity so small banks can fund local activities.

Although the transition economies have had some success in the stabilization phase, the longer-term development of a set of macroeconomic arrangements and policies is a major challenge for the future.

Problems of the Social Safety Net

Safety net issues are both microeconomic and macroeconomic in character. They are especially important during transition, since the collapse of the old order and the initial absence of a new order is likely to increase the demands on many of the safety net programs. Many countries including the United States are reexamining the manner in which to provide broadly defined social benefits, but meanwhile these issues remain critical in the transition economies. Safety net programs include a wide variety of issues such as unemployment benefits, pensions, job retraining, and disability programs.

Although the actual benefits of the socialist safety net may have been overstated, they nevertheless were broad and came to be accepted by many as a basic feature of the social contract. As these countries move toward market arrangements, that contract is bound to change dramatically. Yet support for change must include some measure of social support.

As with other aspects of transition, safety net programs will inevitably differ from one case to another. A number of basic considerations, however, will apply in a variety of programs.

Initial studies have already indicated that standards of living in many of the transition countries are lower or much lower than were first estimated.[15] That fact, along with the decline in output and the sectoral and regional differences in that decline, motivate a need to understand existing living levels and minimal requirements. These conditions will differ; for example, unemployment and rural–urban distinctions in Poland will be different from regional issues in the vast territory of Russia.

With some knowledge of basic economic conditions, it is necessary to define a number of programs that are simple but that appropriately address such specific problems as unemployment. With the initial decline of economic activity, unemployment can be expected to increase, in such countries as Poland, by significant amounts. Safety net provisions may initially differ during the transition and stabilization era from those that are more expedient and effective over the long term.

Safety net programs must meet budgetary requirements. Obviously, the traditional socialist mechanisms will be eliminated and new arrangements implemented that have reasonable and stable sources of funding. Programs must be identified, participation and benefits defined, and record-keeping procedures developed. During the transition, programs will likely change, and the overall level and impact of such programs will differ considerably from the pretransition era. Most importantly, the mechanisms for developing, delivering, and paying for programs will change significantly.

Summary

In this chapter, the focus is on two core aspects of transition; namely, microeconomic issues (privatization and the development of markets) an macroeconomic issues (stabilization, development of a new role for the state, and associated monetary and fiscal arrangements).

Although privatization is a policy issue in a variety of different economic systems driven by both equity and efficiency considerations, the fundamental issue in the transition of the former socialist economies is the creation of private property through mass privatization. While private economic activity arises quickly in the service sector, the privatization of state property—for example, industrial enterprises—presents major challenges. Beyond preparing enterprises for sale, typically through a state property fund, a means for selling the assets must be established. Typical means have been direct sale, auctions or vouchers, the latter a means used to distribute equity more widely among the population.

The typical pattern for large enterprises has been corporatization, or the creation of a corporate structure (for example, a share structure) followed by the sale of shares (privatization) and finally restructuring. The latter step is especially important since it implies not simply a formal change of equity arrangements, but rather the implementation of new corporate decision-making arrangements and procedures to change the manner in which the enterprise operates.

The macroeconomic side of transition involves initial attention to price liberalization and stabilization, both of which are important but difficult for economies emerging from many years of non-market operation in the absence of market-type financial arrangements. Fundamentally, a new role for the state both as a provider of public goods and as a regulator of the newly emerging market economy must evolve. On the fiscal side, the end of a dominant state sector means that new sources of revenue must be found through new western style tax systems. On the expenditure side, the state must shift away from the traditional function of subsidizing loss-making enterprises towards the provision of basic public goods and especially safety net components: for example, unemployment insurance, pension benefits and medical care.

On the monetary side, the appropriate financial institutions must be developed, especially a modern banking system and associated financial markets, such that monetary policies (for example, with regard to the expansion of the money supply) can be developed and implemented. The objective is a fundamental change in patterns of resource use from sectors of low effectiveness to sectors of high effectiveness but with reasonable macroeconomic stability and with growth potential, specifically a reversal of the decline of output typical of the initial stages of transition.

Key Terms

property rights
privatization
efficiency
equity
market failure
government failure
contracting
mass privatization
vouchers
auction

corporatization
employee buyout
restructuring
price liberalization
stabilization
subsidization
monetary policies
fiscal policies
safety net

Notes

1. There is a large and growing literature on privatization. A useful presentation of basic issues can be found in Janet Rothenberg Pack, "Privatization of Public-Sector Services in Theory and Practice," *Journal of Policy Analysis and Management*, 6 (1987), 523–540.
2. Ibid., 528–532.
3. For a discussion of such cases, see, for example, William L. Megginson, Robert C. Nash, and Matthias van Randenborgh, "The Financial and Operating Performance of Newly Privatized Firms: An International Empirical Analysis," *Journal of Finance*, 49 (June 1994), 403–452.
4. See, for example, John B. Goodman and Gary W. Loveman, "Does Privatization Serve the Public Interest?" *Harvard Business Review* (November/December 1992), 26–38; John B. Donahue, *The Privatization Decision* (New York: Basic Books, 1989); Richard L. Worsnop, "Privatization," *CQ Researcher*, 13 (1992), 979–999.
5. Unfortunately, there is relatively little empirical evidence to assist in making the privatization decision in market economies.
6. For a useful discussion of microeconomic issues, see Jan Svejnar, "Microeconomic Issues in the Transition to a Market Economy," *Journal of Economic Perspectives*, 5 (Fall 1991), 123–138. For a general perspective on privatization, see Gerd Schwartz and Paulo Silva Lopes, "Privatization: Expectations, Trade-offs, and Results," *Finance and Development*, 30 (June 1993), 14–17; for a critical view, see Roman Frydman and Andrzej Rapaczynski, "Privatization in Eastern Europe: Is the State Withering Away?" *Finance and Development*, 30 (June 1993), 10–13.
7. There is a useful literature that examines the important cases. For discussion of the Russian case, see Lynn D. Nelson and Irina Y. Kuzes, "Evaluating the Russian Voucher Privatization Program," *Comparative Economic Studies*, 36 (Spring 1994), 55–68; Trevor

Buck, Igor Filatotchev, and Mike Wright, "Employee Buyouts and the Transformation of Russian Industry," *Comparative Economic Studies*, 36 (Summer 1994), 1–15; for a discussion of the Polish case, see Andrew Berg, "The Logistics of Privatization in Poland," in Oliver Jean Blanchard, Kenneth A. Froot, and Jeffrey D. Sachs, eds., *The Transition in Eastern Europe*, vol. 2 (Chicago: University of Chicago Press, 1994), 165–186; for a discussion of the former GDR, see Wendy Carlin and Colin Mayer, "The Treuhandanstalt: Privatization by State and Market," in Oliver Jean Blanchard, Kenneth A. Froot, and Jeffrey D. Sachs, eds., *The Transition in Eastern Europe*, 189–211; for a discussion of the Czech case, see Eva Marikova Leeds, "An Evaluation of the Czech Voucher Program," *Comparative Economic Studies*,

8. See Trevor Buck, Igor Filatotchev, and Mike Wright, "Employee Buyouts and the Transformation of Russian Industry."

9. For a discussion of the background to privatization in the Russian case, see Vladimir Shlapentokh, "Privatization Debates in Russia: 1989–1992," *Comparative Economic Studies*, 35 (Summer 1993), 19–32.

10. Lynn D. Nelson and Irina Y. Kuzes, "Evaluating the Russian Voucher Privatization Program."

11. Vladimir Shlapentokh, "Privatization Debates in Russia: 1989–1992."

12. For a discussion of initial evidence on restructuring, see, for example, Saul Estrin and Xavier Richet, "Industrial Restructuring and Microeconomic Adjustment in Poland: A Cross-Sectoral Approach," *Comparative Economic Studies*, 35 (Winter 1993), 1–20; Trevor Buck, Igor Filatotchev, and Mike Wright, "Employee Buyouts and the Transformation of Russian Industry." For empirical evidence, see William L. Megginson, Robert C. Nash, and Matthias van Randenborgh, "The Financial and Operating Performance of Newly Privatized Firms: An International Empirical Analysis."

13. See, for example, Ronald I. McKinnon, "Financial Controls in the Transition from Classical Socialism to a Market Economy," *Journal of Economic Perspectives*, 5 (Fall 1991), 107–122.

14. The World Bank, Russia: The Banking System During Transition (Washington, D.C.: The World Bank, 1993).

15. See Abram Bergson, "The USSR Before the Fall: How Poor and Why?"

Recommend Readings

A. The Microeconomy

William J. Baumol. "On the Perils of Privatization," *Eastern Economic Journal*, 19 (Fall 1993), 419–440.

Dieter Bös, "Privatization in Europe: A Comparison of Approaches," *Oxford Review of Economic Policy*, 9, 1 (1993), 95–110.

Trevor Buck, Igor Filatotchev and Mike Wright, "Employee Buyouts and the Transformation of Russian Industry," *Comparative Economic Studies*, 36 (Summer 1994), 1–16.

John D. Donahue, *The Privatization Decision* (New York: Basic Books, 1989).

Saul Estrin and Xavier Richet, "Industrial Restructuring and Microeconomic Adjustment in Poland: A Cross-Sectoral Approach," *Comparative Economic Studies*, 35 (Winter 1993), 1–20.

Roman Frydman and Andrzej Rapaczynski, eds., *Privatization in Eastern Europe: Is the State Withering Away?* (New York: Oxford University Press, 1994).

John B. Goodman and Gary W. Loveman, "Does Privatization Serve the Public Interest?" *Harvard Business Review*, (November/December 1992), 26–38.

Barbara G. Katz and Joel Owen, "A 'Big Mac' Approach to Denationalization," *Comparative Economic Studies*, 32 (Fall 1990), 82–92.

Sunita Kikeri, John Nellis, and Mary Shirley, *Privatization: The Lesson of Experience* (Washington, D.C.: The World Bank, 1992).

Raul Laban and Holger C. Wolf, "Large-Scale Privatization in Transition Economies," *American Economic Review*, 83 (December 1993), 1199–1210.

William L. Megginson, Robert C. Nash, and Matthias van Randenborgh, "The Financial and Operating Performance of Newly Privatized Firms: An International Empirical Analysis," *Journal of Finance*, 49 (June 1994), 403–452.

Peter Murrell, "When Privatization Should Be Delayed: The Effect of Communist Legacies on Organizational and Institutional Reforms," *Journal of Comparative Economics*, 17 (1993), 385–406.

———, "Evolution in Economics and in the Economic Reform of Centrally Planned Economies," in Christopher C. Clague and Gordon Rausser, eds., *Emerging Market Economies in Eastern Europe* (Cambridge, Mass.: Blackwell, 1992.

Janet Rothenberg Pack, "Privatization of Public-Sector Services in Theory and Practice," *Journal of Policy Analysis and Management*, 6 (1987), 523–540.

Andras Simon, "Privatization: An Analysis of the Absorption Problem," *Comparative Economic Studies*, 34 (Fall–Winter, 1992), 1–10.

Jan Svejnar, "Microeconomic Issues in the Transition to a Market Economy," *Journal of Economic Perspectives*, 5 (Fall 1991), 123–138.

Lynn D. Nelson and Irina Y. Kuzes, "Evaluating the Russian Voucher Privatization Program," *Comparative Economic Studies*, 36 (Spring 1994), 55–68.

OECD, *Employment and Unemployment Issues in Transition: Conceptual and Measurement Issues* (Paris: OECD, 1993).

———, *Methods of Privatising Large Enterprises* (Paris: OECD, 1993).

———, *Valuation and Privatisation* (Paris: OECD, 1993).

Paul J. J. Welfens, *Private Investment and Foreign Direct Investment in Transforming Economies* (Aldershot, England: Dartmouth Publishing, 1994).

B. The Macroeconomy

Philippe Aghion, Oliver Hart, and John Moore, "The Economics of Bankruptcy Reform," in Oliver Jean Blanchard, Kenneth A. Froot, and Jeffrey D. Sachs, eds., *The Transition in Eastern Europe* vol. 2 (Chicago: University of Chicago Press, 1994), pp. 215–240.

Roger H. Gordon, "Fiscal Policy During the Transition in Eastern Europe," in Oliver Jean Blanchard, Kenneth A. Froot, and Jeffrey D. Sachs, eds., *The Transition in Eastern Europe* vol. 2 (Chicago: University of Chicago Press, 1994), pp. 37–66.

Steve H. Hanke, Lars Jonung, and Kurt Schuler, *Russian Currency and Finance: A Currency Board Approach to Reform* (London and New York: Routledge, 1993).

Hansjorg Herr, ed., *Macroeconomic Problems of Transformation: Stabilization Policies and Restructuring* (Aldershot, England: Edward Elgar, 1994).

Ronald I. McKinnon, "Financial Control in the Transition from Classical Socialism to a Market Economy," *Journal of Economic Perspectives*, 5 (Fall 1991), 107–122.

———, *The Order of Economic Liberalization: Financial Control in the Transition to Market Economy* (Baltimore, The Johns Hopkins University Press, 1991).

Janet Mitchell, "Managerial Discipline, Productivity, and Bankruptcy in Capitalist and Socialist Economies," *Comparative Economic Studies*, 32 (Fall 1990), 93–137.

OECD, *Transformation of the Banking System: Portfolio Restructuring, Privatisation, and the Payment System* (Paris: OECD, 1993).

The World Bank, *Russia: The Banking System During Transition* (Washington, D.C.: The World Bank, 1993).

C. Safety Net Issues

Abram Bergson, "The USSR before the Fall: How Poor and Why? *Journal of Economic Perspectives*, 5 (Fall 1991), 29–44.

Ke-Young Chu and Sanjeev Gupta, "Protecting the Poor: Social Safety Nets during Transition," *Finance and Development*, 30 (June 1993), 24–27.

Christopher Mark Davis, "The Health Sector in the Soviet Union and Russian Economies: From Reform to Fragmentation to Transition," in United States Congress, Joint Economic Committee, *The Former Soviet Union in Transition* vol. 2 (Washington, D.C.: U.S. Government Printing Office, 1993), pp. 852–872.

Peter Diamond, "Pension Reform in a Transition Economy: Notes on Poland and Chile," in Oliver Jean Blanchard, Kenneth A. Froot, and Jeffrey D. Sachs, eds., *The Transition in Eastern Europe*, vol. 2 (Chicago: University of Chicago Press, 1994), pp. 71–103.

Murray Feshbach, "Continuing Negative Health Trends in the Former USSR," in *The Former Soviet Union in Transition*, pp. 840–851.

George Kopits, "Reforming Social Security Systems," *Finance and Development* 30, 2 (June 1993), 21–23.

OECD, *Unemployment in Transition Countries: Transient or Persistent?* (Paris, OECD, 1994).

George Schieber, "International Report: Health Care Financing Reform in Russia and Ukraine," *Health Affairs*, supplement, 1993, 294–99.

15

Problems of Transition: Foreign Trade, Energy, and Agriculture

The previous two chapters analyzed general issues of transition: sequencing, the distinction between macroeconomic and microeconomic aspects of transition, and the role of institutional changes such as privatization. This chapter addresses three specific problems of transition: the liberalization of foreign trade, the transition of production and of energy based on market principles, and the conversion of state and collective agriculture to private agriculture. While much of what has been said about the general issues of transition applies, these sectors have special problems that deserve additional attention.

International Trade During the Transition

Administrative-command economies have encountered acute problems when converting administratively planned trade to trade dictated by market principles. These problems arose largely because the administrative-command economy had not conducted international trade according to market practices, nor had it used the organizational arrangements and policies generally found in market economies. A **foreign trade monopoly**, consisting of a ministry of foreign trade, foreign trade organizations, and specialized banks, was responsible for managing international economic dealings. The national currency of the administrative-command economy was not **convertible**. Instead, **exchange rates** with other currencies were set by fiat, which resulted in domestic prices that had little relationship to world prices. Additionally, the flow of commodities was determined largely by **bilateral trade** agreements. As the administrative-command economies have all strived to achieve self-sufficiency, each has developed a wide range of domestic industries—heavy manufacturing, light manufacturing, and agriculture—and has avoided specialization. The structure of production was not what one would expect, given their different sizes, resource bases, and geographical settings.

The inconvertible currencies, arbitrary domestic prices, and lack of credit facilities dictated that each trading partner balance trade administratively. Therefore, the Soviet Union would sell to Bulgaria exports equal in value to the imports it received from Bulgaria. If either Bulgaria or the Soviet Union wished to decrease its imports to the other, the entire volume of trade would be limited.

The foreign trade monopoly negotiated trade agreements with other countries in both the East and the West, in which the end users or end suppliers were scarcely involved. When a piece of machinery was sold to another country, the domestic producer was paid in local currency at the local price. When a domestic business received a piece of equipment from abroad, that equipment was purchased by a centralized state agency, usually a **foreign trade organization** (FTO) not by procurement officials of the company.

The results of these trading arrangements led to uniformly underutilized trade potential in the administrative-command economies, a trade structure that could not be sustained in a market setting, and the lack of specialization in the domestic economy.

Trade Liberalization During Transition

As the administrative-command economies began their transitions to market arrangements, the old arrangements for foreign trade were among the first to change. The foreign trade monopoly crumbled in the late 1980s along with the planning apparatus. Without a planning system, it was not possible to plan foreign trade, and domestic enterprises pushed for freedom to engage in trade independently. Just as domestic buyers and sellers were free to work together directly, enterprises also gained the right to form their own business relationships abroad. Initially, however, the market-type mechanisms necessary to conduct trade in a new environment did not exist. Not surprisingly in this transition setting, the **volume of trade** actually decreased significantly.[1]

Increased freedom for domestic enterprises to make their own deals in foreign markets accompanied the collapse of the foreign trade monopoly. **Financial discipline** was another casualty as the authority of the state bank eroded. Strict controls over access to foreign exchange were removed, and citizens were increasingly allowed to acquire foreign currencies in private markets. Countries that previously had good payment records now found that often, inexperienced enterprise officials ordered more goods for import than could be paid for with available foreign currency reserves. Foreign debts from the administrative-command era could not be serviced, country credit ratings slipped, and international lenders had to reschedule debts, make emergency loans, and provide other concessions to bridge the shortage of currency.

With the collapse of administrative trade based on **bilateral agreements**, the former administrative-command economies had no choice but to move to trade based on **world-market prices**. For political reasons, sometimes trade continued to be conducted at **preferential prices**—such as trade relationships between Russian and specific former Soviet republics—but the transition saw a rather speedy move to world prices. No longer bound together militarily and politically, the former socialist trading partners saw no reason to part with goods at less than their opportunity cost—that is, the price the goods would command in the world market. Insofar as the prices at which trade had been conducted were artificial, the switch to world prices markedly altered the terms of trade, or the ratio of prices of exports to the prices of imports.

Although prior to the breakup of the Soviet Union there had been debate about who benefitted and who lost from administrative trading practices, the move to world prices had a negative impact on trade in Eastern Europe and the nonenergy-producing republics of the former Soviet Union and worked favorably for Russia and Kazakhstan, both of which are major suppliers of energy. Cheap energy and cheap raw materials were no longer available to the industries of those countries, making the transition to a market economy even more difficult. Table 15.1 shows the effect of the shift to world market prices on the former Soviet republics.

Such rapid shifts in the terms of trade reduced real income in those countries in which terms of trade were deteriorating and raised it in countries with improving terms of trade. The results of these shifts ranged from an 18 percent ceteris paribus increase in Russia's real GDP to a 16 percent decline in Moldava.[2]

TABLE 15.1   The Impact of Changing to World Market Prices: Terms of Trade for Republics of the Former Soviet Union (percentage change, based on 1990 data)

	Percent Change
Armenia	−24%
Azerbaidzhan	− 7%
Belarus	−20%
Estonia	−32%
Georgia	−21%
Kazakhstan	+19%
Kyrgyzstan	+ 1%
Latvia	−24%
Lithuania	−31%
Moldava	−38%
Russia	+79%
Tajikistan	− 7%
Turkmenistan	+50%
Ukraine	−18%
Uzbekistan	− 3%

Source: David Tarr, "The Terms of Trade Effects of Moving to World Prices on the Countries of the Former Soviet Union," *Journal of Comparative Economics*, Vol. 18 (February 1994), 12–13.

The collapse of the Communist bloc was accompanied by the collapse of the **Council for Mutual Economic Assistance (CMEA)**—the organization charged with promoting the economic integration among the administrative-command economies. Political change combined with economic change (particularly the move to world prices) to redirect world trading patterns. In 1953, the Soviet Union accounted for 82 percent of Eastern Europe's trade. By 1985, that had declined to 59 percent. By 1991, the Russian Federation's trade with the former members of the CMEA had fallen to 30 percent.[3] In fact, more than 60 percent of Russia's trade in 1991 was already with the capitalist West. Table 15.2 shows the dramatic swing of trade between the countries of Eastern Europe and the European Union. These figures demonstrate the enormous restructuring of trade that took place during the early years of transition.

The amount of restructuring that took place among the former republics of the Soviet Union was even more substantial. In 1990, more than 80 percent of the trade of the typical former Soviet Republic was with another Soviet republic. By the mid-1990s, these figures had already shifted dramatically. Russia, which had sold more than 60 percent of its exports within the Soviet Union, now sold more than 60 percent outside the former Soviet republics.

The **liberalization of trade** in the former administrative-command economies also required currency arrangements suited to market exchange. It had been argued that the transition would be assisted by a convertible currency. If trade takes place at world-market prices and currency can be freely converted, then factory managers and consumers can readily compare domestic prices with world prices through the exchange rate. When the domestic price differs from the world-market price, valuable economic information is lost.

Some countries of Eastern Europe, such as Poland and Hungary, liberalized restrictions of foreign currency transactions early on. Others, such as Russia and

TABLE 15.2   Restructuring Trade between Eastern Europe and
the European Union (EU)

	Percentage of Trade			
	Imports from EU		Exports to EU	
	1988	1993	1988	1993
Bulgaria	40.5	50.7	23.6	38.7
Czech Republic	26.5	46.3	24.2	46.6
Hungary	25.2	43.0	22.5	46.5
Poland	27.2	54.7	30.3	56.6
Romania	6.2	41.0	24.0	32.2

Source: International Monetary Fund, *World Economic Outlook*, (Washington, D.C.: IMF, May 1994), p. 75.

Ukraine, attempted to restrict such transactions, but economic reality gradually forced them to allow convertibility. Liberalized trade, moreover, created a two-currency economy in those countries that attempted to retain currency restrictions. A sometimes large portion of consumer spending went to the purchase of imported goods in hard currencies, whereas the average citizen continued to purchase domestic goods in domestic currency.

By the mid-1990s, a number of former administrative-command economies had both convertible currencies as well as stable currencies. The three Baltic states introduced their own currencies, which appreciated relative to the dollar and substantially to the Russian ruble. By the mid-1990s, virtually all the former administrative-command economies had convertible currencies. The major differences among these new currencies was whether the convertible currency was stable, relative to Western currencies (such as in the Baltic States), or was depreciating against hard currencies (such as in Russia and Ukraine).

Transition and Trade Policies

The former administrative-command economies must now establish trade policies for a market setting. Under the old system, **tariffs** and **quotas** were irrelevant because planners managed trade. In a market setting, however, each of the former administrative-command economies must determine the wisdom and desirability of protection. The former CMEA members have entered the market era in international trade facing considerable protection against their products. They are competing for the European market—the **European Union**—which has removed most tariffs for member countries. Accordingly, the only choice, particularly for Eastern Europe, appears to be integration into the European Union (EU).[4] The potential for trade increases remain substantial. As of 1989, the countries of Eastern Europe and the Soviet Union were meeting less than half of their export potential to Europe.[5]

Integration into Western trading unions has created problems for both the West and for the former CMEA countries. If the CMEA countries enter into such markets without significant tariff and nontariff-barrier protection, many domestic industries will be unable to compete. The structural distortions from the old regime (too much investment in agriculture and in heavy industry) now mean that many plants and entire industries will have no rationale for existence. Yet membership in the EU requires adoption of rules that do not allow for such protection.

For the West, such as the EU, admission of former CMEA countries requires that the union pay for a portion of the restructuring losses in agriculture and in industry. According to the EU's existing rules, admission of Poland, Hungary, and the Czech Republic to the EU would require some $20 billion in transfer payments to these countries for structural assistance.[6]

Transition and Capital Flows

This examination of the former planned socialist economies has paid little attention to **capital flows** because international trade was largely in goods and services because of the ownership arrangements of these systems. However, the structural transformation of the former CMEA countries requires substantial capital investments. Under the old administrative-command economy, investment finance was provided internally, most of it directly through the state budget. The administrative-command economy operated with strict budgetary discipline. State revenue mainly came from the tax on state enterprises and sales taxes. When central discipline collapsed and production declined during the early phase of transition, state revenue declined and the traditional source of investment finance dried up.

The substantial capital expenses of the transition have made it necessary for the CMEA countries to look to the West for private and public capital. Private capital requires an appropriate investment climate. Public capital—in the form of **grants** and **soft loans**—requires political agreement and consensus.

One of the most difficult challenges of the transition period is to create an investment climate to attract private investment. Political uncertainty, an untested regime of commercial law, and unstable currencies, among other things, deter private investment. Unfortunately, the transition period is indeed characterized by just such phenomena. Moreover, the old system was managed by seasoned bureaucrats who were experienced in such matters, while the transition has necessarily brought to the force new faces who have had little experience with international dealings.

The transition experience of the late 1980s to the mid-1990s has shown that private capital cannot be attracted in reasonable amounts during the early stages of transition. However, once the initial transition difficulties have passed and rules of law have been established, private capital can indeed be attracted. Such has been the case in Hungary, Poland, and the Czech Republic—areas international investors now consider to be promising "developing markets." All three countries have succeeded in attracting **venture capital** and have even experienced stock-market booms (some of which have been followed by busts). The Baltic States have also succeeded in establishing stable currencies and a sufficient reputation for rule of law so that they may be the next "developing market" regions for international investors.

The remaining areas of the former CMEA—the underdeveloped countries of Eastern Europe and the former republics of the Soviet Union—have yet to develop a climate suitable for private international investment. They remain politically unstable, they have not developed stable currencies, they continue to have macroeconomic instability problems, and foreign investors do not feel that there are sufficient legal protections for their investments. Rules and laws change too rapidly, and investments do not appear to be secure. Table 15.3 shows the limited flow of foreign direct investment into Eastern Europe and the former Soviet Union. Only Hungary has succeeded in attracting a reasonable volume of foreign direct investment on both a total and a per capita basis.

An unfavorable climate for private investment means that most of the former CMEA countries depend on public assistance for needed capital. The industrialized West has not been particularly generous with foreign assistance to the region. As of June 1992, the former Soviet republics have drawn a total of $44 billion in economic support from the $96 billion that had been committed between 1990 and 1992.[7] That commitment represents some 0.006 percent of the donor countries' GDP.

TABLE 15.3   Foreign Direct Investment into the former Soviet Union and Eastern Europe and Registered Joint Ventures, 1993

	Foreign Direct Investment and Registered Joint Ventures		
	$ Millions U.S.	$ Per capita	Joint Ventures
Eastern Europe			
Bulgaria	$ 44	$ 5	1200
Czech republic	561	75	3700
Hungary	1200	130	15311
Poland	580	11	6300
Former USSR			
Estonia	86	46	4052
Latvia	50	18	2072
Lithuania	40	7	2638
Kazakhstan	300	15	n.a.
Russia	666	5	5249
Ukraine	225	4	2400
Uzbekistan	100	5	n.a.
Total	4630*	11[†]	

*This figure includes Romania, the Slovak Republic, and the former Yugoslavia.
[†]Dollars per capita.

Source: *European Economy*, Supplement A, no. 3, March 1994, p. 5.

Why has the West been so stingy with its public assistance? First, donors have wished to tie assistance to the commitment to real reform. Assistance granted without such strings as requiring privatization or macroeconomic austerity could be used to slow the pace of transition by supporting failing industries or by preventing prices from rising to world levels. Second, public assistance has been used as a lever to force leaders whose commitment to reform may be half-hearted to make hard political decisions. In 1993, for example, when the liberal Russian government of Egor Gaidar and Boris Fyodorov was removed, Western economic support was put on hold until the new government demonstrated its commitment to reform. Political issues relating to the Chechen issue have further complicated Western aid discussions in 1994 and 1995. Third, most public assistance takes the form of repayable loans. International lenders, even if they are international organizations, want to ensure that the loans will be repaid. International organizations, such as the World Bank and the European Bank for Reconstruction and Development, must examine the commercial viability of projects for which the funds are being committed. They have been deterred by the same factors that deter private investment.

Transition and Energy

The transition to a market-based energy industry creates both general transition and industry-specific problems. The general transition problem is that a market-based system must recognize energy's true opportunity cost—the world-market price. Because the administrative-command economies administratively allocated energy to users at artificially low prices, industrial structures, not surprisingly, used energy inefficiently. Administrative methods, supported by artificial prices, meant that energy-intensive technologies and capital were used in industry and agriculture. A shift to world-market prices in energy would render these industries noncompetitive in a market environment and would severely complicate the transition process.

Specifically, the disruptions caused by the transition have severely reduced energy production in the former Soviet republics of Russia, Azerbaidzhan, and Kazakhstan. If the former Soviet Union had not been the world's largest producer of oil and gas (as well as a major producer of coal), energy resources would not have been treated so cavalierly by the administrative-command economies. That Russia, Kazakhstan, and Azerbaidzhan were such major producers and exporters allowed Soviet planners to use this energy to create an **energy-intensive** industrial base both at home and in the other CMEA countries.

This discussion focuses on the specific transition-related problem of restoring production. The general problem of transition—the correction of distortions in the industrial structure—is addressed elsewhere.

Energy Production Under the Old Regime

Administrative methods were used to manage Soviet mineral and oil/gas resources for more than 60 years. Government bodies, such as the USSR Council of Ministers or the State Planning Commission, working in conjunction with the Communist Party, formulated basic targets for oil and gas industries. These targets were then translated into concrete tasks by the oil and gas ministry, which handed down specific production, supply, and delivery targets through their various departments to the producing enterprises and associations. The state budget supplied investment, and enterprises tended to operate at losses because of the artificially low delivery prices for crude oil and natural gas. A state trade monopoly handled exports, which were purchased from enterprises at low wholesale prices and sold at world-market prices; the difference went into the state budget.

Directors of oil concerns were responsible for meeting output and delivery targets. These directors, who received their material and equipment inputs from unreliable central supply organizations, were little interested in profits or in hard currency sales. They were occasionally promised a small share of hard currency sales, but central authorities usually reneged on these promises. Oil company directors were mainly concerned with keeping their work force in place and meeting government output and delivery targets. Within that framework, the ministry was extremely powerful. It assigned output and delivery targets and allocated supplies and equipment to the enterprises.

Between 1985 and 1991, the administrative-command system broke down. At first the breakdown was gradual, but then it accelerated, especially after 1988. The ministries, which had been the backbone of the system, lost their power over enterprises. Central planning organizations, such as Gosplan, became superfluous.

Enterprises received newfound freedoms, but price controls and continued restrictions on foreign sales and currency accounts prevented them from exercising this freedom. The breakdown of the administrative-command system created the worst of all worlds—the old system that had provided some degree of order but at very low levels of efficiency had disappeared, but no market system had been established in its place. The result was chaos and, in the energy industry, a substantial drop in output.

As the old system collapsed, the state kept key controls that it felt were necessary to prevent total collapse. These controls or levers consisted of **licensing controls** and **currency controls**. In response to the external debt-servicing crisis, confiscatory taxes were levied on all hard-currency earnings; that created a situation in which enterprises capable of earning hard currency were better off selling at inflated domestic prices. Confiscatory taxes on currency basically destroyed the incentive to earn currency, thereby worsening the currency crisis. Investment dried up as the central budget collapsed. The petroleum industry, left without investment, saw its production decline. The lack of attention to repairs and upkeep caused productive wells to shut down and the transportation infrastructure to deteriorate. Table 15.4 shows the decline in Russia's crude-oil production during that period.

The decline in crude-oil production presented Russia and the other petroleum-producing republics with a problem: how to restore and revitalize its oil and gas industry. The general consensus was to create a market-based energy industry that would provide sufficient stability and incentives to attract the billions of dollars of foreign investment and know-how to revitalize the industry. Another opinion suggested restructuring Russia's oil industry to make it capable of operating in a market environment. That internal restructuring was based on the notion that Russia had to create integrated oil companies—companies like Royal Dutch Shell and Exxon that handle the industry from the wellhead to the gas pump. Several such integrated companies were indeed formed in the 1990s and, in fact, one such company, Lukoil, appears to be a growing power in the international petroleum market.

TABLE 15.4   Russia's Crude-Oil Production

	Thousands of Barrels per Day
1985	10,840
1987	11,380
1989	11,440
1990	10,320
1991	9,220
1992	7,900

Source: *Handbook of International Economic Statistics 1993*, p. 127; Charles Malin, "Russian Energy Policy—A View Towards the Future," The Atlantic Council, *Energy Policies for Russia and the Ukraine*, March 1993.

The Legislative Framework

Russia conceded that it needed to enact legislation that would promote a market economy in its petroleum industry. Such legislation would serve as a model for other industries and would create the stable framework necessary to attract foreign investment. The passage of such legislation, however, required resolution of the following problems.[8]

Presumably, one feature of a market-oriented petroleum law would be to allow producers to sell at world prices. Russian oil officials, even those with strong reform leanings, had to consider the impact of a 3,000 or 4,000 percent increase in domestic energy prices (if world prices are used as a standard for domestic prices) on an industrial economy based on cheap energy. As the price of oil was gradually adjusted, some sales would take place at world-market levels, others at controlled prices. Administrative controls would therefore be required to "force" oil producers to meet domestic needs. In that situation, any law that gave energy producers freedom to select output levels and deliveries would drive out voluntary deliveries at the lower domestic price. Some type of administrative regulation had to remain in effect until prices are totally decontrolled.

Petroleum legislation would have to sort out property relations. Even if all mineral resources initially remained public property, intense political battles between the center, the region, and the locality would have to take place before these issues were decided, because local areas always want access to the revenues derived from what they view as local resources such as oil. Indeed, beginning in 1991 a continuous power struggle was waged among the center, region, locality, and even the production associations over the ownership of petroleum or gas deposits. It will be difficult to restore production until property relations are defined, yet the resolution of that issue will determine the distribution of wealth in Russian society. Western investors also cannot be expected to commit substantial funds until they can be sure that property rights are defined.

Russian authorities, even those who strongly believe in market economies, have trouble imagining that markets can allocate resources in a rational manner. There is great fear of the unknown. Can the market really be trusted to get energy to households and to plants in a particular region? What happens when things start going wrong? These are deep and strongly ingrained concerns that are reflected in legislative attitudes toward enterprises. Can these enterprises really be trusted to make the right decisions? Maybe they need to be told what to produce and to whom to sell? Maybe they should have only limited freedom at the margin? Other decisions should be made for them. Under the old system, such fears of enterprise autonomy were legitimate. Managers could not be trusted when prices and the "rules of the game" were irrational. A key test of the desire to go to a market economy is the willingness to give producing enterprises freedom to make output, input, and sales decisions.

Russian authorities believe that monopoly will be a severe problem during the initial phases of market operation of the Russian oil industry. The administrative-command economy created an industry production structure and transportation infrastructure dominated by a few producers. The presence of a monopoly during the early stages, in fact, has been used as a strong argument for going slowly or not going at all. Reform opponents continue to argue that the administrative system must first create a competitive industrial structure before market reforms can take place.

The administrative-command system gave little attention to the efficiency implications of pricing and taxation decisions. After all, decisions were made administratively; accordingly taxation and pricing systems had little effect on economic outcomes. Russian officials have long felt that prices should play a "social" role— widows should not have to pay high prices for coal or fuel oil, consumers should be able to buy meat at one ruble per pound, and so forth. Taxes are to gather revenue not to cause producers or consumers to behave in a rational manner. It will be difficult for Russian authorities to drop the notion that prices and taxes should be considered in terms of their effects on economic efficiency rather than on social concerns.

Although most Russian prices have been decontrolled, price controls remain a fact of life for the Russian petroleum industry. Other prices are less visible to end users and to industrial users than energy prices. Therefore, the political pressure has been strong to retain price controls. In December 1992, the domestic prices of oil and gas were 20 percent and 2 percent, respectively, of the world price. By May 1994, those percentages rose to 38 percent and 33 percent of the world price.[9]

No mineral or oil and gas laws can be written in isolation from other laws that form the legal framework of Russian society. Energy laws must conform to the constitution, to property laws, and to umbrella laws. Rational behavior assumptions embedded in a petroleum law may be based on privatization laws or tax and currency laws that have yet to be finalized. Petroleum laws must therefore be made to fit into the broader matrix of creating the entire legal framework.

The time necessary to pass mineral and petroleum legislation is instructive as a guide to the amount of lag involved in creating necessary legislation for a market transition. Russia's Law on Underground Resources was passed in February 1992 after more than a year's preparation and debate. That law was followed by the passage of concession laws and licensing regulations in 1993. The petroleum law scheduled for passage in 1991 had not been approved by the Russian parliament in mid-1994.

Energy and Foreign Investment

As of mid-1994, Russia had yet to create a stable environment to attract substantial amounts of foreign investment. Although a number of landmark deals were nearing closure, the actual amount of foreign investment in Russia's oil industry remained minimal. The tax regime remains undefined. Without knowing how profits would be taxed, what excise and export fees would be levied, Western companies could not predict the after-tax return on their investment. **Property rights** remained poorly defined with the struggle between the federal, regional, and local governments over property rights continuing. As noted earlier, domestic crude oil and natural gas prices remained well below world-market prices, which meant that administrative interference would remain a fact of life.

Transition: The Problems of Agriculture

The agricultural sector, like energy, also poses an industry-specific transition problem for the former administrative-command economies. Agricultures' transition problems include establishing improved management and ownership arrangements and restructuring to meet the demands of a market economy.

The administrative-command economy has left a lasting imprint on the agricultural sector. Agricultural output had been produced mostly by large state or collective farms and not by private landowners. In the case of the **state farm**, the land was clearly the property of the state and farm workers were employees of the state. In **collective farms**, land was held collectively, but individual workers had no real equity stake in that ownership, nor did they have decision-making power at the local level. Both forms of agricultural production unit were integrated into the state-planning and material–technical supply systems. The state farm received investment funds from the state budget, while the collective farm was more responsible for raising its own investment funds.

The majority of the administrative-command economies had a history of private ownership in agriculture. However, the major republics of the former Soviet Union, such as Russia and the Ukraine, had little experience with private land ownership.

The administrative-command economy also left behind a legacy of relatively high shares of output and a labor force that produced agriculture inefficiently. Although some of the former administrative command economies may have a long-term comparative advantage in agriculture, each of these economies tried to achieve self-sufficiency in agriculture. The result was that despite considerable investment relatively larges share of the labor force were required in agriculture.

Although there were important differences among the various republics, the Soviet model of **collectivization** generally prevailed. However, since the collapse of the Soviet Union, differences between collective and state farms seemed to disappear. These perceptions of an inefficient agriculture dominated by state influence explain why many observers expected agriculture to be an early candidate for transition to new arrangements. Such improvements in production, processing, and distribution of food product could immediately benefit the population therefore generating support for the difficult process of transition. As we know, the story of transition has been different from those expectations. The emphasis instead was placed on industry and services, not agriculture. Nevertheless, the potential impact of the change in agriculture remains great.

The transition problems the agricultural sector must tackle include improving the incentive system, creating private property, and making structural adjustments to improve the efficiency and to reduce the relative share of resources devoted to that sector.[10]

Agriculture: The Contours of Change

In some respects, patterns of change in agriculture are less-well-defined than those in industry.[11] However, in all of the former Soviet-type economies, the role of the state must be reduced, especially in the large state subsidies. Privatization and associated organizational changes will lead to important changes in the decision-making arrangements, especially decisions relating to output determination and input usage. It will also be necessary to develop the infrastructure to support production units, in the form of markets for inputs, social support programs for the rural population, and processing and distribution facilities.

The extent of land privatization in Russia has been limited, though legislation developed in 1991 promoted change in the organizational arrangements of land varying from individual peasant farms to the development of joint-stock arrangements of the former collective and state farms.[12] Thus far, however, the impact of these sorts of changes has been small.[13] In other cases, associated problems of transition are emerging. For example, in the former German Democratic Republic, a relatively stable political environment, the problems of changing ownership arrangements and releasing excess labor from the agricultural sector have presented both social and economic difficulties.[14] In Hungary, a mixed picture of agricultural transition emerges that involves progress in the late 1980s followed by difficulties identifying and developing new property rights, and especially regarding problems of indebtedness.[15] Romania seems to have had some success in the development of new land holdings and organizational arrangements (including forming individual farms into associations), however, the adjustment to emerging market forces has been more difficult.[16]

Thus far, it appears that the transition in agriculture has generally been uneven and difficult. It has not been easy to remove the state's involvement in agriculture production, and even where new organizational arrangements and ownership patterns have emerged, the impact of market forces has been limited and uneven. These early developments suggest that restructuring of the agricultural sector will be a slow and difficult process.

Summary

This chapter has focused on three areas that have had special problems with the transition from plan to market: foreign trade, energy, and agriculture. In all three situations, the special sectoral features of the administrative command era have presented important problems in the transition era.

In foreign trade, the organizational arrangements for conducting trade, the policies followed, and the absence of convertible currencies resulted in a variety of distortions in foreign trade patterns and arrangements. The breakdown of the old order effectively changed and decentralized decision making in the foreign trade sector, leading to the gradual introduction of world-market forces as well as the collapse of bilateral trade agreements and a significant decline in the volume of trade. A major change in foreign arrangements has been the development and implementation of various exchange-rate regimes, which eventually led to convertibility of the currency or its free conversion to foreign currencies at prevailing market rates of exchange.

The liberalization of trade raised new problems: the need to develop tariffs and quotas along with issues relating to capital flows, including foreign direct investment, loans, and aid grants of various types.

Under the old regime, energy production was fully controlled by the state, which provided end users with energy at artificially low prices that created a wasteful energy-intensive technology. However, the demise of the administrative-command economies led to the virtual collapse of the energy sectors. In Russia, which has been a major energy producer, steps were taken to develop the energy sector based on market principles that used foreign capital but that also included substantial state controls over such issues as energy prices.

The transition of agriculture in the former administrative-command economies has been rather different from what had been expected prior to the collapse of the old regimes. In most cases, the Soviet-style model of collective and state farms had been used, although there were important variations in Eastern Europe. However, rather than moving rapidly with agriculture as a vanguard of transition, in most transition cases the focus has been on industry, while agriculture is evolving more slowly.

The tasks involved in the transition of the agricultural sector include reducing the major role the state played during the socialist era, changing ownership and organizational arrangements, and developing the infrastructure necessary for agricultural production (including processing and distribution) to be conducted within the framework of market forces. In most of the contemporary transition cases, progress in agriculture has been slow. Even when new ownership arrangements and new organizational forms have emerged, the development of market forces has been slow and difficult. Restructuring will most likely be both slow and uneven.

Key Terms

foreign trade monopoly
convertible currency
exchange rate
bilateral trade
foreign trade organization (FTO)
volume of trade
financial discipline
bilateral agreement
world-market prices
preferential prices
council of mutual economic assistance (CMEA)

liberalization of trade
tariffs
quotas
European union
capital flows
grants
soft loans
venture capital
energy intensive
licensing controls
currency controls

property rights   collective farm
state farm   collectivization

Notes

1. See Arye Hillman, "The Transition From the CMEA System of International Trade," in
   Michael Keren and Gur Ofer, eds., *Trials of Transition: Economic Reform in the Former
   Communist Bloc* (Boulder, Colorado: Westview Press, 1992), pp. 271–290.
2. David Tarr, "The Terms of Trade Effects of Moving to World Prices on Countries of
   the Former Soviet Union," *Journal of Comparative Economics*, Vol. 18 (February 1994),
   1–24.
3. These figures are from *Handbook of International Economic Statistics* (selected years)
   and from *Narodnoe Khoziaistvo Rossiiskoi Federatsii 1992* (*The National Economy of
   the Russian Federation, 1992*), p. 49.
4. See Paul Welfens, "The EU Facing Economic Opening Up in Eastern Europe: Problems,
   Issues, and Policy Options," Conference on European Integration as a Challenge to
   Industry and Government, University of Muenster, July 8 and 9, 1994.
5. R. Baldwin, *Towards an Integrated Europe* (London CPER, 1994).
6. Welfens, p. 27.
7. *Handbook of International Economic Statistics 1993*, p. 205.
8. This discussion is based on the following sources: "Symposium: The Russian Petroleum
   Legislation Project at the University of Houston Law Center," *Houston Journal of International Law*, vol. 15 (Winter/Spring 1993); George Hardy III, "Energy Law and Policy
   in the Russian Federation: A Western Perspective," Atlantic Council, *Energy Policies
   for the Newly Independent States of the Former Soviet Union*, April 1993.
9. A. Makarov and D. Shapot, "The Basics of Pricing and Taxation Policy in the Russian
   Energy Industries," Atlantic Council, *Energy Policies for Russia and the Ukraine*, July
   1994.
10. For an analysis of East European agriculture in the era prior to transition, see Michael
    L. Boyd, *Organization, Performance & System Choice: East European Agricultural
    Development* (Boulder: Westview Press, 1991).
11. For some observations, see Karen Brooks, J. Luis Guasch, Avishay Braverman, and
    Csaba Csaki, "Agriculture and the Transition to the Market," *Journal of Economic
    Perspectives*, 5 (Fall 1991), 17–32.
12. For a discussion, see S. K. Wegren, "Dilemmas of Agrarian Reform in the Soviet
    Union," *Soviet Studies*, 44, 1 (1992), 3–36; Paul R. Gregory and Robert C. Stuart, *Soviet
    and Post-Soviet Economic Structure and Performance*, 5th ed. (New York:
    HarperCollins, 1994), Chapter 13.
13. For a critical view, see Robert McIntyre, "The Phantom of Transition: Privatization of
    Agriculture in the Former Soviet Union and Eastern Europe," *Comparative Economic
    Studies*, 34 (Fall–Winter 1992), 81–95.
14. Leila Sfeir Lueschen, "Collective Farms in Transition in the Former German Democratic
    Republic," *Comparative Economic Studies*, 36, 2 (Summer 1994), 33–50.
15. Michael Marrese, "Progress in Transforming Hungarian Agriculture," *Comparative
    Economic Studies* 33 (Summer 1991), 159–177.
16. Karen Brooks and Mieke Meurs, "Romanian Land Reform: 1991–1993," *Comparative
    Economic Studies*, 36 (Summer 1994), 17–32.

Recommended Readings

A. International Trade

R. Baldwin, *Towards an Integrated Europe* (London: CPER, 1994).

United States Congress, Joint Economic Committee, *The Former Soviet Union in Transition* vol. 1, part II. (Washington, D.C.: U.S. Government Printing Office, 1993).

Juergen B. Donges and Jurgen Wieners, "Foreign Investment in the Transformation Process of Eastern Europe," *The International Trade Journal* 8, 2 (Summer, 1994), 163–91.

Kenneth A. Froot, "Foreign Direct Investment in Eastern Europe: Some Economic Considerations," in Oliver Jean Blanchard, Kenneth A. Froot, and Jeffrey D. Sachs (eds.), *The Transition in Eastern Europe* vol. 2 (Chicago: University of Chicago Press, 1994), 293–318.

Arye Hillman, "The Transition From the CMEA System of International Trade," in Michael Keren and Gur Ofer (eds.), *Trails of Transition: Economic Reform in the Former Communist Bloc* (Boulder: Westview Press, 1994).

D. Gale Johnson, "Trade Effects of Dismantling the Socialized Agriculture of the Former Soviet Union," *Comparative Economic Studies* 35, 4 (Winter, 1993), 21–32.

John Pinder, *The European Community and Eastern Europe* (New York: Council on Foreign Relations, 1991).

Dani Rodrik, "Foreign Trade in Eastern Europe's Transition: Early Results," in Oliver Jean Blanchard, Kenneth A. Froot and Jeffrey D. Sachs, *The Transition in Eastern Europe* vol. 2 (Chicago: University of Chicago Press, 1994), 319–52.

Alan Smith, *Russia and The World Economy: Problems of Integration* (New York: Routledge, 1993).

David Tarr, "The Terms of Trade Effect of Moving to World Prices on Countries of the Former Soviet Union," *Journal of Comparative Economics* 18, 1 (February, 1994), 1–22.

B. Energy

George Hardy III, "Energy Law and Policy in the Russian Federation: A Western Perspective," *Atlantic Council, Energy Policies for the Newly Independent States of the Former Soviet Union*, April, 1993.

Office of Technology Assessment, *Energy Efficient Technologies for Central and Eastern Europe* (Washington, D.C.: U.S. Government Printing Office, 1993).

A. Makarov and D. Shapot, "The Basics of Pricing and Taxation Policy in the Russian Energy Industries," Atlantic Council, *Energy Policies for Russia and the Ukraine*, July, 1994.

Symposium: The Russian Petroleum Legislation Project at the University of Houston Law Center, *Houston Journal of International Law*, 15, 2 (Winter/Spring, 1993).

United States Congress, Joint Economic Committee, *The Former Soviet Union in Transition* vol. 2, part IIIA (Washington, D.C.: U.S. Government Printing Office, 1993), 461–90.

C. Agriculture

Michael L. Boyd, *Organization, Performance & System Choice: East European Agricultural Development* (Boulder: Westview Press, 1991).

A. Braverman and J. L. Guasch, "Agricultural Reform in Developing Countries: Reflections for Eastern Europe," *American Journal of Agricultural Economics* (December, 1990), 1243–51.

Gregory J. Brock, "Agricultural Productivity in Volgograd Province," *Comparative Economic Studies*, 36, 1 (Spring, 1994), 33–54.

Karen Brooks, J. Luis Guasch, Avishay Braverman, and Csaba Csaki, "Agriculture and the Transition to the Market," *Journal of Economic Perspectives* 5, 4 (Fall, 1991), 149–161.

Karen Brooks and Mike Meurs, "Romanian Land Reform: 1991–1993," *Comparative Economic Studies*, 36, 2 (Summer, 1994), 17–32.

Karen Brooks, "Price Adjustment and Land Valuation in the Soviet Agricultural Reform: A View Using Lithuanian Farm Data," *European Review of Agricultural Economics*, 18 (1991), 19–36.

Elizabeth Clayton, "Agricultural Privatization in Transition Economies," *Comparative Economic Studies* 34, 1 (Spring, 1992), 86–92.

D. Gale Johnson, "Trade Effects of Dismantling the Socialized Agriculture of the Former Soviet Union," *Comparative Economic Studies*, 35, 4 (Winter, 1993), 21–32.

Leila Sfeir Lueschen, "Collective Farms in Transition in the Former German Democratic Republic," *Comparative Economic Studies*, 36, 2 (Summer, 1994), 33–50.

United States Congress, Joint Economic Committee, *The Former Soviet Union in Transition*, vol. 2, part IIIB (Washington, D.C.: U.S. Government Printing Office, 1994), 491–566.

William M. Liefert, Robert B. Koopman and Edward C. Cook, "Agricultural Reform in the Former USSR," *Comparative Economic Studies* 35, 4 (Winter, 1993), 49–68.

Robert McIntyre, "The Phantom of Transition: Privatization of Agriculture in the Former Soviet Union and Eastern Europe," *Comparative Economic Studies* 34, 3–4 (Fall–Winter, 1992), 81–95.

Michael Marrese, "Progress in Transforming Hungarian Agriculture," *Comparative Economic Studies* 33, 2 (Summer 1991), 159–77.

OECD, *Review of Agricultural Policies: Hungary* (Paris: OECD, 1994).

———, *The Soviet Agro-Food System and Agricultural Trade: Prospects for Reform* (Paris: OECD, 1992).

———, *Policy Reform, Economic Growth, and China's Agriculture* (Paris, OECD, 1993).

David J. Sedik, "A Note on Soviet Per Capita Meat Consumption," *Comparative Economic Studies*, 35, 3 (Fall 1993), 39–48.

Don Van Atta, "Declining Soviet/Russian Per Capita Meat Consumption: A Comment," *Comparative Economic Studies* 35, 4 (Winter 1993), 69–71.

PART V

Moving Toward a Market Economy

16

The Russian Economy

The breakup of the Soviet Union at the end of 1991 allowed the 15 Soviet republics to become independent countries of which **Russia** is the largest. In terms of land area, Russia represents roughly 76 percent of the former Soviet land mass, 70 percent of its population, and the bulk of oil production.

Examination of the contemporary Russian economic system is complicated by the fact that, as with other transition cases such as those studied in Chapter 18, the Russian economic system is in a state of change. But because of its size, past development experience, and contemporary political and economic importance, Russia is the most important case of transition from plan to market.

The pattern of study of real-world systems this book has followed examines the natural setting, past development experience, and the contemporary economic system in terms of both performance and restructuring. A similar pattern is followed for Russia, with one exception. The administrative command economy of the Soviet era, which was discussed in Chapter 12, must be understood in order to appreciate the contemporary difficulties of transition.

Russia: The Natural Setting

Russia is by far the largest of the former Soviet republics, and, as a new and separate nation, it remains a country with great economic potential. At the beginning of this decade, Russia had a population of just fewer than 150 million, 75 percent of whom lived in urban settings, and of those, many had substantial educational and career achievements.

The breakup of the Soviet Union changed the balance of resources among the former republics. Russia is now the most wealthy of those republics, because of its substantial supplies of many basic natural resources, ranging from oil to timber and minerals. The issue is not reserves, but rather using those resources in a manner that helps improve the standard of living of the Russian people.

The vast Russian landscape is geographically diverse; its northerly location encompasses wide natural and climatic variations with substantial land areas that are relatively inhospitable. These facts have dictated and will continue to dictate the nature and location of economic activity, especially agricultural production.

The immense size of Russia is important in another respect. As Chapter 12 emphasized, the economic system of the Soviet era was centralized, as was its political power and will to develop and execute economic policies.[1] That centralized system had a major influence on the nature of resource allocation. As Russia moves toward a decentralized market economy, both economic and political power will shift from upper to lower levels. These new emerging arrangements will create a very different sectoral and regional pattern of economic activity than that which previously prevailed. Such changes, however, will emerge slowly over a long span of years.

Russia: Economic Reform

The discussion of the administrative command economy in Chapter 12 emphasized that this system was in place for many years, since 1928. Thus, to the extent that resource allocation patterns of Russia in, say, 1991 did not reflect those of market forces, major changes could be anticipated. Moreover, one might expect such changes more difficult to develop and to implement in Russia (and for that matter in the other former Soviet republics) than in Eastern Europe where the planned socialist economic system lasted a relatively short time. The impact of the past on the transition process and the way one case differs from another remains to be seen.

For the Russian economy, change began before the events of the late 1980s and early 1990s. Important changes took place even during the Stalin era; however, Russian economic reform in the post-World War II era focused on regime-directed programs designed to improve the working arrangements of the planned economy. In the late 1950s and early 1960s, a variety of modest reforms were attempted that had relatively little impact on either Soviet working arrangements or economic performance.[2]

The contemporary reform that attracted the most attention was **perestroika** or restructuring, begun with the ascendancy of Mikhail Gorbachev to head the Soviet Union in 1985.[3] This economic reform program, along with its political counterpart of **democratization** and social counterpart of **glasnost**, or openness, brought forth wide-ranging changes in the old Soviet order. Unfortunately, these changes failed to improve economic performance and led to the end of the Soviet economic and political systems. In some respects, the attempted reforms of Perestroika suffered from the same problems associated with earlier Soviet reform efforts. But many viewed these latest reforms as exciting and capable of rationalizing the Soviet economic and political systems in a new era.

Perestroika was motivated by declining performance of the Soviet economy. By the mid-1980s, the Soviet economy, like other planned economies, had years of declining rates of growth and major productivity problems. Declining economic performance was attributed to serious information and incentive problems of the command system. Indeed, when Gorbachev announced the beginnings of Perestroika, he suggested that his new policies would cure what he termed the "period of stagnation" (*zastoia*) that characterized the Brezhnev era, especially during its latter period of the 1970s and 1980s. In addition to emphasizing technological change, by open-ing the economy to the external world and improving internal enterprise decision-making rules, Gorbachev placed great reliance on what he termed the "human factor," an attempt to bring back the enthusiasm displayed by the Soviet citizens in the early 1930s. However, with many years of unkept economic promises, stimulat-ing the population to greater effort would prove to be impossible.

Unlike earlier superficial reforms, perestroika was of greater significance be-cause it was **radical economic reform**, combined with an opening of Soviet society (glasnost) and increased citizen participation through democratization. The sense that this economic reform was genuine initially created enthusiasm for change.

Although the first years of perestroika had no comprehensive reform program and could be described as "tinkering," those years soon produced major legislative acts that were designed to make fundamental changes in areas of the command economy.[4] It was soon apparent that the era of perestroika would be different from the superficial programs of the past.

Possibly the most fundamental aspects of perestroika were the changes in enterprise rules, the reduced role of the state in the guidance of enterprises, and the increased freedoms in foreign trade.[5] The legislation of perestroika made state enter-prises self-financing, semi-independent production units that enjoyed new autonomy as a result of state orders replacing plan directives. Enterprises received greater freedom to set their own prices, and contracting among enterprises replaced the material–technical supply system. Cooperative enterprises took up the slack in the lagging retail and service sectors. In the foreign trade sector, the structure of trading organizations was simplified and the monopoly of the Ministry of Foreign Trade ended.[6] Enterprises were granted the right to directly enter foreign trade. In addition, legislation permitted the development of joint ventures between Soviet and Western firms.

Through the late 1980s, a great deal of new legislation passed. For example, foreign trade was markedly liberalized on such critical issues as foreign ownership, repatriation of profits, and joint management arrangements. In other areas, such as the development of cooperatives and new land laws, the new legislation was very conservative. Initially, the cooperatives were limited to small service-sector opera-tions that were severely limited in hiring labor or having access to capital. Gorba-chev showed little interest in the concept of private property and price reform, both of which were critical to making real changes in the allocation procedures.

Although one can criticize perestroika as less than a complete, poorly sequenced and coordinated reform program (for example, reform of decision-making arrange-ments without price reform), nevertheless if the legislative decrees had been fully implemented, they would have changed the nature of the Soviet economy. However, traditional problems of resistance to reform emerged as managers implemented some changes and ignored others. Indeed, there was so much legislation during this period that it became difficult to know which rules and laws applied to what cases. The result was an attempt to implement changes that could not be successful in isolation. The traditional system began to disintegrate, and toward the end of the decade re-trenchment was attempted. The net result of perestroika was the worst of all worlds.

It destroyed the old system without creating a cohesive new one. By the end of the 1980s, confusion prevailed.

Table 16.1 presents some basic performance indicators for the perestroika era. Although the economy improved somewhat during the first two years of perestroika, the reform began to crumble in 1989. At the time, observers attributed declining performance to the incomplete nature of the reform, overemphasis on the human factor, sequencing problems, and implementation lags. The Soviet command system was markedly weakened during these years, even though re-centralization was attempted in response to lagging performance in the latter part of the decade.

The beginning of the new decade was a time of pivotal economic and political change. Through 1990, the discussion was increasingly on *transition* rather than reform, as major transition programs, such as the so-called 500-day plans, were developed and discussed.[7] Although these plans were limited in many ways, they were very different from earlier reform programs, because they were reasonable comprehensive and they specified a specific timetable, including the sequencing of key changes. In addition, they called for fundamental change in such areas as prices and privatization. Put another way, these transition programs fundamentally envisioned a shift to a market economy (transition) rather than reform of existing institutions.

The performance problems of the Soviet economy became increasingly more serious in 1990 and 1991. Following the coup of August 19, 1991, Mikhail Gorbachev resigned as head of the Communist Party on August 25, effectively bringing the power of that body to an end. Thereafter, the republics of the Soviet Union began to declare their independence from Moscow, and by December of 1991, the Soviet Union came to an end. Boris Yeltsin, the leader of a new Russia, had been active on the economic front and was prepared to move quickly in the new era.

TABLE 16.1　The Soviet Economy under Perestroika

	Average annual rate of growth				
	1986	1987	1988	1989	1990
Gross national product[a]	4.1	.3	2.2	1.4	−2.0
Per capita consumption[b]	−2.1	0.4	3.0	3.2	
Consumer price index:					
（1980 = 100）	111.0	116.0	119.0	122.0	139.0
Soviet exports[c]	97.0	107.7	110.7	109.3	104.1
Soviet imports[c]	88.9	96.0	107.3	114.7	120.9
Net hard-currency debt[d]	20.9	26.4	26.8	36.1	45.4

[a] GNP is measured by sector of origin at factor cost in 1982 prices.
[b] 1982 established prices.
[c] Includes all trade, in billions of current U.S. dollars.
[d] Gross debt minus assets in Western banks, in billions of curent U.S. dollars.

Source: Directorate of Intelligence, *Handbook of Economic Statistics 1990* (Washington, D.C.: CIA, 1990), and *Beyond Perestroika: The Soviet Economy in Crisis* (Washington, D.C.: CIA, 1991).

Russia: The Transition to Markets

As the Soviet Union entered its final days in 1991, Boris Yeltsin's influence became increasingly apparent. By October 1991, Yeltsin had unveiled a **transition** plan that focused on macroeconomic **stabilization**, the freeing of prices, the expansion of foreign trade, and the privatization of factories.[8] These steps were fundamentally more aggressive than those Gorbachev developed under perestroika, though during the early months of transition, political turmoil and a generally recalcitrant population limited the transition process and its initial achievements.[9] It is important to reemphasize, that political stability is a critical necessity in order to fully implement transition programs. Political stability in the Russian case has been precarious at the central level as well as at the regional and local levels.

In January 1992, there was a general **liberalization of prices**, with important exceptions, such as in the energy sector. At the same time, foreign exchange was liberalized, trade restrictions removed, and an effort made to achieve budget balance through new taxes and restrictions on expenditures. These programs bore the stamp of Deputy Prime Minister Egor Gaidar, who Yeltsin named as economic czar. Although an attempt was made to index wages, the general result was inevitable: significant, though highly varied price increases that roughly doubled money wages but that led to a significant decline in real wages. Initial changes in the state budget and an initially very restrictive monetary policy resulted in an immediate but temporary shortage of rubles.

Decrees, beginning in late 1991, started the privatization of industry and services, with changes in agriculture handled separately in an April 1992 decree.[10] The transition to privatization was initially slow and uneven; however, in October 1992 the Russian government began issuing vouchers, and the privatization process sped up significantly through 1993 and 1994.[11]

From a macroeconomic perspective, the initial stages of transition were difficult. The end of the administrative command economy placed enterprises in an awkward position. With the gradual elimination of state orders and the collapse of interrepublic trade, enterprise activity plummeted while inventories increased.[12] Traditional sources of state revenue declined sharply in the absence of a western-style system of taxation. At the same time, subsidies continued, and enterprises, unable to pay their bills, accumulated large amounts of interenterprise debt.

The early stages of transition were difficult because market-type guidance mechanisms were being introduced (market prices for both inputs and outputs); enterprises were increasingly being required to respond to these signals, and yet they would have to do so with little or no market infrastructure. Transition for the banking sector has been especially difficult. The Central Bank of Russia took over *Gosbank*, which closed in late 1991.[13] The Central Bank created the Savings Bank of Russia (*Sberbank*) as the main holder of citizen deposits. In addition to the savings bank, two large specialized banks emerged during the early stages of transition: *Promstroibank* for industry and *Rosselkhozbank* for agriculture. Although the number of commercial banks has sharply increased, reform in the banking sector remains incomplete.[14]

An important component of transition has been the changing role of the state budget. On the revenue side, there has been a continuing attempt to shift away from levies on state-owned enterprises to a Western-style system of income and excise taxation. But without such a system in place and with enterprise performance plummeting, it is not surprising that declining budget revenues became an immediate problem. Not only were revenue sources collapsing, but taxation discipline was also deteriorating as regional and local authorities failed to turn over tax collections to the central authority.

On the expenditure side, the state continued subsidies and used the close connection between enterprises and banks to sustain directed credit programs. This type of activity in the special transition environment sustained inappropriate government spending at inappropriate levels. In addition, sustaining benefits in the safety net programs remained important. The major political battle over transition policy focused on the state budget. "Shock therapy" advocates such as Gaidar favored tight money and balanced budgets; however, those who espoused slower reform preferred continued subsidies and easy credit. The net result was a rapid expansion of the money supply to support the budget deficit. Inflation accelerated to near hyperinflation rates. A variety of forces drove up prices, such as the initial structural disequilibrium in the economy, aggregate excess demand, and monetary expansion.[15] Isolating the impact of different forces is difficult, though the initial disequilibrium would have led to a one-time adjustment, not to a sustained increase in the aggregate price level.

The Russian Economy: Performance, Restructuring, and Sectoral Issues

This discussion of transition economies has emphasized the distinction between such performance indicators as economic growth, and longer-term restructuring indicators, such as structural shifts and privatization. Although Russia is only in the early stages of transition, it is important to learn from available preliminary evidence. Let's first turn to a discussion of basic performance indicators, which is followed by an examination of restructuring patterns.

Performance

Table 16.2 presents basic performance indicators for the contemporary Russian economy. Although accurate data in a transition era is very difficult to generate and interpret, these data nevertheless provide some guidance as to trends in the Russian economy.

Although estimates differ, as expected, output dropped significantly. The understandable decline in investment was especially sharp in 1992. These patterns represent a significant slowdown in the activity of large state enterprises and have been partially offset by the smaller emerging private sector. These reductions in industrial output have continued through 1994.

TABLE 16.2 Russia: Basic Performance Trends

	1988	1989	1990	1991	1992	1993	1994	1995
Real GDP (% change)	n.a.	n.a.	n.a.	−9	−19	−12	−8.0	−2.0
Investment (% change; Constant Prices)	7.7	4.1	0.1	−11.0	−45.0	−10.0	−10.0	−5.0
Retail Prices (end period)	n.a.	n.a.	n.a.	143.9	2318	940	550	200
Money Supply (end period)	14.0	14.6	17.6	77.0	814	435	n.a.	n.a.
Unemployment Rate (end of year)				0.1	0.8	1.1	n.a.	n.a.
Exchange Rate (year end; rubles per U.S. dollar)	0.6	0.6	1.7	1.7	415.0	1247.0	n.a.	n.a.

n.a. = not available

Sources: Data through 1993 from *Economics of Transition* 2, 1 (1994), 123; projections through 1994 and 1995 from The Economist Intelligence Unit, *Russia: 2nd Quarter 1994* (London: The Economist), 9.

Prices, which were liberalized in January 1992, were expected to increase significantly, in part from excess demand and also from the preexisting distortion of prices. Prices did, in fact, increase sharply in both 1992 and again during 1993, and although prices of both producer and consumer goods have continued to increase through 1994, the increases have been less drastic than in earlier years.

There has been considerable discussion and debate about living standards in the post-Soviet era. Generally, indicators of standards of living levels are not very reliable, making firm conclusions difficult. The available data on unemployment indicate a low level, but much of the decline in employment has resulted from extended leaves. Also, part-time employment is widespread as is the holding of several jobs by one individual. Thus unemployment may actually be much higher than those figures officially reported.

Although money wages have risen, prices have increased considerably faster and real wages have declined severely. As expected, changes in the distribution of income occurred, and the proportion of the labor force in the lower end of the distribution increased especially. Although difficult to verify, it is likely that the gap between rich and poor has widened significantly.

Most of these trends were anticipated and the pattern of changes over time provide some encouragement; however, when these data are compared with similar data for Hungary and Poland, the latter seem to have made it past the economic trough more quickly than Russia, but with more evidence of such costs as high levels of unemployment.

Restructuring

Ultimately, the success of transition depends on restructuring—that is, the shift from the command economy to market arrangements. There are, however, problems in assessing restructuring. First, the time frame is unclear. The nature of the privatization process will have a major impact on the distribution of wealth. Societies cannot be expected to resolve such a fundamental issue quickly. Second, generating accurate data is difficult in a time of transition. This comment has been frequently reiterated in this book, yet it must be taken seriously. Some would justifiably argue that many of the numbers examined during transition, at best, represent broad trends. At worst, they represent inaccurate pictures that are becoming more so over time. For example, when firms are privatized, basic definitions become complex issues, and new tax arrangements create strong incentives to avoid accurate reporting. For small cooperative firms or for retail and service-sector operations, reporting problems are especially serious. Data, for example, on the share of total output from the private sector must be suspect, and yet the private sector should be an important and growing component of total output. In that sense, even basic output series and especially short-term shifts in those series may be misleading.

Ideally, it would be useful to know about the role of the state in the new Russian economy, the expansion of the private sector, and the impact of both on the structure of the Russian economy. While the effect of privatization will take time to discover, the pace of privatization, while initially quite slow, has accelerated significantly in 1993 and 1994. Privatization has proceeded most rapidly in the service sector, and even where the privatization of large companies has proceeded successfully, the restructuring (or the conversion of businesses that had been involved in military production) has been much more difficult.

Sectoral Issues

The process of transition will affect every sector of the Russian economy, including the urban, defense, energy, or agricultural sectors. Of special interest, however, are developments in agriculture and in foreign trade.

Many Western observers have viewed the rural economy as a likely starting point for the shift from plan to market. The transitions of the former Soviet and Eastern European republics have generally not followed this pattern, and thus differ markedly in this (and other respects) from the changes that have occurred in China.[16]

Although Gorbachev was reticent to move ahead with privatization in Russia, Yeltsin moved aggressively toward privatization in all sectors except agriculture. By the end of 1991, legislation had emerged that provided a number of options that collective and state farms could use to implement change. Individual peasant farms could emerge, **joint stock companies** could be formed, producer cooperatives could be established, or farms could remain essentially the same.

Judged by the amount of land that has been privatized, change has been very slow. At the same time, much of the conversion of state and collective farms to joint stock companies has been primarily an action on paper, though decision-making arrangements on farms have changed.

Although agricultural output has declined, it has not been as severe as the decline of total output, mostly because of the sharper decline in industrial output. Moreover, the liberalization of prices in 1992 and the gradual emergence of markets seems to have eliminated what had been perceived as a serious lack of food products.

One of the important developments of the Russian transition has been the change in the foreign trade sector.[17] Chapter 12 has already described the peculiar nature and impact of foreign trade arrangements and policies during the administrative command era. But even during the Gorbachev era, significant changes in the Soviet trade regime did not resolve Gorbachev's complaints about the lack of access to world technology and the need for diversification of Soviet exports. Put another way, Russia entered the era of transition with serious distortions and imbalances in the foreign trade sector.

In addition to an outmoded and inappropriate set of foreign trade arrangements and policies, any movement of the Russian economy toward an open posture in foreign trade would necessitate a **convertible ruble**, or the ability to exchange the ruble for foreign currencies. However, in the face of price liberalization, newly created financial markets, and a general lack of legal infrastructure, a changing regime of multiple exchange rates gradually emerged that provided increasing degrees of access to foreign currencies that were in part supported by a stabilization fund from the International Monetary Fund. As in other cases, market forces have increasingly pushed Russia to a convertible ruble, albeit one that has depreciated rapidly over time.

During the transition era, two other developments have seriously hampered smooth adjustment. First, trade among the former Soviet republics collapsed as the republics became independent and gradually began introducing their own independent national currencies. Although discussion of a "ruble zone" would continue, in fact close integration of Russia with other former republics was sustained only in limited cases, such as Belarus. Second, the socialist system of foreign trade disintegrated.

The net result has been a sharp drop in Russian foreign trade during transition and a significant redirection of that trade. Between 1990 and 1992, the volume of Russian exports fell by roughly 50 percent, while the volume of Russian imports fell by more than 50 percent. There was an understandable reduction in trade with former CMEA countries that was greater than that with non-CMEA countries.

The nature of trade arrangements during transition has created a great deal of discussion. The central issue involves determining which foreign trade arrangements and policies will contribute the most to a rebuilding of the Russian economy. As with other transition issues, the messages from historical experience are not always clear. Moreover, the issue of external assistance plays an important part in this discussion.

Assistance from the West has been broadly focused and very modest in aggregate value. Much of the debate over such aid has focused on the difficulties of guaranteeing that it will have a positive impact on a turbulent political environment. Much Western aid has been linked to politically painful domestic issues, such as reductions in the budget deficit or a freeing of energy prices. Additionally, such aid with "strings attached" has provided ammunition for nationalistic forces that complain about foreign encroachment on domestic Russian sovereignty.

Summary

Russia became a new and independent nation in December 1991 after the breakup of the Soviet Union. As the largest of the Soviet republics, Russia includes roughly 76 percent of the land mass of the former Soviet Union and 70 percent of its population.

Russia is a country of vast size and significant economic potential. There are many natural resources, including oil, timber, and minerals, with which Russia is more than adequately endowed. Russia's northerly location includes a challenging natural environment as well as large areas of excellent agricultural land.

Although the administrative command economy existed in Russia (and the other Soviet republics) for many years, economic reform was also part of the economic landscape. Beginning in the late 1950s and early 1960s, various Soviet leaders attempted to modify the systemic arrangements to stem a falling rate of economic growth and serious productivity problems. While these attempts at reform generally failed, they would be dwarfed by the policies of Mikhail Gorbachev, who became the Soviet president in 1985.

Under the leadership of Mikhail Gorbachev, the Soviet Union embarked on a program of restructuring (perestroika) and openness (glasnost). Beginning with legislation in 1986, Gorbachev attempted to modify the working arrangements of the economy to stimulate the role of decision making at the enterprise level, improve technology, and open the Soviet economy to foreign markets and capital. Along with a series of reform proposals, Gorbachev relied heavily on the "human factor" to stimulate citizen participation.

Although there were short-term improvements, *perestroika* failed for reasons that plagued earlier unsuccessful reforms: for example, poor design, lack of complementary reform components, and bureaucratic resistance. By 1990, with the economy slipping, it was clear than the path would be transition or the movement towards a new economic system.

With the dissolution of the Soviet Union in December 1991, Russia, under the leadership of Boris Yeltsin, pursued a path of economic change designed to release and rationalize prices, eliminate the state monopoly, open the economy, and privatize the means of production.

The results through 1994 have been generally predictable, mixed, yet generally positive. The release of controlled prices and the expansion of the money supply to reduce a large budget deficit has made inflation a serious problem. At the same time, output has fallen sharply though with recent improvements in the rate of fall. While money wages have risen, real wages have fallen and much of the population, poverty has become a way of life.

As we enter the second half of the 1990s, much has been done yet much remains to be done. Unquestionably prices have more meaning than before, and privatization has produced a reasonable supply response especially for basic consumer goods and services. Although privatization has proceeded, the development of a market infrastructure and the modernization of the banking system has yet to occur.

Sectoral changes in the Russian economy remain uneven. Agricultural output has fallen and restructuring has largely involved the creation of joint stock companies for collective and state farms and slowly emerging changes in decision-making arrangements.

The sharp reduction of trade among the former republics and the disintegration of the socialist foreign trade structure both led to a reduction of the volume of Russian foreign trade and a redirection of remaining trade away from former CMEA partners. At the same time, new trade arrangements and a convertible ruble are gradually emerging amid frequently changing legal and institutional arrangements.

Key Terms

Russia	radical economic reform	joint stock company
perestroika	transition	convertible ruble
glasnost	stabilization	
democratization	price liberalization	

Notes

1. For an in-depth look at the Soviet economy and the post-Soviet era, see Paul R. Gregory and Robert C. Stuart, *Soviet and Post-Soviet Economic Structure and Performance* (New York: HarperCollins, 1994).
2. For a detailed discussion of economic reform, see Paul R. Gregory and Robert C. Stuart, *Soviet and Post-Soviet Economic Structure and Performance*, Chapters 12 and 13.
3. Understandably, a great deal has been written about the Gorbachev era. For an introduction to the literature, see Joseph L. Wieczynski, ed., *The Gorbachev Encyclopedia* (Salt Lake City: Charles Schlacks, Jr., 1993).
4. A useful discussion of the early years of perestroika can be found in E. A. Hewett, *Reforming The Soviet Economy* (Washington, D.C.: The Brookings Institution, 1988).
5. Changes in enterprise arrangements are discussed in R. E. Ericson, "The New Enterprise Law," *The Harriman Forum* vol. 1 (February 1988).
6. For a discussion of initial changes, see, for example, D. Thorniley, "Reforming the Soviet Foreign Trade Structure and Adapting to Change," in NATO, Directorate of Economic Affairs, *Soviet Economic Reforms: Implementation Underway* (Brussels: NATO, 1989), 157–184.
7. A. Aslund, *Gorbachev's Struggle for Economic Reform*, rev. ed. (London: Pinter Publishers, 1991).
8. For an excellent survey of the early transition era, see J. H. Noren, "The Russian Economic Reform: Progress and Prospects," *Soviet Economy*, 8, 1 (1992), 3–41.
9. Ibid.
10. For a discussion of change in agriculture, see R. J. Mcintyre, "The Phantom of Transition: Privatization of Agriculture in the Former Soviet Union and Eastern Europe," *Comparative Economic Studies* 34, (Fall–Winter 1992), 81–95; S. K. Wegren, "Private Farming and Agrarian Reform in Russia," *Problems of Communism* 41, 3 (1992), 107–121.
11. Privatization vouchers were issued with a face value of 10,000 rubles at a time when the average monthly salary was roughly 12,000 rubles. By the middle of 1994, most small-scale activities were privatized, and roughly three-quarters of medium and large-scale enterprises were privatized.
12. The collapse of trade among the former republics was a serious factor contributing to the decline of output. For a discussion of this issue, see J. H. Noren and R. Watson, "Interrepublican Economic Relations After the Disintegration of the USSR," *Soviet Economy*, 8 (April–June 1992), 89–129; A. McAuley, "Costs and benefits of De-Integration in the USSR," *Most*, 2 (1991), 51–61.
13. For a useful discussion of the reforms in the banking sector, see The World Bank, *Russia: The Banking System in Transition* (Washington, D.C.: The World Bank, 1993).
14. The World Bank, *Russia: The Banking System in Transition* emphasizes the need to phase out directed credit arrangements and to introduce the International Standard Bank (ISB) program.
15. Recall that prior to the dissolution of the Soviet Union, there was great concern about "monetary overhang," its magnitude, and potential equity considerations. Sharp price increases largely eliminated this problem.
16. While agriculture was a subject of major focus during the Soviet era, it has received much less attention in the post-Soviet era. For an early discussion of privatization, see R. J. Mcintyre, "The Phantom of Transition: Privatization of Agriculture in the Former Soviet Union and Eastern Europe," *Comparative Economic Studies*, 34 (Fall/Winter

1992), 81–95; for a discussion of the food issue, see S. S. Nellow, "The Food Situation in the Ex-Soviet Republics," *Soviet Studies*, 44, 5 (1992), 857–880; for a general discussion, see S. K. Wegren, "Private Farming and Agrarian Reform in Russia," *Problems of Communism*, 41, 3 (1992), 107–121.

17. Considerable attention has been focused on foreign trade issues. For a general survey of the past and the present, see Alan Smith, *Russia and the World Economy: Problems of Integration* (London and New York: Routledge, 1993).

Recommended Readings

The Soviet Era

Paul R. Gregory and Robert C. Stuart, *Soviet and Post-Soviet Economic Structure and Performance*, 5th ed. (New York: HarperCollins, 1994).

Tania Konn, ed., *Soviet Studies Guide* (London and New Jersey: Bowker-Saur, 1992).

Perestroika

Anders Aslund, *Gorbachev's Struggle for Economic Reform*, rev. ed. (London: Pinter Publishers, 1991).

Padma Desai, *Perestroika in Perspective* (Princeton, N.J.: Princeton University Press, 1991).

Ed. A. Hewett, *Reforming the Soviet Economy* (Washington, D.C.: The Brookings Institution, 1988).

William Moskoff, *Hard Times: Impoverishment and Protest in the Perestroika Years* (Armonk, N.Y.: M. E. Sharpe, 1993).

Joseph L. Wieczynski, ed., *The Gorbachev Encyclopedia* (Salt Lake City: Charles Schlacks, Jr., 1993).

Transition

Anders Aslund, ed., *Economic Transformation in Russia* (London: Pinter Publishers, 1994).

Olivier Jean Blanchard, Henneth A. Froot, and Jeffrey D. Sachs, *The Transition in Eastern Europe*, Vols. 1 and 2 (Chicago and London: University of Chicago Press, 1994).

Central Intelligence Agency, *Measuring Russia's Emerging Private Sector* (Washington, D.C.: CIA, 1992).

J. Hahn, "Attitudes Towards Reform Among Provincial Russian Politicians," *Post-Soviet Affairs*, 9, 1 (1993), 66–85.

B. W. Ickes and Randi Ryterman, "The Enterprise Arrears Crisis in Russia," *Post-Soviet Affairs*, 8, 4 (1992), 331–361.

Peter Murrell, et. al., "Symposium on Economic Transition in the Soviet Union and Eastern Europe," *Journal of Economic Perspectives*, 5 (Fall 1991), 3–162.

James H. Noren, "The Russian Economic Reform: Progress and Prospects," *Soviet Economy* 8, 1 (1992), 3–41.

Kenneth K. Koford, et. al., "Symposium: Economic Reform in Eastern Europe and the Former Soviet Union," *Eastern Economic Journal*, 19 (Summer 1993), 329–393.

R. J. Mcintyre, "The Phantom of Transition: Privatization of Agriculture in the Former Soviet Union and Eastern Europe," *Comparative Economic Studies*, 34 (Fall/Winter 1992), 81–95.

Lynn D. Nelson and Irina Y. Kuzes, "Evaluation the Russian Voucher Privatization Program," *Comparative Economic Studies*, 36 (Spring 1994) 55–68.

Andrei Schleifer and Robert W. Vishny "Privatization in Russia: First Steps," in Oliver Jean Blanchard, Kenneth A. Froot and Jeffrey D. Sachs, *The Transition in Eastern Europe*, vol. 2 (Chicago: University of Chicago Press, 1994), 137–160.

Alan Smith, *Russia and Ther World Economy: Problems of Integration* (London and New York: Routledge, 1993).

Robert C. Stuart and Paul R. Gregory, *The Russian Economy: Past, Present and Future* (New York: HarperCollins, 1995).

United States Congress, Joint Economic Committee, *The Former Soviet Union in Transition*, Vols. 1 and 2 (Washington, D.C.: U.S. Government Printing Office, 1993).

S. Sk. Wegren, "Private Farming and Agrarian Reform in Russia," *Problems of Communism*, 41, 3 (1992), 107–121.

The World Bank, *Russian Economic Reform: Crossing the Threshold of Structural Change* (Washington, D.C.: The World Bank, 1992).

———, *Russia: The Banking System During Transition* (Washington, D.C.: The World Bank, 1993).

Data and Commentary

Central Intelligence Agency, *Handbook of International Statistics* (Washington, D.C.: CIA, annual).

———, *World Fact Book* (Washington, D.C.: CIA, annual).

The Economist, Intelligence Unit, *Quarterly Reports* (London: The Economist Quarterly).

The Economics of Transition: Reports and Statistical Data (Oxford: Oxford University Press).

Institute of the World Economy and International Relations (IMEMO), *Russian Economic Monitor* (Moscow: IMEMO, monthly).

International Monetary Fund, *International Financial Statistics: Supplement on Countries of the Former Soviet Union* (Washington, D.C.: International Monetary Fund, 1993).

Russian Economic Trends (Lawrence, Kansas: Whurr Publishers, quarterly).

OECD, *Short-Term Economic Indicators: Transition Economies* (Paris: OECD, quarterly).

———, *National Accounts for the Former Soviet Union* (Paris: OECD, 1993).

———, *Transformation of the Banking System: Portfolio Restructuring, Privatisation, and the Payment System* (Paris: OECD, 1993).

———, *Trends and Policies in Privatisation* (Paris: OECD, biannual).

Jan Vanous, ed., *PlanEcon Reports* (Washington, D.C.: PlanEcon, various).

Jaclyn Y. Shend, *Agricultural Statistics of the Former USSR Republics and the Baltic States* (Washington, D.C.: U.S. Department of Agriculture, 1993).

The World Bank, *Historically Planned Economies 1993: A Guide to the Data* (Washington, D.C.: The World Bank, 1993).

———, *Russia: The Banking System During Transition* (Washington, D.C.: The World Bank, 1993).

———, *Russian Economic Reform* (Washington, D.C.: The World Bank, 1992).

17

China: Socialism, Planning, Markets, and Development

China has fascinated the west for centuries. Economists are interested in modern China for three principal reasons. First, the characteristics of Chinese industrialization distinguish it from other cases that we have examined. After the Chinese Communist party came to power in 1949, a period of socialist industrialization began. The Chinese applied the Soviet model, with alterations, in a highly underdeveloped setting.[1] Second, the easing of Chinese-American hostilities in the early 1970s sharply expanded communication between the two countries.[2] This era has provided Americans a long-denied opportunity to examine the Chinese system on a firsthand basis. This opportunity was enriched in the late 1970s and early 1980s when the Chinese began to release more information about their economy.[3] In spite of a difficult political situation in China in the late 1980s, interaction with the West was sustained. The result has been a sharply expanded and productive dialogue, considerably enhancing our knowledge of the Chinese economy. Third, the post-Mao era has seen major changes in the Chinese economic system. These changes are of great interest, not only for their impact on Chinese development, but also for the enrichment they provide to our understanding of the traditional Soviet model of development. China in the 1990s is clearly a different model of change, and that deserves close attention in light of the demise of the Soviet Union and other similar socialist systems.

For more than a decade, China has been one of the world's most rapidly growing economies. Unlike the planned socialist economies of the Soviet Union and Eastern Europe, China casts as image of success and progress. Unlike the former Soviet Union and Eastern Europe, which chose democracy over the communist party monopoly, the Chinese communist party has remained the controlling force in China. In China, the communist party, it can be said, has directed the progress of economic reform from above. China also shows the effects of opening a planned socialist system to the world economy, while retaining the monopoly of its communist party.

China, therefore, represents an alternative to the ongoing reforms in the former Soviet Union and Eastern Europe—a path that combines political and economic liberalization with an opening of the economy to the outside world while the communist party retains political control.

The Setting

First, China is a very large country by any definition. It is sobering to compare China with Canada, another large country. Canada, with a population of approximately 25 million, has a land area of 3.8 million square miles. China, with a population of slightly more than one billion, has a land area of just over 3.6 million square miles. Indeed, if the Chinese population should continue to increase at the average annual rate of 2.1 percent of the past two decades, a new Canada, in terms of population, would arise in China roughly every fifteen months![4] Both land and population are resources that can contribute to economic development, but people must eat, and considerable portions of China's land are inappropriate for increasing the food supply, at least in the absence of capital investment.

Second, China is a resource-rich country, but, once again, its resources must be exploited to support economic development. Although coal is a major source of energy, only recently has China undertaken a major effort to utilize its oil riches. In addition, sharp variations in climate and fertility, along with large areas of rough terrain, require large amounts of capital to raise agricultural output, despite China's vast land area.

Third, China remains a poor country despite rapid growth. Substantial economic progress has been made since the industrialization drive began in the early 1950s, but China in the early 1990s had a per capita income of about $500 or above.[5] China's per capita income, though above that of its immediate neighbors India and Pakistan, ranks well below that of Taiwan, South Korea, and Hong Kong. China's major goals are still industrialization and economic development.

Finally, a nonsystemic feature is the unique Chinese historical experience. China is the oldest existing civilization in the world, a source of great pride to the Chinese people. While there are numerous ethnic minorities in China (primarily in the western part of the country), the dominant nationality group is the *han* nationality. The Chinese language comprises many varying dialects; the Mandarin dialect is dominant. The rich heritage of the Chinese people is an important if unmeasurable influence on their attitudes toward and participation in the modernization process.

China and the Soviet Model

The economic, social, and cultural differences between China and the other socialist countries are striking. To the extent that we wish to make comparisons between China, with its low income, and, say, the United States, with its high income, great caution must be taken. Comparisons of China with India, or even contemporary China with the Soviet Union of the 1930s, make more sense. Even in this latter comparison it is important to note that China in 1949 was probably much more backward than Russia in 1917.

In looking at the problems that Chinese leaders and planners faced in adapting the **Soviet model**, we raise several key questions: How could the Chinese economy, in the absence of the advantages enjoyed by Russian leaders in 1917 (a basic industrial capacity, a transportation network, and so on), institute a planned socialist economic system in a large and very poor peasant economy? In developing such a planned socialist economy, what modifications of the Soviet model had to be made to account for the very large Chinese population, its relative poverty, and its primarily rural character? To what extent would the Chinese natural resource base support industrial development, especially in view of sharp regional disparities and the likelihood that foreign trade would play a relatively small role? Could the Soviet model of rapid industrialization, used twenty years earlier under rather different circumstances, be transplanted in whole or in part to the Chinese case?

China at the time of the 1949 revolution was a classic LDC: low per capita income, significant population pressure on arable land and other resources, and an absence of institutions appropriate for economic development. China, with a land mass slightly larger than the United States and about half the Soviet Union, and with a population roughly four times the United States and about three-and-one-half times the Soviet Union, began in 1949 to implement the Soviet model, with substantive modifications. The result was economic growth and development that has been interrupted when ideological and political factors gained supremacy over economic factors.

Chinese economic development can best be understood in terms of its historical evolution since 1949 and, in particular, as a modification of the Soviet model of economic development. What we wish to learn from the Chinese experience is, above all, the extent to which planned socialism is a suitable vehicle for economic development in a large and poor country.

The History of Planning in China

The Beginnings of Industrialization: The 1950s

The Chinese People's Republic was proclaimed by Mao Zedong in 1949. Between 1949 and 1952 a period of consolidation ensued. Two main goals were sought. First, the redistribution of land to individual households was implemented in preparation for ultimate collectivization. The latter, however, was to be pursued without undue haste. Second, nationalization and consolidation of the holdings in industry took place in preparation for the development of national economic planning. Other steps were taken—financial reform, educational reform, and other changes deemed necessary to stabilize the economy in preparation for the beginning of the first five-year plan in 1953. However, the basic steps were toward changing the ownership base and the means of guiding the economy. In this respect, China's first steps were much like those of the Soviet Union in the aftermath of the revolution.

The Chinese experience with change in the rural sector must be compared with the Soviet experience of the late 1920s and early 1930s, especially inasmuch as Soviet collectivization brought with it a number of important negative consequences.[6] Did the Chinese leadership modify the Soviet approach? On the surface, both countries utilized initial land reform and similar experimental forms of organization—the elimination of class differences at a rapid pace, the distribution of machinery and equipment through centralized facilities, and pressure to hold down rural food consumption. At the same time, there were differences. Possibly the most important achievement was the avoidance of substantial destruction of cattle, facilities, and equipment in China.[7] The extremes of the Soviet model were avoided. Possibly the Chinese countryside was better prepared in terms of ideological and organizational factors, though certainly not in terms of machinery and equipment. Also, the state farm, a key feature of the Soviet experience, was not introduced until later in China.

The Chinese adopted the basic Soviet model of land reform and subsequent collectivization; the differences, however, were sufficient to preclude the extreme negative consequences experienced in the Soviet Union. However, the success of Chinese collectivization in transferring resources to the needs of industrialization remains an open question, just as it remains an open issue in the former Soviet Union.

The Planning Apparatus

The second important policy of the early years was the nationalization of industry and the development of a system of national economic planning. During the early 1950s there was a gradual transition from private industry toward socialist industry —certainly more gradual than in the Soviet Union after 1928. The shift from private to socialist industry in China was targeted to be slow, though toward the latter part of the first five-year plan it proved to be rapid. The pattern of change was from private ownership to elementary state capitalism, then to advanced state capitalism, and finally to socialist industry.[8] By 1955, 68 percent of the gross value of output was accounted for by state industry and only 16 percent by joint state–private enterprises.[9] Indeed, even handicraft production was brought under state control in moves reminiscent of the excessive nationalization of Soviet war communism. Thus, although the plans for the socialist transformation in both agriculture and industry called for a relatively gradual pace, the experience in 1955–1956 demonstrated that ideology and political considerations could accelerate the rate of change.

Soviet leaders learned from their experiences between 1917 and 1928 that if the market is to be abolished, a substitute mechanism must be developed for economic activity to continue in a coordinated fashion. The Chinese planning structure, put in place in the early 1950s and subsequently modified, was initially similar to the Soviet model.[10] The basic unit of production activity was the enterprise. As in the Soviet Union, a dual party–state administrative structure drew up and implemented (and often interrupted) five-year plans for both agriculture and industry. Chinese plans are formulated largely by the State Planning Commission, which like Gosplan in the Soviet Union, operated through an industrial ministry system communicating with regional and enterprise officials and ultimately assembling a plan. Once it was approved by the State Council, that plan became law for all enterprises.

Inevitably, this system produced problems similar to those found in the Soviet case—imbalance and shortages, poor quality, late plans, and deviation of results from targets. Chinese thinking on reform began to surface in the mid-1950s, but it was overshadowed by the political and ideological upheavals of the late 1950s.

The early 1950s was a period of unrest. After the liberal **Hundred Flowers Campaign** (1956–1957), during which there was open discussion and criticism of the system, the **Great Leap Forward** was launched (1958–1960).[11] The Great Leap was a massive resurgence of ideology, which replaced rationality. Campaigns were instigated with revolutionary fervor to emphasize a new role for the peasantry, especially through small-scale industry in the countryside and the introduction of communes. Development of water resources was also stressed. A brutal campaign against the educated elite was conducted.

For a variety of economic, political, and ideological reasons, the Great Leap was abandoned by 1960, but the commune system, introduced in 1958, remained.[12] The **Rural Peoples Communes** were initially set up as very large units combining a number of collectives (advanced cooperatives) to produce agricultural and handicraft products and to serve as local units of government. The original communes (roughly 26,000 in number and averaging about 4,600 households each) faced difficulties. Agricultural units encompassing some 50,000 households were too difficult to coordinate, and individual incentives were overshadowed by the size of the collective. Subsequent modifications improved the commune system.

The First Ten Years

How can we appraise the first ten years of the Chinese industrialization experience? As one observer noted: "In general, it can be said that during 1953–1957, the Chinese followed the broad outlines of the Stalinist strategy of selective growth under conditions of austerity with three important qualifications."[13] First, less pressure was placed on the agricultural sector, possibly in recognition of the important underlying element of the Chinese case: a large, rural, poor population. Presumably the Chinese leaders had learned from the Soviet experience with rapid collectivization, for despite many similarities between the two cases, the extreme costs of the Soviet case were avoided in China.

Second, unlike the Soviet case, where state resources were directed toward the agricultural sector through state farms, Machine Tractor Stations, and so on, agriculture in the early years of the new Chinese regime was largely self-financed. This may have reflected the much lower level of economic development in China in 1949 than in the Soviet Union in 1928.[14]

Third, the Chinese relied heavily on the state enterprise as a revenue source for state investment funds. In 1953, for example, revenue from state enterprises accounted for roughly 35 percent of total budgetary revenue; this figure rose to 46 percent by 1957. In comparison, by far the most important source of budgetary revenue in the early years of Soviet industrialization was the turnover tax, and revenues from enterprises played a minor role. The decision not to rely on taxes forced from the peasants reflected the planners' realization that such a policy could not be applied to a subsistence agriculture.

During the 1950s, the Chinese generally followed the Soviet "industry first" strategy. Between 1953 and 1957, heavy industry in China absorbed an average of 85 percent of industrial investment. At the same time, only 8 percent of state investment was devoted to agriculture, while aggregate investment accounted for roughly 20 to 25 percent of the national product.[15] These figures suggest a relatively high rate of accumulation for a poor country (though not nearly so high as the comparable rate for the Soviet Union in the early 1930s), with emphasis on industry in general and heavy industry in particular.

China's economic performance during the 1950s was generally strong, though uneven. There was an impressive doubling of GNP per capita, a ninefold increase in industrial production, and a modest increase in agricultural production. Overall, the early years were ones of consolidation. The first five-year plan witnessed substantial growth of production; the latter part of the 1950s saw a mixture of progress and retrogression in both industry and agriculture.

The striking feature of Chinese economic performance in the 1950s was the impact of ideological disruptions. Chinese GNP grew at an annual rate of 6 percent from 1952 to 1956.[16] The 1958 level of GNP, however, was not regained until 1963. Thus the Great Leap Forward caused an enormous setback in Chinese growth.

The Great Leap Forward was abandoned in the late 1950s at a time when relations between China and the Soviet Union were deteriorating rapidly. The ideological and economic break between the two countries was almost complete by 1960. Although the role of outside aid in the Chinese development experience was minimal, the Soviet contribution was important in the early years, especially in the area of technical assistance. The break would prove to be a sobering experience for Chinese leaders and planners.

The 1960s: Development and Disruption

Like the earlier decade, the 1960s can be conveniently divided into two very different periods: moderation in the early 1960s and upheaval in the late 1960s.

The early 1960s was a period of relative calm in which there was a tendency to look toward balance in economic development, modernization in the agricultural sector, and recovery from the aftermath of the Great Leap. In industry, the 1960s was a period of rather substantial reform—a movement away from the overwhelming importance of gross output (the major success indicator of the 1950s) toward quality in production and the elimination of major deficiencies in the planning system.

In a sense, both central control and local initiative were variables to be changed. The center tried to put pressure on enterprises to improve quality, to be concerned with efficiency, and to enhance the role of technical expertise in the decision-making process. At the same time, there was a tendency to shift many decisions, especially minor ones, to the local level. For example, local industrial establishments were set up to serve local (especially rural) needs. Although the emphasis on enterprise efficiency and profitability came under sharp attack during the **Cultural Revolution** of the late 1960s, in the 1960s the Chinese industrial structure was modified to suit peculiar Chinese conditions, and the modifications for the most part withstood later upheavals.

During the early 1960s, new emphasis was placed on agriculture's role in the economy and on the need for mechanization and reorganization in that sector. The communes underwent substantial change. Because communes were found to be too large, the intermediate (brigade) and lower-level (team) units assumed new importance. Emphasis on nonmaterial rewards, a hallmark of the earlier commune system, was changed in favor of material incentives and the reintroduction of private plots. Although the number of communes was reduced during the 1960s, their role in the social, cultural, and political affairs of the countryside remained intact through the 1970s.

In addition to organizational changes and policy shifts, the 1960s witnessed a widespread educational campaign among the Chinese people. There was an effort to re-educate the population in the ways of Mao. This campaign laid the foundations for the Cultural Revolution.

If the early 1960s was a period of rationality—reform and change along a well-defined continuum—the opposite could be said of the Cultural Revolution of 1966–1969. The Cultural Revolution, difficult for the Western observer to fully comprehend, was an upheaval of ideas, an abandonment of much that had preceded it. Emanating from a Communist party struggle, the Cultural Revolution was not a debate over economic ideas. In fact, its disastrous disruption of economic activity became apparent only later. However, although economic activity was substantially disturbed, the basic organizational arrangements in industry and in agriculture do not seem to have been altered in significant ways.

Like the Great Leap, the Cultural Revolution had a devastating effect on output. Disruption was so great that meaningful GNP estimates during the Cultural Revolution are not available. GNP failed to increase between 1965 and 1970, a loss of output equal to or more severe than that of the Great Leap.[17]

The Contemporary Chinese Economy

The early 1970s was a period of recovery from the events of the Cultural Revolution.[18] Western scholars have argued that the Cultural Revolution was a major setback for the Chinese economy. Furthermore, any immediate attempt to return to normalcy would be interrupted by events of the early and mid-1970s. Zhou Enlai, an advocate of a moderate path of industrialization, died in early 1976. The following September, Mao Zedong, the father of the revolution and an advocate of continuing the revolutionary mentality, died. Shortly thereafter, in October 1976, the **"Gang of Four,"** representing the revolutionary left and espousing a continuation of the Stalinist mode of industrialization, were arrested amid great ideological fervor.[19] These events paved the way for what would be fundamental changes in the Chinese economic system and its policies.

In 1978, a ten-year plan for the modernization of China was announced by Hua Guofeng. This plan, to cover 1975 through 1985, was to pursue the **"Four Modernizations"**—industry, agriculture, science and technology, and defense. The initial plan was grandiose, projecting an average annual rate of growth of industrial output of 10 percent, and agricultural output of 4 to 5 percent. The emphasis would be traditional—industry, especially heavy industry, was placed at the forefront.

By the end of 1978, however, imbalances in the Chinese economy led to an emphasis on economic reform that, in effect, scrapped the ten-year plan. One-year plans were announced and in 1982 a five-plan was announced for 1981 through 1985.

By the end of the 1970s, the problems of the Stalinist industrialization model were evident. Material incentives were inadequate, accumulation was emphasized, and heavy industry was the focus of economic policy. As a result, problems began growing in areas such as energy, transportation, and consumer goods. However, the reforms announced in the late 1970s (ultimately under the **"eight-point program"**) would turn out to be fundamental, making 1978 a year of pivotal importance and fundamentally changing the direction of the Chinese economy.

China: The Pursuit of Markets

Beginning in the late 1970s, China pursued economic reform in four major areas: agriculture, service, foreign trade, and industry.[20] Although the reforms are by no means complete as we enter the second half of the 1990s, there is agreement that the Chinese economy has made significant and substantial moves toward becoming a market economy. Although it is not unusual to hear about contemporary economic and political problems, such as the macroeconomic instability of the early 1990s, on balance, the reforms have been strikingly successful, as judged by contemporary Chinese economic performance.

Prior to 1978, the commune was the best-known unit of organization in agriculture.[21] Basic economic activity was in the hands of the **production team**, which comprised a number of households within a village. Production teams would combine to form a brigade, and brigades would combine to form a commune. Above the commune, the county was the state unit responsible for directing agricultural activity. It played a major role in implementing the national economic plan administered by the Ministry of Agriculture and Forestry.[22]

The commune had a reward system not unlike that used in the collective farms of the former Soviet Union prior to 1966. Individuals would accumulate points for daily work done, with the ultimate reward based on residual income, which consisted of revenues less expenses.

The **contract responsibility system** was introduced in the late 1970s.[23] The release of local agricultural markets and the contracting by the state with households for the sale of major crops effectively brought collectivization to an end. The system for distributing output changed, as did the ability of households to purchase inputs. Although restrictions remained on the availability of land for household farming, by the early 1980s, the commune and production-team arrangements had virtually disappeared.[24] In effect, on both the output and the input side of Chinese agriculture, markets dominated.

The impact these changes had on agricultural performance was immediate and dramatic, though by the latter part of the 1980s there had been some retrenchment to slower rates of growth of output. Indeed, the accompanying structural changes in agriculture and in the 1990s continued the discussion of the basic issue of property rights.

A second major area of change in the Chinese economy was in the service sector. Prior to 1978, Stalinist priorities prevailed; however, as an example of substantive change, between 1978 and 1981, the share of total investment devoted to heavy industry fell from 54.7 percent to 40.3 percent, a sharp drop in a very short span of time.[25] Indeed, the average annual rate of growth of services was 6.1 percent between 1970 and 1980, and 11.2 percent between 1980 and 1991.[26] Finally, the labor force in the service sector doubled from 48.7 million in 1978 to 99.5 million in 1988.[27] What accounted for this dramatic change in the service sector?

China, like other planned socialist economies had essentially prohibited the development of the service sector largely through outright prohibitions. Beginning in the late 1970s, however, these rules were substantially relaxed, which resulted in a sharp and sudden increase in service-sector activity. Entry was easy, markets were functioning, and large amounts of capital investment were, for the most part, unnecessary.

A third and critical area of reform has been the foreign-trade sector. Again, China in the 1970s was typical of the planned socialist economic systems. Trade was centralized and fully controlled by the state. Beginning in the late 1970s, the regulations pertaining to foreign trade were relaxed and businesses were encouraged to import and export using decentralized market arrangements. Exportation has been especially important in developing arrangements to encourage the sale of manufactured goods in foreign markets and to stimulate foreign direct investment in China.

The issue of convertibility remains unresolved, though the sequence of steps taken in China resemble other cases. From an initial posture of total state control, dual channels were effectively implemented to combine continuing state control with "foreign exchange adjustment centers," where access to foreign currency was possible at, essentially, market-determined rates.

The final and possibly most limited focus of economic reform has been in the industrial sector. Beginning in the mid-1980s, again after a long history of state controls and a soft budget constraint, rules governing enterprise behavior changed. On the production side, enterprises shifted away from old gross output indicators to profitability and other market-type indicators. Meanwhile, firms could purchase inputs in markets at market-determined prices. For many enterprises, the rules of the game had changed in major ways.

If there has been a limitation on enterprise reform, it pertains to the large state enterprises that, even in the mid-1990s, remain wedded to old ways, despite changing rules and regulations.[28] In part, the difficulties stem from ambivalence about the establishment of full private-property rights, much less a problem in the case of small-scale industry.

If one examines these reforms in both form and results, they are impressive. But, reforms are, after all, set within the larger economy and must be judged against their contribution to aggregate economic performance.

The Chinese Economy: Reform and Performance

An important component of reform has been an increased availability of empirical evidence on the performance of the Chinese economy. Table 17.1 assembles basic performance indicators to illuminate the story of the reform era. Although a breakdown of growth rates by shorter subperiods would illustrate a series of cyclical fluctuations, the overall performance of the reform era has been impressive.

Comparing the decade of the 1980s with the decade of the 1970s reveals significant improvements in growth performance of aggregate output, especially in agriculture and in services. Foreign trade expanded rapidly as did foreign direct investment in China. For example, on an annual basis between 1979 and 1982, $1.5 billion, U.S., were contracted, and $.29 billion were actually used. By 1992, that amount reached $58.12 billion and $11.01 billion, U.S., for commitments and utilizations, respectively.[29] Although studies of Chinese factor productivity reveal varying results, it is reasonable to suggest that after a long period of stagnation, total factor productivity for industry improved during the 1980s in both the state and the nonstate sectors.

Beyond the immediate components of economic reform and the basic changes in output, the Chinese economy exhibited considerable cyclical variation during the 1980s and 1990s. After a period of significant expansion in the early 1980s, rates of growth of output declined during the remainder of the decade, with a concomitant growth of inflationary pressures and a negative trade balance from the mid-1980s through the end of the decade. Although there were favorable trends in a number of these indicators as the 1980s came to an end, rapid economic growth and inflationary pressures in the early 1990s again necessitated steps to bring an overheated economy under control.[30]

TABLE 17.1   China: The Reform Era

	Average Annual Rate of Growth	
	1970–1980	1980–1991
Gross Domestic Product	5.2	9.4
Agriculture	2.6	5.7
Industry	7.8	11.0
Services	6.1	11.2
Foreign Trade		
Exports	8.7	11.5
Imports	11.3	9.5

Source: World Bank, *World Development Report 1993* (New York: Oxford University Press, 1993), various Tables.

The Chinese Economy: Reform in Perspective

Clearly, economic reform in China is a story of major importance in the 1980s and 1990s. In light of the demise of many of the major planned socialist economic systems, it is surprising to witness such changes within the context of what has been a planned socialist economy. In many respects, China represents a path thought relevant to, but largely ignored by, other such systems, for example, the decollectivization of agriculture and the expansion of the service sector. The Chinese reform differs from that of the former Soviet Union and Eastern Europe in another sense. Democratization of the political sphere has not been allowed in China. The market reform is being carried out prior to the creation of democratic institutions. At the same time, from a variety of perspectives, the Chinese case is very different because, for example, the country is facing serious population growth and needs to utilize a rapidly increasing labor force as well as improve its standard of living. What is next for economic reform in China?

Probably the most critical aspects of continuing successful reform will be creating the underpinnings or infrastructure necessary to sustain reasonably stable economic growth and development. Clearly the instruments of macroeconomic management—the banking system and money markets, the fiscal system, and especially the control of government revenues and expenditures—need to be perfected. All have been partially to blame for cyclical instability in recent years.

Finally, while the problems of establishing private property rights in agriculture have been discussed, the problems of developing a legal infrastructure are broader and more complex but equally important if business in China is to survive and prosper in the next decade.

Summary

China is an important example of economic growth and development, in which the traditional Soviet model has been applied in a very large but poor country characterized by significant regional diversity and an abundance of natural resources. Since the beginnings of Chinese socialism under Mao Zedong in 1949, analysts have been interested in both the application of the Soviet model and the importance of ideology in explaining policy and systemic changes.

During the first decade of socialism in China, the basic Soviet model was implemented, including the socialization of agriculture, nationalization, and the development of a system of central planning. Although there were deviations from the Soviet experience, a feature of the 1950s was the presence of substantial ideological deviations, notably the Great Leap Forward campaign of the mid and late 1950s.

While the first half of the 1960s was a period of relative tranquility, the latter half gave way to major disruption resulting from the Cultural Revolution. Although

the ideological upheaval of this era had a significant impact on the overall performance of the Chinese economy, its basic organizational arrangements seemed to
undergo relatively little change.

After a period of recovery in the early 1970s, a number of important events
occurred, notably the deaths of the most important Chinese leaders of the early
years: Zhou Enlai and Mao Zedong. By that time, many of the problems plaguing
the Soviet Union were also evident in China, which had had a long and persistent
application of the Stalinist model of industrialization. That model emphasized heavy
industry with high investment ratios and minimal attention to incentives, especially
in agriculture.

The changes of the mid-1970s, however, would usher in a new era characterized
by dramatic and sustained changes in agriculture, industry, service, and international
trade. Beginning with an effective end to collectivization, markets were introduced
in a meaningful way, and the rural population responded with sharp increases in
agricultural output.

The service sector began to grow rapidly, which expanded the importance of
private economic activity in the Chinese economy. At the same time, there were
important changes in the rules governing industrial enterprises, emphasizing both
the output and the input of market forces. Finally, departing from the rigidities of
the Soviet model, foreign-trade regulations were substantially altered, opening up
the Chinese economy for significant expansion of both exports and imports and an
influx of direct foreign investment.

Since the post-1978 reform era, the Chinese economy has moved significantly
toward the market model. Although there have been cyclical problems, the generally
positive economic performance has paved the way for the continuation of reform
and especially for the development of a basic infrastructure necessary for the long-
term evolution of markets.

Key Terms

Soviet model	Gang of Four
Hundred Flowers Campaign	Four Modernizations
Great Leap Forward	eight-point program
Rural Peoples Communes	production team
Cultural Revolution	contract responsibility system

Notes

1. Although cross-country comparison of GNP must be interpreted with caution, a per
   capita gross national product of $131 (measured in 1980 dollars) must rank China as a
   very poor country on the eve of the socialist industrialization drive. For a useful long-
   term comparison of basic economic and developmental indicators, see Arthur G. Ashbrook, Jr., "China: Economic Modernization and Long-Term Performance," in U.S.

Congress, Joint Economic Committee, *China Under the Four Modernizations*, Part 2, Section V (Washington, D.C.: Government Printing Office, 1982), pp. 151–368.

2. For a detailed discussion of the path of Sino-American normalization, see Joint Economic Committee, *China Under the Four Modernizations*, Part 1, pp. 171–223.

3. For a discussion, see K. Chao, "The China-Watchers Tested," *The China Quarterly*, 81 (1980), 97–104; Erik Dirksen, "Chinese Industrial Productivity in an International Context," *World Development*, 11 (April 1983), 381–387. Since 1982, China has published an annual statistical handbook.

4. For recent population estimates from the Chinese census, see "Chinese Population Census—1982," *Communist Affairs—Documents and Analysis*, 2 (July 1983), 319–321; for greater detail, see John S. Aird, "Recent Demographic Data from China: Problems and Prospects," in Joint Economic Committee, *China Under the Four Modernizations*, Part 1, pp. 171–223. For an update, see Kaun-I Chen, "China's Food Policy and Population," *Current History*, 86 (September 1981), 257–260, 274–276. The population of China in 1989 was estimated to be 1,102.4 million with an annual growth rate of 1.4 percent. See *Handbook of Economic Statistics 1990* (Washington, D.C.: CIA, 1990), Table 3.

5. *Handbook of International Economic Statistics 1992* gives China's per capita GNP from $315 to $3000. Most studies place China's GNP per capita within the $500 to $2000 range (p. 10).

6. Although collectivization may have been a factor in the consolidation of Soviet power in the countryside, recent evidence suggests that collectivization had little influence on the magnitude of the surplus shifted into the industrialization effort. For evidence, see James R. Millar, "Mass Collectivization and the Contribution of Soviet Agriculture to the First Five-Year Plan: A Review Article," *Slavic Review*, 33 (December 1974), 750–766.

7. There was some unrest and disruption in China, but markedly less than that which occurred in the Soviet Union. For a comparison, see Jan S. Prybyla, *The Political Economy of Communist China* (Scranton, Pa.: International Textbook, 1970), Ch. 5.

8. For a discussion of the transitional phases, see Prybyla, *The Political Economy of Communist China*.

9. Ibid., p. 175.

10. For a useful outline of the basic features of the Chinese administrative structure and changes through time, see Thomas G. Rawski, "China's Industrial System," in U.S. Congress, Joint Economic Committee, *China: A Reassessment of the Economy* (Washington, D.C.: Government Printing Office, 1975), pp. 175–198. For a recent comparison of the Chinese experience and the Soviet experience, see Robert F. Dernberger, "The Chinese Search for the Path of Self-Sustained Growth in the 1980s: An Assessment," in Joint Economic Committee, *China Under the Four Modernizations*, Part 1, pp. 19–76.

11. For a discussion of this period, see Roderick MacFarquhar, *The Hundred Flowers Campaign and the Chinese Intellectuals* (New York: Praeger, 1960).

12. For a discussion of the early commune, see Kenneth R. Walker, "Organization of Agricultural Production," in Alexander Eckstein, Walter Galenson, and Ta-Chung Liu, eds., *Economic Trends in Communist China* (Chicago: Aldine, 1968), pp. 440–452. For a study of the private sector, see Kenneth R. Walker, *Planning in Chinese Agriculture: Socialization and the Private Sector, 1956–1962* (Chicago: Aldine, 1965). For an update of organizational changes into the 1970s, see Frederick W. Crook, "The Commune System in the People's Republic of China, 1963–74," in Joint Economic Committee, *China: A Reassessment of the Economy*, pp. 366–410; a useful recent source is Frederic M. Surls

and Francis C. Tuan, "China's Agriculture in the Eighties," in Joint Economic Committee, *China Under the Four Modernizations*, Part 1, pp. 419–448.

13. Prybyla, *The Political Economy of Communist China*, pp. 144–145.

14. For example, in terms of agricultural performance, we might make the following crude comparison. In China in 1949, grain production was 0.20 metric ton per capita; in the Soviet Union in 1928–1929, grain production was 0.47 metric ton per capita. Chinese data are from Ashbrook, "China: Economic Modernization and Long-Term Performance," p. 104; Paul R. Gregory and Robert C. Stuart, *Soviet Economic Structure and Performance*, 3rd. ed. (New York: Harper & Row, 1986), p. 244; and TsSU (Central Statistical Administration), *Naselenie SSSR 1973* (Moscow: Statistika, 1975), p. 7.

15. These data are from Prybyla, *The Political Economy of Communist China*, pp. 135 ff.

16. Subramanian Swamy, "Economic Growth in China and India 1952–1970: A Comparative Appraisal," *Economic Development and Cultural Change*, 21 (July 1973), 62.

17. Ibid.

18. An excellent survey of these years can be found in Dernberger, "The Chinese Search for the Path of Self-Sustained Growth," pp. 19–76.

19. For a discussion of the revolutionary left in the economic context, see Robert F. Dernberger and David Fasenfest, "China's Post-Mao Economic Future," in U.S. Congress, Joint Economic Committee, *Chinese Economy Post-Mao* (Washington, D.C.: Government Printing Office, 1978), pp. 3–47.

20. There is a great deal of literature pertaining to the contemporary Chinese economy. For a useful survey of contemporary events, see Dwight Perkins, "Completing China's Move to the Market," *Journal of Economic Perspectives*, 8 (Spring 1994), 23–46; Gary H. Jefferson and Thomas G. Rawski, "Enterprise Reform in Chinese Industry," *Journal of Economic Perspectives*, 8 (Spring 1994), 47–70; Shahid Yusuf, "China's Macroeconomic Performance and Management During Transition, *Journal of Economic Perspectives*, 8 (Spring 1994), 71–92; "China's Economic Reforms: Structural and Welfare Aspects," *American Economic Review Papers and Proceedings*, 84 (May 1994), 266–284; *China: Statistical Yearbook 1993* (Bejing: State Statistical Bureau of the Peoples Republic of China, 1993).

21. Frederick W. Crook, "The Commune System in the People's Republic of China, 1963–1974," in U.S. Congress, Joint Economic Committee, China: A Reassessment of the Economy (Washington, D.C.: U.S. Government Printing Office, 1975), 411–437.

22. For a discussion of pre-reform arrangements, see, for example, Henry J. Groen and James A. Kilpatrick, "China's Agricultural Production," in U.S. Congress Joint Economic Committee, Chinese Economy Under Post-Mao, vol. 1 (Washington, D.C.: Government Printing Office, 1978), pp. 607–652.

23. For a discussion of changes in the rural economy, see for example Kuan-I Chen, "China's Changing Agricultural System," *Current History*, 82 (September 1983), 259–263, 277–278; Kuan-I Chen, "China's Food Policy and Population," 257–260, 274–276; Yak-Yeow Kueh, "China's New Agricultural-Policy Program: Major Economic Consequences, 1979–1983," *Journal of Comparative Economics*, 8 (December 1984), 353–375; Nicholas R. Lardy, *Agriculture in China's Modern Economic Development* (Cambridge, England: Cambridge University Press, 1983); Dwight Perkins and Shahid Yusuf, *Rural Development in China* (Baltimore: The Johns Hopkins University Press, 1984); Kenneth R. Walker, "Chinese Agriculture During the Period of Readjustment, 1978–83," *China Quarterly*, 100 (December 1984), 783–812; Kenneth R. Walker, *Food Grain Procurement and Consumption in China* (Cambridge, England: Cambridge University Press, 1984); Peter Nolan and Dong Fureng, eds., *Market Forces in China*

(London: Zed Books Ltd., 1990); Anthony Y. C. Koo, "The Contract Responsibility System: Transition from a Planned to a Market Economy," *Economic Development and Cultural Change*, 38 (July 1990), 797–820.

24. Dwight Perkins, "Completing China's Move to the Market," 26.
25. Chu-yuan Cheng, "China's Industrialization and Economic Development," *Current History*, 82 (September 1983), 266.
26. World Bank, *World Development Report 1993* (New York: Oxford University Press, 1993), Table 2.
27. Dwight Perkins, "Completing China's Move to the Market," 30.
28. See Gary H. Jefferson and Thomas G. Rawski, "Enterprise Reform in Chinese Industry."
29. Dwight Perkins, "Completing China's Move to the Market," Table 4.
30. Directorate of Intelligence, *China's Economy in 1992 and 1993: Grappling with the Risks of Rapid Economic Growth* (Washington, D.C.: CIA, 1993).

Recommended Readings

General Works

Richard Baum, ed., *China's Four Modernizations: The New Technological Revolution* (Boulder, Colo.: Westview Press, 1980).

Chu-yuan Cheng, *China's Economic Development: Growth and Structural Change* (Boulder, Colo.: Westview Press, 1982).

Gregory Chow, *The Chinese Economy* (New York: Harper & Row, 1984).

Robert F. Dernberger, ed., *China's Development Experience in Comparative Perspective* (Cambridge, Mass.: Harvard University Press, 1980).

Audrey Donnithorne, *China's Economic System* (New York: Praeger, 1967).

Alexander Eckstein, *China's Economic Development: The Interplay of Scarcity and Ideology* (Ann Arbor: University of Michigan Press, 1975).

———, *China's Economic Revolution* (New York: Cambridge University Press, 1977).

———, *Communist China's Economic Growth and Foreign Trade* (New York: McGraw-Hill, 1969).

Alexander Eckstein, Walter Galenson, and Ta-Chung Liu, eds., *Economic Trends in Communist China* (Chicago: Aldine, 1968).

Christopher Howe, *China's Economy: A Basic Guide* (New York: Basic Books, 1978).

Gary H. Jefferson and Wenyi Yu, "The Impact of Reform on Socialist Enterprises in Transition: Structure, Conduct, and Performance in Chinese Industry," *Journal of Comparative Economics*, 15 (January 1991), 45–54.

Thomas P. Lyons, *Economic Integration and Planning in Maoist China* (New York: Columbia University Press, 1987).

Nicholas Lardy, *Economic Growth and Distribution in China* (New York: Cambridge University Press, 1979).

Jan S. Prybyla, *The Chinese Economy: Problems and Policies*, 2nd. ed. (Columbia: University of South Carolina Press, 1981).

———, *The Political Economy of Communist China* (Scranton, Pa.: International Textbook, 1970).

Carl Riskin, *China's Political Economy* (New York: Oxford University Press, 1987).

Kai Yuen Tsui, "China's Regional Inequality, 1952–1985," *Journal of Comparative Economics*, 15 (March 1991), 1–21.

U.S. Congress, Joint Economic Committee, *China: A Reassessment of the Economy* (Washington, D.C.: Government Printing Office, 1975).

———, *China Under the Four Modernizations* (Washington, D.C.: Government Printing Office, 1982).

———, *Chinese Economy Post-Mao* (Washington, D.C.: Government Printing Office, 1978).

———, *An Economic Profile of Mainland China*, Vols. I and II (Washington, D.C.: Government Printing Office, 1967).

———, *China's Economic Dilemmas in the 1990s: The Problems of Reforms, Modernization, and Interdependence*, Vols. 1 and 2 (Washington, D.C.: Government Printing Office, 1991).

The Rural Economy

William A. Byrd and Lin Qingsong, eds., *China's Rural Industry* (New York: Oxford University Press, 1991).

Kang Chao, *Man and Land in Chinese History: An Economic Analysis* (Stanford: Stanford University Press, 1987).

Kuan-I Chen, "China's Food Policy and Population," *Current History*, 86 (September 1987), 257–260, 274–276.

Yak-Yeow Kueh, "China's New Agricultural-Policy Program: Major Economic Consequences, 1979–1983," *Journal of Comparative Economics*, 8 (December 1984), 353–375.

Nicholas R. Lardy, *Agriculture in China's Modern Economic Development* (Cambridge, England: Cambridge University Press, 1983).

Victor Nee and Frank W. Young, "Peasant Entrepreneurs in China's 'Second Economy': An Institutional Analysis," *Economic Development and Cultural Change*, 37 (January 1991), 293–310.

Dwight H. Perkins, *Agricultural Development in China, 1368–1968* (Chicago: University of Chicago Press, 1969).

———, ed., *Rural Small-Scale Industry in the People's Republic of China* (Berkeley: University of California Press, 1977).

Economic Reform

Willam A. Byrd, ed., *Chinese Industrial Firms under Reform* (Oxford: Oxford University Press, 1992).

Richard Conroy, *Technological Change in China* (Paris: OECD, 1992).

Kang Chen, Gary H. Jefferson, and Inderjit Singh, "Lessons from China's Economic Reform," *Journal of Comparative Economics*, 16 (1992), 201–225.

Directorate of Intelligence, *The Chinese Economy in 1991 and 1992: Pressure to Revisit Reform Mounts* (Washington, D.C.: Central Intelligence Agency, 1992).

———, *China's Economy in 1992 and 1993: Grappling with the Risks of Rapid Economic Growth* (Washington, D.C.: Central Intelligence Agency, 1993).

Qimiao Fan and Peter Nolan, *China's Economic Reforms* (New York: St. Martin's Press, 1994).

Joseph Fewsmith, *Dilemmas of Reform in China* (Armonk, N.Y.: M.E. Sharpe, 1994).

David Granick, *Chinese State Enterprises: A Regional Property Rights Analysis* (Chicago: University of Chicago Press, 1990).

Keith Griffin and Zhao Renwei, eds., *The Distribution of Income in China* (New York: St. Martins Press, 1993).

Gary H. Jefferson and Thomas G. Rawski, "Enterprise Reform in Chinese Industry," *Journal of Economic Perspectives*, 8 (Spring 1994), 47–70.

Gary H. Jefferson, Thomas G. Rawski, and Yuxin Zheng, "Growth, Efficiency, and Convergence in China's State and Collective Industry," *Economic Development and Cultural Change* 40 (1992a), 239–266.

Hsueh Jien-tsung, Sung Yun-wing and Yu Jingyuan, *Studies on Economic Reform and Development in in The Peoples Republic of China* (New York: St. Martin's Press, 1993).

Deborah A. Kaple, *Dream of a Red Factory* (New York: Oxford University Press, 1994).

Anthony Y. C. Koo, "The Contract Responsibility System: Transition From a Planned to a Market Economy," *Economic Development and Cultural Change* 38 (July 1990), 797–820.

Deepak Lah, "The Failure of The Three Envelopes: The Analytics and Political Economy of the Reform of Chinese State-Owned Enterprises" *European Economic Review* 34 (September 1990), 1213–1231.

Ike Mathur and Chen Jui-Sheng, *Strategies for Joint Ventures in The People's Republic of China* (New York: Praeger, 1987).

Barry Naughton, *Growing Out of The Plan: Chinese Economic Reform, 1978–1993* (New York: Cambridge University Press, 1993).

Ole Odgaard, *Private Enterprises in Rural China* (Brookfield, Vermont: Ashgate Publishing Company, 1992).

Dwight H. Perkins, "Completing China's Move to a Market Economy," *Journal of Economic Perspectives*, 8 (Spring 1994), 23–46.

Elizabeth J. Perry and Christine Wong, *The Political Economy of Reform in Post-Mao China* (Cambridge, Mass.: Harvard University Press, 1987).

Jan S. Prybyla, "Mainland China's Economic System: A Study in Contradictions," *Issues & Studies* 30, 8 (August, 1994), 1–30.

Susan L. Shirk, *The Political Logic of Economic Reform in China* (Berkeley: University of California Press, 1993).

Clement Tisdell, *Economic Development in The Context of China* (New York: St. Martin's Press, 1993).

George Totten and Zhou Shulian, eds., *China's Economic Reform* (Boulder: Westview Press, 1992).

Lim Wei and Arnold Chao, eds., *China's Economic Reforms* (Philadelphia: University of Pennsylvania Press, 1983).

Gordon White, The Politics of Economic Reform in Chinese Industry: The Introduction of The Labour Contract System," *The China Quarterly*, 11 (September 1987), 365–389.

Christine P. Wong, "The Economics of Shortages and Problems of Reform in Chinese Industry," *Journal of Comparative Economics*, 10 (December 1986), 363–387.

Shahid Yusuf, "China's Macroeconomic Performance and Management During Transition," *Journal of Economic Perspectives*, 8 (Spring 1994), 71–92.

18

Eastern Europe: Poland, Hungary and the Czech Republic

Chapter 4 examined the broad issues of how economic systems change. Section IV focused closely on the issues of transition, particularly emphasizing the basic concerns facing contemporary economies, especially those of the former Soviet Union and Eastern Europe. Although fundamental transition issues can be identified and discussed, our examination of Russia and China has indicated that transition patterns deviate considerably in differing real-world settings. Such is certainly the case in the countries of Eastern Europe, which is the subject of this chapter.

Although it is difficult to discuss the basic transition issues in isolation from real-world cases, the discussions in Section IV were designed to present contemporary economic thinking on transition and to focus only limited attention on real-world cases. As this discussion of Eastern Europe begins, it is important to understand how these countries differ from those previously studied, and how these differences have and will continue to affect the transition process.

The East European Setting

Prior to the era of glasnost and perestroika in the mid- and late-1980s, the Soviet Union had not been a leader in the sphere of economic reform and change in the planned socialist economic systems. At the same time, within political constraints, Eastern European countries, such as Hungary, pursued **economic reform** so they would be in a different position as transition began in earnest in the early 1990s. Although the Soviet Union had been the political and economic model for Eastern Europe after World War II, important differences had developed between the Soviet Union and the systems of Eastern Europe by the mid-1980s.

The first difference centers on the economic history of Eastern Europe, which was very different from that of the Soviet Union. The Soviet Union imposed its political and economic systems on Eastern Europe, and, with the possible exception of Yugoslavia, their arrangements followed the **Soviet model** very closely. The means of production were nationalized, agriculture was collectivized, and balance planning was the primary mechanism for allocating resources. Within a few years after World War II, the economic systems of Eastern Europe closely resembled that of the Soviet Union.

Second, at the time of the breakdown that led to transition in the early 1990s, the nations of Eastern Europe had been functioning under the Soviet model for roughly 35 years, a relatively short period. In contrast, the political and economic arrangements in the Soviet Union had been in place since the late 1920s, a much longer time. Thus the characteristics of the command economy had much less time to take hold, which made both the memory and the impact of market forces much stronger in Eastern Europe than in the Soviet Union.

Third, although there was a great deal of discussion in the Soviet Union in the 1920s regarding the nature of economic growth and development and the appropriateness of alternative strategies, no such discussion occurred in Eastern Europe. Indeed, in the early 1950s the countries of Eastern Europe were at a very different starting point than that of the Soviet Union in 1928. These differences were important then and became important again in the 1990s as these countries reverted to market arrangements.

Fourth, most of the countries of Eastern Europe differed from one another, but most important, they differed fundamentally from the Soviet Union. Most were relatively small, resource poor, and were, of necessity, reliant on foreign trade for any development strategy. If planned socialist systems were trade averse, the impact of such a policy must have been significantly more in these relatively small trade-oriented nations.

Fifth, there were significant differences among the Eastern European nations regarding the level of rigor with which the Soviet model was applied and thus the extent of reform and change during the plan era. For example, one might contrast Albania, always considered a rigid Stalinist model, with Yugoslavia, a country that broke with the planned socialist model relatively soon after its attempted implementation. In the middle were the economic situations in Hungary and the Czech republic, each of which were different. Hungary began to experiment with economic reform in the late 1960s, while political repression in Czechoslovakia limited the extent and meaning of economic reform.

Finally, the countries of Eastern Europe differ significantly from the former Soviet Union (and the now independent countries) in yet another important dimension: their cultural, religious, and ethnic composition and the historical experiences based on those differences. Although critical exceptions do occur (such as the violent situation in Yugoslavia), many countries of Eastern Europe have a measure of ethnic and religious harmony that can provide the basis for political consensus and the stability necessary for economic change.

When examining the cases focused on in this chapter, it is important to consider the impact of these forces on the success and the failure of the transition process.

Eastern Europe: Selecting the Cases

This chapter pays special attention to Poland, Hungary, and the Czech Republic, which were chosen a variety of factors. Because these countries were better able to pursue transition, they have had greater success than other Eastern European countries. Foreign trade was much more important for these countries than for other Eastern European countries. In addition, Hungary had pursued economic reform for decades, and prior to the end of the planned socialist era, Poland had a strong political opposition through the Solidarity movement.

Despite differences, the treatment of Poland, Hungary, and the Czech Republic here will include a brief discussion of the background of each country followed by an examination of how the transition process unfolded and how the early results were achieved.

Poland: From Plan to Market via Shock Therapy

Until the Solidarity Party won the parliamentary elections in Poland in the summer of 1989, the Polish economy had been, in the post–World War II era, a typical planned socialist economic system molded after the Soviet model.[1] State ownership predominated, industry was emphasized, and although reform was attempted at various stages it was largely unsuccessful. Rates of growth of output declined over the years along with recurring shortages, inflation, and an understandably declining work ethic.

The initial years of transition—1990 and 1991—were critical. The approach, dubbed "shock therapy," was sudden, as opposed to the more **gradualist approach** other countries used. In a nutshell, prices were generally freed, the growth of the money supply was controlled, the zloty was made convertible into hard currencies, and steps were taken to control wage increases. Initially, the Polish approach was considered unique, though the shock therapy approach is not without critics.[2] Before examining the Polish transition experience in greater detail, some background is necessary.

Poland: The Setting

By European standards, Poland is a large country. With a land area just over 300,000 square kilometers, it is just over half the size of France. Moreover, with a population of approximately 38 million, Poland is 68 percent the size of France in terms of population.

Poland can be characterized as a relatively homogenous society, a factor that greatly facilitates economic reform and transition. Although there are urban–rural differentials in standards of living, 95 percent of Poland's population is Catholic and 98.7 percent is ethnically Polish, leaving only a few minority groups.

Urbanization and industrialization have clearly changed the nature of Polish life and customs, and yet the strength of the church, family, and folk ties have been sustained. That clear measure of identity has made social and economic change easier to implement than would otherwise be possible.

In terms of natural resources, Poland is a country with considerable regional diversity, though major portions of the land are not especially fertile, and environmental decay remains a serious problem. Poland's main source of energy is coal, but it also has some basic minerals and some deposits of oil and natural gas.

Poland: The Command Economy

The Polish command system was established immediately after World War II and closely resembled that of the Soviet Union.[3]

The 1980s began with roughly three years of martial law and new reform attempts under the military leadership of General Wojciech Jaruzelski. These attempts were somewhat similar to ones proposed in the 1950s; however, analysis of the economic reforms of the 1980s suggests that their impact was limited and that the Polish economy was not converted to market socialist arrangements during the 1980s. Serious changes, however, would begin at the end of that decade.

From the data presented in Table 18.1, the economic difficulties of the 1980s are evident.[4] Growth of output experienced serious fluctuations after secular declines in earlier years. The volume of industrial employment fell by roughly 20 percent in the 1980s, and inflation became a serious problem, which worsened to hyperinflation in 1989. The Polish external hard-currency debt roughly doubled during that decade. These economic difficulties prepared the way for the beginnings of transition in 1990.

Polish Transition: "Shock Therapy" in Practice

The Polish reform program officially began on January 1, 1990, several months after the collapse of its communist government.[5] At that time, the economy was in a state of disequilibrium. Although the exact magnitude of the monetary overhang has been the subject of debate, money wage increases were out of control, there was a significant budget deficit, and hyperinflation was rampant. The initial program consisted of four components: fiscal control and the elimination of the budget deficit, control of domestic credit expansion, limits to the growth of wages, and convertibility of the zloty.

By autumn 1989, most price controls were lifted on producer and consumer goods, rationing was ended, public spending was reduced, and the zloty was devalued. In early 1990, the reduction of subsidies to state enterprises further reduced the state budget. Plans were being made to implement a positive real rate of interest and to use the market to signal real changes in the value of the zloty. Foreign trade was becoming a key component of the transition program. In January 1990 the government set the exchange rate at 9500 zloty to the dollar, roughly the rate on the black market, and the government also established **convertibility**. Many trade restrictions were eliminated and internal exchanges were established to handle the

TABLE 18.1 The Polish Economy: The 1980s

| | | | Average Annual Rate of Growth | | | | | |
	1971–1980	1981–1985	1987	1988	1989	1990	1991	1992
Real Gross Domestic Product	3.6	.6	-1.5	2.3	-1.6	-9.6	-7.6	-1.5
Real Gross Domestic Product per Capita	2.6	-.3	-2.0	2.0	-2.0	-9.8	-8.1	-1.7
Consumer Price Index (1980 = 100)	—	—	575	938	3325	—	—	—

Sources: Directorate of Intelligence, *Handbook of International Statistics 1992* (Washington, D.C: CIA, 1992), Table 13; *Handbook of International Statistics 1993*, Tables 8 and 9.

buying and selling of hard currencies. Although these changes resulted in domestic inflation, the initial price increases were temporary and the exchange rate of the zloty was reasonable. Wage indexation and a new tax on wage increases that exceeded established guidelines partly controlled wage increases.

In mid-1990, a **privatization** law was passed and a Ministry of Ownership Change was established to oversee the privatization process. Although the process of privatization turned out to be complicated, the initial steps proceeded in a familiar fashion, focusing on the gradual privatization of large state enterprises through the initial establishment of corporations, the auctioning of smaller enterprises, and the development of small new enterprises through reduced entry restrictions, a process already begun in the late 1980s.

In practice, privatization was uneven largely because it proceeded primarily for services and small-scale industry, not the large state enterprises. Moreover, the role of local authorities and the level of worker participation in new arrangements were controversial issues. Although private employment was reportedly 45 percent of total employment (including agriculture) at the end of 1991, privatization in the state sector still lagged. This lack of progress motivated the creation of an Industrial Restructuring Agency and the beginning of privatization in the state sector through the establishment of stock funds and a voucher system. These policies were designed to offset problems typical of large-scale privatizations in Eastern Europe, specifically the absence of capital markets and the limited savings of potential individual investors.

Although privatization has been slow in the major state sector, it would be wrong to conclude that changes have not been made. Apparently there have been considerable changes in the management system of these now-private companies, largely through the active operation of workers' councils established in the 1980s. According to one study, by the end of 1990, half of the managers of these private enterprises were reconfirmed by the councils and 40 percent were new managers.[6]

Prior to the beginning of the transition in Poland, the agricultural sector was predominantly private. By the end of the 1980s, 75 percent of arable land was in private hands, and 85 percent of net agricultural output was generated in the private sector. During the command era, however, private Polish agriculture did not have adequate access to inputs in policy setting that favored the socialized sector. Thus modernization of a technologically backward but private agriculture has become the focus of agricultural development in Poland during transition.

Not surprisingly, 1990 the Polish economy suffered a significant decline in output. Having said that, there is little agreement on just how serious the decline had been, and the nature of the underlying causes. Obviously, one would expect the performance in the state and private sectors to be different, though isolation of these sectors has been difficult. Much of the decline was in the state sector because of a decline in demand, changing enterprise rules, and other factors that made conducting economic activity difficult, such as the disruption of the supply system and the problem of obtaining credits.

Beyond the difficulties of 1990, the collapse of the socialist bloc trading arrangements at the beginning of 1991 created serious problems for Eastern European nations. Trade essentially collapsed and the move for Polish/Soviet trade from zloty/ruble exchanges to hard currency exchanges began. In Poland, there was considerable debate over the causes of this decline and especially about the potential role of domestic macroeconomic policies. In any event, the collapse of CMEA trade was a serious problem for all of the countries concerned.

As Table 18.4 on page 443 indicates, Polish output began to grow at relatively rapid rates in the 1990s. Inflation dropped to an annual rate of 25 percent, though unemployment remained stubbornly high at around 15 percent of the labor force.

What generalizations can be drawn from the Polish experience with shock therapy? Although a longer span of years would provide a better perspective on the economic events in Poland, the initial outcomes show that while there was an initial collapse of output and rising inflation during the period of rapid transformation, Poland was able to return to positive output growth and to limit inflation more quickly than other transforming economies. Although the rate of unemployment increased significantly during the transformation, the level of Polish unemployment was not unusually high relative to that of other transforming economies. But as in other transition cases, the Polish outcome results from a variety of conditioning forces, which are more complex than simple shock therapy.

Hungary: The New Economic Mechanism and Transition

Unlike most East European economic systems functioning through the Soviet model, Hungary has made early attempts to implement economic reform. Prior to 1968, Hungary was a typical centrally planned socialist economic system. Beginning in 1968, Hungary tried to introduce the most radical economic reform attempted at the time by a planned socialist economy (with the exception of Yugoslavia). Although the program—the **New Economic Mechanism (NEM)**—was only partially successful, some of the changes implemented may have facilitated the subsequent transition to markets when the communist government collapsed. But in other dimensions, such as its geographic size and the importance of foreign trade, Hungary has been prototypical of the East European experience.

Hungary: The Setting

Hungary has a land area approximately 92,000 square kilometers, slightly larger than the state of Indiana, with a population of roughly 11 million, equaling that of the state of Illinois. Although Hungary has limited natural sources of fuel, it does have certain amounts of coal, oil, and a number of minerals, including substantial bauxite deposits.

From a geographic perspective, Hungary is a flat country with good land and a favorable climate for farming. As in other areas of Eastern Europe, in the period since World War II, Hungary experienced considerable shifts in population, from rural to urban locations and from agricultural to industrial and service activities. Today, roughly half of the Hungarian population lives in urban areas.

Hungary is not a particularly prosperous nation. Most estimates of the Hungarian output, or output per capita, place it in the middle of the East European countries, wealthier than Bulgaria, Yugoslavia, and certainly Albania, but behind the former German Democratic Republic (GDR) and the Czech Republic. The per capita income of Hungary is close to that of Greece.

The Hungarian Command Economy: Implementation and Reform

The postwar reconstruction of the Hungarian economy began modestly in 1945.[7] Before the implementation of a three-year plan in 1947 (to cover the years 1947 through 1949), the main policies were currency stabilization, changes in the nature of rural landholding, and the beginnings of nationalization. A system of economic planning was established, and investment shares increased sharply. Although balanced development had been envisioned, that prospect came to an end in the early 1950s when the Soviet model was implemented.

A number of basic problems plagued the Hungarian economy during these early years that were partly a result of the command system. There were problems with labor supply, specifically low productivity and limited ability to offset this problem with new labor from rural areas. Waste and imbalance were considerable, especially in the material supply system. Excess demand for investment left construction unfinished and traditional facilities neglected.

Beginning in the mid-1960s, Hungarian leaders began discussing economic reform, which culminated in the NEM program, announced in 1969.[8] That program sought to combine traditional state control of the major sectors of economic activity with increasing reliance on market-type forces to assist in routine decision-making activity. Put another way, the NEM was an attempt to decentralize decision making in the Hungarian command economy. That sort of change would come from a reduction in the number of targets promulgated by central planners. In many cases, compulsory output targets ended when enterprise managers began relying on local market forces especially for coordinating interenterprise activities.

In addition to changes in the plan and its guidance rules, were changes in the use of financial indicators. Profits became more important and would be a source of enterprise financing and decentralized incentives for managers and workers. Local flexibility would be limited by state guidelines, but within these guidelines would be flexibility in areas such as wages and profits.

Foreign trade reform was another major component of the NEM. Firms were able to engage directly in foreign trade and changes were made to facilitate such a process. Price flexibility was even suggested to allow changes in foreign prices to influence domestic Hungarian prices.

Observers of planned socialist economies were very interested in the NEM for several reasons: First, it was announced shortly after the announcement of Aleksei Kosygin's largely unsuccessful and more conservative reform program of 1965 in the Soviet Union. In addition, it was clearly an alternative to the sorts of changes envisioned in the former GDR. And finally, it seemed to represent a major attempt to implement what had been suggested many years earlier by Oskar Lange—namely central control of major economic issues combined with local control of the daily functioning of the economy.

Although most observers would probably argue that the NEM program was unsuccessful, it nevertheless had an impact on the Hungarian economy. There were, however, a variety of familiar problems.

First, these types of reforms, and NEM was no exception, met with political constraints. Real limits were imposed on how much central power could actually be delegated to lower levels. That fact, combined with traditional political rigidities, limited the extent to which change could be made.

Second, any reform of planned socialist systems always encountered difficulties. Combining plan and market proved to be difficult. Moreover, any reform would be implemented from the given economic structure, which was often not suited to a market environment.

Third, the **implementation of reform** in these systems implied acceptance of goals and outcomes that the political leaders usually found unacceptable. If the labor market were to function, there had to be mobility and unemployment. If prices were to be freed, inflation would be likely. These results were generally unacceptable to the leaders of the planned systems.

As time passed, it was evident that the NEM would not be implemented as originally designed. Although some argue that the Hungarian economy had been decentralized to some degree, it was considerably less so than the extent to which it had been originally envisioned. In fact, state control of the economy increased. For example, taxes and subsidies were introduced to protect the Hungarian economy from the influence of world market forces, which was the opposite of that envisioned in the original NEM blueprint. The net result for Hungary was an economy facing rather typical problems in the 1980s—worsening performance and a growing debt.

Although Hungary was able to translate past improvements in economic performance into a better standard of living, performance slipped in the 1970s and 1980s (see Table 18.2). Inflationary pressures (though not as serious as those in Poland) plagued the Hungarian economy along with internal microeconomic imbalances and a growing **external hard-currency debt**. Although the volume of that debt was roughly half that of Poland, it had doubled in size in the 1980s.

Hungarian leaders responded to these economic difficulties by implementing policies designed to sustain the standard of living while bringing the trade balance under control. A stabilization program was introduced, and Hungary joined the International Monetary Fund in the early 1980s. Controls were implemented to limit imports and to expand exports. Investment was to be constrained by the state budget and the growth of consumption constrained through wage limitations. While some change took place (for example, adjustments in prices), the persistence of Soviet-type controls limited its nature and extent and left the Hungarian economy with a wide range of unresolved economic problems as the Communist era came to an end.

TABLE 18.2 The Hungarian Economy: The 1980s

			Average Annual Rate of Growth					
	1971–1980	1981–1985	1987	1988	1989	1990	1991	1992
Real Gross Domestic Product	2.7	.3	1.5	1.5	-2.3	-6.8	-6.8	-7.8
Real Gross Domestic Product per Capita	2.1	.9	1.8	3.5	-2.1	-6.8	-5.9	-7.8
Consumer Price Index (1980 = 100)	—	—	164	184	240	—	—	—

Sources: Directorate of Intelligence, *Handbook of International Statistics 1992* (Washington, D.C: CIA, 1992), Table 13; *Handbook of International Statistics 1993*, Tables 8 and 9.

Hungary: Gradual Transition to Markets

Transition in Hungary has been different from other cases. Not only has it been gradual, but it also has not been based on a **"grand design"** and it began earlier and under different circumstances from those which prevailed in Poland.[9] Inflation did not necessitate immediate stabilization measures, though issues relating to foreign trade assumed importance partly because of the size of Hungary's hard-currency debt as well as the collapse of the CMEA in 1990.

The beginning of transition is generally dated to 1985, although this is hard to pinpoint without a specific reform program. Since that time, a series of ongoing policy and systemic changes has occurred that shifted the Hungarian economy toward a market economy. But these changes have taken place on a sequential and continually changing basis. Understandably, the changes have been in expected areas, namely privatization, macro- and micro-economic policies, and foreign trade.

Beginning in the 1980s, the means for selecting enterprise managers changed when enterprises themselves began exercising a voice.[10] This managerial revolution not only changed personnel, it also changed the decision-making environment and began to change the way in which enterprise managers functioned. Thereafter, in 1988 the Company Act was passed, and in 1990 the State Property Agency was created. Privatization mainly began on a small scale in services and related areas and proceeded slowly from there. While fewer than 10 percent of the GDP originated in the private sector in 1985, the private sector share captured 20 to 30 percent by 1991. In the early 1990s, a serious effort began to formalize the legal structure, especially to isolate the state enterprises in corporate form.

Throughout the late 1980s and into the 1990s, efforts have begun to change the role of government in the Hungarian economy.[11] The share of subsidies decreased by more than half (from 15 to 7 percent of GDP) between 1985 and 1991. Efforts also began to redefine income maintenance programs, and prices were gradually freed. As a result, unemployment increased and real wages declined.

Although Hungary began its transition era with a large external and growing debt, assistance was provided and, in spite of the virtual collapse of CMEA trade in the early 1990s, a reduction of imports and significant increases in exports especially in Western markets caused a major decline in the current account deficit between 1989 and 1991. On the capital account, the increase in private transfers and the sizable inflow of foreign capital were both extremely beneficial.

The Czech Republic: Planning, Politics, and Transition

In 1993, the Czech Republic was formed when the former Czechoslovakia was divided into the Czech and the Slovak republics. Throughout the period after World War II and until the end of the 1980s, the economic arrangements of Czechoslovakia were similar to other East European economies—a planned socialist system that followed the Stalinist model. However, in addition to its political and economic differences, Czechoslovakia was, in the late 1940s, much more developed than other East European economies, though there were significant regional differences because industrialization was mainly confined to the Czech lands.

Although the case of Czechoslovakia was different in some respects, the long period of central planning culminated in an economy with distortions and declining performance similar to those found elsewhere. For convenience, the Czech history will be described as it was, namely by looking at the issues relating to Czechoslovakia. Later a discussion on transition deals with the issues facing a separate Czech Republic.

Czechoslovakia: Natural Setting

Czechoslovakia has a land area of just more than 125,000 square kilometers, somewhat larger than that of New York State. Although Czechoslovakia is strategically located with a moderate climate and good agricultural lands, its industry, which was developed during the plan era, is outmoded, and in spite of a quality labor force, its close link with the economy of the former Soviet Union has limited the ability of Czechoslovakia to compete in world markets.

Czechoslovakia is deficient in energy supplies and raw materials, and like many other contemporary East European nations, environmental disruption is a serious problem. To understand the contemporary transition to markets that began in late 1989 and early 1990, the basic elements of the former command system are discussed.

Czechoslovakia: The Command Experience

The Communist Party of Czechoslovakia took control of the country in 1948.[12] Immediately afterwards, the Soviet model was introduced along with the nationalization of property, the collectivization of agriculture, the familiar priorities of high investment focused on industry, and a reorientation of foreign trade toward the Soviet Union and other East European countries.

Although the initial plan years yielded good economic growth, early attempts in the mid-1950s to decentralize the economy were abandoned until the late 1960s. After a period of markedly slower growth rates in the early and mid-1960s, there were serious reform discussions. These discussions centered on the concept of market socialism and a plan for significantly decentralizing decision making along with important market influences.

A new reform leader, Alexander Dubček, encouraged the new directions of the late 1960s. Moreover, the substantial popular support for both economic and political reform was important to Dubček's position. This receptivity to economic and political reform culminated in what was called the Prague Spring of 1968. The outcome of the Prague Spring is well known. Alarmed by potential democratization,

Moscow ordered Warsaw Pact troops to invade, bringing an immediate end to the reform and a recentralization of the economy.

Although some piecemeal reform efforts were made in the 1970s, that decade and the one following were difficult times for Czechoslovakia, similar to those experienced by Poland and Hungary. Czechoslovakia had to import energy, and it faced serious problems in after the 1973 era of OPEC. In addition to the serious impact rising costs had on domestic industry, they also significantly lessened Czechoslovakia's ability to compete in foreign markets.

The data in Table 18.3 tell a familiar story. There were, however, some exceptions. Although the Czech economic performance fluctuated and underwent significant slowdowns during the 1970s and 1980s, Czechoslovakia, unlike Poland, began the subsequent transition era with a very small external hard-currency debt. This was largely due to conservative financial management. Inflation was also limited. In a sense, that history put the economy of Czechoslovakia in an interesting position at the beginning of transition. Some of the adverse indicators common in other countries (inflation and external debt) were absent, even though the economy of Czechoslovakia had been significantly repressed after the Prague Spring of 1968.

Czechoslovakia: Transition and Political Change

At the beginning of 1987, a major program of economic reform was announced.[13] This program resembled earlier reform attempts, and yet it was more modest in character. Initial implementation was also modest, until the events of late 1989 and the free elections of 1990 that brought communist power to an end. While the transition government announced its intention to move toward the creation of a market economy, it was not until late 1990, after considerable discussion, that a transition plan was announced. But transition steps did not begin in earnest until early 1991.

In January of that year, producer and consumer prices were liberalized and the koruna was devalued. Changes in the exchange rate of the koruna vis-à-vis other currencies would be determined by a tie or peg to a basket of five western currencies. In addition, a surcharge was placed on imports and steps were taken to control the growth of wages. These changes were made within the context of a set of stabilization policies and the pursuit of privatization. As in other transition cases, much attention was focused on privatization in the Czech and Slovak republics.

Privatization began in Czechoslovakia in three broad forms: restitution, small-scale privatization through auctions in 1990, and finally in 1991, **voucher privatization** as a part of a large-scale privatization initiative instituted by the Ministry of Finance.[14] In addition to direct sales and sales of enterprises being converted to joint stock operations, individual access to property was achieved through the voucher system. Citizens could purchase vouchers with investment points that they could use later for bidding on enterprises listed for privatization. The bidding could be made directly with public announcement of the results, or it could be made through investment diversification funds, which are mechanisms used to encourage diversification.

TABLE 18.3 The Economy of Czechoslovakia: The 1980s

			Average Annual Rate of Growth					
	1971–1980	1981–1985	1987	1988	1989	1990	1991	1992
Real Gross Domestic Product	2.8	1.2	.5	2.2	.7	-2.8	-14.8	-5.3
Real Gross Domestic Product per Capita	2.0	1.0	-1.	2.2	.7	-3.4	-14.6	-5.3
Consumer Price Index (1980 = 100)	—	—	110	112	114	—	—	—

Sources: Directorate of Intelligence, *Handbook of International Statistics 1992* (Washington, D.C: CIA, 1992), Table 13; *Handbook of International Statistics 1993*, Tables 8 and 9.

In the initial stages of privatization, a majority of citizens chose to invest through the investment diversification funds. The Czech voucher system has been praised for providing citizens with a quick means of privatization. But in the absence of developed financial markets, there have been problems with restructuring, management, and the sale of remaining stock in privatizing firms. Thus, while much of the population has participated in exchanging most of the points for shares, the bulk of privatized firms have been unable to sell all their shares. Although preparations began earlier, the Prague Stock Exchange did not begin operations until the spring of 1993. Moreover, the separation of the Czech and Slovak republics inevitably complicated the process of privatization. In particular, the two countries began to pursue different approaches to privatization; the Czech Republic continued using the voucher approach while the Slovak Republic preferred more traditional approaches.

Beyond the pursuit of the basic objectives of transition, substantial efforts were made in 1991 and 1992 to change the pattern of government spending (such as reducing subsidies to enterprises) and to develop domestic financial markets and a new social safety net. That safety net is important in light of early reductions in the standard of living, even though levels of unemployment in the Czech Republic have not been high and support for serious transition measures has always been substantial. Probably the most important item on the agenda for the mid-1990s is restructuring, to take place in a setting of generally restrictive economic policies.

Eastern Europe: Transition, Performance, and Restructuring

Thus far, the three major transition situations in Poland, Hungary, and the Czech Republic have been examined in light of each country's background prior to transition and the basic components of transition. Despite broad similarities among these cases, there were also differences at the start of transition as well as differences among the policies and systemic changes implemented. Although it is far too early to provide a substantive assessment of the outcomes in such cases as these, it is useful to take a preliminary glance at the numbers that are available.

Table 18.4 presents basic performance data. The pattern of decline in output is evident in all three countries, though the pattern and the depth of the decline differs. If the numbers are reasonably accurate, Poland suffered the least decline and has recovered most quickly. From the standpoint of the consumer, it is clear that Poland faced the most serious inflation problem, though all three countries have been able to bring inflation under better control. While unemployment has increased significantly in all cases, it is least serious in the Czech Republic. Finally, the decrease in the value of the domestic currency relative to the U.S. dollar has been strikingly similar in all three cases, the most stable case being the Czech Republic.

Although the data in Table 18.4 indicate important changes in these economies and a measure of hardship for the population, they could arguably represent

TABLE 18.4 Poland, Hungary, and the Czech Republic, 1988–1995 (percentage change)

	1988	1989	1990	1991	1992	1993	1994	1995
GDP (Constant Prices)								
Poland	4.1	0.2	-11.6	-7.6	1.0	4.0	4.0	3.0
Hungary	-0.4	0.7	-3.5	-11.9	-4.4	-1.6	1.0	2.0
Czech Republic	2.5	1.4	-0.4	-14.2	-7.1	-1.0	2.0	5.0
Consumer Prices (Annual Average)								
Poland	60.2	251.1	585.8	70.3	43.0	35.3	30.0	25.0
Hungary	16.5	17.0	28.9	35.0	23.0	22.5	19.0	17.0
Czech Republic	0.2	2.3	10.8	56.7	11.1	20.8	11.0	10.0
Unemployment Rate (year end)								
Poland	0.0	0.1	6.1	11.8	13.6	15.7	16.0	15.0
Hungary	n.a.	0.3	2.5	8.0	12.3	12.1	11.0	11.0
Czech Republic	n.a.		0.8	4.1	2.6	4.0	5.0	7.0
Exchange Rate (end of year)								
Poland (zloty per U.S. $)	503.0	6500	9500	10583	13631	18136	n.a.	n.a.
Hungary (forint per U.S. $)	52.5	62.5	61.5	75.6	84.0	101.8	n.a.	n.a.
Czech Republic (crowns per U.S. $)	14.3	14.3	28.0	27.8	28.9	29.8	n.a.	n.a.

n.a. = not available

Source: *Economics of Transition 2* (March 1994), Tables 3, 4, 5; projections for 1994 and 1995 from OECD, "Developments in Selected Non-OECD Countries," *Economic Outlook*, J5 (June 1994), 115–117.

considerable success for the transition process as well as for the policies designed to stabilize the economy, limit the extent of downturn, and begin a pattern of recovery.

Although short-term performance is important for the success of transition and for defining new social contracts, ultimately the success of **restructuring** is most important for these economies to become integrated into the world economy. Although restructuring will take many years, it is useful to examine preliminary changes while bearing in mind the limitations of available data.

Table 18.5 presents data for examining basic trends in restructuring. It is evident from the share of GDP derived from the private sector that privatization has proceeded in all cases, though in each instance progress has been quite different. Moreover, considering that the initial stages of privatization are in some sense the easiest (privatization of small-scale service operations compared with large-scale industrial enterprises), much remains to be done.

If, in fact, the Soviet model of the pretransition era left a distorted structure that unduly emphasized the industrial sector, **sectoral shares** (measured, for example, by output or labor force) would be expected to change. Here the evidence is mixed, though the span of time is very short and measurement problems are serious. Poland has experienced a significant decline in industry, while the decline in Hungary has been modest, and the change in the Czech Republic perverse.

A major thrust of transition programs is the introduction of markets and, one could anticipate, a reduction of the role of government in the economy. The role of the government is, however, complex. First, the functions of government and its ability to perform these functions are likely to change during the transition process and might well be different from the functions anticipated in a stable post-transition setting. Second, while both revenues and expenditures change during transition, the net outcome is not always clear. With the collapse of the state sector, revenue sources are likely to decline as there is a movement away from direct accumulation through enterprises toward a system of western-style taxation. Such changes take time to implement. On the expenditure side, infrastructure needs may be postponed, though adjustments in social service programs may be necessary during the transition process. Third, government responsibilities are likely to decentralize to regional and local levels. This process takes time and is difficult to measure accurately.

The budget data assembled in Table 18.5 are not comparable across the three country cases, though all could be considered as appropriate proxies for government involvement in the economy. So considered, it is striking that in Poland and the Czech Republic, where government is declining in importance, the changes have been modest, although the period of time under consideration is, in fact, very short.

It is perhaps not very meaningful to attempt generalizations based on the evidence gathered on these the three cases. With some exceptions, much of the evidence is directionally consistent with our prior expectations, though the magnitude of change is generally not large. Although specific differences could be cited in each case, there is no clear-cut evidence to promote one model of transition over another. A longer span of time is required to make such judgments.

TABLE 18.5 Poland, Hungary, and the Czech Republic, 1988–1993

	1988	1989	1990	1991	1992	1993
GDP: private sector share (%)						
Poland	n.a.	28.6	30.9	30.0	40.0	45.0
Hungary	n.a.	<10.0	10–20	20–30	n.a.	n.a.
GDP: Share derived from industry (%)						
Poland	50.6	49.5	43.6	39.2	39.6	n.a.
Hungary	30.9	30.1	28.8	26.8	26.0	n.a.
Czech Republic	59.9	59.6	63.2	67.7	n.a.	n.a.
State Budget outlays (% of GDP)						
Poland (state budget outlays: all levels)	37.0	36.9	36.7	33.0	33.4	32.5
Hungary (central government outlays)	50.0	49.5	47.5	54.9	54.1	54.6
Czech Republic (general government expenditure)	59.6	64.5	60.1	54.2	52.8	47.0

Sources: *Economics of Transition* 2 (March 1994), Tables 3, 4, 5; Private Sector data for Hungary from Kemal Dervis and Timothy Condon, "Hungary—Partial Success and Remaining Challenges: The Emergence of a 'Gradualist' Success Story?" in Oliver Jean Blanchard, Kenneth A. Froot, and Jeffrey D. Sachs, *The Transition in Eastern Europe*, Vol. 1 (Chicago: University of Chicago Press, 1994), p. 125.

Summary

This chapter has examined the cases of transition in Poland, Hungary, and the Czech Republic. All three cases were examined using a similar approach, which involved each country's natural setting, its background during the era of planned socialism, the transition, and finally the outcomes of basic performance and restructuring indicators.

All three revealed striking similarities as well as interesting and important differences. These similarities and differences are important for an understanding of the economic situation of these countries in the 1990s.

Poland, Hungary, and the Czech Republic are all relatively small, poor countries with few natural resources. All had been market economies with differing levels of economic development prior to World War II and the subsequent adoption of the Soviet model. In all cases, this communist model included a new set of political arrangements under a dictatorship, collectivization of agriculture, nationalization of the means of production, and the implementation of central planning as the dominant mechanism for resource allocation.

In all cases, several attempts were made to reform the economic systems beginning in the middle and late 1950s. However, while these reform attempts generally failed, their origins differed among these countries, and in the end, so did their impact.

From the perspective of performance, the Soviet model created a variety of familiar distortions in these systems: the expansion of industry and de-emphasis on consumption and services in general and the reorientation of foreign trade away from Western market economies toward the Soviet bloc countries functioning through the CMEA. Although reform movements of the 1960s and thereafter did little to offset lagging performance, the impact of these attempts at reform differed.

The Czech Republic after the Prague Spring of 1968 was a planned socialist economy with little change. Meanwhile, unsuccessful reform attempts continued into the 1980s in Poland. The most interesting reform was the New Economic Mechanism (NEM), which originated in Hungary in 1968 with varying and limited degrees of implementation thereafter.

The essential elements of transition included macroeconomic stabilization, privatization and the freeing of prices and a reorientation of foreign trade away from the former Socialist trade bloc toward the West. Although the degree of implementation of such policies has differed in the cases examined, all pursued a market economy with Poland doing so through the "shock therapy" approach or the rapid implementation of a specific set of transition policies. Hungary and the Czech Republic, however, pursued a "gradualist" approach with pragmatic modification of policies that were implemented on an ongoing basis.

Although performance and transition outcomes (restructuring) have varied, these three countries all experienced significant decreases of output along with inflationary pressures. However, in all cases, the output declines have been reversed, inflation has been controlled, and the currency has been made convertible, resulting in changing patterns of foreign trade.

Key Terms

economic reform

Soviet model

Solidarity

shock therapy

gradualist approach

convertibility

privatization

CMEA

New Economic Mechanism (NEM)

implementation of reform

external hard-currency debt

transition

grand design

voucher privatization

restructuring

sectoral shares

Notes

1. A great deal has been written about the command experience in Poland. The publications of the Joint Economic Committee provide a useful set of papers, in particular, United States Congress, Joint Economic Committee, *East European Economies Post-Helsinki* (Washington, D.C.: U.S. Government Printing Office, 1977); United States Congress, Joint Economic Committee, *East European Economic Assessment* (Washington, D.C.: U.S. Government Printing Office, 1981); United States Congress, Joint Economic Committee, *East European Economies: Slow Growth in the 1980s* (Washington, D.C.: U.S. Government Printing Office, 1985).

2. For an interesting survey perspective, see, for example, Jozef M. van Brabant, "Lessons from the Wholesale Transformations in the East," *Journal of Comparative Economics*, 35 (Winter 1993), 73–102; see also Norbert Funke, "Timing and Sequencing of Reforms: Competing Views and the Role of Credibility," *Kyklos* 3 (1993), 337–362.

3. In addition to the sources cited in note 1, a summary discussion of Polish economic reforms can be found in Raphael Shen, *Economic Reform in Poland and Czechoslovakia* (Westport, Conn.: Praeger, 1993).

4. For a discussion of Poland on the eve of transition, see, for example, David Lipton and Jeffrey Sachs, "Creating a Market Economy in Eastern Europe," *Brookings Papers on Economic Activity*, 1 (1990), 75–147; Stanislaw Wellisz, "Poland Under 'Solidarity' Rule," *Journal of Economic Perspectives*, 5 (Fall 1991), 211–217.

5. This discussion is based on Andrew Berg and Oliver Jean Blanchard, "Stabilization and Transition: Poland, 1990–91," in Oliver Jean Blanchard, Kenneth A. Froot, and Jeffrey D. Sachs, eds., *The Transition in Eastern Europe*, vol. 1 (Chicago: University of Chicago Press, 1994), 51–91; John P. Bonin, "On The Way to Privatizing Commercial Banks: Poland and Hungary Take Different Roads," *Comparative Economic Studies* 35 (Winter 1993), 103–120; Jeffrey Sachs and David Lipton, "Poland's Economic Reform," *Foreign Affairs*, 69 (Summer 1990), 47–66; Saul Estrin and Xavier Richet, "Industrial Restructuring and Microeconomic Adjustment in Poland: A Cross-Sectoral Approach," *Comparative Economic Studies* 35 (Winter 1993), 1–19; John P. Farrell, ed., "The Economic Transformation in Eastern Europe," *Comparative Economic Studies* 33 (Summer 1991), 1–77; S. Gomilka, "Polish Economic Reform, 1990–91: Principles, Policies and Outcomes," *Cambridge Journal of Economics* 16 (September 1992), 355–372; Alain de Crombrugghe and David Lipton, "The Government Budget and the Economic Transformation of Poland," in Oliver Jean Blanchard, Kenneth A. Froot, and Jeffrey Sachs, *The Transition in Eastern Europe*, vol. 2 (Chicago: University of Chicago Press, 1994), 111–133.

6. Andrew Berg and Oliver Jean Blanchard, "Stabilization and Transition: Poland, 1990–91," 69–70; see also Zbigniew M. Fallenbuchl, "Polish Privatization Policy," *Comparative Economic Studies* 33 (Summer 1991), 53–69; M. Shaffer, "The Polish State-Owned Enterprise Sector and the Recession of 1990," *Comparative Economic Studies* 34 (Spring 1992), 58–85; Andrew Berg, "The Logistics of Privatization in Poland," in Oliver Jean Blanchard, Kenneth A. Froot, and Jeffrey D. Sachs, *The Transition in Eastern Europe.* vol. 2 (Chicago: University of Chicago Press, 1994), 165–186.

7. For a discussion of the Hungarian economy after World War II, see the publications of the United States Congress, Joint Economic Committee cited in note 1.

8. P. G. Hare, H. K. Radice, and N. Swain, eds., *Hungary: A Decade of Economic Reform* (London: Allen and Unwin, 1981); Bela Csikos-Nagy, "The Hungarian Economic Reform after Ten Years," *Soviet Studies,* 30 (October 1978), 540–546; Bela Balassa, "The Hungarian Economic Reform, 1968–83," *Banca Nazionale del Lavoro Quarterly Review* 145 (June 1983), 163–184; Bela Balassa, "Reforming the New Economic Mechanism in Hungary," *Journal of Comparative Economics,* 7, 3 (1983), 253–276; J. Kornai, "The Hungarian Reform Process: Visions, Hopes, and Reality," *Journal of Economic Literature* 24 (1986), 1687–1737; J. Kornai, *Contradictions and Dilemmas* (Cambridge, Mass.: The MIT Press, 1986).

9. This discussion is based on Kemal Davis and Timothy Condon, "Hungary—Partial Successes and Remaining Challenges: The Emergence of a 'Gradualist' Success Story?" in Oliver Jean Blanchard, Kenneth A. Froot, and Jeffrey D. Sachs, eds., *The Transition in Eastern Europe,* vol. 1 (Chicago: University of Chicago Press, 1994), 123–153; D. M. Newberry, "Tax reform, Trade Liberalization, and Industrial Restructuring in Hungary," *European Economy* 43 (March 1990), 67–96; Erzsebet Szalai, "Integration of Special Interests in the Hungarian Economy: The Struggle between Large Companies and the Party and State Bureaucracy," *Journal of Comparative Economics,* 15 (June 1991), 107–124; P. G. Hare, "Hungary: In Transition to a Market Economy," *Journal of Economic Perspectives,* 5, 4 (1991), 195–202; Janos Kornai, *The Road to a Free Economy* (New York: Norton, 1990).

10. Kemal Davis and Timothy Condon, "Hungary—Partial Successes and Remaining Challenges," 138–141.

11. Ibid., 141–148.

12. For a discussion of the post–World War II era in Czechoslovakia, see the publications of the United States Congress, Joint Economic Committee, cited in Note 1.

13. This discussion is based on Karel Dyba and Jan Svejnar, "Stabilization and Transition in Czechoslovakia," in Oliver Jean Blanchard, Kenneth A. Froot, and Jeffrey D. Sachs, eds., *The Transition in Eastern Europe,* vol. 1 (Chicago: University of Chicago Press, 1994), 93–122; Jan Svejnar and Miroslav Singer, "Using Vouchers to Privatize an Economy: The Czech and Slovak Case," *Economic of Transition,* 2 (March 1994), 43–70; Raphael Shen, *Economic Reform in Poland and Czechoslovakia* (Westport. Conn.: Praeger, 1993); Josef C. Brada, "The Economic Transition of Czechoslovakia from Plan to Market," *Journal of Economic Perspectives,* 5 (Fall 1991), 171–177; Karel Dyba and Jan Svejnar, "Czechoslovakia: Recent Economic Developments and Prospects," *American Economic Review Papers and Proceedings,* 81 (May 1991), 185–190; Eva Marikova Leeds, "Voucher Privatization in Czechoslovakia," *Comparative Economic Studies,* 35 (Fall 1993), 19–38.

14. For an excellent discussion of privatization, see Jan Svejnar and Miroslav Singer, "Using Vouchers to Privatize an Economy: The Czech and Slovak Case," Eva Marikova Leeds, "Voucher Privatization in Czechoslovakia," and Karel Dyba and Jan Svejnar, "Stabilization and Transition in Czechoslovakia," 113–116.

Recommended Readings

General Sources

Anthony B. Atkinson and John Micklewright, *Economic Transformation in Eastern Europe and the Distribution of Income* (Cambridge: Cambridge University Press, 1992).

Mario Baldassarri, Luigi Paganetto, and Edmund S. Phelps, eds., *Privatization Processes in Eastern Europe* (New York: St. Martin's Press, 1993).

Oliver Jean Blanchard, Kenneth A. Froot, and Jeffrey D. Sachs, eds., *The Transition in Eastern Europe: Country Studies*, vol. 1 (Chicago: University of Chicago Press, 1994).

———, *The Transition in Eastern Europe: Restructuring*, Vol. 2 (Chicago: University of Chicago Press, 1994).

Michael L. Boyd, *Organization, Performance, and System Choice: East European Agricultural Development* (Boulder: Westview Press, 1991).

Jozef M. van Brabant, *Economic Integration in Eastern Europe* (New York: Routledge, 1989).

———, ed., *The New Eastern Europe and the World Economy* (Boulder: Westview, 1993).

Hans van Ees and Harry Garretsen, "The Theoretical Foundation of the Reform in Eastern Europe: Big Bang versus Gradualism and the Limitations of Neo-Classical Economic Theory," *Economic Systems* 18, (March 1994), 1–13.

John P. Farrell, ed., "The Economic Transition in Eastern Europe," *Comparative Economic Studies*, 33 (Summer 1991), 1–177.

Daniel S. Fogel, ed., *Managing in Emerging Market Economies: Cases from Czech and Slovak Republics* (Boulder: Westview, 1994).

Petr Hanel, "Trade Liberalization in Czechoslovakia, Hungary, and Poland through 1991: A Survey," *Comparative Economic Studies*, 34 (Fall–Winter 1992), 34–53.

C. Clague and G. Rausser, eds., *The Emergence of Market Economies in Eastern Europe* (Cambridge: Blackwell, 1992).

Michael Kaser, ed., *The Economic History of Eastern Europe 1919–1975*, vols. I–III (Oxford: Clarendon Press, 1986).

Michael Keren and Gur Ofer, eds., *Trails of Transition: Economic Reform in the Former Communist Bloc* (Boulder: Westview Press, 1992).

A. Schipke and A. M. Taylor, eds., *The Economics of Transformation* (New York: Springer-Verlag, 1994).

Raphael Shen, *Economic Reform in Poland and Czechoslovakia* (Westport, Conn.: Praeger, 1993).

Jozef M. van Brabant, "Lessons from the Wholesale Transformations in the East," *Comparative Economic Studies*, 35 (Winter 1993), 73–102.

Kenneth J. Koford, et al., "Symposium: Economic Reform in Eastern Europe and the Former Soviet Union," *Eastern Economic Journal*, 19 (Summer 1993), 329–393.

Poland

Andrew Berg and Oliver Jean Blanchard, "Stabilization and Transition: Poland, 1990–91," in Oliver Jean Blanchard, Kenneth A. Froot, and Jeffrey D. Sachs, eds., *The Transition in Eastern Europe*, vol. 1 (Chicago: University of Chicago Press, 1994), 51–91.

John P. Bonin, "On The Way to Privatizing Commercial Banks: Poland and Hungary Take Different Roads," *Comparative Economic Studies*, 35 (Winter 1993), 103–120.

Saul Estrin and Xavier Richet, "Industrial Adjustment and Restructuring in Poland: A Cross-Sectoral Approach," *Comparative Economic Studies*, 35 (Winter 1993), 1–20.

Zbigniew M. Fallenbuchl, "Polish Privatization Policy," *Comparative Economic Studies*, 33 (Summer 1991), 53–69.

Irena Grosfeld, "Prospects for Privatization in Poland," *European Economy*, 43 (March 1990), 139–158.

David Lipton and Jeffrey Sachs, "Creating a Market Economy in Poland," *Brookings Papers on Economic Activity*, 1 (1990).

Jan Mujzel, "Polish Economic Reforms and the Dilemma of Privatization," *Comparative Economic Studies*, 33 (Summer 1991), 29–52.

Leon Podkaminer, "Estimates of Disequilibria in Poland's Consumer Markets 1965–1978," *Review of Economics and Statistics*, 62 (August 1982), 423–432.

D. M. Nuti, "Internal and International Aspects of Monetary Disequilibrium in Poland," *European Economy*, 43 (March 1990), 169–182.

Jeffrey Sachs and David Lipton, "Poland's Economic Reform," *Foreign Affairs*, 69 (Summer 1990), 47–66.

Jeffrey Sachs, "Poland's Big Bang: A First Report Card," *The International Economy*, (January/February 1991), 40–43.

Mark Schaeffer, "State-Owned Enterprises in Poland: Taxation, Subsidization and Competition Policies," *European Economy*, 43 (March 1990).

Richard Portes, "Introduction to Economic Transformation in Hungary and Poland," *European Economy*, 43 (March 1990).

Hungary

Jan Adam, "Work Teams: A New Phenomenon in Income Distribution in Hungary," *Comparative Economic Studies*, 31 (Spring 1989), 46–65.

James Angresano, "A Mixed Economy in Hungary? Lessons from the Swedish Experience," *Comparative Economic Studies*, 34 (Spring 1992), 41–57.

Josef C. Brada, Inderjit Singh, and Adam Torok, *Firms Afloat and Firms Adrift: Hungarian Industry and Economic Transition*, (Armonk: M. E. Sharpe, 1993).

Kemal Davis and Timothy Condon, "Hungary—Partial Successes and Remaining Challenges: The Emergence of a 'Gradualist' Success Story? in Oliver Jean Blanchard, Kenneth A. Froot, and Jeffrey D. Sachs, eds., *The Transition in Eastern Europe*, vol. 1. (Chicago: University of Chicago Press, 1994), 123–153.

A. L. Hillman, "Macroeconomic Policy in Hungary and its Microeconomic Implications," *European Economy*, 43 (March 1990), 55–60.

Janos Kornai, *The Road to a Free Economy* (New York: Norton, 1990).

D. M. Newberry, "Tax Reform, Trade Liberalization, and Industrial Restructuring in Hungary," *European Economy*, 43 (March 1990), 67–96.

Gabor Oblath and David Tarr, "The Terms-of-Trade Effects from the Elimination of State Trading in Soviet–Hungarian Trade," *Journal of Comparative Economics*, 16 (March 1992), 75–93.

Erzsebet Szalai, "Integration of Special Interests in the Hungarian Economy: The Struggle Between Large Companies and the Party and State Bureaucracy," *Journal of Comparative Economics*, 15 (June 1991), 284–303.

I. Szekely, "The Reform of the Hungarian Financial System," *European Economy*, 43 (March 1990), 107–124.

The Czech Republic

Josef C. Brada, "The Economic Transition of Czechoslovakia from Plan to Market ," *Journal of Economic Perspectives*, 5 (Fall 1991), 171–177.

Karel Dyba and Jan Svejnar, "Czechoslovakia: Recent Economic Developments and Prospects," *American Economic Review Papers and Proceedings*, 81 (May 1991), 185–190.

————, "Stabilization and Transition in Czechoslovakia," in Oliver Jean Blanchard, Kenneth A. Froot, and Jeffrey D. Sachs, eds., *The Transition in Eastern Europe*, vol, 1 (Chicago: University of Chicago Press, 1994), 93–122.

John Ham, Jan Svejnar, and Katherine Terrell, "The Emergence of Unemployment in the Czech and Slovak Republics," *Comparative Economic Studies*, 35 (Winter 1993), 121–134.

Eva Marikova Leeds, "Voucher Privatization in Czechoslovakia," *Comparative Economic Studies*, 35 (Fall 1993), 19–38.

Jan Svejnar and Miroslav Singer, "Using Vouchers to Privatize an Economy: The Czech and Slovak Case," *Economics of Transition*, 2 (March 1994), 43–70.

Tito Boevi, " 'Transitional' Unemployment," *Economics of Transition*, 2 (March 1994), 1–26.

PART **VI**

Prospects for the Future

19

Comparing Economic Systems: Trends and Prospects

The demise of the Soviet Union and the planned socialist economic systems fundamentally altered the way in which we approach the comparison of economic systems. Although economic systems had always undergone change, it was generally assumed that change was not fundamental and significant, and that the classic variants of planned socialism and market capitalism would, at least for the foreseeable future, be sustained.

From the vantage point of the mid-1990s, one could characterize the changes in the field of comparative economic systems in a variety of ways. However, several important and overriding changes deserve our attention.

First, past comparisons of different economic systems have always been cast in terms of stylized variants, especially that of centrally planned socialism with market capitalism. Although such comparisons remain important, the spectrum of systems has now become more significant than polar extremes. But it is important to realize that simply desiring a broader, more complex approach does not mean that such an objective can be quickly realized. In a sense, systems have changed more rapidly than our ability to analyze that change, a situation quite different from that of the 1970s. The case of reform and transition is instructive. Reform of socialist economic systems was generally considered limited and ineffective, understood with traditional tools of analysis. Transition and restructuring, on the other hand, are the dominant systems phenomena of the 1990s. However, a systematic body of economic theory for analyzing and understanding contemporary transition. is, as yet, unavailable.

Second, analysts of the planned socialist systems always realized the necessity for moving beyond the traditional bounds of basic neoclassical economic theory to understand different systems and system change. Now, however, such a posture is widely accepted. Thus, the inclusion of, for example, principal-agent problems and information theory in neoclassical theory fundamentally affects the study of different economic systems. But before we can applaud the application of new tools to old problems, research must be done.

455

Third, past analysis of different economic systems was comfortable because the stylized variants were similar and could be studied as whole units. Now, however, system components and mechanisms can vary widely from one case to another making simple classification schemes much less useful than they once were.

Fourth, the impact of real-world events, while exciting and meaningful, can be much less useful than many would surmise. For example, those who studied the Soviet Union were accustomed to a veil of secrecy shrouding data that was inappropriately distorted or simply useless. Has the demise of that country as a political and economic entity changed all this? For a variety of reasons, the quality of the information has improved in some cases, but elsewhere it simply has not. To the extent that the data involve economic history in a very difficult contemporary setting of transition, improvement will be slow. Focusing on the present and the future is now a priority, not reconstructing the past.

Finally, quite apart from the dramatic changes in the socialist order, forces beyond these former countries' borders—be they changes in international objectives, changes in trading arrangements, or increasing concern for the environment—will remain important well into the next century. There is indeed a new world order, but it is an order that, in this final decade of the twentieth century, is in process of being constructed. These broader forces will influence and be influenced by system differences.

Although it is not possible to summarize the content of a book in a few pages, it is useful to review the basic themes as seen through past and contemporary research. The objective, in summarizing these themes, is to make them clear and at the same time use them to interpret the sorts of changes anticipated through the remainder of this decade.

A Summary of Themes

In this book, three closely related themes have been developed and examined. First, what is the nature of an economic system, and how can the system be isolated and identified both in theory and in the real world? Second, what is the relationship between an economic system and observable economic outcomes in real-world settings? The assumption underlying this line of investigation argues that economic systems and system differences matter, and that these differences and their impact on different outcomes can be observed in theory and in practice. Thus the economic system becomes an input that is variable and hence capable of being manipulated to alter future outcomes. Third, how do outcomes differ among economic systems, and in what ways can we systematically observe and understand these differences?

To examine these issues, we chose a framework of simple system models that we used to understand real-world variants, looking for both similarities and differences. We then compared the performance of different real-world systems using a variety of commonly used performance indicators, such as economic growth. Ultimately, we tried to generalize about our system models from the real-world experience.

Our examination of differing systems was couched within the traditional labels of capitalism and socialism with appropriate refinements. These labels are a useful way to classify systems, as they are in scientific literature, which is largely developed along these lines and is generally familiar. But we observed that the system mechanisms or components were, in fact, more important than the names attached to the overall economic system. In our examination of the Soviet case, usually described as centrally planned socialism, our interest was in the centralized nature of the plan mechanism as a way to organize economic activity. This mechanism could be and has been used in other settings characterized by different name tags.

What is an economic system? Traditionally, economic systems are defined as the organizational arrangements used to allocate resources in a given country or geographic setting. Systems are usually classified in terms of four major characteristics: the mechanism for generating and using information for decision making (plan or market), the level of decision making (centralized or decentralized), the property holding arrangements (public or private), and the system of incentives (material or moral). Immediately it must be observed that real-world systems are typically mixed systems in which one finds combinations of mechanisms rather than extremes. Most observers, however, would argue that these differences do matter in understandable and observable ways.

Probably the most fundamental organizational difference among real-world systems is the use of plan, market, or some mixture of both for resource allocation. Plan and market are fundamentally different, though in real-world settings, we encounter mixed systems where some elements of both are present. A plan is a document prepared by some planning agency that directs enterprises to produce desired goods and services using inputs as directed. The choice of what to produce and how to produce it may be derived from some exercise of consumer sovereignty, but more likely, in planned systems, state directives dominate. The market, on the other hand, brings together producers and consumers on a decentralized basis through the forces of supply and demand and the price system. Both demanders and suppliers influence prices, which provide a source of information as they change over time in response to underlying forces. Although government may intervene in a market economy to regulate economic activity or to produce public goods, such a system is not a planned economy. A fundamental difference between the two mechanisms is the issue of **control**. In the planned economy, the state can, if it wishes, exercise control over the nature of economic activity, implying that in such systems, outcomes will be different than where such control is not exercised. Is there any basis to believe that such central control will be desired?

Central control of economic activity may arise for a variety of reasons. The political system could be a dictatorship. The political system could be a democratic and pluralistic system but one in which some segments of the economy are directed by the state. Yet another variant is the French type of system involves a system of planning, but rather than **directive** planning, **indicative** planning is used. That system uses plan targets to induce system participation and to disseminate useful information, but it eliminates any measure of coercion over participants.

Although there is no one-to-one correlation between planning arrangements and socialism as an ideology, much socialist thought implies policy imperatives that would only be possible in settings with strong incentives and/or measures of state control. Understandably, in most socialist systems the state has played a strong role, though the particular mechanisms for exercising that strength have varied considerably. The case of savings and investment in the Soviet Union is instructive. Socialist thought suggests the need for a high level of savings and investment. Both were manipulated directly by the state, in the Soviet case, to achieve that result. An advocate of this mechanism would argue that higher rates of savings and investment are justified to improve the standard of living of subsequent generations to a greater degree than would otherwise be possible. Ultimately, we may judge the state control by its success in achieving the desired objective. But assessing that objective—that is, which generation should benefit and to what degree—is a subjective matter.

The second important system difference is the location of property rights. Indeed, as we observed, socialism is traditionally cast in terms of public ownership in order to facilitate such basic socialist objectives as a more egalitarian distribution of income than is normally found under capitalism. State ownership of property not only implies state control of the use of that property, but most importantly, it implies state control over the benefits that accrue from the property.

Third, levels of decision making are important yet difficult to isolate and classify. Again, the extremes of full centralization and full decentralization are understandable, yet in the real world, mixed systems are encountered. However, as we look at various mixed systems, it is evident that decision-making levels differ and accordingly the degree of state control differs.

Finally, incentives are important to motivate participants to achieve desired societal objectives. Although incentive arrangements vary widely from one economy to another, the degree of differentiation, from largest to smallest reward, is the most intractable issue. To motivate individuals to achieve desired objectives, what degree of income differential is necessary? Relating these differences to outcomes is complex and not well understood.

Systematic Change

One of the most dramatic developments in the field of comparative economic systems has been the rediscovery of change. In the past, change in socialist systems was viewed as regime directed, slow, and uninteresting. In capitalist systems, change was viewed as substantially decentralized through the market, but to the neoclassical economist it was also slow and generally uninteresting. Thus it was argued that market structure mattered, but within a particular setting the companies were black boxes.

As we look at systemic change in the 1990s, our task is considerably more complex. We may still rely on the grand theories such as Marxism–Leninism, the teaching of economic development, or the contemporary boundaries of evolutionary economics. In the main, however, we do not understand change well, whether it is discussed as economic reform in China or as transition in the former Soviet Union. The latter is particularly intractable because we have never really thought about the evolution from plan to market, but rather based on real world experience we have focused on the reverse.

The essence of transition is changing the economic system, in the contemporary cases from plan to market through privatization, including decentralization of decision making, the use of market-type regulatory devices in the macro and micro spheres, and finally differentiated material rewards.

Thus far we have focused on the economic system and its impact on resource allocation. We have emphasized that while basic relationships between system mechanisms and selected outcomes can be observed in real-world settings, in fact the establishment of these relationships is difficult. There are a wide variety of reasons—conceptual, methodological, and statistical—for these difficulties. But, ultimately, a major difficulty arises from the fact that different economic systems arise in different settings and follow different policies. Moreover, the functioning of the economic system is clearly conditioned by such factors as ideology, cultural characteristics of the population, and geographic considerations. However, understanding the interaction between the economic system and the nonsystem characteristics is difficult and has been a matter of great importance in the 1990s.

Beyond the Economic System

Why are we concerned about those influences that lie beyond the economic system? Nonsystem factors, such as policies and environmental issues, influence outcomes, but in part they do so through interaction with systemic factors. Thus, as we assess system elements and consider their adoption in new settings or the manner in which different policies are being implemented, the interaction of system and nonsystem factors becomes important. But it is difficult, in the absence of controlled experiments, to discover the nature of these interactions.

Consider the well-known case of unemployment in the Soviet Union. Soviet leaders persistently argued that unemployment, an important outcome, was eradicated, claiming that the basic characteristics of the socialist system made eradication both desirable and inevitable. Although we could argue about the existence of frictional unemployment in the Soviet Union, most Western economists would argue that there was little unemployment in the system in the traditional meaning of the term but, that this outcome is not inevitable in a planned socialist economic system.

Was the achievement of full employment in the Soviet Union an outcome of the economic system, or was it a policy that could be changed if the leadership desired? Unfortunately, knowing the "facts" does not always help us isolate one factor from another. Soviet enterprises faced no hard budget constraints and paid little attention to cost reduction. Moreover, low productivity and uneven technological advances created a demand for labor as planners envisioned increases in output.

Soviet leaders pledged the elimination of unemployment and created rules to make the dismissal of unnecessary labor very difficult. In this setting, it is not really surprising to find no unemployment. Moreover, this outcome would be viewed positively by many Soviet citizens whether or not the system had "really" eliminated unemployment.

Unemployment in other socialist systems, such as Yugoslavia, was serious. But because the Soviet system was centralized, a particular policy objective (in this case full employment) could be enforced, even at the expense of efficiency. The United States also has a policy on full employment, namely the Full Employment Act of 1946, and yet in the absence of political will and the mechanisms to implement this act, efficiency wins over unnecessary labor. Thus the American economy achieved greater efficiency vis-à-vis the Soviet system, but it did at the associated cost of unemployment. Whether such a policy was reasonable in the Soviet context is a separate issue, though economists would probably argue that the lack of efficiency in the Soviet system was a major factor that contributed to its economic difficulties.

Historically, there has been a tendency to identify system and nonsystem influences according to measurable means. Indeed, this issue remains central to our analysis of system factors in the 1990s as we increasingly focus on mixed systems as opposed to pure models. But most observers of the Chinese economy would argue that ideology was a major driving force for change in the decades of the 1950s through the 1970s.

Consider another case, as yet not discussed, namely Cuba. Cuba is a small tropical island economy following the traditional Soviet model. Part of that model is a substantial degree of trade avoidance. Could an island economy such as Cuba avoid trade? Certainly. If it were possible to compare Cuba with market economies similar except for their economic system, we might find that Cuba still fits the trade-aversion model. However, compared with other planned socialist economic systems, we would probably not expect Cuba to follow a policy of trade aversion.

An important aspect of the relationship between system and nonsystem characteristics is the matter of transition. Although no simple relationship exists between system and nonsystem features and the success of transition, some generalizations may be possible. For example, systematic change seems easier in those countries that have higher levels of economic development. In addition, countries with more open economies, where foreign trade has had a structural impact, seem better able to cope with change. Put another way, it may be argued that as a system moves closer to the newly chosen variant, the easier the transition becomes.

In sum, system features are likely influenced by nonsystem features, though the relation between both and the outcomes observed is seldom clear. Most observers would argue that both Germany and Japan are influenced by a strong but nonquantifiable work ethic and a sense of discipline. China has been strongly influenced by ideology, while Yugoslavia has been influenced and disrupted by regional and ethnic factionalism. Because these influences are not readily measured, they tend not to enter the equation when differing economic systems and related outcomes are analyzed.

Economic Systems: Development and Convergence

The reader must now be aware of the close relationship between comparative economic systems and economic development. The difference, however, rests largely with the fact that economic development focuses on the evolution of an economy through sectoral supply-and-demand forces and technological change. This focus leads to a structural transformation from a primarily agricultural (rural) society to a primarily industrial (urban) society. The development literature focuses on the means of bringing inputs into the production process, ensuring accumulation, and ultimately increasing per capita incomes. Why such change comes about and why it is limited to a relatively small proportion of the world's population is largely unexplained. Much of the analysis of growth and development is cast within traditional neoclassical economic theory in the absence of reference to organizational (system) arrangements. The major difference between a development perspective and a systems perspective is the latter's focus on differing organizational arrangements as an important force influencing the allocation of resources.

If we believe that the economic system matters, identifying and isolating the systemic features in particular settings would be an important though difficult task. The traditional approach examines patterns of economic growth and development in market economies to observe historical regularities. Indeed, as we have emphasized, there are observable regularities. Moreover, similar analysis of planned socialist systems have also revealed regularities, though they differ in some respects from those found in market systems.

The planned socialist economic systems (compared with market capitalist systems at similar levels of development) stress capital-intensive factor proportions in heavy industry, downplay service-oriented activities, devote substantial labor resources to agriculture, and envision a controlled role for foreign trade, while emphasizing its contribution to growth rather than immediate consumer well-being. Consumption shares are low, replacing private consumption with communal consumption. Investment ratios are high, and the system facilitates the concentration of that investment in key sectors, especially industry and heavy industry. High employment levels are sustained through persistent underemployment.

In almost all instances, the socialist pattern of economic development is directionally consistent with the market capitalist pattern. What distinguishes the socialist from the capitalist development pattern is the speed and the magnitude of the shifts. Viewed over time, the planned socialist systems compressed into a decade or so what it took capitalist systems fifty years or more to accomplish. Viewed in a cross-sectional context, socialist societies tended to attain allocation patterns typical of capitalist societies at much higher levels of economic development.

Although it is useful to make these sorts of comparisons, the contemporary demise of the planned socialist economic systems suggests that comparisons should be made with care. Specifically, although we have argued that name tags are useful for identifying system types, it may be more appropriate to analyze the use of ystem mechanisms, for example, in systems where planning is or is not used, ownership arrangements differ as do policies on the distribution of income. Apparently, there are a wide variety of patterns for examining industrialization, many of which would move beyond the simple planned socialist–market capitalist pattern that we have pursued in this book.

A second aspect of capitalist–socialist comparisons involves the time element. Many of the comparisons made here are limited by the number of cases and by a relatively short span of time. With the recent demise of major planned socialist systems (the former Soviet Union) and the radical change of others (China), it will be difficult to assess the relevance of the convergence hypothesis.

The convergence hypothesis focuses on the existence of basic regularities in the process of economic growth and economic development; such regularities include factory work, urbanization, and interest groups. Thus it has been argued that, while the mechanisms and the results of the allocation process may differ at various times, the underlying regularities will eventually prevail, lessening the observed differences.

Although a variety of interpretations of the convergence hypothesis have been made, it has not been reinterpreted in terms of the developments of the 1990s. In a sense, the demise of the planned socialist economic systems might be thought of as the ultimate proof that the proponents of convergence were correct. There does, however, exist sufficient differences in economic systems and related outcomes to suggest that a more sophisticated investigation is necessary.

Economic Systems: The Future

Throughout this book we have emphasized the importance of fundamental changes in the field of comparative economic systems. Will the field exist, let us say, in ten years, or will it be subsumed by other fields of economics, such as economic development? The history of methods in the discipline of economics is important but beyond the scope of this book; however, a number of observations about the field of comparative economic systems seem relevant.

First, economic systems have always differed and will continue to differ. That they differ in more subtle but possibly approachable ways complicates the task of the comparative economist, but it does not lessen the importance of the issues at hand. Is planning useful in less developed countries? To what extent can privatization be beneficial, and can privatization be combined with elements of planning where the latter may be desirable?

Second, economic systems exist in real-world settings. These settings differ in important ways, and yet our understanding of these differences is quite primitive. What is the impact of cultural and ethnic differences on economic development?

Third, economies throughout the world face a variety of persistent problems, such as inflation and unemployment. Can we examine different systems that are functioning in different settings to learn about optimal organizational arrangements as objectives and circumstances differ?

Fourth, much of the world remains in poverty. Can we learn from the experiences of differing economic systems, both successful and unsuccessful, about the means to lessen this poverty? Clearly, it is not just the economic system that must be considered, but rather a multidimensional approach must be taken to combine the most effective factors in a given case.

Finally, while many of the planned socialist economic systems collapsed from political inertia with economic underpinnings, their economic future remains uncertain. It would be folly to believe that these systems will systematically and steadily move toward the market. Some will follow such a path, while others will do so much more slowly, and others still may make little if any progress in the attempt to develop new organizational arrangements. The pattern of transition itself deserves attention for the messages that it can send to the poor nations of the world.

Possibly the most encouraging aspect of contemporary change is the willingness to reassess our approaches to the study of differing economic systems. The limits of neoclassical economic theory are clearly evident, preparing a path for a much broader and hopefully a much richer analysis of how economic development and economic progress can be experienced in a wide variety of settings with differing organizational arrangements.

Index